DATE DUE

TION

Meyer Weinberg

INTEGRATED EDUCATION

A READER

THE GLENCOE PRESS
A Division of the Macmillan Company
Beverly Hills, California
Collier-Macmillan Ltd., London

First printing, 1968.

Library of Congress catalog card number: 68-19321

The Glencoe Press
A Division of the Macmillan Company.
Collier-Macmillan Canada, Ltd., Toronto, Canada

Printed in the United States of America.

Preface

In 1963, nine years after the supreme court held that racial discrimination in public education is unconstitutional and eight years after the court required all deliberate speed in effectuating transition to nondiscriminatory school systems, racial integration in the public schools of the United States seemed to be of interest only to civil-rights activists and, in a negative way, to segregationists. Some small advances had been made, to be sure, but relatively few American citizens had focused attention on problems relevant to integrated education. In that year, 1963, the first issue of the magazine *Integrated Education* was published.

The magazine was started by seven classroom teachers in Chicago who were eager to learn about new ideas and developments concerning school integration. They hoped to apply this knowledge to the schools in which they worked. Instead of becoming a repository of articles reprinted from other publications—as the founders thought it might—the awful truth dawned: There were no other periodicals devoted to school integration and so there were virtually no articles to reprint. Unexpectedly, then, *Integrated Education* was forced to become a source of original articles. With the slimmest of budgets and numerous volunteers, the magazine gained much moral support and even some subscribers. Ideas for articles now come from an extensive editorial correspondence, a close reading of the research literature, the educational press, conference papers, and occasionally, submitted articles.

In the eventful years that followed the founding of the magazine, more and more educators and other leaders in public and private sectors in the United States turned attention to inadequacies, inequities, and deficiencies of our system of public education. As the editor of *Integrated Education* magazine since its founding, I have had the privilege of helping to chronicle that growing awareness. In the years since 1963, the magazine has become a prime source of news, analysis, ideas, and research information relevant to the school integration movement. It is a matter of some pride to have provided for many outstanding minds a forum through which they could address the crucial problems attending the search for equal educational opportunity.

The present book, also titled *Integrated Education,* consists of a selection from the articles, addresses, and documents that have been published in the magazine. The process of selection was not easy, and many pertinent items were reluctantly omitted because of space limitations.

I wish to thank the members of the editorial advisory board of *Integrated Education* magazine for their continuing support and cooperation: Mathew Ahmann, Herbert Blumer (chairman), Horace Mann Bond, Kenneth B. Clark, Charles Cogen, Robert Coles, Martin Deutsch, Dan W. Dodson, Leslie W. Dunbar, G. W. Foster, Jr., John Hope Franklin, Edmund W. Gordon, Jacob Landers, August Meier, Guichard Parris, Thomas F. Pettigrew, Frank Riessman, Patricia C. Sexton, June Shagaloff, Neil V. Sullivan, Jacob J. Weinstein, and Max Wolff.

The present volume is another evidence of their trust in and encouragement of the magazine's contribution to the struggle for integrated education.

Finally, my thanks to Gladys Hamilton for her usual excellent typing of the present manuscript.

MEYER WEINBERG

Chicago, December 1967.

Table of Contents

Part Four: Prospects for Change 169

Part Five: The Contribution of Research 241

Introduction

Integrated education can produce better schools and better human beings. America has never needed both more desperately than now.

An integrated school system would be one that encouraged every child to achieve his utmost, without regard to race, and which consciously planned toward that end. Integration could degenerate into a slogan or a panacea. In fact, however, it remains a rational response to the challenge posed by those great contemporary destroyers: racism and privilege. The fate of millions of children is bound up with the questions of whether our society will demand that the schools serve to unify rather than divide America.

Educators have in fact become increasingly concerned with such critical questions. Over the past five years or so, a new energy has infused the educational scene. What significant trends have become evident?

Educational deprivation.—Much experimentation and research have dealt with the plight of the child whose immediate environmental circumstances are considered to be unfavorable to school achievement. Many workers in the field stress the child's subculture as the dominant influence on the approach to the school learning situation. Evaluations of the precise importance of that influence differ, with some authorities regarding a child's home and family deprivation as a virtual bar to equal school achievement, while others view the deprivation as a handicap within the power of the school to overcome.[1] Still others view the subculture of deprivation as a source of positive aids to learning if only the school will seek to utilize them.[2]

Concern with educational deprivation led to consideration of the problem of compensation. Compensatory education, for the most part, was originally designed to

---

[1] See "American Education Today."
[2] See "Ebb and Flow in the School Integration Movement."

. remedy individual shortcomings, by such means as tutoring, the assignment of special personnel, and the provision of health and other technical services. Later, however, greater stress was placed on the need to reorganize the school for more effective compensatory learning. In neither instance were adequate resources invested to effect significant changes.

School desegregation.—For nearly a decade after the 1954 supreme court school decision, the destruction of existing patterns of segregation was emphasized. Civil rights advocates held out for the physical presence of Negro children among white children. This interest fostered open enrollment, the Princeton Plan of pairing nearby schools, redrawing of attendance-area lines of single schools, and similar techniques.[3] Two observations can be made: (1) Only limited successes in desegregation were recorded, and in some cases a worsening of segregation followed limited attempts to desegregate; and (2) virtually no attention was paid to the subsequent quality of classroom instruction.

In time, civil rights concern focused on the classroom. Both segregation and integration came increasingly to be viewed as processes to be planned out of or into the everyday classroom routine. The segregative consequences of ability grouping and the track system could be felt even in a formally desegregated school. Patterns of faculty assignment could encourage or discourage pupil desegregation. Student extracurricular activities were seen in their broad importance for equal opportunity.[4]

Most important, by the mid-1960s, the school integration movement had intersected the interests of the compensatory education movement. More and more, educational deprivation was seen as a consequence of racial segregation. This realization was reflected in federal court decisions which required not only desegregation but also a definite program of compensatory education.[5] The achievement of both desegregation and compensatory programs was thereby made more probable.

The urban school system.—Six out of seven American school children attend public schools, most of them in urban centers. A large number of the private schools are also in cities. American education is thus urban education; and the urban school system is the most meaningful unit of analysis.

Virtually every large urban school system is made up of two subsystems: one, attended predominantly by middle-class whites, succeeds in teaching children at least the basic skills of reading; the other, attended by Negroes, Spanish Americans, and poor whites, fails—by all quantitative measures—to teach the basic skills.[6] Over the nation, more and more children have received less and less adequate education. By the mid-1960s, more than half the public-school population in many large cities were Negro and other minority students; and in each of these cities, the school system was in deep trouble.[7] The failings of urban education were too widespread to be explained by purely local factors and too profound to be remedied by compensatory instruction for laggard individuals. New currents of teacher organization, community insistence, and political opportunity began to merge into a real wave of school reform, the effects

---

[3]See "The Allen Report on New York City Schools."
[4]See "School Integration and Absorption of Newcomers."
[5]See "The Washington, D.C., School Case."
[6]See "The Right to Read—A Straight Path to Integration."
[7]See "The Allen Report on New York City Schools," and "The Chicago Title VI Complaint to H.E.W."

of which cannot yet be assessed. We should remember, too, that it is as much the spirit of urban education as its structure that needs reform. Historically, America's urban school systems never tried to educate all the children of all the people.[8]

The role of the judiciary.—The Brown decision of 1954 was handed down in an era of open, legal segregation, primarily of the sort found in the South and rural areas. Little progress was made in implementing the decision, at least until about 1962. In southern courts, judges tended to demand only the legal minimum of compliance. In the North, the doctrine of *de facto* segregation immobilized courts as school boards acknowledged the existence of school segregation but denied any responsibility for remedying its consequences.[9]

Starting in 1962, state courts—especially in New York and New Jersey—began to legitimize school board actions to outlaw segregation however it was caused. Here and there, judges reached into school systems to assert judicial authority over everyday school matters such as teacher assignment, building plans, provision of remedial education, and attendance boundary lines.

Federal courts were asked to decide if school boards had an affirmative constitutional obligation to desegregate, whether or not the initial segregation had been deliberate. From 1955 to 1965, federal district and appeals courts were almost unanimous in answering in the negative. In 1965, however, the tide began to turn. The U.S. court of appeals in the fifth circuit led the way in the South. In 1966 and 1967 it explicitly declared that the Brown ruling required affirmative action to integrate and not merely to avoid segregation. In 1967, the U.S. district court in Washington, D.C., decided a case involving the District of Columbia public schools. The court struck down a number of discriminatory practices, most of which were at the time still standard in many northern and western school systems.[10]

Through 1967, the U.S. supreme court, for its part, had yet to declare a policy on the type of school segregation that existed in northern urban centers. The court had refused to review lower court decisions that ruled (1) a school board could regulate school attendance boundary lines to maximize racial balance regardless of the neighborhood school system; and (2) a school board could maintain a neighborhood school system even if racial imbalance resulted.

The role of legislation.—State legislatures began to assert an interest in some problems of urban education. In 1965, Massachusetts became the first state to legislate a combination of financial incentives and penalties to encourage local boards of education to establish racially balanced schools.[11] Many states have enacted laws requiring that ethnic minorities, especially the Negro American, be truthfully represented in textbooks.[12] Other states have adopted policy statements on behalf of school integration.

In 1964, Congress passed the Civil Right Act and included two sections of special significance for schools. Title IV provides federal funds to help school boards to manage the transition to desegregation. Title VI forbids the use of federal funds for

---

[8]See "Desegregating City Schools" and "New Forces in Educational Decision Making."
[9]See "*De Facto* Segregation: Fact or Artifact?"
[10]See "The Washington, D.C., School Case."
[11]See "The Massachusetts Law on Racial Balance."
[12]See "California Law on Teaching Negro History."

racially discriminatory purposes.[13] In the South, Title VI had an immediate and significant impact on numerical progress in desegregation. In the North, however, Title VI was not interpreted by federal authorities as clearly applying to what is called *de facto* segregation and, therefore, it contributed little to northern desegregation efforts. Nevertheless, the growing federal involvement in school affairs has resulted in an expanding debate.

Changing geography of segregation.—Since the 1954 Brown decision, Americans have learned a new geography lesson—racial segregation is by no means a regional problem. Northern school segregation has proved no more easily eradicable than segregation elsewhere. No large northern or western city can show substantially more progress in desegregation than can any large southern city.

In the South, meanwhile, growing urbanization led to changed forms of school segregation.[14] Extreme forms of educational deprivation were still common in the South long after the Brown ruling, perhaps the most notorious occurring in Prince Edward County, where Negro children were deprived of all public schooling for five years.[15] On the other hand, here and there in the Deep South there were surprising instances of integrated educational experiences.[16]

There has been increasing realization that school segregation is less a regional than a national problem. This realization formed a basis for action on the national level, especially through the congress and the federal courts.

New community-school relations.—The ferment in urban education in large measure resulted from ever more insistent demands for effective schooling that were voiced by parents of disadvantaged children. These components of the urban community are not new; that their voice may begin to be heard—even heeded—is indeed novel. Their protests focus attention on the inadequacies of the neighborhood school, which has no educational justification in the most deprived neighborhoods. Parents in these areas are most insistent on progress. What appears to them as the raising of their aspirational ceiling seems to critics to be nothing but blowing the roof off the house. In truth, there will be much more raising and blowing.

Parent organization in the ghetto emerged as a new constructive, if unsettling, force.[17] Organized parents, even if they are clear about their aims, cannot achieve more direct controls over the school or school system in the absence of cooperation with teacher groups.[18] This factor may be the single most dynamic element on the contemporary school scene.[19]

Changing school practices.—The crisis in urban education is a crisis of traditional practices. Rare is the practice that remains untouched by the new currents of aspiration and concern.

School districting, limited only by custom to the corporate limits of cities and counties, is being regarded in a larger geographical perspective.[20] The Great High

---

[13] See "The Chicago Title VI Complaint to H.E.W."

[14] See "*De Facto* Segregation, Southern Style."

[15] See "Family and Educational Experiences of Displaced Negro Children."

[16] See "Beyond Tokenism: Reverse Integration in Albany, Georgia."

[17] See "New Forces Operating in Educational Decision Making."

[18] See "The Issues at I.S. 201: A View from the Parents' Committee."

[19] See "Ebb and Flow in the School Integration Movement."

[20] See "Metropolitan Planning for Education."

Schools planned for Pittsburgh and similar enormous educational complexes proposed for many other cities are expected to provide high-quality education to integrated student populations numbering as many as 30,000.[21] The techniques and concepts of urban planning are being applied in a broadening way to school problems.[22] Recruitment of teachers is being placed within a more realistic and challenging framework of specific needs of ghetto schools.[23] The educational significance of integration could be removed from the realm of speculation by examination of functioning integrated school situations.[24]

The world scene.—Color, minority status, and educational disadvantage are closely associated in many countries of the world. Within the former colonies of western powers can usually be found a heritage of social inferiority deeply imbedded in the schools. The sudden opportunity for comparatively large numbers to attend schools and colleges brings everywhere a crush on existing facilities. Where rising educational aspirations are deliberately frustrated by government policy, the entire social system is under serious threat.[25] Isolated cultural minorities, arising after a long history of non-concern by authorities, are only starting to organize themselves to demand new opportunities.[26] But even in a modern industrial country such as England, allocation of educational resources by color is becoming a national problem.[27]

American education must plan for significant changes of unprecedented scope and depth. A context of urgency presses upon schoolmen what are sometimes only partly-clarified goals. But deprivation long denied, joined with a new-born self-assertion, cannot be expected to be patient, too. The contemporary schoolman will probably have to become conversant, at the least, with changing currents in the civil rights movement and with life in the minority communities, as well as with pedagogical reforms that can be readily applied.

---

[21] See "The Educational Park."

[22] See "Planning and the Neighborhood School" and "Integrated Integration."

[23] See "Take Up the Challenge"; "Self Selection of Student Teachers" and "Securing Teachers for Slum Schools."

[24] See "Classroom Grouping and Integration"; "Day-to-Day Problems of School Integration"; "Some Effects of Segregation and Desegregation in the Schools"; and "Learning Effects of Segregation in New Rochelle."

[25] See "Education for Africans in South Africa."

[26] See "Aboriginal Education in Australia"; "Education of the Canadian Indian and Eskimo"; and "Socially Handicapped—The Maoris of New Zealand."

See "School Integration in England."

Part One

The General Problem

In 1860, some two and a half centuries after settlement of the Jamestown Colony, America's public school system was rudimentary and incomplete. The average school year lasted less than three months. Except for occasional cultural islands in the South, only northern white children had even a minimal opportunity to learn at public expense. Negroes were subjected to a system of compulsory ignorance; teaching a slave to read was illegal throughout the South. The census of 1860 revealed literacy rates in the nation of 55 percent for whites and 10 percent for Negroes, slave and free.

During the half-century following the Civil War, the public schools were greatly extended and strengthened. In the South, elementary education became widely available though profoundly differentiated in quantity and quality between white and Negro children. Secondary education started to emerge in public school systems.

By 1920, school systems of metropolitan centers in both North and South had accommodated themselves well to the inflow of European immigrants. Public education in New York took place in an immigrant school system; the majority of New York City students before World War I were foreign-born. Their parents were poor, often illiterate even in their native languages, and came from peasant or village backgrounds. The parents could readily find jobs—with long hours and low pay, to be sure—in the many types of work requiring physical strength or dexterity but not formal education. As the economy generated numerous white-collar and semitechnical jobs, children of immigrants found a ready market for the skills they had learned in the public schools. The European immigrants, then, became urban Americans during a period when the U.S. economy was expanding. Their children flocked to schools whose quality was rising and whose accessibility was broadening.

It was otherwise for Negro Americans. Even after the Civil War they were denied many of the benefits of the developing public school system. Assigned to separate and inferior schools, their educational accomplishments were extraordinary only in comparison with the almost total deprivation under slavery.

The contemporary organization of American education still reflects this traditional structure of deprivation. Negroes, Spanish Americans, American Indians, and poor whites all share the burden within the context of urban life. Seventy-five percent of Negro Americans, 80 percent of Mexican Americans, and almost all Puerto Ricans live in cities; and the American Indian is heading cityward, as is the white mountaineer.

How can we make the public schools once again into centers of opportunity while divesting them of the straitjacket of racial inequality? It is this central question of American education that is dealt with in the following section.

AMERICAN EDUCATION TODAY

Kenneth B. Clark, *professor of psychology, City University of New York, served as chairman for the education group at the planning session of the White House Conference "To Fulfill These Rights," held on November 16-18, 1965. Following is part of the text of an agenda paper presented to that education group. Dr. Clark is currently president of the Metropolitan Applied Research Center, an organization working toward significant social changes in our great cities. He recently became a member of the New York State Board of Regents. Dr. Clark is a member of the editorial advisory board of* INTEGRATED EDUCATION *magazine.*

It is now clear that American public education is organized and functions along social and economic class lines. A biracial public school system, wherein approximately 90 percent of American children attend segregated schools, is one of the clearest manifestations of this fact. The difficulties encountered in attempting to desegregate public schoolf in the South as well as in the North point to the tenacity of the forces seeking to prevent any basic change in the system.

The class and social organization of American public schools consistently makes for a lower quality of education in the less privileged schools. The schools attended by Negro and poor children have less adequate educational facilities than those attended by more privileged children. Teachers tend to resist assignment in Negro and other underprivileged schools and generally function less adequately in these schools; they are less adequately supervised and they tend to see their students as less capable of

From *Integrated Education,* **December 1965/January 1966. Reprinted by permission of the author.**

learning. The parents of the children in these schools are usually unable to bring about any positive changes in the conditions of these schools.

The educational inefficiency which characterizes these schools results in: (1) marked cumulative academic retardation in a disproportionately high percentage of the children who attend these schools; the process begins in the third or fourth grade and increases through the eighth grade; (2) a high percentage of dropouts in the junior and senior high schools; these students are characteristically unequipped academically and occupationally for a constructive role in society; and (3) a pattern of rejection and despair and hopelessness resulting in massive human wastage.

Given these conditions, American public schools have helped to block economic mobility for some and have tended to intensify class distinctions in our society. To the extent they do this they are not fulfilling their historic function of facilitating mobility among Americans.

In effect, the public schools have become captives of the middle class in our society. The controlling middle class has not as a rule geared the schools' programs to aiding others to move into the middle class. It might even be possible to interpret the role of the controlling middle class in some school situations as that of using the public schools to block further mobility.

What are the implications of this existing educational anomaly? It is a serious question whether the nation can afford the continuation of the wastage of human resources at this period of world history. We cannot conclusively demonstrate a relation between educational malfunctioning and other symptoms of personal and social pathology such as crime, delinquency, and urban decay, but there is strong suggestive evidence that these are correlates.

Increasing industrialization and automation of our economy will demand larger numbers of skilled and educated workers and fewer uneducated workers. The manpower needs of contemporary America require society to pay the added burden of reeducating the miseducated. This is a double taxation. To the costs of inefficient public education should be added some of the costs of crime and family instability and some of the consequences of an artificial constriction of the labor and consumer market.

Beyond these material disadvantages are the human costs inherent in the thwarting of the demand for equality of educational opportunity. This thwarting contributes significantly to a cycle of socioeconomic pathology—poor education, menial jobs, unemployment, family instability, group and personal powerlessness.

The obstacles that interfere with the attainment of efficient public education fall into many categories. Among those obstacles are those that reflect historical premises and dogmas about education, administrative realities, and psychological assumptions and prejudices.

The historical premises and dogmas include such notions as the inviolability of the neighborhood school concept—a notion which might include the belief that schools should be economically and racially homogeneous.

In evaluating these historical premises as a basis for the reorganization of school systems to meet contemporary needs, one is required to determine as realistically as possible the relative advantages of neighborhood schools versus the disadvantages of racially homogeneous schools that are educationally inefficient.

The administrative barriers involve such problems as those incurred in the transportation of children from residential neighborhoods to other areas of the city.

Here again the issue is one of the relative advantages of maintaining the educationai *status quo* versus the gains that come from following the strong imperatives for change.

The residual psychological and intellectual biases take many forms and probably underlie the apparent inability of society to resolve many of the historical and administrative problems related to providing quality public education. Initially, the academic retardation of Negro children was explained in terms of their inherent racial inferiority. The existence of segregated schools was supported either by law or explained in terms of the existence of segregated neighborhoods. More recently, this justification of segregated schools by theories of racial inferiority and by tradition and law has given way to a more subtle rationale and basis for continued inefficient education. Among the examples of such rationalizations and support are the theories of "cultural deprivation" and the related beliefs and assertions that the culturally determined educational inferiority of Negro children will impair the ability of white children to learn if they are taught in the same classes. It is assumed that because of their background, Negro children and their parents are poorly motivated for academic achievement, and that these children will not only be unable to compete with white children but will also retard the educational development of the white children. The implicit, and at times explicit, assumption of the theories and programs stressing cultural deprivation is that the environmental deficits, which Negro children bring with them to school, make it difficult, if not impossible, for them to be educated either in racially homogeneous or racially heterogeneous schools. This point of view, intentionally or not, tends to support the pervasive rejection of Negro children and obscures and intensifies the basic problem of providing quality education for all.

There are more flagrant sources of opposition to effective desegregation of American public schools. White citizens groups in the South, parents and taxpayers groups in the North, and boards of education controlled by whites who identify either overtly or covertly with the more vehement opposition to change, are examples of effective resistance. School officials and professional educators have defaulted in their educational responsibility for providing educational leadership. They have tended, for the most part, to go along with what they believe to be the level of community readiness and the "political realities." They have been accessories to the development and use of various subterfuges, and devices that give the appearance of change but little substance. They have failed to present the problem of the need for school reorganization in educational terms. This failure seems equally true of individual teachers and teachers' organizations. In some instances, teachers, textbooks, and other teaching materials have contributed to racism in education—or have failed to counter it.

Representatives of those who are the chief or most obvious victims of racially determined educational deficiency have attempted to bring about change in the organization of American public education by a variety of methods. Chief among the methods used are litigation, negotiations with school boards and school officials, and direct action such as boycotts and sit-ins.

The ten years since the supreme court decision of 1954* have been marked primarily by token desegregation in border states, minimal desegregation in the Deep

*[Editor's Note: See Appendix A, "Text of Supreme Court Rulings (*Brown* v. *Board of Education. . . .)*."]

South, and paradoxically the spread of *de facto* segregation in the North. Within the past year, federal civil rights legislation has sought to accelerate public school desegregation through the use of Title VI of the 1964 Civil Rights Act. There remains a serious question as to whether the compliance requirements for federal aid to localities will be so loosely interpreted as to be virtually meaningless in attaining this goal. The reversal of the United States Commissioner of Education's decision to withhold aid from the Chicago school system is a serious omen that Title VI can become a mockery.*

This evidence strongly suggests the need for sustained and increased pressure on the part of civil rights agencies, if the intent of the Brown decision is not to be thwarted and evaded by tokenism and other devices. So far there appears to be no serious attempt to bring about large scale desegregation of American public schools. There seems little awareness of the need to reorganize public education as a whole to obtain maximum educational efficiency for all children.

Instead, there has developed within the past three or four years a plethora of special educational projects that seem to stem from and reflect an acceptance of the cultural deprivation explanation of the problem. These "enrichment" programs, "special summer programs," and preschool programs demonstrate that when Negro children from any socioeconomic level are taught efficiently they learn, generally at the same rate as other children. However, these programs must also be understood as a contemporary version of "separate but equal" education.

All special programs of this kind do some good, help some children, and underline the inadequacy of their regular education. But, they obscure the basic fact that underprivileged children are being systematically shortchanged in their regular segregated and inferior schools. The crucial issue is the extent to which the uncritical acceptance of these programs reflects a commitment to continue segregated education.

EBB AND FLOW IN THE SCHOOL INTEGRATION MOVEMENT

Frank Riessman, *author of* The Culturally Deprived Child *(Harper & Row, 1962) and other books, is professor of educational sociology at New York University. This address was delivered in Chicago on October 29, 1966, to a conference sponsored by the Teachers for Integrated Schools and Teachers Resource Action Council. Presently, Dr. Riessman is heading a Center for New Careers at NYU. He is a member of the editorial advisory board of* INTEGRATED EDUCATION *magazine.*

At the moment we are in a period of ebb in the integration movement in the United States. The backlash simply means that many people who had an anti-integration position were relatively silent only because the consensus seemed to be

From *Integrated Education,* **October/November 1966. Reprinted by permission of the author.**

*[Editor's Note: In October, 1965, political pressure trom Chicago succeeded in reversing a federal decision to defer federal aid to Chicago schools pending a full investigation of racial discrimination in the public schools; see "The Chicago Title VI Complaint to H.E.W." in this volume.]

moving in the other direction. These quietly anti-integration people have become noisily anti-integration; people whose position was in the middle have become quieter; and a larger section of the friends of integration have become confused and are in retreat. I think this is the kind of shift that has taken place along the entire continuum, including government.

It is a basic principle in any political analysis to be very careful not to escalate an ebb, not to overreact to it, not to assume it is going to be enduring, not to build up this defeat, as some people are in fact doing today. In so exaggerating they are contributing toward it unwittingly. In a sense, you must remain calm and take a look around to see what can be done. I am terribly troubled by people who think the backlash is the real character of Americans coming out and that the integration movement is taking a long-term defeat. I do not think that is true. I think it is a temporary defeat and that we will rebound from it; my whole educational planning is in that direction.

Effects of Movement

Looking at the integration development in the United States over the last ten years, its principal contribution has been its approach to a major objective. That major objective, however, has not been integrated education. Rather, the movement has achieved a great increase in concern and funding for education in general, and particularly the education of the disadvantaged. This is best seen in the Elementary and Secondary Education Act [1965]; particularly in Title I and Title III we have the possibilities of innovational developments which, while they are not yet in practice, may soon open the doors to a significant revolution in education. And I think the major impetus producing this, along with the competition of the sputnik, has been the demand of the integration movement that the school stop blaming the child and his family and start producing a significant, meaningful education. Francis Keppel* accepted this view very fully as a basic model, and I believe Harold Howe† accepts it as strongly. So before we view ourselves as soundly beaten I think it is important to recognize that we did achieve some very important things.

On the other hand, we did not produce anything like integrated or even desegregated school systems. We made only very modest advances in this area. Small percentages have been desegregated, there are a few paired schools, there is some open enrollment, there are many human relations courses for teachers, there has been talk about educational parks, and a few are in the process of being developed. But all in all, there has been largely token reaction. A number of decisive errors were committed in attempting to develop integrated education. We ought to learn from these errors.

The most important lesson to learn is that the integrated sector of education has to have the best educational program in America. We have to put the major resources, the major funding, the major rewards, the major new construction, and the best-trained teachers into a program in which *everyone will significantly and powerfully benefit in an integrated quality school system.* When you have that kind of school system, everyone will want to be a part of it. But it has to be the best school system around. The country's public and private school system is terrible. The private

---

*[Editor's Note: One-time U.S. Commissioner of Education and later chairman of the board of directors of the General Learning Corporation.]

†[Editor's Note: U.S. Commissioner of Education.]

school system can never beat the public school system if we do anywhere near the proper job in the latter. Federal funds are fundamental to the task. I am not suggesting merely the old formulation that we have to take the profit out of segregation; that is a negative way of looking at it. *I want to put the profit into integration.* I want a multiclass win, potentially an all-class win, with almost everybody benefiting from integrated education. This has to be planned and has to be paid for. Conceivably, it might not be super-expensive. In my opinion, the present costs of school systems are ridiculous. We mismanage them so badly, administer them so terribly, that if you gave over a school system as Christopher Jencks* and others have been suggesting to a college or a business or a labor union or a community group to run, I think you would soon find that it could be run a lot cheaper and a lot more effectively.

But my major point is that integrated education has to be developed on a basis of a coherent plan and that it has to be supported by ample federal funds. Local funds will not do it because if you use local taxes, the complaint will be heard that some are paying for the education of others. Too much of what has been happening in the development of integration in the United States has made it look like somebody has to lose by integration. So, in Chicago the Poles and Italians think they are going to lose. In other towns, the Puerto Ricans or the traditional American working class thinks it is going to lose. In other places, the middle class thinks it is going to lose. The fancy rationale of the liberal white American says that the school system is deteriorating and that while Negro children are catching up, his white children are being held back.

So we have to make terribly sure that nobody or practically nobody loses. I keep saying practically because there probably are some people who will lose. There usually are in any wide coalition. I want to minimize the number who will lose. I disagree very much that we have to take any power from somebody and give it to somebody else in order to have effective integration.

Role of Teachers

It is impossible to overstress the significance of the teachers and their organizations in this new coalition. The coalition must include the parents, the children, the teachers, the professionals who are involved as consultants, the new nonprofessionals, and technicians. One of the most positive things taking place in New York is the development around Intermediate School 201 in Harlem of a magnificent new unity of the parents† and some professionals, but unfortunately not the teachers. That is the key to the present impasse. A new trend has appeared: The teacher is the new scapegoat. Instead of the board of education, the "power structure," "Wall Street," capitalism, or Washington, it is now the little teacher—the little teacher who does not want to be transferred into Harlem. He is terrible. He does not like the idea of a transfer and his union does not like the idea of a transfer, and so they are awful. I just want to say that I do not think they are awful and I do think that is a bad way to build a coalition. *I would not want to transfer anybody to Harlem. I would want to take the teachers who are now in Harlem and make them the best teachers in America.* Long

---

*[Editor's Note: A contributing editor of *New Republic* and a free-lance writer on education and civil rights.]

†[Editor's Note: See also Dorothy S. Jones, "The Issues at I.S. 201: A View from the Parents' Committee" in this volume.]

years of experience in our very regressive school system do not necessarily improve teaching ability. I do not want your "experienced" teachers. I want to take all kinds of new teachers and build the training right into the Harlem schools because I do not expect these teachers have gotten it in their graduate schools or in their undergraduate training. I would build a coalition exactly around this kind of proposal. What I am suggesting about this coalition is that the teachers have to be a key part of it.

It is interesting that in a teaching audience like this—in contrast to what people will tell you about teachers—teachers will actually applaud when you tell them the frank truth about how they have gone through a school system which has actually hurt their teaching. People told me when I wrote the book, *The Culturally Deprived Child,*[1] that the book was antiteacher, and that teachers would hate it. The leading people on boards of education refused to say positive things about it because they said the book was antiteacher. Essentially, that has not turned out to be true.* Teachers are not disturbed by the fact that it is critical about teaching and they have not run away from the criticism. It is really the higher incompetents who pretend to speak for the teachers who really fear the criticism. The teachers know exactly what is going on in the classroom and know that they have not been helped to teach; nor have they been permitted to teach. So teachers do not need telling that they have yet to learn a great deal in twenty years of teaching. In fact, if these experienced teachers are brought into Harlem schools they must be retrained. I would want to draw on some of the positive things they have learned, of course, but I would not want to assume that because they have been in the schools for a long time they have learned a lot that made them very efficient teachers.

Integrated and Quality

An integrated quality school system, if it is to benefit all children, must embody two basic ideas. First of all, you must get away from the idea that bringing children up to grade norms is quality education. It is not. The grade norms are absurdly low and, as Dr. Aaron Lipton has suggested, the whole point is that we want to bring out the children's potential, which is a lot better than those grade norms.† The grade norms are based on the way children have been taught—and I know that is bad—so I am not in the least impressed by bringing children up to grade norms. My friends sometimes tell me that it would be nice to bring Negro children in segregated schools up to white norms of reading. And I have constantly said that I do not object to their trying for that goal, but I think it is a pretty low goal. That is not quality education at all, compared with what we know about technologies of improving children's learning.

The second basic point is the whole principle of accountability which has to be introduced into the schools and which many people fear. Let me put this into perspective. People who are trying to build segregated quality schools of Harlem these days tell me that the major things these schools need are Negro principals, Negro teachers, and the teaching of Negro history. These are, of course, excellent objectives. Nevertheless, you could put all those things into the school and not get better

---

[1] Harper & Row, 1962.

*[Editor's Note: In support of this statement, see Patrick J. Groff, "Culturally Deprived Children: Opinions of Teachers on the Views of Riessman" *Exceptional Children,* October, 1964.

†[Editor's Note: See "Day-to-Day Problems of Integration" in this volume.]

education. Do not think you have won an educational victory if you merely change the number of Negroes teaching in the schools. In Washington, D.C., schools, for example, there are many schools with high percentages of Negro teachers, and these are not by any means any better schools educationally. The children do not learn any better. So do not permit any substitution for the direct result you want.

It is educational accountability we should seek. That includes a wide range of things on which parents will need professional help in evaluating. The improvement on reading scores and achievement scores is a minimum. I want to also improve the child's *ability to learn—learning how to learn.* The child's attitude toward learning is very important to improve. Attitude is no substitute for learning, of course. I want to get the whole package—improved achievement, improved learning ability, improved interest in learning, so that the child can resist fall-back, so that he does not fall back when he gets a bad teacher next term or when he moves out of the neighborhood. These children move a great deal. You must build a great deal of learning power into them.

You probably know from the very recent Max Wolff study of Operation Head Start[2] that the improvements are rapidly diluted as soon as the children get into the regular school system. Our schools know how to destroy progress very quickly and efficiently. It is a sad fact that I had much earlier predicted just such an outcome in Operation Head Start. The shortcomings of the schools have to be dealt with in their place—in the schools. You cannot substitute preschool learning or any special stimulation for changing the schools themselves.

In the educational attempts that we have seen in the integration field during the last number of years, one reason why we have not been more successful is that the emphasis has been on the human relations workshops for teachers. They are, I think, quite limited. I have taught them, too, so I can say it readily. What they do not do is teach teachers how to teach; and they do not teach them how to teach within the new context of desegregated classes and desegregated schools. This is what the teachers desperately want and this is what they have not received. This is part of the total point that I am making. To make quality desegregated education the best in the country, we do not need human relations workshops or exhortation about the morality of integration. What is really needed is educational program, new curriculum, new technology, new assistants in the classrooms, and how to use all these efficiently. You also need teaching machines, and to learn how to use them. And perhaps most of all we need to let the teachers in on decision making in the schools. I am not saying that to you just because you are teachers; I say it to everybody, even principals. Principals really run schools, you know. Frequently, it is they who overpower the schools and the teachers, and exclude the teachers from decision making.

I am calling here for planning the most advanced kind of educational programs. I happen to think that they would be placed best in the context of the educational park. If there were a concerted demand on the part of the teachers, parents, and the integration movement for an intensive development of educational parks, I think there would be strong federal support for them. I think *an educational park movement* should become a major proposal of integration groups. And while I am at it I would

---

[2] Max Wolff and Annie Stein, "Head Start Six Months Later," *Phi Delta Kappan*, March, 1967.

like to say that I think integration groups should make proposals. I do not think they should accept the posture which they frequently have adopted: "We've told you what's wrong, fellow, and it's your fault. Get with it and straighten it out. If you don't, I'm going to be back there with a demonstration next week. We can't help you work it out. —It's not our responsibility—it's yours." Well, that is a stupid surrender. It might be a very principled position; I am not sure that it is, but it is tactically ludicrous. What happens is that you leave the job of proposing plans in the hands of ineffectual people who frequently do not have the same goals you have. Their objective frequently is how to find a plan that will either fool you for a while (Operation Head Start was exactly that) or will divert you. They usually produce the plan which has the least difficulty in it but is by no means the best plan.

I perfectly well understand that not every integration leader and every person involved in the integration movement is going to sit down and make a plan, but I think there again comes the coalition, the team, where you seek out the best professional consultation in the country that you can get—and you can get it. Dr. Kenneth Clark helped devise that plan for I.S. 201 in Harlem, with a group of educational experts. The point I am making is that civil rights leaders have to be involved in developing specific proposals so that you do not get a watered-down proposal from the boards of education, saying, "Oh, yes, we like educational parks. We'll plan one for ten years." And that is exactly what they have done. They have a couple on the drawing boards, and they are doing them poorly. As Max Wolff points out, you could develop an educational park in three to six months, phasing in the school buildings that already exist, moving toward the ultimate construction.* You do not have to wait ten years. Nor is it necessarily expensive. It might be the framework in which we pull in the best educational innovation that can be organized.

I would include a very judicious use of programmed learning directed toward individual instruction in skills. But in order to make programmed learning effective you have to contact children first; you have to get them interested in looking at the learning program; thus, you need some excellent contact-teaching techniques such as the use of games, role-playing, etc., contact techniques for getting the child interested. Incidentally, there are some contact teachers who are excellent but they do not get any further than initial contact. They get the child interested, but he does not learn much after that. But these contact specialists have a significant place in the reorganization of the educational system. I would use movies for contact, educational TV, and so on. Then turn them loose on the educational programs. Once you are involved you can go very fast. And then we could have some teachers who are specialists on teaching children how to learn, helping them to learn. Teachers should be trained very rapidly in everything we know about teaching children how to learn, including school know-how; how to take tests; how to study; how to listen; how to make notes. You find, by the way, that children's ability to learn also increases marvelously by the use of helper-principle; that is, when a child teaches another child, both youngsters improve, both the child teacher and the child receiving the help. These are the kinds of things I would want to introduce in this new exciting kind of school.

I would also use lots of nonprofessional aides. These aides have been taught how to function as remedial reading assistants. D. G. Ellson developed a technique for

---

*[Editor's Note: See "The Educational Park" in this volume.]

doing this that requires only ten hours of instruction for the aide.* Teachers should be able to obtain reading aides, nonprofessionals, who have had no advanced education but who can assist teachers in the classroom on a remedial basis while the teachers work with other groups. They can provide important assistance, especially in view of the manpower shortage among teachers. We need many of these assistants in the schools and we need to develop something more for them; that is, a career line for them. Large numbers of poor people and minority people should be hired in these positions as teacher aides and their services should be combined with further education to enable them to become assistant teachers, associate teachers, and finally full-fledged teachers. We now have colleges around the country—and some of your community colleges in and around Chicago might be very interested in such plans—where they send in a clinical professor. He goes into the field and works with the teacher aides, helps to train them, helps to pattern courses for them for college credit such as early childhood education. This allows them to move up, to get further jobs, get credit for the job experience and in five or six years, we hope, become full-fledged teachers. I cannot tell you that that has happened, because it has just begun, but it is the main idea in the new "careers for the poor" concept.†

The point I am making is that the hiring of minority-group people from the neighborhood to work within the school, with a chance to move up, may be a very significant approach to integrated education. Moreover, it helps the teacher get rid of many nonprofessional tasks which you know all teachers perform: taking attendance, helping children on with their boots, running moving picture machines, taking students on trips. We have listed some seventy-three such teacher tasks,‡ only one of which is teaching. We would like to see them have a little more time for teaching and a little less for some of these other tasks which we feel we can train other people to perform rather rapidly. This is the kind of new school of the very near future that I am talking about. In New York City, they are planning for an ideal school in the year 2000. I wish they would plan one for next year.

In the integrated quality schools we are talking about here, you would want to have an intensive after-school program to help the children who are behind in reading, for example. Frequently, they will be Negro. Recently, I was working in a paired school program where I was proposing this plan. A Negro parent got up and said: "I don't like that after-school program you're talking about; I think it is going to be segregated." I replied: "I think it is going to be quite segregated—not completely, but I think it is going to be largely black." And they said, "Really?" "Yes, but I think it's going to lead to a powerfully improved, integrated school through all of the rest of the day. And I think anybody can go to that after-school program who needs help. I'm not going to restrict it to Negroes by any means." Questions like these have to be

---

*[Editor's Note: See D. G. Ellson, Larry Barber, T. L. Engle, and Leonard Kampwerth, "Programed Tutoring: A Teaching Aid and a Research Tool," *Reading Research Quarterly*, Vol. 1, No. 1 (1965).]

†[Editor's Note: See Arthur Pearl and Frank Riessman, *New Careers for the Poor: The Non-Professional Revolution*. New York: Free Press, 1965.]

‡[Editor's Note: A systematic statement can be found in Frank Riessman, "Issues in Training the New Nonprofessional," *Poverty and Human Resources Abstracts*, September-October, 1967, pp. 5-17.]

faced honestly, and I think the parents were very willing to see it at that point. They realized they were being a bit mechanical in their first formulations.

Principals and Principles

Significantly, also, I think that we are going to have to recruit and train large numbers of Negro principals and teachers. In New York, however, school authorities report that they have a lot of trouble finding Negro principals. They looked around for people who were potential candidates, and trained them to take the tests and so on, but not enough of them passed these fabulous tests that have been developed. I suggest as a temporary alternative that we might try on-the-job training. How about having a Negro *principal-intern* work in one of the schools alongside a principal for a year and then phase into the job or at least be evaluated for it? You could waive the examination. I know that will trouble some traditionalists, but we have to start to think about the difference between credentials and qualifications. The principals who are in the schools today certainly have the credentials; too many, however, do not have the qualifications. I am sorry to say these are the ones holding on to the traditional routine for dear life.

My favorite illustration of this is a recent event in the New York schools. You may recall the case of the long-haired high school students. A high school principal said, "You ought to cut that hair; get with it, buddy." The boys did not want to cut their hair and there was a big argument about. Finally, the superintendent of schools, in one of his most heroic and breathtaking stands, opposed the principal and said long hair was all right. Don't you think the principals' association in New York got together to defend the principal as having had the right to get the kids to cut their hair? It is interesting how people use the concept "rights" in a nonsensical manner. The next thing we may expect to see is principals picketing the board of education, demanding their rights to stop people from having their hair long. Many principals just don't know what time it is. I would seriously take their behavior as an index of their incompetency. This is the kind of thing that goes on in the school system. So I am not impressed by the tests that admit principals like that one. I begin to wonder whether we should not use the tests inversely: Principals who fail those tests might be better people to put in charge.

Separate, Unequal

There is an increasingly powerful trend toward accepting segregated schools on both sides of the fence. Many of the white and working middle-class goups which have always been ready to accept segregated schools are now being joined by Negro separationists who are calling for quality segregated education. Of course, this is not just occurring in New York but it is getting quite a lot of press in New York as you may well know. A lot of people have come to believe that this is the best that can be achieved and have, with unbelievable speed, capitulated to the idea. I am not at all sure it is possible to have much quality segregated education. Apart from this, however, I think it is a tremendous capitulation to the backlash. I think that the people who are supporting it are deceiving themselves and deceiving other people by putting it in a militant garb. The whole black power stance holds that this position is very militant, activist, and aggressive. I think it is a highly reactionary one, and a very dangerous turnback in the society. In New York, many of the very same people who previously demanded militantly instantaneous integrated education are now willing to accept, with this new militant garb, so-called quality segregated education.

I know of no place in America where Negroes have obtained quality segregated education. I do know that in the schools where desegregation is occurring, there has been a distinct improvement in the educational performance of Negro children. This has most recently been pointed out in the Coleman study.[3] Nationwide data gathered for the Office of Education indicated that regardless of other deficiencies in the situation, Negro children definitely improve in the integrated school situation while white children did not suffer.[4] The overall data indicate that the typical white fear—of white children suffering while Negro children are catching up—is just not true. The Negro children are catching up in those schools and they are by no means great schools. I do not know of much data which shows this is happening in segregated schools.

I think it is certainly true that not every school in every school system in the United States can immediately become integrated. In central Harlem it is ridiculous to talk about immediate integration and therefore one may have, temporarily, quality segregated education. I would like to warn against making a virtue of what seems to be a necessity. In looking at something that is hard to do, let us not make it impossible to do. A number of realistic plans have been suggested, even in that situation. Large numbers of schools on the fringes of Harlem could be, without busing, integrated into educational parks. In central Harlem this is not immediately possible. But I certainly think that while one might accept quality segregated education situations, one should not sacrifice for a minute the basic goal of working toward integrated quality education. Where it is at the moment practically impossible, you can phase to permit segregated quality education. Make sure, however, that you get as much *quality* there as possible. My own guess is that you will not easily get much quality. I think that it is much more likely that the major funds in the country will be provided largely for white people and will go for an educational system in which white children benefit. My whole point has been that you must produce an educational system in which both groups benefit powerfully. That is why the educational park and integrated educational plans are the key. Consequently, I disagree with my separationist friends who believe it is going to be relatively easy to get this quality segregated education in Harlem.

Some believers in quality segregated education think people are going to give money out of fear of riots. To think you can get far with fear money is a misunderstanding as well as bad tactics. You get much more money *when everybody is going to benefit—when conscience and benefit work together.* I think it is most tactically meaningful to combine conscience, ideology, and benefits for all groups. Quality segregated education, then, is a temporary phase, one that may be temporarily necessary. Do not by any means build it up.

Ancient Immigrants

I do not at all subscribe to the popular theory nowadays that Negroes are first going to organize themselves as Negroes and will ultimately be absorbed in other

---

[3] James S. Coleman, *et al., Equality of Educational Opportunity*, 2 vols., U.S. Government Printing Office, Washington, D.C., 1966.

[4] *Ibid.* Vol. 1, pp. 29, 307, 331.

groups in the society. I call this an immigrant theory of history. The immigrant theory of history is that the other immigrant groups in America, such as the Poles and Italians, did absorb. I would like to point out, though, that while the Jews, Poles, and Italians were doing that, the Negroes were already around for three hundred years. The Negroes were there, and in much, much larger numbers than all the Poles, Jews, and Italians put together. So anybody who tells you that the Negroes are going through some kind of phase, like the Irish did to become policemen, should take a second look at history.

The significant thing is that Negroes are demanding the most progressive actions in society, and in coalition with a large number of other groups can win those progressive things for all Americans. Separated from them they are not going to win anything. Essentially what is needed to make the coalition real is a job program; a major job and career program which would hire millions of poor people. A million poor people being hired as aides for the school system and for the welfare program would cost five billion dollars, which is not a lot of money. These jobs for nonprofessionals would produce a fantastic change in the society where people help other people, help professionals, help themselves, earn a living, and move out of poverty.

While fighting for integrated education, we must, unhappily, also fight for quality segregated education. I want to point out that there are a number of specific dangers to keep in mind. Booker T. Washington long ago called for quality segregated education and you know what we got. What we really need is a *basic educational leap for Negroes and minority groups in America.* My own hunch is that you are going to get a bigger relative improvement in the white segregated group. There is a great deal of self-deception developing among people in this area.

I also want to reiterate that the new involvement of the community in education is a very exciting new trend, and it is again reflected in the I.S. 201 situation in Harlem. When you have accountability, you are demanding that the school move toward increasing integration, increasing improvement of grades, and learning how to learn—you demand that the school do this and you make the schools live up to this. You do not demand instantaneous integration, that the whole thing be achieved overnight; that can only lead to disillusionment. The new community involvement is part of *a new bill of rights* that includes the right to a job, a career, and an income, and I think it is very crucial. But I want to warn that we may get a good deal of community involvement, become optimistic, get a few things changed, but the children may not improve their education. You have got to keep their eye on the education ball. We have got to demand of the schools, specific accountability, specific improvements of various kinds in phases—at designated points in time. It is not sufficient improvement to say that teachers are getting in-service training, that there are Negro principals, and Negro history is being taught. That is good, all those things are good; but they must lead to educational improvement, and this has to be measured and evaluated. I would like to warn the community movement in a sense to keep their eye very much on classroom improvement.

Let me close with the reiteration of the theme that I have been trying to stress. I do not think integrated education in America is by any means dead; I do not think the backlash is going to be long-lived; I think there is a need to move on to a much higher level that we failed to attain in our first integration effort. We are going to need to work for wide coalitions, with large numbers of people in society benefiting measurably from integration. I mean benefiting quite specifically in terms of obtaining specific educational improvement in the public school system, that no middle-class white child is getting in the private school system. If we build more meaningful jobs for minority groups, then white workers, who fear being automated out of jobs and are now afraid of the Negro, will not be afraid of him. As you move toward fuller employment, not simply expanding the economy, but by producing public service jobs in the public sector, you provide a good for everybody. You provide jobs for everybody if those people work as school aides, welfare aides, health aides, or research aides; you improve the service for everybody, you push up wages for everybody, and you break the back of the economic fear of integration. And this is what has been missing—the moral dimension alone is not sufficient. *You must make integration economically and educationally advantageous.* You must demand funds and organization for this. The school system would then have to produce the best educational programs, and not human relations workshops, in the integrated schools. The expense would come out of essentially federal funds which increasingly are going to be moved toward expenditures in welfare and education. I think we have to arouse the integration movement and demand those funds which have to be spent. When this kind of philosophy permeates the entire integration movement, I think you will quickly overturn the backlash that has been developing, and the kind of lukewarmness that has developed with a great many people. The major emphasis that I am calling for is the reactivation of the movement for integrated quality education.

NEW FORCES OPERATING IN EDUCATIONAL DECISION MAKING

Dan W. Dodson *is the director of the Center for Human Relations, New York University. The following selection was originally an address presented on December 2, 1966, to the Fifteenth Annual Working Conference of the New York State Citizens Committee for Public Schools. For many years Dr. Dodson was editor of the pioneer publication* Journal of Educational Sociology. *He has conducted numerous studies of school segregation and authored many remedial plans for specific communities. Dr. Dodson is a member of the editorial advisory board of* INTEGRATED EDUCATION *magazine.*

All of us are beginning to examine the context in which educational decisions are made in the community and in the state. We are beginning to look at the changing relationships that are taking place, changing relationships that directly affect the decisions that are being made and the way in which they are being made. These forces not only impinge on the educational decisions, but on the whole decision-making process in our society.

Fundamentally, these are changing relationships occasioned by the shifting of power relationships in the community. They represent a growing understanding of the function of power and its use in decision making at local community levels.

It is no secret that by and large the schools have been the handmaiden of the power arrangement of the community, and their programs, their mythology, their

From *Integrated Education,* **June/July 1967. Reprinted by permission of the author.**

rituals, and their methodology are validated on and perfected and implemented through this power arrangement.

Heretofore, the greatest competency of a superintendent was to be able to play golf so that he could meet the power structure of the community on the links and make the decisions that directed the schools' programs in his community.

This is no longer so. Increasingly, there is a shuffling of power arrangements and, by and large, this is where we are caught in the hassles we face at the community level.

Not the least of these shuffles, of course, is that which has been occasioned by the shift in population. All of us have had the experience of these changing power patterns as populations have shifted.

I lived in Yonkers during the 1950's when Education Commissioner James E. Allen, Jr., threatened to withhold funds unless they acted to improve their schools. The move from New York to this suburb had begun. "Beyond the Alps" was the way they referred to that section in the eastern part of Yonkers that was across the ridge from the Hudson, where tremendous new growth and development was taking place. The city fathers were slow in getting around to provide the educational assistance for this new group. This out-migration from the city they referred to as the "Bronxification of Yonkers." To the old timers, it meant a new population coming into the community, as had happened in all the stable, staid little communities of the suburbs.

It meant new groups challenging power arrangements in the community. It created the kinds of conflicts that have made us all sensitive to this function of power and the redistribution of power as populations change.

Most dramatic of these population changes, of course, has been that of the great metropolitan inner cities. Here we have the dramatic out-migrations to the suburbs of middle-class people, who are primarily white. We have had the in-migration of minority, ethnically identifiable peoples—Negroes and Puerto Ricans for the most part. With this has come, of course, the shifting of power.

Our new challenge is to the structure of education as it has attempted to serve communities wherever they may be. But most dramatic has been the thrust of the marginal citizen, the newcomer as he is turning to political leverage to alter the power arrangements of the community, for, by and large, politics is the major way through which power is redistributed in a democratic society.

And if you have the suffrage, if you have the ballot, you can ultimately make alliances, and with astuteness in the use of the ballot you can challenge the power arrangements politically. If you do not have it (or do not use it), the alternative is to take to the street, and this is what we have had, of course, in the civil rights revolution where people did not have access to the ballot or the immediate sophistication to use its leverage against the majority.

But one of the most dramatic things in America today, in my judgment, is taking place in these large cities, as the newcomer is finding increased political sophistication and is restructuring the time-honored arrangements of the society. The power patterns that have been those of traditional status and economic privilege are coming to be challenged by this new-found power through politics.

I need only to remind you of the way this had happened on the national scene to suggest its significance in all these local communites. When Truman was elected by such a narrow margin and carried such states as Illinois, California, and Ohio by such narrow margins, the significance of the Negro vote in closely contested political elections was plainly evident. Consequently, it was not extraordinary that the supreme court found it could now reverse the *Plessy v. Ferguson* decision of 1896. It was understandable that it could, in the *Baker v. Carr* decision,* rule that the time-honored rural domination of these urban places was unconstitutional. This election of Truman brought the executive arm of government into the civil rights picture. The recognition of this emerging political power in the six most populous states, where this narrow margin existed between the two political parties, ultimately changed the whole pattern of American life.

If you believe that the whole civil rights interest and concern is the result of a change of heart of the American people rather than this change of political power, look at the backlash. Look at the fact that, with perhaps a half-dozen exceptions, no civil rights issue has been put on the statute books by popular referendum. Every time you have asked the people if they wanted to mix, they overwhelmingly have said no. Or, look at the Indian who does not have the power and does not have the leverage, and you get something of what is involved in this restructuring of power relations.

In our own community of New York, where I live, the last mayoralty election is tremendously to the point and suggestive of the growing sophistication of the use of the ballot. Ninety percent of the Negroes and Puerto Ricans are registered Democrats; yet there was enough splitting of ballots in Bedford-Stuyvesant and Harlem that Lindsay was elected mayor although the rest of the city government was Democratic. Or in Virginia, where 90 percent of the vote went to the Johnson ticket a few years back, 90 percent went against the Byrd machine in the same district and defeated the Byrd machine there in all except young Harry Byrd's candidacy. This is suggestive of the kind of sophistication that is coming with this new-found power for a new group.

Caught in the throes of urban life, urbanization, developing this kind of sophistication in bringing pressure to bear, political pressure to redistribute power, these groups are exhibiting one of the most exciting things, I think, that is happening in America today. I wish I had time to talk a little bit about this. Let me just say quickly a kind of thing I think significant.

I have just been working with George Stoddard on a study of the socioeconomic background of the Borough of Brooklyn for the Brooklyn Institute of Arts and Science.

In 1960, 71.6 percent of the people living in that borough were either foreign-born, children of foreign-born, Negro or Puerto Rican. Of a 2.6 million population— the fourth largest concentration of people in the country, following New York City, Chicago, and Los Angeles—71.6 percent of this population was new and marginal to the inner city. Between 1950 and 1964, Brooklyn exported roughly a fourth of its white population to the suburbs. How many middle-class Negroes were also exported, I do not know. But if you can see and feel this motion in the cities then you can understand. See the input of the great inner cities: this raw stuff of human nature—human material—these marginal newcomers anchored to lesser loyalties, less educated, more despised, hated, driven by whatever brought them to the cities. See the export: these well-sandpapered people who are now able to live in the suburbs

---

*[Editor's Note: A case decided by the U.S. supreme court in 1962 holding that a federal issue existed when a state legislature failed to reapportion seats for 61 years and thus left some districts under- and some over-represented.]

and fit the suburban image. Then you can understand this involvement, this transmutation that is taking place in the great encounter, that is taking place between input and output. I think you would say that this is the most dramatic and exciting thing that is happening in American life.

It is where the human estate is being changed and out of it is coming something magnificent and wonderful. The major things we see, of course, are the gang fights and the muggings. We do not see as goodness this great thing that is happening. With it is coming sophistication in dealing with these inner city problems—and they are going to be dealt with. Middle-class whites can try to escape this encounter out there in the suburbs, but with the leverage these groups are beginning to develop, not only in this state but in the nation, it is certain that the resource with which the cities can carry out their function is going to be provided one way or another. You might as well understand this and understand the realism of it.

It also means that as this sophistication is taking place, we are moving to deal with the problems of the community on a shared power base rather than on the basis of the power structure of yesteryear making decisions for "these people." And I mean by "these people" not only these newcomers and marginal people but also everybody for whom decisions were made in these years past.

Out of it is coming the type of great encounter that we are caught up in over Intermediate School 201 in Manhattan, the encounter over the problems of the suburban communities in Long Island and Westchester like the Malvernes, the Wyandanches or the Greenburgh No. 8's, or wherever they are. People who yesteryear had the decisions made for them are coming to stand in their dignity or selfhood and say, "We demand to be accepted as peers in the decision-making process and you are no longer going to make the decisions for us. We are going to be involved in the decision making."

This is pretty hard on a superintendent of schools and for some boards of education, especially the elected boards that are elected by the majority with majority rule. The politically appointed boards have to be a little more amenable to the new and emerging power.

We are coming now to new forces that are involved in the decision making. One of the forces is this emerging population that says, "We are tired of having the decisions made for us. We are going to demand that you share power with us and politically we are going to require it." If they cannot do it otherwise, and where the disparity cannot be dealt with through politics, they have been taking it to the street.

Within the school another new force is being exerted. Teachers have been second-class citizens in this process through these years. Decisions were made for them. In very few instances were their interests and needs considered by the powers that be. Very rapidly now the teachers' groups are organizing and demanding that they, too, be allowed to come to the communal decision-mapping table on matters of education as peers in the process.

Thus, the board of education cannot take its cue any longer from the economic and social status arrangements of the community alone, but is going to have to take into account not only the interests of the emerging people, but also the interests of the people who are presiding over the classrooms. This is a new dimension and it is hard for some to take because, you know, you get cozy with the power arrangements and it is easier to live in a familiar situation. So that when you come to an I.S. 201 situation, for instance, you have the emergence of a community group challenging the kind of education the community is offering, challenging the very basic issue of whether you can provide quality education there. They are saying fundamentally that if racism is so great in our communities that you cannot desegregate the schools, then is it not too great for white teachers sent into ghettos essentially as carpetbaggers, sent into the communities from outside as control agents, is not such racism too great for these white teachers to elicit creatively from our children? If so, how do we come to the encounter and work this thing out? Furthermore, the emerging people are saying, when a decision is imminent here come the teachers walking in with their organized power and vetoing the proposal.

The boards of education and superintendents of schools are not any longer trying to pacify groups, but are coming into a new role—the role of negotiator, trader, referee, umpire, whatever you want to call it, but whose great skill in the future will need to be much more that of political science, as they learn how to deal with these power blocks who come to confrontation with each other in the community on an organized basis.

The backlashers, the forelashers, and everybody else come to communal decision making on a power basis. They meet as peers in an honest relationship in which one is not going to be manipulated by the other, but where they come as peers in power. They sit down at the conference table or whatever kind of places we provide for them (and we need to think about what kinds of places these are) to make decisions that will be shared power decisions rather than one segment of the community making the decisions for everybody.

This is the realism, I believe, of the kind of era into which we are moving. It is an era in which the skill and ingenuity of dealing with the process through which we are going needs to be enhanced. The skills of human relations are needed as we negotiate these things. The capacity to interpret in the process the significance and meaning of education so that children are not hurt in the process must be tremendously stepped up.

I submit that out of this shift of power is coming something that is precious in spite of all the disruption it is creating in these communities. People really learn attitudes, I believe, when they are really caught up in the significant encounters in which they have to learn to a purpose.

I was looking the other day at the data collected by one of the denominations on attitudes they expressed on race and matters of this sort. It is one of the older, better disciplined denominations with a better religious education program. These data had been broken down by inner city, suburb, great plains and so on. I would submit to you that—on the basis of these data—these parishioners by and large believed the opposite of what the church had been teaching since time immemorial. The great learning which does come, comes from being caught up in the significant encounters in which we have to validate our position against the others.

I was recently up one night until midnight at a meeting of the Inkster School District outside Detroit. Here is a little place just beyond Dearborn where years ago Ford brought some Negro workers. Through the years they developed almost a solid Negro community with only a few whites. And they were arguing on this issue. Whites had not turned out to meetings. This is a reversed role, because Negroes are in the majority out there, so they are meeting power arrangements in a different way. Whites had not turned out—they showed about the same apathy that Negroes are accused of having elsewhere—until their interests were threatened. Then the whites turned out in about equal numbers and the dialogue went on, a very significant dialogue, until twelve o'clock at night. People who were involved in it were tremendously impressed with the amount of growth and the amount of understanding that came out of this confrontation, just because people were caught up in this significant type of encounter.

Underlying Inkster's problem and others we will have to deal with, is the antiquated political structure that denies the majority political leverage. I do not mean, now, just racial minorities, but I mean any groups that are caught up in this kind of thing.

I am impressed, for instance, with the problems of Hartsdale and Greenburgh No. 8 in Westchester. How do you get two school districts which should merge to do so? But one district has Negroes in it; consequently, the other does not want to be identified with them. So you put it to a vote. Well! They are not going to vote themselves into one district. This structure makes it impossible to achieve quality education on any viable basis. Around the suburbs of New York, unless it is going to be a checkerboard arrangement, black and white—black in this one where they happen to get in somewhere—the whites in the other who seal themselves off in these little political turfs which the Negro could not get into with a blowtorch—unless you are going to have this sort of thing, these political boundaries have to be altered. I do not believe they can remain in the test of time as viable situations. I do not believe they can be dealt with by the approaches we have today. I think we are going to have to face up to this, even if the court ultimately has to say that this is a violation of the rights of some. Judge Skelly Wright has already intimated that he believes the courts could not overlook too long this suburban-urban inequality of opportunity occasioned by political segregation in the suburbs.*

It is not only the race factor I am talking about. It is the kind of thing that Inkster is in relation to Dearborn. It is the relation of a Levittown in Long Island, completely saturated with low-income housing which is filled with children, to communities with middle- and high-cost housing. In Levittown our projections indicated—and I have not checked to see if these projections have held up—that by 1963 they would have a tax base of less than $2500 per child on which to provide their community services for their children in a state whose comparable tax base at the time was $15,000 per child.

These inequalities of educational opportunity rise from the kind of political boundaries that exist. They preclude people using their political leverage to change the situation. Here, somehow, we have got to find a way to help to ventilate this. I think it is one of the things to which we need to address ourselves.

I do not believe that you can have the inequality of education that exists between some of these communities side by each, and have the dominant group live in unshared privilege without its becoming fundamentally corrupting. I think the problem of dealing with this in these years ahead—some of you who are in some of these cozy places are going to have to take a new look at it—because some way, the power leverage in this state, at least of the newly emerged groups, newly emerging

---

*[Editor's Note: See "The Washington, D.C., School Case" in this volume.]

power blocs, I believe is going to bring you to the confrontation in the near future. Consequently, it seems to me that the big issue on which we are grappling today is this issue of power leverage and how we restructure the society. And it means that we are moving through political action to do a lot of these things where we have the access to the ballot.

It means on the other hand how the group itself, how any group, can make its interests felt in the communal decision making.

As we become increasingly interdependent in this society, it becomes possible for the smallest group among us to create sufficient disruption, if it so desires, to bring the rest to heel. This operates internally as well as locally. Very rapidly the art of destruction is going to be great enough and cheap enough and plentiful enough that the smallest nation among us can blow the rest off the face of the earth.

And no longer is the kind of force that England used to hold an empire together—on which the sun never set—going to be the pattern that holds a world together. Increasingly, the least among us is going to be able to demand a seat at the conference table and require that the total of interests work through shared relationships for the totality.

We had better be learning these skills in these local communities as we come to these great confrontations with each other. We had better realize that the smallest power among us can create disruption enough to block the whole.

The New York subway drivers, for instance, demonstrated it to us in New York in a hurry. They created enough dysfunction in a highly complicated, intricate system that it brought the totality to heel.

Out of this, I believe, comes the new concept of selfhood for man when no one is then compromised in integrity of his selfhood because he feels himself powerless. Increasingly, as he demonstrates his capacity to use power, he shakes off the apathies that have characterized so much of our inner city slums and begins to move in participation and take the responsibilities that go with it. In this context it seems to me new forces are emerging that are going to require our boards of education and superintendents of schools to move into new approaches to the issue of decision making. If children are not going to get hurt in this process, we are going to have to develop new skills with which to approach this conflict of interests. People must honestly come to face each other and honestly say that we have our differences and ask how we reconcile and compromise and how do we work them out to some sort of viable solution.

From this process will come a new sense of education. It will not be that we are doing something for "those people." All the community will feel that it is involved in the dynamics of the decision-making process and a new sense of worth will emerge from it.

This may be threatening to some who feel that their status is jeopardized. It may be there will be a lot of backbiting and all the stereotypes that are always slung around about "these people not being capable of decision making." These are attempts to discredit them, of course, in the demands of what they want. There is no guarantee that sometimes groups with new-found power are not going to abuse it. They have no corner on the market because power has been abused by everybody who has ever had it. But America has a great skill in socializing power that is used in arbitrary and capricious ways. We have a great capacity for dealing with it in the democratic society. The Pure Food and Drug Act and the Interstate Commerce Commission or our Fair Employment Practices Act say you shall not abuse the power. If it is abused, it is socialized.

Men will be tremendously threatened because they fear that groups with new-found power will not make responsible decisions. But I would submit to you that there cannot be responsible decisions until there is responsibility for making the decisions. The growth and responsibility come out of taking the responsibility, and you see this in tremendously exciting ways as you see these "little people" moving into the mainstream of the community.

But the superintendent of schools and the staff who work with him are going to also have to understand this and understand how to work with it in new dimensions if we are going to avoid a lot of flack in these years ahead as the establishment of education is brought to this new encounter. It is going to be a wholesome thing for the establishment, as well as a learning experience for those who are underneath.

I say only one other thing. In the process of these new groups reaching for power, there will emerge a new morality that will bring our living arrangements more in line with our protestations. We have given lip service to a lot of this in the past. But the great documents by which we live were not written by people who were on top of the power heap of the society, writing rationalizations as to why they deserved to be there and stay there. They were written by the people who were making the upreach to selfhood and challenging the power patterns of the society.

And those who were on top abused the power. Henry Lloyd once said: "Seldom does the new conscience when it seeks a teacher to declare to men what is wrong, find him in the dignitaries of the church, the state, the culture that is. The higher the rank, the closer the tie that binds these to what is but ought not to be."

The only guarantee we have that there will be a new morality that will check all this movement toward privilege and pulling apart into some suburb, or check the use of power to create prestige patterns, is for the little people to learn how also to use power—the people who have not been in on the decision making to be there, and to require that the decisions be made on a new basis in the future. I am confident that out of this will come a goodness that all of us will recognize in the years ahead—although it may be a process now that may be a hair shirt to us.

DESEGREGATING CITY SCHOOLS

John H. Fischer *is president of Teachers College, Columbia University. Below is the text of an address to the School Administrators Conference, a meeting co-sponsored by the National Urban League and Teachers College, Columbia University, and held on June 17, 1966. At the time of the Brown decision in 1954, Dr. Fischer was superintendent of schools in Baltimore and supervised the disestablishment of legal segregation in that city. He is now a member—along with Kenneth B. Clark—of an advisory committee on integration policy to New York State Education Commissioner James E. Allen, Jr., and in that capacity helped to prepare "The Allen Report on New York City Schools," which appears in this volume.*

From *Integrated Education,* **December 1966/January 1967. Reprinted by permission of the author.**

Assuring all American children equal access to good education has never been easy, and it is not easy now, but the conditions in which the effort must be carried forward are vastly more favorable now than they have been. For one thing, in both our own country and the rest of the world the attitude toward education is more serious—one might almost call it more desperate—than ever before.

A generation ago when George Counts asked, "Dare the schools build a new social order?" the question was considered as little more than the extravagant language of a visionary liberal. Whatever it was the country needed in the depths of the depression, few expected to find it in the schools.

But that depression itself, the wars that followed, the technological revolution, and now, most recently, a massive and worldwide social upheaval have put a different face upon the matter.

President Johnson summarized the shift when he said that "one great truth" he had learned is that "the answer for all of our national problems, the answer for all the problems of the world comes down when you really analyze it to one simple word—education." In one sense the President only echoes in his own words what all his predecessors have said in theirs about the dependency of democracy on popular education, but Mr. Johnson is not content merely to talk about that relationship. Sensing and leading the mood of the country, he has made the improvement of education and the extension of access to it a cornerstone of his entire domestic policy, and most recently has proposed also a strong new program of international education.

The significance of what has happened since the end of World War II, and particularly since 1954, is that we have begun seriously to consider the full implications of the relationship between democracy and education in more than institutional terms. We are facing up squarely to the fundamental proposition that to limit a man's education is to limit his freedom. This is what the problem of school desegregation in its broadest meaning is all about.

What is required, therefore, is much more than the mere proclamation of a new policy of equality. To be sure, the educational opportunities of Negro Americans must be equalized with those of their white neighbors, but equalization must be accompanied by prompt and vigorous action to improve the Negro's access to those opportunities and, further, to increase the inducement most Negroes now have to use the opportunities. Until, in all three respects, the American of Negro ancestry enjoys full parity with his white neighbor, the Negro citizen will inevitably continue to depress the composite level of American society, and that society will continue to depress his standing as a man.

In a world in which education is essential to virtually every form of social, economic, political, and personal advancement, it is pointless to argue that the schools need only follow the lead of other segments of society. The schools will perform their functions more effectively, of course, if they enjoy the support of a favorable community climate, but the absence of such a climate can never be considered an adequate excuse for the schools' failure to stand for what is educationally sound and morally defensible. Those charged with the leadership of educational policy and practice carry a very special responsibility. But those who lead other important segments of public and private activity bear comparable obligations to support school board members and the professional educators when they offer sound leadership.

In approaching the educational task, it may be well to consider some salient facts. One is that a school which enrolls largely Negro students is almost universally considered to be of lower status and less desirable than one that is attended wholly or mainly by white students. Regardless of the quality of the building, the competence of the staff, or the size of classes a school composed of three-fourths Negro children is viewed by both races, almost without exception, as inferior to one in which the proportions are reversed. Whether such appraisals are present is beside the point. The schools that are known as Negro schools are so often inferior in fact that such generalized attitudes must be expected to persist even though good schools can occasionally be found in Negro neighborhoods. The point is that genuinely first-rate schools in Negro communities have been so scarce that anyone who wishes to demonstrate that an institution known as a Negro school can produce first-rate results must be prepared to accept a substantial burden of proof. A second fact closely related to this first one is the unfortunate psychological effect upon the individual child of belonging to a school where every pupil knows that, regardless of his personal attainments, the group with which he is identified is viewed as less able, less successful, and less acceptable than the majority of the community. This impact upon the self-image and motivation of the child is perhaps the most tragic outcome of segregated education. It emphasizes the dual need for immediate steps to achieve wherever possible a more favorable balance of races in the schools and for strenuous efforts to upgrade to full respectability and status every school in which enrollment cannot soon be balanced.

The action of the supreme court in striking down the legal basis of segregation in 1954* marked the climax of an obviously necessary first campaign, but the new problems which followed the Brown decision are even more complex than those which preceded it. The task now is not only to end segregation but to correct the effect it has produced. It is useless to debate whether *de jure* or *de facto* segregation is the worse evil. It was the supreme court that ruled "separate schools are inherently unequal" and led the court to strike down the laws supporting such schools. To argue now that although the statutes have been declared unjust the fact is acceptable requires a curious twist of logic indeed.

It would be irresponsible, however, to attempt to deal with a problem so deeply rooted in practice and custom and so often due to causes beyond the school's control without taking full account of its complexity. No solution is likely to be effective unless it is based on a realistic appraisal of the forces and factors involved. Yet, however complicated the situation or its final solutions may be, the clearly essential first step is a firm and forthright confrontation of the problem.

Some of the bitterest attacks on school authorities have been brought on not so much by the failure to integrate every school as by their apparent unwillingness to accept racial integration as a desirable educational goal. To justify this position, the argument is offered that the only acceptable policy is simple and complete non-discrimination, that unless the school is color-blind the spirit of the Brown decision and the Fourteenth Amendment is violated. What this approach overlooks or attempts to evade is that the consequences of earlier discrimination cannot be ended

---

*[Editor's Note: See Appendix A, "Text of Supreme Court Rulings (*Brown v. Board of Education.* . . .)."]

merely by ceasing the practices that produced them. Without corrective action the earlier effects will inevitably persist. The equal treatment of unequals, it was pointed out long ago, produces neither equity nor justice.

A second justification commonly offered for not taking positive action to integrate schools is the lack of evidence that better racial balance leads to better learning. It must be conceded that solid, objective evidence on this question is difficult if not impossible to find. But even if sound statistical data were available, they could not be expected to furnish per se an adequate basis for policy. The purpose of school integration is not merely or even primarily to raise the quantitative indices of scholastic achievement among Negro children, although such gains are obviously desirable. The main objective is rather to alter the character and the quality of the opportunities all children can enjoy, to provide them with incentives to succeed, and to foster a sense of intergroup acceptance in ways that are impossible when schools or students are racially, culturally, and socially isolated. The simplest statement of the situation to which school policy must respond is that few Negro American children now can grow up under conditions comparable with those available to white children. Of all the means for improving this situation that are subject to public control the most powerful is the public school. The Negro child must have a chance to be educated in a school where it is clear not only to him but to everybody else that he is not segregated and where his undisputed right to membership is acknowledged by his peers and by his elders of both races.

The most important social policies, including quite particularly educational policies, have never been based on scientific evidence but on a sense of what is equitable, just, and morally right. Our system of universal education was established not because research showed that the country would profit from it but because we were committed to the principles of equal opportunity and personal fulfillment. Our now widespread programs of special education for mentally and physically handicapped children were established not for scientific but for humanitarian reasons. Every major policy decision affecting education has been taken on grounds of its moral, social, and political desirability. It is after policy action is taken that science, technology, and professional skill are called upon to devise the most efficient and effective procedures for translating purpose into practice.

To be sure, some important gains in learning may come rather quickly in newly integrated schools, but lasting changes in the deep-seated behavior patterns of children and parents of both races cannot realistically be expected to occur overnight. What a school can boast of following the first grading period after integration is far less important than what happens to the quality of living in America during the next generation. Of course school integration will be needed and also more economic opportunities. Recently there have been improvements in the general social condition of Negro Americans, but the absence of adequate effort elsewhere only increases the urgency that prompt and energetic action be taken by the school.

The effort to identify and define *de facto* segregation has led to the concept of racial balance. While no single ratio of races can be established as universally right, there is no doubt that when the number or proportion of Negro children in a school exceeds a certain level, the school becomes less acceptable to both white and Negro parents. The point at which that shift begins is not clear, nor are the reasons for the variation adequately understood, but the results that typically follow are all too familiar: an accelerated exodus of white families, an influx of Negroes, increased enrollment, frequently to the point of overcrowding; growing dissatisfaction among teachers; and the replacement of veterans by inexperienced or unqualified junior instructors.

There are no fully satisfactory measures of segregation or imbalance but several tests are applicable. The simplest is to ask whether a particular school is viewed by the community as a Negro school. Whether the school is assumed to belong to a Negro neighborhood or merely to be the one that Negroes "just happen" to attend, whether it has been provided especially for a Negro population or has gradually acquired a student body disproportionately composed of Negroes, the typical consequences of segregation can be predicted.

In gauging the degree of segregation or imbalance, the percentage or number of Negro students in a given building is ordinarily less important than the relation of the school to the entire system of which it is a part. It is not the number involved, but the substantial isolation of Negro and white students from each other which implies differences in status and prevents the association that is the indispensable basis for mutual understanding and acceptance.

The problem of definition and the establishment of formulae cannot be wholly avoided, but these are less important matters than creating and retaining student bodies that will be considered acceptably integrated by the largest possible number of persons in both races. Universal approval of any such scheme represents unattainable perfection, but no plan for integration can be sustained unless it is supported by substantial elements of both the majority and the minority.

The plain fact is that there can be no integration without pupils of different races. Any plan, therefore, which increases the movement of white pupils out of the public schools will defeat the purpose it is intended to serve. On the other hand, unless the plan advances the process of integration at a realistic rate it is certainly futile and probably illegal.

A number of administrative procedures for promoting school integration have been devised and each has some merit. The free choice plan, the so-called Princeton plan for pairing schools, the comprehensive reorganization of attendance areas and feeder patterns all are applicable and useful in certain situations.

The most promising—and the boldest—scheme yet proposed for achieving a more durable balance of races in public schools is the educational park, which would assemble on a single large site children from an attendance area broad enough to include a substantial number of both majority and minority children. It would also make possible the diversity of program and the concentration of services needed to serve a widely varied student body. The educational park requires, however, a radical departure from past practice and major commitments of space, money, and program direction.

Yet another approach now being discussed but not yet tried is the merger or redefinition of entire school districts. The purpose is to counteract the effect of arbitrary lines that often deny children access to schools that they might otherwise attend. One sentence in the Brown decision seems to bear directly on this problem: "Such an opportunity [to obtain an education], where the state has undertaken to provide it," the supreme court said, "is a right that must be made available to all on equal terms."

When a boundary separating school districts results in obvious educational inequity, it seems pertinent to ask whether the state, which drew the line, is not required to erase it or redraw it if such action is necessary to establish the "equal terms" to which the court referred.

It is not my purpose to discuss any of these approaches in detail, but rather to emphasize that there is no single plan, no magic key by which instant integration can be achieved. No one familiar with the reality of the problem could for one moment believe that there is a panacea, nor could anyone acting in good faith promise to deliver one.

What is required is neither insistence on a particular method nor resistance to it, but rather a common and resolute willingness to face up to the urgency to end the destructive divisiveness that still plagues too many of our communities, and to search for solutions with open minds and dedicated inventiveness. Such determination is obviously easier to describe than to obtain. We are dealing with long-standing prejudices, established practices, and deep-seated apprehensions. But it must be made clear to all our people that we cannot expect to attain our full strength as a democracy while any group of our citizens is denied free and complete access to the benefits which are the proper birthright of our entire people.

One friend of mine well experienced in this field claims that there are no hard barriers to the attainment of school integration but rather a vast and dense fog that delays and frustrates effective action. I think he is right, and I am convinced that this cloud of uncertainty, insecurity, fear, and plain inertia will be dispelled only where the necessary leadership is forthcoming. This is not to say that one or a few firm-minded individuals can work a miracle. It is rather to argue that the broadscale public understanding and support which are needed cannot be expected to develop until a nucleus of intelligent, well-informed, and capable leaders accepts the responsibility for clarifying the issues, illuminating the possibilities, and proposing forthright action.

Much of that leadership, for both legal and psychological reasons, must be furnished by school boards and superintendents. Although every member of the school staff has an indispensable part to play, those who have the duty to set top policy and to see that it is carried out must be able and willing to project the goals and the programs by which they are to be attained.

But even the ablest and most dedicated school board and staff cannot successfully mount any educational program without the support of substantial and powerful elements in the community. The creation of a public school system that will assure every pupil equal access to excellent instruction is not the business solely of the school authorities. It must be approached rather as a task of comprehensive community planning in which many public and private agencies will be involved.

It must begin with an imaginative and bold appraisal of what a first-rate system of public schools, well staffed, well supported, and well integrated, might plan in the social, economic, and cultural advancement of the community. A second step will be to project the parts that agencies other than the schools can play in the total effort, to identify their roles, and to determine how their work and the schools' can best be interrelated. A third step is to estimate the resources required in manpower, facilities, and money; to adapt the magnitude of the effort to the resources available; to schedule the timing of development to the predictable flow of resources, and to maintain at every phase a balanced plan of operation. The fourth and possibly the most important part of such an approach must be the willingness of all concerned to make and to meet commitments of policy, resources, and action. What I am proposing would mean for many organizations a new relationship to the public schools, and it would require on the part of some school systems a quite different posture toward the community. It would entail a sharp departure from the tradition of autonomy that has characterized much of school administration since the turn of the century. The relative independence of public schools from other governmental and private agencies, although a rational and wise response to the hazards of partisan political control, has in some places separated the schools too sharply from other community concerns.

The fact that the public schools belong to the people and are established to serve the public interest imposes obligations on the people as well as the schools. In the past, many groups and individuals have expressed their interest in public education chiefly in the form of criticism, finding fault with what was being done, and attacking those whom they held accountable for error. Others have seen the schools as instruments for promoting their own special interests and have not hesitated to apply heavy pressure to shape the school to conform to their own predispositions. Any public agency, and the schools most particularly, must expect criticism and pressure. The best of them do expect it, and frequently are able to use it in constructive ways. But while every institution, for its own good and for the public interest, needs external criticism, no sound institution has ever been built by criticism alone.

What is called for now is a new coordination of community support for the schools and their purposes, a clearer identification of the common interests of a wide variety of organizations and forces, and a deliberate effort on the part of all such forces and agencies to bring their collective influence and resources to bear, not in competition for control of the school but in cooperation to support it.

It goes without saying that if this is to happen, labor and industrial establishments must become vigorous participants in the process. The relationship between strong schools and a strong economy is often talked about but too seldom taken with complete seriousness by business leaders and major taxpayers. Despite genuine progress in smaller communities where forward-looking industrial corporations view the improvement of schools as a necessary and desirable long-range investment, in the larger cities such constructive interest is more notable for its absence than its presence. The time has come for the business leaders in the metropolitan centers to appraise realistically the relation between high quality schools for all children and the long-term well-being of the city.

But it will be necessary for other groups also to become major participants in educational development. I think here particularly of the civil rights groups, which have especially powerful contributions to make. In the past, many of these groups, too, have used their energy chiefly to point out what was wrong and have refused to join forces with school people to establish and support more promising programs. The groups in our society that are most concerned about promoting equality of opportunity must be willing to turn from the easier task to build the institutions and programs that are required. This calls for a readiness to temper dramatic demands for special attention with a broader awareness of the total community interest. It requires recognition of the common obligation of all citizens and all groups to share the duty to maintain public institutions at the same time that they exercise the right to criticize them.

I speak of this relationship here because the part that the Urban League has played in the support of public education might well serve as a model for other community groups. My specific suggestion now is that this gathering be used as a beginning point from which further action might be taken to mobilize community resources, to identify the problems that must be met, and to lay out the steps needed to achieve high quality integrated schools and to assure every pupil free and equal access to them.

No city in this country can reasonably expect its future as a place to live to be any better than the education its young people are receiving today. Any school system that subjects part of its children to the repression and indignity of ghetto schools while others are given the stimulation and security of a sound school environment is only accumulating further trouble for the future. The correction of such inequities must have the highest priority on the agenda of the school board among the tasks of the schools and every other governmental agency and private group that can help.

The time for action is now. A substantial part of the necessary leadership is in this room. The question for all of us is what we mean to do about it.

TWO SUPERINTENDENTS DISCUSS INTEGRATION: INTERVIEW

Studs Terkel *is author of* Division Street: America *(Pantheon, 1967). This article is an edited interview with Neil V. Sullivan and Gregory Coffin by Mr. Terkel, made for Chicago radio station WFMT on June 3, 1967. Mr. Terkel has received national and international recognition for his outstanding work in radio.*

TERKEL: How did it begin, Dr. Sullivan? You were superintendent of schools at a rather posh community in Long Island?

SULLIVAN: Yes, probably the richest community on Long Island, the gold coast close to Old Westbury and Oyster Bay. It had this marvelous school system where people wanted excellence and I was brought in to try to develop it with them, and we did. Yet, I grew tired of it; and in time I became involved in civil rights. I was a friend of the Kennedys dating back to post-World War II, and in 1963 they asked me if I would become involved in Prince Edward County. As this was through Robert Kennedy I was delighted to do it, and they gave me an assignment.

TERKEL: That story—now that story. You were doing pretty well, even the way you begin that story in your book, *Bound for Freedom.* ¹ A man was asking you about a contributing editor to an educational magazine. Life was pretty good; you were going on vacation. Then came the call from Washington. Tell us about Prince Edward County first.

SULLIVAN: Well, Prince Edward County is located in South Side Virginia; the South Side is where the Negroes are. Close to Appomatox, a stone's throw away from Jefferson's birthplace and Monticello; the home of Patrick Henry; not too far away from Lee's birthplace. All the great heritage of Virginia is wrapped up in this country

From *Integrated Education.* **August/September 1967. Reprinted by permission of the author and radio station WFMT.**

¹Neil V. Sullivan, *et al., Bound for Freedom,* Little, Brown and Company, New York, 1965.

and the surrounding counties of Appomatox and the Lee area. So rich in cultural background; poor, however, as far as the Negro in his economy is concerned. The average Negro family in that area earns less than $1,500 a year.

TERKEL: Tobacco country.

SULLIVAN: Tobacco country, but poor tobacco country; not cigarette tobacco but pipe tobacco and chewing tobacco. That isn't going too big in the country. So they are very poor people, destitute. Incidentally, they are still in segregated schools in Virginia. There is no integration, despite the Brown decision* and despite the changes in the educational philosophy in the state. South Side Virginia is still a segregated country. So I'm talking about poor people, but people who are rich in heritage, people who have made a tremendous contribution—I'm talking about the Negro people now, because these were the people who slipped through Lee's Army of Northern Virginia and joined Grant's army; many of them died in the Civil War.

TERKEL: This is a fascinating history, now—rich in heritage. And back to the Prince Edward County case. This case became celebrated because in 1958 the establishment in that area decided that rather than abide by the Brown decision of 1954—integration—they would close all public schools.

SULLIVAN: It was an incredible decision, one that was devastating to the Negroes for a generation in the area, and unpardonable. The men who made that decision deserve, as far as I am concerned, to be in jail.

TERKEL: And as far as the white kids are concerned, they had to pay, too?

SULLIVAN: They paid a price. They went to secondhand schools in back of churches, without certificated teachers.

TERKEL: In a moment, we are going to be joined by Dr. Gregory Coffin, a colleague of Dr. Sullivan, who is the superintendent of schools here in Evanston. But continue the story, Dr. Sullivan.

SULLIVAN: Most people do not realize that the Brown case was one of three cases decided at the same time. One of the other cases involved Mr. Francis Griffin, a Baptist minister in Prince Edward County, dynamic president of NAACP in Virginia, who had a five-year-old son, Skippy. He enrolled Skippy in the public school. He had the courage to do that. But Skippy never attended school. Skippy grew up and was with me in the supreme court chambers in 1963 when the supreme court ordered the board of supervisors to reopen the public schools. But this all started, you see, in 1951, in Prince Edward County, when a thousand Negro kids said, "We're fed up with what we have. We're going on strike." This, incidentally, was the first student strike that I know of in the United States. It led to the Brown decision. It led to the closing of the schools in Prince Edward County in 1958. It led to violence. It brought me to Prince Edward County four years later.

TERKEL: You were down there. Now you accepted the job—to do what? There were no schools except for the few kids who were able to attend paid schools.

SULLIVAN: That's right, but in the meantime this became the *cause célèbre* in the South. Southern racists poured millions of dollars into Prince Edward County to fight NAACP in the court case. It went to the supreme court on three different occasions. But during this period the South built beautiful schools in Prince Edward County for the white children. They built a fabulous secondary school and called it Prince Edward

---

*[Editor's Note: See Appendix A, "Text of Supreme Court Rulings (*Brown* v. *Board of Education*, . . .).”]

Academy. They bought beautiful buses; they had fine equipment and they took care of the white children.

TERKEL: Did they have to pay for this, though?

SULLIVAN: Their parents paid, but there were tremendous subsidies being poured in, and in addition the state of Virginia in its gracious fashion gave each parent state aid. We all pay taxes in Virginia, but the money went to the white parents.

TERKEL: And yet eventually when that great moment came for the convocation at the free public schools that you opened—integrated primarily—it was Governor Darden who made the commencement address?

SULLIVAN: It was. A most gracious gentleman, in the spirit and heart of Thomas Jefferson, Governor Darden, a great man.

TERKEL: What did you find when you arrived in Prince Edward County?

SULLIVAN: We found youngsters who had lost the ability to communicate, children who didn't know they had a second name, children who had learned to read in 1957 but who had lost the ability to read; young teenagers who had migrated across the country and slept in the subways of New York City who came back to the opening of school; frightened young creatures who had been on farmland and had never ridden a bus. They had never been to Farmville, the county seat. This is what I found—destitute youngsters who were afraid to speak, who couldn't read.

TERKEL: And then something happened at that first graduation, when was that?

SULLIVAN: It was twelve months later. We did graduate about thirty students and at that time some of them were to go on to college.

TERKEL: I want to ask Dr. Sullivan about some of the teachers and a few white kids who went there and their experience, and also, of course, of your current work at Berkeley, California. But Dr. Gregory Coffin, in your case, you came to Evanston from Darien, Connecticut, and there you did something quite unprecedented.

COFFIN: Darien is a very affluent suburb about thirty miles out of New York, inhabited by management people from New York; the average income according to one study was $20,000 a year. A unique feature of Darien, however, is the fact that it is one of the few communities in the country where gentlemen's agreements still prevail. So that Darien is inhabited by a homogeneous population. There are no Negroes in Darien. According to one survey, there are fifty Jewish families, but when a friend and I got together one night and tried to count them we could only count about ten. Primarily WASPs, then; and there is a small Italian element, which is Catholic. I used to kid about the fact that they couldn't build a wall around them to keep them out because they were the people who three generations ago built the railroad and so they are really natives; there would not be a Darien had it not been for the people who built the railroads.

TERKEL: But in the middle of this, in this atmosphere, you did something quite unprecedented as far as teachers are concerned.

COFFIN: Yes. We started a couple of programs, both teacher and student exchange programs, with Harlem. I think the genesis of this may be of some interest. I lived about a block from school. I had four youngsters in school. My youngsters would go to school in the morning, go by a bus stop and the bus would come in and unload; half a dozen to a dozen Negroes would get off. Then, at night, when they came home from school they would see these same people get on the buses, and this was really their only contact with Negroes. And so, despite what we try to teach them in school, in the curriculum, about the equality of people, the whole idea that people could achieve given an opportunity to achieve, all of their direct experience was contrary to their vicarious experience. And direct experience is a far better teacher than vicarious experience. So, after this experience—and this was probably a year or so after I had gone to Darien—I decided that this was wrong and that we ought to do something about this.

I was talking about this with Calvin Gross, who was at that time superintendent in New York City, and musing about how we could change this. I liked Darien but I didn't like certain aspects of life in Darien, especially for my four kids. We came up with an idea that we might exchange some teachers initially so that we could demonstrate to youngsters in a very visible way that given the opportunity a Negro would achieve the same professional status that the whites in Darien achieved. Then we carried this a step further and exchanged youngsters.

TERKEL: What was the reaction when you first suggested this idea, that Negro teachers would come from Harlem to teach the white kids, the materially privileged white kids in Darien and some of the Darien teachers would go to Harlem?

COFFIN: The board of education adopted this program on a nine-to-zero vote. That is, when we proposed the program for the exchanges, the board was unanimous in its agreement. After we started the program, we started to get some kickback, some backlash, and gradually there was a swelling amount of backlash. However, all of the people who were directly involved in the program, that is, teachers and the students that these teachers were teaching and the parents of these youngsters, were all very enthusiastic about it. So that we managed to move along actually for two years and then it was after that I left Darien. But we ran the program for two years, expanded it in the second year for teachers and youngsters. There was some growing resentment, not so much growing resentment in terms of more people, but many of the apathetic or totally uninformed people were beginning to come to the fore and make noises. So we had big crowds at board meetings and in two successive board elections people who were anti- this program got on the board. When I left Darien, instead of the nine-to-zero vote we had a thin five-to-four vote for supporting any kind of a program of this sort. My guess is that after this last election last November the vote would go the other way.

TERKEL: The other way, despite the experiment. Do you have any idea of the reactions of the kids themselves? Toward the Negro teachers?

COFFIN: Yes, the youngsters were tremendously enthusiastic, even after having these teachers for just four or five weeks—they came in for four or five weeks at a stretch, and youngsters were most enthusiastic about the teachers—obviously the teachers were very carefully selected (this was very important to the program). Our teachers who went into Harlem were very enthusiastic about their experiences there. We broke down many stereotypes on both ends.

TERKEL: The whole thing is very interesting. So here is the case of teachers and students both in Harlem and in Darien being obviously rewarded and excited—

COFFIN: It's very obvious that if we could do things throughout the country—and lots of these kinds of things are being done now—with the present generation of school kids, hopefully the next generation won't create Dariens. There will be no reason to do it. We could create a wholly different attitude toward what a community should be.

TERKEL: So we leave—as they do in soap operas—so we leave Gregory Coffin in Darien and come to Evanston, which is as you know the home of the WCTU and a center of rock-ribbed conservatism. We will ask the superintendent of schools about that, but turn to Dr. Sullivan now. And Prince Edward County, Virginia. This is rather interesting. Dr. Coffin was talking about the problems that arose in Darien as a result of his integrated teacher-student program. So we come to Prince Edward—the kids had been away from school for four years, shy, frightened, terrified—those are the Negro kids you're talking about.

SULLIVAN: The Negro kids—that was the student body—we had three frightened white youngsters, too—one was the son of the dean of the teachers' college in the community who was a very articulate Caucasian.

TERKEL: Dean Moss?

SULLIVAN: That's right, quite a hero who had fought the establishment in Prince Edward County alone with Francis Griffin for a period of ten years and who had suffered greatly during this period, had great physical damage resulting from this to the family. A very, very brave, a great man in this whole story.

TERKEL: And then there was a poor tobacco farmer named Abernathy.

SULLIVAN: Right, Right. The Abernathys had one daughter, Letitia, seven years of age, and the Abernathys decided that to them right was right; and therefore they would not go to the private academy that had been set up. They believed in free public education, so when the free schools were opened the Abernathys registered Letitia and then their troubles began. All the problems that could be heaped on one poor farmer by his neighbors went on for this period of a year when I was there, and it has continued. They have long memories, these Virginians in rural, South Side Virginia, and they made life almost unbearable for these wonderful people. However, I think the Abernathys were the great gainers because they found friends in the Negro community that they never had before. Letitia had more friends than all the Caucasian kids in Prince Edward County put together.

The poor whites in the South are the great losers. Their education is neglected, but they are militant as far as the Negro is concerned and as far as integration is concerned. They are the great losers in this struggle.

TERKEL: I was thinking about your recruiting of teachers. Here, the story that Dr. Sullivan tells about coming there and finding those neglected schools having to recruit staff. Among them was this elderly white teacher who was retired—Etta Bailey?

SULLIVAN: Yes.

TERKEL: There's a most moving story.

SULLIVAN: Miss Bailey, 72 years of age, retired in Richmond, was an eminently successful teacher, recognized by her peers as one of the truly great innovators in the South. When she came to be interviewed she said she was a loser all her life because she had never had an opportunity to work with Negro children. Richmond was a segregated city. Could she have that privilege? Of course, the doors were opened wide to the Etta Baileys. This was a Peace Corps type of operation. We didn't care how old they were or where they went to school or what type of certificate they had or even if they had one. We were looking for people who had a commitment to this cause. Etta Bailey, 72 years of age, was typical of my staff.

TERKEL: And of course most of your staff was Negro.

SULLIVAN: Yes, that's correct. And the Negro staff came across the country from California, came from Alabama, and actually most of them from New York and Washington.

TERKEL: Dr. Coffin.

COFFIN: There's an interesting sidelight on that. Dr. Sullivan had some of the same kind of flack in the backwoods of his East Williston, Long Island, community that I was getting in Darien.

TERKEL: That's East Williston, before he went to Virginia.

COFFIN: While he was in Virginia. I happened to be taking a course, a seminar, at the Harvard Club in New York, and a man from East Williston, a business executive, was in the course. I was talking at the time about some of the things we were doing in Darien, and this fellow took off one night on their superintendent, "that guy" Sullivan.

TERKEL: Neil Sullivan.

COFFIN: Neil Sullivan, who was down here and they hoped he would stay down there in Prince Edward County and not come back to East Williston. So he had some of the same people going in the backwoods that I had going for me in Darien.

TERKEL: So you were invited here, in our neck of the woods, to the largest suburb in the world, the largest small city, Evanston. You did something quite unprecedented in Darien, with this exchange of teachers black, and white, and now Evanston. But it was a very logical thing.

COFFIN: I think, Mr. Terkel, that you have a stereotyped image of Evanston.

TERKEL: Evanston is changing?

COFFIN: Evanston may have been a rock-ribbed conservative kind of community, but this has not been my experience there. Evanston is a very proud community. It's quite heterogeneous, it's very proud, and it is very anxious to solve its problems. It would like to solve its problems by itself without the state or the federal government or any outside participation. And so I think one of the reasons I was invited to go to Evanston was because the school board in Evanston felt that maybe I could help Evanston solve its problem, which was a problem of rather tight *de facto* segregation in the center of the city.

TERKEL: How long have you been in Evanston now?

COFFIN: Just a year.

TERKEL: Just a year. I have to ask about your observations thus far. The fact that the committee chose you, Dr. Coffin, is certainly a credit to that part of the establishment.

COFFIN: They were concerned, I think, with two things. They were anxious to solve their *de facto* segregation problem and had been working on this for five years before I came. I wasn't the champion to step in and solve this thing. Actually, I just moved in at the time when we were right on the brink of a solution. But they were also interested in the kind of high-quality education for all boys and girls that we were offering in Darien. Darien has its limitations, and certainly its limitations revolve around this whole problem of prejudice and things of that sort. But despite this, Darien's educational system and educational output in terms of the achievement of boys and girls and what they did with their educations afterward ranked very high. Evanston aspires for all of its kids, both Negro and white (they have 21 percent Negro), the best possible education. So this was the combination they were looking for, and they thought I had it—I hope this proves to be the case.

TERKEL: Dr. Sullivan, we are turning again to you. You left Prince Edward County. (By the way, the story, *Bound for Freedom,* was published by Little, Brown. I think it is not just a moving story but full of incredible insights.) You were talking about when you left the situation, then you were invited to Berkeley, California, but first Virginia.

SULLIVAN: We had a fantastic year. Any time, as Dr. Coffin knows, you have a faculty that is willing to work eighteen hours a day, seven days a week, you have it made. And these people were committed to the education of children. The salaries, incidentally, were low in Prince Edward County. We were paying on the average of $5,000 a year. They came there to teach children. They came to try to erase this terrible sin that had been committed. They gave a year of their lives, they do not regret it, I don't regret it, and the accomplishments were extraordinary. Now, I'm not a salesman for compensatory education. I don't think it's the answer to the Negro problem in America. I think that you must go all the way in compensatory education—we haven't gone far enough. But this was truly an effort in compensatory education, to make up for educational blight for four years and we succeeded as far as the achievement was concerned. These kids achieved.

However, they still lived in isolation. They were desolate youngsters. And we enriched their lives by giving them the type of program that has never been given in American public education; after all, it was not unusual for these kids to spend a week at the United Nations or in Washington, and their friends were the Kennedys. You know, it's rather nice to think that Jackie will drop in and see you. So it was romance, but it was also great compensatory education; and achievement test results indicated that we were successful. However, we didn't change the power structure of South Side Virginia. We were spending somewhere in the neighborhood of $2,000 per capita on these kids. When we left, they reverted to an expenditure of about $125 to $175. Our class size was in the neighborhood of fifteen to twenty; it suddenly jumped the next year to thirty-five to forty. All the enriched courses we gave the youngsters in the fine arts were eliminated, the fine language courses were eliminated, so I am not optimistic about education in the rural South. I tend to believe that the federal government must play a larger role, a more active one. I was terribly dismayed to learn recently that Mr. Howe, our U.S. commissioner, is no longer going to have the authority to enforce Title VI of the Civil Rights Act. I think that this is a horrible decision.

TERKEL: Title VI is . . .?

SULLIVAN: The enforcement clause for federal moneys. This was what happened here in 1965 in Chicago—the Keppel incident. And moving this away from the U.S. commissioner, taking his power of enforcement away, I think just gives the South and the North, cities like Chicago, a free hand . . .

TERKEL: In one of your articles, you talk about changing a kid's cultural pattern—say this is wrong, like "I is going," the teacher says, "Oh, that's wrong," whereas the good teacher says, "There is another way of saying it."

SULLIVAN: There are two languages we have to teach, and one is the child's language. We begin there, and we work with him, you know, and not *for* him. Through this there develops an *esprit de corps* that starts with the child, and he's a member of the team.

TERKEL: Doesn't this lead into the question, Gregory Coffin, of who is disadvantaged? Are they, quote-unquote, to be like us, the majority, Caucasian group, or is it a question of mutual learning, of richness of both backgrounds?

COFFIN: It's certainly both, and this is the whole thesis of the program in Darien. There was an element of cultural deprivation in their rather thin culture of Darien and the associations they had as they grew up.

Youngsters' attitudes, basic attitudes, are formed very early so that it's at this stage in the child's life in school that we have to provide him with experiences which will enable him to come out with healthy attitudes. In Evanston, if I made any kind of unique contribution, it was by introducing the notion that not only did we have the problem of *de facto* segregation in the Negro Foster and Dewey schools, but we had the problem of *de facto* segregation in at least ten other elementary schools, which were segregated white schools. And these youngsters were missing out on a phase of their education which they shouldn't miss out on and which could be relatively easily corrected. In our integration program, all of our schools will be integrated. We are not just trying to eliminate *de facto* segregation, in the all-Negro Foster school, or at 65 percent Negro Dewey school—we want to integrate all the schools. This we will do in September, where the range will be from 17 percent to 25 percent Negro, and there will be Negroes, this range of Negro population, in every school. And many of these schools, of course, have never had a Negro student in them.

TERKEL: What were the reactions—are you able to tell so far the reactions in some of the white schools where Negroes entered?

COFFIN: Evanston has had for three years now a voluntary enrollment program which has integrated several of the schools which wouldn't otherwise be integrated. Actually, not all of the schools will be integrated until September, 1967. The reaction overall has been very favorable. We have had our opposition and we know that there is still opposition. However, I sense that there's a growing body of support for the total program, and I sense that part of this comes out of community pride, this idea of solving one's problem. We have had very favorable publicity about the program. We appreciate the efforts of Chicago news media, the newspapers and other news media, and I think that as people become more aware of what we're doing and just why we're doing it there's a sense of community pride which is bringing more and more people on the side of strong support for the program.

TERKEL: We swing from Evanston back to Neil Sullivan, and leaving Virginia a new challenge. So now the free schools are there to stay, aren't they?

SULLIVAN: No, actually the U.S. supreme court decision of 1964[2] was a very interesting decision, in which it decided that no community, as long as a neighboring community in the state afforded public education, could ever close its public schools. This was a very crucial supreme court decision. So Prince Edward County was forced to reopen its public schools, but these public schools now are Negro schools, so the free school was a one-year John F. Kennedy project. This was as long as we had anticipated being there. The court made its decision—we left. But today in Prince Edward County there are public schools for Negroes, private schools for Caucasians.

TERKEL: So there is a reversion here. It's interesting. Since Dr. Coffin left at the time of reversion taking place there to old hardened attitudes, you get the basest reality, and you are in a sense also in Prince Edward County.

COFFIN: This question has been raised with me a number of times. I have given one answer but I'm not at all sure the answer is correct. If you start a program and do

[2]*Griffin* v. *Prince Edward County School Board*, 377 U.S. 218 (1964).

something for a limited period of time, in this case in Prince Edward County for a year and these exchange programs in Darien for a couple of years, and then the basic power structure takes over, and they revert to type so to speak. Have you really made a contribution? I don't know. I'd be curious to know what Neil thinks about it.

SULLIVAN: Well, I certainly do agree with you that a one-year project would leave a great deal to be desired when you evaluate it ten years later. However, the Prince Edward project was unique because it broke the pattern. This was the challenge. Could a community, could a state, close its public schools? As far as the kids were concerned, they had one great year. I do think retrogression started the day after we left.

TERKEL: And does this raise another question to you, that of time, but something else must change along with it? Here are two committed educators, two superintendents of schools, Neil Sullivan and Gregory Coffin, and you have staffs that are equally committed to an idea that is very human and civilized in the only way we can live in the twentieth century. Yet, doesn't it raise another question? Something else must change, too.

SULLIVAN: Yes, and I think this did occur in Prince Edward County. I can give you a couple of examples. As you read in *Bound for Freedom,* I could not get a house in the community. I not only had the problem of working with Negroes, but I happen to be a Catholic, and when you put these two things together you have an impossible situation. My only Caucasian friend, who helped me out here, was a Jew. He was a merchant, and he was to suffer all the great indignity that could be heaped on one man's head for his friendship with me. So attitudes have to change. While I paint rather a dismal picture of a power structure of Prince Edward County, I think I do it correctly. Public opinion is controlled by a newspaper, by an editor, Barry Wall, who was hard and firm and refused to give an inch. But what happened in Prince Edward County was integrated living. We have Negroes living with whites and this has changed the attitude, I think, of many of the Caucasians in that community. Prince Edward County will never be quite the same. The establishment must give way.

TERKEL: Now a new challenge for Neil Sullivan. A new chapter in Berkeley, California. How did this come to be?

SULLIVAN: Well, Berkeley in many ways, I think, is similar to Evanston. Berkeley wanted to do something. Berkeley had a heart. Berkeley had a desire to integrate its schools. Berkeley wanted to do the right things, morally and legally. And they wanted to bring in an educator who was committed to integration. No fooling around about this thing. They searched the country and interviewed many men. Incidentally, there are a lot of guys with the same commitment that Dr. Coffin and I have. We're not too unique. If a community will search hard enough, it will find the Coffins. They are not, of course, in great abundance.

TERKEL: May I ask you this question, Dr. Sullivan. Were you invited last year as a candidate here by the Chicago Board of Education?

SULLIVAN: No, I was not.

TERKEL: Let's continue, shall we? With the subject of Berkeley.

SULLIVAN: Yes. Berkeley was looking for a school superintendent who had knowledge of and interest in the education of a total school population. I'd like to point out that Berkeley has a Negro population of 43 percent. This is a substantial

Negro community. It has in its student body the sons and daughters of the great Nobel prize winners who teach at this fabulous University of California at Berkeley. One tenth of our kids in the Berkeley school system fall within the one tenth of 1 percent of the elite intellectual families in the country. So we have this desire in Berkeley to have quality education but also integrated education.

TERKEL: I want to make this clear about Berkeley. In the minds of most Americans outside California, outside of Berkeley, we think of it as the home of the University of California primarily, and militant students. But Berkeley is an industrial city.

SULLIVAN: It certainly is. It's just part of megalopolis, that's all. You can't tell Berkeley from Oakland, other than that there is a philosophical wall between Berkeley and Oakland that I would be happy to describe for you. But Berkeley is just part of a tremendous burgeoning [San Francisco] Bay-Area community now over three million people. We're a small part of it. The community is, with its student body, 150,000 bodies.

COFFIN: Another interesting parallel there. Neil mentioned a philosophical wall. There's a philosophical wall between Evanston and the rest of the North Shore, too.

TERKEL: Would you mind just touching on that for just a minute?

COFFIN: Well, the fact that Evanston as a North Shore suburb is unique in that it has heterogenity in its population—it has a Negro population in the schools as I have indicated of 21 percent. The minute you go north of Evanston into Wilmette and then up the line to Kenilworth, Winnetka, and Highland Park you find virtually pure white suburbs. There must be a philosophical wall to create that kind of a demography along the North Shore, since the North Shore communities are really packed quite close together.

TERKEL: This observation made by Gregory Coffin, of philosophical walls, I imagine this is true in every part of the country, similar and yet with basic differences.

SULLIVAN: There is no question; Dr. Coffin is correct. His Darien, my East Williston, Boston's Newton—you go across the country and you will find the same barriers that he has just described.

TERKEL: But these walls, too, are seemingly of the same pattern, economic and cultural. Again, in the mind of a midwesterner, Berkeley and Oakland are almost the same.

SULLIVAN: That's correct. But those of us who live in California know that the dichotomy that exists between these two cities is so distinguishable, there is no doubt in the minds of the people in the two cities what's going on in both. As far as concerns education, as far as the police, as far as civic attitude toward its people, as far as human relations, there is a Berkeley, there is an Oakland. These are almost incompatible communities.

TERKEL: As Gregory Coffin was saying I'm sure to people outside the Midwest, outside of Chicago, Evanston is identical with Winnetka.

COFFIN: This is the impression I had when I was back on the east coast, where I spent all of my life. I had heard about the Evanston schools for as long as I had been in the education business. They have a great reputation and have had for over fifty years. And I just assumed that Evanston, Wilmette, and Winnetka were all the same. You have to be here to realize that there is a tremendous difference. There's a difference in the attitude of the people. We've heard recently of a few incidents where people who had moved up the North Shore, farther up where you can get more land for the money and perhaps more housing in some of the communities, are now moving back. A few people have moved back because they are interested in having their kids grow up in a heterogeneous situation.

TERKEL: We have two educators here, two courageous and distinguished educators, and we are talking suddenly not so much about schools, we are talking about housing now.

SULLIVAN: We must stop the flight of the Caucasians from the city. We need these people in Chicago. We need them in Evanston, we need them in every American city. Now he has indicated to you that he sees a trend in Evanston, the return of some of the Caucasian people to an integrated school system. I can tell you it happened in Berkeley, too. The Caucasians are coming back to Berkeley for the first time in ten years. They've been leaving steadily for ten years: its reversed.

TERKEL: Let me point out one of the reasons. The fact is that when you, Neil Sullivan, and your colleagues are integrating schools, this development is occurring.

SULLIVAN: That's right. When we started to integrate, now over three years ago, there was a movement of the Caucasians out. They were afraid of two things, and let's face it. They were afraid of violence in the schools and they were afraid of loss of achievement for their children. Now these are real things and you've got to face up to them. And you've got to prove with facts that these things aren't going to occur. If we're going to have more violence in our schools, if the Caucasian child is going to suffer, then I would oppose integration. The facts are these two things do not happen. There is not a loss of Caucasian achievement in the Berkeley schools; rather, it has been accelerated. There was less violence in all of our Berkeley schools. We carefully evaluated this, but whether we evaluate it or not, parents know what goes on, kids know what is going on. They are coming back in large numbers to the Berkeley schools. We do have a problem in housing.

COFFIN: Just to bear out what Neil says, last night I came from a meeting at Illinois Beach State Park, where a group of our teachers had assembled to make final plans for an institute we are running this summer for three hundred of our teachers, financed by Title IV of the Civil Rights Act. Although the focus of the institute is on integrated education; that is, the kind of things we were talking about before: language patterns, mannerisms, and the things which connote condescension to the Negro child—very subconscious things that the white teacher does who does not talk to Negro youngsters—the real end result here is that the teachers, after this five-week institute, will be better prepared to teach *all* youngsters. So, actually, the educational fare of all of the kids will go up, will be improved, even though the *raison d'être* for having the institute is integration.

TERKEL: It comes to that. It comes to the benefit of the white child in getting him out of what I call his spiritual deprivation, spiritual ghetto.

SULLIVAN: Dr. Coffin has mentioned this earlier. One of the great losers certainly is the Caucasian child who lives in isolation. To break this wall down through integration, we are suddenly giving this child an opportunity to live in one world. And that really is the purpose of this whole thing. We don't want anyone to live in isolation, either Negro or Caucasian.

TERKEL: The question of housing actually becomes a factor here, doesn't it?

SULLIVAN: It certainly does when realtors refuse to operate in a fair manner.

TERKEL: So this leads to a question, a key one for two educators, Neil Sullivan and Gregory Coffin. In the supreme court there are judges, there is some enlightenment. At the same time, year after year of myth, conditioning, unnamed fears, fear of the stranger, are overwhelming factors for the average man.

SULLIVAN: Sure, and we have to attack the myths. This isn't easy. Incidentally, I'd like to share this responsibility with other civic leaders. I think that school administrators, the Coffins around the country and guys like Briggs in Cleveland, courageously fight this thing. And city hall is perfectly willing to let the school administrator do all the fighting. I want them to get into this thing with me. I'd like for the mayor, alderman, and all the fellows to join in.

TERKEL: You're talking now about Berkeley, California.

SULLIVAN: I'm talking about the United States of America. I'm talking about cabinet members, I'm talking about governors, I'm talking about senators. I don't like the attitude of some of these distinguished people. I met with a cabinet member within the month, who indicated to me that the answer to the problem in America was strong neighborhood schools and that he would break down this pattern of integration by open housing. I just don't want to wait a hundred years.

TERKEL: There's something just—not wanting to wait a hundred years in Berkeley. We pick up a vote in California of two to one against open housing, fair housing. And yet there was a referendum in your city, Berkeley. Now you were selected by a vote of nine to one to come there, right. Now something has happened. Now what has happened?

SULLIVAN: Well, I went out there in the spring and worked with the group on a plan of integration and developed the plan with them and we started its implementation in September of the year I arrived. Now, it was a five-member board and not nine-member, and of these five members, before I arrived in September three had left Berkeley. So I now had a two-member board and they were to elect a third member so we could conduct business. But the Parents for Neighborhood Schools decided to have a recall election and remove the two incumbents.

TERKEL: The neighborhood school group is against . . .

SULLIVAN: As far as I am concerned, I think that they are against progress. We had a very spirited election in which I think about 70,000 people cast ballots, and the two incumbents won a resounding victory. We were concerned, because people were voting on integration in Berkeley; let's not kid ourselves. This was the question, "Shall we or shall we not integrate our schools?" and we won a resounding victory. Incidentally, Oakland, our neighbor to the south, has lost election after election, tax elections, bond elections; and Berkeley in the middle between Richmond and Oakland wins these elections. Now as we are moving ahead toward integration, people are voting more money for us, retaining board members, while our neighboring cities are turning these things down.

TERKEL: This raises a key question, Gregory Coffin. Here are two communities next to one another, very close. Are they so basically different, when we come down to it?

COFFIN: The value systems of the people that live in these communities are different. This is why they go there to live. There was a migration, as I understand it, from Evanston for a while. I understand and I know a number of families that have moved out and farther up the North Shore, and I mentioned the fact that some families are moving in the reverse direction now. The people that move out are people who are running away. They're the people who are afraid, and they're afraid of all kinds of things, but they are afraid, so they move out, so they congregate in one community, and the people who are not afraid and have a different code of values stay. We have weekly phone calls from people on the east coast who have been transferred to Chicago, saying, "We have heard about your schools. Tell us more about them." They more and more frequently mention the aspect of what is the population of the schools, are they heterogeneous or homogeneous. They could pick from any of fifty suburbs around Chicago, and they decide that Evanston is the place they want to be because this is the kind of atmosphere they want their kids to grow up in.

SULLIVAN: I definitely believe this. As far as the west coast is concerned, in the Bay Area, the racial composition in Oakland and Berkeley is the same. Oakland refuses to do anything about school integration. The Negroes constantly vote down any increase in taxes. They are completely disappointed and discouraged with the establishment. They won't give them more money to run the schools. Now what happens? They are the losers, obviously in poor education, but believe me, the Caucasian kids are the big losers.

COFFIN: We have a contrasting situation, too. It is not next door, but there is an Illinois city called Waukegan, which has a population not unlike ours in many respects. It is unlike ours in some respects, but they have a *de facto* segregation Negro situation. I have been to Waukegan, talking with groups up there and I am convinced that our situation *vis-à-vis* Waukegan is like Neil's with Berkeley and Oakland. One community wants to do something to solve its problems and the other community wants to preserve the status quo.

TERKEL: This subject comes back to "Are these people so basically different, I'll say of Oakland as against Berkeley, or Evanston as against Waukegan?" Or, isn't there a question, too, of a certain step being taken by the establishment of these cities and a choice of certain educators?

SULLIVAN: I definitely think so. The image of your school is the image of your board of education.

TERKEL: The image of the board of education is the image of the power structure.

SULLIVAN: Absolutely.

TERKEL: Anything else you would care to say, Gregory?

COFFIN: I would say the image of the board of education is the image of the city-wide power structure.

BIBLIOGRAPHY FOR PART ONE

Abrams, Charles. *The City Is the Frontier.* New York: Harper & Row, 1965.

Anderson, Arnold. "Inequalities in Schooling in the South," *American Journal of Sociology* (May 1955).

Baldwin, James. "A Talk to Teachers," *Saturday Review* (Dec. 21, 1963).

Bennett, Lerone, Jr. *The Negro Mood.* Chicago: Johnson, 1964.

Brink, William, and Louis Harris. *Black and White.* New York: Simon and Schuster, 1967.

Cass, James. "Do We Really Want Equality?" *Saturday Review* (Dec. 17, 1966).

Coleman, James S., and others. *Equality of Educational Opportunity.* Washington, D.C.: Government Printing Office, 1966.

Davis, John P. (ed.) *The American Negro Reference Book.* Englewood Cliffs (N.J.): Prentice-Hall, 1965.

Dentler, Robert A. "Barriers to Northern School Desegregation," *Daedalus* (Winter 1966).

Erikson, Erik H. "The Concept of Identity in Race Relations: Notes and Queries," *Daedalus* (Winter 1966).

Farmer, James. *Freedom—When?* New York: Random House, 1966.

Heller, Celia S. *Mexican American Youth: Forgotten Youth at the Crossroads.* New York: Random House, 1966.

Keppel, Francis. *The Necessary Revolution in American Education.* New York: Harper & Row, 1966.

King, Martin Luther. "Education and Equality," *Integrated Education* (June-July 1964).

Monserrat, Joseph. "School Integration: A Puerto Rican View," *Integrated Education* (October-November 1963).

Moynihan, Daniel P. [Interview]. "Moynihan Believes Class Is the Issue," *Southern Education Report* (May 1967).

Nam, C. B., and others. *Inequalities in Educational Opportunities: A Demographic Analysis of Educational Differences in the Population.* Tallahassee: Florida State University, 1966.

Newman, Dorothy K., and others. *The Negroes in the United States: Their Economic and Social Situation.* Washington, D.C.: Government Printing Office, 1966.

Pearl, Arthur. "Are You Sure Pupils Are Better Off at School?" *Nation's Schools* (August 1966).

Pettigrew, Thomas F. *Profile of the Negro American.* Princeton, (N.J.): Van Nostrand, 1964.

Rose, Arnold. *De Facto School Segregation.* New York: The National Conference of Christians and Jews, 1964.

Schafer, Walter E., and Kenneth Polk. "Delinquency and the Schools," Appendix M in The President's Commission on Law Enforcement and Administration of Justice, *Juvenile Delinquency and Youth Crime.* Washington, D.C.: Government Printing Office, 1967.

Sexton, Patricia C. *The American School: Its Social Context.* Englewood Cliffs (N.J.): Prentice-Hall, 1967.

Shapiro, Elliott. "The Dynamics of Self-Deception," *Phi Delta Kappan* (March, 1967).

Taeuber, Karl E., and Alma F. Taeuber. *Negroes in Cities: Residential Segregation and Neighborhood Change.* Chicago: Aldine, 1965.

Yinger, J. M. *A Minority Group in American Society.* New York: McGraw-Hill, 1965.

Part Two

Places and Practices

The many forms of deprivation and discrimination that exist in American schools can be found in the school systems of the great cities, whose racial composition has changed significantly since the end of World War II. The affluent whites move to the suburbs; the affluent Negroes are not permitted to follow suit; and the poverty-stricken Negroes continue to reside in spreading ghettos whose contours are guided for the most part by urban real estate interests.

As the population patterns of the cities change, boards of education and school administrators have generally patterned attendance lines after population lines. Consequently, school segregation and deprivation have tended increasingly to take on the appearance of inevitability.

In city after city, studies have revealed the following about public school systems:

1. Negro schools are more crowded, are staffed with less-experienced teachers, offer a narrower range of courses, and exhibit sharply lower academic achievement levels.
2. Negro children and teachers are concentrated in predominantly Negro schools, while location of sites and decisions to expand existing facilities generally result in intensification of patterns of segregation.
3. Where deliberate efforts are made by school authorities to maintain segregation, they regard it as more important to channel white students away from Negro schools than to permit a few Negro children to enter a previously white school.

Comparable differentials are found for situations involving whites and other minorities; however, the degree of Negro segregation is unmatched by the others.

Selections in the following section illustrate the similarities and diversities of segregated education in the American metropolitan complexes. It is the diversities that are usually slighted. Both New York and Chicago, as you will see, are typical segregated cities. Yet, there are important differences between the two.

There is less segregation, both residential and school, in New York than in Chicago.

New York school authorities have been more ready to admit certain shortcomings; citizen groups have been far more articulate; and many more desegregative devices have been tried. In Chicago's school system, only half as large, there has been much less effort to escape the constrictions of a strict neighborhood school policy. The dominant political leadership of Chicago has been an effective force in maintaining racial boundaries. In New York, the Negro community has been more or less effectively organized for some years—in the late 1950s, for example, a strong movement for integration emerged in Harlem. In Chicago, the same development occurred only a decade later.

There is a changing social landscape in the South. Pettigrew describes the growth of metropolitan urban communities and their accompaniments of residential and **de facto** segregation in the South. Thus, the South is rapidly joining the North in reproducing what was once correctly regarded as "northern type" segregation. Mrs. Wasserman writes about a new kind of interracial cooperation, new in that it is cooperation among equals across the color line.

THE ALLEN REPORT ON NEW YORK CITY SCHOOLS

Complete text of report by the State Education Commission's Advisory Committee on Human Relations and Community Tensions, Desegregating the Public Schools of New York City, May 12, 1964. At the time, the State Commissioner of Education was Dr. James E. Allen, Jr. Members of his Advisory Committee were Judah Cahn, Rabbi, Metropolitan Synagogue; Kenneth B. Clark, professor of psychology at the College of the City of New York; and John H. Fischer, chairman, president, Teachers College, Columbia University. The report was prepared with the assistance of the Institute of Urban Studies, Teachers College, Columbia University. The introduction and statistical appendixes have been omitted here.

Efforts to improve teaching and other school services are a necessary part of any sound effort to desegregate the schools. Desegregation without improved instruction could produce equal but poor education for all. On the other hand, improved instruction without real desegregation could not contradict the fact that when schooling has been separate, even if only *de facto*, it has almost invariably meant *de facto*, unequal education.

Superintendent Calvin Gross stated in December, 1963:

The entire school integration program may be summarized under two headings: the achievement of equality of education and vocational opportunity for all children, and particularly those of minority group status; and the promotion of ethnic integration. These two complementary approaches have formed the warp and woof of efforts to improve the education of Negro and Puerto Rican children in New York City—efforts which have absorbed a major share of energy of the school system for more than nine years.

From *Integrated Education,* **August/September 1964.**

Throughout its work our committee has been concerned with both objectives, but this report deals chiefly with the promoting of ethnic integration. We prefer, however, to speak of desegregation rather than integration or ethnic balance, since the segregated school is the evidence of the difficulty and must therefore be the target of the corrective effort.

The earliest possible elimination of *de facto* school segregation should be the overriding concern of all responsible groups and authorities.

The aim of this report is to evaluate past programs and current plans for ethnic desegregation of the New York City public schools and to propose further steps to that end. If these steps are to succeed they must be accompanied by immediate, far reaching, and intensive new efforts to raise the quality of instruction in all the schools, beginning with those now most urgently in need of improvement.

We are aware of and appreciate the various actions of the board of education to improve instruction in public schools in depressed areas, to recruit more teachers from minority groups, to consider Negro and Puerto Rican personnel for advancement to administrative positions, and to introduce remedial, guidance, and other special services into the system as counterforces to the effects of increasing segregation over the last several years. Many of these efforts are commendable. Some are like several of our recommendations in intent, if not in substance or scope.

We believe that such improvements are essential *but must be combined with effective steps toward desegregation.* This report confines its evaluation for the most part to desegregation policies; and, while we have reviewed past efforts of the board to desegregate, we are also concerned with educational programs that advance beyond where the system is at this time. We have assumed that the board's present efforts at improving instruction and personnel will continue.

Defining Public School Segregation[1]

In developing this evaluation, we sought an unequivocal definition of the ethnically segregated public school. After considering alternatives, we chose to define a public school in *New York City* as ethnically segregated if, in 1963, it enrolled less than 10 percent Negroes and/or Puerto Rican of if it enrolled less than 10 percent from other groups. For clarity we refer to others as White, despite the imprecision. (The terms Puerto Rican and White are most doubtful, since most Puerto Ricans were classified as Whites in the 1960 Census. Our use of "Whites" ignores the fact that the word "Other" included Oriental-Americans, Indian-Americans, etc. Nevertheless, we employ the three terms, Negro, Puerto Rican, and White on the ground that they are fairly accurate and commonly understood.) Three types of schools result from this definition:

1. *White Type.* A *white* type school is one enrolling more than 90 percent Others, here termed Whites, and fewer than 10 percent Negroes or Puerto Rican pupils. This, under our definition is a *segregated* school.

2. *Desegregated Type.* A *desegregated* school is one enrolling fewer than 90 percent Negro and Puerto Rican pupils, and 10 percent or more Whites. By our definition, this school is desegregated since at least 10 percent of its students are Negroes and Puerto Ricans and another 10 percent at least, are Whites.

---

[1] Note: Our data in this report refer to regular, day-type elementary and secondary schools. "600" and other special schools are excluded. This, and the periodic regrouping of schools, explain differences in our figures that appear in one or two places in this report.

3. *Negro-Puerto Rican Type*. A school enrolling more th..n 90 percent Negro and Puerto Rican pupils is defined as a *segregated* school of the Negro-Puerto Rican type, because less than 10 percent of the student body is White.

Our definition is exact, if arbitrary, and seems to us reasonable in the light of the present facts in New York City. A criterion of larger magnitude in a city in which more than *half* the first and second graders are Negro or Puerto Rican would be unrealistic. Moreover, if a larger interval were accepted, it would not greatly affect the critical category of Negro-Puerto Rican type segregated schools: Under the criterion of 10 percent we used, 22 percent of the elementary schools in the city were minority segregated in 1963. Under a 20 percent criterion, this increases to 29 percent; and under a 30 percent criterion, this increases to 31 percent. Thus our 10 percent standard contains 131 elementary schools, while the apparently much wider 30 percent criterion would include 183. Our standard includes nearly three fourths of this 183. The 10 percent standard, incidentally, was the one used in the Public Education Association's 1954 study of the New York schools, and it was employed most recently in a distinguished analysis of segregation in the Chicago public schools.

Early Desegregation Efforts

The New York City Board of Education in 1954 appointed a committee to examine the racial composition of the public schools and to recommend actions to achieve racial integration. This committee recommended in 1958 that three mechanisms be employed: zoning, site selection and construction, and pupil redistribution. An advisory council on zoning was subsequently formed, but there is no evidence that it effected any lasting results, although several new schools were built and some older ones modernized in ethnically mixed as opposed to segregated neighborhoods. The commission's recommendations on the redistribution of pupils through "permissive zoning" and busing were not implemented.

Open Enrollment in New York City

On the basis of experience during 1959 with the transporting of children from schools in the heavily segregated Bedford-Stuyvesant section of Brooklyn to mixed schools in Queens, the board of education introduced a plan for Open Enrollment.

The board introduced a larger Open Enrollment program which permitted students with the consent of their parents to transfer out of segregated schools by the fall of 1963. A total of roughly 16,000 students were affected or less than 1 percent of all students in the public system as a whole, or about 3 percent of the Negro and Puerto Rican student population.

Open Enrollment has had no significant effect on the extent of segregation. It *cannot* have, as it depends wholly upon voluntary choice among Negro and Puerto Rican parents. In September, 1963, for example, when the program was revised and enlarged, about 110,000 elementary pupils were offered the opportunity to transfer. Of this number, about 2,000 applied, and some 1,800 were in fact transferred—an impact of less than 2 percent of those given the option.

Zoning

The board made about a hundred changes in district and school zones in order to stimulate desegregation between 1959 and 1963. In addition, the board permitted more than six hundred individual exceptions, called zoning variances, for high school attendance in the same period. These changes, together with those summarized above, constitute *all* notable efforts by the board and its staff as of 1963 to reduce the level of *de facto* segregation among students in the city's public schools.

Evaluating Effects of Past Efforts

Data have been gathered on the ethnic composition of the schools only since 1958. If past efforts of the board have affected the level of segregation, the effect should be measurable—however slight—by comparing the 1958 data with those from 1963. (Any change in school segregation noted in our figures must be qualified. First, the underlying data are to some degree inaccurate, since they are based on visual judgments of classroom teachers as to each child's ethnicity. Secondly, about 5 percent on *any* increase in segregation is attributable to ethnic changes in school and city populations. Thus, if schools changed in percent segregated from 10 percent [1958] to 20 percent [1963], we would estimate that half of this change was inevitable. Had they declined from 20 percent to 10 percent, we would conclude that board efforts might have had up to a 5 percent effect.)

The fraction of Negro-Puerto Rican type segregated schools in New York City increased over the five years from 12 percent to 22 percent at the elementary level, from 10 percent to 19 percent at the junior high level, and from 0 percent to 2 percent at the senior high school level.

About three fourths of the city's schools did not change in percent Negro or Puerto Rican during the same period. Among the one fourth that did change, however, nearly all increased very substantially in percent Negro or Puerto Rican. *Despite Open Enrollment, rezoning, and associated efforts, segregation, city wide, has not been reduced. On the contrary, the overall level of segregation has increased.*

No act of the board of education from 1958 through 1962, with a single small exception, has had a measurable effect on the degree of school segregation. This exception may be at the senior high school level. Although there are White type segregated high schools, as of 1963 only one high school was clearly identifiable as a Negro-Puerto Rican type segregated school. This is the Girls' High School in Brooklyn, which, under the board's recent plan, will be abandoned. Benjamin Franklin High School, which was 11 percent White in 1963, has also received board attention in an effort to improve its situation.

About seventy-eight public schools below the high school level became segregated between 1958 and 1963. (The number will vary slightly depending upon the classification of certain schools that were combined during the period.) A judgment as to whether board efforts *slowed* the rate of school segregation in this period would require more detailed data from the years 1953 through 1963, but *our impression is that, not a single elementary or junior high school that was changing toward segregation after 1958 by virtue of residential changes and the transfer of whites into parochial and private schools was prevented from becoming segregated by board action.* There were schools whose composition was changed toward desegregation during this period, but they appear to be located in neighborhoods where urban renewal, relocation and redevelopment involved the displacement of families. Of the board's desegregation activities (during this period) only the Open Enrollment program was large in scale. It affected only previously segregated schools—and even there, too few pupils to modify the trends.

Evaluation of 1964-1970 School Building Program

The board has adopted a program for erecting new buildings and renovating old ones during the next six years and beyond. Of the forty-four projected for action in 1964 and 1965, about twenty are located at points *outside* existing, overcrowded residential ghettos. A statement in explanation of the site selections prepared by the board's planning and research division helps interpret this fact:

> A more helpful perspective would be achieved if we viewed the budget from the vantage point of providing desperately needed additional accommodations to achieve a full day in badly overcrowded areas of the city. From this viewpoint, the board of education is recognizing these needs and taking steps to satisfy them.

The school building program as presently set forth reinforces substantially the historic pattern of building on sites within the most segregated areas. This is the case chiefly in Negro residential areas, but it is also true in some mainly white neighborhoods, and thus helps to intensify both forms of segregation.

To date, desegregation has not been a main factor in the programming of construction and physical renovation. Building plans have developed in response to population increase, age and quality of existing plant, transport conditions, and site availability. If the purpose to desegregate was considered at all, it apparently was ranked in importance below these other considerations.

Evaluation of the Free Choice Transfer Policy

The board announced, late in 1963, a Free Choice Transfer Policy. This permits any child in a school with a "high" percentage of Negro or Puerto Ricans to transfer, at his parent's request, to any other school where space is available.

This policy improves upon the Open Enrollment plan. The board intends, for instance, to define space available "liberally," that is, at something more than 100 percent of rated capacity. In addition, the standard for a "high percentage" of minority students will be lowered "progressively" over the years. And, unlike the Open Enrollment plan, once a school qualifies under the new policy, any student in it may apply for a transfer.

In our judgment, the Free Choice Transfer Policy, whatever its other merits, and we think it has some, will probably have no city-wide effect on the level of segregation. It is an optional, not a required program. It puts the burden for desegregation entirely on the voluntary and individual decisions of Negro and Puerto Rican parents. A handful of whites may elect to use the programs, but generally the policy will tend to operate in but one direction: minority children will transfer out of Negro-Puerto Rican type segregated schools. The total enrollment of such schools may decline a bit, but they will not gain white students and therefore will not be desegregated as a result of the policy.

Evaluation of the Junior High School Feeder Pattern Changes

The board of education plans to change the pattern of elementary schools feeding into junior high schools. Specifically, the board proposed ten such changes and then reduced this number to six, out of a total of 132 regular junior high schools.

The number of Negro-Puerto Rican type junior high schools in the city increased from twelve in 1958, to twenty-five in 1963; or from 10 percent to 19 percent of all junior highs. At the same time the White type junior high schools declined from 43 percent to 22 percent. In numbers of students, about 45 percent of the city's Negro and Puerto Rican youths attended segregated junior high schools in 1963.

The six Feeder Pattern Changes proposed by the board would *reduce* the percent of segregated junior high schools from the present 41 percent to 39 percent. At this rate of desegregation, and ignoring natural population changes in the interval, the junior high school system would be desegregated by about the year 2010.

If a great effort were made to desegregate the twenty-five junior high schools which are now Negro-Puerto Rican type schools, the new policy could make a difference within a single decade. Such an effort is not proposed by the board of education.

Evaluation of Pairing Proposals

The chief innovation made by the board in 1964, was the location of twenty-one areas where elementary schools might be paired. Under this policy, two schools in proximity would be so organized that each building would be used for selected grades for all pupils in the combined zones of the two schools.

In 1958, 12 percent of all elementary schools were Negro-Puerto Rican segregated, compared with 22 percent in 1963. If all twenty-one of the pairings proposed by the board were to be introduced at once in 1964-65, this fraction of 22 percent would drop to 21 percent. *The pairing proposal thus would reduce minority school segregation in the city by 1 percent if introduced all at once.* Not only have many of the proposed sites been withdrawn following local opposition, however, but the board proposed to make only four such pairings in September, 1964.

Summary of Evaluation of Board Proposals and Efforts

We must conclude that nothing undertaken by the New York City Board of Education since 1954, and nothing proposed since 1963, has contributed or will contribute in any meaningful degree to desegregating the public schools of the city. Each past effort, each current plan, and each projected proposal is either not aimed at reducing segregation or is developed in too limited a fashion to stimulate even slight progress toward desegregation.

Our data suggest that present conditions and immediate possibilities are relatively most favorable at the senior high school level. Here, the system is two-thirds desegregated. However, nearly one third of the high schools continue to be of the White type. Many of these are the most advantaged schools in the system, and board policies have not addressed the task of desegregating these "choice" institutions.

At the elementary school level, the board has done nothing and proposed no plan that would reduce current levels, or stem the rising tide of segregation.

With no special policies, Negro-Puerto Rican type segregated elementary schools will tend to grow from 22 percent of all the schools in 1963 to 31 percent in 1970, to perhaps 38 percent in 1975. We estimate that the pairing of some twenty elementary schools a year—presuming a very active extension of the board plan—would yield a system that would still be 24 percent minority segregated in 1970.

The feeder changes proposed for junior high schools would have merit, if the proposed annual rate of change were increased by about three times, and if chief attention were given to minority rather than to White type segregated schools.

Some Underlying Forces

Before advancing alternative suggestions, we wish to describe the population changes which have historically characterized the social situation in New York City, and are likely to do so in the future. Any planning on so vital an educational issue as desegregation should be done, we believe, on the basis of full knowledge of the total community situation.

Public school ethnic segregation is less severe in New York City than in most major central cities such as Philadelphia, Chicago, and Detroit. In Chicago, for example, 37 percent of all elementary schools were Negro type segregated in 1963, compared with 22 percent in New York City; and 18 percent of the high schools were Negro segregated, compared with 2 percent in New York City.

The ethnic minorities are numerically larger in New York City; and residential segregation is different in pattern. Chicago's population was 23 percent nonwhite in 1960, where New York City's was 22 percent Negro and Puerto Rican. However, the numerically smaller Chicago minority was crowded for the most part into *one* elongated "Black Belt." New York City's ghettos are more dispersed; indeed, there are seven large, circle-shaped ghettos in noncontiguous areas. In any case, *de facto* school segregation is not unique to New York City. It is rather a major social problem in most large and many smaller northern metropolitan communities.

De facto segregation in public schools cannot be attributed to intentional policies of the board of education in New York City. Given the prevalence of the neighborhood school principle under which urban public schools are organized, and which continues to be preferred by most parents, school segregation is a by-product of patterns of segregation in settlement and housing.

Two great migrations form the basis for public school segregation in New York City today. The greater of the two is the movement of Negroes from the South. In 1910, 89 percent of the nation's Negro population resided in the South. In the same year, only about 100,000 or 1 percent of the total resided in the New York metropolitan area. By 1960, nearly 1.3 million Negroes, or about 6 percent of the nation's Negro population, had settled here. In the fifty years from 1910 to 1960, while the number of Negroes in the United States approximately doubled, the number of Negroes in the New York urban area multiplied *ten times.*

The second great migration has been the movement into the city and its area of Puerto Ricans. The Puerto Rican population grew from less than 1 percent to nearly 6 percent of the urban area population between 1940 and 1960. Both migrations will continue, though at a decreasing rate, for the rest of this century.

As the Negro and Puerto Rican populations in New York City have increased, other groups have spread outward to the perimeters of the city and into its suburbs. This change also continues. *About one fifth of the city population was Negro and Puerto Rican in 1960. About one fourth will be in 1965; the fraction may expand to one third by 1970.*

The 20 percent Negro and Puerto Rican residents of the city in 1960 were crowded into extremely overpopulated, segregated sections of the city. The Puerto Ricans have dispersed gradually since 1955, but Negroes continue to be confined chiefly to seven residential ghettos. New little islands have started elsewhere, but real dispersion is rare.

For the public schools, this situation is intensified by more than the departure of whites, or more advantaged groups, from the city. Residential segregation and a rapid thinning of whites is further confounded by the fact that New York City parents have the option of choice among public, private and parochial schools. Because the latter are overwhelmingly white in composition, and because the number of these schools has grown substantially since 1950, the overall fraction of Negroes and Puerto Ricans in the public schools far exceeds their representation in the city population at large. The percentage of minority children is also larger in thelower grades than at the upper levels. In the Bronx, for example, in 1960 when 25 percent of all residents were Negro or Puerto Rican, 43 percent of the students in the public schools were of those groups. In the elementary schools, 51 percent were from the two minorities. This difference is attributable not so much to size of family or birthrate (as is often believed), but rather to the fact that the more recently arrived households of Negroes and Puerto Ricans are younger than their white neighbors, and therefore have younger children.

Three present population trends are likely to continue to affect New York City no matter what policies are adopted for the public schools. First, the proportion of public school pupils who are Negro and Puerto Rican will continue to increase. *We estimate that minority pupils will exceed 50 percent in 1965, 66 percent in 1970, and 70 percent in 1975.* Secondly, these increases will be differentially distributed. The Manhattan schools already have 73 percent Negro and Puerto Rican pupils. The Queens schools will not reach the 40 percent to 50 percent interval until about 1980. Third, within each borough, unless unforeseen changes occur, this increase will continue to take place under patterns of residential segregation. As White type segregated schools remain persistently under-utilized in many places, Negro-Puerto Rican type segregated schools will continue to become overcrowded.

All three trends add to the difficulty of forming a policy for effective desegregation. The continuing overall decrease in the white component of the school population further reduces the possibility of easy improvement. Moreover, the wide differences in the various sections of the city require different policies in different sections. Most painfully, overcrowding in the residential ghettos makes many efforts to desegregate futile, for distance and population concentration work against nearly all forms of redistribution. Many features of this population process are beyond the control of either the board of education or any other agency of city government.

White New Yorkers do not move out of the city simply because of prejudice. White migration to the suburbs results from many economic, social, and familial forces. The migration *out of the region, largely white,* is a response to the rapid rates of growth in the west and southwest areas of the nation.

An increase in the ratio of Negroes and Puerto Ricans to whites in city public schools helps to *precipitate* movement out of the public schools and out of the city. When ethnic imbalance occurs, all three broad ethnic groups lose, educationally and socially. As the rate of immigration rises or imbalance reaches a certain level in relation the the distribution of residents in the neighborhood around a public school, non-Puerto Rican and other whites tend to remove their children from it and minority segregation inevitably follows.

This pattern of white exodus from the public schools has proceeded in Washington, D.C., Newark, New Jersey, and perhaps elsewhere, to the point of near-total segregation. In less than ten years, for example, the Washington public school pupil population changed from about one-third to more than three-fourths Negro. They may well be nine-tenths Negro by 1970.

The trend toward school segregation has been and will continue to be slower in New York City. There are several reasons for this prediction. New York City is much larger than Washington and Newark, and its adults are employed in much more widely diversified occupations. For these and other economic structural reasons, New York City can absorb a numerically greater amount of ethnic change than other cities without the change being reflected as dramatically or extremely in overall statistics. New York City can also "hold" a greater proportion of its white families for a longer period than can other cities.

Another important consideration is the balance between private and public schools. About 70 percent of the city's white students were in public schools in 1960, compared with 86 percent of its Negro students. Stated another way, there are about 1.4 million white and Negro students enrolled in schools in New York City. Of these, about 400,000 are in private and parochial schools; and of these, only 32,000 (less than 10 percent) are Negroes.

Most of the 32,000 are in schools operated under the auspices of Roman Catholic and Episcopal Churches, which together account for nearly three fourths of the city's private school students.

Our data lead us to predict that, in the absence of significant efforts by the board of education and other groups and agencies, the New York City public schools by 1980 will enroll about 70 percent to 75 percent Negro and Puerto Rican pupils and that the proportion may be expected to stabilize at that level.

Even though no action by the board of education can prevent the growth of minority population, wise and intelligent policies can contribute substantially to preventing extreme school segregation. What occurs when firm preventive steps are not taken is all too obvious: when a city school system moves from ethnic balance to extreme segregation, the quality of its instructional services is undermined as support, both lay and professional, declines. Aggressive policies designed to desegregate the schools and improve instruction simultaneously can, in contrast, make such a period of ethnic change one of *heightened* confidence in public education.

The options available to New York City are not unlimited but they are real. Total desegregation of all schools, for example, is simply not attainable in the foreseeable future and neither planning nor pressure can change that fact. Yet if nothing more is done, or too little is attempted, the outcome will inevitably be more extensive and more extreme segregation and a larger number of poor schools. More can be done, however, and should be. With thoughtful planning, bold policies and vigorous action, there are sound reasons to believe that the spread of segregation can be slowed, its severity reduced, and the effectiveness of school programs substantially improved.

Findings and Recommendations

By the definition used in this report, the proportion of segregated schools in the public school system may be expected to increase between 1963 and 1975, from 22 percent to 38 percent and the elementary level, from 19 percent to 29 percent at the junior high school level, and from 2 percent to 6 percent at the high school level, *unless* steps far more comprehensive and effective than those currently proposed by the board of education are taken promptly.

Some remedies that have been suggested are both impractical and educationally undesirable. Among these is long-distance transportation of elementary school pupils. This device appears to promise the greatest immediate change in *de facto* segregation, but in many cases it is more likely to have a negative effect. Residential segregation in Brooklyn, for example, is so extreme that some 70,000 Negro and Puerto Rican children, ages five through eleven, would have to be transported twice daily on trips as long as that from Brighton Beach to Fulton Street, some ten miles or fifty city bus minutes away. In Manhattan, because of an even higher proportion of Negro and Puerto Rican children, even greater amounts of transport would not effect integration. The same condition holds (but in a lesser degree) for the Bronx and Queens.

Persuaded by the fact, however, that *there are steps which could be taken by the board to desegregate the public schools*, we sought ways to reduce segregation and at the same time improve education. As our earlier interpretation of the city ethnic trends reveals, we believe that part of the educational desirability of any plan at this time must be its *mutual* acceptance by both minority groups and whites. It should be obvious, but does not always appear to be, that integration is impossible without white pupils. No plan can be acceptable, therefore, which increases the movement of white pupils out of the public schools. Neither is it acceptable, however, unless it contributes to desegregation. Our criteria for devising proposals are therefore these: (1) genuine, prompt reduction of school segregation; (2) improvement in the quality of educational services; and (3) retention and, if possible, attraction of more white pupils.

It is our considered judgment that a major reorganization of the school system is required in order to achieve within a period of the next ten to fifteen years the twin goals of high quality schools and the greatest possible degree of desegregation.

The data on the ethnic composition of schools indicate most clearly that even a comprehensive desegregation plan will not eliminate all segregated schools. Our proposals will, however, reduce the number of them and retard the spread of segregation. They will also increase the proportion of Negro, Puerto Rican, and white children who will have the opportunity for integrated experience in good schools.

High Schools

The maximum degree of desegregation can now be achieved at the high school level. This possibility can be realized by the more effective use of existing plants and the strategic selection of sites for new buildings. Toward this end, the board of education should introduce a large-scale program of construction and development of *four-year comprehensive high schools*.

We recommend that these high schools include grades nine through twelve, absorbing ninth grades now assigned to junior high schools. We recommend further that to accommodate the ninth-grade students, and to relieve overcrowding from the already anticipated increases in grades ten, eleven, and twelve, the high school construction program be revised.

Most of the new four-year comprehensive high schools should be located at sites in the north Bronx and in predominantly white neighborhoods in Brooklyn and Queens. These are the three boroughs that are now moving most rapidly toward predominantly Negro and Puerto Rican public school populations. Within ten years, therefore, comprehensive high schools located in now white neighborhoods will, in all likelihood, be centers of desegregated communities outside the ghetto. *The first step to be taken would be to revise the planned locations of the five high schools projected by the board of education for construction in 1964 and 1965. At least four of these are now projected for location in heavily segregated residential areas.*

Comprehensive schools on well selected sites would provide a significant counterforce to the present slow but evident trend toward segregated high schools. They will do this by redistributing students now segregated by reason either of their residence or of the curricula they are presently pursuing. At present 78 percent of the pupils in academic high schools are whites, while only 52 percent of the pupils in vocational high schools are whites. The programs of the new high schools should be planned to assure a suitably high level of general education for all students. Such vocational courses as are to be continued should be distributed among the comprehensive schools rather than concentrated in wholly specialized vocational units. While some special-purpose schools may well be justified, the policy should be to eliminate those at which attendance seems to imply a stigma, or which show a trend toward increasing racial homogeneity.

We recommend further that all high schools should be open to all students on a city-wide basis with no restrictions except those needed to prevent the overcrowding of particular schools.

In short, this proposal would seek to promote the desegregation of the high schools and to meet the educational needs of all groups by introducing schools that are neither too general nor too specialized to adapt to changing occupational and cultural conditions. An additional advantage of including the ninth grade in the high schools is that this grade contains a larger proportion of minority students than the tenth through twelfth grades. The four-year organization will accordingly yield a better ethnic balance and will increase the number of students who will have the opportunity for integrated educational experience.

The Middle School

In order to extend the process of desegregation to the lower grades and at the same time improve the educational opportunities for children we recommend the establishment of new *middle schools* to include grades seven and eight of the present junior high schools and grades five and six of the present elementary schools. At present there are twenty-five Negro-Puerto Rican type segregated junior high schools; there are twenty-nine White type segregated junior high schools. The junior high schools represent a concentration and intensification of the effects of segregation.

For the immediate future most middle schools should be located in former junior high schools renovated for their new purpose. Their ethnic mixtures, especially in the ghetto fringe areas, can approach desegregation because students would be drawn from predominantly white as well as predominantly Negro and Puerto Rican elementary schools, and because increased equity of distribution will make this possible.

All of the segregated junior high schools should be eliminated immediately. Of the twenty-five in this group, more than half are situated in the deep centers of the several residential ghettos. Elimination of junior high schools should begin at the fringes of the ghettos, going in as deeply as transportation and the effective organization of the complexes described later will allow. Over the period from 1965 through 1970, the abolition of junior high schools could make a substantial contribution, particularly to preventing future growth in the number of upper level ghetto schools. Even while some segregation will remain in the middle schools, it might be possible to so organize the cluster of primary schools which feed each middle school in order to increase the racial heterogeneity of most of these middle schools. (See discussion of Educational Complex below.)

The program of the middle school should be planned to meet the educational needs of older children through increasingly diversified and specialized instruction. The upper grades of the middle school would be expected to resemble the better parts of the junior high school. Giving the seventh and eighth grades the status of being the senior members of their school communities may be expected to reduce some of the adjustment problems that have so long plagued the junior high school. Middle school students would also begin their exposure to secondary education earlier, yet not be subjected to the undesirable poor models provided by so many ninth graders in the current junior high school system, models of antagonism and indifference toward school induced by the onset of adolescence combined with a lack of preparation for, or hope about, movement into senior high school. Middle schools and four-year comprehensive high schools may in combination contribute to reducing the city-wide problem of drop-outs from high school. The middle schools provide strong programs of guidance and such other special services as may be needed and should give close attention to both the special aptitudes and the handicaps of its pupils. As has been pointed out, junior high school buildings may be converted for the use of these units. In the newer plants, relatively few physical changes should be necessary.

The middle school as envisioned in this proposal would receive its students from a combined and clustered set of between two and six primary schools, as described below.

Primary Schools

We recommend that a new school unit be established to include the first four grades, the kindergarten, and as soon as they can be added, one or two years of prekindergarten education. The prekindergarten programs should be added first in those neighborhoods where the need is greatest. The primary unit should be centered in the neighborhood and as close as possible to the homes of the children attending it.

Wherever possible, a unit should not enroll more than five hundred pupils although where larger buildings are used, as will be necessary in many cases, two or more such units might well be organized in the same building. The reason for proposing relatively small groups is to make it possible for the young child to feel himself a member of his school group, to make it possible for the faculty of the unit to work together as a close-knit organization and to enable the parents of the school to work closely with it on a continuous and intensive basis.

The primary unit should be organized on a nongraded basis so as to facilitate the continuous progress of pupils as individuals without arbitrary barriers of grade placement and time limits. Such an arrangement should also add to the possibility of introducing forms of coordinated or team teaching, variable grouping of pupils and the imaginative use of space, materials, and teaching devices.

The program of the school should be planned to serve both the general educational needs of young children and any special requirements of children in its own neighborhood. The parents should be involved in many ways, including service as volunteers or where feasible as part-time or full-time paid assistants. Close liaison should be maintained with the homes through the services of counselors, school social workers, and classroom teachers when they are adequately prepared for this additional duty. Parent education programs should also be developed as a part of the program of the local school, with appropriate staff assistance by specialists.

These neighborhood units will inevitably in many cases be segregated. We recognize the disadvantage of that condition but believe that it is offset by the superior opportunities for teaching and guidance that such a school offers. Since in many neighborhoods integration can be achieved only at the expense of large amounts of travel time and the transfer of a child to a school far from his own home, we believe that on balance the neighborhood primary unit is the more desirable arrangement.

The Educational Complex

Neighborhood primary schools and nearby middle schools should be combined into clusters that, for want of a more descriptive term, we shall call *educational complexes*. An educational complex will be composed of from two to five primary schools and one or two middle schools. The new organizations should be created first wherever they will contribute to desegregation or better integration. . . .

An educational complex should be administered by a *senior administrator*, who should be given authority and autonomy to develop a program which meets appropriate city-wide standards but is also directly relevant to the needs of the locality. Primary schools within the complex should share among themselves facilities and special staff and should be coordinated to encourage frequent association among students and parents from the several units. Within the educational complex teachers will be better able to help children from diverse ethnic backgrounds to become acquainted with one another. Parent-teacher and parent-school relations should be built on the bases of both the individual school and the complex. The children—and their parents—will thus gain the dual benefits of a school close to home and of membership in a larger, more diverse educational and social community. The concept of the educational complex arises in part from the view that the means of education and much of their control should be centered locally.

Although it may not be possible to desegregate all primary schools, ultimately most of them should be integrated educationally. This will aid the better preparation of students for life and study in the middle school; it will more nearly equalize resources; and it will give the staff in the primary schools new opportunities for innovation and originality in their work.

It may be useful to illustrate the arrangement and operation of schools under our proposals. In District 8 in Manhattan, P.S. 75, P.S. 84, and P.S. 166 are currently desegregated elementary schools in transition toward partial White type segregated. They are located near one another and near Junior High School 118. These units would become an educational complex under our recommendations, the ninth graders from 118 being reassigned to the reorganized comprehensive high schools situated outside a ghetto area. Fifth and sixth graders from 75, 84, and 166 would be picked up at designated assembly points and *transported by shuttle bus* to middle school 118, a trip requiring not more than ten to fifteen minutes, or *the average time it now takes children to walk to school*. This policy will prevail in as many instances as possible.

Another illustration: P.S. 189, 219, 156, 175, and 183, in Districts 41 and 42 of ͏ Brooklyn, are located near one another, and near Junior High School 252. The entire group is proceeding toward Negro-Puerto Rican type school segregation, for these schools are on the fringe of the rapidly enlarging Bedford-Stuyvesant community. If no changes are introduced, it is predictable that Junior High School 252 will have less than 10 percent white students by 1970, rather than the present 40 percent white. The board of education proposed for this area a Princeton type pairing of P.S. 156 with P.S. 210. This would desegregate *one* elementary school but would leave the other schools in the immediate area vulnerable to rapid and extreme segregation. Our plan, in contrast, would mean that the youngest primary children would go to their nearby elementary schools. Thus, P.S. 210 would remain predominantly white and P.S. 156 predominantly Negro and Puerto Rican. Both sets of parents would, however, be encouraged to *stay on* in the community because a good, stable, and desegregated middle school was at hand.

We recommend further that, as soon as possible, the middle schools should be located in educational parks so situated as to provide children in as many parts of the city as is feasible, the experience of attending a genuinely integrated school during their middle school years. We recognize that for reasons previously pointed out, it may not be possible for some time to assure every child such an experience, but our objective is to bring it about for the greatest possible number. This we think can be accomplished by locating groups of middle schools on large sites designed to accommodate perhaps 15,000 children with administrative units organized so that each child will be a member of a school enrolling 500 to 1,000 pupils. The most practical location for such schools would be in areas where a suitable number of minority group children can be drawn from existing ghetto neighborhoods into parks which will also enroll children from white neighborhoods.

Equalizing Facilities

Good physical facilities are no substitute for good teaching but they are powerful auxiliaries to it. Obviously, there are limits on the speed with which New York City can reconstruct its gigantic collection of more than a thousand buildings. Many of them are deteriorating and it is essential that more be done to improve the buildings and equipment of the school system, especially in the depressed and segregated neighborhoods. This condition requires immediate and sustained attention.

As of 1963, in spite of the fact that the board erected many new schools in the last five years (twenty-six as replacements for schools within ghettos), Negro and Puerto Rican segregated schools as a group were still, on the average, the oldest in the city, formed the greatest number of overcrowded buildings, and included the greatest number of buildings in need of modernization or installation of essential facilities.

Staffing the Classroom

Desegregation and the prevention of further school segregation alike hinge upon the creation of public schools so excellent that parents of all ethnic groups will enroll, their children with confidence and pride. This condition hinges upon recruitment, certification, supervision, and retention of outstanding classroom teachers.

Without good teaching, desegregation is educationally meaningless. Moreover it becomes increasingly impossible to achieve as parents lose confidence in their public schools and as those with higher economic, occupational, and educational attainment can achieve the means to move away. Authentic desegregation is impossible without the progressive provision of improved instruction in the public schools. The proposals for modifying the organization of levels in the schools and for the clustering of units form a basis for such improvement. A major reconstruction of the sort outlined will introduce *new incentives* for such teachers. The new educational complexes can become centers within which exciting professional activity and development is both possible and encouraged. We would go further, however. Many practices of the present city system must be changed drastically if more good teachers are to be employed, attracted to assignments in heavily mixed schools, and retained while they mature toward professional excellence.

For example, more Negro and Puerto Rican teachers and administrators must be recruited and advanced in responsibility as rapidly as their performance justifies. Although the school system does not close any of its positions to members of minority groups, Negroes have had more difficulty than others progressing through the system's hierarchy.

It should be possible to find more than the present group of fewer than ten Negroes who are competent to handle some of the system's more than 1,200 administrative positions. Surely more than the present two or three Negroes are capable of outstanding service among the 800 principalships.

It is not enough that selection stardards be high and objective. An equally important question is whether they are sufficiently relevant and flexible to obtain people with the qualities most needed in the schools.

We propose, therefore, greater flexibility in the recruitment and examination of school staff members. The board of examiners since 1960 has placed somewhat less emphasis on written test performance. This reform should be continued and intensified.

We also propose greater flexibility in the design of the teacher's day. The reports persist that teachers and other staff members are overburdened by paperwork, lack of clerical and technical support, and are subjected to unprofessional regulations that unduly restrict their performance.

The proposed reorganization should be used as an opportunity to correct these conditions. With the development of educational complexes, middle schools, and comprehensive high schools, considerable decentralization will be possible. Within system-wide policies to assure high minimum standards of administration, teaching, pupil services, and community relations, decentralization can release administrators and teachers from standardized requirements. The local initiative and responsible freedom essential to good schools must be more actively encouraged.

At present, a spurious "reward structure" exists within the staffing pattern of the New York schools. Through it, less experienced and less competent teachers are assigned to the least "desirable" yet professionally most demanding depressed area schools. As the teacher gains experience and demonstrates competence, his mobility upward usually means mobility away from the pupils with the greatest need for skilled help. The classrooms that most urgently need the best teachers are thus most often deprived of them.

With the assignment of a teacher to one of the proposed complexes such transfers would be unnecessary. Within a complex teachers will be able to work with a variety of types of pupils or colleagues. No complex need be a "hardship post" or "ghetto outpost." They can become centers of professional excitement and growth.

This prospect will not be realized, however, merely by changing the organization of schools within the complexes. Serious and sustained efforts will have to be made to achieve equitable assignment of staff, competent supervision, strong support structure, a release from constrictions on local and individual initiative, and maximum racial heterogeneity.

Training Teachers

While the board becomes more flexible and imaginative in its personnel recruitment efforts, as we believe it has since 1961, it must also look more closely at its *training* resources.

For example, arrangements must be made so that student teachers may take their practice in schools that are well mixed ethnically, and even predominantly Negro and Puerto Rican. To accomplish this, the college auspices under which the professional education occurs must be strengthened substantially. Virtually every one of the city's public and private higher educational institutions has experimented with programs for teachers planning to enter big city schools. Most of these efforts remain underfinanced; only a few are more than tentative pilot projects; and too few provide any solid basis for close cooperation with the public school system.

In order for these new programs in teacher preparation to succeed, more than a few courses in urban sociology are needed. State and federal as well as city funds must be channeled into cooperative reasearch and development activities to involve colleges and universities more effectively on the work of the urban school system. The major training institutions should not be devoted as consistently as they have been to the preparation of teachers for suburbia.

Preprimary Programs

Harvard psychologist Thomas Pettigrew has commented, "Fourteen generations of Negro talent have already been wasted by American society; our technological society cannot afford to waste yet another." If the talents of the young are to be cultivated and preserved, the process must, under modern conditions, not only take longer; it must also start sooner. The outstanding educational program necessary to prevent further segregation of schools and children in New York, moreover, depends upon high levels of aspiration and school type achievement among a larger proportion of children. The talents of New York City children must, therefore, be cultivated earlier than ever before. Only a new, *city-wide* program of prekindergarten education will stimulate this change.

There are two reasons why we urge that the board of education introduce on a large scale basis a preprimary program of instruction. First, it is at this level that what we have elsewhere called *compensatory* education can have a significant impact. The materially or socially deprived child can gain most from extra enrichment at the age of three or four. This program is both compensatory and preventative. It would cost less and have greater benefits than remedial programs for adolescent dropouts.

We recommend that the pilot projects in preprimary instruction be adopted progressively throughout the city, beginning first within the educational complexes and in the centers of ghetto areas. The board of education should be encouraged to cooperate closely in this activity with the City Department of Welfare's Division of Infant Day Care Centers, which can provide additional starting points for this program.

Special Schools

Few objective data are available on the programs of the special schools but, what evidence we do have suggests that these schools, particularly the "600" schools, have grown at a rapid pace in recent years. The functions they are designed to serve remain vague. We could find, for example, no clear statement of the present curriculum for these schools. And the available data indicate a disproportionate number of minority group students in these schools. The plans for the newer programs for special students seem, in Junior Guidance classes and After-School programs, similarly unclear.

Special schools seem often to be set up deliberately outside the neighborhood where their students live. The rationale offered is to release the child from his antagonistic surroundings without embarrassing him by special placement in his own neighborhood schools. Actually, this arrangement also removes the child from his family, neighborhood, peers, and normal school experience. Although he is officially defined as a special problem, he is also treated as if he were autonomous and responsible enough to *commute* to a distant school. The arrangement, to say the least, raises serious questions.

Similar questions must be raised about educational provisions for the mentally retarded. Gerhart Saenger, in his report, *Factors Influencing the Institutionalization of Mentally Retarded Individuals in New York City,* said in 1960 that "more than half of the recently institutionalized low grade retarded children came from Puerto Rican and Negro families, even though these groups together make up slightly less than one quarter of the population of the city." Saenger also identifies probable serious errors in the diagnostic and referral systems leading up to institutionalization.

The total numbers of disturbed, maladjusted, and retarded students in the city's public schools are very small compared with the total student population, yet we believe that the *educational quality* of a school system can be assessed to an important degree by the treatment it affords the most disadvantaged, the needy, and deviant groups of children and youth. We do not have adequate facts about special educational programs in the city. It appears that such information has not been secured by the school system itself.

We therefore propose that objective, independent studies be made of the care and schooling of special students in the city's public school system, and the results published. We also propose that *special educational programs be closely related to the neighborhood primary school and the middle school.* Children with emotional and social handicaps should increasingly be dealt with as those with physical handicaps are. If a student is not principally an invalid, a medical patient, or a hazard to his schoolmates, he should be educated with his peers or at least within the same school building. If the child's primary problem is medical or one requiring custody, the responsibility for him should rest with an agency other than the school.

Fiscal Responsibility

These proposals are advanced as a *minimum* program of changes that are necessary if the board is to reduce and prevent school segregation. The proposals may be modified in their particulars, but their combined magnitude and import is, if anything, an understatement of what must be done to achieve desegregation in New York City schools.

Can the New York City public school system, already burdened with excessive fiscal problems, achieve these goals? One response is the logic of crisis: As Commissioner Allen wrote about New York's school system in 1962, "In many ways, possibly in most ways, the future of the metropolis is being written in its classrooms today. Unless what is being done now is done better, and unless much, much more is done than is now being done, that future will be a bleak one in many respects."

The second answer is that more is at stake in New York City than the future well-being of a single city. The public school students of this community form more than one third of the total public school enrollment of New York State. A large part of the state's responsibility for the welfare of its youth is concentrated here.

The third consideration is that among all the great cities of the North, New York's public schools stand a better social chance of achieving authentic desegregation than possibly any of the others. This city is comparatively free of the forces of social and political reaction against full civil rights. This city has a heritage of cultural innovation and educational progress. If school segregation cannot be fought effectively here, if the public school children of New York City must be relegated to second-class status for lack of energy and effort, the nation will have reason to despair.

In view of the enormity of both the problem and the possibilities, *we propose that both the state and federal governments be urged to demonstrate their deep involvement through progressive increases in fiscal support. When municipal initiatives toward substantial change are demonstrated, and as they are introduced, substantial financial assistance and technical cooperation will be essential.* It is doubtful that without large-scale additional state and federal support, the necessary reforms can even be successfully begun, much less thoroughly completed.

The Test of School Desegregation

An effective program of desegregation will be very costly. It will require funds not available from within the public economy of New York City, to be sure. Yet, there are steps that can be taken by the board of education and by the superintendent of schools and by others that will not require extra funds. *Decisions and actions on these, we suggest, should become the test of whether the city's educational policy makers seriously intend to reduce and to prevent further segregation.*

The fact that outside support must be obtained to accelerate desegregation should not become a reason for inaction. Indeed, it is probable that when the board of education initiates its own revised program, significant outside help will materialize. The steps that can be taken now and over the coming year without additional outside funds include the following:

1. The five high schools already projected by the board for construction and already capitalized could be relocated outside minority ghettos and redesigned to become comprehensive high schools. This would set the precedent for future secondary school contruction.
2. Junior high schools feeding the new comprehensive high schools, other new junior high schools for construction, and other selected junior highs . . . should be chosen

for conversion into middle schools. This conversion could be accomplished, we believe, without great extra expense within the next year. Later, additional conversions would require further funds.

3. A first series of educational complexes could be created around the newly formed middle schools cited above. These would require complicated administrative and faculty reorganization but no important addition to expenditures.

4. Openings for Negro and Puerto Rican teachers and administrators can be widened immediately without extra expense.

5. Greater flexibility and autonomy can be provided to the principals and their staffs within the new educational complexes.

6. Newly strengthened cooperation between teacher-training institutions and the board can be developed over the next year with no important additional expenditures of funds.

7. Studies and policy reviews of the organization of special educational services, especially for the socially maladjusted and the mentally retarded, can be initiated at no important additional cost.

Prompt decisions and vigorous action on these items will demonstrate the clarity of purpose, the firmness of commitment, and the determination to succeed that the entire community is waiting to witness and eager to applaud.

Brief Summary of Report

Findings

1. Puerto Rican, Negro, and other students in public schools in New York City suffer extensive and serious ethnic segregation.

2. This segregation increased between 1958 and 1963, and will continue to increase over the next ten to fifteen years, unless deliberate policies are introduced to reduce current levels and prevent future increases in segregation.

3. The board of education has made efforts between 1954 and the present which were intended to reduce segregation. These efforts have had *no* measurable effect upon the overall number of students attending segregated schools or upon the number of segregated schools in the system.

4. Early in 1964, the board of education introduced new proposals intended to aid in desegregating the public schools. The new proposals, considered singly and in combination, would not reduce current levels of school segregation or prevent future increases.

5. Ethnic segregation cannot be wholly eliminated from the schools of New York City in the foreseeable future, but the adoption of wise and intelligent policies can reduce segregation substantially. The basic requirement is a deep and sustained commitment on the part of the board and its staff to the purpose of reducing segregation throughout the city at the earliest time and at the fastest possible rate.

6. The adopted building program of the board does *not* treat *desegregation* as a main factor in choosing sites, although this factor could be utilized.

7. Wise and intelligent policies to foster desegregation must include intensified efforts to raise the quality of school program and teaching in New York City schools to the highest level, which is to say a degree of excellence second to none in the United States. The purpose of desegregation and increased excellence must be pursued simultaneously. They are absolutely interdependent.

8. The real accomplishment of both objectives is a complicated, costly, and difficult undertaking. It is far beyond what many advocates of change have seemed willing to recognize or acknowledge. Basic changes in the present organization of the school grades and the revision of construction programs are essential to desegregation and improvement, as are new concepts of recruitment, faculty involvement, curriculum design, pupil services, administrative operation, plant use, and interschool communication.

Recommendations

1. Comprehensive four-year high schools should be built at points well outside existing ethnic ghettos, to be attended by commuting youths from points all over the city as well as by local residents.
2. Fifth- through eighth-grade middle schools should replace junior high schools ultimately in the entire system. The purpose of these units should be to furnish improved instruction for older children. They should be so located as to provide for as many children as possible an experience in an integrated school. Shuttle buses should be used to reach these middle schools.
3. Primary units extending from prekindergarten classes through the fourth grade should replace existing elementary schools. These units would still be neighborhood schools, but they would be organized differently and would feed into the middle schools. Many existing elementary schools could be reorganized to contain two or more primary units.
4. Educational complexes should be formed, consisting of from two to six primary units clustered around the middle schools. These should be managed by a single administrator, with assistant administrators in the separate unit buildings. The complexes should integrate educational activities, improve the distribution of facilities and resources, and promote communication between faculties, parents, and students from diverse ethnic backgrounds. Complexes should have a high degree of organizational autonomy over their programs.
5. Eventually, educational parks housed in newly developed structures on cleared sites should replace single middle schools with their educational complexes.
6. Facilities should be equalized in every wáy, so that mainly Puerto Rican and Negro schools in the city will *not* continue to be older, more overcrowded, and in greater need of installation of essential facilities than other schools.
7. The new organization of the system should be utilized to stabilize and improve the staffing of the schools. The middle schools and clustered primary units with their new autonomy should be used to attract and retain the best teachers and administrators.
8. Board programs to improve recruitment and advancement of minority group teachers and other personnel should be extended and intensified. As part of this, training relations between the system and local teacher-training institutions must be greatly strengthened.
9. Preprimary programs of instruction should be introduced on a city-wide basis, serving children as young as three years.
10. Special schools and programs, particularly those for maladjusted and retarded students, should be studied independently and the findings should be made public. A stronger policy for retaining more such students in their regular schools should be pursued.

11. State and federal support, fiscal and administrative, should be provided to the city to accomplish these necessary changes. This support should begin after the board of education has demonstrated its new initiative and commitment by taking some of the steps toward desegregation which do not involve additional municipal expenditures.

Our proposals do, we trust, make plain the fact that substantial forces must be reckoned with and redirected if desegregation is to be achieved. If these proposals are adopted and implemented we are confident they will effect some immediate desegregation. More importantly, they would help prevent an increase in the rate of segregation within the schools. To accomplish this, however, they would have to be introduced promptly, progressively, and in an ever more extensive network during the next five years.

RACIAL AND ETHNIC SURVEY OF CALIFORNIA PUBLIC SCHOOLS

Frederic R. Gunsky *is consultant in intergroup relations, California State Department of Education. This work presents the major findings of the first statewide ethnic census.*

California has completed the most comprehensive racial and ethnic survey of public school pupils and employees undertaken by any state, and is preparing to conduct a second survey in the fall of 1967. The results of the October, 1966, survey, presented to the State Board of Education in two reports (March and June, 1967), already have served as the catalyst for renewed efforts to reduce *de facto* segregation in the public school system of the nation's most populous state.

One in four of the children enrolled in California schools is a member of a minority group. Proportions vary greatly, however, in different parts of the state. There are school districts that are predominantly Negro, or Spanish surname, or Anglo-Caucasian, and there are also individual schools in mixed districts that are predominantly or entirely composed of one ethnic group.

Because remedies are limited by the fact that local school districts operate within their own boundaries under the policy determinations of local boards of education, the first survey report's analysis of the extent of segregation was based on the deviation of each school from the average composition of its own district as a whole. This approach does not take into account the existence within Los Angeles County, for example, of many school districts without a single Negro pupil, of other districts that are less than 1 percent Negro and are contiguous to districts that are 62 percent and 70 percent Negro, and of at least two districts that are 99 percent Anglo-Caucasian and two that are 87 percent and 93 percent Negro. Nor does it point to the massive concentrations in Los Angeles County of Spanish surname (largely Mexican American) pupils in certain school districts and their virtual absence from others.

Even so, measuring imbalance only by the standard of each district's own racial and ethnic composition, the California Board of Education was confronted with

From *Integrated Education,* **June/July 1967. Reprinted by permission of the author.**

evidence of hundreds of public schools outside the limits of "mixed" composition as defined by the State Commission on Equal Opportunities in Education.

Of 1,276 schools in the state's eight largest school districts—all urban or suburban, and each with enrollment of more than 50,000—419 were found to be mixed, 440 to have a high concentration of minorities, and 417 to have a high concentration of the Anglo majority group. A sample of the state's other 567 districts that have more than one elementary or secondary school showed fewer minority pupils and less minority segregation, but serious problems in many districts.

Dorman L. Commons, president of the state board, commented that California has not been "walking fast enough to keep up with itself" in its efforts to integrate schools and that the survey results comprise a "frightening report."

The report presented in March was focused on the distribution of pupils. It emphasized that Negroes are most severely affected by *de facto* segregation or racial isolation; that California's largest ethnic minority, Mexican Americans and others of Spanish surname, is often isolated in schools with relatively few pupils of the Anglo majority; that these problems are most acute in the metropolitan areas, where most of the Negro and Spanish surname people are; and that differences between central cities and suburbs mean that most California children, like most children in other states, attend school with other children of the same racial or ethnic group—minorities with minorities, and majority with majority.

Spanish surname pupils comprise more than 13 percent of the state's total elementary and high school enrollment, Negro pupils more than 8 percent. The survey identified three other minority groups which together accounted for about 3 percent of the total: Chinese, Japanese, and Korean, more than 2 percent; American Indian, 0.25 percent; and other nonwhite, 0.61 percent.

Seventeen of the state's fifty-eight counties—those designated as metropolitan in the 1960 U.S. Census of Population—have 85 percent of all Spanish surname pupils and 95 percent of all Negro pupils. These minorities, much more than most students in the majority group, turn up in statistical categories associated with educational handicaps and disadvantages. They are more heavily reported in special education classes (including those for children classified as mentally retarded or emotionally disturbed) and in compensatory education target schools. Their smaller percentages in high schools and in junior colleges suggest a higher dropout rate and the failure of many of them to go on to higher education.

The California survey, essentially a head count, included more than 5 million students and about 300,000 positions in school employment. The schools and administrative units which were covered carry out the public education program from kindergarten through grade fourteen. Reports were submitted by the school districts through the offices of county superintendents of schools to the Bureau of Intergroup Relations in the State Department of Education. There, by use of electronic data processing, tabulations were made concerning the numbers, percentages and locations of adults, pupils enrolled in special education, and all other pupils, as well as certificated and classified employees, teacher aides and community aides, in six racial and ethnic groups: Spanish surname; other white; Negro; Chinese, Japanese, and Korean; American Indian; and other nonwhite.

Requested by the State Commission on Equal Opportunities in Education, the survey was made at the direction of the State Board of Education. Some local boards questioned the legality or propriety of such a racial and ethnic count, but in the end only six school districts, with 1.2 percent of the statewide enrollment at the K-12 level, failed to participate. All junior colleges, reporting 549,537 students, took part in the survey.

At the heart of the inquiry was the question of the extent of racial and ethnic separation or isolation among pupils and employees in the public schools. According to the formula suggested by the Commission on Equal Opportunities in Education, a school is considered mixed and potentially integrated when it is within 15 percentage points, plus or minus, of the average percentage of each racial and ethnic group in the school district as a whole. Outside that 30 percent range for the total of all minority groups, it is a majority or minority school. Any school outside that range, for any racial or ethnic group, is considered imbalanced, contrary to the policy adopted by the State Board of Education in 1962.

Applying the Commission's formula as an integration scale in the study of two large samples of schools, the Intergroup Relations staff found that in the eight largest districts, 85 percent of the Negro pupils, 57 percent of the Spanish surname pupils, and 6 percent of the other white pupils attend minority schools. Twelve percent of the Negro pupils, 28 percent of the Spanish surname pupils, and 39 percent of the other white pupils attend mixed schools.

The sample of schools in the other districts (many of them with few or no minorities) indicated that 59 percent of the Negro pupils, 30 percent of the Spanish surname pupils, and 5 percent of the other white pupils attend minority schools, and that 38 percent of the Negro pupils, 63 percent of the Spanish surname pupils and 83 percent of the other white pupils attend schools which are within 15 percent, plus or minus, of their own district majority-minority ethnic composition.

Since receiving the first survey report, the California Board of Education has approved the making of a second survey in 1967 and has asked the department of education to make the data available for purposes of scholarly research, especially in order to correlate the findings with data on curriculum, achievement, and other school-related problems. The board also has directed a letter to every local school district emphasizing the responsibility of governing boards to take steps to avoid and eliminate the segregation of pupils. Currently under study is a proposal by the Commission on Equal Opportunities in Education to revise and strengthen Administrative Code regulations on this subject.

Part two of the survey report, submitted to the state board in June, 1967, is concerned with the racial and ethnic distribution of school employees. Among the findings:

While 75 percent of pupils at the K-12 level are Anglo-Caucasian, members of that group hold 91 percent of the teaching positions, 96 percent of the principalships, and 93 percent of other certificated positions.

At the junior college level 83 percent of the students, 95 percent of the teachers, and 99 percent of the administrators are Anglos.

None of the minorities is represented in total school employment in proportion to its part in the pupil population. The lowest ratio is that of the Spanish surname group, next lowest is Negro.

From 1940 to the present there has been a slow but steady increase in the proportion of minority teachers in California. From 0.2 percent in the 1940 U.S.

Census, the Negro teacher percentage rose to nearly 4.0 in the 1966 survey; the other nonwhite percentage rose from 0.7 to more than 2.0.

In the eight largest districts, district percentages of Negro certificated personnel range from 0.38 to 15.98; Spanish surname from 0.71 to 2.68; and Chinese, Japanese, and Korean from 0.39 to 4.37.

A single district employs more than half of the state's Negro certificated personnel and one third of the state's Chinese, Japanese, and Korean certificated personnel.

Negro teachers and principals are seldom assigned to majority schools. A larger proportion of Negroes than of other groups is assigned to minority schools.

Spanish surname people in California comprise the largest of minorities, but Spanish surname certificated and classified employees are fewer than those who are Negro, and relatively fewer than the Chinese, Japanese, and Koreans.

DE FACTO SEGREGATION SOUTHERN STYLE

Thomas F. Pettigrew, *professor of social psychology, Harvard University, is the author of* A Profile of the Negro American *(Van Nostrand, 1964). During 1965-1967, he served as chief social science consultant for the U.S. Commission on Civil Rights study* Racial Isolation in the Public Schools. *He has done research on racial factors in the American South and North, as well as in South Africa. Dr. Pettigrew is a member of the editorial advisory board of* INTEGRATED EDUCATION *magazine.*

Whenever southern liberals, black and white, gather to discuss "The Question," someone inevitably introduces a grand vision for the future. The South, runs the argument, will shortly catch up and surpass the rest of the nation in the thoroughness of its racial integration. The reasoning behind this vision is straightforward. White and Negro southerners are not strangers; they are both products of the same subculture. They share a common history and a common religion, while white and Negro northerners often share neither. Nor is intimate interracial contact anything new for the South. Consequently, the giant step from formal desegregation to informal integration should take place in the South with great swiftness.

The southern liberal vision for the future should give pause to champions of integrated education in the North, for it is not without merit. There are, however, a few cantankerous flies in the ointment. These flies all concern the establishment in the South of *de facto* segregation, the idea for which came from watching how Yankees "managed" their race problems. The new strategies of southern segregationists have an unpleasantly familiar ring to any northerner enmeshed in the struggle to overcome *de facto* segregation. Consequently, the most forthright discussion of these strategies to date—the Civil Rights Commission's *Civil Rights U.S.A: Public Schools Southern States 1962*[1]—has a relevance for Americans interested in integrated education, North and South.

From *Integrated Education,* **October/November 1963. Reprinted by permission of the author.**

[1]U.S. Government Printing Office, 1962.

Lower Court Trends

This report is a tightly written, 217-page document consisting of five parts. The first reviews the emerging lower court definitions of "a prompt and reasonable start" and "all deliberate speed." Naturally, there have been conflicting interpretations between federal court circuits and even within a single circuit. But the report perceives several definite and consistent trends evolving. Any school board start prior to a suit, for example, is highly regarded by the courts; plans offered by such boards are generally given lenient acceptance. Delaying school boards, however, have an increasingly difficult time winning approval for their plans. Good faith is the critical criterion, and no action prior to a suit is becoming regarded as evidence that the school board is operating in bad faith. The application of this principle to northern cases should prove interesting, considering the refusal of the school administrations of such major cities as Boston and Chicago, until very recently, to admit even the existence of *de facto* segregation.

The constitutional fate of the South's pupil placement acts is especially crucial. Ingeniously designed to bar class suits and provide a near-endless series of administrative delays, these laws form one of the "moderate" segregationists' most serious barriers to the dreams of southern liberals. Here, too, after some time-consuming backing and filling, the federal courts are exhibiting growing impatience. Even in those courts which continue to sanction pupil placement acts as proper desegregation plans, the Civil Rights Commission detects a distinct dissatisfaction with the administration of these acts. Decisions since the report appeared confirm this conclusion.*

1962 also witnessed a series of court refusals to interpret grade-a-year plans as meeting the "all deliberate speed" test. Had these plans been offered in the 1950's, there is little doubt they would have won the enthusiastic approval of federal courts throughout the South. But almost a decade after the supreme court's 1954 desegregation decision,† grade-a-year tokenism is well past its time. To accept these plans now, reason many courts, is tantamount to rewarding intransigence of the past. Increasingly, southern federal courts are requiring school systems to move with the speed necessary to achieve the desegregation level of comparable systems which initiated their program earlier.

Transfer rules often become bones of contention in northern *de facto* segregation disputes; hence, the validity of southern-style transfer provisions is of special interest to northern observers. These so-called "safety-valve" measures provide that any child may be granted a transfer from a school in which he is among a racial minority. At the time the commission report was drafted, lower courts were generally sanctioning such provisions. But on June 3, 1963, the supreme court rejected such transfer rules.‡ This decision has important implications for a number of northern situations.

"The Northern Plan" in Action

The remaining four sections of the southern school report deal with educational desegregation in Kentucky, North Carolina, Tennessee, and Virginia. Five lawyers

---

*[See, especially, the supreme court ruling in *Watson* v. *City of Memphis,* 373 U.S. 526 (1963).]

† [Editor's Note: See Appendix A, "Text of Supreme Court Rulings (*Brown* v. *Board of Education,* . . .)."]

‡ [*Maxwell* v. *County Board of Education of Davidson County, Tenn.,* 83 S. Ct. 1405.]

are the authors, and a legal tone generally prevails. Yet the problems discussed largely involve education, sociology, and psychology. One wonders when the vast resources of American education and behaviorial science will finally be tapped by the commission in its vital work.

It is this specific case material—especially that involving such cities as Louisville, Nashville, Richmond, and Norfolk—that will bring a shock of recognition to northern readers. Consider the 1961 *de facto* segregation of Louisville schools. About three out of every four Negro high school students attended the one virtually all-Negro institution. Two out of every three Negroes at the junior high level attended the three nearly all-Negro institutions. And elementary schools are in rapid transition. In just two years, from 1959 to 1961, one elementary school shifted from two-thirds white to almost three-fifths Negro; another changed from over half white to three-fourths Negro; and a third went from one-third white to 94 percent Negro.

The northern cast to Louisville's school problems extends beyond racial statistics. All-Negro schools have suffered since desegregation from the loss of both their best teachers and students to predominantly white schools (though the student selection factor has declined somewhat, in part because several biracial high schools have failed to grant a single college scholarship to a Negro). At desegregated schools, social functions create special administrative concern. The report asserts a cautious return to school dances would be abruptly discontinued if Negro and white children began to dance together.

Two of the most serious problems posed by *de facto* segregation everywhere are highlighted in Louisville. The first is the manner in which segregation begets segregation. The report provides striking data to demonstrate that Negro high schoolers generally prefer integrated education only if they have experienced it in lower grades. The majority of Negroes in each of the three almost all-Negro junior highs chose the almost all-Negro high school, while a majority (ranging from 58 percent to 100 percent) of the Negroes in each of the nine biracial junior highs chose biracial high schools.

The second problem concerns the unemployment of the city's Negro youth. "Only a handful of Negroes" are among the roughly 1,000 Louisville youth in apprenticeship programs. And a 1962 survey of the 1960 graduates of the virtually all-Negro high school revealed an unemployment rate almost three times that of the other high schools (more than 25 percent compared with an average of 10 percent).

Four factors—a grade-a-year plan, a minority transfer rule, Negro reticence, and housing segregation—combine to maintain Nashville's *de facto* segregation of schools. After five years of "desegregation," the city boasts 270 Negroes in biracial schools, about 2 percent of the Negro enrollment. The first three of these factors, however, are waning in importance. Half of the grades are technically desegregated (fall of 1963); the supreme court has specifically overturned Nashville's transfer rule; and there are indications of less Negro reluctance to participate (in 1961, roughly 20 percent of the eligible Negroes attended previously all-white schools, as compared to only 13 percent in 1960). Soon Nashville segregationists will have to rely primarily upon the pure "northern plan"—the exploitation of housing patterns—to sustain its *de facto* segregation.

Nashville and Richmond have both hit upon annexation of suburbs as a means of reducing their large and politically potent Negro percentages. To be sure, there are excellent reasons involving metropolitan efficiency for these annexations, but many proponents in these cities blithely admit that racial considerations are paramount. Nashville has succeeded in carrying out its plan, but Richmond is still in the courts trying to achieve its annexation over suburban resistance.

This attempt to "gain more time" in race relations is typical of Richmond's hesitant approach. Otherwise talented school administrators meekly obey the state's segregationist pupil placement board in every conceivable particular and take care not to offend the city's far right-wing newspapers. The first two years of token school desegregation witnessed only thirty-six Negro children attending biracial schools— barely one seventh of 1 percent of the system's Negroes.

(Since the report appeared, a major foundation has aided in perpetuating this *de facto* segregation—an event that will hardly surprise northern integrationists. In June of 1963, the Ford Foundation announced the award of $500,000 to the Richmond School Board for an intensive forty-month educational program designed to raise the academic achievement of the city's underprivileged school children. The next day the city's newspapers reassured their white readers the Yankee money would not rock the racial boat. The program began with two special summer centers—one exclusively for whites, the other exclusively for Negroes. This rigidly segregated project, incidentally, is ironically billed as "improving human resources through education.")

Concludes the commission report candidly: "The real problem in Richmond is not the desegregation of schools, nor any particular type of desegregation at all. Its difficulties lie in the belief of the white citizen that Richmond has a Negro problem. It is the presence of the Negro in large numbers that makes Richmond's whites tense. . . . [they] fear 'engulfment' . . . Richmond must recognize its problems are big-city problems, and not Negro problems. Big-city problems can be aggravated by race issues. And one way to aggravate them is to continue to preach that you have a race problem." To this, the writer, born and reared in Richmond and a product of its public school system, can only add, "*Amen!*"

The extent of *de facto* school segregation in Virginia's largest city, Norfolk, is similar to that of Richmond. In its first three years of school desegregation, the city had only fifty Negroes in biracial classes—about one fourth of 1 percent of the system's Negroes. Norfolk accomplished this tokenism in spite of firm pressure from its federal district judge and a court order to disregard the state's pupil placement board. The city has its own placement criteria: achievement test performance, "ability to adjust," and place of residence. In assigning students to schools, only Negro test scores are considered and the test of residential proximity is rigorously applied.

Honors go to Norfolk for executing "the northern plan" to the point of caricature. To strengthen its exploitation of existing housing patterns, many of the city's new schools are small, three-to-four room structures for the first three-to-four grades. These little boxes are carefully located to maximize *de facto* school segregation. At one point, Norfolk's city council considered a proposal for constructing sixty-eight of these tiny and inefficient schools. Negroes joked the city would soon provide a separate school for every Negro child in his own backyard.

Norfolk's emulation of northern segregationist strategy is unique only in its extremity. Though the commission's report does not provide further examples, the great majority of the region's largest cities are currently planning their communities on ghetto principles. But using residential segregation as a substitute for a legal segregation is often not as easily managed in southern cities as in New York or Chicago. Charleston, South Carolina, Macon, Georgia, and New Orleans have much less separation of the races by residence than comparable northern cities. Yet where there's a will, reason southern white supremacists, there's a way. "Modern" city planning means strategic placement of new public facilities; it means the development of residential patterns along racial lines by ingenious employment of federal urban renewal funds and local real estate board cooperation; it means, in short, *de facto* segregation.

Conclusion

Token school desegregation in the South is not just a foot-dragging device; its greatest danger lies in its establishment of *de facto* segregation modeled directly after many northern situations. The presumed need for "time," for which southern "moderates" have so long and effectively pleaded, has resulted in a decade of delay. The time thus granted has not generally led to good-faith resolutions of real problems; rather, the ten years have typically been used to erect racial barriers which closely resemble those of New York, Chicago, Detroit, and Boston.

Americans who work for integrated education in the North should realize the broader significance of their efforts. Just as housing segregation, special transfer provisions, and job discrimination in the North have provided a negative model for southern segregationists, so, too, can the destruction of these same barriers serve as a positive model for southern integrationists. Years ago it was fashionable to point out that racial segregation was not just a southern, but a national, concern. Now, as the South's formal separation evolves into informal separation, it can just as truthfully be said that *de facto* segregation is not just a northern concern.

BEYOND TOKENISM: REVERSE INTEGRATION IN ALBANY, GEORGIA

Miriam Wasserman, *formerly on the faculty of Spelman College, Atlanta, is a free-lance educational consultant who was educational consultant for the Albany, Georgia, Tutorial Project during the summer of 1965 and educational director of the Dougherty County Summer Head Start Program during the summer of 1967.*

"When you set up something that is better than anything they've got, the white people are going to come to it."—Speaker at a community planning meeting in Selma, Alabama.

The Court's 1954 qualification that *even though the physical facilities and other tangible factors may be equal,* segregation in public schools deprives minority children of equal educational opportunities is plainly irrelevant in most southern states: *separate physical facilities and other tangible factors have never been and, in the nature of past and present power arrangements, cannot be equal.* The resurgent

From *Integrated Education,* **June/July 1967. Reprinted by permission of the author.**

segregationists of the turn of the century did not establish institutional duality in order to admit equality but in order to lock in inequality.[1]

They succeeded. The cost paid is expressed in the familiar nonjoke that the only way the "cracker" can keep the "nigger" in the gutter is to get down there with him or—with more dignity—in Martin Luther King's frequent warning that if one of us is unfree, all of us are.

By almost every index of educational adequacy we have, the systems of the southern states measure up short.[2] Only to the Negro children and parents whose educational institutions are even more improverished can the average southern school system look like a castle worth fighting to get into. As I write, Governors Wallace, Maddox, Johnson, and McKeithen are still standing guard at the moat. If and when they surrender to court decrees, increasing numbers of Negro children will begin to cross over into schools desperately in need of more equipment, more books, better-paid and better-trained teachers, and the spontaneity and creativity without which all those assets remain mere things.

---

[1]"The fact is we didn't know what they had in their schools till some of our kids started to go there," said a Negro minister at an Albany, Georgia, meeting of parents getting ready to exercise "freedom of choice."

Item: In 1963-64, 13 percent of the white high school students in Georgia were attending schools not accredited by the Southern Association; 42 percent of the Negro students were attending such schools.

Item: In 1913 the Julius Rosenwald Fund began to provide building grants for Southern Negro schools. By 1932 these funds accounted for 15 percent of the money spent on Negro school construction in the states affected; another 17 percent came from private Negro contributors. Still, the per pupil value of Negro school property was 20 percent of that of white school property.

Item: From the April, 1967, report of the Georgia Council on Human Relations comes the following information: "Last month, members of the Houston County Chapter of the Council, SCLC, and NAACP investigated the school system. A casual walk through the elementary schools showed the differences. In the white elementary schools, new TV sets are mounted at the front of each room while in the Negro schools, some TV sets are said to be available in the storage room. The few seen in classrooms looked much older than the ones in the white schools. One of the white high schools had lockers in the halls for books and clothes lockers in the gymnasium, while the Negro high school had no lockers. A white high school had five science laboratory rooms while the Negro school had only one. The white school had four rooms full of typewriters while the Negro had only one. The white high school library was much larger than the library in a Negro school that covered twelve grades. An even greater shock was that twenty-two courses are taught at the white high school that are not taught at the Negro school!"

[2]In 1964-65, the low-ranking states in per-pupil school expenditures were: Alabama, Arkansas, Georgia, Kentucky, Mississippi, North Carolina, South Carolina, Tennessee, and West Virginia. To eliminate the downward pull of Negro schools and get a fairer estimate of "white" Southern education, we may compare the highest-spending school district of each state; the low-ranking states in 1947-49 were: Alabama, Maine, Mississippi, North Carolina, South Carolina, and Arkansas.

The low-ranking states in percentage of ninth graders who eventually graduate from high school are: Alabama, Georgia, Mississippi, New Mexico, North Carolina, South Carolina, and Texas.

In 1964-65, the average salary of classroom teachers for the country as a whole was $6,220. In Alabama, it was $4,700; in Georgia, $5,050; in Louisiana, $5,175; in Mississippi, $4,103; in North Carolina, $5,022; and in South Carolina, $4,500.

Meanwhile, in Albany, Georgia, a Negro community that had been kept separate and unequal for generations has for two years been providing educational experiences as far superior to those of the white schools as the white schools' have been to the Negro schools'. And in the last eight months, native whites have been participating in these experiences as a minority group, but a minority group that is accepted matter-of-factly and in numbers beyond tokenism. So while the governors are blustering at the front gate, the defending knights are defecting through the back windows.

Howard Zinn described Albany in 1962 as "wide-avenued and clean, a commercial center for southwest Georgia, trading corn, cattle, and pecans, attracting tourists, new industry, and travelers heading toward Florida. 'Tenth fastest booming city in the U.S.A.,' the man at the Chamber of Commerce said proudly. 'There's the rating—in black and white.' "[3]

Black and white were barely on speaking terms when I first went to Albany three years later—no violence, but just about no communication.[4] The city had closed down all recreation facilities and sold the "white" swimming pool to the New England-born owner of the bitterly segregationist Albany *Herald*, who resold it to a group that proceeded to operate it as a private club; they offered to sell the Negro pool to the Negroes, but no one bid. So all summer long black children stood in the dusty, unpaved streets and watched their mothers being chauffeured away by white ladies to houses on the clean, broad avenues where they tended the white ladies' children for ten dollars to twenty dollars a week—public buses had just been put back into operation after a three-year lockout against integrated seating, and many people did not yet know where to catch the bus or where it went.

Federal money was hanging over the horizon like a good rain cloud after a drought, but the city of Albany, county seat of Dougherty County, wasn't having any. The city fathers appointed no boards, drew up no proposals to bring the poverty program to Albany. A county official later explained to me that "the people didn't care to have the federal government coming in and telling them what to do"; he said, "the stigma of the federal government ruins just about anything." He also said that "they" (lexical successor to "nigras") wanted to do it "through their own organization, so we let them." Sargent Shriver had from the first been serious about requiring integration in OEO programs, and word of this was already around.

School integration was lagging. Prominent southwest Georgia civil rights attorney C.B. King (not related except in brotherhood to Martin Luther) had had to carry a stingy district court decision to the fifth circuit court to achieve a very limited "freedom-of-choice" plan for the first, second, and twelfth grades, and he was preparing to go back to court to gain admittance for the dozen integrating twelfth graders to the school band and athletic activities. Withal, there had been progress. Only three years before, Dougherty County Sheriff Campbell had beaten Attorney King over the head with a walking stick and then bragged to Howard Zinn, "I let him

---

[3]Howard Zinn, *Albany: A Study in National Responsibility*, Southern Regional Council, Atlanta, Georgia, 1962.

[4]"Our big trouble is we haven't talked to each other enough," said a speaker at a parents' meeting in Albany recently. "So we don't understand each other. So our children have got to wrestle with each other till they get to it."

know he's a damn nigger. I'm a white man and he's a damn nigger." Now the Dougherty County officials courteously requested of Attorney King that he inform them of the Negroes' grievances before going to court, and they desegregated the band and teams without court order.

In that summer of 1965 the leaders of the white community were not yet sufficiently recovered from their shock of disbelief and hurt experienced at the militant testing of public facilities by the Albany Movement to be willing to work in community with Negroes except under court order or threat of court order. The leaders of the Albany Movement, however, had sufficiently recovered from the beatings and jailings they had experienced to be up and ready for the next round. They organized the Doughery County Resources Development Association, Inc., and sent letters to top county and city officials, to white businessmen, and to other prominent (white) citizens asking for an audience to discuss the possibilities of the Economic Opportunity Act. The letter pointed to the needs of the community and said that an OEO program could bring help to "All of the citizens of Albany, Dougherty County, Georgia." They received either no replies or curt postcards of refusal.

Then, in a community and an area and a nation where privileged institutions had heretofore always been white institutions—and where the Negro population might or might not be granted parallel, unequal institutions—the Dougherty County Resources Development Association moved to establish privileged institutions for Negroes, using federal money, under a law which forbade the creation of parallel facilities for whites, equal or unequal. They submitted a proposal for a $190,000 community action program to consist of five Head Start centers, five tutorial centers, and two neighborhood service centers. The proposal pointed out that the average annual family income of Negroes in Dougherty County was $2,500; that the only nearby state park with swimming facilities was open to Negro use in theory only; that many Negro children enter school not knowing even how to hold a pencil; and that many drop out of school after a few years not knowing much more than how to hold a pencil.

The purpose of the nursery school would be "to offer an environment where children can gain feelings of confidence, pride, and worth in themselves. The activities must be geared to enable the child to accumulate feelings of success and a positive self-image. Three learning areas will be stressed: language development, concept formation, and perceptual discrimination."

The tutorial program proposed "to organize the community so that various groups can help other groups to raise their aims and achievements. We think that parents can be taught to help children, college students can help high school students, and we can all learn by communicating with and teaching one another more than we have been doing."

The Head Start program and the tutorial program which began in the summer of 1965—the former with federal funds, the latter without—did actually build upon these earnest words.

The blocks, paints, songs, pictures, books, dolls, sand tables, hot lunches, and joy that entered the lives of 135 five-year-olds in Albany that summer were proteins and vitamins for half-starved souls. At one center, housed in a rambling private house, ten- and twelve-year-olds from the neighborhood came begging daily to sit on the floor with the "littlies" and play with the blocks and dolls. The teachers— professionals and mother-helpers—were lit with a love and enthusiasm for an educational process that most of them, bounded by the concepts of the conventional education which had been their only experience, could not even have created as daydreams.

The tutorial program, although somewhat marred by a number of factors including a tone of "school-teacherishness" and the tutors' disappointment at not being paid as expected, did succeed in pushing out the boundaries in a number of respects. There were about two hundred professional teachers, mothers, college students, and high school students from the community who were designated tutors, and about a thousand children ages six to fourteen or fifteen who were designated tutees. Efforts to make the learning process reciprocal focused on the tutor seminar at which tutors dealt with one another's problems in teaching techniques, discipline, content, and so on; gave demonstration lessons for which their colleagues served first as class and then as critics; took turns writing up seminar minutes; and often revealed by their own reactions—such as reluctance to speak for fear of giving wrong answers—some of the learning difficulties under which their tutees were laboring. Parent-tutor meetings consisted of discussion of common child-rearing or community problems, rather than the passive attention to a program or a speaker which so often characterizes PTA meetings. Actual tutorial sessions ranged from very dull and inept to very stimulating and creative, with some of the warmest and freest performances being given by the mothers and young students.

These judgments are made by an outsider with perhaps unrealistic standards of creative, interesting teaching; the participants expressed their judgment by attending faithfully all summer, the tutors without pay and the tutees without a compulsory attendance law.[5] It is hard to believe that adults, adolescents, and children would vote with their feet like that for the educational experiences which the public school system of Dougherty County (or of most other communities) offers.

But, unlike and superior to the Albany schools as they were in other respects, the Albany Head Start program and the Albany tutorial program were like the public schools in being wholly segregated operations. The Dougherty County Resources Board had four white members in a total of seventy-odd; one was the California-born white assistant of Attorney King; one was his wife, colleague of Mrs. C. B. King; two were Catholic priests. And the white Dougherty County superintendent of schools participated to the extent of allowing the Negro community to use their schools for tutorial and Head Start centers. That was all.

There were no local whites as teachers or as pupils in either program. There are many poor white families in Albany. They live in close proximity to, often across the street from or backyard-to-backyard with, Negro families. They had spurned participation in the programs to the extent of setting their dogs after Negro recruiters for Head Start on one occasion.

After an absence of a year and half, early in 1967, I came back to Albany to observe the programs. Both programs were funded and operating year-round. As I

---

[5] A report on the project to the Dougherty County Resources Board directors says: "There is no doubt that the Project has succeeded in answering some felt need in the community. We have had hundreds more applicants than we now have places for tutees. Parents report children dressed and ready for 'school' hours before opening time. Every day new children turn up at the centers and say, 'I want to come to the school.' "

drove into town, I saw Negro and white children playing together in the front yard of what I knew to be a "white" school two blocks from the main thoroughfare. I stopped at the corner, backed up, and looked again: I saw Negro and white childi ;n playing together in the front yard of a "white" school. In Albany, Georgia.

In the fall of 1966, again responding to pressures from Attorney King, the board had opened the "freedom-of-choice" plan to all grades. The conservatism of the measure was attested by the fact that only about six hundred to seven hundred Negro children were attending formerly all-white schools, leaving something over 90 percent in all-Negro schools, and that staffs were still entirely segregated. The superintendent of schools, asked about staff integration, said he thought Albany wasn't "going to do it, not in a hundred years." He also said that while the people of Albany were by-and-large law-abiding, "white folks are not going to integrate unless they have to."

Many of the integrating Negro children were attending the Broad Street School, where I saw the children playing together, making the student body about 45 percent Negro. When the integrated school opened in the fall, the principal very firmly turned down a request from a parent that the "two races be assigned separate commodes"; but she agreed to discontinue evening meetings of the Parent Teacher Association in favor of an arrangement whereby parents would visit individually in the afternoons and so, she explains, have more time for conferences with the teachers. (Many Negro mothers, it may be observed, are busy preparing dinners in white ladies' kitchens during the late afternoons.) On the whole the principal gives the impression of bearing up quite staunchly under something of a burden.

One half hour after the end of the regular school day at Broad Street, 150 children and 12 staff members assemble for an hour and a half to two hours of tutorial. Of the 150 children, 65 are white, 85 are Negro; 6 staff members are white, 6 are Negro. Staff members are paid; the children attend voluntarily. Although many would-be tutees have been turned away, the ratio of children to tutors is still higher than the staff likes. News of the singing, the crayoning, the trips, the outside games played with an energetic male college student, the records and the films, and undoubtedly the freedom to move about the room spreads about during the school day; and children whose teachers say they do not "need" tutoring show by their insistence on attending that they do need what is being offered. The superintendent of schools by-and-large approves of the tutoring program but thinks that for it to be really effective it would have to be integrated more closely with the regular school program and attendance would have to be made compulsory.

A significant element in the tutorial program is parent participation. Evening meetings of parents, staff, and children present programs, refreshments, and oppor-tunities for socializing. White and Negro parents both helped provide transportation for an Easter outing held at a nearby (formerly Negro) state park. The loneliness of the poor,[6] and their generous readiness to depart from social scientists' stereotypes, were demonstrated for me by the warm pleasure with which a very poor and ill-educated white mother of nine recalled some of these events. She was a good

---

[6]The Director of the community center of the program told me, "One afternoon a white boy came by when there was a party, and he just kept coming back. I have never seen a child so hungry for activities."

negative test of the poor-white stereotype. When a local businessman had come to warn her against continuing to allow nearby Negro children to play with her children in her yard, she had sent him packing. She had two little children enrolled in the Head Start program and hoped to get a job there as a parent helper. Several of her older children were in the tutorial program because they "cried to go," although their teachers said they did not need tutoring. I tried to explore her view of the stereotype: she said she supposed some people are just "narrer-minded."

Another, somewhat more self-conscious deviant from the stereotype is Mrs. Willis, the white, southern head tutor of the Broad Street program. She was raised on one of those small struggling farms in which if every child is to eat, every child must help to plant and pick. A respected teacher in Albany for ten years and mother of two children, she volunteered to teach in the summer Head Start program in 1966, pitting her determination to "serve" against her husband's reluctance and her friends' and associates' horror. Known as a dedicated teacher, she has been instrumental in recruiting other white parents and teachers for both programs. And her friends are beginning to come back, saying, "So you really did mean what you said you wanted to do."

She says she has "a good feeling" about her work in both programs and admires the competence of some of her Negro colleagues. Like almost everyone else who knows her, she especially admires Carol King.

Carol King, Attorney King's wife, is director of Head Start, one component of the Dougherty County Community Action Program. It was she who ran from the dogs on a white street two summers ago. The executive director of the entire program is Mrs. Elza L. Jackson; she has two masters degrees, one in library science, but was refused employment in the Dougherty County school system after her militant participation in the Albany Movement. Mrs. Eulah Boles is director of the tutorial program; formerly a civilian employee at a nearby Air Force base, for years she valiantly battled the Dougherty County school system, which seemed to her to be spending all the federal funds for impacted areas on the white schools. These three ladies were the dominating figures at a staff conference I attended of tutors from all seven tutorial centers, including, conspicuously, the six white tutors from the Broad Street center. If it had not been that everyone else was playing it so cool, I would have stopped, backed up, and looked again. In Albany, Georgia!

Mrs. Willis stopped Mrs. King at the close of the meeting to talk about training of teachers for the 1967 summer Head Start, an eight-week expansion of the year-round project. There have been over nine hundred applications for seventy staff openings during the summer, about half of them white and numbers from other Deep South states. About half the teachers and half the children in the summer program will be white. At present there are about fifteen white children scattered among the three Head Start centers whose enrollment totals seventy children. There are four regular teachers, all Negro, and ten subprofessionals, four white. Most of the subprofessionals and one of the teachers are parents of children enrolled in the program. Next fall, when two new centers open, one in a mixed neighborhood and one in a white school, there will be a higher proportion of whites in the program.

An exhilarating spirit of participation in a creative common endeavor enlivens the entire Head Start program: three mother-teachers, one white, are going back to school, two at the high school level; at two centers children and teachers have planted vegetable gardens; at another two five-year-old girls are in the kitchen with the cook cutting out biscuits for the noon dinner; they are disappointed that Mrs. King is not staying to eat at their school today; the head teacher, a father in his thirties, has spent long after hours building extra equipment for the expanded summer program; both professional and subprofessional teachers leave at intervals for training sessions at Tuskegee Institute and at Peabody College and word comes back that they have taught as much as they have learned. There is a community here of white and black, of adult and child, of teaching and learning whose equal one would go a long way, North or South, to see.

In the summer of 1967 each center opened a parents' room—furnished with a coffee pot, comfortable chairs, tables, and sewing machines—and a nursery—furnished with cribs, bottles, and toddler toys. In the nursery, aides and teen-agers from the Neighborhood Youth Corps fed, diapered, rocked, and cooed at pre-Head Start infants and toddlers brought by visiting mothers. In the parents' room the mothers gathered to sew for themselves and for the program, to help in classroom emergencies, and to escape from lonely kitchens and lonely lives into the conviviality of shared concerns and activities. The mothers were black and white. Once a week a Negro sewing teacher attended each center and taught the ladies how to lay out and cut their patterns and turn their seams. One of the most conscientious helpers in the parents' rooms was a local white eighteen-year-old social service aide just graduated from high school and bound for theological seminary in September.

The program also initiated a series of community meetings preparatory to a new election to the Dougherty County Board of Trustees. Poor whites and poor Negroes came together and began by reciting their grievances to each other. The whites said that in the "rich" neighborhoods, the grass in the parks got cut, mosquitoes got sprayed away, school yards had equipment. The Negroes said that in the "white" schools children received band instruments and team uniforms and new books. Probably not since the time of young Tom Watson, among whose followers must have been some forebears of these very men and women, had blacks and whites in Southwest Georgia so confronted each other. The group moved on to inviting "their" city commissioner to attend one of their meetings and respond to their grievances. The commissioner, who *represents* this poor community but is *elected by* the Albany voters at large—a neat bit of democratic legerdemain executed after Negroes began to vote in large numbers—was politely evasive. The lady chairman—obese, determined, smart, poor, white—laughingly reported his elaborate rationalizations for refusing to attend an integrated meeting. Another lady—obese, determined, smart, poor, black (in short, her sister)—spoke up, "I could talk to him. He's a nice man. He'd listen to me because my mama nursed him." The next day they went together to the commissioner.

Here in the South and throughout the country the dubious and the reluctant like the sound of the refrain, "You can't change peoples' minds and hearts by legislation."

Maybe so, maybe not. But you can by quality education.

THE CHICAGO TITLE VI COMPLAINT TO H.E.W.

On July 4 and 27, 1965, the Coordinating Council of Community Organizations (CCCO) of Chicago submitted a complaint to the U.S. Office of Education. CCCO charged that the Chicago board of education was in violation of Title VI of the Civil Rights Act of 1964; that it was using federal funds in a racially discriminatory way. On September 30, 1965, the Office of Education notified the Illinois State Superintendent of Public Instruction that there was reason to believe some of the charges were true and that transfer of new federal funds to Chicago was being deferred . On October 5, 1965, the deferral was ended and the Chicago school board agreed to study certain charges and report to H.E.W. on these charges within sixty days.

On October 4, 1965, Education Commissioner Francis Keppel had stated that the CCCO complaint was "the most detailed and documented of any complaint received by the Department of Health, Education and Welfare so far." He added: "In the case of Chicago, complaints other than de facto *segregation have been made, and it is in regard to some of these that new commitments of funds are being deferred at this time."*

Following is the complete text of the complaint, consisting of two separate documents.

THE JULY 4, 1965, DOCUMENT

Honorable Francis Keppel
Commissioner of Education
U.S. Department of Health, Education
    and Welfare
Washington, D.C.

Dear Commissioner Keppel:

The undersigned respectfully submit to you charges that the Board of Education of the City of Chicago (Illinois), Frank M. Whiston, president, Benjamin C. Willis, general superintendent, stands in violation of Title VI, Sec. 601, of the Civil Rights Act of 1964, and should, henceforth, be deprived of any and all federal assistance currently being received, and any currently under consideration.

Title VI, Sec. 601, states that: "No person in the United States shall, on the grounds of race, color or national origin, be excluded from participation in, be deprived of the benefits of, or be subjected to discrimination under any program or activity receiving Federal assistance."

We hold that the Board of Education of the City of Chicago operates a public school system that is, in fact and by its own statistics, segregated and discriminatory on a racial basis, and that the education offered Chicago's Negro children is not only separate from, but inferior in quality to, that offered white children.

We charge that the Board of Education of the City of Chicago is also in violation of the "Guidelines" issued by the U.S. Department of Health, Education and

From *Integrated Education,* **December 1965/January 1966.**

Welfare, which are designed to assure compliance with Article VI of the 1964 Civil Rights Act by agencies and organizations receiving federal funds.

We charge further that the Chicago Board of Education collaborates with certain trade unions in the operation of Washburne Trade School, a skilled-trade apprentice-training program that maintains a policy of Negro exclusion, thereby limiting greatly the opportunity of Negro youth to receive the training necessary for them to compete in the skilled labor market.

In support of these charges we offer a brief study of the public debate on school segregation in Chicago, documented primarily by official publications of the U.S. Civil Rights Commission, the Advisory Panel on Integration of the (Chicago) Public Schools, the Chicago Urban League, plus proceedings of the Chicago board of education, legal documents filed against that body, and various additional commentary on the public record.

While debate has taken place on the question of segregation in Chicago schools since the late 1940's, it was not until 1961 that the issue belatedly received widespread public attention based on the alleged violations of the Fourteenth Amendment to the U.S. Constitution. Much of the relevant documentation had been gathered prior to the filing of those suits, but most of the information pertinent to the charges we bring stems from the events following filing of the case of *Webb* v. *Board of Education of the City of Chicago* (Civ. No 61 C 1569 D.C.N.D. Ill.) in September, 1961.

As a result of an out-of-court settlement of said case, the Chicago school board agreed to create a panel of educators to conduct a study of segregation in the schools. This was the Advisory Panel on Integration of the Public Schools, which on March 31, 1964, issued its report to the Board of Education of the City of Chicago, known popularly as the "Hauser Report," after its chairman, Philip M. Hauser.

Meanwhile, in 1962, the document *Civil Rights U.S.A. Public Schools North and West, 1962*, staff reports submitted to the U.S. Commission on Civil Rights (referred to hereafter as the *Civil Rights Report*) was published by the U.S. Government Printing Office. Part Four, dealing with Chicago, identified a substantial number of the issues and problems. We shall quote liberally from both of the above publications in this presentation.

The Chicago board of education in October, 1963, published a "Racial Head Count," and in November, 1964, published a "Student Survey," breaking down the official enrollment of students on a racial basis. The former made public for the first time the precise statistics defining racial segregation in Chicago schools.

[These are] the raw data on Chicago school segregation and will be cited here, since [they] confirm officially the results of previous studies such as those cited in the *Civil Rights Report*.

In 1963, the total enrollment in the public schools was 507,592 children of which 239,630 were Negro, 254,320 were white, and 13,642 designated as "other."

There were 471 public schools, including 430 elementary and 41 high schools. In this presentation, following current accepted terminology, schools having populations of 100 percent of one race are termed "absolutely segregated," and those having populations of 90.0 to 99.9 percent of one race are termed "segregated."

The Chicago board of education disclosed in 1963 that 44 elementary schools (10.2 percent) were absolutely segregated-Negro; 105 schools (24.4 percent) were segregated-Negro; 52 schools (12.1 percent) were absolutely segregated-white, and

150 schools (34.9 percent) were segregated-white. Seventy-nine elementary schools (18.4 percent) were considered integrated.

Of the high schools, 1 (2.4 percent) was absolutely segregated-Negro; 7 (17.1 percent) were segregated-Negro; 5 (12.2 percent) were absolutely segregated-white; 17 (41.5 percent) were segregated-white, and 11 (26.8 percent) were integrated.

Thus, 81.6 percent of Chicago's elementary schools and 73.2 percent of its high schools were designated as either absolutely segregated or segregated during the school year 1963-64.

In 1964-65, with the addition of 10 new elementary schools and 2 new secondary schools, accommodating an increase of 14,812 Negro pupils on both elementary and secondary levels, and a decrease of 642 white and 264 "other" pupils, segregation in the Chicago schools was shown to have increased: absolutely segregated and segregated elementary schools now constitute 82.3 percent of the total and both categories of segregated high schools now constitute 74.4 percent of the total.

More than 90 percent of Chicago's Negro children attend segregated schools.

Of great significance are both the statistics on segregation and the increase in segregated schooling in this city. A complete breakdown, with careful detailed analysis, is contained in "Public School Segregation: City of Chicago, 1963-1964 and 1964-1965," a Chicago Urban League Research Report. This document contains a full set of tables and narrative discussion of the situation which we shall not duplicate in this petition.

We ask, however, that special attention be given to the statistics pertaining to branch schools and upper-grade centers, which show an even more marked segregation, because they are relevant to discussion below on the use of branches and upper grade centers as tools to introduce and perpetuate segregation.

With the factual existence of segregation established, two questions arise: Is the situation deliberate and has it been consciously perpetuated? Second, has the situation resulted in unequal quality of education and otherwise damaged the children of one or both races?

As stated, we believe the answer to both questions is affirmative, and shall outline below our documentation.

Regarding the question of deliberate segregation, such charges have been officially denied by the school board. When segregation was finally acknowledged, it was officially attributed to racial housing patterns throughout the city and beyond control of the board. However, the Second Amended Complaint in the case of *Webb v. Board of Education of the City of Chicago,* 1964 (Civ. No. 63 C 1895 D.C.N.D. Ill.), alleges that the board of education has acted in concert with the Chicago Real Estate Board, which has pursued a deliberate pattern of restriction of Negro residence within the city, and " . . . has acted to create racial segregation in the public schools to coincide with residential racial segregation in the City of Chicago."

Further, we charge that it is the official but unwritten policy of the Chicago Housing Authority to segregate public housing on a racial basis, and the school board has acted in concert with this city agency to establish "neighborhood" schools in areas of public housing projects that are deliberately zoned to follow the racial lines of their tenancy.

Further, we charge that school boundaries have been drawn, redrawn, and gerrymandered to follow patterns of racial change in Chicago neighborhoods and to maintain a policy of segregation and Negro containment. Some of the complex maneuvers in this area are described in the *Civil Rights Report*, pp. 209-215, and in the *Handbook of [Chicago] School Segregation*," Coordinating Council of Community Organizations, 1963, pp. 28, 30-32.

In 1963, the Illinois State Legislature passed the Armstrong Act, amending the state school code. It requires that school boards shall not build schools " . . . in such a manner as to promote segregation or separation of children in public schools because of color, race or nationality." It also requires that " . . . as soon as practicable, and from time to time thereafter, the board shall change or revise existing [attendance] units or create new units in a manner which will take into consideration the prevention of segregation, and the elimination of separation of children in the public schools because of color, race or nationality."

While the school board has repeatedly insisted that school segregation is not of its own making, it has lobbied against earlier versions of the Armstrong bill. On March 25, 1959, the board voted eight to one against that year's version of the Act. (*Proceedings*, Board of Education, City of Chicago 1959-1960, p. 1646.)

No effort has, as of this writing, been made to comply with the Armstrong Act, despite the fact that adequate time existed between the law's passage and the beginning of the following school year.

If housing segregation is not of the school board's making, and if its claims of innocence on the issues of school district gerrymandering are valid, then why has it gone on record against such ameliorative legislation, and not made a single move to comply with a two-year-old state law requiring that districts be redrawn to promote integration? As you will note in the Urban League Report, and as the Hauser Report notes especially regarding "upper-grade centers" (p. 64), segregation has increased in our schools precisely during the period since the Armstrong law has been in force.

Additionally, we charge the Chicago school board and administration with having introduced and perpetuated school segregation through the process of constructing new schools in locations that would assure all-Negro or all-white populations. The Armstrong Act's injunction against this practice was in all likelihood stimulated by the Chicago practices, particularly during the tenure of the present general superintendent. (The late Representative Charles Armstrong was a Chicago legislator.)

According to the *Civil Rights Report*, when new schools are constructed in the heart of the Negro neighborhoods, " . . . the program has the effect of preserving the segregated character of these schools." The report then notes that more than 200 new school buildings or additions to buildings were completed between the years 1951 and 1962, and shows maps indicating " . . . most of this building was in the Negro residential area . . . " (pp. 189-190).

Supplementing the construction of new buildings in segregated areas of residence is the use of mobile classrooms as another instrument to perpetuate segregated school patterns. Pages 196-7 of the *Civil Rights Report* are devoted to a study of this use, and cite a prointegration school board member's prophetic remarks, "Trailer classrooms will become the symbols of segregation."

Indeed, a year after the report was published, community protests centered on construction of a mobile-classroom campus brought the issue to nationwide attention as the so-called "Willis Wagons" were equated with segregation and the policies of the chief administrator of the school system.

Yet another device used to contain the Negro pupils within the boundaries of Negro-segregated schools has been the creation of "upper-grade centers," housing the seventh and eighth grades. These centers, which circumvent long-established board policy against junior high schools, would, under ordinary circumstances, be expected to have a more integrated population than elementary schools, since they draw students from a wider geographic base.

However, the Hauser Report (p. 64) states that such is not the case. According to the report, "Only 2 of the city's 26 upper-grade centers have an integrated student body." Close examination shows the geographic placement of these centers, which must be interpreted as deliberate placement in areas that could serve only segregated populations. These centers also showed a marked increase in segregated populations from school year 1963-64 to 1964-65, as documented in the Urban League report.

Similarly, the creation of segregated "branch" schools serves the same ends. These are discussed in the aboved-cited reports and the "Handbook of School Segregation." It has also been charged in the 1964 brief of *Webb* v. *Board of Education*, that these branches have been placed in vacant space in white-segregated elementary and high schools so as to prevent the use of that space for transfer of Negro pupils from nearby overcrowded Negro-segregated elementary and high schools.

The "feeder plans," designating schools that send pupils to the various branch or upper-grade centers, are also contrived to assure segregation in the upper-grade centers, as well as assure the flow out to segregated high schools, again perpetuating the condition.

Added to the above issues of school construction, mobile classrooms, upper-grade centers and branch schools, is the question of existing unutilized classroom space throughout the school system. Despite the massive building program, schools remain overcrowded by the admission of board, superintendent, and concerned persons who are both favorable to and critical of school policies and administration. A 1961 report of the Urban League asserted that there were 382 unused classrooms throughout the school system. (Cited in *Civil Rights Report*, p. 200.) The general superintendent has consistently claimed far fewer. Heated public debate, estimates from independent surveys, official reports from the administration, demands of the board itself for an accurate count of unused classrooms, statements, counter-statements and considerable statistical juggling are reported in the aptly titled "The Empty Desk Imbroglio," pp. 198-204 of the *Civil Rights Report*. The conclusion was then that no accurate count of genuine unused or available classroom space had been produced by the superintendent, who was under board directive to so report.

The question, at this writing, is still unresolved. Newer reports have come from the administration, some of which have been interpreted as indicating that the original Urban League estimate was correct—or possibly even low. However, a full and complete report, satisfactory to either the board of education or the concerned citizen organizations, has yet to be issued.

We charge that this question has been evaded and hedged because it would tend to show certain available classroom space would not only relieve the unfortunate overcrowding of many schools, but would begin to produce a more integrated situation in certain schools if boundaries were redrawn only slightly to accom.nodate the student population—or if transfer policies were not so rigid as at present.

On the issue of transfers, it should be noted that Chicago's basically inflexible plan of assigning pupils to schools only in their "neighborhoods" has prevented any important cracking of racial lines. Most of the documents offered in exhibit here* discuss this policy and recognize it as the most immediate impediment to desegregation. While it should be noted that various limited forms of transfer for the alleged purpose of relieving overcrowding have been offered by the administration, they have been voluntary and so highly restrictive in detail as to permit no appreciable integration. In sum, such efforts indicate to us no good faith in implementing any of the various transfer programs that have been proposed to help desegregate Chicago schools.

It would be redundant at this point in history to point out to the U.S. Office of Education the numerous deleterious effects of segregation on Negro children specifically, and the social and educational benefits of integration for the white child. These have been pointed out by educators, psychologists, psychiatrists, sociologists, social workers, and specialists in the many other branches of behavioral and social sciences. They have been recognized by the courts, by the U.S. Department of Health, Education, and Welfare, and are the premises of many recent laws of this nation.

We would, however, point out some of the gross inequities that exist in the Chicago public school system as a direct result of school segregation. It is the existence of these inequities, as a matter of fact, recognized by some white parents, that results in existing antagonism to plans for desegregation. These white citizens, assuming the highest motives on their part, and eliminating the die-hard segregationist-racist element, fear that integration of their schools will result in lower standards of education for their children. An outline of these inequities tends to support these fears, though we maintain that a solution will only fully be achieved through a uniform upgrading of the school system as it becomes fully integrated.

First, Negro schools, despite the fact that they are larger, tend to be more overcrowded than white schools, according to the Hauser Report (pp. 52-54), and have a higher number of pupils per teacher than do white schools. The mean figure per elementary school classroom shows 29.7 pupils in the white classroom, 34.0 in the integrated school classroom, and 34.4 in the Negro school classroom.

Second, the question of quality education can be judged strongly on the proportion of uncertificated teachers on a school's staff, according to the *Civil Rights Report* (p. 224), which shows that white schools had an average of 12 percent noncertificated teachers, integrated schools had a corresponding average of 23 percent noncertificated teachers, and Negro schools an average of 27 percent noncertificated teachers. This evidence is largely corroborated in the Hauser Report (p. 74): "It is apparent that teachers in Negro schools are younger and have less formal education and that the teaching staff in these schools has a much higher turnover."

The school board also systematically discriminates against Negro children in the matter of supplying substitute teachers when regularly assigned teachers are not available.

---

*[Editor's Note: Exhibits attached to the complaint are not included here.]

During the week of March 29-April 2, 1965, the Chicago Teachers Union conducted a survey of classrooms in which teaching vacancies were not filled by substitutes. In other words, children in these classrooms had no teacher at all or were sent to already-crowded classrooms in which the teacher had no prior knowledge of the new children.

The CTU found that "approximately 40 percent of the teaching positions vacant . . . due to the absence of the teacher were not filled by substitutes." (Letter by CTU President John M. Fewkes to Board of Education, May 18, 1965, published in *Chicago Union Teacher*, May, 1965.)

What the CTU did not report was the further fact that the situation was *three times* as bad in Negro school districts as in white school districts. A Negro district is here defined as one with 80 percent or more Negro students in grade schools, and a white district as one with 80 percent or more students in grade schools.

The table is the resulting distribution of classrooms that did not have teachers in the sample week.

School Districts	Average percentage of Negroes in grade schools	Average percentage of class-rooms not covered by substitutes
White 1-6, 12, 17	2.0	19.8
Negro 8, 9, 11, 13, 14 16, 20, 21	90.4	59.2

There is no reason to doubt that the present pattern has existed for many years.

Third, on the question of vital supplementary facilities, according to the Hauser Report (p. 76) Negro schools have proportionately fewer libraries, adjustment rooms, and auditoriums.

Fourth, on curriculum, again according to the Hauser Report (pp. 78-79), the number of Negro high schools offering honors and/or advanced placement courses in English, chemistry, biology, algebra, geometry, physics, and U.S. history, was substantially lower than the number of white high schools offering those courses.

Finally, the virtually total absence of statistics on achievement levels of Chicago schools, *broken down on a school-by-school basis*, makes us highly suspicious of the total quality of the school system, and especially of that in Negro schools. Concerned organizations have long sought school-by-school information on the median achievement levels in reading, arithmetic, etc., but none has been forthcoming from the superintendent.

Guarded and highly incomplete citywide and district-by-district reports have been issued, indicating Chicago pupils to be performing just at or below the national averages, with the lower scores in the identifiably Negro school districts, but these have been simple barometers and do not tell the full story. (See Hauser Report, pp. 81-85.)

The only concrete piece of information available was taken from the records of Forrestville North Upper-Grade Center, a Negro school. It showed that the median reading level of the eighth-grade graduating class of 1963 was fifth grade. Of 749 pupils, 397 (53 percent) had second-to-fifth grade reading levels; 207 (27 percent) had sixth and seventh grade reading levels, and 145 (19 percent) had eighth grade or higher reading levels (*Handbook of Chicago School Segregation*, p. 33).

If this is indicative, as well it may be, of the entire system, it is small wonder that the administration is so loath to publish such damning information.

The Chicago school board's inaction in this regard might be contrasted with that of New York City, which has announced that it will make available its school-by-school academic achievement scores, starting in October, 1965, to all responsible organizations.

These are simply a few highlights extracted from these authoritative reports. We urge your perusal of the full texts of these attached exhibits* in order to gain a complete and rounded picture of discriminatory practices in Chicago schools. Many of the raw statistics and much of the the language of these documents will bring home to you even more strongly the continued situation of "separate and unequal" education in this city.

There is yet to be considered the problem of staff segregation, a further point showing probable racial discrimination. According to the Hauser Report (p. 68), 15 percent of the city's high school teachers are Negro. The majority are assigned to six Negro schools, where the staff is 70 percent Negro. Nineteen schools classed as segregated-white have only 10 Negro teachers out of a total of 1,913 teachers. The report indicates that a similar pattern exists in the elementary schools.

Further, there is only one Negro principal assigned to a non-Negro school. Meanwhile, numerous vacancies have opened and no Negro principal assigned since January, 1963.

These simple statements of fact underline what is believed to be an unwritten policy of staff segregation. We have at the present time no conclusive documentation of such a policy, but informal firsthand reports of teachers, Negro and white, would indicate that such does exist. The issue merits your consideration and further investigation.

Before continuing with a chronology of events succeeding the issuance of the Hauser Report, we should like to focus special attention on the situation at Washburne Trade School, which provides training programs, in cooperation with trade unions, for students who are employed in and are apprenticed to the trades. Failure to achieve admission can result in exclusion from the trades. It is the only such school in a city having a simple majority of Negro pupils in the public schools, yet the racial head count of 1963 showed Washburne's enrollment to be 97 percent white and 2.5 percent Negro! The Hauser Report (p. 21) found it " ... shocking that some unions in Chicago do not admit Negroes as apprentices and that the public school system cooperates with these unions in providing apprenticeship training programs."

The *Civil Rights Report* also deals at length with this situation (p. 208). It is our understanding that a complaint has been filed with your office on this situation. We incorporate it into our petition here as a supporting motion.

In establishing the Hauser panel, the Chicago board of education described its purpose as follows: " ... To analyze and study the school system in particular regard to schools attended entirely or predominantly by Negroes, define any problems that

---

*[Editor's Note: Exhibits attached to the complaint are not included here.]

result therefrom, and formulate and report to this board as soon as may be conveniently possible a plan by which any educational, psychological, and emotional problems or inequities in the school system that prevail may best be eliminated," and further to "promptly take such action as it may determine is appropriate or required to work toward a resolution of any problems and any inequities found to exist." (Hauser Report, p. vii.)

On February 13, 1964, six weeks before the Hauser panel completed its report, the board adopted a policy statement on integration that said in part: " ... We reaffirm [sic] and publicly declare a policy of racial integration. We shall endeavor to effect the development of a continuous program to achieve this goal."

When the Hauser Report was issued on March 31, 1964, its clear statements on the existence of segregation and its corresponding inequities (as cited above) were made public, along with 13 major recommendations. In April, the report was adopted "in principle" by the board. The general superintendent failed to make such an endorsement. No effort was made by the board to promote acceptance of the report by administrators or teachers. At no time did the board direct the general superintendent to engage in such action, nor did the general superintendent ever do so.

Some five months after submission of the report, Hauser stated in the periodical *Integrated Education*, "Very little has yet been accomplished in the way of implementing the report. ... Of the 13 recommendations made, almost one-fourth of one has been implemented."[1] He referred here to establishment of a biracial "Friends of the Chicago Schools" Committee (Hauser Report, p. 38), which was to help gain community support for the integration program. (On June 22, 1965, four prominent members of the committee resigned in protest of the "misleading" and "rubber stamp" role of the group, according to the Chicago *Sun-Times*, June 23, 1965.)

In April, 1965, one year after the report was submitted, Hauser publicly declared his conviction that only a change in the general superintendency would activate his panel's recommendations. On May 27, the general superintendent was rehired.

Meanwhile, in November, 1964, an official survey of the schools, conducted by Dr. Robert J. Havighurst, with the general superintendent on the panel, was submitted to the school board. (*The Public Schools of Chicago, A Survey*, by Robert J. Havighurst for the Board of Education of the City of Chicago.) The report contained 22 major recommendations, several of which dealt with desegregation, in addition to improvement of education. In an address to the Men's Club of Sinai Temple in Chicago on May 26, 1965, Havighurst said that only one of the survey's recommendations had been formally considered and acted upon by the board. The recommendation was purely an administrative matter, not related to desegregation or educational upgrading. Havighurst also said that the school board had neither requested nor directed the general superintendent to make an explicit commitment with respect to each of the major recommendations.

At this writing we are met by still another crisis bordering on an emergency. The school board's decision to rehire the general superintendent for another 18 months now confronts us with the impending passage of his plan to reorganize all Chicago school districts. This plan, if passed, will tend to lock in and reinforce the segregated situation.

[1]Philip M. Hauser, "Dynamic Inaction in Chicago Schools," *Integrated Education*, October/November 1964, p. 44.

When a public body such as the school board draws boundary lines such as it has in the past, and is likely to do again, that produce segregation, then what we have is not *de facto* segregation—it is *de jure* segregation. We maintain that such is the case here.

Mr. Commissioner, Chicago's schools are segregated and unequal because of racial discrimination, and are thus in violation of the 1964 Civil Rights Act. Copious evidence and testimony, of which we have alluded to only a small but significant portion, [have] demonstrated this to the Board of Education of the City of Chicago and to the citizens of Chicago. The board has not only failed to take any action to remedy the situation, but it has gone against the recommendations of church, community, civil rights, education leaders, and civic organizations by rehiring a general superintendent who is widely believed to be a major architect of methods to perpetuate segregation in Northern urban communities.

We are reluctant to submit this to petition the federal government to withhold further funds from the Chicago board of education, because we realize that short-term harm to certain programs can occur through suspension of funds. But we are persuaded that far greater damage will be done if the present situation is permitted to continue. We are further persuaded that the ways and means of creating and perpetuating segregation in Chicago may become the handbook for southern communities seeking to evade the 1954 supreme court ruling. We are confident that federal intervention in this matter, through the withholding of funds, will help underline the high fiscal cost, as well as the immeasurable social cost, of segregation to Chicago and to the rest of the nation.

> Respectfully submitted,
> ALBERT A. RABY, Convenor
> Coordinating Council of
> Community Organizations

THE JULY 27, 1965, DOCUMENT

The Chicago Board of Education has deliberately segregated the city's public school system. This can be seen from an examination of: (1) the general pattern of use of the community's educational resources; (2) gerrymandering of school attendance boundaries; (3) legislative lobbying by the board against state legislation that could force it to reduce or prevent segregation; and (4) maintenance of an apprenticeship-training program that excludes all but a tiny, token Negro representation.

General Patterns

Over a period of years the board of education response to the shifting population was such that by 1950, there was overcrowding in areas where there were Negroes, and empty rooms where there were whites. The school board could have opened the underutilized white schools in order to relieve the overcrowded Negro schools. Their refusal to do so was deliberate. After refusing, the board then claimed it had no alternative except to build new segregated schools in the Negro ghetto. Clearly it created that alternative and then proceeded to "select" it.

The school board could have chosen the first alternative, that is, fill up the white schools—but it did not. The Chicago school board deliberately chose to segregate.

But was there much space available in the white schools?

Table 1, "Fifty Years of Enrollment in the Chicago Public Schools, 1914-1964," sums up part of the story. It shows that enrollment rose from 292,823 in 1914 to a high

Table 1

FIFTY YEARS OF ENROLLMENT IN THE CHICAGO PUBLIC SCHOOLS, 1914-1964*

Year	Elementary	High School	Total
1914-5	268.259	24.564	292.823
1915-6	273.121	28.351	301.472
1916-7	270.681	29.907	300.588
1917-8	276.754	30.560	307.314
1918-9	276.812	31.347	308.159
1919-20	288.719	34.611	323.330
1920-1	302.610	37.442	340.052
1921-2	316.291	44.713	361.004
1922-3	325.122	50.562	375.684
1923-4	341.057	53.352	394.409
1924-5	345.870	62.553	408.423
1925-6	347.466	70.033	417.499
1926-7	349.996	78.875	428.871
1927-8	350.956	93.212	444.168
1928-9	345.829	104.603	450.432
1929-30	343.336	109.458	452.794
1930-1	338.738	123.696	462.434
1931-2	329.298	137.189	466.487
1932-3	325.401	147.388	472.789
1933-4	340.543	119.337	459.880
1934-5	334.207	123.507	457.714
1935-6	328.169	127.791	455.960
1936-7	321.476	126.961	448.428
1937-8	309.594	129.545	455.960
1938-9	299.920	135.820	435.740
1939-40	290.443	137.343	427.786
1940-1	280.993	134.537	415.530
1941-2	273.821	125.261	399.082
1942-3	264.651	116.296	380.947
1943-4	254.865	108.854	363.719
1944-5	246.263	107.856	354.119
1945-6	240.696	106.029	346.725
1946-7	242.589	102.316	344.905
1947-8	250.486	95.569	346.055
1948-9	257.165	90.934	348.099
1949-50	259.933	90.962	350.895
1950-1	261.127	89.652	350.779
1951-2	266.942	89.269	356.211
1952-3	279.267	88.467	367.734
1953-4	290.469	86.954	377.423
1954-5	302.976	87.635	390.611
1955-6	312.299	87.312	399.611
1956-7	323.315	90.887	414.202
1957-8	329.444	95.609	424.053
1958-9	340.577	97.626	438.203
1959-60	354.724	96.552	451.276
1960-1	368.736	97.004	465.740
1961-2	377.331	103.509	480.840
1962-3	389.591	112.200	501.791
1963-4	396.981	123.974	520.955

*Source: Chicago Board of Education, **Fact and Figures,** May, 1963; p. 12; and September, 1964, p. 24. These figures are for average daily membership. From 1924-5 to 1932-3, high school figures include junior high school enrollment.

of 472,789 in 1932. It shows further that after 1932 enrollment fell to a low of 344,905 in 1946 and rose to a new high of 520,955 in 1963. In other words, today's total enrollment is only somewhat larger than it was in 1932. That enrollment, moreover, is now about one-half Negro whereas in 1932 it was approximately one-tenth.

Furthermore, as is well known, there was a net exodus of 424,345 whites from Chicago between 1930 and 1960. A considerable number of the remaining whites sent their children to the expanding parochial schools.

The white population to be educated in Chicago's public schools is much smaller now than in 1932. The school board, however, chose to allocate to this declining group exclusive and ample schools. As the U.S. Commission on Civil Rights staff commented in December, 1963: "The tenacity with which Chicago confined its Negro pupils to neighborhood schools, and refused to rezone attendance areas on the fringes of the concentrated Negro residential areas or to relax its no-transfer-from-zone-of-residence rules is well known."[1]

For a generation, the city's Negro children were burdened with an extra handicap—double-shift classes. As Map 1, "Double-shift, Cumulative Burden, 1950-1961" shows, by far the greatest sufferers from double-shift were Negroes. Once having decided to exclude Negro children from the emptying white schools, the school board chose to reduce the amount of schooling they could receive even in Negro schools. A number of Negro children who were thus penalized during the years 1950-1961 are now themselves parents. Is it any wonder that their fresh and bitter memories make them determined to see that their children receive a good education?

Map 2, "Racial Patterns of School Mobiles, 1962"—demonstrates that the school board used mobiles as it used double-shifts—to contain Negro children in ghetto schools.

The school board has refused to direct the general superintendent to submit an accurate definitive room-count. The latest version of a room-count was made by the general superintendent in November, 1964. How vague and indecisive it was can be judged from the following colloquy between school board members Warren Bacon, Bernard Friedman, Cyrus H. Adams III, and General Superintendent Benjamin C. Willis:

Bacon: "In the light of the figures released Tuesday, some 703 vacant classrooms are available."
Adams: "There are likely to be about 93.5 classrooms vacant. . . . "
Friedman: "Are there 703 vacant classrooms available to students in the city, Dr. Willis?"
Willis: "I think there are 275, approximately."[2]

This vain effort joined a long train of similar vain efforts made during the preceding three years. A reasonable interpretation of these events is that the school board does not wish to reveal the extent of underutilization which was made inevitable by its exclusionist policies.

By the same token the relative overcrowding of Negro schools was also made inevitable. The effects of that choice—less learning, poorer conditions of space and equipment, and impoverished curriculum, and more—were as inevitable. The school board has chosen to use the entire community's resources for the greater benefit of only one part of the community. This it has done consciously and deliberately.

---

[1]U.S. Commission on Civil Rights, 1963 Staff Report, *Public Education* (Washington, D.C.: Government Printing Office, 1964), p. 85.

[2]Private transcript of board of education meeting, November 12, 1964.

MAP 1. Double-Shift, Cumulative Burden, 1950-1961

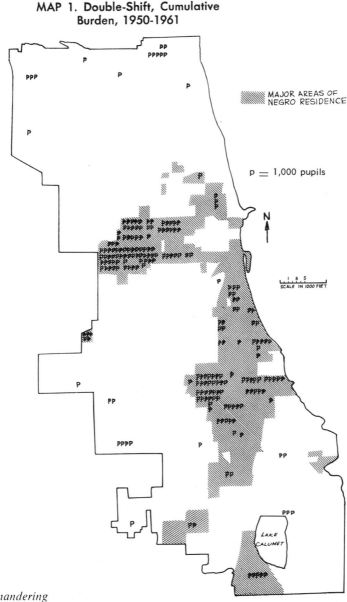

MAJOR AREAS OF NEGRO RESIDENCE

P = 1,000 pupils

N

SCALE IN 1000 FEET

LAKE CALUMET

Gerrymandering

According to *Webster's New International Dictionary*, 2nd edition, the word "gerrymander" means "to divide into ... districts ... in an unnatural and unfair way with a view to give ... an advantage ... or for some other improper purpose. Hence, to manipulate ... in order to gain an unfair advantage ... " A school gerrymander means the arrangement of school attendance boundaries to include children of one type who receive a special advantage and exclude others who thereby are deprived of that advantage.

MAP 2. Racial Patterns of School
Mobiles, 1962

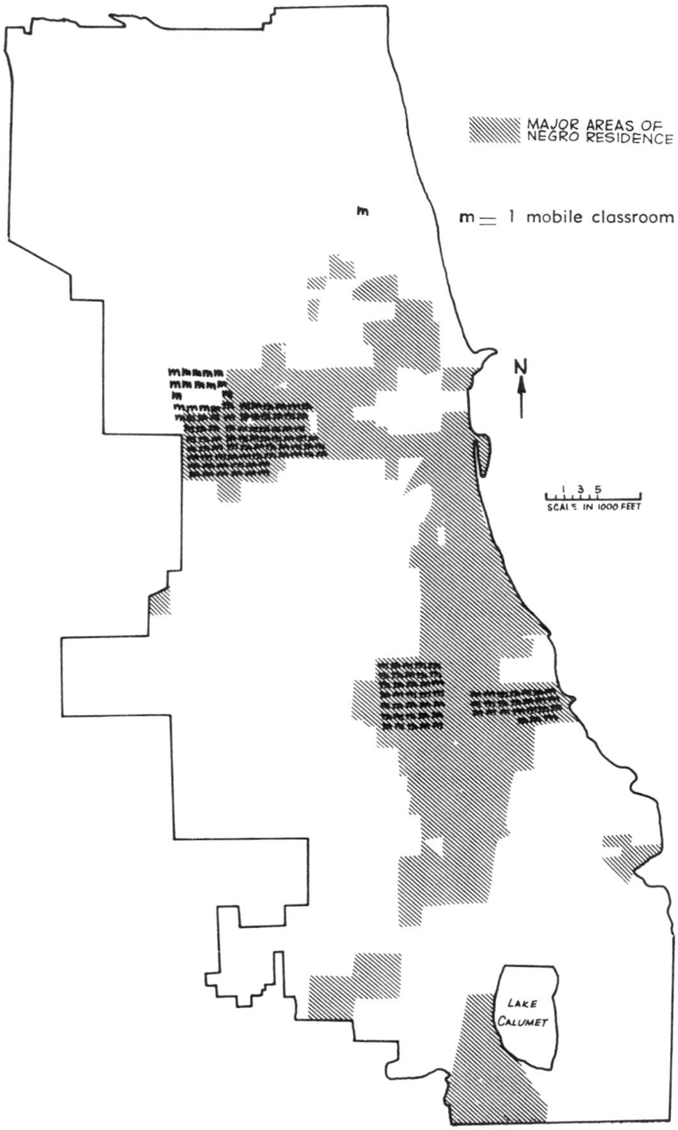

MAJOR AREAS OF
NEGRO RESIDENCE

m = 1 mobile classroom

N

1 3 5
SCALE IN 1000 FEET

LAKE
CALUMET

Mr. Anthony Celebrezze, Secretary of the U.S. Department of Health, Education and Welfare, has testified: "Basically, racial imbalance in any community comes
because of school district lines."[3] There is more than a suggestion in this statement by

---

[3]U.S. Congress, 88th, 1st session, House of Representatives, Committee on the Judiciary,
Subcommittee No. 5, *Hearings ... Civil Rights ...* , Parts 1-4, Serial No. 4, (Washington,
D.C.: Government Printing Office, 1963-1964), II, p. 1514.

a former mayor of Cleveland that the hand that draws attendance boundary lines may largely determine the amount of school segregation. When asked by a congressman whether federal funds could be cut off from a school board that created racial imbalance, Secretary Celebrezze replied: "If we come to the conclusion after due investigation, after due hearings, that they are using [attendance] district boundaries as a device to promote segregation, and we have the law or the authority, which we probably don't have now, then we would have a right to cut off funds."[4] (The secretary was testifying on the bill that became the Civil Rights Act of 1964. Title VI gives the secretary such authority.)

In November, 1963, the Illinois State Superintendent of Public Instruction, Ray Page, wrote:

> There is no law in this state which requires that a school (attendance system), developed on the neighborhood school plan, *honestly and conscientiously constructed with no intention or purpose to segregate the races,* must be destroyed or abandoned because the resulting effect is to have a racial imbalance in certain schools where the district is populated almost entirely by Negroes or whites.[5] (Italics added.)

Implicitly, Mr. Page seems to say that racial gerrymandering would not qualify as an "honest and conscientious" system. Inferred under Illinois state law, in case of demonstrated gerrymandering, the state superintendent would have to refuse state aid to the school board involved. In fact, however, he has not.

The end result of large-scale gerrymandering is to make the ghetto school a trap for Negro children. Stigmatized socially, and deliberately deprived by the school board, Negro schools increasingly fail to serve the needs of children. Classes are permitted to grow larger, the teaching staff becomes less stable, learning achievement becomes less evident. Any effort to permit children to escape such a trap is met by the cry of "neighborhood school." What may have been perfectly innocuous boundary lines years ago, now become bars to prevent escape. The failure to redistrict ghetto schools is deliberate to restrict educational opportunity. It is the sense used here, gerrymandering. . . . The contention was made [above] that the entire school system is, in a sense, gerrymandered. Let us now examine two specific current cases of gerrymandering. [See Map 3, "The Riverdale Gerrymander," and Map 4, "The Orr Gerrymander."] This examination is followed by a listing of twenty additional cases. We present these as worthy of further study. Because of the press of time we have not been able to describe them in detail.

The Riverdale Gerrymander—The Riverdale Elementary School, 13233 South Prairie Street, was built in 1937 in a very sparsely populated area of the city. Attended exclusively by white children from the immediate neighborhood, its graduates went to Fenger High School, some four miles to the north; no nearer high school being then available. Riverdale, rarely enrolling more than 100 or so students, was classified as a branch of white Pullman Elementary School, a "feeder" to white Fenger High School.

During World War II, Altgeld Gardens, an extensive all-Negro public housing project, was built adjacent to the Riverdale district. Between 1945 and 1960, four

[4]*Ibid,* p. 151.
[5]*Decision, In The Matter of Petition of Certain Residents of School District 14 of the City of Chicago, Complaining of Segregation in the Chicago Public School System,* November 19, 1963, p. 11.

MAP 3. The Riverdale Gerrymander

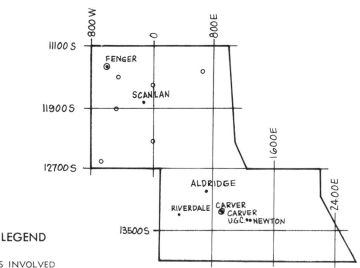

LEGEND

⊚ HIGH SCHOOLS INVOLVED

• GRADE SCHOOLS INVOLVED

o SCHOOLS NOT KNOWN TO BE
  INVOLVED

MAP 4. The Orr Gerrymander

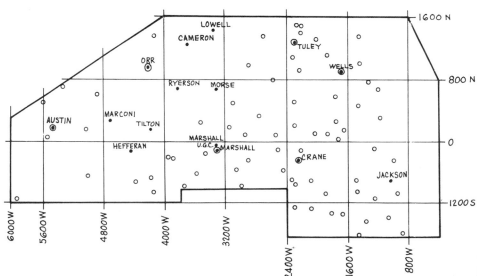

schools were built within the confines of the project; all project children attended these schools. They are:

Carver Primary School, 909 East 132nd Street, built in 1945.

Carver High School, (and later, also Upper-Grade Center), 801 East 133rd Street, built in 1949.

Newton Elementary School, 901 East 133rd Street, built in 1955.

Aldridge Elementary School, 630 East 131st Street, built in 1960.

After 1945 and 1949, the board of education initiated two attendance-districting principles in the general region which are still in force today. (1) No part of the Altgeld project is included in the attendance area of Riverdale school, and (2) although Riverdale school is located five blocks from Carver High School, its graduates attend Fenger High School, *three miles away*.

The mechanism whereby such an extraordinary procedure occurs is that Riverdale is a branch of 98.4 percent white Scanlan, four miles away, a feeder into Fenger. Thus, Riverdale school has been a clear case of gerrymandering since this time. The motive—racial segregation—is plain. In the 1964 school board racial count, the schools under discussion showed the following percentages of Negro pupils: Riverdale, 0.0; Fenger, 4.8; Carver UGC, 99.0; Carver Primary, 100.0; Aldridge, 100.0; Newton, 100.0; and Carver High, 100.0.

When Carver High was built, in 1949, a few white families lived interspersed outside the Altgeld project. The school board took two actions to segregate racially the children of these families. First, a "neutral" area was created, to cover the whole area, *excluding* Altgeld Gardens. Persons living in the "neutral" area could send the children to Riverdale or Carver Primary. Needless to say, no Negroes ended up in Riverdale and no whites ended up in Carver. The "neutral" area was neutral in every respect but race. Second, on September 6, 1949, the school board created a "neutral" area for Fenger High School. All persons living in the general area, again excluding Altgeld Gardens, could use Carver High or Fenger. Apparently without exception, Negroes in the neutral area "chose" Carver and whites, Fenger. Thus, Carver High School attendance district was in effect completely encircled by Fenger's district.

In 1955, an official publication of the school board misrepresented the gerrymander on a map.[6] In August of that year, General Superintendent Willis distributed a map showing Riverdale school as a feeder to Carver High School. The map gave no indication that Riverdale was a feeder of Fenger.

When were the neutral areas abolished? It is difficult to say, although evidence points to 1958. By that year a number of housing trailers had been removed from the area slightly north of Altgeld Gardens. These had been the principal source of Negro families in the "neutral" areas. As a result of the removal, segregation could be effected without "neutral" areas; Fenger was redistricted accordingly.

On July 8, 1964, Superintendent Willis presented a proposal to the school board regarding the attendance boundaries.[7] The changes contemplated: (1) requiring Riverdale seventh- and eight-grade students to attend Carver Upper-Grade Center; (2) placement of the Riverdale-Altgeld Gardens area with Carver High School district, thus making Riverdale a feeder to Carver instead of Fenger; and (3) placing

[6]See *Educational Progress*, September, 1955.

[7]*Proceedings* of the Chicago Board of Education, July 8, 1964, pp. 67-68; Report No. 72364-C.

within the Riverdale attendance district the new Negro-populated Golden Gates development, adjacent to Riverdale and Altgeld Gardens.

The changes were significant. The Riverdale-Scanlan-Fenger gerrymander would have ended and Riverdale would gradually cease being a white preserve.

But the changes never occurred. On July 8, 1964, the day the proposal was made, two board members moved to defer the matter until the following meeting. On August 12, 1964, the matter was again deferred. On August 26, a third deferral was obtained. On September 9, 1964, the item was withdrawn at the request of the general superintendent.

On October 14, 1964, Superintendent Willis made a new proposal which was referred immediately to a committee of the board. It was adopted by the board on October 27, 1964.[8] The new proposal once again designated Riverdale as a branch of Scanlan, and so Riverdale graduates are still eligible to enter Fenger but not Carver High. In addition, part of the Golden Gate development was districted into Riverdale. Residents report, however, that not a single Negro child was enrolled in Riverdale during 1964-1965.

Riverdale is a stark symbol of deliberate segregation and educational deprivation. During the years of the most severe overcrowding in the Altgeld schools, with double shifts in the project schools, Riverdale suffered no overcrowding. It never had double shifts. In 1964, class size, according to Superintendent Willis, was as follows in the area's schools: Aldridge, 33.1; Carver Primary, 32.8; Carver U.G.C., 32.7; Newton, 32.7; and Riverdale, 16.8.[9]

One should recall our earlier definition of a gerrymander: "To manipulate . . . in order to gain an unfair advantage." Such manipulation is obvious in this case. It cannot be charged to geographical or housing factors. The board used its public authority to effect racial discrimination.

A Westside Story—In 1962, the board of education opened Orr High School "Unit" in the Orr Elementary School building, 1040 North Keeler Avenue. The "unit" shared the principal of Marshall High School. In 1964, it received its own principal. The "unit" was not a branch of any other high school, although the school board listed it in a manner of a branch (e.g., in the documents relating to the racial head count). A curious feature of the "unit" was the fact that while physically it was in Administrative District 4, it was listed in school board sources as in District 8 at times and in District 4 at other times.

Indications are strong that the new school was started, in large part, as a white school to please parents of white children then enrolled in a predominantly Negro Marshall. Thus, the attendance area of Orr "unit" was drawn to include, as feeders, Morse, Cameron, Ryerson elementary schools. These were the last three white feeder schools for Marshall, which was now fated to become a completely black school fed by completely black elementary schools. If the aim had been to relieve the overcrowding at Marshall—which was extreme, while Orr "unit" was underutilized—both integration and efficient space utilization could have been served by shifting certain Negro feeder schools from Marshall to Orr. Distance was not a factor.

---

[8]*Proceedings* of the Chicago Board of Education, October 27, 1964; Report No. 72594.
[9]*Ibid.*

In June, 1963, Governor Otto J. Kerner of Illinois signed the Armstrong Bill. It required that school boards locate school buildings so as to avoid segregation, and stipulated that school boards must periodically redistrict attendance areas so as to minimize segregation.

On July 10, 1963, the Chicago school board adopted board Report 71354-E, establishing the gerrymandered Orr attendance district described above. On July 30, 1963, the author of the Armstrong Act testified before the school board and warned that straightforward and decisive action against segregated site locations and districting was required by the act.

On May 27, 1964, Superintendent Willis presented a series of proposals to the board; all were included in Report 72221-B. It was deferred until June 10, 1964, and then adopted. He reported that enrollment could not be expanded any further at Tuley (1.2 percent Negro), Crane (91.1 percent), and Marshall (93.6 percent). Room was available at Austin (0.0 percent Negro) and Orr (1.8 percent Negro).

Good administrative practice suggests that in the light of this, reallocation of space could easily be combined with increased integration. Crane and Marshall were both Negro-segregated and overcrowded. Two proposals were related to Crane. Six students, presumedly white, were permitted to attend Tuley High School even though they lived just on the Crane side of the Tuley-Crane boundary. If, as we assume, these students were white, then the move decreased integration.

A ninth-grade branch, capacity of 500, was created at Jackson Elementary (5.5 percent Negro). This relieved Crane and seemed to increase integration.

How is integration affected by the Jackson branch? In October, 1964, it enrolled 388 Negroes and 40 whites, or 89.4 percent Negro. Meanwhile, in the same building, in the elementary classrooms, only 5.5 percent of the students were Negro. Observers report that no integration at all occurred in practice between Jackson's elementary and high school children. They arrived and left at different times; ate at separate times; played at separate times. They had nothing to do with each other.

With new and virtually all-Negro Faraday Elementary School about to open directly across the street from Marshall, forty classrooms in Marshall that had been used for the waiting elementary students were now to be returned for high school use. (In October, 1964, accordingly, enrollment rose in Marshall from 4,490 to 5,066. That same month, the racial head count showed Marshall to be 97.6 percent Negro—up four percentage points in a year). During the school year 1963-1964, nearby Orr enrolled 501 white students. Perhaps as many as 250 came from former Marshall feeder schools. Their absence from Marshall was crucial in making this a virtually all-Negro school.

The Willis proposals of May 27, 1964, also provided that two Marshall feeder schools, Marconi (40.0 percent Negro) and Hefferan (94.1 percent Negro), be made into feeders for Austin High School (0.0 percent Negro). Austin was to receive some 130 students from these new feeders in September, 1964. This would increase integration. Out of a total enrollment of 3,195, somewhat fewer than 130 would be Negro. Needless to say, Marshall became even more segregated by the loss of Marconi.

Superintendent Willis also proposed two changes in Orr's boundaries. Lowell, a feeder for Tuley High School, was made a feeder for Orr. Lowell was 0.9 percent Negro, and a few blocks to the south—mostly nonresidential park property—were added to the Orr attendance area. "These changes," Superintenden Willis told the school board, "could increase the ratio of Negro pupils at Orr, which is presently very small."[10] As a matter of fact, however, a grand total of 7 Negro students was added as a result of these changes. In 1963, 9 of a total enrollment of 511 were Negro; in 1964, it was 16 out of 644. Such tokenism does not merit the name "integration."

In the superintendent's report of October 24, 1963, ("Use of Facilities, High School Buildings"), Orr had been reported operating at 18.2 percent under capacity. Here was an excellent opportunity to use classroom space and to integrate at the same time by switching a Marshall feeder school to Orr. Tilton, 57.3 percent Negro, would have been a judicious choice.

Instead, as we have seen, Lowell (0.9 percent Negro), a Tuley feeder, was made into an Orr feeder. Ostensibly, Lowell was chosen, according to Superintendent Willis, "to reduce overcrowding at . . . Tuley . . . "[11] This aim could have been accomplished more easily by redistricting Tuley's easternmost feeder to Wells High School; both Tuley and Wells are in the same district. (In 1963, Wells was only 10.9 percent over capacity and 11.8 percent in 1964. In 1964, Tuley was 114.6 percent over capacity.) Had this been done, Lowell could have remained with Tuley and an integrated or Negro Marshall feeder could have been districted into Orr.

It may be noted in conclusion that the 1964 school board budget provided for a large-scale addition to Orr. By 1966 or thereabouts, Orr will be a full four-year high school. It will continue to be the pivot of planned segregation of the west side and near northwest side of Chicago. The board must be challenged for its persistent violation of the Illinois Armstrong Act and the U.S. Civil Rights Act of 1964.

Twenty Cases for Further Study.—1. *Austin High School,* 231 N. Pine Avenue (5440 West), School District 4.

Was Austin partially demolished in 1959 and later districted to keep Negroes out? The only explanation given in the *Proceedings* (June 24, 1959, p. 2080) of the board of education for the demolition was that there was enough room left in the remainder to accommodate the students. Yet shortly afterwards a branch was opened in an elementary school. For some years the contiguous Negro high school, Marshall, has been crowded far beyond the city average; yet Austin, with its branch, remained at capacity.

2. *Prosser Vocational High School,* 2184 N. Long Avenue (5400 West), School District 4.

Was Prosser built to segregate? Earlier there had been only one west side vocational school, Manley, 2935 W. Polk Street (800 South), which of necessity either was or would have become integrated. Now there is white Prosser, opened in 1959; and Negro Cregier, 1829 W. Grenshaw (1120 South), renovated from an elementary school. When Prosser was budgeted, its location was not given and the National Association for the Advancement of Colored People had some difficulty finding out where it was. They protested in their testimony at the budget hearing that unless carefully districted, it would certainly be segregated. It has tool-and-die apprentices; Cregier has none. Prosser is much less crowded than Cregier.

---

[10]**Proceedings of the Chicago Board of Education,** May 27, 1964, p. 2390.
[11]*Ibid.*

3. *Waller High School*, 2039 N. Orchard Street (700 West), School District 7.

Why is this high school about five times as crowded as Wells, 936 N. Ashland (1600 West) to which some of its feeder schools were formerly districted? Is Wells now being resegregated white and Waller, Negro?

4. *Jenner*, 1009 N. Cleveland Avenue (460 West), School District 7.

Why were two additions made to create this oversized elementary school serving a nearly all Negro public housing project when the board of education owned nearby sites and was even renting out a school building for private school use?

5. *Manley*, Kg.-6, and Upper-Grade Center, 2935 W. Polk Street (800 South), School District 8.

Why was Manley Vocational High School converted into an oversized elementary school with 2,500 pupils under one principal?

6. *Sumner*, Kg.-8, 715 S. Kildare Avenue (4300 West), School District 8.

At this crowded elementary school on the expanding edge of the Negro ghetto, twenty-six mobile units have been on the playground for three years. The next school west, May, at 512 S. LaVergne Avenue (5000 West), probably nearly all white in 1962, has an ample campus on which the mobiles could easily have been accommodated for integration. Here, where the Upper-Grade Center could have been formed to reduce crowding as well as for educational purposes, the school remains Kg.-8.

7. *McKinley Upper-Grade Center*, 2040 W. Adams Street (200 South), School District 9.

This elementary school, formerly a high school, was converted to the first upper-grade center in 1954. In 1964, McKinley was 96.8 percent Negro. It has probably been Negro from its inception as a center. Immediately north of McKinley and its feeder schools are white Tuley High School, 1313 N. Claremont Avenue (2325 West), School District 6, and its white feeder schools. Tuley is crowded even with two branches. The upper-grade centers were established partly to relieve crowding. Therefore the nearby white schools, not being crowded, were not included in McKinley Upper-Grade Center. But had McKinley remained a high school it could have been redistricted with Tuley. Negro Emerson Branch of McKinley, 1700 West Walnut Street (230 North), is less than a mile from white Otis, 525 N. Armour Street (1550 West), and from white Talcott, 1840 W. Ohio Street, (600 North).

8. *Burns*, Kg.-8, 2524 S. Central Park Avenue (3600 West), School District 10.

From within the former boundary lines of Burns Elementary School have emerged in 1962 and 1964, two Negro elementary schools: Crown, 2128 S. St. Louis Avenue (3500 West) and Paderewski, 2221 S. Lawndale Avenue (3700 West). Burns changed from 60.5 percent to 19.5 percent Negro from 1963 to 1964. Many questions come to mind about this process of new building. Were Crown and Paderewski built for an illegally high housing density due to failure to enforce the building code? Why were there practically no white children in them? Why did they open more crowded than Burns?

9. Hearst, Kg.-8, 4640 S. Lamon Avenue (4900 West), School District 10.

This is a school serving a public housing project, LeClaire Courts, built on vacant land in a white area. It opened in 1950 with 90 percent white occupants. It had an extension in 1953. By 1962, LeClaire Courts was 90 percent Negro, the extension, 81 percent Negro.

Although Hearst School remained integrated (only 62.0 percent Negro in 1964), it suffered the fate of its Negro rather than its white component. The four white public housing projects in Chicago—Lawndale Gardens, Lathrop Homes, Trumbull Park Homes, and Bridgeport Homes—never had crowded schools. But nearly all the Negro projects (and by 1964, 92 percent of those in Chicago public housing projects were Negro) had crowded schools, most of them on double shift at one time or another; and very large schools, often isolated from the surrounding community. Hearst School was on a double shift in 1957 and 1958 and in 1963 had an average class size of 43.3 pupils per classroom.

10. *Baum Branch of Twain*, Kg.-6, 4950 S. LaPorte Avenue, (4934 West), School District 10.

Within a few blocks of Hearst a seven room branch of Twain, 5131 S. Linder Avenue (5440 West), was built and opened in 1962. Baum Branch has no Negro pupils. It seems to have been built to avoid taking any pupils from Hearst which was also crowded, as well as its parent school, Twain. Instead of making Baum an integrated school, it was built as a small branch; and another addition was built on Hearst.

11. *Pershing*, Kg.-6, 3113 S. Rhodes Avenue (500 East), School District 11.

This school seems to point, not to a racial, but to a class gerrymander. At the same time the insignificant amount of school integration produced by the urban renewal effort and money is disappointing.

When large financial interests built Lake Meadows and Prairie Shores on publicly cleared land, the board of education put up a new small school, Pershing, with 12 classrooms. A block away, Douglas, 3200 S. Calumet Avenue (317 East), had less than 35 per classroom in 1958, when Pershing opened. By 1963, Douglas had only 24.2 per classroom, with 1,729 pupils in 71 rooms. If, instead of building Pershing, the board of education had split up Douglas into two moderate-sized schools for the benefit of all the pupils and had made the few children of Lake Meadows and Prairie Shores a part of the surrounding community, democracy and equality of educational opportunity might have been advanced. While Pershing is technically integrated if the 90/10 formula is followed, since it is 11.4 percent white, the extent of integration is small. On October 7, 1964, there were present 31 white pupils, 233 Negro, and 9 others, Douglas had 2 white pupils; 1,805 Negro.

12. *Holden Branch of Tilden High School*, 1104 W. 31st Street (3100 South), School District 21.

Holden Branch was once a branch of Englewood High School, 6201 S. Stewart Avenue (400 West). When Englewood became Negro, Holden became a branch of white Kelly High School, 4136 S. California Ave., (2800 West). In 1964, for reasons unknown to us, it was made a branch of Tilden High School, 4747 S. Union Avenue

(700 West). Why was not Holden made a branch of Negro Phillips High School, 244 E. Pershing Road (3900 South), the nearest high school to it? This would have been especially appropriate in 1964 since Abbott, the branch of Phillips, 3630 S. Wells Street (200 West), was underpopulated, whereas Holden Branch was crowded with 503 students in instructional areas with a capacity of only 325.

13. *Beethoven*, Kg.-6, 25 W. 47th Street (4700 South), School District 13.

This segregated Negro school opened in 1962, crowded and overflowing into Taylor Homes Public Housing Project apartments needed for housing. In 1964, it still had 2,478 pupils under one principal, including 518 in 12 units of the Chicago Housing Authority apartments. Its upper grades go to upper-grade centers eastward into the Negro ghetto. West of Beethoven is a white school, Graham, 4436 S. Union Avenue (700 West), Kg.-8; and immediately west is Tilden High School, 4747 S. Union Avenue (700 West), 40.2 percent Negro in 1964.

14. *Harlan High School*, 9652 S. Michigan Avenue (100 East), School District 16.

This high school opened in 1958 and 1960, itself integrated, but thus resegregating Calumet High School, 8131 S. May Street (1100 West), and Fenger High School, 11220 S. Wallace Street (600 West), white. Even at its opening, although it was itself integrated, it caused a net increase in segregation. Calumet meanwhile became reintegrated in another direction; but Fenger remains segregated white to the present time, while Harlan itself became 90 percent Negro in 1964. The Chicago Board of Education built Calumet in a U shape in anticipation of population increases. An addition to Calumet instead of Harlan would have been less expensive and would have increased integration.

15. *Oglesby*, Kg.-8, 7646 S. Green Street (832 West), School District 16.

By refusal to redistrict or to transfer on an equitable basis, this school was made into a trap on the edge of the Negro ghetto. The next school west and south of it is Cook, 8150 S. Bishop Street (1550 West). In 1962, Cook, as a receiving school in the permissive transfer program, could not receive more students than would leave it at 30 per classroom; Oglesby as a crowded sending school, could not send students until it rose above 40 per classroom. By 1963, Cook, 3.1 percent Negro, had 25.7 pupils per classroom; Oglesby, 89.3 percent Negro, 44.1 pupils per classroom. In 1964, Cook was 9.7 percent Negro, 29.0 per classroom; Oglesby, 96.8 percent Negro, 46.3 per classroom, including ten mobile units.

16. *Morgan Park High School Branches Clissold and Shoop*: Clissold, 2350 W. 110th Place (11000 South) Kg.-8; Shoop, 1460 W. 112th Street (11200 South) Kg.-8, School District 18.

Morgan Park High School, 1744 W. Pryor Avenue (11200 South, 1650 West), has been physically integrated in its student body. In 1964, it was 31.3 percent Negro. Near it is an integrated elementary school, Esmond, 1865 W. Montvale Avenue (11300 South), which was once a branch of Morgan Park High School. For some years now, however, Morgan Park has had two completely segregated branches, Clissold, with 311 white students and Shoop with 108 Negro students. The elementary part of Clissold has 31.6 pupils per classroom; Shoop, 37.2.

17. *Whistler*, Kg.-6, 11513 S. Ada Street (1326 West), School District 18.

Whistler opened in 1958. In 1964, including its branch of mobile units, Whistler, 100 percent Negro, had 1,457 pupils, at 43.8 per classroom in the main building.

West Pullman Branch, 100 percent white, built in 1953 with an addition in 1957, 12151 S. Racine Avenue (1200 West), Kg.-2, had, in 1964, 158 pupils at 32.7 per classroom.

The southern boundary of Whistler ends at the end of the uninhabited area south of the Negro ghetto; the northern boundary of West Pullman Branch begins at that point.

18. *Chalmers*, Kg.-6, 2745 W. Roosevelt Road (1200 South), School District 19.

The recent history of this school might be studied to learn whether the neighborhood school or race is decisive for districting.

During the four school years 1956 through 1959, the old Chalmers on the same site as the above, was on double shift while about four blocks away from it in the same North Lawndale community area, even in the same census tract, parted only by a street which ran through the districts of several other nearby schools, was a white school, Plamondon, which probably had room enough to have taken Chalmers off shift and to have kept it off shift. Plamondon, Kg.-8, 1525 S. Washtenaw Avenue (2700 West), in 1963 had 391 pupils. By that time it was 9.4 percent Negro; Chalmers, replaced by a new building in 1960, was 95.3 percent Negro. The two schools were not redistricted. The upper grades of Chalmers now attend a Negro upper-grade center.

In 1952, Chalmers and Plamondon had the same principal. At issue also is the question of how much room Plamondon did have. As it is still standing, this could be ascertained.

19. *Hammond*, Kg.-6, 2819 W. 21st Place (2100 South), School District 19.

Hammond is a small white school with no Negro pupils. Prior to 1961, when it was partially demolished, it was larger than nearby 100 percent Negro Pope, 1852 S. Albany Avenue (3100 West). Pope, like most of the schools in North Lawndale, was crowded. For six years, from 1956 through 1961, it was on double shift. Yet it was never redistricted with Hammond which had only a few children in a larger building.

20. *Spry Upper-Grade Center*, 2400 S. Marshall Blvd., (2883 West), School District 19.

In the same building is Spry, Kg.-6. The Kg.-6 grades of Spry are composed almost exclusively of white pupils. Of 669 pupils in 1964, 0.9 percent or 5 pupils were Negro and present on the day of the racial count. In Spry Upper-Grade Center, however, 62.9 percent of 621 enrolled were Negro.

Spry is one of the few racially integrated upper-grade centers. But the question must be raised whether a much greater number of pupils could not have been, and cannot now be, integrated than under the present arrangements. McCormick, 2712 S. Sawyer Avenue (3230 West), Kg.-8, has no Negro pupils and does not send its upper grades to Spry. Only two white schools and only parts of two Negro schools participate in the integrated center.

Could not mobiles be placed on the Hammond campus and some paired arrangements worked out with Pope? Perhaps there should be an educational park on the extensive Harrison High School campus, 2850 W. 24th Street, Blvd. (2400 South), which is near Spry.

Legislative Lobbying

Repeatedly, the Chicago board of education has asserted that school segregation is merely a reflection of residential segregation. A more accurate statement would be that school organization may be affected by residential segregation. Precisely how the schools are affected is, in part, a matter that is up to the schools. Nor is this all. The schools may—indeed, should—work for the reduction of residential segregation. It goes without saying that the schools ought to welcome assistance in freeing themselves from the constrictions of segregation.

California is a good example. In the fall of 1964, a statewide referendum was to be held on whether or not to discontinue all state laws forbidding discrimination in the sale of residential property. Were the referendum to pass, residential segregation could be expected to increase and thus further complicate the state government's efforts to achieve school integration. The State Commission on Equal Opportunities in Education wrote to all school boards in the state: "The State Board of Education's policy, which is directed toward the elimination of existing *de facto* school segregation and curbing any tendency toward its growth, will be more difficult to translate into practice if the initiative is adopted."[12] This was a responsible exercise of a public obligation. State education authorities put their weight where it would count. That the measure passed anyway does not change matters.

The Chicago school board, however, did the very opposite. On March 25, 1959, by a vote of eight to one, it opposed a bill later to become the Armstrong Act* which would have required all school boards in the state to redistrict attendance zones periodically to reduce segregation.[13] One might think a local school board would welcome such a concrete measure. Chicago school authorities, on the contrary, did not even remain neutral, which would have been consistent with the board's theory that school segregation just happened to happen and thus need not be helped along. Instead, it did legislative battle against a potentially beneficial measure.

The school board did this officially and, of course, consciously. It thus acted irresponsibly with respect to its obligation toward all children.

This same irresponsibility can be seen in the repeated failure of the Chicago board of education to support the passage of legislation that would ease the pressures of school segregation. Such has been the case with open housing or fair employment practice bills. The legislative theory of the Chicago school board appears to be: Oppose it if it is for school integration, be neutral if it is for equal housing or employment opportunities.

Washburne

Over a period of years, an apprentice-training program that is racially discriminatory has been operated by the Chicago school board. In October, 1961, a representative of the school board testified before a subcommittee of the U.S. House

[12]*Integrated Education,* August-September, 1964, p. 4.

[13]*Proceedings* of the Chicago Board of Education, March 25, 1959, p. 1646.

*[Editor's Note: This Act would also have required the location of new school buildings so as to minimize segregation.]

Committee on Education and Labor and held—as the present general superintendent still holds—that the board had no control over the selection of apprentices. Representative Roman C. Pucinski responded: "I just cannot understand how you can state to this committee that you have no control over this program. There are three parties involved in this program and you are one of those three."[14] In 1962 a report to the U.S. Commission on Civil Rights stated: "The surrender of a public function to private organizations in this manner is difficult to justify."[15] In 1964, the Hauser Report stated: "The panel finds it shocking that some unions in Chicago do not admit Negroes as apprentices and that the public school system cooperates with these unions in providing apprenticeship training programs for them."[16] On January 26, 1965, school board vice-president Thomas J. Murray asked: "Why don't federal agencies do this job of delving into this, instead of the board of education? Why put this onus on us? They give us the money, it is their job to find out who or which union discriminates, if any."[17]

The Chicago Commission on Human Relations has taken an increasingly prominent role in the Washburne matter. On June 5, 1964, in a letter to board president Frank M. Whiston, the commission noted that discrimination by the joint apprenticeship committee and unions continued. Accordingly, it requested that the board of education withdraw funds and facilities from those unions. A year later, on July 6, 1965, the commission again urged the board to bar the unions from Washburne. Eight days later, the board passed a motion to deny discriminatory unions access to Washburne. Any union, however, could continue to use Washburne if it submitted a "written notice" signed by two chiefs of the union, that "personnel practices and policies of the union" were in accordance with the Civil Rights Act of 1964 and that the union did "not discriminate against Negroes" or other minority groups.

The school board has consciously and officially supported the racially discriminatory program at Washburne. It rejected, repeatedly, demands by citizens groups such as the Negro American Labor Council, the NAACP, and others for relief from this illegal program. Its latest action was perfunctory and is merely a new way of perpetuating the present control of the apprenticeship program. There is utterly no way that the board can police the arrangement it has now created. There is no reason to think the board wishes to police it.

Conclusion

Neither segregation nor integration just "happens."[18] Each is deliberately installed or prevented. The school board, acting under advice of its general superintendent, pursues a deliberate policy of segregation. This deliberate or official

---

[14]Quoted in letter from Ely M. Aaron to Frank M. Whiston, June 5, 1964. Mr. Aaron is Chairman of the Commission on Human Relations of the City of Chicago and Mr. Whiston is President of the Chicago Board of Education.

[15]*Ibid.*

[16]*Ibid.*

[17]Private transcript of meeting of school board committee on Washburne, January 26, 1965.

[18]Meyer Weinberg, "De Facto Segregation: Fact or Artifact?" *Integrated Education*, April, 1963. [See also pp. 150 ff. of this volume.]

segregation is exemplified in numerous cases as illustrated herein, and these cases are but illustrations of the general policy and pattern.

The pattern can be found in matters that are not touched in the present report, including the distribution of faculty, student reading materials, and repeated failures of the board to implement recommendations derived from studies the board itself had requested.

Ultimately, the board will have to undo the harm it has caused. This will require an official and factual dedication to integration. It will require painstaking planning to achieve the goal the state law enjoins upon all school boards: "Provide all children of this state . . . a good common school education." We will need to explore constructive experiences of other communities, to use promising tools such as educational parks, to make the schools truly public by insisting that the board cease its irresponsible racism.

But in order to go forward at all we must first face reality. Deliberate segregation is an ugly reality. To ignore it is to consign other generations of children to planned deprivation. If neither the local nor state government will strike down such racial discrimination, then the federal government must do so.

METROPOLITAN PLANNING FOR EDUCATION

Herman R. Goldberg *is superintendent of schools, Rochester, New York. The following includes the major part of remarks made by Dr. Goldberg as a participant at a conference of the Harvard chapter of Pi Lambda Theta, Harvard Graduate School of Education, on December 11, 1965.*

When New York State Commissioner of Education Dr. James E. Allen directed all New York state school systems to submit plans for alleviating racial imbalance, our board of education promptly declared itself ready and willing to act. Acknowledgment was made of the desirability of intercultural understanding in a democratic society and of the responsibility of the schools for fostering this understanding through arranging for continuous direct contact of children of different backgrounds—more lasting contact than exchange visits, interschool choirs, art and athletic efforts, and other important, useful, eye-opening yet fleeting, intermittent and transitory experiences.

Our Open Enrollment Plan went into effect in February, 1964. The response of inner-city parents to the announcement of this plan negated the frequently heard statement that Negroes are apathetic and will not try to help themselves or their children. Over 1,500 parents said, "Yes"—indicating their desire for participation in the new procedure by asking for a different school experience for their children. We were able to accommodate, at the outset, five hundred children from inner-city schools. This has been raised to more than seven hundred since the start of the program. As a result of this plan, each of our forty-three elementary schools now has some Negro pupils. In New York state, 90 percent reimbursement for bus transportation for children living more than one and a half miles from school is available. The board of education approved transportation without cost to the families concerned for the Open Enrollment Plan. This has helped make the program successful.

From *Integrated Education*, April/May 1966. Reprinted by permission of the author.

Although some opposed this plan, it received wide approval from the Rochester community. We were challenged in a court suit, defeated in the Trial Term, but the plan was allowed to stand througha statesman-like directive of the Appellate Division of the New York State Supreme Court which said, in effect, if the plaintiffs protest the proximity of a Negro child to their children, we point to the supreme court decision, *Brown* v. *Topeka, Shawnee County, Kansas, Board of Education*—the landmark decision of 1954.*

Another approach to the problem of racial imbalance is our Voluntary Extended Home Zone, or Triad Plan. Three neighborhood schools that are contiguous to each other were grouped together, making one attendance zone instead of three. Children who live anywhere in this enlarged zone could apply to go to any one of the three schools. However, children who live in the home school zone were not displaced. One hundred fifty-nine children received access to a different school through this plan. We feel that the Triad Plan helped to preserve the basic values of the traditional neighborhood school policy while at the same time meeting the objection that this neighborhood policy—rigidly adhered to—supports and preserves racial segregation. Under this plan the neighborhood is enlarged, not destroyed, and children may transfer to one of the other schools in the zone, which will still be within walking distance of their homes. We have three of these Triad zones in operation, and the program has been successful.

Several thousand parents received letters asking their consideration of the Triad Plan. I feel an important part of the educational process of changing attitudes took place in family-type seminars where parents and children together discussed the idea, and perhaps got to the broader sociological issues involved, reducing them to an individual family and individual child setting. Such concomitant learnings are not to be belittled.

In addition to these programs, which provide access to other schools, we have stepped up our services to inner-city schools. Many in these sections of the city are saying, "Good schools and good teachers; these are the most important things." And we agree with this, too. Some of the best teaching in our city is being conducted in these deprived neighborhoods, and the pupils are benefiting from the dedication of teachers to whom the challenge of improving the chances of a child's successful future is the irresistible force that guides their lives. We find that more teachers ask to be transferred into these schools than out of them.

Extensive and important involvement in preschool programs, development of vocational and occupational opportunities and stepped-up compensatory programs were made available at the same time as Open Enrollment and the Triad Plan were started.

Apparently the commitment and effort of the determined school board, superintendent and staff not to be pushed into a situation which would have turned the entire school system into turmoil because of precipitous, arbitrary action, and at the same time the refusal to vacillate or withdraw from plans carefully made, reaches the ears, eyes, hearts, and consciences of suburban school boards and school officials.

My telephone rang one day. It was the president of a school board of one of Rochester's suburbs, West Irondequoit—a school district of about six thousand

---

*[Editor's Note: See Appendix A, "Text of Supreme Court Rulings (*Brown* v. *Board of Education*, . . .)."]

pupils, all white but a half dozen, inviting me to confer with his board and superintendent. He indicated that they had been watching the events in the city closely, and that they wanted to talk to me about the stand and commitment we had made and to explore other possible approaches.

And may I say right here that in considering a metropolitan approach to racial imbalance, it would be placing too great a strain on reality to expect suburban districts to be interested in cooperation with an urban school system if that school system had not yet itself moved forward within the city proper. I feel that if Rochester had dragged its feet early in its planning, there never would have been a phone call from West Irondequoit. It is clear to me that the most important clue to a desire to cooperate with an urban system is the evaluation of the commitment of the urban school system in the eyes of the suburbanites. You cannot get interest on a bank account if you do not make a deposit.

The West Irondequoit schools came to realize that in their culturally advantaged schools they were depriving their children of a rich cultural experience and understanding of the basic principles of democracy. The New York State Advisory Commission on Human Relations put it this way: "A child who has learned from experience to understand and appreciate people of races other than his own has a sounder basis for both his education and his life." And the West Irondequoit School Board stated in its April, 1965, *Newsletter*: "The Board believes that the presence in a single school of children from varied racial, cultural, socioeconomic, and religious backgrounds is an important element in the preparation of young people for active participation in the social and political affairs of our democracy."

This experience with metropolitan education was implemented this past September, the culmination of more than a year of planning and cooperation among West Irondequoit and Rochester school staffs and boards of education. The suburban school board notified us that they would accept twenty-five children from the inner city of Rochester into their schools, stepping this up to a total of three hundred by adding twenty-five first graders each year for the next twelve years.

The selection of children was made on the basis of pupil readiness, teachers' opinion that the pupils could benefit from the experience, and of course parents' willingness to have their children participate. Preliminary participations included informational meetings for Irondequoit teachers as well as exchange meetings of Irondequoit and city teachers and observation in city schools. In the city there were parents' conferences to discuss details and explain the purposes of the plan.

Costs of the program, tuition and transportation, are borne by reimbursed funds—one half from the state and one half from federal sources.

The pupils attend six different primary schools in the suburban system. In four different settings, three pupils are together; in two classrooms four pupils are together; in two other situations two pupils were added to the suburban classes. This adds up to twenty-four. One pupil moved after the program started.

The funds to be supplied by New York State are coming from the Department of Research of the State Education Department, and accordingly, we had to develop an acceptable evaluation process. The staff of the College of Education at the University of Rochester has been most helpful in developing the evaluative plan, working with our Planning and Research Department, and a graduate student at the University of Rochester assigned as coordinator of the project for the West Irondequoit schools.

While it is still much too soon for any kind of definitive evaluation, the program is working smoothly and seems to be justifying our most sanguine hopes. The children love it; the Irondequoit children wait eagerly for the bus each morning to be sure their new friends will be in school that day.

One of the early comments we have heard, which has made this a very natural kind of situation, is that the teachers and pupils got down to work immediately when school began in September, avoiding the ballyhoo of special arrangements and with no leaning over backward to program special accommodations, welcoming ceremonies, or cookie and ice cream inducements, when what was required was getting down immediately to the task of daily learning.

The parents of these children children have come faithfully to the PTA meetings of the suburban schools, and they were made welcome. Some children have been invited home for lunch with their new classmates. Many of the parents are invited to coffee hours, and eagerly accept the invitations. Commissioner Allen has called the plan a "giant step forward" in improving cultural relations, and has sent letters of commendation to both school boards.

But this first step was not taken without protest or peril. A group of dissidents in the suburban community filed a lawsuit against the suburban superintendent and school board, my school board and me. They contended that they had not been fully informed of the board's plans, and that such a program should have been approved only by referendum. They appealed to the state commissioner, who granted them a hearing. At the same time they sued in court for an injunction to stop the implementation of the plan. This time the Trial Term did not turn against us. The judge, in this decision, declared that the two boards of education had acted in accordance with the education law, and that they had the right to formulate public policy and make administrative decisions in regard to education without a referendum. He stated further that this plan was in no way discriminatory. The plea for an injunction was denied.

It was pointed out during the planning stages of this interdistrict cooperation that many school districts have taken pride over the years in their participation in better international understanding, derived from the Teen-Age Diplomat program. Communities for years have enjoyed and learned much from the blue-eyed blond Swedish high school girl, the boy from Greece with the Apollo profile, the very black boy from Ghana with the cultured English accent, the Italian boy whom no one expected to turn out to be a fair-haired, blue-eyed young man even though he came from Milan in northern Italy—most expected him to be just like last year's Italian teenager, the one with the dark hair, eyes, and skin that characterize the Neapolitan. Many of these youngsters challenged stereotyped ideas of their countries both in looks and in their descriptions of home. Now, as we embarked on our first programs of racial integration, we were about to break down other stereotyped notions, as well as prejudices acquired through generations of insufficient knowledge of and contact with people of other cultures among our American neighbors.

It was pointed out that the long-time acceptance of the Teen-Age Diplomat program should not in any way be diminished, but rather enhanced by the program between West Irondequoit and Rochester, which was really bringing this international concept to immediate neighbors—and may I add a humorous personal note here. My son, a high school junior and a member of his school's soccer team, came home one evening after an inglorious defeat on the field and begged his father, as superintendent of schools, to establish an Open Enrollment Plan for high school soccer players, declaring that all the good Hungarian, Italian, and Greek soccer players were concentrated on three of the nine high school teams. I have given his idea some thought but—first things first.

Other suburban cooperation has been going on in Rochester for the past two years.

First to ask for participation was the Brighton Number 1 School District, a suburb adjacent to Rochester on the south. In 1964, we were invited to send twenty-five children to their summer school. Children in grades three to six were selected from one of our inner-city schools. The funds needed for transportation and tuition were raised by both sending and receiving schools' Parent-Teacher Associations. The program was very successful, and was expanded to thirty-five children the second year. This summer forty-two children from the city will participate, and the expenses will now be paid from funds already approved under Title 1 of the Elementary and Secondary Education Act of 1965.

Three independent private schools, Harley, Columbia, and Allendale, have notified me that they wish to enroll Negro pupils. One school (Harley) has already accepted six children; the others are presently arranging scholarship funds.

The State University College at Brockport, in its new campus school, nineteen miles west of Rochester, has invited seventy-five inner-city children to its 1966 summer session. Administrators at the college feel that their campus school, in this suburban town, is not representative of the communities to which they send many of their graduates, and so this effort will make more realistic the preservice training of teachers.

Such metropolitan cooperation is essential if the problems of poverty and racial imbalance are to be conquered. Incentive legislation on the state level is required to give encouragement to those who see the need to pioneer in this area.

The major costs in such a program are tuition and transportation. Under present state law, the receiving school district must charge tuition or be open to a taxpayer's suit. The heavy financial demand on urban schools does not permit them to pay the total cost alone. Moreover, the problem of racial imbalance is one in which the entire state has a stake, and solutions should be supported by all citizens of the state.

Legislation is needed which would permit the state to pay the tuition and transportation costs for pupil transfer plans among school districts when such plans are for the purpose of improving intercultural understanding and reducing racial imbalance. Receiving school districts would continue to receive state aid on the incoming students so that the full cost of educating such children would be absorbed by the state. Such legislation should be permissive and would probably represent only a small financial outlay by the state at the outset. We have stated that we would be happy to lend our experience in helping to draft such legislation.

Fortunately, not all our changes have taken so long, or if they have, there has been a steady, continued progress toward the ultimate goal. To take just one example, look at the changes in our school buildings. There was a time when the city planners (not the educators) gave the architect the length, width, and height required of the building and the number of children expected, and told him to go ahead and build it. The results were somewhat like Noah and his ark—Noah getting the cubic measurements from on high and then being left to collect and house the pairs of living things in his vessel as best he could. Today we consider first the educational objectives to be met in the new school, then the many areas of learning and how they can best be placed to the advantage of the students, then the various aspects of the curriculum. The architect is given a résumé of these educational specifications and needs, and he designs a building around them.

The most significant change from our attitudes of the past needs to concern the children themselves. We used to think of them in groups: exactly-alike minds into which we crammed or pounded a preset amount of knowledge in a certain amount of time. Those who resisted were seated at the back of the room and ignored. Those who did not absorb at a set rate of speed were "kept back" and put through the same procedure all over again the next year. Harvey McMains of American Telephone and Telegraph told a story recently which illustrates the point well. An old-timer, tobacco-chewing army sergeant asked a batch of recruits why the sabre he was carrying was curved. One of the privates was a bright MIT student who volunteered that the swing of the arm, with the shoulder as a fulcrum, needed such and such an arc to have the proper swing to behead an opponent. The sergeant looked him up and down, spat a few times, shook his head, spat again, and said in a disgusted voice, "This *here* sabre is curved because it has to fit into this *here* scabbard." Society has given today's superintendent a sword of a different shape but has yet to adjust his scabbard.

And the urban superintendent has a bigger menu, too! Among the responsibilities accepted by public education are others which bring with them their own sets of problems: toddler-to-old-age instruction, the teaching of moral and spiritual values (but, don't be too *moral* for the pupil *won't* listen and don't be too *spiritual* for the courts *will* listen), occupational training and retraining for an automated society, and the ones receiving the most publicity today: the elimination of *de facto* segregation and teaching of the culturally different child. Like the aims of "we" that I mentioned a few minutes ago, these are interrelated, each requiring different techniques but aiming for the same ultimate result.

Some of the help we need to accomplish our purposes has already started coming to us. Society is saying "We'll give you the money; now you just have to do something about all these problems." This is a big step; society's acceptance of change and understanding of what we are trying to accomplish are absolutely essential to our success.

The greatly augmented interest of state and federal governments will prove another giant step forward in our progress. From a small beginning through the provisions of the Northwest Ordinance of 1787, the federal government has now jumped into education with both feet, as evidenced in the Elementary and Secondary Education Act of 1965. This will provide us with resources and instructional materials, supplementary educational centers and services, educational research and training on a large scale, and funds for carrying out long-sought compensatory programs in individual school districts.

The dissemination of information should also include clear and encouraging reports to the general public of our progress and our aims. We must not risk delay or defeat because a poorly informed public is confused or reluctant, or afraid, simply because it lacks understanding. The attention of the public at the moment has been distracted by the tumult and the shouting over the concerns for school integration and improving conditions for the culturally different. These are important, but there are many other avenues of educational development. So let us hope for the day when the balance of publicity reflects the additional good being proposed and accomplished, rather than just the concerns and fears of change in this one area. And let's not be afraid of some smoke surrounding change. I am reminded of the words of the commentator at a concert of the London Philharmonic Orchestra at a Royal Albert Hall performance of Tchaikovsky's 1812 Overture, referring to the cannon blasts near the rousing close of the work—*"There will be a bit of smoke about the gallery; don't be alarmed."*

Some innovations will be smoky, some even may show a bit of flame as they are developed. We must keep calm and try to keep others calm—and we may find that innovations work when prepared for properly.

As the concept of metropolitanization of education expands, it should be kept in mind that a large city school district has much to offer its neighbors in the way of specialized services that the smaller systems cannot or do not wish to add to their programs. Thus, the city can give as well as get. For example, Rochester has several programs—and has had for many decades—which are available to both adults and children in surrounding districts. For at least forty years we have had classes for handicapped children to which suburban children have always been admitted on a tuition basis. Our technical and industrial high school draws out-of-district pupils. An extensive adult education program, which had a class attendance of more than 10,000 last year, includes residents from many nearby communities. Now, as you have heard today, there can be some flow of students to the suburbs. . . .

Triple-powered devices are coming back into style. The Boeing 727 jet has three matched engines. It is the first of its kind since the old Ford trimotor. The Russian troika has also been known for its triple source of power—three matched horses. And I feel that the solution to *de facto* segregation needs triple matched sources, too—three horses if you will. The name of the first horse is Education; the second, Housing; and the third, Jobs. But the sled society is asking us to pull these days at times seems to be powered by one horse and two ponies. Anyone for two more horses?

BIBLIOGRAPHY FOR PART TWO

Advisory Panel on Integration of the Public Schools. *Report to the Board of Education, City of Chicago* [The "Hauser Report"]. Chicago: Board of Education, 1964.

Blake, Elias, Jr. "The Track System in Washington, D.C.," *Integrated Education* (April-May 1965).

Caughey, John W. *Segregation Blights Our Schools: An Analysis Based on the 1966 Official Report on Racial and Ethnic Distribution School by School Throughout the Los Angeles System.* Los Angeles: Quail Books, 1967.

Caughey, John W., and Laree Caughey. *School Segregation on Our Doorstep: The Los Angeles Story.* Los Angeles: Quail Books, 1966.

Commission on Professional Rights and Responsibilities. *Baltimore, Maryland. Change and Contrast—The Children and the Public Schools.* Washington, D.C.: National Education Association, 1967.

Committee on Race and Education. *Race and Equal Educational Opportunity in Portland's Public Schools.* Portland (Ore.): Board of Education, 1964.

East Harlem Project and City Commission on Human Rights. *Releasing Human Potential. A Study of East Harlem-Yorkville School Bus Transfer.* New York: City Commission on Human Rights, 1962.

Gittell, Marilyn. *Participants and Participation: A Study of School Policy in New York City.* New York: Center for Urban Education, 1967.

Goldberg, Herman R. *Desegregation of the Elementary Schools. Special Report to the Board of Education, February, 1967.* Rochester [N.Y.] City School District.

Havighurst, Robert J. *The Public Schools of Chicago: A Survey.* Chicago Board of Education, 1964.

Kaplan, John. "Segregation Litigation and the Schools—Part III: The Gary Litigation," *Northwestern University Law Review* (May-June 1964).

Meredith, James. *Three Years in Mississippi.* Bloomington: University of Indiana Press, 1966.

Mizell, M. Hayes. "School Desegregation in South Carolina," *Integrated Education* (December 1966-January 1967).

National Commission on Professional Rights and Responsibilities. *Detroit, Michigan: A Study of Barriers to Equal Educational Opportunity in a Large City.* Washington, D.C.: National Education Association, March, 1967.

Pennsylvania Human Relations Commission. "Pennsylvania's Affirmative Integration Policy," *Integrated Education* (August-September 1964).

Pois, Joseph. *The School Boards Crisis: A Chicago Case Study.* Chicago: Aldine, 1964.

Schrag, Peter. *Village School Downtown. Politics and Education: A Boston Report.* Boston: Beacon Press, 1967.

Smith, Bob. *They Closed Their Schools: Prince Edward County, Virginia, 1951-1964.* Chapel Hill: University of North Carolina Press, 1965.

Swanson, Bert E. *The Struggle for Equality: School Integration Controversy in New York City.* New York: Hobbs, Dorman, 1966.

Trillin, Calvin. *An Education in Georgia: The Integration of Charlayne Hunter and Hamilton Holmes.* New York: Viking, 1964.

U.S. Commission on Civil Rights. "Education," Exhibit No. 34 in *Hearing Before the . . . Commission . . . in Cleveland, Ohio, April 1-7, 1966,* pp. 750-763. Washington, D.C.: Government Printing Office, 1966.

U.S. Congress, 89th, 2d sess., House of Representatives, Committee on Education and Labor. *A Task Force Study of the Public School System in the District of Columbia as It Relates to the War on Poverty.* Washington, D.C.: Government Printing Office, 1966.

Part Three

Points at Issue

American education may well be on the verge of taking its greatest step forward since the inception of the public schools. The forces of tradition and change clash as every facet of the schools undergoes scrutiny and reconsideration. If, therefore, the educational scene has come to resemble a debating forum, one should hardly expect otherwise. It would be unrealistic to anticipate significant change without conflict. Indeed, it is the very conflict itself that makes the change possible.

Some of the issues raised by articles in this section can be put in question form.

1. **Is a sense of psychological security denied to the Negro child who desegregates a neighborhood and a school? How does one balance—if this is even possible—the psychological gains against the losses?** Haggstrom examines these questions in a context of his own formal research as well as from a review of the research literature.
2. **How can the school administration simultaneously implement programs of instructural improvement and of integration?** Sullivan recounts the operation of a reading improvement program within a context of school integration.
3. **What happens to educational values in a classroom that is deliberately organized to include children of widely varying ability levels, different races, and different socioeconomic classes?** Lipton, reflecting on eight years of experience as a principal of a unique New York state elementary school, reports his positive evaluation.
4. **What are the dimensions of change called for by the eradication of racism from educational systems?** Solomon traces the pervasive strands of racism, and stresses professional commitment as the cardinal factor in change.
5. **Does the neighborhood school have certain advantages that are consonant with the age and residence of young school children?** Blackman measures the advantages customarily attributed to the neighborhood school (e.g., safety, intimacy of parent and school) and ascertains the degree to which these accord with sound planning principles.

6. **To what degree is urban school segregation a result of human agency and to what degree is it an unintended result of population and housing patterns?** Weinberg holds that the concept of **de facto** segregation is defective in that it assumes too sharp a distinction between deliberate and happenstance (or fortuitous) segregation.

7. **How much authority over a public school can be lodged in the hands of an organized community?** Mrs. Jones presents arguments for a community-controlled school; the New York City school board, in its 1966 response to her, rejects the possibility of sharing its authority—a position that underwent some modification within a few months.

SEGREGATION, DESEGREGATION, AND NEGRO PERSONALITY

Warren C. Haggstrom *is associate professor, School of Social Welfare, University of California, Los Angeles. While teaching at Syracuse University, Dr. Haggstrom was very active in community movements.*

Segregated Negro housing and education in the northern United States have survived a wide variety of sustained assaults. It has become increasingly apparent that segregated institutions create biracial vested interests which have been able successfully to resist desegregation efforts. As racial integration continues to elude its proponents, there has developed a revival of support for the practice of improving separate Negro schools, social agencies, recreation centers, housing projects and other facilities now, with the assumption that such measures will help Negroes to be more ready to enter the presently superior "white" institutions at some (unspecified) later date.

A number of questions of fact are relevant to this practical issue. Can opportunities be so improved for segregated Negroes in American society that they will suffer no disadvantages solely by virtue of their race? Is James B. Conant correct in his belief that "satisfactory education can be provided in an all-Negro school through the expenditure of more money for needed staff and facilities?"[1] It is the purpose of the present article to examine answers to one specific question: What are the consequences of racial segregation and desegregation for the psychological functioning of Negroes? And we will begin this examination with an appraisal of the literature relevant to the more general question: What are characteristics of the psychological functioning of American Negroes?

From *Integrated Education,* **October/November 1963. Reprinted by permission of the author.**

[1] *Slums and Suburbs,* McGraw-Hill, New York, 1961, p. 29.

Research Results

How is one to understand the research reports which have been made over the past quarter century? They are nearly unanimous in suggesting personality damage to Negroes, usually as a direct or indirect consequence of racial discrimination. Still, one cannot decide scientific questions by majority vote, and it should be remembered that the social scientists of an earlier day were nearly unanimous in holding that Negro personality deficiencies are innate. The weight of social scientific opinion may still be greatly affected by ideology as well as evidence.

It is also apparent that studies of individuals typically do not support unique interpretations. Further, clinical and experimental research has been based on relatively tiny samples which include a disproportionate number of school children and middle-class Negroes and very few from the large mass of lower-class Negro adults. The studies to date cannot claim to be based on a representative sampling of the Negro population.

Suppose, however, that we accept these and other methodological criticisms as valid. The fact remains that such a high proportion of studies are most naturally interpreted by hypotheses about direct or indirect psychological damage to Negroes from racial discrimination that it is very difficult to conceive of an alternative view which would account for all the evidence. For that reason we will assume here the general validity of this very broad interpretation and next inquire: Does Negro personality damage stem to any extent from racial segregation alone as distinguished from other kinds of racial discrimination?

A majority of (but not all) social scientists probably are inclined to believe that segregation is damaging to Negro personality, and they relate that belief to evidence. There are a number of suggested rationales concerning how such damage might occur. To some extent research directly and indirectly supports the same conclusion. However, many of the same objections considered in the previous section are also applicable here, and there are additional problems in attempting to distinguish segregation from other causal antecedents of personality damage to Negroes. In several cases replication of research projects is necessary to provide further support for the research conclusions. There should be more sophisticated research designed to understand the consequences of segregation in groups other than Negroes, and, especially, some attempt to determine how the effects of segregation vary in relation to the conditions (e.g., voluntary or involuntary; legal or *de facto*; with or without equal status groups, etc.) under which the segregation takes place, as well as how segregation differentially affects members of various social subsystems (e.g., family or peer groups).

However, taking the literature as a whole into account, at this point the evidence seems clearly to support the hypothesis that segregation itself adversely affects Negro personality. Although the accumulation of knowledge may alter the picture at a later date, no alternative hypothesis seems as plausible today.

Desegregation and Personality

If we assume that segregation is harmful to Negro personality, what about *de*segregation? A number of studies provide support for the belief that the *process* of desegregation, that is, the movement of Negroes from segregated to desegregated social systems, is likely to be psychologically beneficial to Negroes. But in relation to some portions of the literature, this conclusion is not so well substantiated as may be supposed. For example, if we were to consider published expert opinion alone, as it is based solely on clinical experience, and also to restrict ourselves to considerations of residential desegregation, our conclusion would tend in the direction of supposing that the desegregation process is likely to work to the disadvantage of Negro personality. It is the overall trend of the published research data, whether clinical or experimental, that seems definitely inclined in favor of the hypothesis that the desegregation process in general is of positive psychological value to the Negroes involved. On the other hand, the likelihood remains that nowhere in the United States today can Negroes escape some personality injury.

A study by Staten W. Webster illustrates the necessity of avoiding the assumption that school desegregation will immediately affect the attitudes of white children to the advantage of Negroes or even increase the number of interracial friendships. After six months of integration in a junior high school in which three hundred Negro children had entered a white school, this investigator found that attitudes of children prior to integration were not associated with the development of interracial friendship, that Negro children tended to be more accepting of whites than previously, and that white children became less accepting of Negroes.[2]

There are several methodological problems connected with this study. In particular, in view of other research suggesting that classroom race cleavage normally increases with the passage of time at the sixth- and seventh-grade levels, the author cannot properly interpret the decreased acceptance of Negroes by white children as resulting from interracial contact. It is important also to remember that the research literature suggests that Negro children benefit in a number of ways from direct comparisons and competition with white children *regardless of the attitudes of white children toward them.* Thus, the extent of interracial friendships cannot be taken as an appropriate index of the consequences of desegregation for Negro personality. On the other hand, bearing all these reservations in mind, the fact remains that placing a Negro child in a desegregated school is only the first step of many which will be necessary before he can escape personality damage stemming from his racial membership.

Much of the research concerning the onset of racial awareness, it may be remembered, concerned racially desegregated schools, and provides some support for the view that Negro children may suffer personality damage even in desegrated schools. Kenneth and Mamie Clark even found that Negro children in integrated schools in the North showed more emotion when being required to make racial self-identifications (using dolls) than did segregated Negro children from the South. In a coloring test the same investigators found evidence of greater affective conflict in the northern Negro children (than in southern) as well as a greater tendency for northern children to identify with white colors.[3] This and other research suggests that,

---

[2]Staten W. Webster, "The Influence of Interracial Contact on Social Acceptance in a Newly Integrated School," *Journal of Educational Psychology*, Vol. 52 (1961), pp. 292-296.

[3]Kenneth B. and Mamie P. Clark, "Racial Identification and Preference in Negro Children," in Guy E. Swanson, Theodore M. Newcomb, and Eugene L. Hartley (eds.), *Readings in Social Psychology*, Henry Holt, 1952, pp. 551-560; and "Emotional Factors in Racial Identification and Preference in Negro Children," *Journal of Negro Education*, Vol. 19 (1950), pp. 341-350.

while segregated Negroes are harmed by a relatively secure adoption of an inferior Negro identity, desegregated Negroes are harmed by lack of a secure racial identification.

Residence and School

A recent study by the present author suggests that the psychological destruction to Negro children may be less when they are desegregated by residence *and* school than when they are desegregated by school alone. In the study, it was found in Detroit that residentially desegregated families more often and to a greater extent help children consciously work through problems of their feelings about racial differences than do matched segregated families. "Only in desegrated households was it common for parents to help their young children accept the difference in skin color and understand that they need not feel less worthy because of it. It appears that the fewer racial incidents involving small segregated children lead parents to fail to perceive that racial differences already have meaning to their children. The greater number of incidents in white neighborhoods serve as occasions which lead parents explicitly to express love and esteem to their children *as Negro children.*"[4] It may be that Negro children who live in segregated neighborhoods but attend desegregated schools do not receive the parental support in interpreting racial incidents that is received from residentially desegregated Negro parents.

Brenman described a Negro girl from a residentially desegregated Negro family who grew up tending to use the defense mechanism of denial of her racial identity and who, although she obtained a good professional position, suffered from personality difficulties which Brenman related to desegregation.[5] Kennedy reported that, of two Negro patients, one of whom had grown up in a white neighborhood and the other in a Negro neighborhood, therapy with the one from the white neighborhood failed because of her unusual problems in racial identification, while the other patient improved. However, the desegregated patient not only lived in a white neighborhood, but also in a family which was very hostile to that neighborhood, and it was Kennedy's view that this particularly strong hostile identification with white was the basis of the personality problem.[6] She suggested that the problem could only be solved when Negroes participate in the majority culture but also secure a comfortable racial identification as Negroes.

On the whole, there seems to have been little research concerning possible psychological damage to desegregated Negroes as a consequence of their race. About the only generalization which is supportable is that, while such psychological damage very likely exists, it is also probably less than that consequent upon segregation.

If we assume that segregation hurts Negroes psychologically and that desegration also hurts, but to a lesser extent, how can this assumption be related to practical community decisions?

---

[4]Warren C. Haggstrom, *Self-Esteem and Other Characteristics of Residentially Desegregated Negroes*, unpublished doctoral dissertation, University of Michigan, 1962, pp. 157-158.

[5]Margaret Brenman, "The Relation Between Minority-Group Membership and Group Identification in a Group of Urban Middle Class Negro Girls," *Journal of Social Psychology*, Vol. 11 (1940), pp. 171-197.

[6]Janet A. Kennedy, "Problems Posed in the Analysis of Negro Patients," *Psychiatry*, Vol. 15 (1952), pp. 313-327.

Rejection by Majority

Evidence beyond that which could be considered in this article suggests that the approaching presence of Negroes on a basis of equality threatens the status of white persons, causing them typically either to flee from the presence of the threat (as in the departures from areas of Negro residential infiltration) or to push Negroes from them (as in the creation, directly or indirectly by whites, of segregated Negro institutions). Thus, racial segregation in the United States may be understood as a form of racial discrimination in which the majority white community excludes Negroes completely from social systems in which they might enter interracial social relationships as equals. In spite of the official doctrine of equality, the meaning of segregation is correctly (if partly unconsciously) perceived by Negroes and white alike. In addition the separate Negro institutions are necessarily smaller than their white counterparts, and furnish decreased opportunities for their members. For example, even in principle there is no means of finding such a wide selection of housing in the small Negro neighborhoods as occurs within surrounding white areas in which there are typically at least ten times as many houses. In politics (based on segregated residence) Negroes, although constituting more than 10 percent of the population, can elect no president, no governor, no United States senator, and only a disproportionately small number of United States representatives. There are necessarily restricted possibilities for upward mobility within separate Negro work organizations.

If racial segregation in the United States is institutionalized rejection of Negroes by the majority community *with which those Negroes are identified*, it creates a conflict with Negro personality which is intensified by the necessary relative inferiority of segregated social systems. But these adverse consequences, and especially the visibility of Negro inferiority in segregated institutions, create precisely the conditions which motivate renewed rejection by the majority community.

Even if some institutions (for example, elementary schools) were given facilities equal or superior to their white parallels, the consequence would only be a more salient racial identification for a Negro child who spends his early life in an all-Negro family with all-Negro friends in an all-Negro neighborhood. As the social inferiorities of Negroes are concurrently impressed on him, this stronger racial identification can be expected to increase the force of the threat to his self-esteem. So long as Negroes in the broader society are assigned a lesser social status because of their race, the improvement of some segregated facilities cannot be psychologically beneficial to them.

The problem of ending segregation, however, is affected not only by the institutionalized ways in which white persons ward off Negroes. The presence of Negroes in segregated organizations has led vested interests in segregation to appear within the Negro community. Thus improvement of segregated Negro institutions not only results in psychological damage; it also interferes with the possibility of desegregation by persuading well-intentioned persons that nothing need now be done since Negro facilities are getting better, and by reducing the motivation of Negro leaders (in high positions in the segregated institutions) to seek desegregation. For these reasons, the improvement of segregated Negro institutions, if it is to avoid harm to Negroes, should be accompanied by a rapid promotion of the desegregation process, and by efforts to hold off or minimize white rejection of Negroes until desegregating Negroes can form new interracial relationships of equality.

Overall Goals

In the long run, avoidance of destruction of personality to Negroes through their race will require:

1. Desegregation of all Negroes in presently segregated social systems.
2. Negroes visibly in positions of high status, power, and influence in the United States in rough proportion to their numbers. For example, there should be a visible opportunity for Negro children to become president of the United States, chief justice of the supreme court, chairman of the board of General Motors Corporation, or president of Harvard University. This requirement is necessary if Negroes are to be able to acquire a nonhostile, nonracial identification with the overall society.
3. At present Negro-white social relationships tend to be characterized by white dominance and to occur primarily in work settings. That is, they tend to be role relationships in which Negroes have an inferior position. There will have to be developed interracial primary (e.g., friendship) relations of equality from very early in the lives of Negroes so that they will acquire the skills and opportunities to participate freely as equals in the larger community, and especially in the large work organizations.

The de-discrimination process can probably be facilitated by conventional community organization efforts to coordinate the power structures of the nation and of local communities for such a purpose. But these efforts alone ignore the extent to which Negroes are and see themselves as powerless objects of manipulation from outside the Negro community. The status-anxiety that leads whites to reject interracial egalitarian relationships can be reduced only when Negroes become more nearly equal in general levels of achievement—an equality which can be motivated by provision of additional visible opportunity for Negroes to participate in decisions which affect their lives, by attainment of a general level of personal social power in the Negro community more nearly equal to that of the majority society. The larger community should, therefore, assist and encourage social action efforts by Negroes on their own behalf, if motivation is to be forthcoming from both racial groups to allow the desegregation process to occur.

Summary

1. There is evidence that American Negroes have suffered personality damage through membership in their racial group, and that deleterious influences on Negroes begin in early childhood.
2. There is evidence that racial segregation in itself is psychologically harmful to Negroes.
3. Although the process of racial desegregation is probably beneficial to Negroes, further changes may be necessary to end the psychic damage resulting even to desegregated Negroes from membership in the Negro minority in the United States.
4. Major changes in several areas of American society as well as conditions which will enhance general motivational levels of Negroes are necessary to the attainment of full Negro equality which, in turn, would ensure that no person is psychologically harmed by virtue of being Negro.

THE RIGHT TO READ—A STRAIGHT PATH TO INTEGRATION

Neil V. Sullivan *is superintendent of schools, Berkeley, California. He has also been superintendent in Prince Edward County, Virginia; in Long Island, New York; and in New England. Dr. Sullivan is a member of the editorial advisory board of* INTEGRATED EDUCATION *magazine.*

All children—except those few who are neurologically, physically or emotionally damaged beyond repair—can learn to read. Yet, more than half of our minority children have not been learning to read. *Only the privileged few among our children have been learning to read effectively.* The National Council of Teachers of English recently reported that there are nearly 4,000,000 pupils with reading disabilities in our elementary schools—16 percent of our national elementary school population.[1] I believe, as do other critics, that this estimate is low.

I say that these 4,000,000 not only can learn to read but also that they must be taught to read if they are to be happy, useful citizens. Our minority children must learn to read if they are to be part of the main stream of our society. Reading is the key to learning, to understanding our complex world, to working with one's best skills, to coping with life in general.

Learning to read and school integration go hand-in-hand. School integration is a national mandate. "Reading is the most important subject in our schools," the President's Commission on National Goals has stated.[2] We have gone but a little way toward school integration. Only a few cities—of which Berkeley is one—have been cited by the U.S. Civil Rights Commission's School Integration Study Committee as having made progress, and many more cited as making no progress at all. As a member of that committee, I have seen the situation firsthand.

More than that, every ghetto school is a "bad" school educationally, no matter how much money and effort we pour into it. This was the basic finding of the recent, historic report to the U.S. Congress directed by James T. Coleman for the U.S. Office of Education. This study on "Equality of Educational Opportunity,"* perhaps the most significant in recent years, put it conclusively: Communications skills, reading in particular, are most important areas of learning for the minority child as they are for all children. Armed with these skills, the Negro child can achieve in school, feel and achieve mastery of his fate. As a matter of fact, Negro children achieve better in truly excellent integrated schools than in segregated ghetto schools. Caucasian children do just as well as they do in the all-white school. But up to now, we are neither effectively desegregating our schools nor narrowing reading and achievement gaps. Herein is the prime challenge.

We can be more hopeful about reading than integration. I believe that we are now in the midst of a reading revolution, and I predict this is a revolution that we will win. It is a revolution against prejudice and lack of understanding of children, the rigidity

From *Integrated Education*, **February/March 1967. Reprinted by permission of the author.**

[1]Neila Banton Smith, "An Evaluation of Reading in American Schools," *Proceedings of the Seventh Annual Conference* (May 3-5, 1962, Champaign, Ill.), International Reading Association, 1962, p. 188.

[2]President's Commission on National Goals, *Goals for Americans: Programs for Action in the Sixties,* Prentice-Hall, Inc., New York, 1961, pp. 6,7.

*[Editor's Note: In two volumes, U.S. Government Printing Office, 1966.]

of outworn methods that lock children out from learning, and the failure of teachers' colleges to teach teachers how to teach reading. In our colleges and universities, in institutes, in national meetings by the hundreds, our teachers are told about reading, not how children learn to read, and most importantly, not why they do not learn to read. And in almost one fourth of our teachers' colleges and schools of education they are not preparing teachers in reading methods at all!

Reading experts have been arguing ever since the American Revolution *about* reading. First, phonics came in as the wonderful system, then was blamed because not enough children made sufficient progress. So, out with phonics, in with the "word method," the "look-say" system, which again failed to teach enough children to read. Then in again with phonics, but never the delving into the basic "how"—and the important "why" of nonlearners. Fashionable terms such as "elyxia" and "dyslexia" and "stratosymbolia" sprang up as excuses for children who did not learn.

The experts have thought the solution is simple—find the right method and children will learn to read. It is not simple. Teaching children to read—all children, and especially minority children—requires the use of many methods, adapted to many levels and many rates of learning, and, back of this, the development of understanding, through study and experience and feeling, of the children one is teaching. It requires special reading training for every teacher, no matter what her specialty, and it is a matter concerning the heart as well as the mind.

Here are some simple statements of why minority children are not learning to read. These are taken from a tape recording made in a ghetto school as a teacher questioned a group of fourth graders on their reading problems. The children said: "I got messed up on sounds. They didn't sound like anything." . . . "The words looked like I never saw 'em before—never heard 'em at home." . . . "Some of the books looked funny—not real." . . . "You're scared you'll be wrong and then the teacher won't call on you and you'll just sit there." . . . "You don't know what's going on so you just don't listen—you goof off." . . . "You feel dumb—you just want to get out and go home."

Over and over, they got "messed up," they "goofed off," or they sat there silent, feeling dumb, wanting to go home.

In other words: Insecurity, brought about by fear, or anxiety, or a feeling of guilt; unhappy or unpropitious home conditions; and unsatisfactory relationships with the teacher and other pupils. Add to these hazards the fact that some of these children, instead of being allowed to learn at the level of their current mental age, had been pressured to learn at an unrealistic pace.

What have the teachers' colleges and university schools of education been doing about this crucial situation? Those of the only 76.3 percent that do "prepare" students to teach reading have tended to train them only in the mechanics of reading without any relation to the children many of them will be teaching. Some teacher-training institutions have been sending their students into poverty-area schools for their internships. This is good. This is needed. But they are sending them into the ghettos totally unprepared for what they will find. The professors, most of them, know nothing about disadvantaged children—the way they live, their culture, their patterns of reward and punishment, their anthropology, if you will. They themselves have never come down to the ghettos and looked. They have tended to reject this tremendous population with which many of their graduates will work.

Understanding and involvement are the words. Dr. Elliott Shapiro, the subject of Nat Hentoff's *Our Children Are Dying*,[3] and now on leave from Public School 119 in New York's Harlem, calls it "Teacher Involvement with the Poor," the title of a course he taught in Berkeley last summer in the University of California Extension program. He came to address a teachers' workshop in one of our ghetto schools.

"In the ghetto of the poor," he said, "the child is constantly aware that he does not belong in the main stream of 'the outside.' There is a tremendous feeling of aloneness, of separation."

The child brings this "aloneness" with him into the ghetto school. He feels lost, as though he were in a big department store and had lost his mother. He needs a friendly adult "to take him by the hand."

The reading revolution, as I see it and take part in it, is tackling this "aloneness," this "separation." I can describe it best by what is being done in Berkeley.*

I came to Berkeley in the fall of 1964 from Prince Edward County, Virginia. I had been sent there by the Kennedys, backed by much of the Kennedy Foundation money and that of other foundations, to open up the Free Schools for Negro children who had been deprived of school for four years due to the county's refusal to obey the integration edict. There we packed two and three years' reading learning into one. How? With money, yes; but even more importantly, with committed, understanding teachers who worked around the clock. We used every reading system and combination of systems that worked, and all the materials we could buy. We took the children on field trips locally and even to New York City to visit the World's Fair.

As a result of our efforts in the South, according to Michigan State Psychologist Dr. Robert L. Green,[4] the IQ's of the children advanced six points in a ten-month period.

The reader may say that Prince Edward County is a far different situation from that of Berkeley, "The Athens of the West." In 1964, Berkeley's children had not been deprived of schooling for four years, but many of their essential needs were the same. More than 40 percent of Berkeley's schoolchildren are Negroes whose families live in "the flats," a housing ghetto which I hasten to say is by no means a slum but, rather, an area of neat, well-kept houses and gardens which are cherished. Some families are old Berkeley residents, but most are newcomers who have been pouring into Berkeley during the last eight years from the rural South and urban ghettos in search of a better life. Almost all are poor, unemployed, many mothers must go out to work, many are on the welfare rolls. Their children make up the largest proportion of our nonreaders and, as teenagers, our largest group of school dropouts. Those who do learn to read tend to be two and three years behind the Caucasian "hill" children, some of whom learn to read in kindergarten.

In the fall of 1964, the Berkeley School District was taking important integration steps after a year's study by a citizens' committee and many meetings to study its recommendations. All seventh and eighth graders were being combined into two junior high schools, all ninth graders into one "West Campus" of Berkeley High

---

[3]The Viking Press, Inc., 1966.

[4]Robert L. Green, Louis J. Hoffman, Richard J. Morse, and Robert F. Morgan, *The Educational Status of Children During the First School Year Following Four Years of Little or No Schooling*, College of Education, Michigan State University, East Lansing, Michigan, 1966.

*[Editor's Note: See also "Two Superintendents Discuss Integration: Interview," pp. 29 ff. of this volume]

School which contained all the city's students in the three higher grades. A move to recall the board of education, for its pains, was in process and was overwhelmingly defeated in the April, 1965, vote. In February, 1966, we began busing 230 Negro children from the ghetto to hill schools with a small portion of our Elementary and Secondary Education Act-Title I funds, more than half a million dollars, granted at that time. This "token" integration, to reduce class size in the ghetto schools, was done by community consensus and has been evaluated as highly successful.

All of these steps, however, are interim measures. Total integration is the goal. Hopefully, we will accomplish this through educational parks, where all the children of certain age and grade levels in the city will be taught together in a great center shared by the community. The board has now asked our Master Plan Committee to study moving toward the first educational park. We shall soon present the plan to the public for consideration.

No segregated school reflecting small neighborhood conditions can be a good school. True integration, however, will not be brought about by desegregation alone. The disadvantaged minority child in the desegregated school will continue to be discriminated against, set apart and isolated if he cannot read—or cannot read as well as his fellows. Equal ability to read is implicit in integration.

In 1964, the Berkeley schools started scheduling extra time for reading wherever needed; to double or triple it even at the expense of other subjects. We singled out reading specialists, promoted team teaching, encouraged nongraded programs. Whenever any community group has asked me to make a speech, or to come to lunch, I have talked about reading. I have gone into the schools and taught reading, as have others of my fellow administrators.

Now, in the fall of 1966, we are broadening and deepening our emphasis on reading. The school tax increase we won last June has helped us do this. The Elementary and Secondary Education Act-Title I grant has been a boon to the ghetto schools. We have had two highly successful summers of Head Start, launching children into the schools wanting to learn to read. We have reduced class size, hired more teachers and specialists. We have established an attractive, refurbished library, staffed by a teacher-librarian, in each of our schools. We have paperback sales, a bookmobile that draws up to the school gates, and "home-made" books in the children's words and out of their own experience. Six buses afford many field trips. School resource volunteers and other volunteers work with children one-to-one or in small groups.

We keep our school libraries open into the late afternoon and during evening hours. We require some students to attend school for a longer day by having them report an hour early in the morning. We open our schools in the evening and volunteers help students with their homework. Class size has been reduced from about twenty-nine to about twenty-two. In-service courses in reading for the total teaching staff are held—and teachers are urged to attend them. When we say that every teacher, no matter what his grade or specialty, must be a teacher of reading, we must make the training available.

I suggest we drop the term "remedial reading." Let's just call it reading. All teachers are remedial—there to provide remedies for the troubled reader. One of our ghetto schools is making a strong attack on reading problems by its team diagnostic program. The principal has divided the six grades into three "circuits," each supported by a "resource team"—one headed by himself as he goes into the classrooms of his circuit, teaches with the teacher, discovers needs and fills them from his resource team; one by the vice-principal; and one by the program coordinator. They find out the needs, then pool all resources available, and as a working team bring all their resources to bear on problems. In the grade five and six circuit, eight reading groups—ranging from the "groping group" to the group being primed for college—have been developed. Eight teachers are taking reading courses at night at a nearby college.

An exciting event in another ghetto school, as I write, is the publication of a "home-made" book—not a mimeographed production such as many of our schools are making, but a beautiful hard-cover book—*On The Go: Boys and Girls Exploring the Bay Area*[5]—made (with the help of Elementary and Secondary Education Act funds) by second graders who went on a series of field trips with their teachers and a professional photographer. Back in class next day, the children looked at the pictures and talked about what they had seen and how they had felt, while the teachers took down their words. *On the Go* will soon be in our Berkeley schools and libraries, and will be available to other schools and the public.

Last summer we experimented with many teaching methods and materials in a language arts and mathematics workshop with two hundred first, second, and third graders, mainly Negro youngsters, selected as "intelligent but nonachieving." Team teaching prevailed, three teachers to a classroom. There were no bells. Snacks could be enjoyed during study time. There were rugs on the floor to sit on, and big movable tables. Every method and all materials available were tested and those found good were used. After each session with the children, teachers compared notes on their experiences and observations, sorting out what ways and means they had found most effective. The most important finding was how the children blossomed and how they learned in an atmosphere of informality, warmth, happiness, and love.

"Reinforcement" is our word here in Berkeley, where Dr. Jerome J. Gilbert, principal of Columbus School whose enrollment is mostly Negro children, and eight teachers have created the "Berkeley Easy Reading Program" now just going into use. Although usable everywhere, it takes into consideration especially the disadvantaged child who has been burdened by "negative reinforcement"—the feeling that he must be changed, remolded, repaired to fit suddenly into the middle-class pattern and middle-class English; that if he cannot do this, he less bright, less capable, has less potential. Dr. Gilbert and his reading committee of teachers know "why" many of their pupils were not learning to read. They knew, for one thing, that reading must be taught these children through the first two grades as a "second language."

Originally, the intent of the project was to add reinforcement exercises and activities to the best standard commercial reading program they could find and to adapt it to the nongraded concept of pacing instruction to the learner's needs. But they did not find any standard program that would do what they wanted. . . . The material in the printed manual was not the language of the ghetto child, not about his experiences and his world.

They decided to develop their own curriculum, using what they found good in the commercial systems for reinforcement of *their* reinforcement procedure—this and all

---

[5]Sheryl Burke, Virginia Hadsell, Marie Kane, and Grethel Newcom, *On the Go*, Berkeley (California) Unified School District, 1966.

good available supplementary materials—homemade books, Bank Street books,* and 150 paperbacks which Dr. Gilbert lumps under "anthropology."

Each commercial system they analyzed was designed on the assumption that one unit of effort applied to one unit of materials will produce a given amount of achievement. Their concept, however, is based upon the idea that children vary in their ability to learn to decode and to comprehend and that many materials must be available to provide for this variation in learning rates. They also saw that no single commercial program adequately teaches children to acquire the structure of the larger society, the ability to think complexly and abstractly, the skills of listening and the motor perceptual skills related to reading, writing, and thinking.

They built a vocabulary real to the child, supporting this beginning with an extensive vocabulary from many sources—Bank Street Books for one, also homemade books, paperbacks, etc.—all this prepared in advance for the child's use. The first part of the program is "Initial Teaching Procedures and Materials," with accompanying "Reinforcement Procedures and Materials." One lesson, for example, deals with "Texture and Taste." There is a "surprise box" to which children have brought familiar objects which are related to sounds and words. The child reaches in and says, "I have a doll's dress—it feels soft," or "I have a rock. It feels hard and rough." The second division concerns "Comprehension—Main Idea, Facts and Relationships, Interpreting Characters, Events, Settings, Making Inferences, Vocabulary," and here the reinforcement materials are not toys or simple objects but the dictionary, the encyclopedia, maps and charts, and the skillful use of questioning and discussion.

Implicit in Berkeley's Easy Reading is the philosophy and technique behind teaching Standard English as a second language or, more precisely as a second dialect. Dr. H. J. Maves, Assistant Superintendent in Charge of Instruction, who supervises our homemade ventures, calls this phenomenon "bidialectism" rather than "bilingualism."

"To a certain extent we are teaching children Standard English by foreign language methods," says Dr. Maves. "We are adapting foreign language techniques to the teaching of a second dialect. Our position is that we do little or no correcting of the child's dialect which he uses in his home or neighborhood, but that we teach him to shift to Standard English in school. *We must realize that a person's dialect is one of his most intimate possessions.*"

An example in Berkeley: A firstgrader says "I is goin'." Does the teacher reply, "No, Johnny, that's wrong"? No, without comment she writes it on the board as Johnny said it. Then she asks the class, "Is there another way of saying this?" and when one answers, or she suggests, "I am going," she writes that on the board also. She simply points out, "This is one way—this is another."

"We must not judge or humiliate the child," says Dr. Gilbert. "We must let him speak spontaneously. After a few years he will know several 'dialects,' one used at home, one at school and in the 'outside' working world. He will have learned to slip from one to another as the situation demands." Again, "reinforcement"—Dr. Gilbert's word, the word we must all put into action to teach children to read. It is a

---

*[Editor's Note: The Bank Street Readers, published by Macmillan, range from preprimers through a third reader. They were written by specialists at the Bank Street College of Education in New York City and stress the integrated, urban dimension of community life.]

science, a set of techniques, but science and its techniques will not do it unless understanding and involvement with the child's world are included. Dr. Gilʰert introduces the new reading curriculum with this statement: "It is hoped that the teaching of reading will offer joy to the teacher, and that the learning of reading will be happy and satisfying to our children."

These are the goals for the learning of reading—"happiness," "satisfaction," and a skill for successful work and lifetime pleasure.

In sum, we must attack this problem in many ways, from every angle, all at once. These are the ways:

1. Improve the competence of teachers who teach reading. (Few teacher-training institutions actually take a prospective teacher through the steps of how to teach reading well. Few try or are able to inculcate understanding of the disadvantaged minority child.) Provide a specialist, a "resource team-teacher" for in-service training right in the classroom. Assign teachers by rotation during the school year or the summer to reading clinics where they can be taught the proper techniques.
2. Once teachers are trained for excellence in reading, provide them with the kind of supportive help and instructional materials that will help them in their tasks. (In this day of modern technology, we need not be handicapped by "horse and buggy" texts or materials or equipment.) If we cannot get the materials we need, let's make our own.
3. Train teachers of other disciplines (history, chemistry, mathematics, art) so they can teach children to read the content of their subject areas. We glibly say that every teacher should be a teacher of reading, but we do not give the appropriate training to bring it about.
4. Reevaluate the techniques and procedures that have failed to teach reading to a disproportionate number of our minority children who have ability to learn but are either dropping out of school or graduating with a low level of literacy. Find new ways to teach. Develop understanding of "why" they have not learned.
5. Do a better job of teaching other communication skills, such as oral expression and effective writing, which are vitally interrelated and affect the child's ability to think and to make intelligent inquiry.

If we can do all these things—and we can—we will have the nation of readers we have been trying to have ever since the American Revolution. Through such means the ghetto child will come to "belong" not only to his home and neighborhood but also to the outside world from which he has been shut out. He will get over the wall. He will no longer feel alone.

Yes, all this and more, while we struggle simultaneously to integrate our schools. For either we will tumble down the ghetto walls or see our world consumed by mutual ghetto, hate, and ignorance.

CLASSROOM GROUPING AND INTEGRATION

Aaron Lipton *was principal of the R. J. Bailey School in Hartsdale, New York, a unit in the Greenburgh School District No. 8. Since 1967 he has been associate professor of education, Pennsylvania State University.*

Our school district, Greenburgh District No. 8, Hartsdale, New York, is

From *Integrated Education*, **February/March 1964. Reprinted by permission of the author.**

comprised of approximately seventeen segregated neighborhoods extending over a 5.05 square mile area. These neighborhoods are located about one mile west of White Plains and about twenty-five miles north of New York City. Some 2,500 students attend schools of the district—65 percent white and 35 percent Negro. The white population is predominantly middle class; the Negro population, upper-lower to lower-middle class with an increasing Negro middle class moving in.

While the school district has been desegregated for more than twelve years, only in the last three years has an integrative process evolved in the educational life of our children and teachers. As part of an overall effort to develop an educational system that will reflect the school as a democratic agency, certain grouping practices emerge which support this effort. Our concern is to work in all curricular areas to raise the levels of functioning of all the children. Our grouping patterns, we believe, will help achieve this goal.

Grouping is a procedure whereby we organize children for instruction. Thus, grouping takes place as a culmination of the consideration of many factors that must be taken into account to provide the proper setting for that instruction. There are a number of basic factors to consider which ultimately direct us to the formation of groups and subgroups within our school: The community as it is reflected in the school; the purpose of instruction; a climate for learning; and how and what children learn. In order to determine the direction we must take in developing meaningful grouping, we need to examine the substance of these factors.

The Community Reflected in the School

Each group or class within a school must have within it complete representation from its community. This means that each class must have children who range in intelligence, academic achievement, socioeconomic level, emotional adjustment, and home background in a manner that reflects the diversity of the community. The reasons for this are basically two: *(1) The omission of any children in terms of home background, race, and socioeconomic status from any classroom sets up a pattern of segregation of one kind or another; and (2) academic, racial, or social segregation is destructive to all groups.* The bright children develop a snobbery which leads to "snobocratic" attitudes rather than democratic ones. The average children lose motivational and inspirational direction by not being placed with bright children who help set a positive academic framework. Slow children tend to have their inadequacy feelings accentuated and their feelings of self-worth worsened by being placed in groups designated exclusively for them. Any attempt to eliminate some brighter children or some slower children from each group merely develops these problems to a greater degree. (A basic approach here must be to develop more positive attitudes in children towards their own levels of achievement and more acceptance and respect for the achievement of others among their peers.)

The community must be called upon constantly to support its schools. Segregation leading to favoritism in grouping ("status" classes) can only lead to a diminution of support and acceptance by the community. It is true that there are groups in the community who withdraw or withhold support from our schools because of a reaction to grouping procedures. This lack of support must be examined carefully in order to assess the varied bases for it. Much of it can be ascribed to basic segregationist attitudes, lack of awareness or information regarding the complexities of the problems, or general disinterest in public schools matters. (The uniqueness of our school district—an integrated school system serving a number of segregated communities—does pose a greater complex of problems than is ordinarily presented to the educator and his community.) This one factor does present many problems, but its challenge in a democratic society cannot be overlooked.

One of the major problems inherent in our system revolves around the wide ranges of cultural backgrounds, behavioral patterns and standards, and achievement levels and standards. It is in the perception of these differences and the acceptance or rejection of them wherein much of our problem lies. Our task is twofold here: to try to change the perception of the differences, and to try continually to raise levels and standards of the school population.

The Purposes of Instruction

We seek to provide each child with academic and social knowledge, skills and understandings that will develop attitudes and substance to make him an effective citizen functioning to his fullest academic and social potential. Thus, we provide equal opportunity for every child in our system. We cannot presume to provide an equal education for all children because of inherent differences in human beings and the varying potentials that exist. Equal opportunity can be provided only in a setting that reflects the total community. As a school we must direct our attention to providing as many academic and social tools, techniques, skills, and understandings as possible. Questions have been raised regarding the opportunities and possibilities for providing these learnings within classrooms that reflect the total community (wide-range grouping). Questions concerning the limitations of time and energy of teachers in dealing with the number of children's academic and social levels have been raised as well as the effect of such ranges on achievement. While there are studies of many depths and orientations regarding grouping, it may be generally stated that studies of grouping and comparative performance show no significant advantage for bright children grouped with their fellow bright children over bright children scattered through the school system.

Yet, many administrators have stated that something is accomplished by "homogeneous" or "narrow-range" grouping. The narrow-range group is more "teachable" than the "random" group for the average teacher. But this procedure matches the weaknesses of teachers rather than the facts of educability, and brings in its trail the danger of stereotyping the average child at a level of performance far below his true capacities. Teachers who are capable of working in different ways with children of differing abilities and interests will succeed equally well with the homogeneous and the heterogeneous group. Teachers who can handle only the textbook program will not be very successful with either group.

One additional comment arises here in terms of our grouping as it relates to our community. Generally, people who live in homogeneous communities and send their children to neighborhood schools may accept the research on grouping and the emphasis on the importance and role of the teacher. In our situation, however, questions have been raised regarding the even wider than normal ranges of academic and social-cultural backgrounds than exist elsewhere; and the difficulty of meeting the needs of children who in each class reflect these very wide ranges. Are we asking too much of teachers to teach this wide a range? Is there some loss suffered by one group or another because of this range?

We must consider this problem in its historical perspective in terms of recognizing a historical reality—the need to provide more adequate education to children whose parents and grandparents have long been deprived of it. This focus on history will in the long run be beneficial to all children and adults who participate in this program.

In a sense, our district is faced with two of the major controversial problems in education today—integration and the trend toward narrow-range grouping. The solutions to these problems are incompatible. That is, we cannot have integration (of any kind) and narrow-range grouping at the same time.

Our thesis is, however, that grouping on a narrower-range basis is not an answer. The answer to providing the best possible education to our children lies elsewhere.

A Climate for Learning

In the final analysis, in any grouping procedure the teacher is the backbone of the education system. The teacher sets the climate for learning by her academic knowledge, her own interest and motivation—in addition to her own understanding, sensitivity, perception, and acceptance of children.

Obtaining and retaining excellent teachers is much more the problem that the question of grouping. The staff at the Bailey School is becoming more and more that kind of excellent group of teachers who manifest dedication to the principles of meeting individual needs within an integrated setting.

Within the framework of this quality of staff, certain problems arise relating to personality of teacher and child which must be resolved in order to develop a compatible group available for learning. Each teacher has something positive to offer to certain children, and each teacher could have difficulty in relating to certain traits in children. It must be stated that, basically, a teacher who accepts a position in our district assumes the responsibility for teaching any child in the district. Acceptance of this responsibility, however, does not militate against the possibility of some teacher-child conflict and the possibility of class changes.

Teacher differences are reflected in many ways. For example, some teachers may be more able to be emotionally involved with children, yet some children may not be able to accept this involvement. The class climate can thus become too "warm" for the child. Some teachers may be concrete in their behavior, actions, and thinking. They may do very well with children who have difficulty with conceptualizing processes. Contrariwise, teachers who are able to generalize well and think abstractly may have great difficulty dealing with children who cannot think abstractly. Some teachers impart an attitude of fear of the children. Children with certain difficulties "pick up" or are sensitive to such fear and react negatively and constantly test such teachers. Some teachers are authoritarian in attitude and action.

Certain children become repressive and more disturbed by such personality characteristics. Some teachers are very calm and even and set a tone of quiet in their classrooms. Some teachers are uninvolved emotionally and certain children can benefit from this lack of involvement, while others are too needy of a loving adult figure to derive positive elements from such a relationship.

Generally, teachers relate to children as human beings and the basic component of the right climate for learning stems from the positive factors and elements in each teacher's relationship with each child.

The basic relationship established between teacher and child is the essence of the learning situation. The academic or behavioral level of the child is not the *sine qua non* of grouping. Some children do well with some teachers regardless of the level of their functioning. Some children do poorly with some teachers despite their functioning above "grade-level."

Beyond the teacher-child relationship as a basis for establishing a climate for learning, the group or peer level relationship is also important. Sometimes the source of increased and practically intolerable problem behavior comes from the group psychological constellations. In those cases very often the simple device of a change or removal from the group does away with the problem altogether.

In reference to the problems of teacher-pupil and pupil-pupil relationships, it was necessary to make only four changes out of over four hundred children in terms of group problems, and three changes in terms of teacher-pupil relationships since September, 1961. Requests for teachers are made periodically at the beginning, middle, or end of the year by parents—usually in terms of the "halo" effect acquired by certain teachers in the community, but rarely with any real understanding of the dynamics of the relationships that may develop between the teacher and the child.

Any placement decision is in the principal's hands and it may or may not be in accord with the request, depending upon each situation. Final authority rests with the principal.

The Achievement Record

Tables 1 and 2 illustrate two points. Table 1 shows that most of our children have gained above the normal amount in reading over a year's period within a grouping procedure which provides each class with a wide range of ability and functioning levels. Table 2 shows achievement-differentials between white and Negro children that are largely a reflection of the socioeconomic backgrounds of the children.

How and What Children Learn

Relating our purposes for instruction to achievement goals and grouping requires that we consider how and what each child needs to learn in order to recognize which components are important to children's achievement operations. Children learn by experiencing and by integrating these experiences into their apperceptive mass. They experience by seeing, hearing, smelling, touching, and feeling. A good teacher attempts to provide each child with curricular experiences that permit the use of as many senses as possible in terms of the material being presented.

Some children are exposed continuously to a variety of materials but do not experience any of it because of their own constellation of problems. A good teacher is sensitive to the results of the lack of these children's learning abilities. The good teacher will help a child break down the walls that separate him from his external environment and will, with help from others, too, free him to experience and to learn.

Many teachers expose children to a wealth of information and material. Oftentimes, mere exposure is enough for a majority of children. It is the child who cannot profit from this exposure about whom concern is expressed. His behavior reflects defensive maneuvering which keeps him from learning and also could make him a behavior problem and a "difficult" child to handle. It is these "difficult" children who cause us to raise questions about grouping.

Table 1

GROUPING AT R. J. BAILEY SCHOOL

Class	I.Q. Range	Grade-level Reading Achievement [a]	Average Gains in Grade-level Reading Achievement [b] (Norm: 0.9)		
			All Children	Top-Level Group [c]	Low-level Group [d]
4B	82-134	1.6- 5.7	0.9	1.5	0.7
4E	80-144	1.6- 7.2	1.1	1.4	0.7
4M	85-135	1.8- 7.9	1.2	1.9	0.6
5M	78-139	2.0- 7.9	1.8	2.4	1.7
5B	79-137	2.2- 7.6	2.1	2.6	1.4
5G	79-126	1.9- 7.2	1.5	2.1	1.0
5C	79-140	2.4- 7.9	1.9	2.4	1.7
5W	75-131	1.7- 7.9	1.4	1.6	1.5
5K	78-138	2.0- 7.7	1.7	1.9	1.1
5R	78-137	2.6- 7.7	1.9	2.5	1.4
5S	78-131	2.6- 7.4	1.1	1.5	1.1
6G	85-141	3.0-10.0	1.3	1.8	1.2
6V	75-130	3.0-10.0	1.9	2.4	1.1
6S	75-145	3.6-10.0	1.2	1.2	1.0
6T	77-130	3.2-10.0	1.4	1.0	1.8
6W	76-125	3.1- 9.2	1.4	1.6	0.9
6F	77-134	3.3-10.0	1.8	2.1	1.2

[a] September 1962 reading scores.
[b] From September 1962 to May 1963.
[c] One year or more *above* grade level.
[d] One year or more *below* grade level.

Table 2

RACIAL DATA BY GRADE AND ACHIEVEMENT

Class	Total Number of Students	Top-level Group [a]		Low-level Group [b]	
		White	Negro	White	Negro
4B	22	3	1	5	9
4E	23	4	2	4	10
4M	23	3	2	3	7
5M	21	5	1	3	10
5B	23	5	2	3	8
5G	23	6	2	4	7
5C	24	5	2	3	8
5W	23	3	3	3	9
5K	23	4	1	2	9
5R	24	5	1	3	8
5S	23	5	2	3	8
6G	23	9	4	2	6
6V	22	8	2	4	4
6S	24	9	3	4	4
6T	22	8	2	2	5
6W	22	7	2	3	4
6F	23	7	4	3	4

[a] One year or more *above* grade level in reading achievement.
[b] One year or more *below* grade level in reading achievement.

Grouping then becomes an *exclusion* process—how to eliminate the problem child. Except in extreme cases, however, our energies must be focused on *inclusion*. The approach must be manifold to ameliorate this situation.

1. More psychological (therapeutic as well as diagnostic) services must be provided.
2. Prevention must be a key to the program.
3. Prevention begins at the pre-kindergarten or kindergarten level.
4. Adequate diagnosis of each child's needs and modes of learning must be a major part of each teacher's program.
5. Grouping practices must be consistent throughout the elementary school; class size must be consistent with grouping patterns.
6. Expectations of children must be raised both academically and behaviorally (children often behave in a way that reflects their thoughts of what an adult expects of them).
7. Increasingly higher academic and social standards for each individual must be set in order to develop an educational and psychological climate which would raise the self-concept and adequacy feelings of each child.
8. The community must be involved at every level to gain and maintain support for a program which is designed to eliminate unnecessary conflict, tensions, and hostilities among the various socioeconomic racial groups that interfere with children's learning potential.
9. Our goal is to achieve a class and school setting that allows for acceptance and understanding, correct diagnostic procedures, rich curricular experiences, and the elimination of situations that develop ego-deteriorating experiences.

The question of what we learn is also important. Implicit in what has been said is the fact that we focus on the needs and levels of *our* children. In addition, we present not watered-down curricula but a richer curriculum to augment the backgrounds of all of our children. This means an increased emphasis on:

1. Improving the ability of each child to communicate on a verbal level with adults and his peers.
2. Involving the child in more depth experiences in understanding his physical world.
3. Improving each child's understanding of himself in relation to others.
4. Improving the child's ability to think critically, judge effectively, and to act from fact rather than prejudice.
5. Providing experiences to each child in the arts, to enrich his background and association with cultural media.

These elements of a curriculum are presented as a basis from which our staff has been working and needs to continue working. They are presented as the real issues with which we must cope. All of our children need to learn as much as can be provided to them. Our obligation to the children within the concept of a democratic ideal requires that we deal with them in terms of providing a curriculum which will be absorbed increasingly more adequately as we understand children better, as we provide increasingly more perceptive, intelligent, and accepting teachers, and as we continue to focus more sharply on what our problems are and what we can do about them.

INTEGRATION AND THE EDUCATORS

Benjamin Solomon *is assistant professor of education at Chicago State College and research associate at the Industrial Relations Center of the University of Chicago. His special research interests are the power structure in education and white-collar unionism.*

My aim is to deal with the tactics, strategies, and goals of school integration movements in northern and western communities, and to consider some of their implications for educators. It is hoped that this article will also help the concerned groups to formulate comprehensive and fundamental goals for school integration and to better understand the nature of tactics that would be the most effective toward attaining these goals. In the discussion that follows, I will occasionally refer to Chicago only because it is the city with which I am most acquainted and because it is perhaps an extreme case among large nonsouthern cities.

I would like first to summarize key aspects of this article:

- The cause of integration is the cause of education. Educational philosophy and practice must incorporate concepts of integration in their cores. Integration cannot be viewed merely as an outside force with only a circumstantial bearing on education.
- Commitment of mind and emotion by the teacher is the touchstone and dynamic of education. The most far-reaching aim of community integration movements thus must be to affect personal commitment of educators.
- The words "cause" and "commitment" are used advisedly. Education, rejecting neutrality or passivity, is, if anything, a positive force. Neutrality offers no solution to the problems of the education of Negro or any children. These problems evolved historically in the context of city ghettos and require for their solution large-scale and comprehensive changes in organization and administration of schools and in education theory and practice. Such problems, difficult at best, will not be solved without a strongly affirmative approach by teachers and administrators.
- To bring about change, the integration movement must shake up existing patterns—the values, attitudes, habits, and relationships that together constitute a pattern of weak and inadequate commitment to the education of minority-group children—and must encourage the shaping of a new pattern that incorporates a deeper and enriched commitment to education. To do this, school integration forces must go beneath the surface of mechanical compliance or the provision of merely material means—they must seek to influence the very spirit of the educational process.
- It is most common to view integration as an *end*. It is important that full depth, richness, and scope be given to this end and to understand that it involves much more than the physical mixing of the races in the same school or classroom.
- Integration can also be viewed as a *means or method* by which to attain further integration. Specific steps such as interracial classrooms serve not only to achieve part of the aims of integration but, also, to break new ground for further advances.

From *Integrated Education,* **August 1963, Reprinted by permission of the author.**

- Integration in education must proceed until it has reached its full, logical development. An integration movement that stops short may only serve to create a new set of problems, which will be blamed on integration. But the problems that will arise at each step can then be seen as the problems of progress if they are placed in the context of a comprehensive integration program.

Personal Commitment

Much of modern life revolves around use of mechanical and impersonal means. In sharp contrast, education is personal in aim and process. The commitment of the teacher—his will to teach—is the motive force in the educational process. It is the necessary condition for the contribution of mental, emotional, and moral energies to assist the complex unfolding of the child's capacities.

A lesser degree of commitment implies a relatively shallow and limited educational process. If a teacher does not want to teach, he can easily succeed. And if his attitude is but neutral or one of mild concern, he will take only small advantage of the child's capacities for development.

The importance of personal commitment is heightened when one considers that the aims of education are never fully achieved. To the teacher with an affirmative approach, education is a constant process of striving—striving to achieve the maximum development of the child's potential to learn. It is an adventure into the unknown, since the limits of the child's capacities are never fully explored. The educator's task is to help the child approach ever closer to these limits.

Thus, learning should not be conceived as merely a mechanical process for the imparting of facts and reasoning skills. In actuality, the learning process takes place in a climate of complex, subtle human relationships in which motivation, values, and character traits greatly condition the outcomes. One must ask: In what ways is the teacher humanly involved—what does he give to it of intellect, imagination, integrity, of illumination, of a living example to stimulate and nurture the unformed potential of the child? How does the teacher, interacting with the child, affect his desire to learn, his respect and love for knowledge, his standards of work and work discipline, his sense of integrity in the search for knowledge? How does the teacher touch the imagination of the child, help him gain the excitement of the breakthrough to new intellectual horizons, help him gain the confidence which will sustain him through the sometimes traumatic grappling with new ideas?

Commitment must be more than perfunctory. Nor can we assume that anything like the full promise of education is automatically realized by the existence of a public school system. Public school systems can go through the outward motions of education (often with an exasperating mastery of the technique) while largely ignoring the heart of the learning process. The results in such cases are mediocre—or worse.

What about the community and its commitment to education? Undoubtedly, the community's will to educate its children has a profound effect on the personal affirmation of teachers and administrators and on the quality of education. But the human spirit that infuses education, whether that of the community or of the professional personnel, must be viewed as the product of many interacting forces, of the understandings, interests, and preferences of many groups. For those with a concern for education, the chief questions are: How to influence commitment? How to enrich it, how to give it more depth and scope, how to give it a more powerful expression?

Only inferior education can result where the commitment among professional personnel to the education of minority-group children is less than it is to other children—no matter what other aspects of the education system are equalized. Thus, the school integration movement must seek to exert its most fundamental influence at the core of the educational process, the personal involvement of teachers and administrators.

Tactics and Goals

The school integration movement in northern and western cities originated in the protests of Negro parents against the existing system of *segregated and inferior* education. They demand *integrated and improved* education.

The major response to these pressures has been twofold: (1) resistance to integration steps, and (2) some actions to improve education in the Negro areas. For example, in Chicago, a major part of the building program recently has been in Negro areas. But Negro children were denied the use of an apparently large number of empty classrooms in all-white neighborhoods. We may sum up this response as *segregated but improved.* (The question still remains as to how much an improvement is a new school?)

This combination of resistance and concessionary improvement programs has a persuasive effect on many persons and needs to be carefully evaluated in the light of a comprehensive view of the means and aims of school integration movements.

Any serious integration movement must expect to encounter resistance because of the attitudes and practices which prevail in many white communities. Social scientists have recognized that conflict is an inevitable part of change and, in fact, that conflict can be channeled to help bring about desirable social change. The proposal of an integration program will bring into the open resistance which was there in any case. Once brought into the open, it becomes possible to deal with it. Every effort should be made, of course, to give a constructive and educational shaping to the ensuing conflict. The means of doing this are various and can only be briefly noted.

Rational discussion, carried on by whatever channels, is very much to the benefit of the school integration movement. To aid in making such discussion possible, the effort should consistently be made to pierce barriers by invoking common human compassion and moral and ethical values. Clergymen are more ready than ever before to help in such endeavors. Of a different order but often important are legal steps to enforce rights to nondiscriminatory education. Political action and legislation are, of course, other important instruments.

Underlying all this, there must exist the aroused and organized pressures of the minority community, pressures which it must at times express boldly and demonstratively. Any basic solution must involve capturing on a consistent basis the attention of the dominant white community. The only way to do this is through integration pressures and specific integration steps. The educational problems of Negro children must be transported out of the ghetto and into the schools and neighborhoods throughout the city. In the ghetto these problems will be ignored; removed from the ghetto they will receive attention.

Concessions

It may be said that focusing on integration will mean sacrificing concessions which might be granted under the *segregated but improved* approach. Ironically, perhaps, few in the way of such "concessions" are likely to be lost. The motive behind the concessionary approach is, after all, to divert the pressures while retaining a segregated school system. The means are sufficient amelioration within the framework of ghetto education to reduce Negro community pressures to a "normal" level. Once integration pressures are weakened, the likelihood is that interest in the education of Negro children will diminish. Thus, collaboration with the *improvement* approach represents inferior tactics.

Segregated but improved does not in any way summarize the educational goals held by advocates of school integration. By and large, the former approach caters to sentiments hostile to placing Negro and white children in the same classrooms or Negro teachers and administrators in schools in white neighborhoods. It in no way gets at the vital educational questions, neither those pertaining to the educational needs of Negro and white children nor those pertaining to the problem of unequal commitment among educators and in the community.

In contrast, it may be well to state some of the general elements of the integration standpoint. As the supreme court pointed out in its 1954 decision,* a segregated school system could not give equal education since the fact of segregation alone—even if all else were equal—would have harmful psychological effects on Negro children. The fabric of segregation is interwoven with the theory of inferiority of Negroes. Exposure to the workings of this viewpoint in the very classrooms where he is supposed to develop his capacities—a viewpoint which represents a denial of his humanness—will often have a numbing effect on the child's desire to learn and on the level of his aspirations. He will soon learn, if he does not know at the start, that a successful career must be carved out in a white world for which he is being given little preparation for confident participation. Indeed, his school situation is an everyday reaffirmation of rejection of this white world.

In contrast, integrated education means acceptance as an equal human being; it brings within reach experience about the larger world beyond the ghetto; and it gives point to pursuing educational goals whose fulfillment must be achieved in this larger world.

It has also been noted that integrated education has great potential benefits for white children. Knowing Negroes as classmates and friends or as teachers and administrators will help destroy false stereotypes easily acquired in the all-white community. If education means the search for the truth, integrated schooling will help the white child find out what is true in one of the most vital areas of modern life. It will lay the goundwork for improvement in the processes of democracy and help prepare future white adults to live in a new kind of world now coming into being—one in which colored peoples count as much as white.

Turning now to the schools, what are the aims and strategies of integration groups and what should the roles and responsibilities of professional personnel be? We shall first discuss the top leadership, using Chicago as an example.

That the issue of segregated education arose in Chicago's schools should occasion no surprise.† As in other northern cities, a ghetto pattern has developed for the large and growing Negro population. This pattern is both an expression of and a means for

---

*[Editor's Note: See Appendix A, "Text of Supreme Court Rulings (*Brown* v *Board* of Education, ...).")]

†[See also "The Chicago Title VI Complaint to H.E.W.," pp. 79 ff. of this volume.]

the perpetuation of the racist myth that imbues the minds and emotions of important parts of the white population. It should be noted that school segregation is not simply a circumstance of the prevailing residential segregation but includes also values, attitudes, practices, and policies, many of them informal, which are thoroughly incorporated into the operation of the school system as part of the ongoing larger pattern of segregation in the city.

Top Leadership

As in other cities, the Chicago school system is organized on a centralized basis, with the board of education and the superintendent making policy and controlling its execution. *If* there were a positive integration program we would in the first instance expect to see it shown in the top leadership and overall policies of the system. Certain questions can be raised which seek to ascertain whether there is such a program and what the commitment of the leadership is to the education of Negro children and to integration.

- Have the board and the superintendent shown a moral and intellectual identification with the educational needs of minority-group children and with the educational significance of integration? Has such identification been perceived by principals and classroom teachers so as to have a positive effect on their attitudes and understandings?
- Have they promoted public discussion of segregated schooling in order to point out its harmful educational consequences and thereby gain support for a program of school integration?
- Have they enunciated the goal of meeting fully the educational needs of minority-group children, necessarily including integration, together with a definite and comprehensive program for fulfilling these needs and a specified timetable by which the program would accomplish its aims?
- Has the need for resources been spelled out and have definite requests for undertaking the program been vigorously pursued?
- Has the superintendent launched a searching discussion of the educational issue of integration among the vast professional staff, and have support and encouragement gone out to those teachers and administrators who are most ready to bring about the changes required by integration?
- Has he made it clear to teachers and administrators that segregationist attitudes and practices are unprofessional, immoral, and in the case of certain practices, illegal?
- Has he encouraged the assignment of Negro teachers and administrators to the all-white sections of the city?
- Has he given leadership within professional organizations on behalf of integrated education and has he shown that he is willing to work with professional organizations in integration endeavors?
- Have the board and the superintendent developed strong bonds of sympathy and effective working relationships with the Negro community, particularly with the most active sectors in the fight for integrated education? Likewise, have such bonds been developed with the broader community educational organizations that are most concerned to bring about integrated and improved education?

The program, the attitudes, and the commitment implied in the above questions have been clearly lacking in Chicago. It is probable that t.,e answer in many other cities will also be negative, though perhaps to a lesser degree.

There is no question of the significance of a negative position among the top officials of the school system. Full and genuine integration requires an intellectual and moral leadership and the adoption and application of a wide range of policies and practices, persistently and intelligently applied throughout the school system. Given the centralized organization of public school systems, a higher leadership opposed to or apathetic about integration can easily prevent any progress. This would be even truer where a large part of the teaching staff was at best indifferent to integration.

A major objective of the integration movement, therefore, must be a top administration with a strong commitment to integration, one willing to take a forceful initiative throughout the school system in eliminating segregation practices. Until such a leadership is installed, the gains achievable by integration groups can only be limited, piecemeal, and precarious.

Teachers and Integration

Though segregation would clearly seem to be inconsistent with any meaningful professional credo, there are few instances of serious and persistent organized protests to segregated education among teachers in northern and western cities. The widespread accommodation by teachers to *de facto* segregation suggests a limited belief in the educability of Negro children; lack of encouragement of high aspirations; acceptance of low standards, inferior physical conditions, lack of supplies, and the like; ignorance of or even collaboration with anti-Negro bias in curriculum and materials; lack of understanding of or concern for the impact of segregation on the education of Negro or white children.

Major efforts at reorientation and re-education of teachers and principals are needed if the full educational possibilities of integration are to be realized. We have already discussed the key role that higher administration of the school system can play in helping to bring about such change. School integration movements can also influence teachers through the changes they can bring about in community values and goals and, also by directly working with and encouraging teacher organizations to take an active part in creating a fully integrated school system. One important aspect would be the full integration of the teaching staff in all parts of the system. The ultimate aim must be a school system in which the professional personnel are deeply imbued with the spirit and aims of integrated education.

It must be expected that many teachers will resist integration, while still others will be indifferent. Nevertheless, anything short of a positive approach to integrated classrooms is a presumption of lesser commitment to the education of Negro children. A teacher opposed to "mixed" classrooms typically will express concern over the supposed deleterious effects on white children and will complain that educational principles are violated and difficult educational problems are created. On the other hand, such a teacher will rarely have anything to say about the educational benefits to children from steps toward school integration, nor will he apply much imagination or ingenuity to coping with problems that do arise. In many cases, what actually underlies much of the opposition is a real anxiety about the social implications, in and out of the classroom, of white and Negro children as classmates. The source of such anxieties is, of course, the fact that the segregated community has not allowed the development of normal relationships between Negro and white people. Even teachers who have intellectually broken with the segregation pattern may fear integration because of the lack of experience with integrated situations and lack of knowledge of the positive benefits which may ensue from integration.

Upset Patterns

The most effective context for change must be created if the pattern of accommodation and even collaboration with segregation by teachers is to be upset. This context must be based on the actual fact of integrated classrooms. We have noted earlier that physical integration is a first, not the last, step in achieving full integration. It should be equally stressed that such physical integration is the crucial beginning point for a process of change.

For some teachers, mixed classrooms will represent a traumatic experience, while others will be relatively ready for the change. But for all, the questions around school integration will be concrete and unavoidable. Whatever their feelings, once classroom integration is established, teachers will to a much lesser degree than hitherto be able to set aside the Negro child in a pattern of segregated schools, inferior standards, and limited belief in his educability. This will be especially so if the community school integration movement is strong and expresses comprehensive aims, if the top administration of the school system gives firm leadership, and if important organized groups of teachers make clear in policy and activity their support for integrated education.

The dynamic possibilities stem from the fact that being seated alongside his white classmate represents a living demonstration of the equal claim of the Negro child on the commitment of the teacher. In the integrated classroom the Negro child is a daily reminder of the human force of the Negro community and of those outside of it who believe in equal education—a reminder of what innumerable Negro mothers and fathers are saying to the teacher and principal: "Our children are human. You must establish this in your mind's eye and show it in your relationship with our children. You must believe in our children's humanity because, if you don't, you will not have the desire to help our children to learn as much as they are capable of learning."

When viewed in the context of a comprehensive integration program, a major effect of integration measures will be to open up a whole new frontier of professional development. Teachers will become involved, as they otherwise would not, in significant sociological and psychological aspects of learning theory, in problems of curriculum content and techniques of the organization of the school system, of relationships between the school and community, and of the role and responsibilities of educators. Education, much more than before, will be linked constructively with important currents in our urban communities.

The teacher, by overcoming past barriers and starting to view in serious fashion education for Negro children, will develop a belief in the educability of the Negro child and in the dynamic educational significance of an integrated school system. He will realize that equal respect and dignity are due the Negro child, his parents, the Negro community, and its history. He will be concerned about understanding the cultural background of Negro children so that he might take this into account in designing educational procedures and he will examine textbooks and curricula for bias and omission and make the necessary rectification. He will understand the problems white children and parents might have in viewing integrated schools and will strive to help them cope with these problems in a constructive manner.

When the initiative for integration is largely taken over by teachers and their organizations, when they are imbued with commitment to and understanding of the need for integrated education, then we will know that integration has established its roots deep in the educational process.

A Broader View

There is not space here to discuss the application of this framework to a variety of issues and problems. One of the most important is how to increase student integration, given the segregated housing patterns. Another, not unrelated, question stems from the general middle-class orientation of our public schools and the tendency to group pupils on an "ability" basis. It can only be said that insofar as integration is accepted as a basic educational value and goal, it will be found feasible to take many specific steps towards its achievement. Obstacles in the form of false postures of "neutrality" on racial matters and outcries that sacred educational principles are being violated will vanish as integration takes its place as one of the key considerations in the shaping of the educational process.

It is worth considering some of the implications for education of a school system which attempts to function in segregated halves. A lesser or unequal commitment to the education of Negro children is a corruption of those qualities which are most essential to the work of educators. This corruption, while it may fester in and affect mainly the Negro sector, will nevertheless spread throughout the school system. Teachers who stand by while a large group of children suffer from inferior educational conditions are allowing the stunting of just those sensibilities most important for work with any children. White educators who view early career assignments to Negro schools as a sentence which must be endured for a period may not be able easily to resume the process of professional development whey they finally transfer to white schools. All those who tie their standards of expected performance to city-wide averages are accepting standards lowered by the inferior education in Negro areas. Every professional person who accepts the notion that Negro children cannot learn has made it easier for himself to lose some degree of confidence in the ability of white children to learn. Restrictions on the movement of Negro staff members limit their ability to develop or to contribute and create disunity in the staff. Inevitably, the process is one in which all are dragged down to the standards and concepts deemed acceptable for minority groups under a system of segregation.

The startling implication can be drawn that the pressures of the integration movement, emanating mainly from the lowliest group in the big city, may have ramifying effects of greatest importance for all American education. These pressures originate in the increasing depth of feeling among Negro parents of the need for equal education for their children. Their main cutting edge is directly into the core question of a school system—the desire of its professional staff to help the children to learn. If formed effectively, these pressures can create a ferment among educators, one which forces an overdue reexamination of their roles and which involves them in major educational challenges. But the activity of mind and heart evoked by the integration issue will surely flow over to a whole range of other problems which beset American education. The salvation which the integration movement carries to the larger community is its refusal to accept the status quo and its pressures on educators to think deeply and feel strongly about their work. Negro parents may start by asking for "equal" education through integrated schools. The final consequences of their efforts may instead be a much higher caliber of education for all—Negro and whites.

Public education is the main repository of the community's hopes for the future. Education is concerned with human attributes which can be conveyed only by teachers who can and want to convey these attributes. Citizens and educators must together create a new framework for education in our cities—one which provides a context for teacher and student in which the best potentialities of both may be most fully evoked.

PLANNING AND THE NEIGHBORHOOD SCHOOL

Allan Blackman *is city planner, School of Public Health, University of California, Berkeley. This article is expanded from a talk given March 21, 1964, to the American Institute of Planners, California Chapter, Northern Section.*

The "neighborhood unit" as a planning concept has been cogently attacked on a number of occasions during the past twenty years. Despite these attacks, the idea of a neighborhood remains among the cherished values of most urban planners. "From Atlantic to Pacific and from Canada to Mexico, the basic Perry neighborhood unit, with only minor modifications, has served as the development module."[1]

Part of the reason that the attacks have been ignored was succinctly stated in December, 1960, by the American Society of Planning Officials Planning Advisory Service. Its Information Report No. 141 stated: "Without arguing the validity of the overall Isaacs-led critique, it is safe to say that the attack was measurably weakened by the absence of a concrete alternative proposal."[2] The report goes on to assert that "... it appears that much of the momentum of the opposition movement has been exhausted."[3]

While the opposition movement among planners may be exhausted, recent events in New York, Chicago, Berkeley, and elsewhere make it clear that there is a new, vigorous opposition stemming from the civil rights movement. This new opposition is not concerned with the entire neighborhood unit idea. It is concerned with the neighborhood school which Clarence A. Perry proposed as the social and design focal point of the neighborhood unit.[4] The new opposition proposes a definite social alternative, the racially integrated school.

Given the powerful legal and political attacks now being made upon the neighborhood school idea, it is the duty of the planning profession to reconsider its

From *Integrated Education,* **August/September 1964. Reprinted by permission of the author.**

[1] American Society of Planning Officials, *Neighborhood Boundaries*, Planning Advisory Service Information Report No. 141, Chicago, 1961, p. 8.

[2] *Ibid.,* p. 7.

[3] *Ibid.,* p. 8.

[4] Clarence Arthur Perry, "The Neighborhood Unit," *Regional Survey of New York and Its Environs,* Vol. VII, 1929.

commitment to this form of school organization. We still have the time to try to develop alternative forms of school organization that can satisfy the goals of educators, planners and the civil rights movement. If we do not try, we may be forced to accept alternatives, developed in the heat of political battles, that satisfy no one. As part of this reconsideration, I should like to raise the following questions: What are the purposes and values of the neighborhood school? Are the values of the neighborhood school more important than the values of racial integration of schools? Can we achieve both the goals of the neighborhood school and the goal of racial integration? What are the alternative forms of school organization?

The Purposes of the Neighborhood School

The neighborhood school attempts to achieve four key goals.

1. The neighborhood school provides the cheapest, safest and fastest means of transporting the child from home to school. The farther a school is from the home, the more time is spent in the transportation process, the more streets, especially major streets which must be crossed by the walking child, and the more we feel obliged to transport the child with expensive public transportation.

2. Many educators believe schools should be small.[5] The neighborhood form of organization helps keep them small.

3. "Educators believe that young children benefit from the security that comes from learning and living in the same, familiar environment."[6] They feel that children should be able to have their classmates as after-school playmates and that they should be able to return to school for after-school classes and programs.[7]

4. This major purpose is quite complex but best summarized by saying that educators want a close relationship between the school and the family. "The neighborhood school should, and often does, serve as an invitation to parents to know, confide in, and work with its staff. This offers a good chance for constructive community pressures on the central school administration and the political authorities for local school improvements."[8] Thus the neighborhood school can reflect the values and goals of the community it serves, and can gain that community's loyalty and support. Stated from a different perspective, the neighborhood school is a reflection of the belief that education should be locally controlled.

An Evaluation of the Goals of the Neighborhood School

The Transportation Problem

The transportation problems that the neighborhood school attempts to solve should be divided into four separate problems of safety, walking distance, and cost.

Time.—Minimizing the amount of time spent going from home to school is

---

[5]N. L. Engelhardt, N. L. Engelhardt, Jr., and Stanton Legget, *Planning Elementary School Buildings,* 1953, p. 178.

[6]Wylie H. Davis, "St. Louis," *Civil Rights U.S.A.: Public Schools—Cities in the North and West—1962,* Superintendent of Documents, Washington, D.C., p. 277, n. 62; Fred Hechinger, "Neighborhood School Concept," *The New York Times,* June 26, 1963.

[7]Patricia Cayo Sexton, *Education and Income: Inequities in Our Public Schools,* The Viking Press, New York, 1961, p. 115.

[8]Hechinger, *op. cit.*

important both to avoid wasting time and to avoid fatiguing the child. Most educators say an elementary school child should not spend more than thirty minutes getting to school, a secondary child should not spend more than an hour. The time factor does not appear to be an important determinant of the neighborhood school since in thirty minutes a child can walk or bike considerably more than three quarters of a mile. If a child is driven to school, he can probably go from four to ten miles in thirty minutes.[9]

Safety.—The safety of children going to and from school is extremely important, of course. The concern for safety appears to be a key factor in determining standards for walking distances. It appears to be assumed that the danger of accidents increases directly with the distance a child walks and the number of major intersections he crosses. Are these assumptions correct? Is not the child's safety more related to the types of traffic situations he confronts rather than the distances he walks? Is not a child safer crossing a major intersection with traffic controls than a minor intersection without controls? I raise these points as questions because I have not yet had the opportunity to investigate what research there has been on this matter. Furthermore, if safety is paramount, children should be driven from home to school since the parents' car, public transportation, or a school bus are all probably safer than any walking trip on even the safest streets.

Walking distance.—Walking distance as a factor separate from the time and safety factors is a problem only if the distance is so great that the child becomes fatigued.

Most educators say an elementary school child should not walk more than three quarters of a mile, a secondary child not more than two miles. I doubt that these distances tire children. I doubt that even a thirty-minute walk could so tire a child as to interfere with classwork.

Cost.—We rightly begrudge the cost of transporting children to school because we would rather spend the money for the more important factors of education such as salaries, buildings, and books. However, where educational goals can be achieved only by transportation to distant schools, Americans have generally paid the cost, the time cost as well as the money cost. In Philadelphia, all crippled children are bused to one school where they receive a special education they could not possibly get in any other form of school. For some children, the trip takes more than an hour. In all rural areas, we pay the cost of buses because we know that farm children can get a good education only in large, centrally located schools. Parents who believe in private schools also willingly pay the transportation cost. The largest illustration, of course, is the parochial school which in many instances requires use of public transportation or school buses. Roman Catholic parents have also paid the cost. The point made by these examples is that where educational goals can be achieved only by transporting children to relatively distant schools, the cost of such transportation has been paid.

Clearly, alternatives to the neighborhood school should involve as little transportation cost as possible. Unfortunately, the only forms of transportation generally considered are no-cost walking or very high-cost school buses. Other alternatives should be considered. Even young children safely can use and have used public transportation, presumably at less cost than special school buses. Organized car pools

---

[9]*Guide for Planning School Plants*, National Council on School House Construction, 1958.

manned by parents can be developed. (Many parents already drive their children even to the closest schools.)[10]

The School Size Problem

The second goal of the neighborhood school is to keep schools small. It is important to realize that school size is not a function of location but of organization. If the ideal size for an elementary school unit is four hundred pupils, and if we have a central location drawing two thousand pupils, there is no reason why we cannot build five separate buildings at the one location or why we cannot, even in one building, create five school units. Some so-called "tracking" systems have been attacked just because they create educationally and socially separate schools in one school building.[11]

In reading what educators say about the question of school size, I have been impressed by the fact that big schools are confused with overcrowded schools.[12] Bad planning, bad luck or inadequate expenditures for facilities can overcrowd or overuse a small neighborhood school just as they can a large school.

Elementary schools with five hundred or fewer pupils are generally considered ideal. This standard appears to reflect the subjective judgment of educators rather than any objective measures of efficiency or educational accomplishment.[13] In contrast an Arkansas school study states: " . . . in practice it is difficult to determine just what the maximum limits should be. Few national guideposts are available for help in setting enrollment limits."[14] I have concluded that with proper planning and administration and with adequate operating budgets, we could have much larger schools. As one authority on the subject has stated, "When a school plant is actually planned in every detail to care for the enrollment it houses, the question of optimum size is settled."[15]

The fact that larger schools may not be undesirable is extremely important because frequently the small size of neighborhood units is determined not by any of the other factors discussed in this report but simply by the factor of small school size.

A historical note is interesting in this discussion of school size. In 1929, when Clarence A. Perry first wrote about the neighborhood unit, he considered elementary schools with sixty classrooms and 1,200 or more pupils as desirable.[16]

---

[10]Nathan Glazer and Daniel Patrick Moynihan, *Beyond the Melting Pot: The Negroes, Puerto Ricans, Jews, Italians, and Irish of New York City.* M.I.T. Press, Cambridge (Mass.), 1963.

[11]John S. Hadsell, *De Facto Segregation in the Berkeley Public Schools,* De Facto Segregation Study Committee, Berkeley (Calif.) Unified School District, 1963; Sexton, *op. cit.;* Frank Riessman, *The Culturally Deprived Child,* Harper and Row, New York, 1962.

[12]Engelhardt, Engelhardt, and Leggett, *op. cit., p. 178.*

[13]Frank W. Hubbard, "How Big Is a Good School," *Elementary School Buildings—Design for Learning,* Department of Elementary School Principals, National Education Association; *Proposed Standards for Public Educational Facilities,* Comprehensive Planning Division, Detroit City Plan Commission, 1960; *Guide . . . School Plants, op. cit.,* p. 45.

[14]*Standards for School Planning,* Pulaski County (Little Rock, Ark.) Metropolitan Area School Planning Project, 1957.

[15]N. L. Engelhardt, N. L. Engelhardt, Jr., and Stanton Leggett, *Planning Secondary School Buildings,* 1949, p. 53.

[16]Perry, *op. cit.*

Child Security

The third goal of the neighborhood school is providing the child with a sense of security by having the school as part of the home environment. The factors which make a child feel secure at school are varied and complex. I doubt that the physical location of the school or the physical separation of home and school are important in establishing this security. Two recent studies[17] have pointed out that lower-class students feel quite insecure in school, indeed feel alienated in school, even though the school is close to home. These feelings of insecurity result from the attitude of the lower-class home toward education and the attitude of the schools toward the lower-class child. At least in the case of the lower-class children whose home environments frequently are insecure and depressing, it could be argued that they would benefit more from a school located in a different environment. Lower-class children frequently have home environments that provide an inadequate and un-stimulating range of experiences, and for these children new experiences and varied experiences may be more important needs than security.

The problems of the middle-class child are not the same as those of the lower-class child but this does not mean that even the middle-class child feels secure in school simply because of the physical location of the school. Again it is relevant to point to the children who presently attend schools not physically close to their homes. I have yet to discover evidence that crippled children, rural children, private school children, or parochial school children feel insecure simply because of the distant location of their schools.

Parent Support of Schools

The fourth goal of the neighborhood school is a close relationship between the school and the family. Here again the evidence indicates that this close relationship is not simply a question of physical proximity. A close relationship between school and home is important at the secondary school level and it is achieved even though the secondary school is much farther from the home than the elementary school. Again we have the example of the private schools, parochial schools, and other non-neighborhood schools. In many of these schools I suspect there is a closer relationship between school and parents than there is in the neighborhood school.

The crucial factor in establishing closeness between home and school is the ability of the home to control the standards, atmosphere, and the goals of the school. This control is generally exercised through the school board and the school district. The centrally located academic high schools and demonstration elementary schools are examples of parents creating non-neighborhood schools with which they have a close relationship through pressure on a school board. The relationship is close because the parents can politically control the character of the schools.

Even though there is no necessity to achieve parental control through physical proximity of school and home, it is the case that in most northern and western communities control actually has been achieved by locating the schools close to the home. Because of this pattern in the North and the West, arguments against integration based on a defense of the neighborhood school frequently reflect the fear of white, middle-class parents that they will lose control if the neighborhood school is eliminated.

---

[17]Riessman, *op. cit.;* Sexton, *op. cit.*

Why do parents want control? To a considerable extent they want it for its own sake. In a democracy all citizens would like to feel they can control their destiny, especially as it is affected by such an important institution as the school. In addition, the white, middle-class parent wants control to achieve goals of specific content concerned with the quality, quantity, and character of education. These goals include the imparting of social and class education by the school.

Frequently, if not generally, the white middle class has had few positive ideas of what it wanted to achieve; but it has had one very definite idea. It has wanted to keep its children's schools from being dominated by Negroes, by the children of the slums, by lower-class and deprived children of all sorts. The white middle class fears these children because it feels they will lower the educational and social standards of their own children. (That these fears may be ill-founded is irrelevant; the white middle class has acted on the basis of these fears.)

To prevent this domination has meant to segregate, but the separation of the slum children from the white middle-class children could not be accomplished in the North and the West as it had been in the South. The way of accomplishing this separation indirectly was residential segregation in conjunction with the neighborhood school concept. This combination has allowed the white middle class to retain the control it desired.

Where the white middle class has remained in the big cities, having their schools within their neighborhoods has made these schools easily identifiable and has permitted the school boards to give them special favors. If the neighborhood changed social composition, the school (i.e. the teachers, the children, the special facilities, and the special favors) could move with the parents to their new retreat. Most white middle-class parents have fled to the suburbs, of course, where they have established class segregated school districts over which they have intimate control.[18] It seems certain that any alternative to the neighborhood school, any proposals for school integration, must successfully deal with these desires of the middle-class white parents to control the schools.

Negative Consequences of the Neighborhood School

In order to understand why the civil rights movement is attacking the neighborhood school so vehemently, it is important to understand not only the four arguments for the neighborhood school but also the particular ways in which the neighborhood school damages children from lower-income families in general and the Negro children in particular.

Unfair Distribution of Services

One of the most evil consequences of the neighborhood form of school organization is that it has allowed many school systems to seriously slight the educational needs of children from lower-income areas. Documentation of this mistreatment is provided in the book *Education and Income*,[19] by Patricia C. Sexton, Associate Professor of Educational Sociology at New York University. Professor Sexton's book is a study of the Detroit school system. The book demonstrates that by every quantitative and qualitative measure of educational service, schools serving

[18]Riessman, *op. cit.*, Ch. III.
[19]*Op. cit.*

areas with families of below-average income receive significantly inferior treatment as compared with schools serving areas with families of above-average income. In terms of class size, number of substitute teachers, age of school buildings, quantity and quality of school facilities, safety and healthfulness of school site, amount of school play space, and in terms of special services, by all these measures the lower-income schools receive treatment significantly inferior to that given to the upper-income schools. One set of statistics from Professor Sexton's book will do to illustrate the unfair distribution of expenditures in the Detroit school system. Of the schools serving areas with average incomes of less than $5,000, 42 percent serve no free meals or free milk. Of the schools serving areas with average incomes over $9,000, 22 percent serve no free meals or free milk.

One of the significant points of Professor Sexton's book is that the unfair distribution of educational services is not a racial problem, but a class problem. She points out that white areas with below average income receive just as bad educational service as do Negro areas.[20]

The unfair distribution of educational funds in Detroit is not unusual. It can be found in many other if not most other American cities. It is only recently in a few cities such as Oakland and New York that a small effort has begun to give equal or extra help to schools in lower-income areas.

Professor Sexton's book helps explain why many people in the civil rights movement are skeptical of the proposition that what is needed is not school integration but improvement of the schools in the Negro areas. The proposition may be true. But if it is, why have these improvements not been made in the past?

Mobility of Lower-Income Families

The second negative consequence of the neighborhood school relates to the importance of classroom stability. In order to receive an education, the child must stay in one classroom long enough to establish the needed relationship with one teacher. The importance of this fact is indicated by recent proposals for having children stay with one teacher for the first three grades.[21] But the lower-income family is very mobile, with the result that each time the family moves, the child must change schools. Professor Sexton's study revealed that in Detroit, among children from families with incomes below $5,000, 49 percent either entered or left a school during one semester. In contrast, among children from families with incomes over $9,000, only 17 percent entered or left a school during one semester.[22] Clearly, for children from mobile families the neighborhood school is not a help, it is a hindrance. Such children would be much better off if they were assigned to one school and guaranteed transportation to the school regardless of where their home was.

Residential Segregation Reinforced

A basic problem is that the neighborhood school is a segregated school. The segregated school reinforces and symbolizes residential segregation. It encourages feelings of inferiority and reinforces the low self-image of the culturally deprived child. It is a symbol of society's rejection of the Negro and the lower classes.[23]

---

[20]Sexton, *op. cit.*, p. 16.
[21]*Ibid.*, p. 269.
[22]*Ibid.*, p. 96.
[23]Kenneth B. Clark, *Prejudice and Your Child*, 2nd ed., Beacon Press, Boston, 1963.

Culture Patterns Reinforced

The segregated neighborhood school surrounds the lower-income child with people who have the same problems he has. There are few good examples from which he can learn and gain motivation. He is surrounded by peers who have difficulty reading, who do not look forward to vocational rewards, and who do not have manners and social graces.[24]

Lack of Community Resources

The segregated Negro community and lower-class communities in general do not have the resources to help their schools as do the white middle-class communities. Crushed by the experience of slavery and the past hundred years of prejudice and segregation and southern deprivation, the Negro community does not have the strength of other *immigrant* groups. It lacks the money, the training, the social and political organization.[25]

Environment of Schools

Most books on school planning describe the sort of pleasant environment in which a school should be located. Yet to have a neighborhood school in a lower-income area frequently means to locate a school in an unpleasant environment of dirt, heavy traffic, mixed land uses, and social diseases. This environment is one of the factors that drive good teachers away from such schools.

Alternatives to the Neighborhood School

I believe that the implication of the above analysis is that the neighborhood school is not sacrosanct and that attempts to alter this pattern of school organization cannot be dismissed simply by waving the flag of the neighborhood school idea. Alternative forms of school organization aimed at achieving integration or aimed at achieving better schools must be considered on their merits. What are some alternative forms of school organization?

Larger Neighborhoods

Definition of "neighborhood" as a larger area would retain many of the values of the neighborhood school while, in some specific situations, ameliorating some of the negative consequences. If we simply change our standards for neighborhoods by enlarging schools and increasing walking distances, we can in some situations create integrated neighborhood schools. Rather than design neighborhoods to fit school standards, land planners under this alternative would design neighborhoods to which educators would fit schools.

Educational Parks

The school village or educational park consists of several schools located on one large campus. The idea was originally proposed for New Orleans.[26] Because of the

---

[24]*Education and The Disadvantaged American*, Educational Policies Commission of the National Education Association of the United States, Washington, 1962, p. 31.

[25]Glazer and Moynihan, *op. cit.*

[26]*Planning 1963*, American Society of Planning Officials.

extremely high value of land in the slum areas of New Orleans, it was estimated that construction of schools on cheap suburban land would cost less even with the added cost of busing than would construction on expensive slum land. The idea was not adopted and it is sad to report that New Orleans recently purchased an expensive three-acre site for a junior high school in the slum area. A three-acre site for a junior high is very small by most standards. Can it be seriously argued that this substandard neighborhood school is better than an adequate school outside the neighborhood? The school village, as well as other plans that call for schools to have larger service areas, would help eliminate difficult planning problems that result from trying to estimate population growth for small areas, from the difficulty of keeping neighborhood schools in areas where there is growth, and from the problem of peak enrollments.

The Princeton Plan

Under this plan, two or more schools are treated as one. If there are two schools, all of the children from the enlarged service area go to one school for the first three grades and to the second school for grades four, five, and six. Theoretically, the plan can involve the combination of as many schools as there are grades. As with other plans that create larger schools, the Princeton Plan has educational advantages in that it enables the use of team teaching, specialized teachers, and other devices that require a larger student body.

Open Enrollment

Such plans generally permit Negro children to transfer out of a segregated school to an integrated school which is underutilized.

Abandonment of Slum Schools

Closing of slum schools that are old would promote integration and increase educational quality if the slum children were transported to new schools in white middle-class areas.

Larger School Districts

Redrawing service district boundaries, as in the California plan for county-wide school districts, and site selection procedures aimed at placing new schools in between segregated neighborhoods can achieve integrated schools where there are Negro or lower-income and white middle-class communities in close proximity.

City-wide Schools

As school districts become larger the development of specialized schools will be possible. However, specialized schools, such as the all-academic high school, can promote segregation if their specialty does not draw students from a variety of backgrounds.

Use of School Buses

The busing of children into other areas can accomplish integration. Planners should note that as more children are driven to school or come by public transportation, the criteria for a good school site may change to include a location near an arterial road or a transit line.

Adjunctive Schools

Boarding schools, day schools that hold children from breakfast through dinner, and special summer schools may be necessary for children from unstable families. These schools could be located in integrated areas as adjuncts of regular schools.

School Site Selection

Especially desirable sites might be used as school locations regardless of the location of the homes of the students. Thus schools might be located near transportation terminals, near parks and museum centers, or near industries which can provide vocational students with part-time jobs.

Sites and Population Growth

Schools can be located in areas where population growth is expected while initially serving older areas with declining populations of children who would be bused to the schools.

Transportation Plans

Imaginative transportation plans can also create alternatives to the neighborhood school. What would be the result of having children attend schools near the location of their fathers' jobs with the father driving the child to school and with special programs organized to keep the child until the end of the fathers' work day?

Other References

James Bryant Conant, *Slums and Suburbs*, McGraw Hill Book Company, 1961.

Seymour Martin Lipset, *De Facto Segregation in Berkeley and the Common School Tradition*, (Mimeographed).

Zane Meckler, "De Facto Segregation in California," *California Teachers Association Journal*, January 1963.

American Public Health Association Committee on Hygiene and Housing, *Planning the Neighborhood*, Public Administration Service, Chicago, 1960.

"Race and the Schools," *Council for Civic Unity Newsletter*, October, 1962.

DE FACTO SEGREGATION: FACT OR ARTIFACT?

Meyer Weinberg, *founder and editor of* INTEGRATED EDUCATION *magazine, is associate professor of history and social sciences at Chicago City College. The following editorial appeared in an early issue of the magazine.*

There is something awesome and final about anything said to exist purely as the result of a fact. As well bemoan the wetness that accompanies rain. So, lately we are told, school segregation in northern and western cities is *de facto* segregation—an inescapable consequence of segregated housing patterns.

The logic, however, is suspect for all its neatness: In the South, school segregation has been a matter of law, *de jure*; in the North, a matter of social fact, *de facto*. About the former, we can do something—that is, pass a law or obtain a court

From *Integrated Education* **April 1963. Reprinted by permission of the author.**

decision. But about the latter, legal remedies are irrelevant. No one, let alone school boards or city councils, can be held responsible for righting a situation arising from an ineluctable fact.

But the entire distinction is most unhelpful.

True, so-called *de jure* segregation can be traced back to a statute or an ordinance. But every board of education is a by-law-acting and law-enacting body; it is an agent of the state and has taxing and other powers of a governing body. Its regulations have the force of law. A board of education decision to establish school boundary lines is *de jure*. The exclusion suffered by excluded children is no less real than if it arose out of a state statute or a municipal ordinance.

But, it may be objected, the board did not create the concentration of racial groups in certain geographical areas. Two things may be said in answer. First, while the board did not create the racial concentration, it chose to base attendance lines on that concentration; it need not have done so. Second, the racial concentration did not itself result from a natural and inevitable train of events but was created by deliberate action. The resulting population pattern was not the only conceivable one.

In what sense was the racial housing concentration created by deliberation? Or, was it simply an impersonal, unplanned outcome of vast population movements?

The first large-scale Negro migration to the North occurred during World War I. In northern cities, the migrants often resided in compact areas but many Negroes also lived among whites. In Chicago, a movement arose among real estate interests to restrict the Negroes' freedom of residence. In 1917, Chicago real estate men discussed the advisability of a municipal zoning ordinance that would create a legal Negro district. In that same year, however, the U.S. supreme court rejected just such an ordinance that had been enacted in Louisville, Kentucky (*Buchanan* v. *Warley*, 245 U.S. 60). The court declared racial zoning ordinances to be a denial of due process under the Fourteenth Amendment. The Chicago effort having become impractical, another means was used to accomplish the same end.

In 1917, the Chicago Real Estate Board appointed a committee to examine the matter. The committee proposed "the block method" of Negro housing: "Inasmuch as more territory must be provided [for Negro migrants], it is desired in the interest of all, that each block shall be filled solidly and that further expansion shall be confined to contiguous blocks, and that *the present method of obtaining a single building in scattered blocks,* be discontinued." (Italics added.) This report was adopted. Several months later, the real estate board resolved to "start a propaganda [campaign] through its individual members to recommend owners societies in every white block for the purpose of mutual defense."[1] Note that while segregation was asserted to be "in the interest of all," whites were called upon to organize for self-defense.

When the new real estate policies were adopted, as Harold Baron pointed out in the January, 1963, issue of *Integrated Education,* "between one third and one half of the Negro children attended integrated schools." The new policies sharply reduced the extent of interracial living in Chicago. They also, by the same token, increased the extent of *de facto* segregation in the schools. This *de facto* segregation was anything but fortuitous or innocent of design. Did the board of education object?

---

[1] Quoted in Rose Helper, "The Racial Practices of Real Estate Institutions in Selected Areas of Chicago," unpublished Ph.D. dissertation, University of Chicago, 1958, pp. 2, and 587-588.

The board of education is usually well supplied with members who are intimately aware of housing patterns in Chicago. Real estate men, construction executives, building-trades union officials, and bank executives have sat and still sit—on the board of education. After 1917, these same individuals must have been familiar with the real estate board's segregative policies. As members of the board of education, they can be presumed to have understood the connection between those policies and the rise of segregation in the school system. It is also reasonable to guess that they welcomed the opportunity to cast a vote on the board of education to support the consequences of the policy of the real estate board.

The supreme court's intention in the 1917 Buchanan ruling was evaded by effective informal arrangements initiated by real estate interests. School integration, not then a concern of the court, suffered.

In 1954, the court struck down—or thought it did—school segregation on racial grounds. Legal, or *de jure,* segregation seemed a certain casualty. But in many places, community forces were able to perpetuate much the same situation that had existed prior to 1954.

More than a year after the supreme court's Brown ruling, on June 1, 1955, the St. Louis County Real Estate Board sent a letter to all its active members. The letter included the following announcement: "Our Board of Directors wishes to call to your attention, our rule, that no Member of our Board, may, directly or indirectly, sell to Negroes, or be a party to a sale to Negroes, or finance property for sale to or purchase by Negroes, in any block, unless there are three separate and distinct buildings in such block already occupied by Negroes."[2]

The St. Louis case is complex. Since 1954, when desegregation occurred, *de facto* segregation—or "resegregation"—has increased. Yet, to account for resegregation of the St. Louis schools, one must also consider the segregative policy of the St. Louis County Real Estate Board. Once it has been considered, little remains of the concept of *de facto* segregation as fortuitous segregation.

Northern, as well as southern, school segregation results from conscious decisions. As Wilson Record has pointed out, boards of education "are political entities through which power groups in the community express their interests and preferences."[3] The real estate interest is one of the central power groups in board of education decisions. Boards buy much land and they often have a lot of it to sell; regular commercial channels are used. The material interest of real estate groups is protected by enforcing the racial composition of neighborhoods. The neighborhood school policy helps assure an orderly and high-priced real-estate market.

Both *de facto* and *de jure* segregation are the results of conscious human decision. But the harmful myth to the contrary continues to be believed. In 1959, Kenneth B. Clark warned about the practical menace of the *de facto* argument:

If northern communities are able to preserve segregated schools, with their inequities and inherent damage, by administrative action, neglect, and indifference, merely because they have no laws which stipulate that this should be done, then southern communities may follow this

---

[2]Quoted in Helper, *op. cit.,* p. 606.
[3]"School Board and Negro Teacher in California," *Integrated Education,* April 1963.

example as an effective way of evading the letter and spirit of the May 17th decision of the United States Supreme Court. If this loophole is not removed, then that historic decision would be made hollow.[4]

Clark's apprehension has proved to be well-founded. The northern example *is* being followed.

In the summer of 1960, the segregation movement in Georgia was at the crossroads. A federal court order to desegregate Atlanta schools was to become effective by May, 1961. Other federal court suits threatened to overturn the state's legally segregated school system. In July, 1960, the president of the Georgia Bar Association advocated the repeal of all compulsory school segregation laws. He had not come to favor the abolition of segregation. Instead, as he explained, "where a state by its solemn statutes admits and even brags that enforced segregation is being practiced there is nothing left for the [federal] court to decide and a blanket injunction follows automatically."[5] On the other hand, he noted, where, as in North Carolina and Alabama, there were no state segregation laws, individual Negro children had to prove their ability to pursue studies in a white school (*de facto* white, of course).

The strategy worked. In February, 1961, the governor of Georgia asked for the repeal of virtually all his state's school segregation laws. This was done promptly after he explained the purpose of his request. Since then, Georgia has managed to practice "tokenism." Where segregation is enforced by law there cannot be tokenism; no children of different races may attend the same school. But in the absence of compulsory segregation laws, it becomes possible for a school system to qualify as desegregating, no matter how few children are involved. By July, 1962, the desegregated Atlanta school system had 57,000 white students and 48,500 Negro students. Only 48 Negro students were in schools with white students.

We may expect to read in days to come of how the South is "plagued" with *de facto* segregation. It will be a stratagem. At the same time, housing segregation is growing fastest in southern cities, thus supplying the *de-facto*-ists the argument they have learned from their northern brethren. Professor Karl E. Taeuber, University of Wisconsin sociologist, in a paper read to the American Sociological Association 1962 annual meeting in Washington, D.C., found that in 1960, housing segregation was highest in southern cities while the North Central states had had that distinction in 1940.[6]

The South is learning to practice *de facto* segregation—using the example of the North—while the North is becoming devoted to separate but equal schools—using the example of the South. The historic decision of May 17, 1954, is being evaded on a national scale. Why haggle over words when, as Robert J. Havighurst has stated, only 15 percent of the country's Negro children attend integrated schools, North and

[4]Kenneth B. Clark, *Harlem Works for Better Schools*, Harlem Neighborhoods Association, New York, n.d., p. 12.
[5]*Southern School News*, July, 1960, p. 9.
[6]Karl E. Taeuber, "Negro Residential Segregation: Trends and Measurement," *Social Problems*, Summer 1964. See also Karl E. and Alwa F. Taeuber, *Negroes in Cities: Residential Segregation and Neighborhood Change* (Chicago: Aldine, 1965).

South?[7] Neither chance nor geography can account for this fact. Least of all can it be explained as *de facto* or as *de jure*. It is segregation, it harms every child's "heart and mind," and it must go.

THE ISSUES AT I.S. 201: A VIEW FROM THE PARENTS' COMMITTEE

Dorothy S. Jones *is associate for public education of the Office of Church and Race, Protestant Council of the City of New York. This article is the text of two memoranda, dated September 19, 1966, and October 4, 1966, prepared by the author for the information of the Church and Race Secretariat of the Council.*

Memorandum of September 19, 1966

Despite the extensive press interest and coverage, the controversy around Intermediate School 201, the real story of the issues involved has not—in my opinion—been clearly expressed. I can perhaps do a better job than the public media.

In a sense the 201 story began four years ago when the site for the school was selected. Actually, however, the problem really began twelve years ago, in December, 1954, when the board of education first espoused the concept of an integrated education for the children of the city.

Since 1954, there have been many projects and programs planned to "increase the integration of the schools of the City of New York." In reality, segregated education has increased rapidly over the years. There are in 1966 not only many more segregated schools than there were in 1954, but the percentage of the total population of Negro and Puerto Rican children in the school system attending segregated schools has increased tremendously. The only real gain that has been made during these twelve years is that, thanks to rezoning, voluntary transfer under open enrollment, etc., almost all of the previously all-white schools in the city have a token number of Negro and Puerto Rican students.

During the same period, the equality of education offered to Negro and Puerto Rican children, as reflected in the achievement of these children, has deteriorated. For example, at the time of the February, 1964, school boycott,* some 50 percent of children attending elementary schools in the central Harlem area were reading two to five years below grade level. This fact was one of the causes of the boycott. Today, despite corrective-reading teachers, crash remedial programs, and all the other things that have been done, nearly 85 percent of the children attending elementary schools in the Central Harlem area are reading two to five years below grade level.

---

[7]Robert J. Havighurst, "Social Urban Renewal and the Schools," *Integrated Education*, April 1963, p. 4.

From *Integrated Education,* **October/November 1966. Reprinted by permission of the author.**

*[Editor's Note: On February 3, 1964, the Citywide Committee for Integrated Schools conducted a boycott which resulted in the absence of 464,362 pupils and 3,537 teachers. Led by Rev. Milton A. Galamison, the boycott was directed against what was regarded by civil rights leaders as an excessively slow, vague, and unimaginative school integration plan.]

It is against this background that we must view the situation at 201. In 1962, the board of education decided that there was need for new junior high schools to serve the children in the overcrowded junior high schools of Harlem and East Harlem. The site selected was Park Avenue between 127th and 128th Streets. Selection of the site created great controversy. Integrationists objected because the site would be extremely difficult to integrate—since there was little likelihood that white pupils would be attracted to this area so deep into the ghetto community. Others not concerned with integration still objected to the site: It is adjacent to the New York Central Railroad tracks and surrounded by depressing tenements and store fronts. The board of education promised that one of their most creative architects would be hired to design a building that would be modern and satisfactory, and they guaranteed that the school would be integrated. A year ago it was announced that the school would open in the spring. The building is indeed unique. The second story of the building extends out over the street on concrete pillars providing a covered arcade, with the ground floor set back from the street providing a windowed lobby. Above the lobby there are no windows (eliminating the dreary view from inside, the noise from the railroad, and the problem of vandalism in broken windows), and the building is completely air-conditioned. The architect has already won an award for his design. (Many parents in the community are unimpressed by the design of the building, and unimpressed by the fact that it cost more than five million dollars—the most expensive school in the city. There are already complaints and rumors that with no windows the lighting will not be adequate, the children will all suffer from eyestrain, that air-conditioning all the time is unhealthy, that problems will arise if the air-conditioner fails, etc., etc., etc.)

Last fall a committee of parents whose children would expect to attend the school asked the board of education to describe for them the plans that had been made for integrating the school and the plans for the program. They were assured that the school would be integrated but no details were provided; they were assured that there would be a high-quality educational program, but again no details. Parents who had had experience with Junior High Schools 139 and 133 in Central Harlem, Junior High School 117 and others in East Harlem were reluctant to accept the vague promises of excellence and of integration. The pressed for details. By the beginning of 1966, they finally got an answer on integration: The school would have 50 percent Negro children and 50 percent Puerto Rican children! As they pressed for details of the educational program they were informed that the school would have exciting programs, art programs, the most modern shops in the city, and that the children would learn typing. Parents were concerned about reading, math, social studies, and science. They were not satisfied with the answers.

Opening of the school was set for April 1. A demonstration by parents and community leaders outside the building "persuaded" the board of education to postpone the opening of the school. It was postponed to May 1 and then to June 1; then a summer program was announced and cancelled; finally, we approached the official opening of school—September 12.

During the spring and summer, the now fairly structured, though still informal, committee of parents and community leaders concerned about the school grew weary of fruitless meetings with the school system personnel. They appealed to Mayor John Lindsay and to the State Commissioner of Education James Allen, and were not satisfied with any of the responses. I had been involved in the early controversy about the site, and this summer, at the request of some of the parents, I again began to work with them. In August, I accompanied a delegation to Washington to meet with the United States Commissioner of Education, Harold Howe, II. We spent an hour and a half with him, explaining the entire situation, received his assurance of understanding and his pledge to do whatever was in his power to help in the resolution. He pointed out that he had no direct authority in this instance.

The parents' demand, oversimplified by the press to "either bus in white children or give us total control," are terribly complex. They have said to the board of education: We recognize, that though your policy is quality integrated education, you cannot deliver. Therefore, we know we will have a segregated school. In that case we want a segregated school that will deliver quality education, the kind that will assure our children the opportunity to advance in the world. Given the problems of teacher-attitudes, bureaucracy, and all of the failure to achieve proper education in other schools in the community, the only way we can see of achieving this goal is for the parents and community to have a real role in the selection of staff, the determination of program, and the evaluation of the education in the school. Preston Wilcox, who was then teaching at the Columbia University School of Social Work, helped develop this concept of "accountability" in a paper written some months ago.*

Though these demands had been put before the board of education consistently for at least six months, it was not until the week before school opened that the school system began to discuss them in earnest. They simply did not take them seriously prior to that time.

The agreement not to open the school on regular opening day was crucial to the achievement of what the parents were seeking. By the Friday before school was to open, Lloyd Garrison, president of the board of education, and Bernard Donovan, superintendent of schools, had agreed to the concept of a community council (though they still saw it at that time as purely advisory) but could not understand that, to be truly effective, such a council must begin with the opening of the school. Since they had failed to negotiate seriously until the eleventh hour, it was literally impossible to reach an agreement in time for September 12. The events of the next few days are well known to anyone who has read any New York newspaper, or listened to almost any radio or TV newscast, so I shall not repeat them.

On Monday morning, representatives of the 201 parents-to-be, parents of the elementary schools feeding 201, as well as representatives of those community organizations that had been involved in the controversy elected ten negotiators, two advisors, and thirteen observers to sit with the board of education in the negotiations. Chairman of the negotiating team is Mrs. Helen Testamark, president of the Parents Council of that school district (the Parents Council consists of representatives of the parents of each school in the area); other negotiators include several representatives of local organizations including the Harlem CORE chapter, the United Block Associations in East Harlem, and the Community Association of the East Harlem Triangle. Representatives of other organizations, *now* interested in I.S. 201, have asked for

---

*[Editor's Note: See Preston Wilcox, "One View and One Proposal," *Urban Review*, July 1966.]

seats as observers. Parents have consistently denied such requests, though they have invited everyone to participate in the community-wide reporting sessions held every evening. It is at these sessions that the final decision to accept or reject the settlement will be made. The negotiating team itself is pledged to make no decisions without first consulting parents and community.

Though we are pledged not to reveal the details of the negotiation until we have reached some agreements, I think I am free to report that we are getting a far more positive reaction from the superintendent of schools than anyone at the table had anticipated. The concept of the community council working jointly with the school staff and having what amounts to veto power in the selection of school personnel with the right to participate in the formulating of programs and evaluation of these programs, is what is evolving. Though we have been negotiating with the superintendent, at our request, one or more board members sit in each session. To date, four of the nine members of the board have sat in at least one session (several of them, more than one), so that the board members not only receive their reports from the superintendent, but also have an opportunity to observe at first hand the seriousness with which the parents are approaching what is actually a most revolutionary concept.

This week the children who would have attended Intermediate School 201 have been crowded into the elementary schools from which they had come, under very confusing and disturbing circumstances. It was agreed today, that as of Monday all the children assigned to 201 along with all of the staff assigned to 201, will temporarily hold classes in P.S. 103, at Madison Avenue and 119th Street, a school that has been closed but still has its furniture in it.

This represents a real victory for the parents, because—though the board of education has refused to say that the school will be kept closed indefinitely—there is obviously no intention of bringing youngsters into 201 next week. This means there is a real possibility of concluding successful negotiation without pressures of feeling they are keeping the children from being educated, and have the community council ready to function when the school opens properly.

Memorandum of October 4, 1966

My first report ended on an optimistic note, looking forward to agreement and solution of the controversy. Superintendent of Schools Bernard E. Donovan had presented to the parents a set of proposals which were discussed with the various groups and individuals in the community who were interested in the 201 situation, and which were agreed to at a meeting on Saturday, September 17.

The agreement was as follows:

> There would be established a community education council (details of this below), which would work with persons designated by the superintendent and board of education jointly on the question of Intermediate School 201 in the following areas.
>
> *Personnel*
>
> A. The parties would jointly establish the criteria for all posts in the school.
> B. Both parties would recommend individuals who would meet these qualifications; with the proviso that if either party had serious objection to an individual proposed by the other, that individual would not be appointed.

Program

A. The parties would jointly define and spell out a proper program for I.S. 201, and
B. Would jointly see to the carrying out of this program.

Fiscal

Parties would jointly explore possibilities of contracting to community agencies certain aspects of the program of the school.

Evaluation

The parties would jointly set up an evaluative procedure for the school, working toward a periodic evaluation of the program of the school.

The Community Education Council would have been composed of representatives elected by the parents of I.S. 201, and its feeder elementary schools, representatives of community organizations selected by the parents and a few nonschool-system professionals selected by all the others. It would have sought a foundation grant to hire a full-time administrator, plus clerical staff, to coordinate the day-to-day activity of the council, and to act as liaison with the personnel appointed by the school system as its liaison.

As of the end of the meeting on Saturday, all that remained for the negotiators to settle in order that the school could be open and functioning was the question of the principal. There was agreement between Dr. Donovan and the members of the negotiation team that there would be no attempt at present to change any of the other personnel of the school. However—for all the reasons spelled out in my first report—there was strong feeling on the part of the parent and community representation negotiators that a new image in the person of the principal must be established. Having in mind the state and city anti-discrimination laws, Dr. Donovan could not, of course, pledge to appoint a Negro or a Puerto Rican. It was agreed that the appointment would be of a "mutually agreed upon person." There was tacit acceptance of the fact that only a Negro or a Puerto Rican would be a "mutually agreed upon person."

I reported previously that it had been agreed that temporarily the children would gather at old P.S. 103 in order that they could have a better temporary program than had been available in the elementary schools from which they had come. This would be for no more than three days, while negotiations hopefully would be brought to a successful conclusion. No one anticipated any difficulty at this point. The announcement that the 201 teachers would refuse to go into P.S. 103 came as a shock. In an attempt to head off this teacher action, I was able to reach some of the union leadership by telephone that day. Though some of the leadership was sympathetic, it developed that it was impossible to stop the action. Had there been time actually to sit down with the teachers at that point, I think we might have developed a better rapport and understanding.

In any case, on Monday morning, many of the children reported to P.S 103—most of the teachers did not. The district superintendent was able to send enough people into 103 to maintain order during the day. Dr. Donovan was expected to telephone Mrs. Edwards, a representative of the committee, to give her a list of names from which the new principal might be chosen. Meanwhile, the parents and community representatives were also preparing to submit names. Hopefully, one of these names would be agreed upon at the one o'clock session. The total agreement then could be ratified and announced.

Unfortunately, things did not work out quite that way. Dr. Donovan telephoned shortly before 11:00 A.M. to tell Mrs. Edwards that he would like to meet immediately with the members of the negotiating team. She was able to assemble us in her living room in less than an hour, and Dr. Donovan arrived to announce that the board of education wanted him to open 201 the following morning with Mr. Lisser still as principal. He said that the rest of the agreement could go through, but that Mr. Lisser had to remain as principal and the school had to open the next morning. The parents protested that while they, too, would be willing to have the school open the next morning, the appointment of a principal reflecting the right kind of image for the children, known to be in tune with the community, and able to work effectively with the Community Education Council was a necessary prerequisite to any agreement on the part of the parents to send the children back to school. Dr. Donovan asked that we take no action until after we had met with him at one o'clock. We agreed.

By this time, we learned that the 201 teaching staff was, at that moment, meeting at the school. We asked for and received permission to meet with them. The meeting was a good one in the sense that, for the first time, I think, the parents and the teachers began to understand one another. The representatives of the negotiating team assured the teachers that they had no quarrel with them, were not anxious to fight them, and explained that the move of the teachers to oppose 103 came as a shock and was difficult to understand. The teachers in turn explained that (1) they had not realized that the parents had requested that 103 be used; and (2) they felt their move was in support of the parents. As one o'clock approached, we explained that we had to go upstairs to meet with Dr. Donovan and promised to return afterwards to continue the discussion with the teachers.

At the opening of the session with Dr. Donovan, he announced that Mr. Lisser had, "*of his own volition,* requested that he be reassigned elsewhere." This left the way open for the assignment of a principal who would be acceptable to the community as well as to the board of education. It was agreed that, since someone had to be in charge of the school when it opened the next day, Mrs. Beryl Bansfield, the ranking assistant principal assigned to the school—who happened also to be Negro—would be acting principal until such time as the negotiating team (acting in the stead of a Community Education Council until such a council could be formed) and the superintendent could agree on an acceptable person for the long-range appointment. The press was called in and Mrs. Testamark, speaking for the parents and community groups, and Dr. Donovan, speaking for the school system, faced the cameras and microphones and the newspaper reporters with their pads and announced the agreement. Mrs. Testamark pledged to bring her daughter to school the next morning—and everyone left happy. We went downstairs to wait for our opportunity to meet with the teachers. Dr. Donovan went into the teachers' meeting, as he had promised, to announce the decision. At that point, it being after four o'clock and I having had no lunch, I went to eat. I called a few people to announce the satisfactory solution of the controversy, then went home. When I arrived home, I turned on the radio and heard a news broadcast reporting that the teaching staff of 201 was urging the board of education not to honor Mr. Lisser's request for reassignment and pledging to boycott the school until he was reinstated. On Tuesday morning, September 20, we had a reversal of what had been the situation the previous week. This time, the *children* were in the school and the *teachers* were out, some picketing the school, some picketing board of education headquarters. Again the district superintendent was able to assign enough personnel from his staff to give sufficient supervision so that the children were in no danger. The parents and community organizations had decided in caucus the evening before *not* to organize a counter-demonstration to either of the teacher demonstrations because they still hoped to avoid a head-on collision with either the teachers in the school or the United Federation of Teachers, with whom at that point they felt they had no quarrel.

That same day, thirty white principals of Central Harlem schools went into a state of panic. They held a meeting from which no formal statement was issued, but from which leaked the rumor that they were going to resign in a body if Mr. Lisser were not reinstated. It seems that these principals feared that the demand for a Negro principal at I.S. 201 and the superintendent's acceptance of this concept meant that they were all likely to be faced with demands that they be replaced. Truth was that no one in their wildest imagining had any such notion. I.S. 201 was to be a pilot project, an experiment. There was no intention to try to change, overnight, the structure of schools in the rest of East and Central Harlem. In fact, it would have been impossible to do so even had anyone wished; the truth is that there are only a handful of Negroes currently eligible for appointment as principal and it will be several years before any of the recently appointed assistant principals would even be eligible to take the principal's examination.

About four o'clock Tuesday, just twenty-four hours after the original agreement was announced, the board of education (significantly, *not* the superintendent) announced that Mr. Lisser had requested that his initial request for reassignment be withdrawn. The board of education had agreed to honor this latest request and he and his teaching staff would all be back in I.S. 201 on Wednesday.

I had arranged earlier in the day with Al Shanker, United Federation of Teachers president, to address a meeting of the 201 staff at the Union's Park Avenue South headquarters at five o'clock. It was as I walked into the meeting room that I heard the news that the board of education had abrogated the agreement. Nonetheless, I had a very good meeting with the teachers—partly, I suppose, because I made no attempt to try to get them to change the position they held. Instead I gave them a thorough picture of the background of the controversy (very similar to my report above), explaining why it had become so important to the negotiating team that a new principal be appointed. Though we reached no agreement, we parted in a friendly manner, with the teachers requesting that whatever happened on Wednesday morning, I come back to talk to them again. I agreed.

On Wednesday, September 21, in the midst of the worst rain New York City has seen since 1903, there was a large and vocal picket line at I.S. 201. The newspapers have devoted many inches of space to what they described as a "take-over" of the fight by the "militant, nationalist, racist forces of the community." This is absolutely false. One of the groups so described, Harlem CORE, led by Roy Innes, had been on the negotiating team from the beginning. The other groups included SNCC, the much-maligned Black Panthers, and other nationalist groups, which, while not sitting at the negotiating table, had long before expressed their interest in and their support for what was happening. They had been standing ready to take whatever action was deemed necessary when called for. These groups, however much people outside Harlem may dislike and/or fear them, are a legitimate part of the Harlem scene. They are known to all of us, not as devils to be feared, but as human individuals whom we know, sometimes agree with, sometimes disagree with, but whose existence and function in the community we recognize. They had not been involved prior to this moment because these are ʿundamentally activist groups—not negotiators. So long as things were proceeding in a positive manner with a hope of solution through the negotiating process, there was no need for them to participate.

The breach of the agreement—and, especially, the way in which it was done—was the signal that now these groups had a role to play. (You will remember that Dr. Donovan came to the negotiating team Monday morning to tell us in person, prior to any public announcement, what the board ordered him to do. When, however, the board decided it would not honor the agreement the superintendent had made, we all heard it from the press. There was no attempt made on the part of the board to reach the members of the team even to give them advance notice of the adverse decision. This was interpreted by many people as an insult not just to the team but to the entire Harlem-East Harlem community.) It was natural, then, that all the activists were involved in that picket line. Though the press tried to project Stokely Carmichael as the "new spokesman" who had "taken over," Mr. Carmichael, every time he spoke to the press, reiterated the fact that he was *not* taking over, that he was simply there in support of the negotiating team. This was true of all the supporting groups—despite press reports to the contrary.

It was that same day that the other members of the team, disturbed and frustrated at the apparent impossibility of getting the true picture reflected in the public communications media, asked me to see if—working through the Protestant Council—I could do any better. With the permission of the Chairman of the Secretariat and the active support of Dr. Potter, arrangements were made for a press conference at 475 Riverside Drive the afternoon of Wednesday, September 21. Dr. Potter and I jointly signed a telegram to Mayor Lindsay urging him to "exert his personal leadership to bring the disputing parties in the I.S. 201 controversy together to seek a solution in the interest of the community and its children." This was released at the press conference. We had radio and TV, one of the wire services and several of the newspapers present. I made a serious attempt to really explain in depth the real issues involved. Considering the efforts that went into it, and the meager results, the press conference cannot be considered an unqualified success. The mayor did indeed intervene the next morning, though not quite in the way we had asked. Unfortunately, he stated his position in support of the princiapl and staff of the school without ever having listened to the community's position. However, he *did* criticize the board of education's inept handling of the entire controversy, and has since been helpful in trying to reach a solution.

On Monday, September 26, I attended a meeting, called by the Rev. J. J. Hicks of St. Mark's Methodist Church at his church, of the Advisory Board of the Harlem Upper Manhattan Church Association. Several members of the negotiating team were present and presented their story. The clergy in attendance were happy to get the real story of 201 and pledged support. They are working on a public statement and are expected to be helpful.

It was at this point that I, personally, almost ceased to function in the controversy for a week. The combination of not enough sleep and too much rain and picketing put me in bed with a nasty cold, restricting my activities to the telephone. It was during this week that several of the leaders of the Negro community who had not been heard from previously began to be involved in an attempt to reach a solution. Percy Sutton, newly elected Borough President of Manhattan, called a meeting at which he, Democratic Leader J. Raymond Jones, Dr. Kenneth Clark, and the members of the negotiating team began to discuss the possibility of an alternative proposal to resolve the impasse. This group met three times and worked out a new proposal, which has now been made public.

It would provide that a board composed of four university representatives from one or two universities in the area, four representatives of parents' and community groups, and one person selected by the other eight would constitute a nine-member operations board for I.S. 201. The school system would contract with that board to run 201 and its feeder elementary schools. Dr. Clark told us at a meeting this evening that the new proposal now has the support not only of the people who were party to drawing it up, but also of Mayor Lindsay, of State Commissioner of Education James Allen, of the Committee on Integration of the Board of Regents (the committee of which Dr. Clark is a member), and *The New York Times*—as indicated by their supporting editorial October 4. This changes the picture considerably. For the first time, now individuals and institutions with power in the city are supporting the concept of parent and community involvement in their local school. Previously the only two groups outside of Harlem endorsing the group's goals had been the Protestant Council and EQUAL (a prointegration citywide organization composed mostly of white parents).

To date, the board of education has not commented on the proposal. They will meet in closed session Wednesday, October 5, to discuss the new proposal. It is difficult to say exactly what the board reaction will be or exactly when they will make it clear.

At this moment, all of the persons concerned about 201 are attempting to collect as many signatures as possible on petitions indicating support during the next forty-eight hours. It is planned that there will be a massive demonstration outside board of education headquarters at 110 Livingston Street at ten o'clock Friday, October 7, at which time a delegation will go into the building and present Lloyd Garrison, president of the board, the signatures that will have been collected by them.

[Editor's Note: During 1967, a number of significant consequences flowed from the above events. In April, the New York school board enlarged the advisory powers of local school boards and increased the amount of local funds under control of district superintendents. In May, seven demonstration projects were authorized whereby parents and staff, with the aid of a university, were to have a large voice in operating their schools, including the employment of principals. In November, the Mayor's Advisory Panel on Decentralization of the New York City Schools recommended near-total decentralization into thirty to sixty community school districts, with each district to be headed by an eleven-person board, a majority of whom would be elected parents.]

References

Bernard Bard, "The Strike That Almost Was," *The Post* (N.Y.), September 24, 1966; reprinted in *United Teacher*, October 7, 1966.

Robert A. Dentler, "In Reply to Preston Wilcox," *Urban Review*, July, 1966.

Sandra Feldman, "I.S. 201—Crisis in Ghetto Schools," *New America*, September 30, 1966.

Rasa Gustaitis, "The Angry Parents of I.S. 201," *Reporter,* November 17, 1966.

"I.S. 201" *New Yorker,* October 1, 1966.

Andrew Kopkind, "Down the Down Staircase. Parents, Teachers, and Public Authorities," *New Republic,* October 22, 1966.

William A. Price, "Harlem School Clash: New View of Integration," *National Guardian,* October 15, 1966.

Albert Shanker, "An Open Letter on 201," *United Teacher,* September, 1966, special edition.

Preston Wilcox, "One View and a Proposal," *Urban Review,* July, 1966. [Written in April, 1966.]

RESPONSE BY THE SCHOOL BOARD

On October 19, 1966, the New York City board of education released the following statement.

I. Background

As far back as 1950 the board declared that:

The education of children will be at its maximum when school, home, and community work together for common objectives—hence the constant need for maximum teamwork among school staffs, parents, and all other forces in the community interested in a better program of education.

Over the years, the board has held to this conviction and has acted on it. The board has encouraged, and collaborated with, parents' associations and volunteer programs. Special board committees have worked with community groups. In setting up the new and strengthened local school boards, the board has provided that their membership be screened by district panels composed one half of parent association representatives and one half of community organization representatives selected by the parents. Universities and colleges have also been involved through special programs sponsored by them in ninety-one schools.

But in disadvantaged areas these and other steps have not brought about enough of the sought-for educational improvement. This state of affairs is the underlying source of the controversy over the administration of I.S. 201. The controversy should not be regarded as an isolated dispute over a single school. The school itself is operating normally. The equipment is the newest and finest in our system; the faculty is integrated and devoted to the school and the principal; many parents appear to be pleased with the start that has been made. Yet discontent and the demand for community participation in the educational process continues. It symbolizes the conviction of many in the community that bold new steps must be taken to upgrade education in the *de facto* segregated schools, and that increased community participation is essential to this end.

Although the board of education in recent years has provided the schools in disadvantaged areas with smaller classes than in other schools, as well as more extensive remedial services, including after-school centers and various special pro-

From *Integrated Education,* October/November 1966.

grams, the fact remains that the degree of retardation in reading and arithmetic and the rate of dropouts in those schools far exceed those in other areas.

Some of the causes of this persistent educational lag are beyond the board's control; as for example, the excessive turnover in student enrollments in many schools, the harmful effect of massive overcrowding in run-down tenements, and the high unemployment among minority groups. The new Human Resources Administration should help greatly to coordinate and amplify the city's efforts to end the ravages of poverty and discrimination. The board has long urged such a step, and will do whatever it can to aid this broader long-term undertaking.

But because a generation of children may be lost, the board cannot wait for environmental changes to ease its task. In determining in which direction it should move, the board must face certain hard facts. In ghetto areas, where many parents are working, parent associations have generally been weak. In part this may have been due to lack of confidence that their demands would be listened to meaningfully, or that promised actions would be carried out. In areas where parent associations are strong, they have been able to serve as a stimulant and to influence and improve the course of school administration. In ghetto areas this educationally and socially useful spur has too often been lacking.

In these areas, distrust of the school system is prevalent. There are frequent charges that teachers lack belief in the educability and potential of the children, and that the children sense this and are damaged by it. There are frequent complaints about the relatively small number of experienced teachers in the disadvantaged areas, and the absence of all but a handful of Negro principals, whose positions would serve as living incentives to the students. These are problems with which the board is actually concerned. Unfortunately, wholesale and generalized public criticisms of teachers have done grave injustice to the many competent and dedicated professionals, both white and Negro, who are in these schools, and to principals who have won the devotion of students and parents alike. In many instances these criticisms have discouraged experienced teachers from remaining in these schools. Nevertheless, lack of confidence is widespread, and the board and the superintendent are under a heavy obligation to correct the weaknesses which undoubtedly exist.

II. Establishment of a City-Wide Task Force

To give the board the assistance it needs in this whole troubled field, the board will immediately appoint a task force composed of educators, public officials, and community leaders who are in the best position to help. It will be called the ' Task Force to Advance Education in Disadvantaged Areas." This is not to be a mere study group. The salient facts are known and can readily be assembled. Prompt answers to questions such as the following should be given.

What are the most practical and fruitful ways of involving parents, community leaders, and universities in the educational process? What different types of plans might be considered? In developing them, what part should be played by district superintendents, local school boards, and parents' associations? Should additional powers be vested in them? What are the overall implications for decentralization? Apart from the greater involvement of these several elements in the work of the schools, what other forward steps can be taken which have not yet been thought of, or have insufficiently been utilized? What would the cost of such steps be? How and when and how fast should they be instituted?

With regard to each of the above areas, what bearing would the answers have on the improvement of education in all schools? For, as we take emergency action with regard to the children in ghetto areas because of their extreme handicaps, it must never be forgotten that there is owing to every child in this city the finest education that is possible. Moreover, the education we provide should, wherever feasible, be in integrated schools so that children of different origins may best be prepared to learn from one another, and to understand and play a useful part in a pluralistic multiracial world. Because of geographical obstacles, many elementary and middle schools in minority group areas may not feasibly be integrated; this places a special obligation on the board to lift their level of performance so that their students may successfully move on into the high schools, now already integrated, and into college, and compete on even terms with children from other neighborhoods.

As noted above, the board recognizes the lack of an adequate number of teachers, principals, and other supervisors from minority groups, and the insufficient supply of experienced teachers in deprived areas. These are longstanding and complex problems toward whose solution the board has been pressing. Some advances have been made during the past year or so, but much remains to be done, and in this connection the board will seek the advice and assistance of the task force.

For service on the task force, the board will invite representatives of the Human Resources Administration, the mayor's office, the civil rights leadership, parents and community organizations, and universities, together with representatives of the United Federation of Teachers, the Council of Supervisory Associations, and the local school boards.

The state commissioner of education has pledged his cooperation in the work of the task force, and will designate a consultant to serve with it. The board will invite the participation as consultants of several nationally known educators, and the service of an outstanding chairman. In order that the task force may be an effective working group, its total membership will not exceed twenty. The board expects to obtain foundation assistance to defray the expenses of the task force, and of the I.S. 201 board described in Part III below.

The board will shortly announce the full makeup of the task force and will convene it promptly thereafter. The task force will be asked to make an interim report within thirty days, and a full report, with specific recommendations for action, within ninety days. The board will ask the task force to continue for the purpose of aiding and evaluating particular programs which the board may institute.

III. I.S. 201

Since the opening of I.S. 201, the board has held a long series of consultations and meetings with various interested groups and individuals, whose assistance has been much appreciated. These have included the state commissioner of education and representatives of the Human Resources Administration and the mayor's office; the borough president; the chairman of the local school board; and persons representing Columbia University, the University of the City of New York, the teaching and supervisory staff, and a number of civic organizations concerned with public education. The board has had the benefit of specific proposals made by representatives of the United Federation of Teachers, the Council of Supervisory Associations, and other staff members; by representatives of the NAACP; and by Dr. Kenneth Clark on behalf of the negotiating committee for I.S. 201, consisting of a group of persons from the area involved who are affiliated with a number of community organizations. The board met with Dr. Clark, and later with the committee; and it has given to their plan prolonged consideration.

The board believes with them that a special local group should be established to concern itself with I.S. 201 and its three feeder schools (P.S. 24, P.S. 68, P.S. 39), as a new and significant step forward in the search for ways and means of upgrading education in ghetto areas. This group will be referred to below as the "201 Board." The board of education has unanimously concluded that the 201 Board, in its functions and composition, should be based on the following principles:

1. The 201 Board will have authority in an advisory capacity to develop and submit to the superintendent and the board of education for appropriate action a broad range of programs for I.S. 201 and the feeder schools. These programs are discussed below.

2. Parents and community representatives should constitute the majority of the 201 Board. In order to promote an effective interchange of knowledge and experience, appropriate teacher and supervisory representation should be involved in the shaping of its programs.

3. The parents and community representatives should be democratically chosen. Parents, for example, could be elected by the parents in each school. Community representatives could be chosen by delegates elected by citizens in the area, along the line of the elections which have been successfully held for neighborhood boards under the antipoverty program. Community leadership should determine the exact process. The board of education stands ready to lend its facilities and give such other help as may be requested.

4. With the board of education's assistance, the 201 Board should arrange with a university or universities of its own choice for professional services to be rendered to the 201 Board in aid of its various functions. The board of education believes that it would be more appropriate, and produce better educational results, for universities to render these services to the 201 Board, than to have voting membership on it.

The board of education regrets that, at its recent meeting with the negotiating committee for I.S. 201, those present were unwilling to discuss the above framework for a plan. The board hopes that consideration will be given to it in the light of what has been set forth in this statement, to which the board wishes to add the following points.

The program of the 201 Board may include: (1) specific goals, standards, and criteria for educational excellence; (2) educational curricula; (3) educational materials, including textbooks; (4) educational techniques and methods, and educational innovations; (5) methods of independently evaluating the performance of the children and the overall effectiveness and quality of the teaching and supervision in the respective schools; (6) development of a training program for closer rapport between the teachers and the community; (7) recognition of persons for employment as community teacher assistants, homework helpers, and guidance assistants; and (8) bringing to the attention of the superintendent and the board of education any facts they deem relevant regarding personnel, it being of course understood that competence and effectiveness of performance in the particular schools are the only criteria on which personnel decisions are to be reached and that these decisions must remain with the board of education.

These functions are in substance those set forth in Dr. Clark's plan, with the exception that the 201 Board cannot be given, as envisaged in that plan, control over the selection and transfer of personnel or authority to direct the work of the school. As a matter of sound educational practice, the board of education could not properly abdicate the responsibilities specifically laid upon it by the education laws; and the commissioner of education has provided the board at its request with a formal opinion of counsel to his department holding that the board cannot lawfully delegate these responsibilities to any other agency (including a university) outside its jurisdiction.

The fact that the 201 Board's functions must remain advisory should not impair its usefulness. The board of education will look to it for fresh ideas, for new and promising educational methods, and for frank evaluation of school performances; and no one will more eagerly hope for the success of its programs.

The city-wide task force will be asked to help the 201 Board with advice and information as requested, and keep in close touch with its operations.

Upon receipt of programs submitted by the 201 Board, the board of education and the superintendent will take action thereon within thirty days, after appropriate consultation with the local school board. The 201 Board and the school staffs will be expected to cooperate in implementing approved programs, and the 201 Board may bring to the attention of the board of education, for immediate action by the latter, any complaints that the programs are not being fully carried out.

The board of education is convinced that the bringing together of parent and community representatives with educators in a continuing service in a local organization, concentrating on the affairs of four related schools, with direct access to the board of education, should be productive of much good. Each group will learn from the other. Each will have a significant status in the affairs of the schools. Their combined views will bring to the board of education new insights into local needs, and fresh educational ideas. If on occasion their views should differ, either group may bring them to the superintendent and the board of education for reconciliation or final judgment. The reports of the 201 Board should have a wide influence, not only with the board of education, but with other concerned officials.

These hoped-for results have led the board of education not to limit its program at this time to I.S. 201. The board will ask the city-wide task force to bring about a parallel experiment or experiments elsewhere in the city, with features which would not necessarily be the same as those contemplated for I.S. 201. From such experimentation other approaches might be tried and stimulating interchanges might take place.

In conclusion, the board shares with the proponents of change in Harlem their aspirations for their children and their hopes for the improvement of the schools. It believes that the initiative which they have taken can bear good fruit if they will now work with us in a sustained effort to achieve the objectives we hold in common.*

---

*[See Editor's Note on p. 162 of this volume.]

BIBLIOGRAPHY FOR PART THREE

Barney, O. Pat, and Lurel D. Hall, "A Study in Discrimination," *Personnel and Guidance Journal* (March 1965).

Carter, Robert L. "De Facto School Segregation: An Examination of the Legal and Constitutional Questions Presented," *Western Reserve Law Review* (April 1965).

Clark, Kenneth B. *Dark Ghetto: An Analysis of the Dilemma of Social Power.* New York: Harper & Row, 1965.

Deutsch, Martin. "Aspects of Ability Grouping," *Integrated Education* (February-March, 1964).

Drinan, Robert F. "Direct Non-Violent Action and the Law," *Integrated Education* (August-September 1964).

Fiss, Owen M. "Racial Imbalance in the Public Schools: The Constitutional Concepts," *Harvard Law Review* (January 1965).

Foster, G. W., Jr. "Color Conscious, Color Blind," *Progressive* (March 1966).

Franseth, Jane, and Rose Koury. *Survey of Research on Grouping as Related to Pupil Learning.* Washington, D.C.: Government Printing Office, 1966.

Gillmor, George W., and Alan L. Gosule, "Duty to Integrate Public Schools? Some Judicial Responses and a Statute," *Boston University Law Review* (Winter 1966).

Greenberg, Jack. *Race Relations and American Law.* New York: Columbia University Press, 1959.

Hentoff, Nat. *The New Equality.* New York: Viking, 1964.

Horowitz, David. "Unseparate But Unequal—The Emerging Fourteenth Amendment Issue in Public Education," 13, *UCLA Law Review* (1966), 114.

Kaplan, John. "Equal Justice in an Unequal World: Equality for the Negro—The Problem of Special Treatment," *Northwestern University Law Review* (July-August 1966).

Kraft, Ivor. " 'Learning How to Learn': Myth or Reality?" *Journal of Negro Education* (Fall 1964).

Lieberman, Myron. "The Civil Rights Fiasco in Public Education," *Phi Delta Kappan* (May 1966).

McKissick, Floyd. "Is Integration Necessary?" *New Republic* (Dec. 3, 1966).

Meranto, Philip. *The Politics of Federal Aid to Education in 1965: A Study in Political Innovation.* Syracuse (N.Y.): Syracuse University Press, 1967.

Piven, Frances Fox, and Richard A. Cloward, "The Case Against Urban Desegregation," *Social Work* (January 1967).

Weinberg, Meyer. *Race and Place: A Legal History of the Neighborhood School.* Washington, D.C.: Government Printing Office, in press.

Part Four

Prospects for Change

The prospects for wholesale change toward greater equality of educational opportunity depend upon a complex of factors. These involve (1) reform within the educational profession itself, (2) changes in the curriculum, (3) innovative organizational change and the development of comprehensive planning techniques, (4) new legislation, and (5) broader judicial doctrines.

Professional reform.—Within the educational profession, the preparation of teachers to teach children in our urban milieu has become a matter of foremost concern. Basic to such preparation is a belief in the ability of all children to profit significantly from an adequate educational program. Another emphasis is upon the need for the teacher to understand the subculture of the student, characterized as it might be by its own language, customs, and life-outlook. Still another stress is upon searching out new techniques of remediation and initial presentation appropriate to children whose previous schooling has often been less than minimal.

Reforms in the training of new teachers are only a beginning. Most teachers, after all, are already on the job; and many of them will need additional training and re-orientation. School administrative personnel and school board members must contribute toward the expansion of educational opportunities. It is difficult to see how genuine changes can occur in the classroom without active and intelligent support from those in top-level administrative and policy-making positions.

Changes in curricula.—Few curricular changes have caught the imagination so much as the increasing attention being paid to the role of the Negro American in our country's history. Fundamental to this kind of change is critical examination of existing instructional materials to unearth traces of racism in the conventional presentation of American history. Less simple to deal with are emotional obstacles that stand in the teacher's way—his own prejudices. There remain, at best, numerous pedagogical problems arising from the integration of seemingly "special" topics such as Negro history into general American history, and we have available very little by way of adequate instructional materials in this area. But the subject makes headway, sometimes under pressure of law. In Michigan and Illinois, state laws require that it be taught. In California, the law penalizes publishers of textbooks who fail to present the subject truthfully.

Organizational change and planning.—Innovative organizational change is exemplified in the widely discussed device of educational parks. Such an installation is a centralized and articulated set of school buildings, embracing as much as kindergarten through junior college, capable of offering an extremely rich educational fare at great economies of scale arising out of consolidation of facilities. As many as 25,000 students might attend school in such a park area and, because the attendance district would necessarily be wide, a heterogeneous student body would be likely.

The educational park, however, cannot be an oasis in a desert of ineffective community life. The greater its contribution to the community and the greater the community's contribution to it, the greater its effectiveness. Preferably, educational parks should be regarded as indispensable ingredients in broader plans for community rehabilitation. Educational parks cannot, for example, create better housing or increase the long-run supply of jobs. But the educational task of the park will be more readily achieved in a context of decent housing and adequate jobs. The educational park must not be considered as a gimmick that will mechanically achieve its formal purpose regardless of the social context of its application.

Legislation.—Legislatures can as easily redefine goals as enforce existing ones. Thus far, no federal legislation has been passed that deals exclusively with school integration, although a few bills have been offered. Title IV and Title VI of the Civil Rights Act of 1964 dealt with schools. In 1965, Representative Adam Clayton Powell introduced a bill entitled "Integrated Education Act of 1965," which would have enacted a system of federal standards, incentives, and penalties; no hearings were held. Several federal laws have been amended so as to restrict the ability of federal agencies to direct the initiation of integration measures.

On the state level, a number of legislatures have enacted formal policy declarations on the educational desirability of racially balanced schools. The Massachusetts Act (see pp. 213-216) was the first legislation that went into financial incentives and penalties or behalf of integration. Many states, New York especially, have adopted statewide administrative policies against school segregation.

As between legislation and administrative policy, the federal government has thus far depended more on the latter. The U.S. Department of Health, Education, and Welfare, in administering Titles IV and VI of the Civil Rights Act, has succeeded in bringing about a very modest degree of desegregation in the southern states. Only recently has H.E.W. concerned itself with northern school segregation.

Judicial doctrine.—During 1954-1955, federal courts labeled separate schools unequal, but just as explicitly held that school boards had no affirmative responsibility to integrate; rather, they needed merely to dismantle the formally separated school systems. Ten years later, some federal appeals courts (especially the fifth circuit in New Orleans) reversed this view in ruling that the precise genesis of school segregation was not so important as the educational deprivation that separation always brought. Thus, one could conclude, so-called **de jure** and **de facto** segregation both must be remedied. Both judicial camps quoted the Brown decision against each other. Meanwhile, the U.S. supreme court declined to rule on the point at issue.

In state courts, almost without exception in the North and the West, judicial doctrines were adjusted to new socio-political realities. The highest courts of New York, New Jersey, Connecticut, and Massachusetts approved the principle that school boards could take race into account if they regarded it essential for educational reasons. The

New Jersey supreme court ruled, in fact, that desegregation must be applied not to single schools here and there but to an entire school system; racial imbalance was a property of a school system rather than of an imbalanced school.

TAKE UP THE CHALLENGE

Harry N. Rivlin *is dean of the School of Education, Fordham University. This article is based on an address to a workshop on "TEPS in Urban Areas," held on October 2-3, 1964, sponsored by the National Commission on Teacher Education and Professional Standards. NCTEPS is affiliated with the National Education Association.*

I am mindful of the four panelists who gave you many worthwhile ideas to take home. I would like to help you by mentioning several ideas to leave behind. One of them is the idea that we have so great a problem that we begin to feel sorry for ourselves. A psychiatrist does not complain because the only people he meets are those who cannot face the ordinary problems of daily living. A social worker has no right to complain if the only people he comes into contact with are those who cannot manage their own family affairs. And we educators have no right to complain if we are dealing with people who are not quite interested in what we would like them to be interested in. We have no right to complain because they are slow learners in school. As a matter of fact, we could wish that they were slow in learning other things, too. Unfortunately, they were selectively slow in their learning. Rather than a feeling of "Are we martyrs in a public cause?" we need to have the feeling that we are a unique profession in several respects. One is that we are the only profession expected to deal with everyone. No dentist is expected to fill a cavity if the person who has it does not come to his office. Not only that, but after the patient gets there, the most common sentence in a dentist's vocabulary is, "Keep your mouth open." We have to teach those who see the school as the avenue to get where they want to go, and we have to teach those who have no respect for anyone, not even themselves. Rather than feel sorry for ourselves, we should be stimulated by the tremendous opportunity we have to do what has to be done.

I would also like to leave behind a whole series of words: culturally handicapped, culturally deprived, educationally handicapped, inner-city children, and you can go right down the list. (If you are afraid of being overweight on the plane, you can drop fifteen pounds right there.) There is a temptation to try to solve the problem by creating a new stereotype. True, in the inner city you have children from impover-

From *Integrated Education,* **February/March 1965. Reprinted by permission of the author.**

ished homes, but you also have children from luxury apartments. There are children in these inner-city homes who get little sympathy or encouragement from their families; other children in these homes get as much affection as you possibly could hope for. Remember, too, that there are Anglo-Saxon middle-class families where there is no great love of learning. Instead of thinking in terms of a stereotype—that these inner-city children are a new breed that has suddenly appeared, a kind of biological sport or mutation—we must consider that we are dealing with youngsters who have varied characteristics and from whom we have to get whatever we can.

I would like to get away from the stereotype of the big city. The big city has slums; it also has luxury apartments. The term *culturally disadvantaged* can be applied just as well to a middle-class youngster who thinks that a newspaper has only a sports section and comics. That youngster is as culturally deprived as any other youngster who does not take advantage of what is before him.

Cultures are not necessarily better or worst. Rather than think of them as being arranged on a scale, let us think of them as being different. (If we were suddenly transported to Argentina, a convention of Argentinian educators might well wonder what to do about the culturally deprived Americans who do not speak Spanish.) What has made America great has been our ability to use a wide variety of cultural contributions from our heterogeneous population.

I would like to discard, too, the idea that urban education is just one tremendous problem. It is true that there are many incompetent teachers in New York, as we were told yesterday. There are many more incompetent teachers in New York than you would find in Oak Creek Canyon. But there are also many more competent teachers in New York than in Oak Creek Canyon. Simply because New York is big, it has more of everything. People in Oak Creek Canyon think they have a traffic jam when there are four cars on Main Street at the same time. New York or any other big city can show them what traffic jams are really like. While the cities have bigger problems because the cities are big, we sometimes forget that they also have tremendous opportunities. The families that moved from Alabama to Chicago took a giant step forward. They moved for the same reasons that people moved away from Ireland and Italy: to go where there were greater opportunities for themselves and for their children. These people are trying for a better life. From among the youngsters will come those who will later supply our pressing manpower needs. In short, though the cities have a problem, they also have an opportunity that we cannot afford to neglect.

While we are talking about the problem as a problem, I would like to refer to what Henry Steel Commager once said about the present method of teaching history. He said, "We teach history through problems, through crises, through headaches." He calls it the headache system of teaching history. It is true that we have had problems and crises, but that is not what made America what it is today. It was what happened as a result of the crises. It was the way in which the headache was relieved and because of what happened between headaches.

We hear, for example, of all the teachers who escape from the big cities as soon as they can, and we hear of all the young teachers who will not accept an appointment to a difficult city school if they can possibly help it. We forget, however, that there are thousands of teachers who are staying the big cities, not because they cannot escape, but because of the satisfactions of teaching youngsters who have so little to offer and who need so much. The same satisfactions just cannot be found in teaching a nice, comfortable, ambitious, middle-class child whose big problem is whether he will get into an Ivy League college or will have to go to one that is not quite Ivy League.

I did my elementary teaching in a school that was about 50 percent Negro, about 50 percent Italian, and about 50 percent almost every other ethnic group. I know it adds up to more than 100 percent, but we were terribly overcrowded. I once took a group of youngsters on a trip to the Museum of Natural History, and then I treated the class to a ride on the upper deck of a Fifth Avenue bus. It cost me about three and a half dollars. I challenge any teacher in Scarsdale, Winnetka, or any other prosperous suburban community to find anything he can do for three and a half dollars that would make that much of an impression on a group of youngsters. There is satisfaction in having one of these youngsters come up and tell you that the music you played was pretty good. There is satisfaction in seeing eyes light up. There is satisfaction in dealing with children where everything you accomplish is, as one of our students put it, pure velvet. While we talk about teachers who are fleeing the schools, may I remind you that one of the teachers here today travels fifteen miles a day in getting from her junior high school in Jamaica to her home in Manhattan, and she passes a great many middle-class schools on the way. While we talk about the problems of those who escape, let us think also of the achievements of the teachers who stay.

It is undoubtedly true that education in the big cities today is markedly different from what it was fifty years ago. Fifty years ago was 1914. And in the fifty years between 1914 and 1964, there has not been a single normal year. I think of a fellow who was making his first trip on the Twentieth Century from New York to Chicago because all planes were grounded by poor weather. When he boarded the train, he said to the porter,"This is the first time I'm taking this trip and I know you're supposed to tip the porter, but I really don't know how much. What is the average tip on this train?" The porter said, "Well, on this train the average tip is five dollars." The next morning when they arrived in Chicago, he gave the porter a five-dollar bill. The porter looked at it and said, "Thank you! That's the first average tip I've ever seen."

Now just look back to 1914. From 1914 to today we have had war years, hot-war years, cold-war years, inflation, depression, automation. As a result, there is a backlog of buildings to be erected, materials to be produced, and professional services to be supplied, and there has been no normal year in which to catch up. One thing of which we have had no shortage is shortcuts, and we are now paying the price for all kinds of shortcuts taken in the past fifty years.

If you look at the difference between our schools today and the schools fifty years ago, you find that we have immigrants. We also had immigrants fifty years ago, but the ones we have today are different. For one thing, they are largely American citizens. I refer to the Puerto Rican as an immigrant, because socially he is. He is moving from one culture to another. I refer to the Negroes who move from the South to the North, and to the whites who move from the South to the North, as immigrants because they, too, are moving from one culture to another. And I refer to our northern Negroes as immigrants because they are now escaping from a population eddy in which they have been trapped for a hundred years and are only now moving into the mainstream of American life.

Dealing with immigrants is not a new problem for urban schools, but these are different days. Fifty years ago we opened the school doors to everybody who wanted to come, and many immigrant youngsters did come. Some of them later became bankers, some became burglars, some became teachers; they went into all phases of American life. For those who did not want to stay in school there were working papers, and for those who had working papers there were jobs to fill. Today we keep everybody in school longer, and those who leave school find that there are few jobs for the unprepared, the unskilled, the unschooled.

To me the biggest difference between the schools of a hundred years ago or fifty years ago and today is that today education is in politics; and the question, for example, of whether or not you bus children is not an educational problem, it is now a political problem. We have to learn how to deal with education as a political issue and how to deal with politics when politics enters education.

As you look at education in our urban centers, there is a great deal that can be done and a great deal that is being done. Let me give you just one illustration of what is being done by superintendents. About two weeks ago, I went to Milwaukee. And with Martin Haberman, who is here, I visited two of the Milwaukee schools to see their Reception Centers in operation. A Reception Center is a special class to which newly arrived children are referred if it appears that they will not get along well in a regular class. After all, a youngster who came from the sixth grade in one of the small schools in the South may not be ready to continue in the sixth grade in Milwaukee. He is referred to a special teacher who works with him until he is ready to go into the regular class. While in Milwaukee, I heard a story that I have not heard anywhere else about any other school in America. A youngster in one of those schools ran away from home. He was away from home for three days, but he was in school every morning. These were the youngsters who came to school before the teacher did. When a summer program was opened in these Reception Centers, the youngsters were there long before the teacher arrived and stayed there long after he had left.

There are steps a superintendent can take and there are steps a teacher can take. Let me give you another illustration from an eastern city that is not represented at this conference. That city, which has eight school districts, decided to organize a class for gifted children in each district. Every principal was told to refer all fifth-grade youngsters in his school who had IQ's above 130 to the central school in that district where they would be organized as a class of gifted children. After the program started it was discovered that in one district there was no such class. Everybody started worrying about what it would look like if there were classes for gifted children in every part of the city except this one. The superintendent, therefore, sent another order to the principals in this district to forget the IQ; every school had to send—I do not remember whether it was two, three, or four fifth graders to a central school in the district to be organized as a class for gifted children. I visited that class. The youngsters were not bright; they all had IQ's far below 130. In fact, they were not bright enough to realize that they were not bright. They were treated like a class of gifted children. And I have never been in a classroom where there was more imagination, more creativity, more originality than in that one. To be sure there was an unusual teacher there.

Most teachers spend a lot of time talking about how to raise the level of aspiration of the children, and then they talk about ways of raising the level of aspiration of their parents. My question is: How do you raise the level of aspiration of the teachers themselves? When this teacher treated the youngsters as though they were bright, they responded in kind. Morris Cohen, when he was a philosophy professor, used to say whenever he was accused of talking over his students' heads, "I never talk over my students' heads. I talk to where their heads ought to be."

As we now talk about raising levels of aspiration, there is a great deal that individual classroom teachers can do. There is even something that colleges can do. You heard at this conference about the Queens College Bridge Project and about the work that Hunter College is doing at Junior High School 120. These are instances where colleges have taken the initiative in attacking a problem in depth and in actually doing something about it. Yet, while teachers can do something and principals can do something and colleges can do something, that is as nothing compared to what you can do when TEPS brings all groups together and says, "Now, what can we do together?"

In recent years, the work with urban schools has led to a rash of multi-discipline conferences. We have all been to some. A sociologist gets up and reads a paper on the sociologist's view of the problem. It is generally a pretty good paper. While he is reading it, the psychologist who is to follow him is not really listening because he is looking at his own paper to see what he needs to change because the sociologist used one of his illustrations. When the sociologist sits down and psychologist gets up, the sociologist does not really listen because he is trying to see what changes he has to make in his paper when he gets home so he can submit it for publication in the conference proceedings.

That is one kind of approach, and I would like to contrast it with the orthopsychiatric approach as used in a child guidance clinic. Clinics have social workers, psychologists, psychiatrists, pediatricians, teachers, and other specialists, but they do not read papers to each other. Instead, they all examine the same child and then they discuss him among themselves until they come up with a tentative diagnosis and a tentative plan of treatment, and then they try it out. About three months later they come back together, and again each one makes his own evaluation of the diagnosis and plan of treatment, but none of them would dare plan the treatment independently of the others.

Can we apply this orthopsychiatric approach to the educational problems of our urban communities? Can we bring together the various disciplines which can contribute to the solution of these problems and have them work together instead of reading papers to each other?

When Toby Kurzband spoke this morning, he said how helpful it was to him as a principal to be able to sit down at these meetings and discuss questions with teachers, not as a principal discusses them with teachers, but as professional colleagues discuss problems when they work together. Through electronics, we have wonderful communication media, but they usually are one-way. A superintendent can get up before a television camera and at one time tell all his teachers what he is thinking, what he is planning, what he dreams, what he hopes, and what he fears. Fortunately for him, he has no way of knowing what his teachers are thinking at that time. What can be done to build two-way communication? What can be done to get ideas from wherever they may originate? What can you do to have these ideas evolved together and then applied together? A great deal is said these days about teacher education. May it be that administrator education is just as important? And may it be that the kinds of conferences that help the teacher may also contribute effectively to the in-service education of a school administrator?

The problems of urban education must be tackled on various levels. There are nationwide aspects that must be approached nationwide. This is where the NCTEPS should take the initiative in bringing together those who should tackle the problems. There are state-wide problems that differ from state to state. Here, the state TEPS commissions have a role to fill. There are local aspects that must be left to local TEPS groups. There are also important aspects that have to be dealt with by individual teachers and principals working with individual children. No single approach on any single level, from that of the teacher in a specific classroom to the most ambitious national program, can solve the pressing problems unless we have effective cooperation on every level.

You have now been here for two days. You came, or at least thought you were coming, to solve the problems of urban education. At the end of a two-day conference, they are still unsolved. We should all be grateful for that, because any problem that can be solved in a two-day conference is not a great one. This is an exceedingly able group, but there are other able people in the United States who have also spent two days with this problem. It is not one to be solved in a short conference. I doubt whether it will be solved in a large conference or a longer one because, basically, what we need now is not so much more talk as more programs. As you listen to what is said about urban education, you hear a rich assortment of adjectives and adverbs. I think we now need verbs, and the verbs are not to be found in a short conference. They will be found after you go back home.

CHANGING ATTITUDES OF SCHOOL PERSONNEL

Wilson Record *is professor of sociology at Portland State College, Portland, Oregon. This paper was delivered at the Tenth Symposium on Race and Education, Michigan State University, May 1964. Dr. Record has made a study of the 1957 school crisis in Little Rock, Arkansas.*

One cannot speak of the attitudes of school personnel without qualification, because what school people think about race or any other issue is subject to wide individual variation. But, although attitudes have not been uniform, it is safe to say that, on the whole, school board members, administrators, teachers, and counselors have been entirely too slow in facing squarely the racial inequities in the American educational system. On this score educators have failed the moral and professional commitment of their calling.

We live in a society that increasingly prescribes education as the passport into the economy, the polity, and the community. Yet the people who run our schools—and therefore serve as guardians of the passport—have been remiss in equalizing the opportunity for acquiring it. By their default educators must accept a large share of the responsibility for narrowing the life chances of perhaps 20 percent of the nation's children.

From *Integrated Education,* **October/November 1964. Reprinted by permission of the author.**

Understanding the attitudes of school personnel—the circumstances in which they have developed and the manner in which they may be changed—is essential for achieving the goals of a democratic educational philosophy, clearly enunciated by the supreme court a decade ago. Had such understanding and its application as public policy been realized during the long and dreary interval since 1954, integration of public schools would be much closer. I do not wish to overestimate the influence that school personnel of even the most dedicated and fair-minded sort could have exerted over the many forces—habit, custom, confusion, and bigotry—that stood in the way of integrated education. But one senses both moral defection and professional failure in the responses of most school personnel to the critical, line-drawing issues brought to the fore by the court's decision, issues voiced time and again, in clear and ringing terms, in community after community, North and South, East and West, by the education-denied and the freedom-deprived groups seeking to claim an American birthright.

Rarely did public school personnel themselves initiate the protests and the court cases which, over a period of some three decades prior to 1954, chipped away at racially segregated education. They were forced to confront the issues; they did not seek them out. With few exceptions, they not only accepted but virtually approved segregated schooling. In doing so they became instruments for propping up a racist society. Schoolmen appeared before the bar not as friends of the court intervening in behalf of education-denied Negroes but as defendants of the established order, which their own public schools helped to create and now fought to uphold. Future historians, looking back on the racial conflicts in education during the past few decades, will express bewilderment at the tragic gap between the moral and professional ideals of school personnel on the one hand and their day-to-day and year-to-year actions on the other. Chronicles will record the opportunity lost, the time dissipated, and humanity wasted. Some historians will footnote—perhaps some novelist will portray in depth—the case of the Negro child who in 1954 entered first grade in a segregated institution, in Chicago or New York or Atlanta, and a decade later terminated his formal schooling without ever having been part of an integrated classroom, without ever experiencing adequate instruction which could mean the difference between his becoming an autonomous man or a dependent drudge in an ever more complex society. Tragedy is the result in the individual case; catastrophe, threatening the whole structure of democratic society, is the inevitable outcome when literally millions of young Negroes suffer the same fate; when millions more will suffer it in the future unless educators bestir themselves—here and now.

Even after the 1954 ruling, most public school personnel assumed a "wait and see" stance, usually proclaiming that in their schools there was no prejudice, no discrimination, no inequities based on race. Presumably the problem of segregated schooling was found only in the South—not in the North, or East, or West—and certainly not in *this* city or in *this* system. Such *"imbalances"* as might exist were written off as a result of time and circumstance, of forces—social, economic, and political—lying entirely outside the school system. Reviewing developments in the immediate post-decision years, one cannot avoid being shocked by the extent to which many school personnel were willing to use delaying tactics in the administrative and judicial arenas and to collaborate with those who wished to perpetuate segregated schools as features of the local social landscape. The many hearings conducted by the

Civil Rights Commission contain convincing, overwhelming evidence that these were not isolated practices resulting from distinctive local conditions but characteristic responses of school personnel across the land. The few instances where school people led the fight for equality of opportunity stand out precisely because they are so few and because they have received so much hopeful public notice. One searches almost in vain for examples of school personnel recognizing their responsibilities in the light of the court decision and taking the initiative to do what they were best equipped in the circumstances to do: educate themselves, the various publics, and their classroom pupils toward the fulfillment of long-neglected obligations.

Many educators today express bewilderment that their position and effort are no more greatly appreciated by education-denied groups, especially Negroes, in whose behalf they claimed to have labored long. Their responses are similar to those of the southern white man who cannot understand why Negroes do not love him for his many sacrifices in their behalf. This white-collar patronization, however, only underscores the schoolman's failure to understand the nature and depth of the Negro's feeling about education, and his determination to become a full citizen by acquiring and using it. The paternalistic attitudes of administrators, teachers, and counselors can only add insult to the deep injury suffered through the centuries by Negroes in American society.

In school integration Negroes are looking for results, not excuses; for actions, not declarations of good intent; for substance, not form. Their skepticism, indeed their mistrust, of school personnel would be substantially less if even now there was clear evidence that the latter understood their problem and on that basis were doing something about it. But what has been the occasion for school action? What lies behind it? More often than not it is the court order, the protest march, the integration rally, the school boycott, perhaps the death of a demonstrator protesting the erection of still another segregated school. It is to fear, to a display of power, that schoolmen have responded. There was a time when Negroes might have appealed to the educators' idealism but no more, no more. Negroes have come to feel that persuasion and negotiation unsupported by organized pressure will produce few changes. The Negro's high regard for education on the one hand and his distrust of educators on the other are clearly evident in the thrust of his pressure and in the tactics he is choosing to break through racial barriers in public schools. To the schoolmen's plea to wait and hope, the Negro's reply is that he has waited too long already and that hope was long ago betrayed by those who could have given it substance.

The foregoing remarks are not an indictment of all educators; there have been happy exceptions. Nor do I take the position that the attitude of the majority cannot be changed. If I thought the educators could not be educated, I would not be here, particularly in this panel discussion. I believe that attitudes are flexible. Furthermore, I am persuaded that even where attitudes of school personnel and other factors in the integration drama cannot be changed fundamentally, their behavioral consequences can be substantially redirected toward socially approved and morally justified ends.

However, the resources of education-denied groups in realizing their aims cannot be tapped readily because of mistrust and the continuing evasion of integration by school personnel. Public schoolmen have not only a past to live down but a professional creed, so clearly implied in the court decision, to live up to.

Attitudes are the creatures of many forces—personal, professional, organizational, and situational—which form the context within which school personnel develop and carry on their specialized tasks. Only if the social, interpersonal, and structural elements in the perspectives of school functionaries are carefully explored can one assay attitudes realistically, or take steps to change them. Focus on attitudes as such is not likely to be rewarding. Even if change is possible, it may take so long that the attack on critical problems in school integration will be tragically postponed and the damage to minority children proliferated. Few school personnel are likely to be struck blind by some great light and, upon recovering, to view school integration in a radically different perspective. And we are no more likely to change their behavior in the future simply by pleading for a change of heart, however desirable that may be as a final condition, than we have been in the past.

The context within which the attitudes of school personnel are formed and altered is invariably complex. It is true that in each administrator, each teacher, each counselor resides a unique person, who brings to his encounter with associates and pupils a psychological makeup different from all others in the past and never to be duplicated in the future. It is equally true, however, that individual diversity is limited by the social context in which it exists. The individual educator is a member of a particular class, a particular race, a particular age group, a particular geographical community which shape and delimit his perspective. The high order of uniformity in the response of schoolmen to the challenge of the color problem is attributable to the fact that they are concentrated in certain social groupings rather than being distributed evenly over the various ranges. The men who run our schools are predominantly middle-aged, middle-class white men.

More than in almost any other professional group, the attitudes of school personnel are influenced by community forces. Administrators, teachers, and counselors are all public employees working in public institution into which a substantial portion of public resources have been poured. Moreover, they are engaged in a vital task, the socialization of the young, whose importance all publics within the community recognize, however much they may disagree on the goals and methods of socialization.

The way school personnel identify the crucial elements of the community will have an important bearing on their conceptions of professional roles, suggesting the limits and forms of change in the schools. Accuracy in definition of the social structure is not readily attained, however. The difficulty of getting essential information and the frequent inability of school personnel to analyze and assimilate it are two barriers, though not necessarily the most important ones; definitions of reality are as much the result of social pressure and emotion as they are of fact and reason. And men, even schoolmen, have been known to deny the existence of what they do not understand, and to proclaim the impossibility of what they do not desire.

In the appraisal of community structures, as a step in changing attitudes of school personnel, sociologists can make a contribution by calling studied attention to the general historical experience of whites and members of racial and ethnic minorities. The aim is not to produce an "accepted" or an official account but to identify those occurrences in the past which bear on present issues and to develop a perspective not unduly pessimistic or optimistic. Changes making for social cohesion and social conflict in intergroup relations can be identified and the possibilities of purposeful change can be scaled against past experience.

Many school personnel are not history-conscious and perhaps should not be expected to be so. There is a strong tendency to assume that race relations patterns are fixed and that what is so firmly rooted in the past cannot be modified. Yet the reader of Woodward's book on Jim Crow[1] or of Logan's works on the Negro in American life[2] cannot help being struck by the fact that post-Civil War patterns of racial segregation were wilfully imposed by powerful white men, frequently against the inclination of other whites and certainly against those of Negroes. Furthermore, we already have in hand a sufficient number of cases of accomplished integration to lend hope to those who would now reduce the heavy levy of history upon the present.

History, I am suggesting, particularly the history of race relations in the local community, can be an instrument for integration of public schools. But it will be useful primarily by indirection, by the way in which it enables school personnel to identify the community and to discern those unique openings through which equitable education opportunities can be initiated.

Sociologists can also interpret for school personnel those mechanisms in the community through which groups assert their interests and seek to control the behavior of their own members as well as that of others. Attitudes of school personnel toward integration depend in part on an assessment of the social forces at play, their components, form, and strength. To say that schoolmen, although they may have had courses in sociology and long experience in the community, understand those forces only slightly is not unfair. They are likely to be conscious of only the more public and articulate forces, ignoring the informal and nonaggressive ones. Thus they miss opportunities to obtain different perspectives on race relations; they fail to tap new and possibly useful resources for integration. For example, I have encountered few educators who were knowledgeable about the church in the Negro community or who saw any possibility of using its resources in solving administrative, teaching, and counseling problems. I have interviewed few counselors who were familiar with the local minority labor market, who saw its limitations and possibilities and its significance for the behavior of their Negro counselees. Moreover, those who have worked with school personnel must be impressed by their unawareness of the roles of other official agencies whose activities have a significant bearing on any move towards school integration.

What I am especially concerned about is the lack of encounter of school principals, teachers, and counselors with members of racial and ethnic minorities on the level of equality and as participants in shaping the activities of the school. Such encounters may not produce understanding or goodwill, but they do have the possibility, much more than do textbooks or administrative rules, of changing attitudes, of forcing the professional to ask again: Who am I? What am I doing here? What ought I to do?

Sociologists can describe the "community power structure," a concept widely used in recent years by civil rights organizations directing their efforts at those groups

[1]C. Vann Woodward, *The Strange Career of Jim Crow*, 2nd ed., Oxford University Press, New York, 1965.
[2]Rayford W. Logan, *Negro in the United States*, D. Van Nostrand Co., Inc., Princeton, N. J., 1957; *Betrayal of the Negro*, P. F. Collier, Inc., New York, 1965.

who heavily influence public policies and public events. How centralized or diffused, how rigid or flexible, how static or changing, how exclusive or representative—these are questions about community power that must be answered by those who would integrate public schools. Wherever public schools are found one finds also the practice of politics and the use of power. School personnel to varying degrees are aware of it, administrators probably more than teachers, and teachers more than counselors. In spite of their claims to the contrary, professional schoolmen are more than the instruments of power directed from the community. They are themselves political actors; they not only respond to but also exercise power. For example, the school administrator who seeks out and uses the advice of a civil rights organization enhances the organization's influence and prestige in the community. This is an exercise of judgment that has specific consequences and direct implications for the patterns of influence and control extending beyond the school.

General attitudes of white publics will certainly be significant for specific attitudes of school personnel toward integration. Most school people are white and upon them falls the responsibility of applying policies at the pay-off place: in the school itself, and in the classroom. Most school personnel are also middle class, if not in origin then certainly in outlook; their class values and status concerns enter into their confrontation of integration issues.

There has been a pronounced tendency for them to assume that other white public attitudes are all of a piece and, possibly, like their own underlying feelings, negative. Such is not the case, of course. In protesting school segregation in community after community outside the South, Negroes have received firm support from predominantly white religious, political and educational organizations; in California, for example, from the Episcopal Youth, the Young Democrats, and American Federation of Teachers.

The skillful use of favorable sentiment among white publics would greatly strengthen school personnel in communities moving toward integrated education. It emphasizes that they do not stand alone and that there are resources on which they can draw. Attitudes, for better or worse, are not granite-like things embedded in the individual and durable until death; they are weakened or strengthened to large degree by the response of other people whom the individual encounters in carrying on his activities, personal, social, and professional.

The success of a school integration program, however, rests importantly upon the initial attitudes of school people—their convictions and willingness to risk social disapproval and public criticism. But there is now, more than at any time since the supreme court decision, a need for white publics to stand up and and be counted, to support school people who, either boldly or timidly, are moving toward integration. The vague resolution about brotherhood, the hopeful declaration that the problem will eventually be solved, the pious appeal to sacred traditions, and the appointment of still another study commission are not enough.

Recently a number of countermovements to integrated education have attracted considerable attention in urban communities outside the South. Their form and strength, exemplified by the one in New York City opposing even the modest desegregation program of Superintendent Gross, have been interpreted by some as a rejection of the principle of integrated education and a marked shift in white attitudes from indifference to hostility. School personnel no doubt have been impressed by these developments, their enthusiasm dampened or their skepticism confirmed. However, I suggest that the main fears of participants in countermovements may not be integration *per se* but a consequent decline in the quality of education, which is something quite different. Integrated education *need not* be and *must not* be inferior. And the answer to such misgivings is not more racially segregated education, which in practice is inferior, but improvement of instruction across the board and a rising quality of learning for all pupils.

School integration efforts must take into account the attitudes of people who man health, welfare, employment, law enforcement, housing, planning, and other public organizations. Here again, public servants reflect a wide range of attitudes toward school integration. Enthusiastic cooperation of other public agencies with the schools would be, of course, a fortunate development. Rarely has it been achieved, for reasons that cannot be fully explored here. The Balkanization of public agencies in urban communities, and the emergence of small bureaucratic enclaves with limited responsibility and limited imagination, are underlying causes. However, these agencies are here, and they will remain for a long time. Certainly, integrated education cannot await a rational consolidation of public units. The wait would be long indeed.

There is not only noncooperation among agencies; much of the time open conflict occurs. Schools are at odds with probation departments about keeping delinquents in the classrooms. Employment services are angry with schools for encroaching on placement functions. Recreation departments feel the schools are against extension of recreational programs to include adult education; and so on. Yet, we know that problems of segregated education cannot best be attacked by the schools alone; it is not enough to reduce the hostility of other agencies to neutrality; the complexities of the problems demand a concerted effort.

School personnel themselves are participants in a bureaucratic system and identified closely with it. They are likely to think first of a proposed program's significance for the school's relations with police, health, welfare, and so on. Predominant here is the bureaucratic and organizational attitude, with moral and professional concerns receding into the background. Hesitation and timidity will be the prominent responses of school personnel wishing to avoid the risks inherent in a bold integration program. Other agencies might take advantage of unfavorable reactions and exploit them to *their* advantage.

However, there are some developments weakening bureaucratic rigidities and hesitant attitudes of personnel. The public school is not the only agency being forced to change its ways. The employment service in having to curtail racial discrimination in referrals and hiring; the police department is having to modify the handling of Negro offenders and the recruiting of new members to the force; the recreation department is having to integrate its playground and swimming pools, and so on. The supreme court decision, by general implication and by subsequent interpretation in specific cases, applies not only to the South but to the nation, not only to schools but to other public agencies.

The primary battleground, however, has been the schools. School people have not only the greatest resources but the largest experience. They are in a strategic position not only to seek *from* but provide support *to* other agencies groping toward integrated policies. By modifying their bureaucratic attitude school personnel may approach probation, recreation, police, and other people and develop a mutual attack on the mutual problem of desegregation of the whole community. It is no compliment to school officials to record that in many cases the initative has come from other agencies. In one large San Francisco Bay Area city, for example, the chief of police, not the superintendent of schools, is the one who has taken *Brown v. Board of Education* seriously and reorganized his program along integrated lines. In the final analysis, the real enemy of school personnel is not members of other public agencies but segregation itself. Those who purport to instruct the young, all the young—to teach, if you will—cannot afford to let their own bureaucratic attitudes obscure the difference.

I turn now to some of the more specific attitudes of school personnel, recognizing again that attitudes vary rather widely and are to no small degree shaped by the functional position of the individual within the school system.

There are four broad categories of personnel—board members, administrators, teachers, and counselors—whose attitudes are significant for integration efforts. An examination in depth of each typical attitude within each category would be highly desirable. Obviously, however, this cannot be attempted in the space available. Accordingly, I shall be somewhat arbitrary in dealing with the few that seem to me most important.

School Board Members

School board members are in key positions to initiate integration programs. Their support is essential in establishing the broad general policies out of which develop precise moves such as the change of attendance boundaries, the construction of new schools, and the development of special resources and services.

The attitudes they bring to the integration issue are not only varied but frequently ill-defined and poorly expressed. But board members are at least public-minded people with more than average concern with happenings in the schools. They can observe school problems directly and draw upon a wealth of official material and advice not ordinarily available to the layman. Even so, board members in community after community have shown a marked lack of sensitivity to the integration issue and a deplorable inability to grasp the feelings of Negroes about local education problems. Especially is this true in places to which large numbers of Negroes have migrated during the past two decades. For examples, local board members frequently propose erection of new schools in Negro ghettos, assuming that Negroes will be content with the new physical plant and appreciative of the board's effort. Or they recommend the appointment of more Negro teachers—and then assign them to predominantly Negro schools. Or they provide a woefully inadequate fund for "compensatory" education programs in ghetto areas. Or they obtain grants from private foundations for bold, experimental programs that are neither bold nor experimental but usually only timid gestures financed from windfall budgets and doomed to end once those funds are no longer available. Each of these moves may be an improvement, but neither separately nor collectively do they seriously bridge the underlying pattern of segregated education; they leave untouched what many Negroes regard as the basic cause of distress.

But board members in nonsouthern communities, however, cannot continue to plead lack of knowledge about the consequences of segregated education or lack of understanding of Negro grievances. The available data on both issues are substantial—and convincing for those willing to examine them carefully.

We must then look elsewhere in assessing the failure of many school board members to act effectively in equalizing education opportunities. Again we come back to the basic attitudes of board members. We should not minimize the school boards' inclusion of people who are bitterly opposed to integration in any form, certainly in the schools. We help none when we account for this attitude as a "lack of understanding" or as a "failure to communicate." These board members, the "bitter-enders," understand all too well and communicate all too clearly.

"Bitter-enders" are not necessarily a small, vocal minority. In some communities they monopolize board positions and in effect control the school system. In others they form an influential bloc and severely limit what the majority may wish to do about segregation and related problems.

The "bitter-ender" publicly justifies his attitude through assertions about race and education that are at once familiar and frightening; familiar because they have been used for decades to support inequality and frightening because they are so inappropriate for the deepening education crisis and can but further inflame an already smoldering issue. "Negroes," he says, "are really not capable of high educational achievement and there is little point in providing better facilities and instruction. They are happier where they are and do not really want to attend integrated schools. In them they would be out of place and feel uncomfortable and would still be segregated on the basis of performance and ability. The causes of unrest among Negroes are the 'hotheads' and 'outsiders' who are stirring up the less sophisticated black citizens who have been content with their place and wanting no change. A few exceptional Negro children may have outstanding potential and these should be encouraged. But the schools, even if integrated, could do little for the others whose low level of culture, if not basic inferiority, will require generations to change if it can be changed at all. To do anything special, or even equal, for Negroes would mean shortchanging other groups of pupils [he means the white middle-class kids], weakening the whole public school system."

On some boards, however, the "bitter-ender" is reaching his own bitter end. He is being replaced by men with less rigid attitudes who realize that something must be done to correct at least the most glaring inequities. The "bitter-ender" is replaced, not changed; he leaves the board feeling no differently about the integration issue than he did at the time when his private attitudes were translated into public policy. The replacement of the "bitter-ender" is essential since his own rigidities prevent change. The instrument for that is politics whether the board be appointive or elective.

The extent to which school personnel should participate in the politics of education is a difficult question, particularly when it comes to eliminating or adding members of the school board. However, it seems to me quite consistent for school personnel to stand firmly on professional principles and on public law, indicating quite clearly what is implied in the position of the "bitter-ender" on the integration issue. However, the critical political initiative will probably have to be taken by the education-denied groups themselves if the "bitter-ender" is to be overcome. They have not only just a right but also an obligation to judge school board members and to act on their conclusions. The minimum response of school personnel to such groups should include providing the widest possible range of official data and full and continuous consultation with their representatives.

The attitude of the conservative school board member is not to be confused with that of the "bitter-ender." The conservative is not a bigot and he is not to be identified with those who call themselves conservatives but behave in the most radical and irresponsible manner with respect to public education and other issues. The conservative board member is open minded; he has a decent regard for the facts and recognizes the reality of social change and the emergence of new social problems. He does not believe, however, that substantial changes in race relations in education can be achieved within a short time or that they can result from the systematic efforts of school boards and school personnel to bring them about. He tends to emphasize the hold of tradition and the substantially irrational elements in the behavior of most people, especially in race relations.

The conservative is also likely to be quite cautious about public school costs. With his social conservatism goes economic conservatism. He may accept an essentially bold integration program if its cost is "reasonable," meaning small. Unfortunately, there is no cut-rate program for integrated education. It is expensive; there is little point in arguing that the necessary tasks can be accomplished without substantially more resources than are currently available. I believe school personnel must make this point emphatically, especially with concerned conservatives who fear deficits much more than they fear desegregation.

The concerned conservative's attitude can be influenced by fact and by logic and by an appeal to his sense of community responsibility. He is likely to view with considerable distaste, however, some civil rights organizations—their demands and their methods of securing them. But he does not kid himself, and his own decency soon comes to the fore. He knows that the cry of "Red" and "Communist" is no substitute for either an analysis of racial injustice in American society or an adequate education program for millions of Negro children. Above all, the conservative knows that one does not escape moral responsibility by pious, self-serving incantations or by falsely labeling those who remind him of his shortcomings.

Many school personnel should feel comfortable with the concerned conservative, for their attitudes are highly similar. With him, they feel that something can be done on the integration issue but not so much as to upset the "neighborhood school" pattern or to shift school boundaries drastically or to introduce bold programs of compensatory education that would substantially alter the long established curriculum. (Parenthetically, one wonders just how even the most uninformed and irresponsible critic of public schools could accuse their personnel of "radicalism.")

The administration-dominated school board member is another type with which most of you are familiar. His position on integration is no "position" at all; that is to say he embodies a kind of vacuous fluidity. On this and other issues he takes his cues from the key administrator, usually the superintendent, who is quick to recognize the man's possible usefulness, and in time probably his patent liabilities. The administration-dominated type is either too lazy or too timid to form an independent position. He sees it not as a public trust but as a private opportunity. School board membership is essentially a means to a higher goal, for basking in the local limelight or stepping upward to another public office. His chief concern is to make no serious mistakes, offend no important group, and avoid being labeled controversial. He believes these aims can best be served by close identification with the chief administrator on whose support he can count in exchange for uncritical loyalty.

The key to the attitude of the administration-dominated type is not the man himself but the administrator who wields a determining influence on his behavior as a board member. The administrator-dominated man has a great deal of faith in "experts" and "specialists," not only to evaluate and carry out policies but to devise them initially. Indeed, he sees the board's function essentially as approving administrative proposals and "interpreting" them to the public.

The response of this type to integration proposals is predictable if the attitudes of the administrators are known. School personnel come to realize this in time by watching board members and administrators consider a series of issues. Those outside the official system soon learn that integrated programs cannot be initiated through the administration-dominated board member. Much time and energy can be saved if the focus is shifted quickly to the people who count, the powerful administrators.

The attitudes of liberal type board members are more diffuse than the three considered above. Liberals agree that segregated education exists, is undesirable, and that school boards have a responsibility for eliminating it. The question is how—in what length of time, with what means, and at what costs? One finds surprising diversity in responses of liberal types; civil rights leaders frequently are startled at the hesitancy of liberals on specific issues that must be faced if integration is to proceed. The liberal type by nature is peculiarly concerned with method, with the consistency of the several available means with long-term goals and basic values. The integration advocate understandably emphasizes goals and is not greatly disturbed if means for attaining them do not always mesh neatly. To the liberal type, who is usually white, the integration advocate's attitude suggests an unbecoming single-mindedness, possibly "extremism," which he fears will endanger the "progress" being made. To the advocate the liberal's preoccupation with method is a mark of weakness, a lack of courage in facing the logical implications of a basic value position and the personal implications, including status, of integrated education.

The liberal type board member, like so many other whites, is frequently only vaguely aware of what is going on in the Negro community. He is not particularly sensitive to the changing collective mood of Negroes and its meaning for their spokesmen to the white community. The integration advocate, on the other hand, fails to understand the limited influence of the liberal board members, who are probably in a minority, and who must work within the framework of an established system that includes many built-in resistances to changes—of any kind.

The liberal type, of course, is a natural to introduce integration measures. Other board members cannot help becoming aware of growing unrest among Negroes and their demands for equal education chances. A certain anxiety has developed in those school boards with which I am familiar; it is likely to increase in the near future. There will develop a situation in which integration proposals will be viewed more hopefully. The liberal with specific measures in hand, can then move boldly with some chance of success; at least he will get a serious hearing.

The four types of board members identified by basic attitudes toward integration are rarely found in pure form. Typologies are useful not because of their symmetry but because they enable us to understand the attitudes of school board members and their bearing on public school integration in specific communities.

The problems of integrated education will challenge school boards across the land for many years to come. Whether elected or appointed, board members will have to confront the harsh facts and issues; there is no easy way out. The board members' attitudes and competencies for this issue should be crucial in their selection. School professionals can instruct board members on many aspects of integration; wiser decisions, hopefully, will be the outcome.

Administrators

On turning to administrative personnel we find a wide range of specialists functioning within varying school systems. Regarding integration, however, there are a few fairly distinct attitudinal types. There is the actively hostile administrator who may have many reasons for being so. Though personal prejudice is at the core, it may be that he fears integrated programs because they are beyond his training and capacity to handle; his failure would mar an otherwise successful professional career. Or he fears that such programs will cause all kinds of internal staff disruptions, even if they do not create additional public relations problems. Or he may feel that introducing such programs is yielding to public pressures and compromising the autonomy of school administrators. Implicit in this attitude is the assumption that neither board members nor spokesmen of education-denied minorities really know what is good for them or for the schools.

My impression is that this type is on the way out. In some communities, however, such administrators are so well entrenched in school system and power structure that they cannot be forced out. Some are changing, not enthusiastically, but nevertheless changing. One superintendent of my acquaintance within a space of three years shifted his position from outright opposition to integration ("to hell with the supreme court; I work for the school board") to studied support of a broad program of integration for Negroes and Mexican Americans. Another is engaged in extensive reading and consultations with social scientists in the nearby university preparatory to initiating a new program this fall. I do not attempt to assess the motives for such changes. The results are more important, and perhaps even the most hostile administrator can be pressured into a substantially new behavioral mold.

The chances for avoiding selection of hostile types will be greatly improved if teacher-training institutions screen applicants more carefully, weighing attitudes about race and ethnic minorities. Further, it will be essential to provide training and experience that will reinforce suitable attitudes and equip officials to express them effectively.

The indifferent administrator is a type whose numbers are shrinking rapidly. Nevertheless, one still finds him in key positions in school systems in which the integration issue must be raised sooner or later. The indifferent type thinks that he will be relatively untouched. Even when there are storm clouds on the horizon, he looks the other way. His lack of knowledge about the Negro community has produced a myopia that blurs the deep feelings and growing needs of frustrated Negro parents and children. By training, and by temperament too, the indifferent administrator is poorly equipped to deal with integration questions. He does not actively seek out minority spokesmen to gain useful information; he does not initiate staff studies to gauge the degree of discrimination in the system; he would not even consider drafting a plan to eliminate inequities. Usually, then, he is caught flat-footed by the demands of Negro organizations. And his reactions, at least initially, only worsen the situation. His lack of concern about minority children can only anger parents who see the inferior education of their offspring as grossly inadequate and a permanent blight on their career chances.

The indifferent type is likely to exclaim: "I can't see what you people (Negroes) are so excited about." The problem then becomes one of how to open his eyes and where to cast the light. The indifferent's subordinates may be in a good position to help, provided they are not also equally unenlightened and unaffected. They can at least describe the racial inequities in the system. Particularly are school principals in a position to underscore the issues. Within the school, teachers, and counselors can look for underlying causes of minority pupil failure and trouble. Why should it be necessary for indifferent administrators to be aroused by court orders, boycotts, mass protests, and other direct action remedies, rather than by their own professional staff members?

In contrast to the hostile and indifferent administrative types are others who want to do something about segregation but who differ in understanding, approach, and emphasis. The first is the "cautious conformist." His attitude is one of fear mingled with a certain guilt about denial of equal access to education. Typically he lacks familiarity with concrete issues, with developments in other communities, with moods of Negroes with whom he has had little or no association. There are few minority pupils now in his district or system. Privately he is relieved that they are concentrated elsewhere.

With so many changes taking place in race relations and education, the cautious conformist cannot rest comfortably. He knows that the issue will one day, sooner or later, confront him. As much as he would like to do so, he cannot simply wait, hoping the time will be long and the confrontation minor. He is moved to some degree by a sense of both professional and personal responsibility. He may initiate inquiries and perhaps develop tentative plans for dealing with the issue. Like the boy scout, he wants to be prepared; unlike the scout, he is not very venturesome.

This type displays attitudes with which you are familiar. You recognize, too, that they have considerable potential for effective integration efforts. The cautious conformist's behavior is a result not only of his personal ambiguities but also of the play of powerful cross-pressures which cannot easily be sorted out and reconciled. Pressures from some white parents, businessmen, and rightist political organizations are for him quite real and persistent. Unless they are countered by civil rights organizations with ideas and plans as well as pressures, the cautious conformist will be slow to move. In this administrator, weakness and wisdom are extremely difficult to isolate. Attitudes at the personal level are quite decent; this must be understood by those who would change his behavior. He can only be alienated by those who interpret caution as meaningless hostility or bureaucratic evasion.

The last of the four types is that *rara avis*, the enthusiastic integrator. He believes changes can come rapidly, even though he knows how slowly bureaucratic wheels customarily turn. He is, let's face it, a minority among administrators. Usually he is younger, more sensitized to the issue, having grown to maturity while integrated education was becoming a large and persistent public issue. Some of his training has at least touched on the problem and perhaps suggested how it can be dealt with. Though youthfulness is no guarantee of an administrator's favorable attitudes, it helps. The young administrator is encountering new challenges before getting "fixed" on controversial issues in school and community.

The enthusiastic integrator must tangle with the established bureaucratic types whose main concerns are organizational stability and risk-avoidance. He may lack knowledge of the ins-and-outs of the bureaucratic structure and of the sentiments and resources of minority communities. The first he will underestimate and the second he will overvalue. He will irritate his associates and evoke mixed reactions from his superiors. However, his enthusiasm itself can be persuasive to the ambivalent and hesitant and it can carry him a considerable distance against outside pressures.

The enthusiast's basic attitudes are quite sound. It is important that they be reinforced by those sharing his goals. He will be strengthened if his effort receives favorable professional and public recognition. For his own career he needs support through promotion, salary increases, and greater responsibilities, possibly direction of a program attacking segregation within the whole system. The "enthusiast" is not the opposite of "realist." It is grossly unfair and question-begging to characterize him as "impractical" or "theoretical" while those who do nothing and prefer bureaucratic comforts are praised as "practical and realistic men who know their business."

There are other attitudinal types within the administrative personnel group. Essentially they are variants of the four already considered; they will not be described at this point.

Teachers

Board members and administrators are key personnel in developing policies and structures for racial desegregation of public schools. But desegregation is not integration; the latter is essential for genuine equality of educational opportunity. Integration depends on practicing administrators, teachers, and counselors carrying out day-to-day tasks in desegregated schools with personal conviction and professional commitment. Of special importance are the attitudes of teachers which we shall next explore in brief typological fashion. (Although the attitudes of counseling and guidance personnel are highly relevant, we will not have time to consider them in any detail.)

Two keys to the attitudes of teachers are their feelings about teaching as a profession and about social status. Those of you familiar with teacher responses to educational inequalities and to desegregation can recall convincing examples of each type to be described. My classification is based on wide observation and on systematic interviewing over a long period in widely varying situations.

One finds some teachers, like board members and administrators, indifferent to integrated education. The indifferent teacher will not be concerned either with race or with other issues in the school and in the profession. For him teaching is a means of obtaining money and time for pursuit of other interests. Status in the profession is not important and he has no great concern with colleague opinion as long as it does not endanger his job (not profession) and income.

His ideas about education are limited; he is concerned with getting through day-to-day tasks with minimum effort and trouble. Social status concerns are not compelling; his "kicks" come from indulgence of highly individualized interests. He has no yardstick for measuring one education problem against another. *De facto* segregation is accepted where it is found; inequities do not strike him as important since education has a low place in his scheme of things. His attitude is neither hostile nor favorable.

He will accept change from segregated to desegregated schools as a matter of course; he will not initiate changes or offer something new for making desegregated classrooms integrated learning communities. He lacks enthusiasm for subject matter and the drive to share it with others, especially with groups with stunted learning motivations.

The indifferent teacher has no animated objections to a desegregated classroom; he will work in "depressed areas" if more money is available and working conditions not particularly objectionable. His basic attitude is not likely to be changed, because he is insensitive to professional pressures and social issues. One may ask why he became a teacher in the first place. But there are a great many of this type in today's public schools; more will join the ranks in spite of better screening norms.

The frightened teacher, for the time being, can contribute no more to integrated education than the indifferent one. He usually comes from a white middle-class background and has had little contact with Negroes.

Familiarity need not produce acceptance, but isolation from the culturally different does produce misgivings and unwarranted fear. The frightened teacher is not necessarily concerned with social status. He is uncertain about coping with new situations, especially those with deep emotional overtones and conflict potentials. His limited awareness of racial and ethnic minorities, largely untested, can be no source of comfort. On the one hand he proposes to "treat all students alike" and on the other he emphasizes the disparities suggested by test scores and performance reports. Adding to his fears are the usual stories and rumors about dire happenings in other schools where desegregation has occurred or is being attempted. Although no desegregation effort about which I know has come off smoothly, much of the experience should reassure the frightened teacher.

This frightened type is concerned not only with doing an effective job but also with his personal dignity and safety in those schools where social disorganization is high and outside conflicts are carried into the classroom. Such anxieties may come to dominate the teacher's outlook and prevent his tackling the instructional task at hand. Then, even the most favorable attitude toward integration as such will be overridden and the teacher's positive contribution lost.

The task here is not one of changing attitudes but of providing those conditions within which the frightened teacher can relax and go about his business. Above all, he must be kept in the school and in the profession; potentially he can make an essential contribution.

The status-striving teacher is also frightened but not for the same reasons. For him teaching is not only a professional activity but also one of the few available means for climbing the social ladder. Teaching is selected because it ranks high in the values of the lower middle class from which the status striver is likely to come and because it is within relatively easy reach as a career. It is not looked upon as a calling or simply as a means of making money. It is an instrument for upward social mobility; if it fails to serve this function, it will be abandoned.

Integrated education is a serious threat to the status striver. He shares the racial antipathies of lower middle-class whites; his own ancestors, immigrants perhaps, are likely to have been poorly rated in the community. His ideal is assignment in an all white middle-class or upper-class school in a suburban community. There he can live as well as work, being recognized as much for what he has and can publicly display as for what he is.

For him avoidance of conflict on public issues is part of conforming behavior leading to social acceptance and confirming hard-won status. He defines the integration issue as controversial and the integrated school situation as threatening. Mixed schools, he concludes, are made up primarily of low-strata people and minorities; to work in them is to endanger social striver self-image and status. An admission of Negro children to his previously all-white school will disturb him. He will as quietly as possible transfer to remaining segregated schools or get out of the system altogether.

If he remains, he will not be very effective since he cannot accept the situation as socially comfortable. This is not to say he is hopeless. He can be influenced by subsequent developments. His preoccupation with status may be reduced. More recognition in the profession precisely for good work in integrated programs will help.

Special counseling and guidance in handling the status-striving teacher in integrated situations will reduce the likelihood of status panic.

We should not minimize the strong social status concerns of many teachers, white and Negro, and their implications for integrated education programs. These teachers can be a cause of low morale and create serious staff disruptions. We should carefully identify those whose status anxieties preclude their doing an effective job, and we should take measures to change or redirect their attitudes.

The custodian type of teacher aims primarily at maintaining order and exercising authority. He is not able to make his subject the focus of pupil attention. Possibly at one time he was enthusiastic about teaching, but prolonged service in a school composed primarily of lower-class and undisciplined pupils has led him to minimize education and to emphasize control.

He gets some satisfaction from exercise of effective custody and is wise in its ways and skilled in keeping the lid on.

He feels that little can be done for racial and ethnic minority pupils because of a depressing acquaintance with them, their parents, associates and the communities in which they live. His attitude is one of weary acceptance of the handicaps his pupils face in breaking the vicious cycle of poverty, poor education, and unemployment. His own demoralization conveys itself to his charges who sense that he has for them no more hope than other adults in their narrow world. The custodian attitude can result from a particular need to impose order and certainty on ambiguous—and danger-ous—situations. This, however, is a matter on which the psychologist is probably best equipped to comment.

As a sociologist, I offer two observations: first, the custodian type can get a fresh perspective by being removed for a time from the slum school and encountering new situations. Second, he has a wealth of valuable experience on which other school personnel can draw and he can take professional pride in making it available to them. His attitude will be improved by teaching in different schools, offsetting the demanding uniformities of single-race, single-class institutions.

The secular missionary teacher differs sharply from the custodian type. Contrary to the title's suggestion, he is not the most effective teacher for integrated education programs. Because of a deep sense of mission toward members of racial and ethnic minorities, he will seek opportunities to work with them in community and classroom. His kind of "acceptance" however is not altogether genuine.

His paternalistic attitude marks the Negro's presumed inferiority in a less harsh but just as emphatic a way. (And if there is one thing the Negro today does not want, it is to be patronized by well-meaning uplifters. He wants respect and he is determined to create those conditions under which it may be gained.)

The secular missionary wants to change converts into something fairly specific, not simply to equip them to find their own way among a number of alternatives. Particularly where Negroes are concerned he fails to understand the values and sentiments.

As a consequence he ignores, even insults, their sense of self-worth. So-called "culturally deprived" Negroes do not necessarily think of themselves as being deprived of or requiring uplift by some self-appointed helper. (They know that they are education denied but that is something quite different.) The same is true for other minorities who see the missionary, secular or otherwise, as much as cause and reminder of their plight as cure for it. The secular missionary's insistence on his own righteousness alienates his associates who feel less worthy in dealing with integrated education issues.

This type can play a worthwhile role by emphasizing segregation issues and providing an example of intense concern. However, unless his attitudes are modified, he will not be effective in the day-to-day integrated setting.

He will substitute moral exhortation for subject matter exposition and focus more on overt form and manners than on the basic topics at hand. The secular missionary must be approached cautiously, especially if he has come lately to the cause. None is so holy or likely to fall from grace so soon.

One other type of teacher whose attitude, in my view, merits more recognition is the teacher's teacher, the professional's professional. He sees his primary task as public service based on competence acquired through training and carried out with standards that are publicly explicit and personally internalized. He interprets *de facto* segregation in light of its bearing on professional goals. He is keenly aware of those conditions, including race relations which bear on the profession's fulfilling its essential objective. And he sees the organized profession of teaching as something more than a trade union preoccupied with wages, hours, and working conditions.

Both the problems of desegregation and integration he views primarily as the responsibility of professionally competent administrators and teachers, with school boards laying down only the broadest policies and providing the resources essential to equaling learning chances. He may not be widely experienced with minority peoples but he can convey confidence by his approach, and a sense that for him race in the classroom is not important.

The professional type is interested in the subject matter he professes and in the conditions essential to imparting knowledge to his pupils. He has discovered that his eagerness to teach it carries a long way even among the so-called "culturally deprived" who are supposed to have little intellectual interest or academic potential. The professional type can be extremely valuable in two ways: he can give a steady focus on the ultimate goals of the education enterprise, and he can provide minority pupils a better sense of their own worth by his faith in their ability to learn.

Counselors

It was my intention initially to examine the changing attitudes of school counselors toward integration, for that is a group I have had opportunity to study in some detail. My failure to give more attention to counselors is not because I regard them as minor players in the integration drama. They can and, no doubt, will play bigger roles as school after school seeks to use its total resources to deal with integration problems.

Briefly, school counselors can be divided into a half dozen or so fairly distinct groups. (1) the administration-bound counselor who is concerned primarily with institutional administrative aspects of counseling and regards himself as an administrator or potential administrator; (2) the amateur psychologist counselor who sees his role as clinician serving clients and the problems of integration as individual psychological issues; (3) the "adjustment" counselor who emphasizes the importance of the individual "accepting" the limits of his situation and fitting into it as best he can, which for the Negro child means *de facto* segregation; (4) the off-beat counselor who rejects many of the values of the dominant white society, including its racist values, and has sympathy and understanding for others who have in another sense been rejected; (5) the authoritarian counselor who is both morally and intellectually rigid and lacking in understanding of minority student sensibilities and who relies primarily on moral admonition in dealing with integration; (6) the jet-propelled counselor who has emerged in recent years primarily as a manpower recruiter for the military and space industry and whose central question for all individuals is: can you build a better bomb or fly to the moon? The detailed components of those types have been considered elsewhere.

Throughout this paper, I have, directly or by implication, suggested steps for defining and changing attitudes of school personnel toward integration. In concluding I wish to suggest some additional measures.

School boards may require some basic changes in form and composition before any effective measures can be taken. This is essentially a broad public and political task on which other school personnel are unable to act directly. However, school personnel are organized; as members of professions and as employees of school systems they do have influence. They can encourage desegregation by developing concrete proposals and by pushing for their adoption. The pose of powerlessness on this issue is at least partially false and it is certainly unbecoming. Knowing the structure and types of members of school boards is essential to effective intervention at the board level. More, I hope can be said on this matter later.

Regarding administrators, it is again important that we recognize the wide range of types and attitudes among them. First, it is essential to understand the system and their roles in it. The limits of their authority and resources, as well as their potentials for integrated education, need careful definition. Much more studied selection of administrative personnel with emphasis on ability to develop integrated programs, is a growing need. Backing up, we need a critical review and modification of administrative curricula in teacher training, intergroup relations, and on specific institutions. Greater emphasis on problems of race relations in schools is an essential but only partial corrective. Backing up still further, we need a keener selection of students for training in school administration.

Heretofore there has been little concern for basic attitudes toward racial and ethnic minorities as a measure of fitness. These attitudes should now be emphasized. More support, technical and moral, for administrators dealing constructively with integration issues is essential. The responsibility of professional organizations here, it seems to me, is quite clear. In the immediate circumstances emergency special or in-service training in race relations for all administrators in a system is highly desirable although not all of them are presently directly affected by integration conflicts. Elimination of certain types of administrators from present positions or even from the system entirely may be essential. This is a possibility that must be faced squarely.

With respect to the attitudes of teachers, some useful steps can be taken immediately. Teacher organizations can drop their extreme caution and broaden their concern about school and community issues. They can insist that members in integration situations adhere to professional principles; they can actively support those teachers who are making a contribution—with protection and with affirmative suggestions.

The importance of careful selection of teacher trainees cannot be exaggerated. We should not ask that they be free of bias or that they be fervently committed to integrated education. But we must insist that they hold no unchangeable attitudes that are basically at odds with professional standards and incompatible with the purposes of public education in a democracy. With careful selection of trainees should go revisions of the curricula they are required to complete. Revision should aim at acquainting the future teacher with the background and character of contemporary race relations; moreover, sustained, firsthand encounter with racial and ethnic minorities in school and community settings must be added.

For those teachers already established in school systems a program of information on developments relating to integration is a minimal need.

Boards and administrators as well as teacher organizations have a heavy responsibility here. Attitudes are likely to be more flexible if the teacher has had access to a continuing flow of information which the school system itself makes available. Specific changes can be anticipated and those affected can have time to "get used" to them. In-service training, not "informational" but in depth, would be an even better way for making up the deficiencies in knowledge and for interpreting more recent developments.

Having said much elsewhere about counselors, I shall say little here except to insist again that more counselors are needed but not more of some of the types to which I have referred briefly. We need counselors with deep sensitivity to individual frailties and potentials, but we need as well those who are able to see the personal frailties in the context of community and social problems, who can mark the difference between an individual problem and a social disorder.

In sum, attitudes of school personnel are not easily changed, but they are not irretrievably fixed. To facilitate integration in public schools, educators should identify those attitudes and seek to modify them, or at least redirect their expression if they are detrimental to public principles of equal education opportunity.

To those of us here, and I hope to many others, the court decision of 1954 was more than a legal opinion. It was a moral challenge; its application by educators requires more than fulfilling bureaucratic obligation or rendering technical service.

Education itself in the final analysis is a moral enterprise, and the education of all to realization of their fullest potential is the great moral obligation we, as teachers, cannot escape.

TEACHING NEGRO HISTORY: AN INTERDISCIPLINARY APPROACH

Robert Bone, *professor of English, Teachers College, Columbia University, is author of* The Negro Novel in America *(Yale Paperback, 1965). This is the text of an address to the American Federation of Teachers Conference on "Racism in Education," December 8, 1966.*

I want to begin by calling your attention to the subtitle of this conference. The title is "Racism in Education," but the subtitle is "Correcting America's Image of the Past." I especially want you to consider that word *image*, so rich in meaning and implication. It suggests, for one thing, that the historian is an image-maker, which is certainly the case. In other words, he is a kind of artist, because it is the man of *imag*-ination who works with images, and is in charge of the image-making function in society. And since the power of images for good or evil is immense, the image-maker—or artist—bears an awesome responsibility. If his images are false, if there is no real correspondence between portrayal and event, then the emotional life of the nation is distorted, and its behavior becomes pathological.

Now, where the Negro is concerned, American historians have been guilty of projecting false images. Of this we have become increasingly aware, as we reassess their work in the light of modern scholarship. But what have been their motives? That is above all what we have to understand. To do so we must grasp the close connection between an image and *feelings*. Because the important thing about an image is its power to arouse strong emotion. In fact, it is not too much to say that the function of images in a society is to guide or direct or channelize the flow of emotion in society. And that is why images are an important means of social control.

To return, then, to our question: why has the white man sought to falsify the image of the Negro over all the long centuries? First, to control the black man's emotions, and especially his feelings about himself, in order to make him incapable of resisting his oppressor. And second—this is every bit as important—to protect the white man from the emotional knowledge of his crimes. Because the twisted image, the stereotype, lets the white man off the hook. If you're doing all that to some kind of a grotesque ape, after all, it's not as if you were doing it to a man.

I make this point about the emotions in order to prepare you, as potential teachers of Negro history, for the emotional resistance you will meet. Not so much in your students, or their parents—although that will surely be a problem—but first of all in yourself. For the main point about the American Negro past is that it is a *painful* past, and to reconstruct that past, in our history classrooms, is to unleash waves of painful emotion. For the white children, guilt and fear. For the Negroes, shame and rage. But in any case painful feelings: that is the point. The result is that everybody runs for cover.

From *Integrated Education,* February/March 1967. Reprinted by permission of the author.

I can testify to this from my own professional experience. Last summer I taught in a special program for high school teachers at Yale University. Twenty experienced teachers from the New England states took part. They took one course in Negro history with Professor Hugh Hawkins of Amherst College, and one course in Negro literature from me. By the end of the summer, we were both on the verge of despair. Nineteen of the twenty teachers were white, and we were about ready to conclude that the job that needs to be done cannot really be done by white teachers. Except, perhaps, in rare instances.

They were learning the facts, all right, but in the crucial area of attitude change, we felt we had very little impact. Some of the younger teachers, five years out of college, were ready, but the older teachers for the most part just weren't with it. The problem is that to teach Negro history well you have to be capable of a very detached stance—I might say a very critical stance—toward the American way of life. You have to see that the society of which you are a part has been guilty of a monstrous crime. And not, so to speak around the edges: like, we're 99.44 percent pure and Christian and democratic, only we did, of course, have slavery. But at the center, at the core of our civilization, we have been, and continue to be, racist, and therefore corrupt—morally compromised. And very few teachers—sometimes I think our teachers last of all—can manage the necessary posture of dissent.

So it's not as if we were dealing with a crash program in chemistry: you don't know any chemistry, but we'll teach it to you in a hurry. Because chemistry is emotionally neutral. But to master Negro history is to have all comfortable, all flattering versions of your country's past suddenly turned inside out. The point is that in the course of learning Negro history, the teachers themselves must be transformed. And change is of course a very painful process. Some people, as you know, would rather fight than switch.

Now comes the commercial. My field of specialization is American Negro literature, and I want to say a few words about the value of this field in overcoming the emotional resistance I have been describing. If you teach Negro history, you will surely stir up some deep emotions, but these emotions will be largely unacknowledged, or disguised as historical argument. They will be present in the classroom, but so to speak, illegitimate. If you teach Negro literature along with the political and economic and social history, you will have this advantage—the emotion will be part of the legitimate subject matter of the course. You can get it out in the open, examine it, draw the students into a direct confrontation with their deepest feelings. Which has got to happen, if we're going to make it, black and white together, in this nation.

I want to urge this conference, in closing, to adopt an adequate concept of Negro history. Your approach should be interdisciplinary, and broad enough to include Negro achievement in music, literature, and the other arts, as well as the more conventional forms of historical study. It would be a great mistake to teach Negro history in isolation from Negro achievement in the arts. That would be to mistake the organization of our school system into various departments—history and social studies over here, literature there, music across the street, and art down the hall—to mistake this perfectly arbitrary system for the cultural reality. For out there, in the real world, you will discover that the American Negro has one, single, unified cultural history, which did not happen in convenient compartments to make things easy for future generations of educators.

We must therefore be concerned with the entire cultural history of the Negro people in America, including their creative response to the circumstances imposed upon them by the whites. We must be concerned with what might be called their emotional history, as recorded in their songs and dances, their novels, poems, and plays. We must enlist our colleagues in the English departments, and the music departments, and the art departments, and arrange a core curriculum, so that these matters can be presented to the students in their proper context.

I stress again the emotional history of the Negro people. That is what the nation needs to understand. That is what we can ignore only at our peril. For only confronting, as whites, the wounds that we have dealt, can we comprehend what is now required of us. And only by confronting, as Negroes, the wounds that have been dealt us, can we finally be free.

THE NEGRO IN AMERICAN HISTORY TEXTBOOKS

Kenneth M. Stampp, Winthrop D. Jordan, Lawrence W. Levine, Robert L. Middlekauff, Charles G. Sellers, and George W. Stocking, Jr.

On March 12, 1964, the California State Board of Education unanimously accepted the report on American history textbooks which had been prepared by a panel of historians from the University of California, Berkeley. The panel reviewed and prepared analyses of textbooks used in California public schools: two for fifth-grade level, three for eighth-grade level, and two for high school level. Their analyses disclosed, according to the panel, "an unhealthy condition in California education." The introduction to the full report is reprinted here.

The undersigned, American historians and members of the History Department of the University of California, Berkeley, have been asked to review the American history textbooks that are most widely used in California from the standpoint of their treatment of Negroes....

We are concerned first of all *as historians* that the history taught in our schools should accurately reflect the best findings of current scholarship. Professional scholars are aware that historical "truth" is an elusive quality. Well into the twentieth century professional scholars themselves were affected by the emotional aftermath of the Civil War, and there was a "northern" and a "southern" interpretation of such sensitive matters as slavery and Reconstruction. In the late nineteenth-century mood of national reconciliation, based on a widespread assumption of racial superiority among whites in both North and South, the "southern" view tended to prevail; and the deference of textbook publishers to the special sensitivities of the southern market has caused it to continue by and large to prevail in textbooks until this day. Meanwhile several generations of scholars, freer of sectional emotions and racist assumptions, through their researches and writings developed a substantially different understanding of many of these matters. Most of the textbooks we have examined reflect views

From *Integrated Education,* **October/November 1964. Reprinted by permission of the authors.**

on racial and sectional themes that have been rejected or drastically modified by the best of current historical scholarship.

We are additionally concerned *as citizens* because these historical distortions help perpetuate and intensify the pattern of racial discrimination which is one of our society's most serious problems. We are concerned not only because much of the material in these books is bad history, but additionally because it is a kind of bad history that reinforces notions among whites of their superiority and among Negroes of their inferiority.

Admittedly there is a danger in assessing historical writing in terms of its social consequences. A laudable desire to combat racism, and especially to bolster self-respect among Negro students, might result in exaggerating Negro contributions and the heroic qualities of Negro figures. In our view this would be an equal distortion of historical truth, and in the long run fail to have the desired social effects.

We do feel, however, that the seriousness of the problem of racism underscores the textbook author's responsibility to portray the Negro's role in American life fully, accurately and without either sentimentality or condescension. There should be a conscious effort to portray outstanding Negro figures selected by the same criterion of historical signifiance applied to non-Negro figures. Even those textbooks that now make some effort in this direction tend to single out men like Booker T. Washington and the minor scientist George Washington Carver, whose attitudes about race relations are least disturbing to conservative whites. Equally or more worthy of inclusion by the standard of historical relevance are men like Denmark Vesey, Nat Turner, Frederick Douglass, W. E. B. DuBois, and the Rev. Martin Luther King.

Always and everywhere our children should be told the truth, and the whole truth, as near as the best current scholarship can bring us to this elusive quality. This means, among other things, not obscuring the harsher aspects of the truth—the fact that Negroes entered American society as slaves, the brutalities of slavery, the racism of the Reconstruction and post-Reconstruction era, and the continuing depth and harshness of the problem of segregation and discrimination.

In the light of these general principles, the greatest defect in the textbooks we have examined is the virtual omission of the Negro. As several of the individual reporters point out, the Negro does not "exist" in the books. The authors of the books must know that there are Negroes in America, and have been since 1619, but they evidently do not care to mention them too frequently. In one book there is no account of slavery in the colonial period; in a second, there is not a single word about Negroes after the Civil War; in a third (composed of documents and substantive chapters), the narrative does not mention Negroes in any connection.

As Ralph Ellison's novel, *Invisible Man*,[1] demonstrates, whites frequently do not "see" Negroes. But Negroes are Americans, their history is part of American history. They need to be "seen" in textbooks. The space given Negro history will, of course, depend in part on the nature of the textbook, and minimum standards of coverage are proposed later in this report. What is especially important is that the discussions of Negroes appear as an integral part of the book. Perfunctory or casual treatment may imply that Negroes are not part of America.

---

[1] Random House, Inc., 1952.

Important aspects of Negro experience, of course, depart from that of many other groups in America. Negroes were not just another immigrant group: no other group could be so readily identified by its color, no other group was so systematically enslaved, and no other group has been subjected to as persistent and virulent discrimination. From the seventeenth century to our own day, Negro life has been filled with violence.

These facts highlight another failing of these textbooks that is almost as distressing as the invisibility of Negroes in them. All the texts play down or ignore the long history of violence between Negroes and whites, suggesting in different ways that racial contacts have been distinguished by a progressive harmony. The tone of a textbook is almost as important as anything it has to say. In their blandness and amoral optimism these books implicitly deny the obvious deprivations suffered by Negroes. In several places they go further, implying approval for the repression of Negroes or patronizing them as being unqualified for life in a free society.

We should now like to suggest in some detail the substantive and interpretive elements relating to Negroes that should be included in textbooks covering the whole period of American history. These suggestions do not reflect any effort to give a special emphasis for the purpose of present-day social effects, but only what is necessary for portraying accurately the Negro's role as understood by current scholarship. We regard the suggested contents as an indispensable minimum at the junior high level. Some compression would doubtless be necessary at the elementary level, while high school treatment should be expanded beyond our suggested content.

Early in the seventeenth century Negroes were brought by force from Africa to the English colonies, and over the next fifty years whites in the colonies reduced them to a slavery that was inherited and perpetual. The Negro incurred debasement because he was different, particularly because he was "heathen," black, and helpless. Other colonials entered types of servitude, but their arrangements were usually contractual, their rights were protected by the state, their physical and moral treatment was much better, and their status was temporary. Not even the American Indian, whose exploitation began in the seventeenth century, was reduced to slavery on a substantial scale. Textbooks should tell this story from its African beginnings, through the slave trade, to the enslavement of the Negro.

As the history of the origin of Negro slavery is important, so also is an understanding of slavery as a mature institution in the eighteenth and nineteenth century. Students should know that it existed in the North until after the Revolution. Textbooks should supply the most important statistics, for example, that in 1860 there were four million slaves in the United States, virtually all located in the South. Although a majority of southern whites held no slaves, one out of every two persons in the South's fourteen million people was either a slave or a member of a slaveholding family.

There should be a full account of the life of the slave, starting from the fact that he was an article of property held for the profit that could be gained from his labor. Recent scholarship has shown that slaves labored in southern factories as well as fields. They were often overworked, and customarily housed, clothed, and fed at only a subsistence level. As a result the slave was often ill, and his life expectancy was shorter than that of the whites around him. His master could punish or sell him at will, and could even kill him with near impunity, since slaves were not allowed to testify against white men. The informal character of slave marriages made for an unstable family life; and the whole pattern of debasement under slavery inflicted psychological and sociological scars from which Negroes still suffer.

Understandably the slave resented, even hated his condition, though he usually disguised his real feelings by subservient behavior designed to protect him from the master's power. Students should be told that slaves often ran away, committed sabotage, and plotted revolts, and that on one occasion a slave, Nat Turner, led a bloody general insurrection against the masters.

Slavery's moral and social evil did not go unremarked in the colonial period. The Quakers, for example, insisted that slavery violated both human dignity and divine law. Not until the Revolution, however, did most Americans become sensitive to the discrepancy between slavery and their professed ideals as embodied in the Declaration of Independence. All the states north of Delaware put the institution on the road to extinction, slavery was banned from the Old Northwest, and the Constitutional Convention opened the way for abolition of the slave trade after 1808. Even in the upper South, where the tobacco economy was languishing, liberal leaders hoped that the general operation of economic forces would eventually permit the abolition of slavery. Instead the developing cotton market revived plantation agriculture. Slaves proved so productive in southern cotton fields that slave-owners shut their ears to any criticism of the institution until the Civil War brought its demise.

Meanwhile antislavery sentiment was growing in the North. Even here racist assumptions caused free Negroes to be segregated and discriminated against; but after 1830 a vocal abolition movement had increasing effect. The efforts of the abolitionists, who included a substantial body of northern free Negroes, deserve serious and sympathetic exposition in textbooks. They are often derided for their occasional extravagance and for their internal disagreements, yet the fact is that they performed an immense service in educating Americans to the moral evils of slavery.

Abolitionists are frequently blamed for the Civil War by people who also insist that slavery had nothing to do with the coming of the war, that indeed the South fought to preserve state rights. Most scholars today agree, however, that slavery, and especially the issue of extending slavery into the territories, was fundamental. Certainly a careful appraisal of the slavery issue in national politics should be included in any textbook covering this period.

When the Civil War came, some 200,000 Negroes participated in the fighting that resulted in their formal emancipation. Following the war they also took an important part in the struggle over southern Reconstruction, which determined whether their emancipation was to be nominal or full. Reconstruction is a controversial issue in American history. The best scholarship today portrays sympathetically the radical Republicans in congress, who opposed Lincoln's and later Johnson's plans for bringing the southern states back into the Union as quickly and painlessly as possible under conservative white leadership. The radicals, this scholarship holds, operated from mixed motives; to be sure, they were interested in maintaining their political advantage, but they also wished to reform the structure of southern life. They especially wanted to help the Negro make himself a full partner in a free society.

It is in treating the Reconstruction state governments in the South that the older scholarship is most distorted by racist assumptions and most pernicious in its present-day effects. Modern scholarship overwhelmingly rejects the myth of Reconstruction as a saturnalia of misgovernment and corruption by ignorant and/or venal carpetbaggers, Negroes, and scalawags. Though the Reconstruction regimes had their quota of corruption, as did other American governmental units in this period, the student needs to know that the radical Republican experiment for a time made progress toward a healthy reconstruction of southern society, that many Negroes served ably in the Reconstruction governments, and that the Reconstruction governments had many constructive accomplishments, particularly the extension of the public school system, and the protection of equal civil and political rights of all.

The experiment in Reconstruction failed after a few years, owing to a growing northern indifference which permitted conservative southern whites to regain control by violence, through such agencies as the Ku Klux Klan. Soon Negroes had been reduced to a kind of unofficial slavery. The vote was taken from them, first by trickery and intimidation and later by amendments to the state constitutions. Denied economic opportunity, many were exploited as sharecroppers, and others in menial jobs. By the end of the century they were born and reared in segregated communities, and lived and died in a state of inequality, isolated from the mainstream of American life. Southern state laws and a disastrous supreme court decision, *Plessy* v. *Ferguson*, helped encase them in segregation.

Segregation and violence continued to characterize race relations in the South during the first half of the twentieth century. The hundreds of lynchings which used to occur annually have almost disappeared, but bombings, burnings, and shootings have increased. A more important change has been the movement of millions of Negroes to the cities and to the North. Here repression has been somewhat more subtle but only somewhat less damaging. Employers and unions relegate most Negroes to menial jobs. They are segregated into ghettos, where they pay high rents for slum housing. Segregated housing means in turn segregated and inferior schools.

The other side of the story is the increasingly vigorous effort, especially by Negroes themselves, to change the situation. The growing Negro vote in crucial northern cities and the cold-war campaign to win the support of the uncommitted nations of the world has made the federal government more responsive to the plight of Negroes. Prodded by the National Association for the Advancement of Colored People (NAACP), the federal courts began to declare in the 1930's and 1940's against racial discrimination in voting, jury service, and educational opportunities. This movement culminated in the Brown decision of 1954 outlawing racial segregation in the public schools. Meanwhile the executive branch of the federal government had begun to move against segregation and discrimination in the armed forces and in civil service employment. Some state legislatures acted against discrimination in housing and employment, and congress took its first cautious steps since Reconstruction to advance civil rights.

In the years since the Brown decision, a civil rights mass movement has taken shape among Negroes, utilizing the tactics of nonviolent direct action to demand immediate and full equality in all areas. The Reverend Martin Luther King led Negroes of Montgomery, Alabama, in a year-long boycott of the city's segregated bus system. Negro college students launched "sit-ins" throughout the South in a movement that ended segregation at lunch counters and other public facilities in hundreds of southern communities. "Freedom Riders" gave effect to court decisions outlawing segregation in transportation facilities. By 1963 mass demonstrations for equality in public facilities, jobs, education, and housing had spread from the South to many northern cities and more than 200,000 joined a "March on Washington" in support of President Kennedy's proposal that congress pass a substantial civil rights bill. These efforts were pursued in the face of mob violence, the arrests of thousands of demonstrators, the assassination of an NAACP leader in Mississippi, and death of four Negro girls in the bombing of a Birmingham church.

This civil rights revolution seems to us to be one of the major historical events of the midtwentieth century and to demand full treatment in any American history textbook. The gains that have been made should be described realistically and not as an ode to the inevitable justice and progress of the democratic system. It should be made clear that the outcome of the civil rights struggle is still in doubt, and that the inequalities are so great as to defy quick remedy by even the most vigorous efforts.

In the midst of this civil rights revolution, historians and educators have a clear responsibility, at the very least, to see to it that the role of Negroes in American life is taught fully and accurately. We have tried to indicate what a minimally full and accurate textbook account should be. Surely the state of California can no longer tolerate textbooks that fall far short of this minimal standard.

CALIFORNIA LAW ON TEACHING NEGRO HISTORY

On July 6, 1965, California Governor Edmund Brown signed into law a series of amendments to the state's Education Code relating to the teaching of Negro history. The amendments were introduced by Los Angeles representative Mervyn Dymally, a former school teacher.

Sec. 7604. The course of study in the elementary schools shall include instruction in the following prescribed branches in the several grades in which each is required pursuant to this article ...: The study of the role and contribution of American Negroes and other ethnic groups in the history of this country and this state shall be an integrated part of the required courses in the history of the United States and California.

Sec. 7700. .... In addition to courses otherwise required by law, the course of study shall require of all pupils in grades 7 to 12, inclusive: (b) Five years of history commencing with grade 7, to include ... a study of the role and contributions of American Negroes and other ethnic groups in the history of this country and this state.

Sec. 9310.5. When adopting the textbooks and teachers' manuals for use in elementary schools for the teaching of courses in civics and the history of the United States and California, the State Board of Education shall include only such textbooks which conform with the required courses and correctly portray the role and contribution of the American Negro and members of other ethnic groups in the total development of the United States and of the State of California.

Sec. 9958. The bond shall further provide that the publisher will pay the cost in a sum not to exceed five hundred dollars ($500) of any investigation of the merits of any textbook in a public high school in the state if a commission of impartial experts finds, after public hearing, that such textbook contained sectarian or denominational doctrine contrary to law, or propaganda injurious in the judgment of the commission, to the schools, or material that does not correctly portray the role and contribution of the American Negro and members of other ethnic groups in the total development of the United States and of the State of California.

Sec. 9959. When, in the judgment of the State Board of Education, there exists sufficient evidence that a textbook offered and sold by a publisher for use as a textbook in any public high school in the state contains sectarian or denominational doctrine contrary to law or contains propaganda injurious to the welfare of the public schools, the board shall cause the book to be investigated by a committee of impartial experts. The committee shall be constituted and shall conduct its investigation under such rules and regulations as may be prescribed by the State Board of Education. If, in the opinion of the committee, the textbook does contain sectarian or denominational doctrine contrary to law or does not correctly portray the role and contribution of the American Negro and members of other ethnic groups in the total development of the United States and of the State of California, the Board of Education may order that the publisher shall cease to offer and sell such textbook for use as a textbook in any public high school in the state. If the State Board of Education shall make such an order, it shall be illegal for any district to purchase copies of such textbook for use as a textbook in any high school or to continue the use of the textbook beyond the close of the current year.

Sec. 10013. [Applies the substance of Sec. 9310.5 to high schools.]

THE CASE FOR NEW DESEGREGATION LEGISLATION

Edward M. Kennedy *is United States Senator from Massachusetts. The text below is part of Senator Kennedy's statement on April 27, 1966, in senate committee hearings on S. 2928, a bill to aid localities in alleviating* de facto *segregation.*

I want to thank the distinguished chairman of the education subcommittee for setting aside time during these important hearings to hear testimony on S. 2928, a bill I introduced in the senate on February 16, 1966. I also want to thank each of the members of the panel which will follow my testimony for taking the time and making the effort to come to Washington today to discuss the problems of *de facto* segregation in our public schools. Each of them has already made valuable contributions in the field of education and I am certain that all of us here in the senate will benefit from hearing their views on this important question.

Any matter affecting the quality of our education and the well-being of our children should concern us seriously. An adequate education is the cornerstone of good citizenship, and in today's complex world, an economic necessity. It is not a privilege to be made available only to a few. It is the indispensable equipment of all free men and their key to equal opportunity. A good education is important for all children. But it is especially vital for the disadvantaged, particularly our Negro citizens.

From *Integrated Education,* June/July 1966. Reprinted by permission of the author.

The American Negro, if he is to have faith in any of our society's institutions, must have faith in our schools. A school is the only institution which, by its very nature, involves a daily effort to give to its students something they did not have before, and make of them something they were not before. Without equal educational opportunities, the American Negro will never obtain the full citizenship which is his birthright. I believe that because of racial imbalance in public schools, many a Negro child today is being denied this opportunity. And once it is denied him, the harmful effects in most cases can never be completely overcome.

With some exceptions, segregation in educational facilities in the North and West does not exist as a result of purposeful official action. But it does exist nonetheless. As a result of a past history of residential segregation combined with a commonly observed school policy of pupil assignment based on place of residence, school systems which are highly segregated *de facto* by color can be found in almost every major city in the North and West.

In my own state of Massachusetts, for example, a study last year by the Massachusetts Advisory Committee on Racial Imbalance and Education found that "most Negro children in Massachusetts attended predominantly Negro schools while the overwhelming majority of white citizens attend schools that are either all white or have fewer than five nonwhite children enrolled." Massachusetts is one example, but by no means the most striking one. The problem of *de facto* school segregation, or racial imbalance, is even more severe in those northern and western states which have a higher percentage of nonwhite citizens than my own state.

Present law does not provide for federal assistance to education programs designed to deal with this problem. Title III of the original administration Civil Rights Bill of 1964 did make specific provision for the inclusion of areas of racial imbalance in all programs, loan, grant, and assistance projects concerned with the study and alleviation of segregation in public education. But these references were eliminated in committee, and the bill as passed provided specifically that "desegregation shall not mean the assignment of students to public schools in order to overcome racial imbalance."

My bill would restore the present law to its original form and permit the same kind of assistance to schools acting to correct *de facto* segregation as it currently makes available to school boards acting to correct *de jure* segregation.

I would now like to discuss in detail each section of Title IV of the Civil Rights Act to show how it would be affected by S. 2928.

Section 402. Presently the commissioner of education is authorized to study and report on the availability of equal education facilities for all individuals in public institutions throughout the nation. My bill would authorize the study of areas of racial imbalance to be included in this report to the President.

Section 403. Under this provision the commissioner would be authorized to render technical assistance to school officials in the preparation, adoption, and implementation of plans for correcting racial imbalance as well as for the desegregation of public schools.

Section 404. The commissioner would be authorized to arrange for the operation of special training institutes designed to improve the ability of personnel who deal with educational problems occasioned by racial imbalance as well as by desegregation in school systems.

Section 405. The commissioner would be authorized to provide for in-service training for teachers and school personnel and the employment of special advisers on problems resulting from racial imbalance as well as from desegregation.

The major limitation of Title IV is its inability to deal with or assist operational programs such as teacher exchanges, busing, and long-range studies, all of which could contribute substantially to the amelioration of immediate and imminently explosive situations. The most important innovation in my bill is the addition to Section 405 of a series of special programs which will allow school officials to obtain federal assistance for dealing with these situations. Included in the special programs would be the development of new curricular materials, the taking of surveys and assessments leading to redistricting of school facilities, teacher exchanges, transportation projects, and supplemental constructions.

The first of these, the development of new curricular materials, is aimed at closing the informational gap between students who were educated in highly segregated schools and the rest of the student population, and at seeking out methods of teaching which appeal to the interests and abilities of culturally deprived children. Three types of curricular materials have been suggested by the Office of Education.

1. Special units for social studies classes dealing with problems of civil rights and civil liberties, emphasizing the historical and cultural contributions of minority groups. New York City school officials have drawn up such a program but have not been able to find enough money for implementing it. They feel that the issues of civil rights can be brought into the lives of Negro and white students on a daily basis through the classroom, and will thereby cease to have fearful or mysterious implications. The school system of Wilmington, Delaware, has also developed a program of curricular materials which would make the study of civic responsibility and community relations a part of the secondary school curriculum.

2. Specific materials such as vocabularies, readers, oral approaches in instruction, books and literature designed to overcome the handicaps suffered by culturally deprived children. These materials would emphasize approaches to learning familiar to the Negro child, and words, pictures, stories, and objects that have been seen and heard in their homes.

3. Illustrations and content, to be included in existing materials, which will develop a self-concept for minority group children. By seeing themselves and the history of their cultures in these materials they will be imbued with a sense of their own importance, and be motivated by their possible contributions to society. In Oak Ridge, Tennessee, for example, school officials have undertaken such a curriculum project but have been unable to find enough money to carry it out. Furthermore, even if a school wished only to make use of such materials, they would be unable to find them, for no agency has taken the time and trouble to develop them for public use.

The second type of special project under my bill is the development of surveys and assessments leading to redistricting and the reallocation of school facilities. There is no question that the ultimate answer for the desegregation of public schools is long-range planning of construction and the eventual implementation of programs for residential and school reorganization in metropolitan areas. Funds under this section of the bill could be used by schools to study the composition and zoning of their established districts, and the use and quality of their facilities. Such studies are essential background for any program leading to long-range building plans, the development of a transportation system that would assist desegregation, and complementing a building program, a more efficient use of existing buildings, and development of new types of school construction. Many school districts have asked for this kind of survey, or for advice on *de facto* consolidation needs, but funds have not been available for them.

A third area covered in Section 405 of my bill is teacher exchange programs. Students need association with teachers, as well as students, of another race. My bill would provide funds for school systems to give special bonuses and incentives to teachers willing to spend time teaching in a "difficult school." Three counties in Florida, as well as areas of Harlem, Cincinnati, and Philadelphia have already inquired about funds for this kind of program. The funds were unobtainable.

The fourth area of concern under this section of the bill is transportation programs such as busing. Any proposal aimed at balancing the racial composition of neighborhoods by open enrollment, pupil transfers, feeder plans, single-grade schools, or pupil dispersal involves the busing of students. Many school officials, including some in my own city of Boston and in Malverne, New York, have been seeking federal help with such programs, to no avail. None of these new methods of integrating school systems can be effectively tested without pilot transportation projects.

The last type of special project involves supplemental construction funds for consolidation of school districts and the creative use of new school designs. The construction envisioned here is not of a comprehensive nature but is a stopgap to provide the greatest use of existing school facilities and short-range building projects. For instance, a small isolated, all-Negro rural school could be closed and integrated with a larger central school by the construction of one additional classroom. A preschool nursery program—vitally important to children with poor home lives— could be extended from four- to three-year-olds by building large, open-space playrooms with separations for group activities. Again, funds under this section could be used to study new design in school construction and for long-range planning of one-grade schools.

My bill includes no coercive measures whatsoever. It merely makes funds available to those school districts that recognize a problem and have designed a program to deal with it.

Mr. Chairman: There is no more serious problem that faces the school systems of the North and West today than the need to guarantee equal educational opportunities to every student regardless of color, race, or religion. President Johnson has recognized the need and has asked the Civil Rights Commission to make an extensive study of the problem and its effect on the children and school districts of the North and West. The Commission has already held hearings in Cleveland. The testimony of the children, teachers, administrators and public officials affirms and expands in tragically personal terms the facts that I have outlined briefly to you. My bill could provide immediate and short-term relief to many such school districts and contribute greatly to the type of investigation presently underway by the Civil Rights Commission.

THE WASHINGTON, D.C., SCHOOL CASE

On January 13, 1966, Julius Hobson filed suit against District of Columbia School Superintendent Carl F. Hansen and the school board. He charged, variously, that the school system was unconstitutionally discriminating on de jure *and* de facto *grounds; and that the board was positively obliged under the constitutional doctrine of equal protection of the laws to remedy the discrimination. On June 19, 1967, the U.S. District Court for the District of Columbia rendered its decision. J. Skelly Wright, U.S. circuit judge, wrote the opinion in* Hobson v. Hansen, Civil Action No. 82-66. *Following are extracts from the full opinion except for the material under the heading "Opinion of the Law," which was written by the editor.*

Findings of Fact

In *Bolling v. Sharpe,* 347 U.S. 497 (1954), the supreme court held that the District of Columbia's racially segregated public school system violated the due process clause of the Fifth Amendment. The present litigation, brought in behalf of Negro as well as poor children generally in the District's public schools, tests the current compliance of those schools with Bolling, its companion case, *Brown v. Board of Education of Topeka,* 347 U.S. 483 (1954), and their progeny. The basic question presented is whether the defendants, the superintendent of schools and the members of the board of education, in the operation of the public school system here, unconstitutionally deprive the District's Negro and poor public school children of their right to equal educational opportunity with the District's white and more affluent public school children. This court concludes that they do.

In support of this conclusion the court makes the following principal findings of fact:

1. Racially and socially homogeneous schools damage the minds and spirit of all children who attend them—the Negro, the white, the poor and the affluent—and block the attainment of the broader goals of democratic education, whether the segregation occurs by law or by fact.
2. The scholastic achievement of the disadvantaged child, Negro and white, is strongly related to the racial and socioeconomic composition of the student body of his school. A racially and socially integrated school environment increases the scholastic achievement of the disadvantaged child of whatever race.
3. The board of education, which is the statutory head of the public schools in the District, is appointed pursuant to a quota system which, until 1962, for over half a century had limited the Negro membership of the nine-man board to three. Since 1962 the Negro quota on the board has been four, one less than a majority. The city of Washington, which is the District of Columbia, presently has a population over 60 percent Negro and a public school population over 90 percent Negro.
4. Adherence to the neighborhood school policy by the school board effectively segregates the Negro and the poor children from the white and more affluent children in most of the District's public schools. This neighborhood school policy is relaxed by the board through the use of optional zones for the purpose of

From *Integrated Education,* **August/September 1967.**

allowing white children, usually affluent white children, "trapped" in a Negro school district, to "escape" to a "white" or more nearly white school, thus making the economic and racial segregation of the public school children more complete than it would otherwise be under a strict neighborhood school assignment plan.

5. The teachers and principals in the public schools are assigned so that generally the race of the faculty is the same as the race of the children. Thus most of the schools can be identified as "Negro" or "white," not only by reference to the predominant race of the children attending, but by the predominant race of the faculty as well. The heaviest concentration of Negro faculty, usually 100 percent, is in the Negro ghetto schools.

6. The median annual per pupil expenditure ($292) in the predominantly (85 percent to 100 percent) Negro elementary schools in the District of Columbia has been a flat $100 below the median annual per pupil expenditure for its predominantly (85 percent to 100 percent) white schools ($392).

7. Generally the "white" schools are underpopulated while the "Negro" schools generally are overcrowded. Moreover, all of the white elementary schools have kindergartens. Some Negro schools are without kindergartens entirely, while other Negro schools operate kindergartens in shifts or consecutive sessions. In addition to being overcrowded and short on kindergarten space, the school buildings in the Negro slums are ancient and run down. Only recently, through the use of impact aid and other federal funds, have the Negro slum schools had sufficient textbooks for the children's use.

8. As they proceed through the Washington school system, the reading scores primarily of the Negro and poor children, but not the white and middle class, fall increasingly behind the national norm. By senior high school the discrepancy reaches several grades.

9. The track system as used in the District's public schools is a form of ability grouping in which students are divided in separate, self-contained curricula or tracks ranging from "Basic" for the slow student to "Honors" for the gifted.

10. The aptitude tests used to assign children to the various tracks are standardized primarily on white middle-class children. Since these tests do not relate to the Negro and disadvantaged child, track assignments based on such tests relegate Negro and disadvantaged children to the lower tracks from which, because of the reduced curricula and the absence of adequate remedial and compensatory education, as well as continued inappropriate testing, the chance of escape is remote.

11. Education in the lower tracks is geared to what Dr. Hansen, the creator of the track system, calls the "blue-collar" student. Thus such children, so stigmatized by inappropriate aptitude-testing procedures, are denied equal opportunity to obtain the white-collar education available to the white and more affluent children.

Other incidental, but highly indicative, findings are as follows: (1) The June 1964-December 1965 study by the Office of the Surgeon General, Army, shows that 55.3 percent of the 18-year-olds from the District of Columbia failed the Armed Services mental test, a higher percentage than any of the fifty states. (2) The average per pupil expenditure in the District's public schools is only slightly below the national average. The 1964-65 Bureau of the Census Report on Governmental Finances shows, however, that the District of Columbia spends less per capita on education generally than all states except Arkansas and Tennessee.

The same report shows that the District of Columbia spends more per capita on police protection than all states without exception. In fact, the District of Columbia spends more than double any state other than Nevada, New York, New Jersey, and California. The inferences, including those bearing on the relationship of the quality of education to crime, which arise from these findings are obvious. Indeed, the National Crime Commission's Task Force Report, *Juvenile Delinquency and Youth Crime,* indicates that the very deficiencies in the District's public school system noted by the record in this case—prejudging, through inappropriate testing, the learning abilities of the disadvantaged child as inferior to the white middle-class child; placing the child in lower tracks for reduced education based on such tests, thus implementing the self-fulfilling prophecy phenomenon inherent in such misjudgments; placing inferior teachers in slum schools; continuing racial and economic segregation of pupils, providing textbooks unrelated to the lives of disadvantaged children; inadequate remedial programs for offsetting initial psychological and social difficulties of the disadvantaged child—all have contributed to the increase in crime, particularly juvenile crime.

In sum, all of the evidence in this case tends to show that the Washington school system is a monument to the cynicism of the power structure which governs the voteless capital of the greatest country on earth.

Opinion of Law*

[The court acknowledged that the school board may have failed to disestablish legal segregation promptly and thoroughly enough after 1954. It held, however, that the plaintiffs failed to prove this; and that it is untimely to try to deal with such a charge so long after the event.

[The court declared appropriate a revived "separate but equal" principle: ". . . If whites and Negroes, or rich and poor, are to be consigned to separate schools, pursuant to whatever policy, the minimum the Constitution will require and guarantee is that for their objectively measurable aspects these schools be run on the basis of real equality, at least unless any inequalities are adequately justified" (p 147). Where for any reason schools are segregated, the least the school board must provide are "materially equal" facilities.

[The court declared that optional attendance zones, as applied in the District, produced "de jure constitutional violations" (p. 152). Another instance of *de jure* segregation cited is teacher segregation: "But if any truth is axiomatic, it is that the Negro *students'* equal protection rights to an integrated faculty cannot be undermined or thwarted by the racially induced preferences of the teachers, who after all are minor public officials whose actions must therefore pass constitutional muster" (p. 156). Segregation of principals is infected "with the identical unconstitutionality" (p. 158).

[The court held that *de facto* segregation in the District " redounds to the academic detriment of Negro students and seriously sets back the working out of racial prejudices" (p. 162). This fact, however, was not held to "conclusively determine its unconstitutionality" (p. 162). While *de facto* segregation is not, as such, unconstitutional, yet its effects must be "carefully scrutinized" for violations of the principle of equal protection for the poor and racial minorities. "What supports this call" for close scrutiny, the court explained, are "our

---

*[Editor's Note: This summary, "Opinion of Law," was written by the editor.]

horror at infflicting any further injury on the Negro, the degree to which the poor and the Negro must rely on the public schools in rescuing themselves from their depressed cultural and economic condition, and also our common need for the schools to serve as the public agency for neutralizing and normalizing race relations in this country" (p. 165).

[Part of the careful scrutiny involves a search for viable alternatives to harmful *de facto* practices. The detriment resulting from *de facto* segregation cannot be justified constitutionally if alternatives to the detrimental condition have not been explored. Remedial alternatives must be sought. The court will consult competent judgment "on whether each specific remedial alternative is circumstantially feasible and within the public interest . . . " (p. 170).

[The track system, holds the court, deprives "the poor and a majority of the Negro students in the District of Columbia of their constitutional right to equal educational opportunities" (p. 170). Children are classified in the tracks not according to ability to learn but according to color and class, factors extraneous to innate ability. The track system thus "amounts to an unlawful discrimination against those students whose educational opportunities are being limited on the erroneous assumption that they are capable of accepting no more" (p. 176).]

Remedy

The remedy to be provided against the discriminatory policies of the defendants' school administration must center primarily on pupil assignment, teacher assignment, and the track system. The overcrowding in the Negro schools results from pupil assignment and the difference in the per pupil expenditure results in the main from the assignment of the more highly paid teachers to the predominantly white schools. Consequently, corrective measures designed to reduce pupil and teacher racial segregation should also reduce overcrowding in the Negro schools as well as the pupil expenditure differential favoring the white children. Pending the implementation of such measures, the court will require that the defendants provide transportation to volunteering children from the overcrowded schools east of the Park to the underpopulated schools west of the Park.

As to the remedy with respect to the track system, the track system simply must be abolished. In practice, if not in concept, it discriminates against the disadvantaged child, particularly the Negro. Designed in 1955 as a means of protecting the school system against the ill effects of integrating with white children the Negro victims of *de jure* separate but unequal education, it has survived to stigmatize the disadvantaged child of whatever race relegated to its lower tracks—from which tracks the possibility of switching upward, because of the absence of compensatory education, is remote.

Even in concept the track system is undemocratic and discriminatory. Its creator admits it is designed to prepare some children for white-collar, and other children for blue-collar jobs. Considering the tests used to determine which children should receive the blue-collar special, and which the white, the danger of children completing their education wearing the wrong collar is far too great for this democracy to tolerate. Moreover, any system of ability grouping which, through failure to include and implement the concept of compensatory education for the disadvantaged child or otherwise, fails in fact to bring the great majority of children into the mainstream of public education, denies the children excluded equal educational opportunity, and thus encounters the constitutional bar.

As has been shown, the defendants' pupil placement policies discriminate unconstitutionally against the Negro and the poor child whether tested by the principles of "separate but equal," *de jure* or *de facto* segregation. The use by the defendants of the neighborhood school policy, intentionally manipulated in some instances to increase segregation, is the primary cause of the pupil assignment discrimination. Because of the ten-to-one ratio of Negro to white children in the public schools of Washington and because the neighborhood policy is accepted and is in general use throughout the United States, the court is not barring its use here at this time.

In preparing the plan to alleviate pupil segregation which the court is ordering the defendants to file, however, the court will require that the defendants consider the advisability of establishing educational parks, particularly at the junior and senior high school levels, school pairing, Princeton and other approaches toward maximun effective integration. Where, because of the density of residential segregation or for other reasons, children in certain areas, particularly the slums, are denied the benefits of an integrated education, the court will require that the plan include compensatory education sufficient at least to overcome the detriment of segregation and thus provide, as nearly as possible, equal educational opportunity to all school children. Since segregation resulting from pupil assignment is so intimately related to school location, the court will require the defendants to include in their plan provision for the application of the principles herein announced to their $300,000,000 building program.

The plan, too, should anticipate the possibility that integration may be accomplished through cooperation with school districts in the metropolitan suburbs. There is no reason to conclude that all Washingtonians who make their homes in Virginia or Maryland accept the heresy that segregated public education is socially realistic and furthers the attainment of the goals of a democratic society. Certainly if the jurisdictions comprising the Washington metropolitan area can cooperate in the establishment of a metropolitan transit authority (see 1 *D.C. Code* pars. 1401-1416 [1961]), the possibility of such cooperation in the field of education should not be denied—at least not without first sounding the pertinent moral and social responsibilities of the parties concerned.

The final question is the remedy this court should forge for curing the illegalities in teacher placement. It is clear, first, that an injunction should be directed against every possibility of willful segregation in the teacher assignment process; if the preferences of principals and teachers are to be relied on at all by the assistant superintendents or any other officer making the assignment, measures must be taken to insure that race does not creep into the expression of preference.

Next, assignment of incoming teachers must proceed on a color-conscious basis to insure substantial and rapid teacher integration in every school. And finally, to the extent that these two measures are unable quickly to achieve sufficient faculty integration in the schools, this court, as it indicated by its discussion above concerning the board's responsibilities in following up on *Bolling* v. *Sharpe*, has no doubt that a substantial reassignment of the present teachers, including tenured staff, will be mandatory. A similar call has been sounded by the Office of Education, whose Title VI guidelines establish that "[e]very school system has a positive duty to make staff assignments and reassignments necessary to eliminate past discriminatory assignment policies" (45 C.F.R. par. 181.3 (d) [1967]); *and see* the discussion and decree in

United States v. *Jefferson County,* 5 Cir., 372 F.2d 836, 892-894, 900 [1967]). In the South, a few courts in their discretion have exacted less inclusive commitments from school boards, relating merely to nonsegregatory future assignments and the encouragement of voluntary transfers;[1] but that does not bind the conscience of other chancellors confronted with other factual situations.

The more complex question is the goal or objective toward which the school system should strive through the various means outlined above. Two federal courts have ordered school systems to proportion Negro and white teachers equally in every school, give or take a small margin of error. *Dowell* v. *School Board,* W. D. Okla., 244 F. Supp. 971 (1965), *affirmed,* 10 Cir., —— F.2d —— (January 23, 1967), *cert. denied,*——U.S.——, 35 U.S.L. Week 3419 (May 29, 1967); *Kier* v. *County School Board,* W.D. Va., 249 F. Supp. 239 (1966). It is true, however, that in Dowell the court assumed the initiative only after the school board defaulted in the obligation assigned it by the court to draw up a faculty desegregation plan, and Kier dealt with a school system with only twenty-five schools, which may make a difference. Still, there is great appeal in the simplicity and thoroughness of such a decree.

These issues of remedy were ignored at trial by counsel for both sides, each intent instead on establishing or refuting the primary constitutional violation. For this reason, and considering the limitations of time, for the 1967-68 school year the court is content to order "substantial" teacher integration in those schools where complete segregation or token integration of faculty has heretofore existed. The court will remit the question of the longer-term goal to the board for first-instance treatment in the plan which the court in its decree will order the board to prepare.

There will be an abundance of opportunity later for adversary argument on the merits and demerits of the ends (and means) concerning teacher integration which the Board decides to propose.

Parting Word

It is regrettable, of course, that in deciding this case this court must act in an area so alien to its expertise. It would be far better indeed for these great social and political problems to be resolved in the political arena by other branches of government. But there are social and political problems which seem at times to defy such resolution. In such situations, under our system, the judiciary must bear a hand and accept its responsibility to assist in the solution where constitutional rights hang in the balance. So it was in *Brown* v. *Board of Education, Bolling* v. *Sharpe,* and *Baker* v. *Carr.* So it is in the South where federal courts are making brave attempts to implement the mandate of Brown. So it is here.

The decree is attached to, and made part of, this opinion.

Decree

It is ORDERED, ADJUDGED and DECREED that the defendants, their agents, officers, employees, and successors, and all those in active concert and participation with them be, and they are hereby, permanently enjoined from discriminating on the basis of racial or economic status in the operation of the District of Columbia public school system.

---

[1]*Clark* v. *Board of Educ.,* 8 Cir., 369 F.2d 661 (1966); *Wheeler* v. *Durham City Bd. of Educ.,* 4 Cir., 363 F.2d 738 (1966).

It is FURTHER ORDERED, ADJUDGED and DECREED that the defendants be, and they are hereby, permanently enjoined from operating the track system in the District of Columbia public schools. It is FURTHER ORDERED that on October 2, 1967, the defendants file in the record in this case a report of their compliance with this order of the court.

It is FURTHER ORDERED, ADJUDGED and DECREED that on October 2, 1967, the defendants herein file in the record in this case for approval by the court a plan of public assignment complying with the principles announced in the court's opinion and the instructions contained in the part styled REMEDY thereof.

It is FURTHER ORDERED, ADJUDGED and DECREED that the defendants, beginning with the school year 1967-68, provide transportation for volunteering children in overcrowded school districts east of Rock Creek Park to underpopulated schools west of the Park. It is FURTHER ORDERED that on October 2, 1967, the defendants file in the record in this case a report of their compliance with this order of the court.

It is FURTHER ORDERED, ADJUDGED and DECREED that, beginning with the school year 1967-68, the following optional zones be abolished: Wilson-Western-Roosevelt; Cardozo-Western; Dunbar-Western; Gordon-MacFarland; Gordon-Banneker; and Powell-Hearst. It is FURTHER ORDERED that on October 2, 1967, the defendants file in the record in this case a report of their compliance with this order of the court.

It is FURTHER ORDERED, ADJUDGED and DECREED that the defendants, beginning with the school year 1967-68, provide substantial teacher integration in the faculty of each school. It is FURTHER ORDERED that on October 2, 1967, the defendants file in the record in this case a report of their compliance with this order of the court.

It is FURTHER ORDERED, ADJUDGED and DECREED that on October 2, 1967, the defendants file in the record in this case for approval by the court a plan of teacher assignment which will fully integrate the faculty of each school pursuant to the principles announced in the court's opinion and the instructions contained in the part styled REMEDY thereof.

It is FURTHER ORDERED, ADJUDGED and DECREED that the United States be, and it is hereby, invited to intervene in these proceedings to assist in the implementation of the decree, to suggest amendments to the decree, and to take whatever other steps it deems appropriate in the interest of public education in the District of Columbia. It is FURTHER ORDERED that the United States be served with a copy of this decree in the manner prescribed by Rule 4(d)(4), *Federal Rules of Civil Procedure.* The parties, of course, may suggest amendments to this decree at any time.

J. SKELLY WRIGHT
United States Circuit Judge

THE MASSACHUSETTS LAW ON RACIAL BALANCE

On August 18, 1965, Massachusetts Governor John A. Volpe signed the nation's first state law to enforce racial balance in schools by a combination of financial penalties and incentives. Following is the text of the law as contained in an advance copy released by the Office of the Secretary of the Commonwealth.

From *Integrated Education,* **August/November 1965.**

CHAPTER 641

THE COMMONWEALTH OF MASSACHUSETTS

In the Year
One Thousand Nine Hundred and Sixty-five

AN ACT PROVIDING FOR THE ELIMINATION OF RACIAL IMBALANCE IN THE PUBLIC SCHOOLS.

Whereas, The deferred operation of this act would tend to defeat its purpose, which is to eliminate forthwith racial imbalance in the public schools, therefore it is hereby declared to be an emergency law, necessary for the immediate preservation of the public convenience.

Be it enacted by the Senate and House of Representatives in General Court assembled, and by the authority of the same, as follows:

SECTION 1. Chapter 71 of the General Laws is hereby amended by inserting after section 37B the following two sections:

Section 37C. It is hereby declared to be the policy of the commonwealth to encourage all school committees to adopt as educational objectives the promotion of racial balance and the correction of existing racial imbalance in the public schools. The prevention or elimination of racial imbalance shall be an objective in all decisions involving the drawing or altering of school attendance lines and the selection of new school sites.

Section 37D. The school committee of each city, town, and district shall, annually, at such time and in such form as the commissioner shall determine, submit statistics sufficient to enable a determination to be made of the percent of nonwhite pupils in all public schools and in each school under the jurisdiction of each such committee. Whenever the state board of education finds that racial imbalance exists in a public school it shall notify in writing the school committee or regional school district committee having jurisdiction over such school that such finding has been made. The school committee shall thereupon prepare a plan to eliminate such racial imbalance and file a copy of such plan with the board. The term "racial imbalance" refers to a ratio between nonwhite and other students in public schools which is sharply out of balance with the racial composition of the society in which nonwhite children study, serve, and work. For the purpose of this section, racial imbalance shall be deemed to exist when the percent of nonwhite students in any public school is in excess of fifty percent of the total number of students in such school.

Said plan shall detail the changes in existing school attendance districts, the location of proposed school sites, the proposed additions to existing school buildings, and other methods for the elimination of racial imbalance. Said plan shall also include projections of the expected racial composition of all public schools. Any plan to detail changes in existing school attendance districts, the locations of proposed new school sites and proposed additions to existing school sites and proposed additions to existing school buildings with the intention of reducing or eliminating racial imbalance, must take into consideration on an equal basis with the above-mentioned intention, the safety of the children involved in traveling from home to school and school to home. Said plan may provide for voluntary cooperation by other cities and towns in rendering assistance and in making available facilities to effectuate said plan.

No school committee or regional school district committee shall be required as part of its plan to transport any pupil to any school outside its jurisdiction or to any school outside the school district established for his neighborhood, if the parent or guardian of such pupil files written objection thereto with such school committee.

Said board may, from time to time, require each school committee to submit to said board a report on the progress of the plan and its implementation.

The supreme judicial and the superior court shall have jurisdiction in equity upon petition of the board of education to enforce the provisions of this section.

SECTION 2. Chapter 15 of the General Laws is hereby amended by inserting after section 1H the following three sections:

Section 1I. The board of education shall provide technical and other assistance in the formulation and execution of plans to eliminate racial imbalance, made pursuant to section thirty-seven D of chapter seventy-one. Whenever the board determines that a school committee or regional school district committee has failed to file a plan in compliance with the provisions of said section, it shall consult with and make specific recommendations for a plan by such school committee or regional school district committee.

If, following the receipt of notification from the board of education that racial imbalance, as defined in section thirty-seven D of chapter seventy-one exists, a school committee or regional school district committee does not show progress within a reasonable time in eliminating racial imbalance in its schools the commissioner of education shall not certify the amount of state aid for such city or town or for such towns which are members of such regional school districts, as required by section nine of chapter seventy, and the school building assistance commission upon receipt of notice from said board that racial imbalance exists shall not approve any project for school construction for such city, town, or regional school district under chapter six hundred and forty-five of the acts of nineteen hundred and forty-eight, as amended, and the commissioner of education may notify the commissioner of corporations and taxation and the comptroller to hold such funds as have been so certified under said section nine but have not been disbursed. The commissioner of education may thereafter upon receipt of a plan acceptable to the board of education notify the commissioner of corporations and taxation and the comptroller to pay any such withheld funds to such city or town in such amounts and at such times as he may designate, and the school building assistance commission upon receipt of notice from said board that a plan acceptable to it has been received may approve such projects.

The school building assistance commission shall, notwithstanding any contrary provision of chapter six hundred and forty-five of the acts of nineteen hundred and forty-eight, as amended, increase the amount of grants for school house construction to sixty-five percent of the approved cost, whenever the board of education is satisfied that the construction or enlargement of a schoolhouse is for the purpose of reducing or eliminating racial imbalance in the school system and so notifies the school building assistance commission.

Section 1J. Within thirty days after (1) a school committee or regional school district committee declines to accept the recommendations submitted to it by the board or (2) the board disapproves a revised plan submitted to it by a school committee or regional school district committee, said committee may file a petition for judicial review in the superior court for the county in which it is located or in the supreme judicial court for Suffolk county. The court may affirm the board's determination of the recommendations submitted by it or its determination of disapproval of a revised plan submitted to it, and order compliance with the recommendations of the board by appropriate decree, or if it finds and rules that the determination by the board is (a) in excess of the statutory authority or jurisdiction of the board, or (b) based upon an error of law, or (c) arbitrary or capricious, an abuse of discretion, or otherwise not in accordance with law, then it may set aside such determination by the board and remand the matter to it for further action.

The supreme judicial and the superior court shall have jurisdiction in equity upon petition of the board of education to order funds withheld as provided in section one I for such period of time as the court may determine.

Section 1K. The board of education, with the advice of the commissioner, shall appoint an advisory committee on racial imbalance and no individual shall be appointed to this advisory committee on racial imbalance who has been listed in any state or federal document as being a member of a communist front organization. The members of the committee shall serve without compensation except that they may be reimbursed for the necessary expenses actually incurred in the performance of their duties.

THE EDUCATIONAL PARK

Max Wolff *is director of research, Migration Division, Commonwealth of Puerto Rico, and senior research sociologist, Center for Urban Education. This is the text of a position paper prepared for the Conference on Education and Racial Imbalance in the City, March 2-3, 1967, sponsored by the Hartford, Connecticut, public schools. Dr. Wolff recently directed a study of how well the educational gains of Head Starters held up after enrollment in kindergartens. (The gains were lost within four months.) Dr. Wolff is a member of the editorial advisory board of* INTEGRATED EDUCATION *magazine.*

QUESTION: How would you define an educational park?

ANSWER: Basically, it is a clustering of educational facilities in a campus-like setting. But a mere cluster of school buildings on one site is *not* automatically an educational park. Centrally organized common facilities serving the schools on the campus are the added essential ingredient of the educational park.

QUESTION: What do you mean by "centrally organized common facilities"?

ANSWER: At present, each neighborhood school must have its own auditorium, gym, library, science room, art and music rooms, and shops if it is to be even moderately well equipped. Each such facility is necessarily modest and is in use only a small fraction of the school week—unless it is used to relieve overcrowding and not for its original purpose at all. Staffing these facilities with subject specialists and librarians is always a financial problem even if the people are available. Few school systems provide more than part-time visiting specialists.

In the educational park, classroom buildings will be small and intimate, keeping the children together in familiar groups, but the gyms, the auditoriums, the science

From *Integrated Education,* **April/May 1967. Reprinted by permission of the author.**

and language facilities, and the art and music buildings will be shared by the children in many classroom buildings. Because a building with classrooms only is drastically less expensive to build than one with large open-space rooms like gyms and auditoriums, construction savings can be realized and used to provide the most modern and imaginative central buildings to serve all the children in the park. The science building, for example, can have both small laboratory rooms and large demonstration theaters. The auditorium building can have a huge theater equipped for professional performances to serve both the park and the adult community. The same building can have small rehearsal rooms, music instruction rooms, and intimate "little theaters."

As another example of common services, imagine a health center for such a park and contrast it with the present "nurse's room" off in a corner of the neighborhood school with a nurse in attendance on Tuesday and Thursday afternoons only. I often wonder what happens to the child who had the bad judgment to get ill on Monday when the nurse is serving at another school. The park's center should have not only an infirmary for emergencies, but an extensive preventive medicine facility and program, testing and following the children's health progress throughout their twelve years at school. Doctors, nurses, psychiatrists, social workers, and guidance people can all be housed here. The local boards of health are often eager to cooperate in running such centers.

These central facilities of all types will be programmed to be in use all of the time, for the children during the day and for the entire community after school hours. Organizing such optimum use of common facilities is child's play for the computer installation—and is educational child's work for the students who will be getting their training in modern computer operation by actually programming the daily operations of the park.

QUESTION: Where will school systems get the teachers to staff these specialized facilities?

ANSWER: Consider these two aspects of the problem. We need specialized, highly skilled teachers and we must also train young teachers coming up in the field. The park provides the opportunity to do both. Master teachers will be in charge of the various specialized programs, supervising and training young teachers. Teaching itself becomes an important learning experience for the new teachers.

In addition, the highly qualified specialist, given the best new equipment and scheduling a full day's work without long interruptions for travel from neighborhood to neighborhood, can benefit a maximum number of children.

Such a combination of excellence in teaching and quality of facilities invites the introduction and testing of innovation, challenging the teacher to delve more deeply into his field as well as into methods of teaching. The specialist today uses his creative imagination just to figure out ways of making do with the frustratingly inadequate facilities in the various schools he must cover. In many cases, it is a daily battle just to maintain the present state of stagnation. To answer your question directly: Whatever specialists or master teachers are available will have the fullest play for their talents, both in working with students and in helping their younger colleagues' professional growth.

QUESTION: What led you to this concept of the educational park?

ANSWER: As a sociologist specializing in community problems, I directed a number of studies dealing with the changing urbia and suburbia. The great movements of people into the cities is a world-wide phenomenon closely related to the current acceleration of industrial development. In highly industrialized countries like ours, this process is far advanced and the cities themselves are spilling over into ever-spreading metropolitan areas covering hundreds of miles. We have all experienced the new problems and tensions that accompany these massive changes. The out-of-city migration of those people who are not hindered by discrimination or socioeconomic standing is followed by the migration of commerce and industry. The others who are forced to stay in the inner city are the tax-poor.

The crisis in the cities is a compound of dwindling revenues and increased need for social services in the old centers and of uncontrolled and unbalanced growth in the new. Intergroup tension rises as the ghetto of the poor is confronted by the ghetto of the rich, the ghetto of the blacks by that of the whites.

The schools reflect all these problems both in the old and the new centers of population. Wherever I was called in to study the local school problems, the central issues that concerned the citizenry were how to modernize the education the children receive within the narrow financial limitations of the local community and how to achieve good racial balance that would relieve intergroup tensions and provide more equality of educational opportunity.

I observed the vitalizing impact of modern shopping centers and industrial parks on the communities and tried to visualize how the school system could become part of this vigorous new growth.

Every one of these community studies made it evident to me that the time for more patches on the old fabric is over. The school is the center of learning and that is its main task. By itself, it cannot solve city problems outside the area of education. However, as a participant in the many democratic processes of the community, it cannot help but affect, in key ways, other spheres of city life.

In my view, the educational park can provide a frame within which a community can approach solutions to the critical problems of stabilizing population changes, of citizen participation in community life and of intergroup tension. It can and should become the cultural center of the community, creating a new focus of communal identification, a rallying-point that counters the centripetal forces breaking the community apart. It will tend to stabilize a changing community particularly in the old centers where fear of declining standards of public education cause flight of those who can afford to move. It can provide the opportunity to promote sound intergroup relationships by bringing together the children (and their families) from the various racial, religious, and socioeconomic clusters in the community.

QUESTION: You have given a partial answer to my next question. At present our school systems build schools in the neighborhood that needs them. Why do you prefer the educational park with pupils from a broader community?

ANSWER: First of all, it is important to remember that the "neighborhood" school is a relatively new urban development. When free compulsory public education was being promoted actively by its proponents before the turn of the century the key purpose of the "common school," as it was called, was to provide equally for the poor and the rich so that all could share equally in the growth of America.

The law contemplates not only that all shall be taught, but that all shall be taught together. They are not only to receive equal quantities of knowledge, but all are to receive it in the same way. All are to approach the same common foundation together; nor can there be any exclusive source for individual or class.

Thus argued Charles Sumner in 1849 in describing the common school. The neighborhood school concept arose in the twenties of this century, responding to the widespread migration of Negroes to the North after World War I. It was given definition in 1926 by Clarence Perry in a study for the New York Regional Planning Association. The South never zoned by neighborhoods until compelled to by the 1954 supreme court decision.

The educational park reintroduces the original concept of the common school. However, there are other important reasons why neighborhood school construction fails to meet our cities' needs. First of all, quality. We have discussed how centralized facilities make possible a new level of educational excellence beyond the reach of the neighborhood school. A second very important consideration is economy.

Nearly every city has some obsolete schools which must be replaced and others that need modernization. All should be equipped to use the most advanced teaching techniques available. To bring all neighborhood schools up to date so that they may render educational services of the highest quality requires more money than any city can possibly afford. Centralized schooling removes existing inequalities among schools and permits continual upgrading of equipment at minimal cost.

The actual number of schools needed is reduced. Today, as neighborhoods gain or lose population with changing residential fashions, some of the existing schools become overutilized, others underutilized. Overcrowding calls for building more schools. Neighborhood school construction means relocating people with all the attendant upheaval and community controversy, especially in densely populated areas. Often the newly built school finds itself underutilized in a few years as the population matures and housing fashion changes. The educational park is more impervious to these intracity population movements. Total city growth can be accommodated by building the educational park from its inception on a site and within a plan that is designed for such growth. New schools can be erected within the park as they are needed on a harmonious, rational plan without disturbing community life.

Another consideration is status. With very few exceptions, the status of the school reflects the status of its neighborhood. "Good" or "bad" neighborhoods are defined by the socioeconomic standing and racial affiliation of the population. Teachers tend to prefer a high-status school to a low-status one because it affects their own status. Thus, as teachers seek positions in higher-status schools, the lower-status schools lose out in attracting and holding the highly qualified teachers they need. The educational park, removed from the individual neighborhood, has its own unique status as a great educational institution and relieves both teachers and parents of the search for the "best" school.

Coming back to the original concept of the common school, I prefer community to neighborhood construction of schools because the former permits integration and the latter tends to prevent it. Permit me for this purpose to call neighborhood schools "ghetto" schools, by which I mean schools that serve any neighborhood with a specific ethnic, racial, or socioeconomic character. Segregated education overlooks the reality of the world, of our country, and even of the specific community. This ignoring of reality harms not only those restricted to certain neighborhoods by law or by custom but also those who enjoy a high degree of freedom of choice. The children of both are ill-equipped to understand the reality of American life when they can see each other only dimly from over the walls of their ghettos.

The educational park is an inclusive frame for public education of the highest quality available equally to all children.

QUESTION: Will it not be extremely wasteful of existing school plant to change from the system of neighborhood schools to one of educational parks? Will it not take many years before such parks can be built, postponing the solution of pressing immediate problems?

ANSWER: If I may answer your second question first, a status quo-minded board of education can use as a pretext for inaction many devices, such as extensive "studies" and even endless community staff discussion of any plan. An alert community will see through such devices and will counteract such abuses of power. Similarly, delays in instituting necessary immediate improvements can be controlled by a watchful citizenry. However, thought should be given to making these immediate changes consistent with the long-range project of building educational parks and not in such a way as to preclude later park construction.

The key to how to do this is the early development of a city-wide skeleton plan that will define in general the areas where parks should be built, a timetable for their construction, and the order of progression of the school grades to be served.

For example, a community may plan to start its park at the fifth-grade level, to include all children from the fifth to the twelfth grades and to continue building, bringing up additional grades below the fifth as new facilities are built. Until the park is actually under construction, one or more of the existing elementary schools might be reorganized into a middle or intermediate school serving several neighborhoods to achieve racial balance or greater specialization during the intervening period. Then, when the park facility is ready, the children in the new middle school enter as a group. No loss of time in solving problems results and the transition to the park, once it is built, is facilitated.

The skeleton plan is essential for still another reason. Since one of the major objectives of the park is to create the bridge that will bring together children from diverse backgrounds, site selection for parks must seek those sites that will be central to the communities to be served, with no inequality in travel time for any of the groups in the park. The selection of a site just because it happens to be cleared and city-owned can result in disaster. It is perfectly possible to misuse the advanced concept of the educational park to solidify school segregation patterns. By building parks on sites that preclude future steps toward desegregation we may isolate whole areas that will be permanently excluded from park development. This is especially true of big cities. A community-wide or city-wide skeleton plan takes all schools into consideration and plans to provide the same high-quality educational park education for every child.

Further, all new schools should be built in the areas designated in the skeleton plan for eventual development as educational parks instead of investing scant construction funds in random neighborhood schools. Thus, the park gradually gets built as money for school construction becomes available according to a rational long-range plan.

Finally, what do we do with the existing schools? Many of them can be immediately used to form the core of the educational park—in instances, for example, where there are good plants already clustered or in near vicinity to each other. All that may need to be done is to change the grades served by these schools or to convert some of the large common rooms to classrooms. As the park grows, in much the same way as a college grows, the local schools that are superseded can be turned over to other educational or recreational uses (Medicare centers, for example) or sold to private investors. In most cities, these older schools are on high-value downtown sites and command good selling prices.

QUESTION: No educational parks exist yet in any major urban center. A number of questions come to mind. Can any city afford to build them with its limited budget? Will the educational park add to the transit problems in our cities? How can we guarantee the safety of pupils traveling to the park and within the park?

ANSWER: The federal government is interested in the idea of central facilities that will serve the whole community and funds are available not only to study educational park possibilities but for actual construction of such facilities. Federal urban renewal funds can also be obtained for school construction. Integration of educational park plans into the city's urban renewal program is often possible and desirable, because the logical areas for educational parks and for urban renewal are often the same, particularly in our smaller cities.

If a city plans to build an educational park instead of continuing the construction of neighborhood schools, it often need use only the very same funds it would ordinarily use for the old type of construction, but make these funds go much further by building classroom buildings and applying to the federal government for help in constructing the central shared facilities that will serve the classroom buildings. The high-cost rooms such as gyms, auditoriums, and so on can be eliminated, and many more children can be provided for by the local community using the same funds allocated for neighborhood school construction. Remember, too, that the educational park requires less overall building. As a pupil's family moves from neighborhood to neighborhood, he still attends the same educational park.

The transit problem is indeed complicated, but not insoluble. Many pupils attending the educational park will live within walking distance. Others, senior high and middle school pupils, have to travel longer now and will continue to do so. The younger children and their parents may need transportation, and special provision for this must be included in any park planning.

Some years ago, despite the protests of many that "it cannot be done," some streets in the heart of our cities were designated as play streets, closed to traffic for certain hours a day. It works. We may find it desirable to make certain streets "school streets" and close them off to general traffic for a brief period each morning and afternoon to use as school transportation arteries for children, teachers, and parents traveling to the educational park and then back home again. Careful site selection for educational parks can limit the ride to and from school, and the ride itself can be used for educational purposes.

The children's safety can be better cared for in the educational park with its own trained police force and a design of ramps and underground passageways which will avoid all traffic approaches to the park. Within the park, traffic will be sharply curtailed and limited to fixed areas, as on any university campus. Safety in the park also includes the concept of the health center we talked about before.

QUESTION: It is already very difficult to interest parents in school activities or to come to parent meetings. If the school is outside the neighborhood, will it not be even harder to get meaningful parent participation?

ANSWER: The educational park will represent more than just the school the children attend: it will be the community's cultural and recreational center. Parents will come for their own adult education or retraining classes, for professional entertainment in the great theater, as well as to attend parent meetings. The pride that the community can have in a great local institution will have a strong drawing power. Special transportation facilities for the appropriate hours of the day can be made available to facilitate travel from various points in the community to the park. Lincoln Center in New York City is now proposing such a "shuttle" serving at certain times.

QUESTION: I kept a central question for last that I know everyone asks in regard to the concept of an educational park. Is it not a gruesome idea to have ten-to-twenty thousand children all in the same park? Who would want his child to become No. 8734? Will the educational park be an educational supermarket?

ANSWER: We already have schools in our big cities that hold nearly 2,000 elementary school children, middle schools for over 3,000 students, and there are some high schools that have over 6,000. The educational park is not "a little bit more of that." It is developed on an entirely different principle. The basic unit in the park is small, protecting the individuality of the child and his teacher better than the present system can. The question is not really the number of children in the park but how the park is organized.

It will be possible, whether the city builds horizontally or vertically, to build classroom buildings for not more than 500 elementary school children, for 800 pupils in the middle grades, and for 1,500 senior high school pupils. The design of the outside of these buildings should be varied and interesting so that the child can identify closely with his unique building. At the same time, he has before him the physical goal of "graduating" into the next higher educational level.

Children identify with their classmates. Their feelings of security in the larger world of school center around the other pupils in their class rather than on the physical classroom. The class will be small and will stay together in its homeroom with its home teacher, separating for the special programs the park provides and coming together again, refreshed and inspired, to compare notes and "show and tell."

The country's demand for quality, economy and equality in education can no longer be met in the old way. The educational park sets the stage for the great advances in education that lie just ahead. Let's get on with it.

DAY-TO-DAY PROBLEMS OF SCHOOL INTEGRATION

Aaron Lipton *was principal of the R. J. Bailey School in Hartsdale, New York, a unit in Greenburgh School District No. 8. This is an edited transcript of a talk given on March 28, 1965, to a meeting in Chicago, co-sponsored by* INTEGRATED EDUCATION *magazine and Teachers for Integrated Schools. Since 1967 Dr. Lipton has been associate professor of education, Pennsylvania State University.*

From *Integrated Education,* **June/July 1965. Reprinted by permission of the author.**

Children from certain socio- and cultural-economic backgrounds have problems in relating to middle-class oriented schools. These problems, however, are reflections not only of their own backgrounds but also of the attitudes of teachers, parents, community administrators, and boards of education. The reactions of children from different cultures are not only a result of their own upbringing but also of the hostility developed by the authorities with whom they are in contact. The problem is to get all the communities in this country to develop a sense of responsibility for the education of all the children. We teachers and principals cannot assume the total burden ourselves. The failure of the country to shoulder this burden is, I think, a reprehensible failure.

There is quite a difference between a district that has 2,500 children and a district such as yours that has 23,000 teachers. Yet, in our microcosm we have done something of national value. I assume that all of you have a feeling of "I want to do something; I want help in doing it." I would like to help you as much as possible in terms of letting you realize that for one thing you are not alone and for another thing your point of view is an admirable and vital one.

We have been desegregated in our system for some time and only in the last five years have we become integrated. Desegregation is an important first step. In order to integrate, you must first physically desegregate. This is a very important step, because once you get there then you can begin to work on involving your children with one another and involving your teachers and other staff with one another. Over the past five years, teacher's attitudes have changed and have been reflected in the children's behavior both academically and socially. Many years ago, the children were grouped by teachers on a racial basis. The Negro children were on one side of the classroom and the white children on the other. As time went on, we began to see that we were cheating the children and that when you cheat one child you cheat all of them. The children needed a better education than they were receiving. Our achievement grades reflected this inadequate education. Then we began to be concerned not about achievement data but children. What is it that keeps them fighting with one another? What is it that keeps them from achieving? What is it that keeps people in the community from relating to one another?

Some years ago there was an attempt at desegregation and some people in the community decided to put money together to buy a house away from a Negro judge who was moving in. This same district recently had a Negro moving in and others moving in later this month. Now this, of course, reflects a change of attitude. The children in our school district have been going to school together for a long time. They were able to see that they were not so different from one another. They were able to see that they could accept one another and live together in peace. They were able to see that they could learn from one another. They were able to see that what each one had to offer was a wonderful thing. The teachers began learning the same way. I must admit that not all teachers learned as willingly and ably as the children. We were fortunate in a sense to be able to change our staff by attrition. Some teachers retired; some other teachers moved into the district; and some other teachers moved out. We now have a dedicated staff, most interested in helping all children.

I think the achievement levels of the children reflect this change of staff attitudes. For example, in 1959 the achievement levels of the children in the upper quartile changed from 1.5 above grade level in the fifth grade to 2.5 above grade level. In 1959 the children were about a year and a half above grade level; in 1963 the same grade showed a 2.5 year lead over the grade level. And the lower quartile showed equally a year's difference in grade from 1959 to 1963. Now this was not because we trained children to take achievement tests; it was because we trained teachers to teach children, and educated the community to accept the fact that all children needed a good education. Now the community itself has reflected this acceptance of integration by never turning down a budget in the last fifteen years, by never electing an antischool member to the board, and by building two brand new schools in the district during the last five years. This says something not only about integration but for a point of view.

Beyond that, there are social gains that have taken place. Children now go to each other's homes. A parent who had been active in trying to buy the house from the Negro judge, had a party in her home last year and she invited a Negro girl to the party. Of course, she did call up all the white parents to find out if it was all right with them, but she did go along. Not only that; but the fight had been taken out of these people, and now there is support, either passive or overt, from seven eighths of the community. There is a very fine group of persons who are actively interested in this educational system.

Just a few things about the children who go to our integrated schools. The children tend to reflect the attitudes of the parents in many ways, until they get to the high school. When they get to the high school they become political activists. Many of them go on picket lines, from the World's Fair to Maryland, on questions revolving around civil rights. They are politically concerned about the status of their fellow student. They are politically concerned about the housing of their fellow students. They are socially concerned about the development of themselves as aware people. In addition to that, they are vitally concerned with something that goes beyond achievement grades. They really have a different feeling, a different attitude from most of the children that you would see in a high school. I think that this is reflected in the fact that they are very much involved in the life around them. And it is one of those things that you really cannot spell out in achievement scores. But you can see it as you walk through the halls in the high school, as you walk through the halls in the elementary school.

I want to underscore the fact, however, that there are still problems that we face. For example, a couple of weeks ago I had an opportunity to meet with eight girls in one of my sixth-grade classes. Four of the girls were white and four were Negro. They told me about a problem that developed on the playground where the white and Negro girls had a little battle about some trivial incident. My approach with children is to let them talk, to find out what they have to say and to see if I can help them see what they are thinking and what they are feeling. After about ten or fifteen minutes of trying to get to the bottom of the problem, I finally said: "You know what I think? I think you girls don't like each other." And one of the Negro girls said, "You're right. I don't like them." So I said to the white girls, "I think I know that Jessie really means this. How do you feel?" "Oh, we like the Negro girls," they said. "I don't think you do, because otherwise you wouldn't act as you do." They began reflecting on this, and they began to see how they were really feeling. The Negro girls began to point out, "We don't like you because you do certain things to us. You talk about us. You call us names, and that's why we hit you." It went on this way until finally they began to appreciate the differences. One girl used the word cute; another one used the word big, and so on, and we begin to get to understand each other. I said, "What do you really mean by this? What you mean is that you don't like it when I walk into the classroom with a white skirt." One of the Negro girls said, "Well, this means that you are trying to be cute, trying to be big." And it was not necessary to tell this white girl not to wear this kind of skirt. It was only necessary to get them to listen to each other, to understand each other. Now, I would say that very nearly all the problems that I have dealt with work out this way, because the children learn to accept one another. They learn to express their feelings.

How does an attitude of fairness get across to children? This has a very important meaning in terms of getting to people who are significantly involved in this whole issue. There must be a way of communicating with those people who are resistive to integration.

One parent called me very defiantly and angrily about the fact that his daughter came home using vile language. His daughter is a sixth-grader and never used this language before, but she was accosted by a Negro girl and all of a sudden she began using vile language. He said, "What are you going to do about it?" I said, "What would you like me to do about it?" He said, "You ought to call that girl into the office and tell her a thing or two." I said, "I will do no such a thing." He said, "You mean you sanction vile language?" I said, "No, I didn't say that at all. I think children use certain language depending on the situation. I think if I tried to control children's language I might take upon myself a job that is insurmountable as well as ludicrous. Besides, the children don't come to school trained to use vile language, and if they do, it must be significant in terms of something that happened between your daughter and this child." He said, "Well, maybe my daughter wasn't all correct." I said, "Well, I looked into the matter already, and I find that your daughter wasn't correct at all." He said, "Well, I don't care what she does, but she shouldn't use vile language. You know why *that* girl used vile language, because that is what she hears at home." I said, "You know what you are really saying is that you don't want your daughter to associate with Negro children. You don't realize that Negro parents themselves have as much concern about children's language as you do." And he said, "Oh, I didn't know that." And was quite taken aback when I said this. His voice and attitude changed completely and he said, "You mean to tell me that this girl's parents are just as concerned as I am? You really mean it?" It sounds naive, I know, but this is true. The man was told that his attitude was really upsetting him rather than the fact that his daughter was using that language, and he wanted to get across to me that the trouble with our school was not anything but integration. Now, in some cases I have told parents that they either have to accept this or move out. There have been some pretty violent reactions from parents, but they did not move out and they have become encouraged by what they have seen.

What I am talking about in a sense is a struggle. The struggle continues in view of what is happening to their children.

We often become overly concerned about the wrong things. We become overly concerned about status, we become overly concerned about achievements, and we become overly concerned about the future of our little Johnny who has to get into Harvard or Yale. At the same time, we are not much concerned about his classmates who may not even get through high school because of defective education. Our experience has led us to believe that children must be put into classes that are designed to be as heterogeneous as possible. In other words, in as small a system as ours—which has 65 percent white and 35 percent Negro children—our system should have in each class 65 percent white children and 35 percent Negro children. If we have 50 percent boys and 50 percent girls in this school, each class should have 50 percent boys and 50 percent girls. If we have 10 children whose IQ's range from 75 to 90 in each section, this should be reflected in each classroom. In other words, every class has within it a wide range of achievement, a wide range of intellectual background, and a wide range of socioeconomic backgrounds, and a reflection of the biracial aspect of the community. Why is this so? When you segregate one child or any number of children from others, you are helping create a self-concept of destruction. You are saying to this child: "You are not really very good or worthwhile or valuable to us, so we are going to put you with all those dummies over there, and when you-all get together over there, then we can teach these children who want to learn." This is exactly what they say as they are grouped this way. I have overheard a junior high school student say to a group of eleven other Negro children, at the time of summer school signing, "Look at all of us; we are all required to go to summer school because we all failed. How come only us colored people fail?" Now, what was he saying? He was saying more than the fact that all these colored children failed, but also something about the attitude of the teachers who failed these children. He was talking about a program which was not geared to them but which was designed to fit the children into the program. And when you have a program that is designed for children to fit into, you are going to have some who are going to be sliced off at either end.

In other words, education must reflect the needs, interests, and abilities of all the children. What we have decided by our program is that in order to develop the best possible education for all, we must have the children in the class which will be dealt with by each teacher. Each teacher, on the basis of small-enough classes, and on the basis of enough material and of a legitimate and worthwhile attitude, has begun to work with the children on the basis of an individualized approach. Individualized programs have begun to be developed in reading, in math, in language arts, and we also have developed programs where children get extra help in remedial reading or enrichment help in science or math. Now, I know one of the problems that you face here is that your class sizes are considerably larger than ours. When I first came to Greenburgh, our class size was thirty to thirty-two. Now it is twenty-five, and next year it will be twenty-three. This did not come about because the board of education simply felt it was nice; it came about because we pulled for it hard, because we went into board meetings and fought for it. We went with data showing that you cannot educate children if you have a whole bunch of them in one place. The job of the teacher is a very, very difficult task. You cannot expect a teacher to do the impossible. It is only next to impossible as it is, and we got the board of education to agree to set up one new class on every grade level, particularly the third, fourth, fifth, and sixth and kindergarten next year, to get the class size down to twenty-three. In some of my classes I shall have twenty-one. Of course, that is because I have some rooms the size of matchboxes, but that really did not affect the board's decision. They really are concerned about the children's education. I may be talking about a different kind of board of education, too, but the board of education is a reflection of the political community (political with a small "p") I think everyone's responsibility cannot be denied in terms of continually fighting to gain better education.

I am struck by the kind of frustration that teachers face. When I speak about Greenburgh, I feel that people think I am in another world; sometimes I feel that I am. Nothing that we accomplished came because some nice, benign people came to us and said, "What would you like us to do now?" Everything came on the basis of a hard-fought struggle. The work must be done by you in order to get people to act. I see this situation as a campaign of action and education and not just inspiration. It is a very vital part of your work. If you do not start acting now or if you fail to continue your actions, your frustration will remain and your ulcers will get worse, and the educational system will deteriorate.

QUESTION: *Does the whole community support integration?*

A vital part of the community. I would say that when I talked about never having lost a budget or a board election, there is a committee for education in the district which is comprised of fifty to a hundred people, and its influence is felt very considerably throughout the district. There is a small group of vituperative people whose hostility and arguments are ludicrous, but I would say that in every district you have a small number of active people and a large number of people who support this small number of people. Keep in mind that no educational system is going to survive unless its professional staff assumes leadership in providing the best possible education. If you get a community that is going to push the professional staff in one direction or in another, and the professional staff is not with or part of the community, then there is nothing to say that the professional staff could not be veered into another direction by another group of people. But the professional staff in our district has, I think, developed leadership, has maintained its leadership, and is increasing its leadership in terms of developing this educational system in the district.

QUESTION: *In your campaign for desegregation and integration, have you had the help of groups like the NAACP and others?*

About one fifth or more of our teaching staff is Negro; we have made a consistent effort over the past number of years to get Negro teachers on the staff and we have been very successful to the point now where the Urban League refuses to send any more Negro teachers because they want to save them for other districts. We are very strong in the leadership in the fight for integration in our district and in other school districts. As far as the NAACP and Urban League are concerned, they call upon us very often to talk to groups and we work very closely together. One of our board members is on the Urban League voter registration organization and other board members are very active in NAACP or Urban League.

QUESTION: *What about the similarity or discrepancy in socioeconomic class between the white and Negro students?*

Originally, there was quite a problem with this. After my first six months as a teacher for disturbed children, I became reading consultant. Some teachers referred only Negro children because they wanted to get them out of their classes and some teachers referred only white children because they wanted to have help. Now, the relationship between the two groups reflected the difference. In other words, teachers would react to the children in terms of their own preconceived attitudes, so that it was reflected in the children's behavior and the children's interpersonal contact. As we worked with this, we began to sense—and get teachers to sense—that the more they accepted all children, the less did this difference become obvious. This is exactly what has happened. One of my teachers came to me the other day and said, "How come you gave me so and so the other day? You know he just came from a training school." So I said, "You are one of the sixth-grade teachers in this school and you are entitled to every child you have. And if you cannot work with these children, or any one child, let me know. And there is something we can do about it. One of the things we can do about it is not to remove the child but see if we can help you get along better and understand the child better." One of the things that I want to point out is that our grouping pattern is one of *in*clusion, not exclusion. As soon as you develop a kind of ability grouping or any kind of selective grouping, you develop a way of excluding children from participation in your educational program. In other words, there is always a cutoff point which tends to eliminate this one or that one. By wide-range grouping, there is no elimination. I have taken children out of classes on occasion—on rare occasions—when I found that personality conflicts have developed either between children or between teacher and child; this, of course, is legitimate. But I will not take a child out because he is not successful, unless I feel that the teacher's attitude is detrimental. Even then I will not take the child out immediately but I will work with the teacher to get him to be more accepting of the child. But these problems are a reflection mostly of the attitudes of teachers and the parents with whom we must work.

QUESTION: *How do you accommodate the differential development of each child without having the brighter children eclipse the others?*

That is a very good question. When I first walked into the school that was formally desegregated, I saw Negro children over here and white children over here, and the teacher called up the bunnies (all the Negro children) and the robins (all the white children), and she had tried to desegregate in her own mind. But what we have done to eliminate this problem is to focus more on individual programs. By individualizing reading programs and by focusing more on interest topics, by focusing more on skill topics, we have gotten teachers to integrate their group without any artificiality. In other words, the teacher with a class of twenty-five will have a dozen children who have difficulty at one time with long division or with phonics or with some other skill in reading. So, while she is working with one child at a time the segregation aspect of it is eliminated because *one child at a time is no longer segregation.* And then when she calls together those five or six children who need help with finding the main idea, those five children can reflect, and usually do, the wide range of the class because the need for finding the main idea, the need of skill, is not a racial need. It is a skill need, and it cuts across the total academic picture because you have children who need help with a certain skill and this number of children is reflective of the total class situation. It is in this way, by grouping in this many-faceted way, that we have tended to eliminate the segregation based on in-track grouping or in-class grouping.

QUESTION: *Aren't there some who tend to come out on top in almost every skill?*

Yes, but that is all right. That does not interfere, because children, when they work on a social studies committee, for example, work as a group or a small group where each child has something to contribute. One child might have a certain aspect of the work which he might be able to contribute and another has something else. But, you see, when we talk about skill we have become very constricted in our discussion of what a skill is. And ordinarily we presume it to be just an academic skill. Some children have a skill that goes far beyond academic skill; they have social skills; they have knowledge of themselves and the world in which they live that other children do not have. They can use this and give other children the benefit of this knowledge and skill which is much more than just an academic skill. This is one of the fruits of our school system; we have tended to view children from a much broader frame of reference than just a cipher on an achievement test.

QUESTION: *Do you have the children help each other?*

Sometimes they do. It depends on what the situation is. I do not encourage it too much, because some teachers would do this all day long. But this is one way in which children can learn more about each other. Our experience is that they learn from each other as well as just exchange information.

QUESTION: *An educator who addressed this group some time ago said that in a mixed grouping the middle-class child has absolutely nothing to learn from a child who comes from a deprived background.*

I will dispute this. As I said, it is when you think of children in an academic frame of reference that you say that the child might not have too much to learn. We think of academic frames of references from a middle-class orientation only. But of course there are other things even within the academic frame of reference that children can learn. Let me cite an example. At teacher was talking about spirit and *esprit de corps*, and she wanted to know from the class: What is the meaning of the word spirit? One Negro child raised his hand and said "Spirit is religion." Well, this is not the answer she wanted. But this opened up a whole new discussion, a whole new discussion about what religion means and what the child meant by religion. He had a lot to contribute about his knowledge of the Bible, to contribute about how he feels about church, and how he feels about his relationship with his minister. This was a kind of learning which the other children did not have. Also, there was the matter of children being able to develop a broader facility with language. There is a matter of the differences in language; children have picked up certain expressions which are very colorful and very rich and which are very significant in terms of enriching the language background of all children. There are other things which we have learned, too. Negro children in our school have a kind of background which has a certain emotional richness to it. Children from deprived backgrounds have learned perhaps more slowly than others but in their learning they make sure to get every facet of the situation the teacher is teaching about. As the teacher explains something on a map, the child learns more slowly because of his style of learning; he will ask questions that other children might not ask for fear of being thought stupid and their eyes will light up because they see that, ah—that is the way to do it. Their own style gets teachers to be more specific in the way they learn, and it is not a style of slowness which is a reflection of low IQ but a style of learning which is in a sense reflective of their own approach. And I think this is something we learn from. As we teachers see children learning in many different ways, we tend to learn from them as well as teach them.

QUESTION: *Do you have any middle-class Negro children, and is there any difference between middle-class Negro children and middle-class white children?*

Actually, this has been a problem for us in the sense that most of our middle-class Negro children are much more like the white children than they are like Negro children of the lower classes. And the most difficult times in the classroom have come in terms of the relationship between lower-class Negro children and middle-class Negro children. The hostility of lower-class Negroes to the middle-class Negroes is rather overt, partly because while the lower-class Negro child is afraid to express too much hostility to the middle-class white child, he is not as afraid to express it toward the middle-class Negro child. So the middle-class Negro child has borne the brunt of a lot of the hostility of the Negro child which is placed on him instead of on the white child. Interestingly enough, however, this is mostly the case with the girls. The middle-class Negro boys fit in very well with both the white boys and the lower-class Negro boys. As a matter of fact, there is very little conflict between the boys of any classes. If a child has a fight with a child on the playground, it is not because he is Negro or white but because somebody took his ball away. And this is a much healthier kind of argument to have. But the girls have much more to be concerned about, and they are concerned because the Negro middle-class girl comes to school with the same kind of dirndl skirt that the white child does, comes to school with her hair combed differently. She tries to be cute like the white girl, and so this goes on and on in terms of developing more and more conflict.

Academically, the Negro middle-class child is under heavy pressure. The middle-class Negro parent particularly wants his child to be unusual academically and, as a result, the pressure on the child is tremendous. Very often, the pressure is greater in terms of expectancy by comparison to potential, because the middle-class Negro parent is expressing his own needs rather than the child's needs. And the problem is that the Negro child is faced with having to identify with his own parents' aspirations on the one hand and his own potential on the other. This disparity has created among boys, mostly, an academic problem. Most of the girls do not suffer from this problem because the parents feel that most of the girls are going to grow up and get married anyway, so what's the difference. But the boys are going to have to be breadwinners. If they are going to be good breadwinners, they must be good in school. So if they are to be good in school you must pressure them, and if you pressure them, you might as well start early. And this is what has happened.

QUESTION: *What about achievement levels?*

Achievement levels reflect this pressure. The achievement levels of many middle-class Negro boys are not as high as the middle-class Negro girls nor as high as the middle-class white children, primarily because of this pressure. The achievement of the middle-class Negro girl is usually higher than that of the Negro boy because of less pressure from the family to succeed over and above the potential.

QUESTION: *Do you involve the parents in any way other than in individual conferences?*

We involve them on the PTA level; we have conferences in the community which are run by PTA. Next month we plan an important conference among our parents in a seminar entitled, "Education in an Integrated School in a Segregated Community." It is a loaded question, one which we have been fighting to talk about for a long time, because we feel that parents themselves have an important responsibility for their own children and for their own children's attitude. The fact is that we have not had this kind of discussion before because parents have not been ready for it. Over a period of years, the attitude of the Negro parents particularly has changed fundamentally in terms of the school. When I first came to Greenburgh, the attitude of Negro parents was, "I will not have anything to do with your school because whenever you call me in it is only to tell me that my child is going to go to jail if I don't do something." And this attitude was reflective of the administration at the time. Negro parents were contacted only as a last resort. And then, of course, when they were contacted and they did not come, the attitude was: "What's the point of calling them anyway; they don't want to come?" Well, if I were a Negro parent, I certainly would not want to come and be told that about my child. We have about nine-tenths participation of the Negro parents because our own attitude reflects the desire to do the best possible for their children. And this is, I think, in very strong evidence.

QUESTION: *Do you use any special teaching devices and techniques?*

I feel strongly that for a learning situation to be most effective you need a very careful diagnostic program and a very strong teacher-pupil relationship on an individual level, as well as teacher participation in group activities. But because of this the skills are most effectively developed on an individual or small group basis. The reading program generally is an individualized program. I feel that a teacher does not need a gimmick necessarily, but needs herself and her own understanding. I am not opposed to providing teachers with adequate materials, however. We do have in most of the classrooms in my building a range of five hundred to eight hundred books: a lot of paperbacks and a lot of hardbacks. We also have a full-time librarian who has a full-time library and a full-time clerk handling the $6,000 library budget annually that I ask for and get from the board of education. My textbook budget is a very good one. We have $7 per child every year, plus $35 per child for every new child who comes in. And this is based on a very realistic figure. I figured out that a set of textbooks cost $35, and that was the figure I used. Use whatever tools are effective and use them with the right attitude.

Periodically, salesmen come into my office with material that they feel is integrated. They say, "I have a book for you." There was one salesman who was in recently. He said, "I have a wonderful book for you. It just came out recently. It's called a science book in intercultural edition." Then he proceeded to open it and said, "Now let's see; where is that picture?" He finally came to the picture he was looking for; it was a picture of a child, but, lo and behold, it was not a Negro child; it was a Puerto Rican child. He said, "Well, I didn't know. I *thought* it was a Negro child. It looks pretty close to it." And that was his contribution to integrated education. But actually many publishers now are getting on the band wagon. Unfortunately, this band wagon has only three wheels. And we have got to get that extra wheel on there to keep it from falling down, because what they have done is to insert a few pictures and call it integrated education. I think this is a very important thing to look at. Our publishers are trying to fool us into thinking that they are joining us when all they are trying to do is soothe our savage breasts.

I'll give you an example. One publisher just came out with a new multiethnic approach in a basal reader. Now, they have an interesting system. They have three books on the fourth grade level and three on the fifth and three on the sixth. There is a low-level fourth grade, a medium-level fourth grade, and a high-level fourth grade—and fifth—and sixth. The low-level fourth grade book has a lot of stories about Negro children in it; the middle textbook has some stories about Negro children; and the high one has none, which is about as blatant a segregationist technique as I can imagine. And I asked the salesman: "By the way, do you sell this book all over?" and he said, "No, this is just a northern edition."

The problem of materials is an on-going one. I think that the publishers need to know how you feel about their books, and they really are responsive. Believe it or not, only a couple of years ago there was no such thing as a picture of a nonwhite child in a book, but the very fact that they are beginning to put pictures shows that they are trying to do something. If we will keep on pressuring them we may be able to get something more. So I think that we have a responsibility in this area as well. I would hope that we would push for it.

QUESTION: *How do you go about determining what grade levels are in each of your classes?*

That is a good question because I think it goes to the heart of the problem of accepting children at their own levels of adjustment and levels of academic ability. There are two things to be said. For one, not all children are in the next number of years going to graduate from any grade necessarily on grade level. For another thing, as long as we are going to be tied to an arbitrary designation of grade level on an achievement test, we are going to hamper the education of our children. There is more to education than achievement levels. If we are going to develop an educational system to meet the needs of all the children, the achievement levels will rise. We cannot conceive of holding children back over a period of years because they are not up to a certain mythical figure as spelled out by achievement tests. On the other hand, as long as we continue practices of segregation and ability grouping, we are going to have children who are not succeeding. And they are failing not only in terms of actual ability level, but in terms of our attitude toward them. And if our attitude toward them is going to be negative, their success is going to be even less. So in a sense there is no way of answering the question in terms of what our system has done except to say that we must develop better attitudes toward all children so that whatever their measure of success will be it will be enough for them to go continually higher. And this is what we try for in our school—to strive continually to meet the needs of every child at every level and to push him toward his potential.

QUESTION: *Here in Chicago the civil rights movement has made one of its demands the release of achievement test scores because we feel we need the evidence that there is a difference in the educational achievement as a result of segregation. How would you suggest we go about—in addition to fighting for integrated education as the only basic answer—conveying the terrible disparity that exists without fighting for the release of such information on the one hand, and without fighting for some standards that must be met in all the schools, which must be common throughout the schools, in order to guarantee at least a minimal effort to equalize educational opportunities?*

That is a good question, because the people down in Norfolk, Virginia, are faced with this dilemma in reverse. The superintendent of schools always published the differences in scores to underscore the fact that Negro children are different and do differently than white children and he says that this proves that we should have them in different schools. Now, what you are saying is that by dint of showing these scores you would demonstrate that segregated education is inadequate. You might have to be careful in order not to "prove" that there is a good reason for segregated education. I think that achievement scores can be so badly abused and poorly used, that I would wonder whether I would even look at this in the beginning because of the way that these things can be misused by any group. For example, we know many reasons why children do not succeed in schools, but those people who do not want to know will distort whatever information they can get. We found that by publishing some of our material we incurred the wrath of some of the local antischool people because they said, "See, all the things we have told you about you have verified for us yourself." And we then began to realize that if we use any data we have to be very careful how we use it. And I would be concerned about not using that, because I feel that it would be abused.

QUESTION: *Some Negro parents are saying in desperation: "We don't care about integration any longer because it seems such an impossibility. Just give us quality schools with high standards." Would you comment?*

Talking mainly about improving the quality of education in the segregated schools is another way of saying we do not really want to get involved with integration. I think that parents are going to be misled if they accept this kind of "quality" education because *this is why the schools are bad in the first place*. Because they are segregated schools. I do not know how you can possibly improve a segregated school except by integrating it.

QUESTION: *Do you have an ungraded program?*

No, we do not. In a sense we have a kind of ungraded program within every classroom. Each teacher works with a child on an individual level. If a child is in fifth grade and is reading at second-grade level, the teacher will work with him on his level; in one class the teacher will have a multilevel approach in most of the subjects.

QUESTION: *You said you had almost segregated communities. And yet you established integrated schools. How do you administer the assignment of children to schools? Do you use busing?*

You have one school that has all the children in the district going to it—kindergarten, one school that has all the children in the whole district going to it for first and second grade, and so on. We bus about 75 percent of the children, and busing costs about $175,000 a year, 90 percent of which is reimbursed by the state. Busing is a major part of any budget in any district in the country. Most school districts bus children, and the bugaboo of busing is another way of saying how can we possibly integrate our schools because our poor children have to ride buses. Don't believe it.

INTEGRATED INTEGRATION

Paul Davidoff *is Director, Urban Planning Program, Hunter College, City University of New York. The article is the text of an address to the NAACP Legal Conference on School Desegregation, October 20-21, 1966.*

The topic assigned to me was that of "indicating in what way one or more proposed solutions to *de facto* segregation can transform the life of the city." I assume that the predictions of good results from the creation of an integrated school system will become some of the major arguments supporting programs leading to integration. But I must admit that I do not believe these will be the most persuasive nor the most urgent arguments in support of integrated education. So what I should like to discuss with you, at least at the start, are some of the transformations in the "life of the city" that will be necessary in order to create solutions to *de facto* segregation.

From *Integrated Education,* **December 1966/January 1967. Reprinted by permission of the author.**

At the outset I should like to warn against our use of terms such as the "life of the city." A city does not have life. The people who live in it or use it have life. It may be said that an institution has life, but, in general, when we speak of the life of a city we refer to a concept that is so muddy as to be devoid of meaning. Now I engage in this discussion for more than abstract academic purposes. I am afraid that when the focus of concern is removed from the individual members of a community, solutions to the perceived problems also shift.

For example, during the past year there has been considerable alarm expressed in the popular magazines about the "urban problem." The establishment of the Department of Housing and Urban Development is both a reflection and a cause of that growing concern. Increasingly, the American public has become aware of the "crisis in our cities." As a city planner, I suppose I should be greatly elated that at long last the public has recognized that more public resources must be allocated to urban areas. But I am not elated for I am afraid that the problem has not been defined properly and that as a result the social changes resulting from the recognition of the urban problem will not be of the type needed to solve what I consider to be the basic problems.

The basic problem in our society is that of social injustice. The problem is created by society's failure to distribute equitably such goods as wealth, income, knowledge, health, shelter, security, and power. Because such a large part of our nation's poor and Negroes live in urban areas, a large part of the nation's social injustice goes on in such areas. That is the real problem in urban areas.

This problem in urban areas, however, cannot be solved separately in each urban area or region. Essentially the problem is national and international. The solution to the problems of poverty and discrimination must be national in scope. Washington, not city hall, will solve the problems in urban areas. This point needs further development.

The proliferation of special agencies dealing with single functions may, instead of leading toward greater equality of opportunity, dissipate energy and result in the maintenance of the status quo.

More specifically, I do not believe that the establishment of HUD, HEW, DOT, OEO, and the future DReC has necessarily been useful for purposes of establishing greater social equity. The establishment of these special-function agencies has resulted in the creation of competing pressures for limited resources in the absence of any strong social and economic plan for the nation's development. No national planning agency exists capable of directing these special-function agencies. The nearest thing we have to such a planning body is the highly secretive Bureau of the Budget. That agency certainly does not do its planning in the open and the public is not made a part of its process of decision making.

The Department of Housing and Urban Development, while focusing on urban problems, is really incapable of solving the major ones. It does not have the power or the mandate to redistribute opportunities more equitably.

The problem which I have just described as existing at the federal level is equally apparent at the local level. Our municipalities have no coordinated social and economic plan for the elimination of poverty and discrimination. The limited planning carried out in municipalities is aimed primarily at physical conditions. The results of this type of planning are all too clear. Urban renewal and zoning and other tools in the planner's kit have been used to enforce rather than destroy racial and economic segregation. Urban renewal too often has meant Negro removal. It is quite clear that in their work in locating new schools and new public housing projects, physical planners have not been strongly motivated to eliminate segregation.

As a matter of fact, if you look at the criteria generally recommended for selection of neighborhood school sites, you will probably not find racial integration mentioned. It is far more typical to find concern with proximity to the potential student body. It could be concluded that those who have recommended school sites have worked in a windowless office.

I would like to take a moment to look at the question of the scope and location of the planning function as it applies in New York City. The new administration's consultant, Mr. Edward Logue, has proposed that city planning be submerged under an agency dealing essentially with housing issues. The alternative to this would be to create a city planning department in the mayor's office directly responsible to the mayor. It is of the utmost importance that this latter solution be given strong support by organizations such as the NAACP. Let me give the reasons for this.

Civil rights groups have not paid much attention to the issue of shape and place within the administration of the planning function. But if we are to avoid piecemeal solutions which in the long run fail to move us toward equalizing opportunities, we will need an agency that can make recommendations for concerted physical, social, and economic action. Even if we dislike the proposals, at least we will know that there exists a forum in which it is possible to plead our case. It will be possible to discuss solutions of a far broader nature than those presently offered on a project-by-project basis.

The Logue proposal for where the planning process should be carried out is essentially an assertion that planning is a relatively unimportant function. Rather than suggesting that city planning must be concerned with education, health, welfare, public safety, and employment as well as with its more traditional concerns—housing, transportation, recreation—the Logue proposal, by placing the planning function in a division of government concerned with housing and development, keeps city planning apart from economic and social planning within the city. This is an archaic notion of how a city should be planned. But far worse than that, it prevents the government planning agency from seeing the different functions carried out in the city as part of a system.

Now, I do not espouse systems analysis for the purpose of being complete or orderly. I propose a systems approach in planning because I believe that it represents a means for a full-scale attack on the many factors which create the large-scale discrimination and poverty within our society. Let me add this; if we can achieve greater social equity more rapidly while our city planners were only concerned with physical problems, or with no problems at all, I would not complain in the least. I am not one to believe that structural changes in municipal administration are going to take us very far in the directions we wish to travel. But I do believe that the development of policy for housing, education, employment, health, and income support must be viewed as a whole.

This has been a long introduction to the problem of what changes are necessary in order to create the possibility for integrated education. I suppose that our long-run objective is to create a society in which integration occurs without its being planned and implemented. That is, we seek to build a society in which the locational distribution of Negroes and whites within a region is identical—a situation in which race or income class does not determine where a person lives.

To achieve this condition it will be necessary to create opportunities for people living in racial or economic ghettos to find housing available at reasonable rents throughout the region in which they live. The implications of this are clear: new low-cost housing as well as low-rent rehabilitated housing should be provided throughout the region, not almost exclusively in existing ghettos.

It is frightening to find so many people speaking today of rebuilding the ghettos. The Demonstration Cities Act is aimed at just this purpose. Logue's proposals for New York City's renewal program speak of improving the conditions within the worst ghetto areas. Liberal senators and newspapers have given their support to improving the ghetto. But a ghetto is a rotten social institution. A ghetto should be destroyed, not improved. Federal funds should be employed to eliminate ghettos rather than to make them permanent. The suggestion that ghettos must be maintained is an admission of indifference to the creation of social equality.

It has been said in response that Negroes must remain together if their political power is to be firmly established. This may be the case. It may be that some Negroes wish to remain within predominantly Negro areas and some prefer to find homes in other parts of the region. Therefore, opportunities should be provided for housing both inside and outside the present ghettos. A ghetto is a place where people are required to live. Clearly, equitable social policy would never require residence in a particular location; it would permit choice among a number of areas—that is part of the meaning of an open society.

But those who call for rebuilding the ghettos without calling for the provision of housing opportunity outside the ghetto for all those who wish to get out, call for the continuation of a closed society, a society in which color and income determine residential opportunities. It may be argued that proposals for rebuilding the ghetto are only short-term remedial measures which will meet present needs. I believe that such arguments can clearly be termed "shit." That is an academic term employed to describe propositions believed to be essentially dishonest.

It is possible today to build government-supported low-cost housing in all sections of urban regions. It is also possible to determine by attitude surveys and by behavior in the face of real choices whether or not present ghetto residents would choose to remain in the ghetto if other opportunities were made available. Making such choices available should be the first order of business in the field of housing.

Now, one reason why ghetto residents might feel constrained to remain in the ghetto is that employment opportunities are not available outside the central city within an urban region. This might imply that job opportunities should be made available outside of the urban core for laborers who now live in ghetto areas. It might also imply the need for low-cost transportation from distant places. Those implications establish the basis for further policy development.

Suppose that a family wanted to get out of the ghetto and to move to a suburban community, but could not because of unemployment or very low income. In such a situation would we require that because of relative poverty such a family had to live in an area set aside for other families with similar problems? We would probably answer by saying that a family should be guaranteed the right to find decent housing in a decent environment in any part of the region they chose, and that its low income would be supplemented sufficiently to enable it to live in comfort and security.

Now, the policies proposed here are not policies for some future date. They are policies that should be actively pursued today. They form a part of a modern liberal platform. It is true that in order to put these policies into effect it would be necessary for our society to turn away from exclusive concern with economic growth and to recognize that the distribution of the nation's wealth was at least as important a factor as the size of its GNP. It seems to me that it would be at least as important to the nation to raise the percentage of the nation's annual income going to the bottom 20 percent or 40 percent of the nation's families as it would be to continue to expand the gross national product. Do you realize that the richest 5 percent of the nation's families receive three times the income received by the nation's poorest 20 percent and the same amount as that received by the nation's poorest 40 percent? It is not only the distribution of income that must be altered. It is also the distribution of years of education, days of health, access to decent shelter, decent transportation, and decent leisure-time activities and vacation resorts. Those who tell us that we can build a great society without altering the present distribution pattern are doing worse than kidding themselves; they are consciously fooling the nation.

Well, after we have adopted the various policies I have recommended, do we need educational parks? We may, but not for purposes of integration. Integration would occur without being created through busing children to educational centers.

If we continue present policies, do we need educational parks for the purpose of creating integration?

If we achieve integration within schools but do not create social and economic equality, will it have been particularly important that children be afforded the opportunity to attend integrated classes? It will be important and it may be one way in which present attitudes can be altered.

Thus, while I would favor present programs to create integrated education, I believe that it is even more urgent that proponents of educational or housing or income support programs attempt a coordinated attack on discrimination and poverty.

One of the first steps in a coordinated attack would be a requirement that all parts of an urban region share in the creation of solutions to present problems. This might be achieved through requirement that as a condition precedent to receiving federal funds for any purpose a locality within a metropolitan region demonstrate two things. First, that it has a workable program for providing a fair share of the region's housing, job, and school opportunities for Negroes and for guaranteeing that such opportunities are provided in integrated situations and for families in poverty. Second, that the community is in fact implementing its workable program. Given the tight enforcement of such a requirement it would not be necessary to specifically require that communities participate in construction of educational parks; some communities might find it expedient to participate in the development of a system of educational parks but others might find alternative means of satisfying the requirement.

It may be more important at this stage to plead for joint effort by all communities in metropolitan regions in solving certain key problems than it is to plead for a single solution to the problem of *de facto* segregation in the schools. I say this because I am almost totally ignorant of the value of educational parks as educational institutions. And I am not alone in this ignorance. Educational parks hold great promise. But it is not yet clear that what is claimed for them could not be achieved as well or almost as well by the present neighborhood school, given the fact of integration in both types of facilities. Thus, I would seek to force communities within metropolitan regions to participate in integrating metropolitan public schools, but I would leave the choice of the solution's exact form to each community.

The major point of this part of my discussion has been that the fight for integration in education must be integrated with other solutions to problems of discrimination and poverty. I would like now to look more specifically at certain problems and opportunities associated with the establishment of educational parks.

The neighborhood school concept had a lot going for it, but in practice, as opposed to theory, the results have not been as great as predicted. A school is but one part and one symbol in a family's life. A neighborhood school may help to develop a community, but much depends on how significant the school appears to members of the community as opposed to other local and nonlocal interests. It will pay to remember this in thinking about the consequences of educational parks.

The educational park can assist in establishing a new type of community, a community far larger in size and population than the community built around a neighborhood school. If developed in such a manner as to permit its use for purposes other than daytime education of children it might serve as a focal point for activity involving families from a large area and from diverse backgrounds. But it is too early to tell whether such interaction would be at all meaningful or significantly different from that which occurs at neighborhood schools.

Successful operation of an educational park system will depend on an efficient transportation system, a system capable of transporting thousands of children rapidly and easily. In a metropolitan area I have been studying recently, it seemed quite clear that most, if not all, of the school population might be transported to school in a time period of under thirty minutes. Of course, significant numbers of children would not need transportation, but most would. Bus or rail transportation for children of junior high school age and up would not seem to present difficulties too different from those they face today. It has been argued, though, that transportation of younger children might involve a good deal of hardship. But it must be pointed out that large numbers of young suburban school children are bused without any great problems. The major difference would be that in a system of educational parks, more children would be bused, their ride would probably be somewhat longer, and the buses would go to few rather than many school sites. This does not suggest that transportation will present insuperable problems.

One part of the transportation issue does raise some difficult questions. In order to establish a good racial balance in each school in a system of educational parks it is necessary that the Negro population, clustered as it usually is in the core of the region, be transported out of the center toward the middle of the region. In such a circumstance the Negro student population may be forced to travel farther than the white population. This may be made even more necessary in order to placate whites who may have great doubts about the benefits of educational parks.

The situation I am describing is not too different from the present case. Busing is all right—sometimes, but "reverse busing" is unpopular. Does this mean that Negro children will have to spend longer periods in transit from home to school and back than whites? One would hope this would not be the case. The situation is bad enough when following a day of integrated education Negroes must enter segregated buses to return to segregated neighborhoods. The awfulness of this two-culture day—the integrated part and the segregated part—is itself ample reason to join the forces working for housing and for educational integration.

One last word about educational parks. A complete system of such parks could have a profound effect on the form of metropolitan regions. In conjunction with parks and other community uses, the educational park system could constitute a green belt around the middle of a metropolitan region. This might lead to naming the institutions the Big Green Schoolhouses.

But a major problem with contemporary city planning has been its too-great concern with physical forms such as green belts and I hesitate to end on such a recommendation. Instead, I would once more urge that thinking about educational forms to serve certain desired educational and social functions should be linked to a larger and more complete program for social actions. And in making this suggestion I want to recommend a particular course of action for the NAACP and for other civil rights groups. I believe that such interest groups should play and can play a greater role in city planning. At present our city planning process is essentially a unitary one, that is, a process in which only one agency prepares plans and in which the public in general can take the plan or leave it. But the process need not remain like this. In a system of plural planning different interest groups would prepare plans for the development of the community, city, region or nation. The plans of such interest groups would be reviewed and debated along with those of the public planning agency.

There is still another reason to invite the civil rights organizations to participate in developing plans for city and metropolitan development. In recent years such organizations have been critics of urban renewal and other methods employed to deprive Negroes of homes and decent opportunities, but our criticism has been essentially negative. The planning process needs to be infused with the positive thoughts of the civil rights movement concerning the future development of the urban areas and, more importantly, the future welfare of the urban population.

BIBLIOGRAPHY FOR PART FOUR

Ablon, Joan, and Joseph W. Reid, Jr. *An Experimental High School Project in Cultural Diversity.* Berkeley: School of Criminology, University of California, 1966.

Anton, Thomas J. *The Politics of State Expenditure in Illinois.* Urbana: University of Illinois Press, 1966.

Balow, Bruce. "The Long-Term Effect of Remedial Reading Instruction," *Reading Teacher* (April 1965).

Barden, John. "The Educational Park," *Nation* (April 20, 1964).

Berube, Maurice R. "Educational Parks: Still a Hope for the Future?" *United Teacher* (June 3, 1967).

Braden, Anne. "The Southern Freedom Movement in Perspective," *Monthly Review* (July-August 1965).

The Children's Academy: A New Concept in School Organization. Mount Vernon (N.Y.): Board of Education, 1966.

Clark, Kenneth B. "Intelligence, the University, and the Society," *American Scholar* (Winter 1966-67).

Crain, Robert L., and Morton Inger. "Urban School Integration: Strategy for Peace," *Saturday Review* (Feb. 18, 1967).

Fischer, John H. "The School Park," in *Racial Isolation in the Public Schools,* Vol. II, Appendix D2. Washington, D.C.: Government Printing Office, 1967.

Goodlad, John I. "Desegregating the Integrated School," in *Racial Isolation in the Public Schools,* Vol. II, Appendix D2.2. Washington, D.C.: Government Printing Office, 1967.

Grieder, Calvin. "Education Parks May Replace the Neighborhood School," *Nation's Schools* (December 1965).

Havighurst, Robert J. *The East Orange Education Plaza: A New Plan for a Modern Community.* Chicago: University of Chicago, 1964.

Havighurst, Robert J., and others. "Metropolitanism: II. What Relevance for Chicago?" *Harvard Graduate School of Education Alumni Association Bulletin* XII, No. 1 (1967).

Howe, Florence. "Mississippi's Freedom Schools: The Politics of Education," *Harvard Education Review* (Spring 1965).

Jacobson, Nathan (ed.) *An Exploration of the Educational Park Concept.* New York: Board of Education, 1964.

Kurland, Norman, and others. "Urban-Suburban Cooperation: A Report," *Integrated Education* (August-September 1966).

Leeson, Jim. "Desegregation Violence, Intimidation, and Protest," *Southern Education Report* (December 1966).

Lortie, Dan C. "Towards Educational Equality: The Teacher and the Educational Park," in *Racial Isolation in the Public Schools,* Vol. II, Appendix D2.4. Washington, D.C.: Government Printing Office, 1967.

Marland, S. P., Jr. "The Education Park Concept in Pittsburgh," *Phi Delta Kappan* (March 1967).

Mauch, James E. "The Education Park," *American School Board Journal* (March 1965).

Plath, Karl R. *Schools within Schools: A Study of High School Organization.* New York: Teachers College, Columbia University, 1965.

Platoff, Joan. "Preschool Prototype: An Integrated, Semi-Cooperative Nursery School," *Young Children* (March 1966).

"The Powell Bill, HR 13079," *Integrated Education* (April-May 1966).

Sherrill, Robert G. "Guidelines to Frustration," *Nation* (Jan. 16, 1967).

Thomas, J. Alan. "The Secondary Education Park: Value Synthesis in Urban School Systems," *Administrator's Notebook* (November 1965).

Trachtenberg, Stephen J. "The Federal Government and School Desegregation," *Changing Education* (Fall 1966).

Wright, J. Skelly. "Public School Desegregation: Legal Remedies for De Facto Segregation," *New York University Law Review* (April 1965).

Part Five

The Contribution of Research

Until 1954, few studies of school desegregation had been made: there was very little to study. Since 1954, many desegregated situations have come into existence. Opponents of school desegregation have ignored this accumulation of experience; and, more or less, so have the proponents of desegregation. In 1966, a high government official, who was asked by a legislator why the federal government financed so little research into desegregation, replied: "The basic problem is there are very few researchers that want to work on it ... " Other inhibiting factors are the political and economic vested interests arrayed against desegregation.

Nevertheless, the volume and the quality of desegregation research are growing. A sampling of that research is contained in this section. The Katz summary is a convenient overall survey.

One value of new research derives from re-examination of old explanations. Levine and Havighurst ask whether the difficulties of desegregation are compounded by certain demographic factors such as a higher birthrate among Negroes. They report that while a higher birthrate undoubtedly played a role in the past, in Kansas City, at least, the Negro birthrate has declined significantly. Thus, the school system has in fact been relieved of a sudden inflow of Negro enrollment, and conditions favorable to desegregation of the schools have been created. Whether the school system and the community would take advantage of the new circumstances to advance desegregation is quite another matter.

Nonstatistical research techniques can be very fruitful. Robert Coles, for example, uses a psychiatric case-study approach with relatively few children. He brings to bear not only his considerable personal insight but a whole body of psychiatric knowledge as well. In addition, he takes into account general factors such as the impact of the civil rights movement and of the family on the individual desegregated child. He is thus led to observe that Negro children in the Cleveland ghetto seem to be less able to cope with the impact of racial segregation than are the southern children he has studied. Perhaps more important. Dr. Coles finds again and again, in both North and South, that segregated Negro children are able to summon up enormous inner reserves and to profit from desegregated schooling even under extraordinary external pressures.

What happens to academic achievement when disadvantaged and hitherto segregated Negro children become classmates of more advantaged white children? In a 1963 study, whose results were repeated elsewhere numerous times in later years, Wolman examined this situation in New Rochelle, New York. About half the students in a Negro school transferred to a white school. At the end of one year, an evaluation of academic achievement was made. Three points were noted: (1) the advantaged white children continued to learn at an accelerated rate; (2) the Negro children, grades one through five, did not gain as much as the whites but neither did their scores **fall,** as did those of Negro children in segregated schools; and (3) kindergarten children who had transferred from the Negro school gained significantly more than did two nontransfer control groups both of which were comparable in terms of socioeconomic status with one also comparable in terms of ethnic composition. Wolman concluded that integration benefits the minority child most if it occurs early in the child's school career. (It is interesting to note that this experiment in integration did not originate in a school board initiative to integrate. Instead, a famous court case had been lost by the school board and the court had directed the board to close down a virtually all-Negro school. It was some of these transferred children who constituted the subjects of Wolman's study.)

Each of the remaining studies in this section exemplifies explorations of important dimensions of school integration and urban education in general.

RESEARCH ON PUBLIC SCHOOL DESEGREGATION

Irwin Katz *is professor of psychology, University of Michigan. This report was prepared for the Research Conference on School Desegregation, Yeshiva University, September 1965, and May 1966, under a grant from the United States Office of Education. Dr. Katz has conducted a number of experiments in the effects of desegregation on learning, and is especially interested in constructing a comprehensive psychological theory of desegregation.*

Segregation must be regarded as a national problem that is not confined to the South.[1] Racial prejudice in the North has given sanction to a pattern of segregation in the public schools which, though different in degree, is not greatly unlike "southern

From *Integrated Education.* **August/September 1966. Reprinted by permission of the author.**

[1] In preparation of this report, the following have been especially useful: R. M. Williams, Jr., "Factors Affecting Reactions to Public School Desegration in American Communities," mimeo., 1964; E. A. Suchman, J. P. Dean, and R. M. Williams, Jr., *Desegration: Some Propositions and Research Suggestions,* ADL, New York, 1958; R. M. Williams, Jr., B. R. Fisher, I. L. Janis, "Educational Desegregation as a Context for Basic Social Science Research," *American Sociological Review,* Vol. 21 (1956), pp. 577-583; S. W. Cook, "Desegregation: A Psychological Analysis," *American Psychologist,* Vol. 12 (1957), pp. 1-13.

style" *de jure* segregation. Dentler points out that school segregation is so pronounced in certain major cities of the North that if public schools are placed on a scale from all white to all Negro, the great majority of them will cluster at the far extremes.

Mixed student bodies are very uncommon.[2] Long notes that until well into the present century, most northern and western states permitted, encouraged, or required school segregation under law. Four northern states did not make segregation illegal till the 1940's, and in the states where it was technically illegal one can show that in many cases it was a result of a deliberate policy of racial districting. By and large, Long concludes, segregation in the North did not "just happen" as a result of occupancy pattern.[3]

Evidence on the extensiveness of northern *de facto* segregation is well-documented in a 1963 report by the National Association of Intergroup Relations Officials.[4] The same report marshals evidence that predominantly Negro schools in the North, like their southern counterparts, are generally inferior in the quality of educational services offered, especially in the large cities. Given these facts, it is clear that the responsibility of the federal government with regard to the furthering of public school integration cannot be limited to any single region of the United States.

In order to decide what types of research are most likely to contribute to the implementation of a governmental policy one must consider the basic principles and objectives of the policy. With respect to school integration, it will be assumed here that, insofar as possible, change efforts should be consistent with the following propositions:

1. The burden of adjusting to desegregation in a community should be shared as equitably as possible by all citizens, rather than being concentrated upon one segment of the total population.
2. The chief responsibility for carrying out desegregation should rest with local school officials and personnel; the change-over should not depend unduly upon the voluntary efforts of those private citizens whose constitutional rights are being violated under the status quo.
3. Since the larger goal of integration is to provide all children with adequate access to the privileges and responsibilities of American society, it should wherever necessary be tied to a general improvement of facilities, staff, and curriculum.
4. In its famous 1954 ruling* the supreme court declared that school segregation was psychologically harmful to Negro children. The implication is that each additional day of forced attendance at segregated Negro schools may contribute further injury to the "heart and minds" of these youngsters. Therefore, unnecessary delays in bringing about change must be regarded by responsible officials as intolerable, and the goal of integration must be pursued with a sense of utmost urgency.

---

[2] R. A. Dentler, "Barriers to Northern School Desegregation," *Daedalus,* Vol. 95, pp. 45-63, Winter 1966.

[3] H. Long, "The Meaning of Segregated Education in the North," mimeo., Talladega College, March 1964, p. 3.

[4] *Public School Segregation and Integration in the North,* special issue of *Journal of Intergroup Relations,* Commission on School Integration, NAIRO, November 1963.

*[Editor's Note: See Appendix A, "Text of Supreme Court Rulings (*Brown* v. *Board of Education,* ...)."]

5. Integration involves more than just racially balanced enrollments. Principals and teachers must be responsive to the needs of those who previously attended inferior segregated schools or who come from disadvantaged homes. But the educational requirements of Negro children should not be used as an excuse for setting up racially segregated classes within biracial schools.

The foregoing considerations are not intended to be exhaustive; they are mentioned merely to suggest some important empirical criteria for evaluating the adequacy of different implementation strategies. Research can provide feedback on the extent to which these and other basic principles and objectives of integration are promoted by local desegregation programs. In addition to this use of research to assess the success of change-over efforts, investigations can increase our knowledge and understanding of the factors that influence the pace of desegregation. Writing on this subject, Pettigrew has stressed the importance of Negro insistence, white resistance, and social structural barriers. It is his view that once token desegregation has taken place, the most critical determinant of the speed of further change is the amount of pressure exerted by the Negro community.[5] Dentler has taken a similar position, on the basis of his own participation in several desegregation programs of small northern cities. He believes that in order for desegregation to become possible politically and educationally, Negroes must protest in a visible, unequivocal manner, and that this protest must "resonate positively with some influential segment of the white population." It also seems plain to him that a very highly stratified class structure will act as a formidable barrier to desegregation. He then suggests another factor: "a clear, sufficiently intense stimulus from state or other extra-local authorities." In the North significant change has tended to occur in the smaller communities only when impetus was provided by strong state educational agencies.[6] La Porte, Beker, and Willie found that, in a middle-sized northern city, pressures from local Negro protest groups and from the state education department were primarily responsible for initiating action on desegregation. A directive from the state education commissioner on racial imbalance seemed to influence the situation by adding pressure on the local board of education and by helping to get the board "off the hook" with more conservative elements in the community.[7]

Research on White Resistance and Related Problems

Cook and others have pointed out that attitudes alone are relatively poor predictors of white people's reactions to desegregation. For example, before integration occurred in the District of Columbia 52 percent of the white adult population were against it, 24 percent were neutral, and only 24 percent were favorable. But except for a brief strike by some students, which was not supported widely by adults, the first steps toward integration were carried out uneventfully. The school superintendent was sufficiently encouraged to speed up the entire process. When respondents in the predesegregation survey were reinterviewed at the end of the school year, it was

[5] T. F. Pettigrew, "Continuing Barriers to Desegregated Education in the South," *Sociology of Education*, Vol. 38 (Winter 1965), pp. 99-111.

[6] Dentler, *op. cit.*

[7] R. La Porte, Jr., J. Beker, and C. V. Willie, "The Evolution of Public Educational Policy, etc.," mimeo., Syracuse University Youth Development Center, 1966.

found that of those who initially disapproved of the supreme court decision, only 29 percent felt that desegregation in Washington was not successful. Experiences in other cities bear out the point that even when there is at the outset widespread feeling against integration, the change-over may be effected smoothly and without incident.[8] Pettigrew has cited evidence that white attitudes tend to become more favorable when desegregation is perceived as a *fait accompli* or as inevitable.[9] Various alternative explanations of this phenomenon readily come to mind: perhaps actual experience, or discussion and reflection, show the imagined dangers of desegregation to be false or exaggerated, or the conflict between reality and the desire for continued segregation generates so much internal tension that the wish is suppressed or abandoned. Research on this problem may yield useful information about the necessary conditions for inducing favorable attitude change. What is particularly needed to improve our understanding of the relationship between attitudes and overt resistance to desegregation is an emphasis upon the psychological sources of segregation feelings and beliefs, rather than—as in the past—upon the attitudes *per se*. To be able to explain why white parents resist racial change in the schools it is necessary to know in what ways they experience such change as threatening to them personally when it involves their own children. Williams has pointed out that any sustained review of the research evidence "will convey a powerful impression of the importance of 'threat' in the entire matter." He discusses the threat of status loss as being particularly potent, since quite often when desegregation occurs the white schools that receive the heaviest influx of Negro students are in working-class or lower middle-class neighborhoods where the social status of residents is at best precarious. For these people there are few if any alternative ways of maintaining status, once the prospective change takes place.

According to Williams, there is a very wide range of possible threats in a proposed move to bring Negro and white children together in the same schools, when they have previously been separated. For example, anxiety may refer to possible increases in cost and taxes, to quality of formal education, to physical safety and comfort (fear of aggression, fear for health condition, hazards of transportation), to social practices (manners, language, etc.), to sexual threats, to status threat to parents *vis-à-vis* their in-group peers, to threat to a categorical sense of superiority, to threat to long-run competitive advantages (jobs, housing, politics, etc.).[10] Investigations are needed to determine how the particular sources of threat to white parents vary, for different socioeconomic groups, with differences in the structure of the white and Negro subcommunities and with regional, demographic, and rural-urban differences. Once research has identified the various specific fears that white people have about integration, it should be possible to assess their validity in the light of actual conditions, and to take appropriate remedial action. Thus, if there is widespread concern about deterioration of scholastic standards, an information campaign could be undertaken to acquaint the population with relevant facts about the impact of desegregation upon the quality of education in comparable communities where the change-over had already occurred, and about the various steps that would be taken in the local school system to preserve or even raise academic standards.

---

[8]Cook, *op. cit.*

[9]Pettigrew, *op. cit.*

[10]Williams, *op. cit.*

In at least one northern community that was studied, white resistance to a "Princeton plan" school pairing did not appear to be inspired by fear of educational deterioration. Rogers and Swanson found that in a high-income, professional neighborhood of New York City, where interest in school affairs had always been high, as reflected in attendance at parents association meetings and other types of activity, a pairing was accomplished smoothly. But in a lower middle-class area, parents who had previously been markedly apathetic about the schools were vehemently opposed to a similar desegregation step. From an analysis of the demographic characteristics of the two areas, the authors concluded that status anxiety was a primary motivating factor in the resisting community. The latter was largely composed of upwardly mobile members of minority cultural groups who had moved to their present homes from ethnic ghetto areas closer to the central city. Because of their limited occupational skills and education they probably had reached the limits of their residential and economic mobility.[11] Similarly, Tumin has reported that "hard core" resisters to integration in Guilford County, North Carolina, tended to be the low men on the economic totem pole who were the least educated, narrowest in social perspective, and most anomic element in the local white population. They were the group that was most vulnerable to Negro competition for jobs and housing, and most likely to bear the brunt of school desegregation.[12]

It is both morally and practically desirable that desegregation be carried out on an equitable basis. Common sense suggests that the wider the range of neighborhoods and socioeconomic groups that can be involved in the initial process, the less intense will be the status threat and the resultant sense of victimization experienced by particular white groups. This proposition can be tested by means of comparative studies in two or more communities that are about to undergo either selective or total-system integration. It would also be worth while to carry out retrospective studies of localities that have already experienced one or the other type of change. Aside from the question of whether they instigate less opposition, it would also be desirable to establish empirically whether system wide change-overs are not more efficient than the piecemeal variety, by virtue of stimulating and permitting a kind of unified, overall planning that is hardly possible when the latter procedure is followed.

An important aspect of the problem of white resistance has to do with the causes of violence and the development of adequate techniques for its control. It is already well established that the public stance of local officials, law enforcement officers, and political leaders can have a decisive influence on whether outbreaks of mass violence will occur. As Vander Zanden observes, the crucial factor governing the incidence or severity of disturbances attendant upon desegregation has "tended to be the determined, unequivocal policy instituted and pursued by authorities and the stern, nontolerant policy inaugurated toward 'agitators' and demonstrators."[13]

Among the problems still in need of study is that of the relationship between the anomic, psychologically alienated condition of certain low-status white groups and

---

[11]D. Rogers and B. Swanson, "White Citizen Response to the Same Integration Plan: Companions of Local School Districts in a Northern City," *Sociological Inquiry*, Vol. 35 (1965) pp. 107-122.

[12]M. Tumin, *Desegregation, Resistance and Readiness*, Princeton University Press, 1958.

[13]J. W. Vander Zanden, *Race Relations in Transition*, Random House, Inc., New York, 1965, p. 80.

the emergence of violent activism. In their study of white resistance to the pairing of schools in New York City, Rogers and Swanson noted "an almost complete absence of intermediate community organizations between the citizenry and the city government. At the risk of oversimplification, the sociopolitical structure of the neighborhood consists of city-wide and local public officials who make major decisions for the area and the large, powerless, alienated, and usually apathetic, though recently very activist, mass." The authors speculated that if the white population had been able to express their interests and grievances through local organizations, "they would have had a built-in safety valve for 'bleeding off' their fears and sense of alienation." If they had had an opportunity to meet with other groups, hear other points of view, and have some of their questions answered, they might even have developed a stake in improving the public schools for all children.[14]

These observations may have bearing upon the situation in the Deep South, where community organizational activity of all kinds is very low as compared with other regions. But at present it is an open question whether Rogers and Swanson's analysis of the relationship between sociopolitical powerlessness and isolation, on the one hand, and emotional activism on the other, can be applied to localities other than the one they studied. From a practical standpoint, it is clear that prolonged open debate about the desirability of desegregating a local school system can have the effect of uniting and strengthening the segregationist elements in the community. On the other hand, there are numerous instances in which desegregation was successfully accomplished in southern and border states with minimal advance publicity or opportunity for discussion. There is a need for research on the factors that govern white responses to relatively open and relatively closed desegregation procedures. Presumably, reactions in the white community can safely be ignored by public officials only when there is good reason to believe that the change-over will not arouse intense feelings of threat and victimization among sizable elements of the population. A particularly harmful type of white opposition is that which takes the form of harassment of Negro children by white students. Permissive attitudes on the part of white parents and school authorities seem to have much to do with its occurrence.

An interesting strategy for studying outbreaks of violence has been recommended by Suchman and co-workers. It involves assigning to special "on tap" field workers the task of going into communities on short notice to do impromptu yet systematic on-the-spot investigations of riots, mob action, etc. Using interview and observational techniques, they would search for significant background conditions that led up to the incidents, and would attempt to describe the full course of events. These studies would be guided by hypotheses derived from more extensive types of community research.[15]

Research on Negro Attitudes About School Desegregation

That Negroes have not pressed vigorously for school integration in the South and North is apparent to all close observers of the civil rights movement. According to Lomax, "NAACP people are hesitant to talk about it, but they are having a most difficult time getting local parents to start integration suits." On the whole, he adds, "Negro parents don't seem to be interested in school desegregation—and not just from fear of reprisals, but simply because school integration isn't something large

---

[14]Rogers and Swanson, op. cit.
[15]Suchman, Dean, and Williams, op. cit.

numbers of Negroes get excited about."[16] Indeed, one has only to recall the stated goals of the major Negro protests and demonstrations of recent years—Montgomery, Birmingham, Selma, and so on—or to examine the writings of Martin Luther King, Whitney Young, and other Negro leaders, to recognize that school integration is not a high-priority target of the Negro revolution. Even in the large cities of the North, civil rights advocates who agitate for an amelioration of *de facto* segregation are disheartened by the lack of grass-roots support. To those who believe that integration is the only feasible way to achieve educational equality for minority group children, the present situation is indeed unfortunate, because numerically meaningful integration is not likely to occur in the foreseeable future except in response to determined Negro pressure.

At first glance the apathy of many Negroes regarding school integration appears to reflect a lack of genuine interest in quality education, for it is certainly true that racial discrimination has long kept Negro education devoid of any real economic utility. Though the job market has improved in recent years, exclusion from white-collar and skilled employment is still a basic fact of life for most nonwhite Americans. However, in their responses to survey questionnaires, Negro parents display a considerable amount of concern about the adequacy of the education their children are receiving in public school. In their study of the Negro community in Tallahassee, Killian and Grigg found that the need for better schools was ranked second in importance in a list of eight sources of dissatisfaction.[17] Looking more closely at the apparent indifference of Negro parents to school integration, one begins to suspect that it is in large measure a manifestation of feelings of threat that are not unlike those experienced by the white resisters—though different in specific content. Negroes may be afraid to expose their children to the open prejudice of white classmates and teachers or to devastating experiences of academic failure. In southern communities where entrance into previously all-white schools is on a "free choice" basis, Negro parents often have realistic fears of official harassment, economic reprisals, and even physical harm. Moreover, southern Negro teachers, who are often the most numerous local Negro professional group, stand a good chance of losing their jobs when school systems become integrated. Killian and Grigg's data indicated that Negroes do not perceive quality education and desegregation as closely connected issues, so that while "better schools" was their second most important public concern, school integration had next to the lowest rank of all eight items. Clearly, Negroes must be made aware through the dissemination of information that separate schools are intrinsically unequal. Widespread desegregation will not become politically possible until large numbers of minority-group parents begin to feel that it is necessary.

The ability of Negroes to bring effective pressure to bear upon local officials will depend upon the level of internal communication, organization, and unity of purpose of the Negro community. Suchman and colleagues observe that the Negro community is "actually a complexly differentiated cluster of subgroups, varying in socioeconomic status, geographic origin, occupational type, intelligence level of children, and attitude toward school desegregation. This internal differentiation is likely to be as complex, if

[16]L. E. Lomax, *The Negro Revolt*, Harper & Row, New York, 1962.

[17]L. Killian and C. Grigg, *Racial Crisis in America*, Prentice-Hall, Englewood Cliffs, 1964.

not more so, than the differentiation within the majority community."[18] Research on minority communities can reveal communication barriers between leaders and the population, and between various segments of the community. For example, in her investigation of the Negro community in a small city in the Middle South, Burgess found that Negro leaders, who favored desegregation, were backed on this issue by 58 percent of the Negro upper class, but by only 60 percent of the middle class and 40 percent of the lower class. Not more than 48 percent of the Negro sample favored immediate desegregation. Thus the most active leaders were "out in front" of their constituency—especially the less educated and lower-income elements—and in danger of being repudiated or censured.[19]

Case studies of Negro communities may reveal various ways in which leaders can improve their relations with different segments of the population. The motives, perceptions, goals, and action strategies of the former can be compared with the attitudes and needs of the latter. Suchman and co-workers favor the use of "action research" techniques in Negro communities. Research personnel would work as "change agents" with community organizations to achieve the following: (1) coordination of minority leadership structures; (2) coordination unification, and the increase of communication channels within the total minority community; and finally, (3) the opening of channels of communication with the white community.[20]

Case Studies of School Desegregation

Case studies in depth of communities with different demographic, economic, and political-social characteristics can contribute much to our understanding of the basic forces that govern the course and the speed of desegregation. These investigations can focus on the processes leading up to the decision to comply with the supreme court ruling, or the processes of the planning and accomplishing of the change-over to nonsegregated schooling, or both sets of processes. The approach is exemplified by the La Porte, Beker, and Willie study of the evolution of a school desegregation policy in a small northern city. Their inquiry included (1) the sequence of action on the issue; (2) the structure and dynamics of "democratic" action in the city; (3) functional relationships among the public, the board of education, and the professional administrators of the school system; (4) the relative contributions of particular individuals and groups to community decisions; and (5) extra-community influences. Their chief sources of information were documents (minutes of meetings, policy statements; reports, etc.); lengthy interviews with key participants (the mayor, members of the board of education, school administrators, heads of citizens' organizations, etc,); and direct hearings.[21] Case studies of this sort are rich sources of insights and hypotheses which can later be tested systematically by means of cross-community studies that utilize a relatively large sample of localities, from which highly specified types of data are obtained.

Dentler observes that barriers to school integration in the North are far less formidable in the smaller cities and suburbs than in the big cities. In the smaller

[18]Suchman, Dean, and Williams, *op. cit.*
[19]M. E. Burgess, *Negro Leadership in a Southern City*. University of North Carolina Press, Chapel Hill, 1960.
[20]Suchman, Dean, and Williams, *op. cit.*
[21]La Porte, Beker, and Willie, *op. cit.*

communities technical solutions are available in abundance, and once the decision to desegregate has been made it is relatively easy to prepare the community and the schools for the change-over. But in the big cities technical solutions are few in number and generally drastic in effect upon both the clientele and the practitioners. Also, problems of communication between the board of education and parents, of new staffing and coordination of effort within the school system, etc., are far more complex. Dentler points out that among the six largest cities in the North, only Detroit has made some progress toward improving the racial balance of schools. "New York City, Chicago, and Philadelphia are more severely segregated today than they were in 1954." The situation calls for systematic case studies of the major metropolises, along the lines of the La Porte *et al.* inquiry. As Dentler puts it, "We must look to the social and cultural bases of northern big city life to understand why so little change has occurred. . . we must take into account the political context and the cultural milieu of urban public education."[22]

Research on Technical Devices for Accomplishing De Facto Desegregation

According to Dentler, several partially adequate technical solutions have been proposed for each of the larger northern cities. The two most promising technical solutions, he remarks, are also the most radical.

> One is the concept of the educational park. Here, big-city systems would abandon neighborhood schools (or use them for very different purposes, such as community centers) and erect consolidated facilities housing from 5,000 to 20,000 students. Such a campus-style institution would be located to draw its students from a very wide residential base, one broad enough, perhaps, to surmount long-term changes in class and ethnic settlements. A second, related idea is to *merge* mainly white suburban school districts with increasingly Negro inner city districts. Districts mergers could be achieved by state authorities and could break through ancient patterns of residential restriction.[23]

The most exciting aspect of the educational park idea is its potential for achieving excellence in public school systems, while at the same time providing a technical means of improving racial balance over wide areas. The park would allow the sharing of physical facilities on a rational basis, provide a wider range of special services— academic, remedial, counseling—than any single school, provide the maximum opportunity for effective decentralization, allow flexible use of teacher skills, and permit greater opportunity for creative innovation such as closed-circuit television, team teaching, language laboratories, and automated equipment. There could also be fiscal gains over and above those resulting from improvements in operational efficiency, for much of the cost of the parks could be paid for by the federal government under Title I of the Urban Renewal Act of 1949. As the first educational parks come into being in various parts of the United States it will be important that their educational and administrative merits and their ability to achieve racially balanced enrollments receive careful and systematic evaluation.

Another promising technical device mentioned by Dentler, the merging of suburban and central-city school districts, could bring about massively favorable changes in the ratios of white to Negro pupils in metropolitan school systems. Cases

---

[22]Dentler, *op. cit.*
[23]*Ibid.*

of this type of redistricting should be assessed for their effect upon residential occupancy patterns, percentage of white pupils who transfer to private schools, staff turnover and morale, scholastic standards, attitudes and organized response of parents.

Research on Compliance of School Officials with Desegregation Plans

Studies of the implementation of desegregation plans must take into account the extent of compliance of field personnel in the school system—assistant superintendents, principals and teachers—with directives from the superintendent. Rogers and Swanson suggest that these personnel, especially the principal, have tremendous impact on the extent of acceptance of white teachers, parents, and pupils of an incoming group of Negroes. The principal and others "may effectively negate, sabotage, or at least water-down an integration plan that was developed after many months, perhaps years, of study and discussion."[24]

Research on "Freedom of Choice" versus Mandatory Integration Plans

Research is needed to evaluate the relative merits of "freedom of choice" and mandatory integration plans in the South. Some civil rights leaders contend that it is unrealistic to expect that Negro parents in the South will ever initiate voluntary transfers of their children to predominantly white schools to any significant extent— that under this procedure integration will probably never become a reality in the Deep South. Lomax and others have argued that having to apply for transfer gives the Negro the feeling of changing schools in order to be with white people. "This is a difficult psychological hurdle for southern Negroes to overcome. The truth is, on the whole, they don't want to be with white people as such. They do want the best schools, however . . . "[25] Requesting transfer also exposes the Negro parent to white displeasure and possible vindictiveness. By slowing down the rate of integration, "free choice" plans also prolong the period that young pioneer pupils remain a small, isolated minority, acutely vulnerable to the debilitating effects of social isolation and rejection by the white majority. Research is needed to show whether mandatory plans can introduce Negro newcomers into previously all-white schools in large enough numbers so that they can provide security for one another, without at the same time arousing a high level of white resistance. Research could also test the proposition that mandatory plans are better than "free choice" in that they allow for rational, system-wide planning with regard to optimal distribution of students in relation to available staff, facilities, and space.

Research on Enlisting Support of Influential Private Citizens

There is increasing evidence of a move on the part of the southern business community toward an accommodation with the civil rights program of the federal government. For example, the Committees of One Hundred in Alabama and Mississippi, consisting of the top one hundred business leaders of each state, have publicly advocated compliance with the Civil Rights Act. While other motives may be involved, economic self-interest is clearly consistent with this change to a more progressive position on racial matters. Research can explore techniques for activating

---

[24]Rogers and Swanson, *op. cit.*
[25]Lomax, *op. cit.*

local business leaders in support of prompt and orderly school integration Perhaps forums and conferences could be organized at colleges and universities on problems of education and local economic development, and talks could be scheduled by visiting federal officers.

Research on the Effects of Desegregation

Among the important areas for research are the effects of desegregation on (1) residential occupancy patterns, (2) parent attitudes and participation in school activities, (3) stability, morale, and attitudes of school staffs, (4) scholastic performance of white and Negro children, (5) social relationships among pupils of same and different races, and (6) self-concept, attitudes, and emotional adjustment of Negro pupils. Ideally, all of these variables should be studied by means of before-and-after research designs with nondesegregated schools as controls.

Experiments can unravel the underlying social dynamics of the biracial classroom and the teaching-learning process. It would be useful to follow up the promising leads of Gottlieb's work on the interracial perceptions of Negro and white pupils and Negro and white teachers in integrated schools.[26] Robert Rosenthal's recent experiment on the effect of teachers' expectations upon the intellectual achievement of their pupils also suggests worthwhile further investigations.[27] In his study, teachers were given fictitious information about the intellectual potentialities of children whose true intelligence was known to the experimenter. At the end of the school year, the IQ's of the children showed changes commensurate with the false information that had previously been given to the teacher. That is, children who the teacher had been told had considerable potentiality for intellectual growth showed large increments in IQ, while those who were supposed to have little potentiality for improvement showed smaller gains or no gains in IQ. Rosenthal's study does not tell us how the teacher's expectations influenced her behavior toward different pupils.

It would be interesting to follow up the Rosenthal experiment with studies in which white adults (teachers) were given different kinds of information about a child (for example, bright-dull, middle class-working class, Negro-white) and then required to teach the child a standard task. Do the differential cues influence the amount of effort expended by the adult in instructing the child, the amount and kinds of reinforcement, unconscious expressions of acceptance or rejection? One might also examine whether the child senses the teacher's attitude toward him, by testing his perception of the teacher after the instructional period. The results of such experiments could be used in the training of new teachers as a means of sensitizing them to the human relations aspects of their future work.

Another problem for investigation has to do with teachers' responsiveness to children's needs as a function of racial differences. White and Negro teachers could be required to observe biracial groups of children and then to report on each child, first at a descriptive level and then at an inferential level where the child's emotional needs and interests were considered. The richness and detail of report, and validity when

[26]David Gottlieb, "Teaching and Students: The Views of Negro and White Teachers," *Sociology of Education*, Summer, 1964.

[27]Unpublished. Reported in a paper, "Changing Children's IQ by Changing Teachers' Expectations," read at the annual meeting of the American Psychological Association, September 2, 1966.

compared with objective information, could be evaluated in relation to the race of the teacher-observer and the race of the object-child. It could be ascertained what teacher characteristics are associated with accuracy of observation of own-race and other-race children. One might also examine the characteristics of teachers whom children like and from whom they learn readily.

In my own research I have examined the relationship between the race of adult testers and the learning ability of Negro boys of grade-school age. I found that the children learned a list of paired associated words more readily from Negro males and females than from white males and females. However, the same boys worked harder for the white testers than for the Negro testers on a simple writing task (drawing X's in small boxes), suggesting that motivation was as high or higher in the presence of the white tester, but that complex verbal ability was impaired. Further research can establish whether the impairment was due to anxiety, and if so of what nature.

Finally, one can study the effects of various types of biracial peer environments upon the learning of Negro children. For example, Negroes can be required to learn a standard verbal task in the presence of white peers who are either friendly or unfriendly in their reactions. With regard to the role of the teacher, situations could be devised in which to study the effectiveness of teachers in inculcating in white children acceptance of Negro peers by means of appropriate modeling of behavior and dispensing of reinforcements.

POPULATION TRENDS AND INCREASED SCHOOL INTEGRATION IN BIG CITIES

Daniel U. Levine *and* **Robert J. Havighurst** *are, respectively, associate director and director, Center for the Study of Metropolitan Problems in Education, University of Missouri at Kansas City.*

The cause of integrated education in the big cities has proved a frustrating one for educators and laymen who believe that segregation is undesirable in a society professing commitment to democratic ideals and traditions. Even in cities in which opinion has been either neutral or relatively positive about integration and in which school officials have joined with community leaders in support of measures to achieve it, few permanent inroads have been made in overcoming segregated patterns in education and housing.

Permissive transfer plans, open enrollment policies, locating new schools on the boundaries between white and Negro neighborhoods, pairing adjacent schools so as to serve differing grade levels, clustering nearby schools into large attendance areas— these and related measures generally have resulted in only a small or temporary reduction in segregated education. Everywhere their impact has been countered by residential patterns which enlarge the Negro ghetto—and with it the number of all-Negro schools—in oppressively limited directions, often leading to the resegregation of schools which had been briefly integrated.

One of the most potent of the underlying forces responsible for widening segregation in the residential and educational patterns in the big cities during the past

From *Integrated Education,* **June/July 1967. Reprinted by permission of the authors.**

two decades has been the large-scale movement of Negroes from the rural south to the urban centers and the naturally high rate of population increase to be expected among this group consisting particularly of relatively young, low-income migrants. During the same period, of course, whites were moving in large numbers from the deteriorating central cities to the more spacious suburban areas. Since the Negro population of the central cities was growing so rapidly, even whites with little or no prejudice toward Negroes expressed fear that an integrated school inevitably signalled an approaching wave of low-income Negroes who would soon constitute a majority in school and community. Seldom willing to send their children to schools in which middle-class whites are not clearly the predominant influence, such parents swelled the numbers of whites who fled to the suburbs. The resulting modal pattern, as demographer Leo F. Schnore has described it in his study of developments in Detroit, has been one in which

> . . . the white population is failing to maintain its numbers in the middle class sections of the city while the nonwhite residents are accumulating there very rapidly; the outer zone of the city is adding to its white population at a much reduced pace, especially that part of the ring which is adjacent to the central city; in absolute numbers almost all of the total increase in the ring is the result of additions to the white population; and finally, these trends could be seen developing at least twenty to thirty years ago and most of them were accentuated during the 'fifties.[1]

Recounting the advantages of the educational park in a paper prepared for the U.S. Commission on Civil Rights, Columbia Teachers College President John H. Fischer recently summarized the effect of this demographic change on desegregation efforts in the schools as follows:

> The steady and continuing expansion of ghettos is clearly evident in almost every central city, yet one desegregation plan after another proposes to build new schools on the obviously temporary borders between white and negro communities or to pair adjacent existing schools in the vain hope of retaining well-balanced student bodies. Even the most superficial glance at occupancy patterns would reveal that only massive changes in housing, migration, birthrates could possibly prevent early resegregation of the schools involved.[2]

Whatever the merits of the educational park, it may be that the pessimism expressed above concerning other desegregation plans in the big cities is no longer as justified as would be indicated by the experience of the past five or ten years. More specifically, there is reason to believe that the period marked by rapid population growth among Negroes in the cities and by seemingly relentless turnover of neighborhoods from predominantly white to predominantly Negro is now coming to an end. Here in Kansas City, Missouri, an accumulating body of data suggests that this has already happened; if so, similar developments may occur in other cities as well.

Whether Fischer's reference to "massive changes" in birthrate and migration patterns accurately describes the situation in Kansas City is, to some degree, a matter

---

[1]Leo F. Schnore, *The Urban Scene: Human Ecology and Demography*. The Free Press, New York, 1965, p. 257.

[2]John H. Fischer, "The School Park," Appendix D-2, 1 in *Racial Isolation in the Public Schools,* Vol. II, U.S. Government Printing Office, Washington, D.C., 1967, p. 254.

of semantics. Regardless of the applicability of the terminology, however, data now available clearly show that the number of Negro children in Kansas City is no longer increasing but rather, if anything, *decreasing*. By extension, the total Negro population of the city almost certainly is no longer growing at the rate it did between 1940 and 1960, if indeed, it is still growing at all.

In a report recently published by the Center for the Study of Metropolitan Problems in Education of the University of Missouri at Kansas City,[3] data from a number of sources reflecting trends in the Negro population of Kansas City were assembled in order to determine whether the number of Negro youngsters in the city was still rising as rapidly as it had between 1955 and 1964, during which time the proportion of Negro youngsters in the School District of Kansas City, Missouri, rose from 22 percent to 38 percent. Examination of these data indicated that

1. The number of births recorded annually to Negro mothers in Kansas City had increased in every year but one between 1947 and 1959, rising from 910 in the former year to 3,161 in the latter. Since 1959, however, the annual number of such births stabilized, and even fell below 3,000 in 1963 and 1965.

2. Among a sample of Negro families interviewed in a 1966 study sponsored by the city planning commission, there were more children seven and eight years of age than in any other two-year sample and the number of youngsters less than three years of age was smaller than in any other three-year sample in the previous twelve years.

3. Among the children in a sample of Kansas City Negro families receiving assistance from the county welfare department, the modal age was five and the number of children in each age group below that age in no case exceeded the respective numbers who were seven or eight years of age.

4. The number of children less than two years of age enumerated in the school district's preschool census as residing in the attendance areas of the nineteen elementary schools, 90 or more percent Negro in 1966, was only 69 percent as large as the number of three- and four-year-olds residing in these same areas. Although sampling procedures may have slightly inflated the latter number as compared with the former, it was concluded that there are significantly fewer Negro youngsters below the age of two than there are in the two-year cohort of youngsters three and four years of age.

5. The kindergarten enrollment in seven predominantly Negro elementary schools, from which nearly two thousand youngsters had been bused to relieve severe overcrowding during the 1965-1966 school year, decreased from 1,325 in the fall of 1965 to 1,274 in the fall of 1966.

If the Negro population of Kansas City were still increasing rapidly, such an increase would have resulted in a continuing rise in the number of young Negro children to be found in the city. Thus, given the fact that all five sources of data indicated that the number of Negro youngsters less than five or six years of age is tending to stabilize or even decline, and in the absence of any evidence to the contrary,

[3]Daniel U. Levine and Robert J. Havighurst, *Population Growth among Negro Citizens in Kansas City, Missouri,* The Center for the Study of Metropolitan Problems in Education, Kansas City, 1967.

it is all but certain that the Negro population of Kansas City is no longer rising rapidly and inexorably as it was between 1940 and 1960.

To explain why the size of the Negro population of Kansas City appears to have stabilized is not very difficult. As was noted above, the rapid increase in the number of Negroes in the cities during the past two decades was due to mass movements out of the rural South on the part of relatively young migrants among whom birthrates could be expected to be very high. None of these causes is now operating with anything resembling its former importance.

There is evidence, in the first place, that recent migration from the rural South to the North is on a much smaller scale than previously,[4] partly because technological and economic change has reduced opportunities for unskilled employment in the big cities and partly because by 1965 there were relatively few Negroes left in many parts of the South to form the human resources pool from which the bulk of this migration has previously been drawn. On this latter point, it is relevant and enlightening to note such estimates as those which have put the total number of Negro tenant farmers remaining in the State of Arkansas in late 1964 at 3,166[5] or which have drawn attention to the fact that very nearly 100 percent of the cotton crop in the Delta region of the South is now picked by machine.[6]

With regard to fertility among the migrants, to expect to find the high birthrate among urban Negroes during the 1950's persisting very long imto the 1960's would be to fail to recognize the facts that

1. The nonwhites who migrated to the cities during the 1940's and 1950's tended to be between the ages of twenty and thirty, so that most of them are now well into their thirties and have already established their families and are no longer producing large numbers of additional children. In Kansas City, for example, the number of Negro women between the ages of twenty and twenty-nine in 1960 was much less than the corresponding number between thirty and thirty-nine (5,805 and 6,810, respectively), a difference that reflected reduced in-migration during the late 1950's and foreshadowed the declining size of the under-six age group which emerged so clearly in our current data on the Negro population in Kansas City.
2. Birthrates tend to fall among newly urbanized groups as they begin to move up the socioeconomic scale.
3. The number of registered births per 1,000 nonwhite women between the ages of fifteen and forty-four in the United States fell from 156 in 1959 to 148.7 in 1962 to 141.5 in 1964.[7]

Returning to a consideration of underlying trends affecting the racial composition of the schools, it should be remembered that Dr. Fischer rightfully cited not only migration and birthrates but also housing patterns as a third factor which has

[4]America at Mid-Decade, U.S. Department of Commerce, Series p. 23, No. 16, March 1966 (revised), U.S. Government Printing Office, Washington, D.C., 1966, p. 11.

[5]*The New York Times,* November 27, 1966.

[6]*The New York Times,* February 13, 1967.

[7]*The Negro in the United States: Their Economic and Social Situation,* U.S. Department of Labor, Bulletin No. 511, June 1966, U.S. Government Printing Office, Washington, D.C., 1966, p. 188.

contributed directly to resegregation in the public schools. As explained above, our data on Kansas City have led us to conclude that the first two factors no longer constitute the potent force toward resegregation that they did just a few years ago. On housing, too, there is reason to take a somewhat more optimistic view than would be warranted if it is simply assumed that newly integrated neighborhoods will tend to resegregate as quickly as in the recent past.

For one thing, the reduced rate of growth among urban Negroes might mean that population pressures are no longer forcing rapid expansion in the size of the ghetto.

Second, in many metropolitan areas, Negroes are beginning to move to the suburbs in significant numbers;[8] while this movement is still small in objective terms, it may constitute a significant breakthrough in that many Negro families who integrate the suburbs would otherwise be relocating in integrated neighborhoods in the cities, and thereby contributing to the rapid resegregation of the latter.

Third, urban renewal projects today seldom necessitate the displacement of large numbers of low-income Negroes as happened in so many cities during the 1950's, partly because urban Negroes are acquiring the political power to block "Negro removal" which fails to recognize the human needs of the people to be bulldozed out to build highways, shopping centers, and other developments sought either by city officials or the local power structure.

Fourth, the tight money situation created by the war in Vietnam as well as by general economic conditions has increased mortgage rates, thereby reducing the previous ease with which whites were able to move to the suburbs. At the same time the stabilization of the Negro population means that Negroes are no longer forced to bid so high on houses which do go on the market. The net result has been to slow the out-migration of whites from newly integrated neighborhoods to the suburbs. (These factors may also be partly responsible for an apparent stiffening against initial integration in some white neighborhoods in Chicago and elsewhere.) While it is true that the mortgage market has begun to ease during 1967, it apparently will be a long time before the pace of building in the suburbs picks up to the level characteristic of the postwar years.

Fifth, and perhaps most important, the suburbanization of many of our metropolitan areas is already far advanced. In the Kansas City area, for example, most of the suburban territory surrounding the central city core is no longer in an early stage of development, as shown by the fact that in 1960 only 42 percent of the area's white population still lived in the city of Kansas City. What this means, in effect, is that while whites who wish to leave the city may need to anticipate locating in ever more distant and less accessible suburban developments, those who are least inclined to remain in the city (particularly in integrated neighborhoods) have long since left it. Similar generalizations undoubtedly apply to many other metropolitan areas, particulary those which, like Kansas City, have a population of one to three or four million people.

To conclude, our studies in Kansas City have convinced us that belief in the inevitability of resegregation in local neighborhoods and schools in many of the big cities may not be as justified as past experience would indicate. Ten or fifteen years from now there may be a new wave of school-age Negro children whose rapidly

---

[8]Jack Star, "Negro in the Suburbs," *Look,* May 16, 1967, p. 51.

increasing numbers make it difficult to maintain stable integrated situations, but, in the meantime, school officials will have a breathing period during which they can work to counteract stereotypes and fears which in themselves are principal causes of resegregation. By then, enough might have been done to break down segregation in other parts of the city and the metropolitan area to allow for the maintenance of integrated schooling over a constantly widening area and a concomitant and permanent reduction in the number and percentage of white and Negro students who attend segregated schools.

Stated more positively, we think that stable integrated education will be a much more feasible goal to work toward during the next few years than has been true in the recent past. The reduced rate of growth of the urban Negro population will soon be reflected in enrollment figures in the public schools, and this stabilization will relieve the pressure which has done so much to resegregate our few integrated schools. Open enrollment, school pairing, careful selection of new school sites, and other policies which have been relatively futile in the past should have a more significant impact in bringing about stable integrated education.

Given the will and the imagination, educators with a real commitment to integration can anticipate that their efforts may well bear fruit to a degree seemingly unattainable in the past decade. In Kansas City, for example, the board of education has been sponsoring special projects (e.g., in-service teacher training, new courses in human relations and in the humanities, the latter taught in association with university personnel) designed to keep whites from leaving a key high school on the verge of resegregation, and these efforts show signs of turning the tide.[9] It is doubtful, however, whether such efforts will continue if board members, educators, and laymen mistakenly believe that resegregation is inevitable. As one would expect, even administrators who support integration are not always acting as vigorously as they might if they were fully convinced that their labors need not be swept away on a continuing tide of resegregation. To some extent, then, educators in the big cities are both victims and perpetrators of a classic example of self-fulfilling prophecy. But, as our data on Kansas City clearly indicate, the formerly realistic basis for this cycle of despair and defeat in working for integrated education is now in the process of withering away.

WHEN NORTHERN SCHOOLS DESEGREGATE

Robert Coles, *research psychiatrist, University Health Service, Harvard University, is author of* Children of Crises *(Little, Brown, 1967). He has conducted numerous study excursions into Atlanta, New Orleans, Boston, Cleveland, and elsewhere. Dr. Coles is a member of the editorial advisory board of* INTEGRATED EDUCATION *magazine.*

For several years I tried to learn how Negro and white children in the South have managed the rather extraordinary social and educational experience that is school desegregation in that region. I worked in New Orleans and Atlanta with Negro

[9]Daniel U. Levine, "School Pioneers Social Change," *Focus/Midwest*, Vol. 5, No. 36 (1967), pp. 10-12.

From *Integrated Education*, **Febuary/March 1966. Reprinted by permission of the author.**

children who were pioneers—at times the whole country watched their difficult and sometimes dangerous struggle. I watched white children slowly accept as "natural" what they had been long told was impossible—the presence of Negroes in their classrooms. Though I spent most of my time in Georgia and Louisiana, I went to other southern states, too, so that I could see how desegregation occurred in a variety of situations: urban or rural; against heavy and noisy opposition, or quietly; when small children were affected, or youths in high school.

All in all I was surprised at how well the Negro children managed the strains they faced—sometimes including riotous mobs—and how gradually but decisively their white classmates accepted them. As a child psychiatrist I expected—perhaps was looking for—emotional disorder in boys and girls under such social stress. I was not only disappointed, but had occasion to reflect upon what really does cause the "symptoms" I failed to see, say, in those four little six-year-old girls who, in 1960, braved threats and jeers to attend boycotted schools in New Orleans. Many of the children I followed rather intensively—and for two years—came from poor homes, sometimes broken homes, from homes mercilessly exposed to every whim of the "economic cycle," not to mention the police or mobs. If they could do as well as they did—and continue to do—then whatever it is that accounts for such endurance is worth our curiosity—particularly in a society whose comfortable, middle-class, suburban (and white) children continue to tax the limits of every child guidance clinic in the nation.

I have no single explanation, no easy answer to why these children survived so handily. Perhaps stress itself is not the issue, but rather its meaning to the child. To Negro children in the South the stress they endured had enormous meaning; it was the beginning of their freedom, and they knew it. Even for white children there was meaning to all the panic and fear they heard at home and on the streets. History was being made. One white youth put it this way: "I'm against this. I was brought up to be; but you have to admit you're in the middle of something important happening. I'll bet I'll be able to tell my children about it; though, of course, by then it may not be so exciting."

In any event, I am continuing to observe Negro and white school children meeting up with one another for the first time, this time in the North, under quite different circumstances. Here in Boston, they are doing so not by federal court order, not in defiance of local tradition, not against the will of aroused crowds, but within the legal and moral traditions of their community. They are urban children, in their bones, so much more so than even those I knew in Atlanta or New Orleans—the South is still rural, and its large cities not yet as massive as those of the North. In the case of the Negroes, they are children who are being bused across the city to secure what their parents—and they, too—feel to be a better education; that is, one obtained in less crowded classrooms, from teachers less harassed and despairing. In the case of the white children, they are boys and girls who—likely as not—have heard their parents' expressed horror at the South's injustice toward the Negro as well as their alarm at the implications of "busing"; the schools to which children are bused will become like the ones they left, crowded, of poor quality, downgraded educationally and—as they will often put it when *they* get ready to say it—"let's face it," socially.

The external or visible stresses then, are different. There is no gross violence. The city or state has no laws against white and Negro children learning together. The churches and newspapers tend to encourage and urge the practice. The community's moral pressure, indeed, the pressure of its history, in the sense of a long abolitionist tradition, both favor whatever is "equal," "fair," and "unprejudiced." Yet, there is unmistakable evidence in many a northern city these days that the desegregation of schools may be as hard, or harder to achieve, and as stubbornly resisted, outside the South as within it. White parents are fighting it—and in some instances making their feelings felt at the polls. A number of legal battles are being fought, with school boards and parents locked in debate and controversy not totally unlike those in the South. Boycotts, demonstrations, counterdemonstrations have plagued a number of northern cities. One distinguished federal jurist, J. Skelly Wright, of the U.S. court of appeals in Washington, D.C., has predicted the eventual necessity of supreme court intervention and decision, unless in some way the opposing viewpoints are brought into some agreement.

In the midst of such social and legal issues, what does happen during school desegregation as it occurs in the North; that is, when children are bused across a city to attend a *de facto* segregated school? In my experience, a lot happens—to both Negro and white children.

The very bus ride gives Negro children vision, a sense of cohesion with one another, and even a feeling of pride. It is *their* bus; it is taking them places they have never seen before, places which, to them, mean a better life in the future. "Since as far as I can remember my mother said it's real good across the city, and now I'm right in the middle and seeing it every day." At ten that girl has a very keen sense of urban sociology.

Certainly, no medical or psychiatric harm can be found in those children who are bused. They like and enjoy the ride. Their ages vary from six to eleven, and they are enthusiastic travelers. Nor are they all from striving, ambitious, middle-class families. Some come from poor homes—their parents are as glad to have them away from home a bit longer as they are to have them in a better school.

"Whether you're poor, or making it, as a Negro you know that somehow we have to get out of our confinement, all of us. They've kept us in jail, and even the best fed ones know it's a jail, because if they try to leave—like a job outside—they get slapped down, for all the money they may have." Those words, from a mother of seven, on relief, show a determination—shared by some but not all Negroes—to leave the ghetto that is essentially not restricted to any one class.

In general what I have found is that children bused across a nothern city do quite well at school, and manage increasingly well with their white classmates. Like their southern counterparts, these Negro children make do astonishingly well in schools clearly better than the ones they have left. They become leaders in both their families and their neighborhoods, sources of information about the "white world," children who have "been there" and return daily with stories to tell—and examples to inspire. Academically, some of these children have not only managed well, but were found to be far brighter than anyone before had realized.

Others have needed tutorial help from college students. The majority have done new and difficult work on their own, and passed their tests well enough to get promoted, and become better educated. "To tell the truth, I think my Jeanne is talking a little white these days; her accent, I mean." Whether there is any glory in that particular achievement, Jeanne and her mother feel more—as the mother says it—"at home with the rest of the American people."

A portion of the rest of the American people feel more at home with Jeanne, too. I have watched white children show these Negro children fear, distrust, suspicion, and occasional outright nastiness. On the whole they were at first silent and guarded, but in a short time increasingly friendly and forgetful of racial distinctions. Friendships have been made, and in general an atmosphere of mutual respect holds between the two groups of children. As one teacher put it, correcting my way of talking: "They're *not* two groups. They're just one—children at school here. I wouldn't have thought it so easy, if it hadn't happened. I suppose after it happens it's easier than before—it's easier to solve a *real* problem than worry about one and be afraid of one that *might* happen."

SELF-SELECTION OF STUDENT TEACHERS

George Langberg *is guidance counselor in the public schools of Ossining, New York.* **Philip Freedman** *is assistant professor of education, Hunter College.*

In recent years a prodigious effort has been made to define, in both educational and psychological terms, the requirements of the "disadvantaged" student. As this effort has continued, it has tended to emphasize the problem of teacher selection, specifically the need to find teachers whose particular characteristics and resources would be responsive to the requirements of the lower socioeconomic classrooms.

So unyielding have been the problems of administrative selection of teachers to schools serving disadvantaged areas that it may be worthwhile to consider alternative proposals for staffing. One such alternative is recruitment based upon volunteer or self-selected applicants. This option has been little employed (although New York City is currently attempting to staff certain designated schools on such a basis) and there is virtually a complete lack of information concerning the consequences of such a self-selection procedure. Considering the importance of the self-selection procedure strategy, the authors attempted a preliminary study of the problem, utilizing an opportunity afforded by an ongoing project of the teacher education department of Hunter College, in the spring semester of 1963.

Description of Experiment

At this time, Hunter College was involved in an effort to staff a "problem" junior high school with student teachers who were willing both to volunteer for the assignment and to remain as appointed teachers to the school subsequent to the completion of their training. It was indicated to all student teachers that those volunteering for this assignment would receive intensive preparation and aid. Student teachers were told that there would be opportunity for face-to-face contact with members of the community served by the school, that provisions for consultation and discussion on all problems would be maximized and that generally, volunteers could be assured that the faculty of both the college and the junior high school were prepared to offer intensive and continuous assistance. Of the fourteen students who

From *Integrated Education,* **August/November, 1965. Reprinted by permission of the authors.**

volunteered for this assignment, ten made themselves available for extensive testing at the beginning of the semester and constituted the volunteer (self-selection) group utilized in this study. A comparison group of twenty-six student teachers who had been administratively assigned to various junior high schools, also presented themselves for testing, thus forming the sample of nonvolunteers.

Three basic hypotheses were entertained about the differences between the two groups. The first was that middle-class students volunteering to operate intensively in a lower-class and racially distinct environment would be found to array themselves on a democratic-authoritarian dimension in a position substantially closer to the democratic locus than that of nonvolunteers. Secondly, it was hypothesized that the volunteers would present greater evidence, both contemporaneously and biographically, of self-confidence, of autonomy, of a receptivity to challenge than would be manifested by nonvolunteers. Finally, it was hypothesized that volunteers would perceive both the "problem" school and their role as an active and reformative one; that the latter would reflect a greater intensity of fear and a more passive and restricted conception of their potential function.

To facilitate the examination of these hypotheses, the following tests were administered to both groups: (1) the Christie 20-item version of the F-Scale; (2) the 22 Gough-Sanford Rigidity Scale, response to which is made in terms of three degrees of agreement or disagreement; (3) a randomly selected 30-item scale drawn from the final form E version of the Rokeach Dogmatism Scale, also a Likert Type test with three degrees of agreement and disagreement as response options; (4) a self-rating scale pertaining to personal history and selected trait characteristics; (5) a projective scale designed to gauge the perception of student teachers with respect to the difficulties of teaching in special service schools; and (6) a scale designed to measure the relative importance of factors that induce student teachers to volunteer for special problem-school assignments.

Test Results

The expectation that volunteers would score significantly lower than nonvolunteers on the dimensions of authoritarianism, dogmatism, and rigidity were borne out by comparison of mean scores between groups.

The significance of the findings can perhaps best be understood by a consideration of the item makeup and hypothesized components of the questionnaires. The Sanford-Gough Rigidity Scale is perhaps conceptually clearest in this regard. Its items, in a more clinical setting, may be regarded as a measure of a disposition towards obsessive compulsive functioning. A sampling of test items provides the following illustrations:

- I do not enjoy having to adapt myself to new and unusual situations.
- I always put on and take off my clothes in the same order.
- I prefer work that requires a great deal of attention to detail.

High scores on such a measure clearly suggest a degree of inflexibility and stereotypy and a strong preference for orderly and manageable situations. Similarly, the Dogmatism Scale, which may perhaps be regarded as a test of rigidification in thought and belief rather than behavior, may be viewed as a measure of a related, if still separate, aspect of adaptable or flexible functioning. The sense of what the

Dogmatism Scale measures is conveyed by a reading of its items, of which the following are illustrative:

- The United States and Russia have nothing in common.
- To compromise with our political opponents is dangerous because it usually leads to the betrayal of our own side.
- In this complicated world of ours the only way we can know what's going on is to rely on leaders or experts who can be trusted.

As to the Christie version of the F-Scale, it is unnecessary to elaborate upon the familiar defining components of the authoritarian dimension that the test presumes to measure. While some degree of ambiguity may complicate the interpretation of responses to the Christie F-Scale, despite its effort to remove response set influences, the relatively high intercorrelations of test scores on the Christie Scale with the Gough-Sanford Rigidity Scale and Dogmatism Scale suggests that all three scales are measuring some common trait characteristic. It seems reasonable to assume that this trait characteristic refers to a particular mode of anxiety management which heavily depends on the reduction of ambiguity and uncertainty and which emphasizes a reliance upon polarization in interpersonal relationships and absolutism in cognitive constructions. Such factors would seem to be essentially restrictive of a teacher's potential functioning, particularly in situations like those presented in the lower socioeconomic classroom where value conflict, behavioral disorganization, and weakened controls make such heavy demands for teacher adaptability.

Biographical and Trait Characteristics

While authoritarianism, rigidity, and dogmatism, as relatively established dimensions, were measurable by available instruments, it was clear that many of the specific impressions that had been gained from informal observation of the student teaching groups could be effectively tapped by utilizing constructed questionnaires and test devices. The devices employed consisted, in the first instance, of a forty-three-item questionnaire consisting of statements dealing with trait and experiential factors to which student teachers were asked to respond by rating each item on a seven-point scale from strong agreement to strong disagreement.

One of the many beliefs that the questionnaire was designed to examine was the notion that volunteers would display a greater degree of self-confidence and self-reliance than would nonvolunteers. Both in their responses to items dealing with developmental experiences and to items characterizing contemporary traits, some corroboration of this notion could be inferred. The pattern of volunteer scores indicates a background characterized by strivings for autonomy, for the early acceptance of childhood challenges, and by a relative freedom from the symptomatic signs of diffidence and fearfulness.

Thus, volunteers found such statements as "My parents urged my early independence" and "As a child I began rather early to do such things as travel myself, etc." to be relatively self-descriptive. By contrast, nonvolunteers reported greater childhood uncertainties, particularly in the character of their interpersonal relationships. Their agreement falls most strongly on such statements as: "It took me a long time to become friendly with children who were strangers to me," "As a child, my fears of going for medical treatment were very strong," and again "As a child, I was shy and easily offended." That these early difficulties may not have entirely been resolved is suggested by the tendency of nonvolunteers to characterize their contemporary relationships as lacking in spontaneity and possessing a degree of contrivance—the statement, "I have to admit to myself that often my interest in people is forced," is among the most discriminating of questionnaire items.

There appear to be consistent differences, too, in the response of volunteer and nonvolunteer to items concerned with individual reactions to difficulty and failure. Thus, the volunteer group, perhaps because of the nature of its aspirations, seems less inclined to forgive its deficiencies ("As a child I could not forget my failures") but less tempted as well to turn aside from situational challenges. Items such as "When I am faced with a difficult problem, I will make a few attempts at solution, but will not continue to knock myself out at it," or "Feelings of despondency following failure sometimes interfere with my further attempts to solve a problem" and "In facing troubling or difficult situations, I feel very much relieved if someone is willing to share some of the burden" are responded to in such a way as to suggest that determination and resiliency are far more significant elements in the volunteer's self-concept than in that of the nonvolunteer. This interpretation should not, however, be over-extended; volunteers appear to be no more persistent or determined at tasks lacking a special quality of challenge than nonvolunteers. Indeed, in more routine circumstances, the volunteer may be in some ways the less dependable performer; it was the *non*volunteer who showed agreement with such items as "I am quite well organized in my work habits," and "I have always handed in assignments on time" while it was the volunteers who answered affirmatively to the statement that "I am very good at starting ambitious projects, but find it difficult to maintain momentum."

Finally, volunteers differentiated themselves from their colleagues in their ratings of items reflecting conscious sympathies and allegiances for the disadvantaged. Their responses indicated their greater attraction to idealistic-humanitarian ventures ("I find the idea of joining the Peace Corps rather attractive") and their early alignment with the less favored individuals ("All through my youth I was a rooter for the underdog"). Parenthetically, it may be noted that the identification was not based on earlier childhood contacts with lower-class groups—volunteers reported no greater association of this sort than did nonvolunteers.

Perceptions of the Special Service School

It seemed reasonable to assume that personality and experiential differences among volunteers and nonvolunteers would be reflected in their perception of the special service school assignment and in their role expectation. Accordingly, student teachers were asked to respond to eleven questions that called for estimating percentages of pupils, teachers, and administrators in special service schools exhibiting certain behaviors or possessing certain specified attitudes and feelings. Inasmuch as student teachers, prior to their assignments, were only slightly if at all, familiar with the actual situation in special service schools, it seemed valid to assume that their answers would be essentially projective, based upon fears and personalized anxieties.

The assumption that fear and anxiety would dissuade many of the students from volunteering was amply supported by the data. The nonvolunteer exaggerated the more formidable aspects of the special service school ambiance—in his estimation of the percentage of the youngsters severely disturbed, in his judgment of the extent of parental lack of concern, and in his view of the degree to which successful teaching is achieved through the adoption of severe, authoritarian patterns. In comparison, the volunteers were consistently more benign in their views of the special service school and appeared less disposed to attribute sharply negative behavior to the pupils of such schools.

The nonvolunteers confronted a school image that was, both broadly and in detail, ominous and threatening, and that involved some anticipation of rejection, resentment, antagonism, and disrespect. Non volunteers, when asked to indicate what percentage of pupils of a special service school would respond in disciplinary situations with insults and threats to their teachers, presented a mean estimate of 30 percent, while the comparable estimate for volunteers was 10 percent. Nonvolunteers perceived 36 percent of the student body as being hostile toward teachers, whereas volunteers judged this hostility to typify only 22 percent of the students. Similarly, it was the nonvolunteers who anticipated the appearance of crude and gross libidinal elements in pupil behaviors, maintaining that 19 percent of students would bring pornographic materials to class as opposed to the more restrained estimate of volunteers that only 7 percent of students would be so sexually overt.

Student-teacher fears such as these seemed unlikely to represent an isolated set of anxieties; it appeared more likely that they expressed entrenched dispositions related to the authoritarian modes of anxiety controls noted for the nonvolunteer group. Some evidence for this viewpoint was found in the relatively high intercorrelation obtained between total scores for projected pupil behavior and scores on the Christie version of the F-Scale. In view of the restricted range on scores on the Christie Scale, a correlation as high as that obtained lent support to the belief that the fears of student teachers were manifestations of central interpersonal perceptions and defense mechanisms.

Still another projective device amplified the character of differences between the groups. Student teachers were presented with a list of eleven proposals designed to enhance the attractiveness of teaching. The proposals embodied commonly proffered suggestions; namely, reduction of class size, salary increases, greater administrative and resource personnel support, and several other somewhat less familiar propositions interpolated so as to provide a sufficient range of options. Subjects were asked to rank these proposals in order of desirability.

Volunteers tended to subordinate those related to the easing of teaching conditions to the proposal that teachers be given a greater choice in the making of educational policy. It seemed clear that volunteers were not preoccupied by their anxieties with respect to the teaching situation; indeed, they seemed to be crowding out such concerns by an activist and reformative zeal. That the least directly advantageous proposal should be the preemptive concern of this group is probably reflective of the earnestness with which the group conceived its role as an articulator of change and to the importance it attached to opportunities to have its voice and ideas heard. By contrast, the nonvolunteer, unarmed by any particular sense of purpose with respect to the special service schools, indicated that his greatest needs were those of reducing the magnitude of classroom problems by such measures as reduction of class size and greater assistance.

The volunteer was also more insistent than the nonvolunteer that he be relieved of nonprofessional duties and much more concerned than the nonvolunteer with the problem of achieving a significant definition of his teaching role. It would seem to follow that the volunteers had certain needs that are diff.;rent from those of individuals appointed in the more conventional manner, and that these involved the desire for a broader dialogue between teacher and administration and for a fuller sense of participation in these substantive elements of special service school planning and experimentation. It is likely that this may be both a source of some strain and a reservoir of opportunity for the special service school.

Directions for Recruitment of Teachers

The evidence thus far reviewed was consistent in its support of the proposition that when student teachers were allowed to volunteer for the type of assignment described in this paper, they did so on the basis of a self-selection process which resulted in distinguishing individuals possessing broadly specifiable characteristics functionally related to the presumptive demands of the special school assignment. Inasmuch as it can be presumed that such assignments call for flexibility, for freedom from prejudicial and authoritarian process, for positive perception of the disadvantaged and lower-class groups, for readiness to react in self-reliant and confident terms, the selective process appeared to urge those students to volunteer who are measurably higher in these characteristics.

The import of such findings may be, therefore, that self-selection can accomplish that which has been largely inaccessible through other means, namely, the fitting of student teaching to the demands of a particular school and school situation. Conversely, the findings imply what has been self-evident to many; namely, that when individuals are randomly assigned to specific schools, some very serious and distressing incompatibilities are likely to arise.

Whatever the advantages of self-selection, however, its utility is dependent upon the number of volunteers that it can produce. As has been indicated, this study suggests that there are many students who are attitudinally ill-equipped to teach the disadvantaged child. Nonetheless, even among the nonvolunteers, there were many who presented positive characteristics and who were distinguishable from volunteers primarily by superficial fearfulness of the special service school situation. Such a group would seem to be a proper target population for extended efforts at recruitment.

It has been suggested that student teachers possess fears which stem, in part, from perceptions that exaggerate those elements of lower-class life that are the most threatening to their conception of a teacher's role and to the self-disciplined modes of interpersonal contact to which they have been accustomed. It would be a rather gross oversight not to recognize that at least part of the fears represents a core of realistic self-doubt that is not to be overcome by an objective portrayal of the special service school situation. These self-doubts are the results of a reasonable recognition of what the special service school pupil demands of his teachers by way of skill, assurance, and insight and of the inevitable difficulty of the student teacher in assessing his ability to measure up to such rigorous demands.

The problem of the teacher-training institution is thus a dual one. It is, in the first instance, the problem of finding an effective format in which the diminution of projected fears of hostility, the eversion of certain sensitivities and guilts, and the verbalization of and reduction of anxieties can occur. It is, secondly—but no less significantly—the problem of providing an effective interpersonal technology, including perhaps a repertoire of responses to categories of disciplinary and disruptive situations. We may need to reexamine our traditional resistance to such a behavioristic view of teacher training; for no less than other professionals, the aspiring teacher must believe that his equipment includes concrete operations for meeting specifiable demands and emergencies. His self-confidence may eventually rest upon just such a belief.

Conclusions

An examination of the process of self-selection in the recruitment of student teachers for special service schools indicated that the process markedly differentiates individuals along personality and attitudinal dimensions presumptively related to teaching effectiveness. The presence of strong fears and anxieties appeared to limit the ability of students to be freely self-selective; some discussion of needed mitigative procedures was attempted.

Although self-selection is perhaps the most important of selection procedures operative in teacher training programs, scant research attention has been given to its study.

Few of the parameters of self-selection have been carefully examined; its validity as measured by performance criteria is largely unknown and efforts designed to increase its reliability have been, in the main, unexplored. In view of its current role and potential utility, these and many other questions concerning the self-selective process press for responsive study and investigation.

SOME EFFECTS OF SEGREGATION AND DESEGREGATION IN THE SCHOOLS

Gerald S. Lesser *is Bigelow professor of education and developmental psychology, Harvard University. In 1964,* **Kristine M. Rosenthal, Sally E. Polkoff,** *and* **Marjorie B. Pfankuch** *were members of the staff of Harvard's Laboratory of Human Development, Graduate School of Education. This article is an expanded version of testimony given on March 21, 1964, before the Massachusetts State Advisory Commission to the U.S. Commission on Civil Rights.*

Discussions of racial segregation in the schools often show a tendency to disintegrate into a series of destructive and vituperative attacks and counterattacks. Frequently, this negative emphasis appears in the effort to identify school conditions that have the least harmful effects or contain the fewest damaging features. It is possible to place such discussions in a more positive, constructive framework by asking at the outset: What are the objectives we hope and expect schools to achieve with children?

What are the goals which we set for our schools? It is only after the aims for children in school have been defined that it becomes meaningful to discuss matters pertaining to the failure of the segregated school to achieve these aims and the ability of the racially balanced school to correct this failure.

From *Integrated Education,* **June/July 1964. Reprinted by permission of the authors.**

There are differences of opinion about the proper role of the school in American society. Teachers may view these objectives somewhat differently from parents. Local school committees may define the goals of schools differently from other professional judgments. A manageable list of educational goals will certainly never be exhaustive, but there perhaps would be common agreement on these objectives.

1. To teach the child certain necessary *academic achievements* such as reading, writing, and the ability to think logically.
2. To help the child develop a realistic and constructive image of himself, a *self-concept* which allows him to regard himself as a capable, contributing member of society.
3. To instill the desire or *motivation to learn.*

For each of these education goals, two kinds of evidence will be presented.

1. Information regarding the differences between Negro and white children in typical segregated school settings.
2. Evidence on the degree to which racial balancing of Negro and white groups appears to correct or reduce the damage to both Negro and white children.

To summarize the observations in advance of giving the available research information, we shall state first, that (in several areas of development) school segregation produces harm to both Negro and white children, and, second, that racially balanced conditions are an effective force in correcting these damaging effects.

Academic Achievement

In the area of academic achievement, there are several studies that reflect upon both the efforts of segregation and racial balance in the schools. The first of these is a study that the senior author and colleagues conducted with young children in New York City during the past five years. Tests were used to assess different aspects of mental ability in children: The child's reasoning ability, his vocabulary and use of words, as well as his ability to deal with numbers and solve problems requiring spatial conceptualization. Evidence indicates that these are the major abilities that allow prediction of the child's performance in school. Each of four hundred children was examined by a trained psychologist for a three- to four-hour period. This study indicates that the child's mental abilities are influenced strongly by his cultural surroundings.

Children studied were from Negro, Puerto Rican, Chinese, and Jewish families in New York City. Each group included children from both racially imbalanced and relatively balanced schools. This is the first finding: For every one of the four abilities measured—verbal ability, reasoning, numerical ability and space conceptualization—the children from the more integrated schools and neighborhoods showed significantly superior performance when compared to the children from racially imbalanced schools and neighborhoods.

Another finding from this study may be described as a "convergence" effect. In the more racially balanced schools, the children from the various ethnic groups show quite similar scores—displaying levels of ability more similar to each other. In contrast, in the racially imbalanced schools, average test scores for each ethnic group remain markedly different. For example, the abilities of the Negro children in racially balanced neighborhoods are comparable to those of other children, whereas in racially imbalanced communities, the test scores of Negro children remain markedly different from those of other ethnic groups.

It is clear that these results cannot unequivocally be attributed to the effects of segregation alone. Other variables, such as social class, are confounded with the degree of racial imbalance. Nevertheless, the conclusion from this research is apparent: *When children attend racially imbalanced schools, their measured mental abilities are significantly inferior to the abilities of children who attend racially balanced schools.*

Another study (Hansen, 1960)* indicates the effects of segregation and desegregation upon the academic achievement of white as well as Negro children. This report from Washington, D.C., includes the following findings:

1. Before the schools in that city were integrated in 1954, the Negro children were inferior in academic achievement to the white children.
2. Integration has been followed by steady and significant gains among both Negro and white children in several different areas of achievement; both Negro and white pupils in Washington schools performed better on objectively measured achievement following desegregation.

Another study that charts the changes in academic performance of both Negro and white children when previously segregated schools become racially balanced was conducted in Louisville (Stallings, 1960). Achievement tests were given to pupils in the second, sixth, and eighth grades for the year prior to desegregation, the year following desegregation, and after the third year of desegregation.

Despite the fact that desegregation of the schools proceeded very rapidly in Louisville, this study concludes that academic standards were maintained; indeed, substantial gains were shown in scholastic achievement, with both Negro and white children making these gains.

Many other studies (e.g., Ferrel, 1959; Public Education Association, 1955; Wolff, 1962, 1963) supply evidence that segregated schools function on lower levels of academic achievement than do other schools in the same educational systems. This inferiority of academic performance in racially imbalanced schools becomes greater as the children progress through the school grades. Deutsch (1960), for example, reports that it is at the first-grade level that the smallest differences between racial groups are observed, and that these differences in academic functioning become more marked in the later grades. By the time children in racially imbalanced schools reach the upper grades, they are academically far behind.

The conclusions from these studies conducted in several different cities with several different age groups are clear:

1. Under segregated school conditions, Negro children are uniformly inferior in academic achievement to white children.
2. The racial balancing of the schools contributes greatly to improving academic achievement of Negro children and, usually, of white children as well.

---

*[Editor's note: See References at end of article for full citations for parenthetical references in text.]

Self-concept

In addition to these observations regarding academic achievement, we shall consider the Negro child's image of himself as a learner, his self-picture or self-concept as it develops under racially imbalanced and balanced conditions. The self-concept of the segregated Negro child differs in several ways from the self-concepts held by other children. The Negro child perceives himself as inferior to others; his self-concept also is less realistic and more confused. In many instances, the perceived antagonism toward Negroes is converted into feelings of self-hatred (see, for examples, Landreth and Johnson, 1953; Trent, 1957).

In order to understand the segregated Negro child's self-concept, it is important to discuss the development of the self-concept of any child, Negro or white. The goals that a child sets for himself, the goals he thinks he can achieve (if he really tries), are affected heavily by the expectations that other people have of him. The educational system—mainly through its teachers—provides the child directly with a sense of what society expects of him. Because it is often a very discouraging job to teach children in segregated schools, a common reaction of teachers in these schools—no matter how well-intentioned they may be—is to reduce their expectations and academic demands upon these children.

Illustrating this is a study (Gottlieb, 1963) in which white teachers of Negro children most often chose the following five categories in describing these children: talkative, lazy, fun-loving, high-strung, and rebellious.

These white teachers of segregated Negro children generally avoided mentioning those qualities which they would consider desirable in the formal classroom setting. They were critical and pessimistic in their prognosis of the academic success of their Negro children. One may argue that these negative appraisals of the Negro child by white teachers only reflect reality but—whether or not these teacher perceptions are realistic—the outcome is the same: The Negro child reflecting the teacher's attitude and those of his society, is likely to perceive himself as unworthy and inept.

When the Negro child notices that not much academic achievement is expected of segregated Negroes, he will come to expect or demand very little of himself. The conditions surrounding the Negro in the racially imbalanced areas and in segregated schools do not encourage academic effort, striving, and vigorous performance; nor do they promote the image in a Negro child's mind that he can ever be a capable, contributing member of American society.

In contrast to the white child or to the Negro child educated in a desegregated setting, the Negro child from a segregated background does not know how to interpret the school situation. He cannot quite understand what the objectives of learning and teaching are, what reactions and responses are expected of him, and what the types of rewards for learning which exist in the typical school can possibly mean. His confidence in himself as a learner is stunted, and he cannot regard school as a place which has any ultimate meaning for his real life outside of school.

The messages communicated to Negro children by our society create not only feelings of inferiority but produce a confused and unrealistic self-image as well. These messages are sharply contradictory. On the one hand, Negro children are told that everyone in America with ambition and effort can be successful; those who fail do so because they do not work hard enough to succeed. Yet segregated Negro children, when they are ambitious, are made to feel that they are resented for being pushy and not keeping in their place.

And then again, if they follow the "know your place" message, they may be more subtly told that this apparent shiftlessness and lack of ambition is final proof of their innate racial inferiority. For the segregated Negro child, it is extremely confusing to try to discover who he is and what society expects of him. The Negro child has little opportunity to measure his own personal worth against the members of other groups. While we cannot wish to deny the Negro child his identity as a Negro, he must also feel that, as a Negro, he has a place in the society beyond his immediate community. The school must contribute to this feeling. By restricting the contact between Negro and white children, the segregated school prevents the Negro child from measuring himself against the children from other groups.

Thus far we have discussed the effects of segregated schools upon the self-concept of Negro children. What of the self-concept of white children? What do they gain or lose by attending schools with Negro children? If we are dedicated to an integrated society, they have much to gain. A segregated school leaves everyone undereducated with respect to living in a multiracial world. Existing prejudices become reinforced in segregated schools. Lacking a diversity of children against whom he can compare himself, the white child, too, develops an unrealistic concept of himself and others.

But it is the destructive effect upon the self-concept of the Negro child that is the more tragic. The stark fact of school segregation instructs the Negro that he is devalued by American society, that he is deemed worthy only of education in schools where other children like himself predominate. The very existence of these segregated schools—no matter what their educational quality—communicates to the Negro child that he is unfit and inferior.

The damaged self-perception is reflected in the Negro child's limited occupational and educational aspirations and plans (see, for examples, Holloway and Berreman, 1959; Rosen, 1959; Stephensen, 1957). One recent study, however, failed to confirm this finding (Gist and Bennett, 1963). The strong aspiration for geographic mobility of Negro adolescents (Gist and Bennett, 1963) is a possible additional expression of the confused self-picture of the Negro child in his normal environment. Other studies (e.g., Radke and Trager, 1950; Stevenson and Stewart, 1958) provide evidence of self-devaluation in the low proportion of Negro children who prefer other Negro children to white children as playmates, companions, and guests.

There is no guarantee, of course, that balanced schools will not also teach Negroes the same destructive lesson.

The point is, however, that the unbalanced school situation is structurally self-defeating; even the most dedicated teachers will encounter severe difficulties in attempting to overcome its effects. The balanced school at least has the opportunity to counteract in part the conflicting and confusing communications of the larger community to the Negro child, to offer him an opportunity to develop a more positive, realistic, and less confused image of himself.

What happens to the self-concepts of Negro and white children when segregated schools desegregate? Unfortunately, studies have not traced changes in self-concept in Negro and white children when segregated schools become progressively more racially balanced. Certain parallels can be drawn, however, between the process of school desegregation and results derived from attempts (e.g., Campbell, Yarrow, and Radke, 1958; Mussen, 1950) to study out-of-school desegregated groups. In a study (Campbell, Yarrow, and Radke, 1958) of a newly integrated summer camp, Negro children were found to under-choose children of their own race, preferring the whites, while the white children over-chose members of their own race. By the end of the camp session, a more balanced situation was achieved; the Negro children chose more Negro friends and the white children, too, were more likely to mention the desire to be friends with a Negro child. It seems, then, that initially the Negro was devalued by members of both races while a more realistic evaluation began to operate after the children had had some exposure to each other and had participated in the same activities.

Motivation to Learn

The child needs a knowledge of society's values and a realistic knowledge of himself and of his potential contribution to society. In addition, he must be motivated to learn how to make this contribution. He must develop both the willingness and the ability to become a contributing member of society. What happens to the child's motivation to learn under segregated and desegregated conditions? One of the studies on this issue (Deutsch, 1960) reports that in segregated schools the Negro children abandoned a problem posed by the teacher as soon as any difficulty was encountered in attempting to solve it. When questioned for an explanation, the children typically responded "Who cares?" or "What does it matter?"

There is much additional evidence (see, for examples, Gottlieb, 1963, Gottlieb and TenHouten, 1963; Lott and Lott, 1963; Mussen, 1953; Riessman, 1962; Rosen, 1959) that segregated conditions weaken the motivation to learn. In a study (Rosen, 1959) comparing the achievement motivation of Negro boys with the motivation to learn of white Protestant, Greek, Jewish, Italian, and French-Canadian boys of the same age, the achievement strivings of the Negro boys were significantly below other groups. This deficiency in motivation to learn found among the Negro boys may be related to their failure to see any relationship among the immediate classroom situation, their lives outside of school, and their expectations regarding their futures.

Also closely related to this lack of motivation is the fact that the rewards for learning offered by our schools and society are not as meaningful for the segregated Negro child as for other children. Typically, the segregated Negro child does not arrive at school equipped with the crucial ideas about the importance of knowledge for its own sake and its value in self-realization. The verbal rewards provided by the teacher which are effective in motivating middle-class white children bear little relationship to the segregated child's life outside of school and consequently have little impact upon him.

How does school desegregation help to strengthen the motivation to learn? Balanced schools are, first of all, capable of offering the Negro child a greater range of rewards than those available in segregated schools. They have both broader and more effective resources available to arouse interest and aspiration. Secondly, racially balanced schools provide the Negro child with an opportunity to see other children responding with excitement and effort to the challenges presented at school. The Negro child in a racially balanced school perceives the effects upon other children of the rewards for learning, begins to value similar rewards, and aspire to them (see Boyd, 1952).

We have referred throughout this review to changes in children when previously segregated schools become more racially balanced. There is, however, a great difference between a racially balanced school and a school that has developed truly integrated conditions. For a research review, the primary implication of a distinction between mere racial balance and integration is this: If the effects of change from segregation to racially balanced conditions are clearly discernible, how much greater would these gains be if changes could be observed from segregated to truly integrated conditions? Studies of authentically integrated schools do not exist, but it is reasonable to expect that the positive results obtained for racially balanced schools would be even more pronounced for basically integrated schools.

Summary

We have discussed the effects of school segregation and desegregation upon both Negro and white children as related to different aims of education: the acquisition of academic skills, the development of a positive self-concept, and the creation of a strong motivation to learn. Although these issues are complex, a relatively direct conclusion summarizes much of the evidence. Segregated schools provide limited opportunities for children to develop to capacity. Racial balancing, on the other hand, by providing an opportunity for association among diverse groups, serves to impart this important lesson—race is no index of human worth.

References

Boyd, G. F., "The Levels of Aspiration of White and Negro Children in a Non-Segregated Elementary School," *Journal of Social Psychology,* Vol. 36 (1952), pp. 191-196.

Campbell, J. D., L. J. Yarrow, and Marian J. Radke, "A Study of Adaptation to a New Social Situation." *Journal of Social Issues,* Vol. 14, No. 1 (1958).

Deutsch, M., *Minority Group Status and Class Status as Related to Social and Personality Factors in Scholastic Achievement,* Society for Applied Anthropology, Ithaca, N.Y., 1960.

Ferrel, G., "A Comparative Study of Sex Differences in School Achievement of White and Negro Children," *Journal of Educational Research,* Vol. 43 (1959), pp. 116-121.

Gist, N. P., and W. S. Bennett, "Aspirations of Negro and White Students," *Social Forces,* Vol. 42 (1963), pp. 40-48.

Gottlieb, D., *Teachers and Students: The Views of Negro and White Teachers,* Michigan State University, East Lansing, 1963.

Gottlieb, D., and W. TenHouten, *Social Alienation: The Case of Negro Youth,* Michigan State University, East Lansing, 1963.

Hansen, C. F., "The Scholastic Performance of Negro and White Pupils in the Integrated Public Schools of the District of Columbia," *Harvard Educational Review,* Vol. 30 (1960), pp. 216-236.

Holloway, R. G., and J. V. Berreman, "The Educational and Occupational Aspirations and Plans of Negro and White Male Elementary School Students," *Pacific Sociological Review* (1959), pp. 56-60.

Landreth, Catherine, and Barbara Johnson, "Young Children's Responses to a Picture and Inset Test Designed to Reveal Reactions to Persons of Different Skin Color," *Child Development,* Vol. 24 (1953) pp. 63-79.

Lott, A. J., and Bernice E. Lott, *Negro and White Youth: A Psychological Study in a Border-State Community,* Holt, Rinehart and Winston, New York, 1963.

Mussen, P. H., "Differences between the TAT Responses of Negro and White Boys," *Journal of Consulting Psychology,* Vol. 17 (1953), pp. 373-376.

Mussen, P. H., "Some Personality and Social Factors Related to Changes in Children's Attitudes toward Negroes," *Journal of Abnormal and Social Psychology,* Vol. 45 (1950), pp. 423-441.

Public Education Association, *The Status of the Public School Education of Negro and Puerto Rican Children in New York City,* Public Education Association, New York, 1955.

Radke, Marian J., and Helen G. Trager, "Children's Perceptions of the Social Roles of Negroes and Whites," *Journal of Psychology,* Vol. 29 (1950), pp. 3-33.

Riessman, F., *The Culturally Deprived Child,* Harper and Row, New York, 1962.

Rosen, B. C., "Race, Ethnicity, and the Achievement Syndrome," *American Sociological Review,* Vol. 24 (1959), pp. 47-60.

Stallings, F. H., "Changes in Academic Achievement since Integration in the Louisville Public Schools," *Second Annual Conference on Education,* Gatlinburg, Tennessee, 1960.

Stephensen, R. M., "Mobility Orientation and Stratification of 1,000 Ninth Graders," *American Sociological Review,* Vol. 22 (1957), pp. 204-212.

Stevenson, H. W., and E. C. Stewart, "A Developmental Study of Racial Awareness in Young Children," *Child Development,* Vol. 29 (1958), pp. 339-409.

Trent, R., "The Relation between Expressed Self-acceptance and Expressed Attitudes toward Negroes and Whites among Negro Children," *Journal of Genetic Psychology,* Vol. 91 (1957), pp. 25-31.

Wolff, M., *A Study of Racial Imbalance in the Plainfield Schools,* Board of Education, Plainfield, N. J.: 1962.

Wolff, M., "Segregation in the Schools of Gary, Indiana," *Journal of Educational Sociology,* Vol. 36 (1963), pp. 251-261.

WHITE CITIZEN RESPONSE TO THE "OPEN ENROLLMENT PROGRAM"

Bert E. Swanson *and* **Clare Montgomery** *teach at Sarah Lawrence College. Mr. Swanson is co-author of the prize-winning* The Rulers and the Ruled: Political Power and Impotence in American Communities (*Wiley, 1964); he is also author of* The Struggle for Equality: School Integration Controversy in New York City (*Hobbs, Dorman, 1966).*

One of the most important methods devised in northern metropolitan centers to eliminate *de facto* school segregation is "open enrollment." This program permits Negro and Puerto Rican students to transfer voluntarily to underutilized white schools. Students are moved from a sending "x" (minority) school, defined as comprising a minority group population of 90 percent for elementary schools and 85

From *Integrated Education,* August/September 1964. Reprinted by permission of the authors.

percent for junior high schools. The "receiving" or "y" (majority) schools comprise 90 percent and 85 percent whites respectively. At present the permissive program in New York City has attracted some 15,000 students since its inception in 1960. A more complex series of additional programs is currently being worked out amid controversy that has seriously split the community. In the long run it is hoped that open enrollment as part of a more comprehensive approach will integrate the city's schools and provide equality of educational opportunity for all students.

The present study examines white-citizen reactions to the open enrollment policy as two busloads of Negro children are transported to an all-white school. It also explores the dynamics of their reactions as well as the possible short- and long-range consequences.

Park is a small, private, planned community of some 5,000 people located within the Greater New York area. Park's inhabitants are attracted by the community's uniform architecture, its layout of streets, trees, and parks, and its generally neat and cared-for appearance. From the beginning, all purchasers in the community have been carefully investigated and every caution taken "to encourage only agreeable, educated, quiet people who might live together in neighborly friendliness and congeniality." This restrictive policy has produced a homogeneous community, predominantly white-collar, upper-middle class, two-thirds of whom earn incomes of $10,000 or more per year at professional and managerial occupations. Nearly half the residents have graduated from or attended college.

Social life in Park centers around the clubs and various churches. The Men's Club, Women's Club, country club, and various church clubs all offer social activities. Park House, a private club restricted to white Christians, caters to young families with children. The youngsters are divided into age groups and much spirited competition goes on within these groups, with achievements being recognized every spring on Award Day. Friendships made at school are very often carried to and furthered in Park House, for there are few families with children who are not members.

For the most part, the local view of life in Park is one of self-satisfaction. It is a comfortable place to live and bring up children. Nevertheless, some who express concern with the character of community life are distressed by the social behavior or misbehavior in Park. As one person put it: "There is a preponderance of instability, alcoholism, divorce, suicide, pregnant brides, and the like."

Another citizen expressed concern with the religious schisms developing in the community life: "Too many people think that because they live in Park they are automatically superior. I wish we could keep the area from being entirely anything——it was no good with no minority groups in it, but it will be no good if it becomes entirely Jewish."

When asked whether they would be disturbed or unhappy if a Negro with the same income and education moved into the same block, half replied, yes.

- "I moved into Park because it is a beautiful and secluded community, one of the finest in the city, and I would be most unhappy."
- "I like the cozy little spot I'm in and don't want it changed."
- "Negroes move in, whites move out, neighborhoods deteriorate."
- "I like to have as neighbors persons with whom I may have social contact, and I do not care to associate socially with Negroes."

Some answered, no.

- " . . . not as long as he does not inflict his way of living upon me; I do not wish to inflict mine on him."
- "By this time he has learned what we would call maturity; it requires not simply income or education, but the absorption of education and breeding to be able to achieve this status."

Introduction of Open Enrollment

Into this community setting the school administrators decided to send two busloads of "minority" students, sixty-five in all, from an all-Negro area some thirty minutes away. The school had been selected because the local principal thought the community was ready for such a program. Also, there was underutilized classroom space; 44 percent of the Park children were in private schools, while another 17 percent attended parochial schools.

The program was introduced to the local parents at an evening parents' association meeting in order that fathers and working mothers might attend. A member of the human relations unit of the board of education explained the purpose of the program and the method to be used, but he received little reaction. The parents later contended that, because the school official was Negro, they were "psychologically paralyzed" and therefore inhibited from voicing their honest opinion about the program. Many parents felt that they were merely told about the program and then sent home. One parent felt that the use of a Negro to introduce the program was "dirty politics" on the part of the board of education and a means of avoiding embarrassing questions.

White Reaction

In order to draw a realistic picture of the community's reaction to the "invasion" of Negro minority students into Park, a sample survey was conducted in the spring of 1963 during the first year of the program.[1] An overwhelming number of respondents (75 percent) were opposed to the open enrollment program. Nearly 60 percent were in strong disagreement; only 3 percent were strongly in favor. These figures are surprising, for citizens of the New York area are considered "tolerant" and "liberal" on the matter of the Negro's role in the community. No explicit official policy has advocated a segregated public school system. The *de facto* system that has developed is the result of residential patterns which segregated families along ethnic lines of race, religion, and nationality. Segregation follows socioeconomic class lines as well.

The actual experience of open enrollment did not improve the evaluation of the program. In fact, negative attitudes increased slightly. One person who initially approved strongly of the program now stated: "I'm in favor of integration, thought it would be good for my children to know Negro children as classmates and good for some Negro children to have the advantages of our underutilized school. However, there should have been some effort to pick Negro children who would be most likely to

---

[1]A questionnaire was left with the head of every fifth household and picked up a week later. The rate of response was 73 percent, with 66 replies from the 90 households. Virtually every respondent (92 percent) had heard of the program before answering the questionnaire.

adjust and benefit from this experience. My children, instead of learning to accept other kids as equals regardless of color, are actually learning that Negro children are slower to learn and more likely to be discipline problems. I can't believe the Negro children are benefiting very much."

Two-thirds of the respondents saw no advantages for either white or Negro children.

Evaluations of Advantages and Disadvantages

Advantages.—Those who believed there were advantages for the white children felt that the program might help to reduce prejudice by showing them that "the color of the Negro's skin is the only difference between them." "It enriches their experience by representing a 'foreign' point of view." "It helps for the children to associate with Negroes before any strong prejudices are developed." "White children in Park usually see Negroes only as domestics and delivery boys. Now they see Negroes as mothers, fathers, and children, in other words as families just like their own."

Most of these advantages were considered to apply to the Negro children as well, for they learn that white children have the same interests and the same school routine. Most respondents felt that advantages for the Negro child took the form primarily of educational opportunities. "He may feel more relaxed with whites since he is now 'allowed' to attend a predominantly white school." "He sees how the other half lives." "It gives the child exposure to normal community discipline." "It is my sincere hope that some of the Negro children will take home the seeds of a better way of life toward which they will aim in planning their own futures."

One respondent felt that the effect was reciprocal: the white person "gets to hate the Negro a little more" and the Negro "gets to hate the white a little more." Another felt that the advantage for the Negro was to give him "a feeling of superiority because he is mixing with 'better class' white children."

Disadvantages.—With regard to possible disadvantages of the program, a variety of answers predicted negative effects for both white and Negro children. "Discipline problems have increased and learning has been decelerated to accommodate the slower child. Disadvantages for the Negro were the long bus ride (10 miles), loss of contact with neighborhood friends, not being able to play together after school, and the use of innocent children for "political ballyhoo." "If honesty is to prevail, there are no advantages to either group. Studies will reveal that the schools in so-called underprivileged areas produce a high number of our leading citizens."

Disadvantages perceived for the white students were

- "There is a lowering of educational standards and standards of decorum."
- "Discipline problems are very disturbing. Also, some children and parents of these children resent handling the same books, holding hands in the playground activities. Vocabulary and manners decrease."
- "I have heard that there was a case of a Negro child molesting a six-year-old child."
- "The situation is obviously synthetic. The white children can easily get the idea that 'we have to make room in our nice school for these unfortunate children.' The Negro children act up because they are 'being helped.' This gives the white child a false impression."

Disadvantages for the Negro children were

- "They are still kept apart from the white children. They live apart, they are bused-in separately, they leave separately, and do not join in after-school activities with their playmates."
- "They are being brought into a better community and are bound to be envious. They cannot visit the friends they make because they are too far away. Their bus is terribly overcrowded. I feel dangerously so. Several children have been injured by behavior-problem children on the bus.
- "They lose contact with old friends, and not too many new ones are available."
- "Normal school discussions about home environment and ways of living may only accentuate differences and flaunt limitations of finances, opportunities, toys, clothes, etc., so that antagonisms are built up in underprivileged children."
- "They are out of their element, socially and economically. No future social relationships will be developed."

Evaluations of Academic Achievement

Half the respondents felt that academic achievement would be lower in integrated classes. A small portion of these had children in the integrated classes and had experienced directly a slowing of the scholastic process. Only two people felt that no change in standards or achievement had occurred during the two years of the program. One quarter could not judge without more information on the Negro children, and only one person thought that achievement would be higher.

Lower Achievement.—

- "My child shows a lack of interest in work, has become a discipline problem, does this (I'm sure) for attention. The teacher spends a great deal of time with Negroes."
- "Time is lost from the educational plan to enforce discipline and settle the children after long bus rides to school and prepare them for the ride home."

Same Achievement.—

- "I think the children are grouped according to intellectual ability. The bright students are in a separate class and given an enriched program."
- "There should be no change if the teaching staff has adjusted normally and with little or no fanfare."

Evaluations of Negro Motivations

Various answers were given as to why the respondents thought Negro parents send their children to Park. Some stated that the parents thought this would offer a better educational experience; some felt that Negroes were forced to send their children; others felt that status was the primary motivation behind the entire situation.

- It is an opportunity for better education, different environment, to have them become more rounded individuals and be able to cope with and help with integration."
- "They want to expose their children to other social attitudes."

- "Because the parents of the problem children lack interest, in some cases it is the principal rather than the parent who is instrumental in sending them."
- "There is a determination on the part of Negro parents to force integration in spite of the inconvenience, expense, etc. This same determination is apparent in the social and business world. In spite of their abilities or the lack of them, they demand a racial balance."
- "I'm certain that many individuals are encouraged to send their children because they are stimulated to do so by many individuals who are politically inclined. Never has a politician had a single solitary concern for the rectitude of his actions."
- "I think there are many sensible Negro mothers who object to this."

Opinions on Integration

Nevertheless, 85 percent of the respondents thought that white and Negro children should attend the same schools. A majority qualified their answers by stating that if the children lived together in an integrated school district they should attend the same school, but that it was more important to attend neighborhood schools than to strive for integration.

Should Attend Separate Schools.—

- "They are happier with their own friends and class—more relaxed and understanding."
- "If Negroes come from similar backgrounds—financial, religious, housing, etc.— then they should go to the same schools as the whites."

Should Attend Same School.—

- "Children should attend their neighborhood schools, regardless of race. This is the democratic principle upon which America was founded."
- "I believe in neighborhood schools, no gerrymandering of districts, no busing in."

Rationales for Types of Schools

A majority of the respondents have sent their children to public school. About half had sent them to private school at some time, and a fifth to parochial school. Half had sent their children to only one type of the aforementioned schools, while one third had sent them to two types and 15 percent to all three. The primary reasons for selecting each kind of school were

Public School.—

- "We are supporting our schools through our taxes and since it is necessary for our children to live with others of all races and creeds, it is important for them to learn how from childhood."
- "Since one lives in a community, one should be educated there with all the children of that community."

Private School.—

- "First grade in private schools has seventeen children, while the same grade in public school has forty-three."

Parochial School.—

- "The parochial school emphasized patriotism and religious activities, which we believe is a good strong foundation to withstand the liberal teachings the children may meet in college which try to tear down all the traditional instruction in church school and at home. This foundation is the bulwark against Communism in today's world."

Public School Changed to Private School.—

- "The inflexibility and shortcomings in public-school instruction convinced us that private schools would meet needs more adequately."
- "They were not learning in the public school and we were tired of teaching them at home and paying for tutors on Saturday."

The type of education had an effect upon the reaction to the open enrollment program. Only those who preferred the public schools strongly favored the program. Parochial school parents almost unanimously opposed (90 percent) the program, while more than three quarters of the private school parents also were opposed. The religious factor appeared similarly important. Only one Catholic and one Jewish family approved the program. The Protestants, who are more likely to send their children to public schools, were slightly more inclined to favor the program.

Consequences

This study portends two main consequences to the open enrollment program. The first is the internal effect upon the school and classroom, where students are placed in the "track" system and classified by achievement and intelligence scores. The Negro students found themselves clustered in the slower track. The effect of integrating the children was noticed primarily during lunch period, as the buses carrying the Negro children arrived after the neighborhood children had gone to their rooms. The Negroes were dismissed from their last classes a few minutes before the rest of the class in order to catch their bus which then stopped at another local elementary school to pick up the Negro children who attended there.

The second consequence of open enrollment was the external impact on the local school district area and the white parents in the receiving school. It is apparent from this study that considerable resistance and latent hostility exist toward the new program. Some parents have taken their children out of the public school and sent them on to private and parochial schools. Yet others have responded by serving as special tutors in a remedial-reading program to assist the newcomers. Some, however, have begun to articulate their opposition to integration and the modification of the neighborhood school concept through such vocal organizations as Parents and Taxpayers (PAT).

Certainly there is a lesson to be learned from the open enrollment program and other methods to bring about equality of educational opportunity and a democratic society through its educational system. The citizen attitudes reported here raise in bold relief the many assumptions of sentiment and willingness of the northern white community to receive Negroes into their neighborhoods. Also, the study raises serious questions as to the ability of school leaders and administrators to create the climate necessary for successful school integration.

A STUDY OF SCHOOL INTEGRATION

Charles V. Willie *is chairman of the sociology department and* **Jerome Beker** *is senior research associate of the Youth Development Center, Syracuse University. This is a statement presented on May 5, 1965, to a public hearing, conducted by the Syracuse School District, on proposals to desegregate the inner-city elementary and junior high schools.*

We would like to present for the board's considerations some preliminary findings from our study of racial integration in four Syracuse public schools. This study is in progress and was started in September, 1964.

The study involves approximately 254 children transferred from Croton, Danforth, Brighton, Prescott, and Madison schools to Edward Smith, Hughes, Levy, and Madison schools.

Of the eight schools in our study, Madison was involved both as a sending and receiving school. Seventy-one percent of the students transferred were Negro, 27 percent white and 2 percent American Indian. These children were transferred as a result of a policy decision by the board of education pertaining to the racial balance of schools and the quality of education.

The federal government indicated an interest in the Syracuse experience and provided a grant through the Office of Education and the National Institute of Mental Health for the Syracuse University Youth Development Center, in cooperation with the Syracuse Public School District, to evaluate this initial program of planned racial integration.

We have developed a comprehensive research design. Observers are on duty in four of the receiving schools with specific instructions to note how the new children are getting along. They spend a minimum of twenty hours per week observing children and recording their observations for careful analysis.

A series of tests were given at the beginning of the school year and will be given at the close of the school year to provide us with factual information of changes in the achievement level of individual students—both new students and host students in receiving schools. Parents will be surveyed this summer to obtain their reactions to the new school and their assessment of the progress of the child during the school year. Finally, the teachers and the observers, who know the children best, have been asked to rate each child's degree of integration in the new school. The teacher-ratings are coming in but are still incomplete. In addition, we cannot give the final word on changes, if any, in achievement level until the results of end-of-the-year tests are analyzed. But we do have the final ratings of our observers.

These observers are mature staff members, not of the Syracuse public schools, but of the youth development center, and therefore in a position to render an impersonal judgment.

(Parenthetically, may I state that we are indeed grateful and appreciative for the fine cooperation by the students, their parents, the teachers, and the administrative staffs of the schools. It is because they have permitted us to observe and to administer selected tests that we are able to provide these facts.)

From *Integrated Education*, **June/July 1965. Reprinted by permission of the authors.**

Our study presents findings about all children who are new in two elementary and two junior high schools—the children who are new because of board of education policy decisions regarding racial balance and quality of education, and the children who are new because their parents moved into the new school district. To our knowledge, this is one of the few studies to compare the social adjustment of all new children. This study should enable us to determine whether problems experienced by Negro children bused to predominantly white schools are associated with their race or whether their problems are those that any new child may experience.

The total population in this study consisted of approximately six hundred new students, one third of whom were new because of policy decisions by the board and two thirds of whom were new because of change in residence by parents. The findings presented here have to do with social adjustment.

Each observer was asked to give his or her opinion on whether the new child had accepted the new school and been accepted by the teachers and pupils so that he acted as a part of that school. The observers were asked to indicate whether the child was well-assimilated, moderately assimilated, or poorly assimilated into the school.

Our overall finding is that about 70 percent of all new children are well assimilated into the four schools studied. This proportion of well-assimilated children is about the same for boys and girls and for whites and nonwhites. Only about one of every ten persons among new students is poorly assimilated. So the general conclusion is that a large majority of the students new to any of the Syracuse public schools should assimilate well.

With reference to age or grade level, we find that new children in elementary school assimilate more easily than junior high youngsters. While the rate of assimilation is high for all, we find that six of every ten new junior high as compared with better than eight of every ten new elementary school pupils are considered to be well assimilated. This finding indicates that assimilation proceeds more rapidly among younger children. As age increases, it would appear that the rate of assimilation for new children decreases.

Nearly one third of the children who were transferred into these four schools due to board policy decisions, designed to improve quality of education, are white. Between 60 percent and 70 percent of the nonwhite and white children are assimilating well; however, the proportion of well-assimilated nonwhite transferred students, which is 67 percent, is slightly higher than the proportion of well-assimilated white transferred students, which is 62 percent. This slight difference between the races may be due to the fact that most of the white youngsters transferred were at the junior high level while Negro youngsters transferred to improve their quality of education were about equally divided between elementary and junior high. (You may recall we found that younger children tend to assimilate more rapidly than older children.) The analysis thus far indicates that age is more importantly related to degree of assimilation than is race.

Finally, we compared all children new to these four schools because they were transferred with children new because their parents moved into the school district. This comparison was made, in part, to determine if the transferred or bused children acted differently because of the neighborhoods from which they came. It has been asserted that children bused into a school district where the income level is different from that of their parents might feel foreign and out of place and that this feeling would hinder their involvement in school activities. Our data cast doubt upon these assertions; we find no evidence to support them. Contrary to these assertions, we find that new children transferred or bused into schools in middle-income neighborhoods have assimilated—that is, they have accepted and been accepted by the teachers and pupils of the schools—at about the same rate as new children who are residents of the neighborhoods in which the schools are located.

Exactly two thirds of the children who are new due to board of education policy of transferring children from the inner city to schools in middle-income neighborhoods are well assimilated; and exactly two thirds of the new children who are residents in these middle-income areas are also well assimilated. This means that one of every three children from the inner city is poorly assimilated but that this proportion is no different from the proportion of middle-income new children who are poorly assimilated into the new school. *Thus, all new children, whether poor or affluent, experience about the same proportion of problems in becoming integrated and assimilated into a new school.*

Based upon these preliminary findings we predict that 60 percent to 70 percent of the students new to any school in the Syracuse Public School District will become well-assimilated in that school during the course of the school year. We further predict that 30 percent to 40 percent of the students new to any school in the Syracuse Public School District will be assimilated moderately or poorly, but that the moderate to poor assimilation will be related to factors other than sex, race, and social class.

Finally, we predict that younger children will assimilate into a new school and become a part of it more readily than older children.

On the basis of our study and analysis, we see no social adjustment problem that might result from transferring children to high achieving schools that may be outside their neighborhood of residence.

Our considered opinion is that white as well as Negro children will receive substantial benefits by attending schools populated by students of diversified backgrounds. Such schools enable the children to come to know all sorts and conditions of persons. Homogeneously white and homogeneously nonwhite schools are inadequate because they tend to limit the students' understandings of the ways of mankind. We submit that the development of such understandings is a fundamental part of education for living in a world of diversity.

SCHOOL AND RACE IN PORTLAND

Clyde DeBerry *is director of the School Desegregation Training and Research Institute, assistant professor, and race and poverty specialist at the University of Oregon.* **Robert E. Agger,** *director of the Institute for Comparative Experimental Research on Behavioral Systems, University of Oregon, is senior author of* The Rulers and the Ruled: Political Power and Impotence in American Communities *(Wiley, 1964). This paper was written privately for the Committee on Race and Education, Portland, Oregon Board of Education and as published here includes a report on a follow-up study conducted eighteen months after the initial study.*

From *Integrated Education,* April/May 1965. Reprinted by permission of the authors.

This report represents an analysis of data collected in two sample surveys conducted simultaneously in May, 1963. One survey sample contains 320 white citizen respondents, selected in a three-stage random sample, representing the adult residents of the Portland School District. The second survey includes sixty-two Negro citizen respondents selected from six contiguous census tracts in and around the area known as the Albina district. In those tracts lived 9,798 Negroes according to the U.S. Census reports for 1960. In addition, the sample includes twenty Negro respondents interviewed because they were drawn in the random sample of 340 citizens so that when added to the Negro sample the total number of respondents became eighty-three, whereas the white sample was reduced in size to the aforementioned 320 respondents. Because of the living patterns in Portland, most of the twenty Negro respondents drawn in the larger random sample survey reside in the aforementioned predominantly Negro census tracts or in tracts adjacent to them.

This report contains sections on the Negro citizen: what he thinks and wants; the white citizens: what they think and want; and the relationships of selected factors, including residential location, to white attitudes on race relations. When the analysis is restricted by the relatively small numbers of respondents in an area of significance or when the data are suggestive of interesting patterns, suggestions are made that such matters might fruitfully be pursued in future large-scale studies. We might note at the outset, as the following section indicates, that we have used the singular for Negro attitudes and the plural for white attitudes in the section titles because of the rather clear consensus on the part of the Negro respondents on certain race relations matters, which is unlikely to change significantly with larger numbers of Negro respondents.

The Negro Citizen

Attitude toward Integration

Are Negro citizens of Portland prejudiced towards white citizens? Do Negroes feel a sense of inferiority, superiority, or equality in regard to whites?

The questions used to measure prejudice are these: So far as intelligence (repeat for morality) is concerned, would you say that, compared to whites, Negroes are by nature: (1) Superior to whites, (2) the same as whites, (3) inferior to whites.

Our findings clearly indicate that there is an overwhelming sense of equality with whites on the part of Negroes. There is a small proportion of Negroes who seem to have developed a sense of biological inferiority, of being born to a racial group that is by nature not only lacking the native-born intelligence of whites but also the latter's morality. A somewhat higher, but still small proportion of Negroes take a posture of superiority to whites, a finding that is not peculiar to Portland alone. Other studies have also indicated that one of the reaction patterns of some frustrated and angry Negroes is to at least respond in such a manner when asked, and the existence of the Black Muslim movement is evidence that such sentiments can become more than a posture or a defensive perspective. A very small proportion of Negroes in the sample, by finding the question difficult to answer, indicates the existence of some confusion about their identity and worth (which proportion might actually be larger if those who responded by saying "equal to whites" on these items had been asked more probing questions). In any event, as we shall see, the general sense of equality that Negroes have vis-à-vis whites is not shared by a substantial proportion of Portland's white citizens.

Do Negroes feel that members of their race ought to live by themselves, or in mixed Negro-white neighborhoods, thereby having Negro children go to school in more integrated neighborhoods?

The question was worded: Do you think that Negroes in the city of Portland ought to live by themselves, or do you think that Negroes ought to live in mixed Negro-white neighborhoods and have their children go to school in more mixed Negro-white schools?

An overwhelming proportion of the Negro respondents (91 percent) feel that Negroes ought to live in integrated rather than segregated neighborhoods. (This compares with the *Newsweek*-Lou Harris poll findings* on Negroes living outside the South for a comparable question that directly asked, "Would you rather live in a neighborhood with Negroes, or in a neighborhood that had both whites and Negroes—if you could find the housing you want and like" to the effect that 75 percent preferred the mixed neighborhood.) The vast majority of Negro citizens in this Portland sample prefer the principle, at least, of nonsegregation in neighborhood living patterns.

Do Negroes feel that it would be better for Negro children to go to schools that have more white pupils?

The question was worded: Because Negroes in Portland live in a very few areas, Negro children tend to go to grade schools that have mostly Negro pupils. Some people have said that it would be better for Negro children to go to schools that have more white pupils. Do you agree or disagree?

Almost eighteen out of every twenty Negroes in the sample felt that Negro children should go to schools that have more white pupils. This feeling is shared by Negroes of every educational level. Thus, the Negro citizens think amazingly alike not only on the matters of segregation in housing (neighborhoods) but also on the matter of *de facto* segregation which was the subject of this question.

Do Negroes want to reduce *de facto* school segregation in Portland through a policy of busing some children to schools outside of their neighborhoods?

The question was worded: How much would you approve or disapprove a policy of transporting some children by bus to schools that may not be the closest ones to their homes in order to reduce the number of almost all Negro grade schools in Portland? (1) strongly approve such a policy, (2) approve such a policy, (3) disapprove such a policy, (4) strongly disapprove of such a policy.

Even without being specific as to whether Negro, white, or both sets of children might be bused, almost three quarters of the Negro respondents (73 percent) approved such a policy, two fifths "strongly." This general disposition to approve such a policy is not shared by one quarter of the Negro respondents, but only one out of twenty Negroes "strongly disapprove" such a policy. One out of six Negro respondents simply disapprove while one out of twenty-five are uncertain. It is apparent that any such policy to effect *de facto* desegregation would be met with widespread approval in the Negro subcommunity on the basis of the predispositions tapped by this question.

---

*[Editor's Note: See William Brink and Louis Harris, *The Negro Revolution in America.* Simon and Schuster, Inc., New York, 1964.]

Characteristics of the Negro Citizen Sample

What are the Negroes in this sample like in regard to a variety of characteristics?

Slightly more than one third of the Negro sample was under thirty-five years of age, 60 percent between thirty-five and sixty-four years, and 5 percent over sixty-five. Almost half made less than $4,000 per year (compared to slightly more than one quarter of the white sample), one third made between $4,000 and $6,000 per year, and 4 percent made more than $10,000 (compared to 14 percent of the white sample). Only 10 percent had any college at all (2 percent having actually graduated with a college degree), while almost one third had eight grades or less of formal schooling. Their occupation structure looks like this: 57 percent of the entire sample was female and 45 percent of those women worked, those having blue-collar jobs outnumbering those with white-collar jobs by a 6:1 ratio. Among the men, 89 percent had blue-collar jobs, none had white-collar jobs, while the remaining 11 percent had business or professional positions. Taking men and women together, we find 5 percent were business or professional men, 4 percent had white-collar positions, 60 percent worked at blue-collar jobs, while 32 percent were housewives. Thirty-eight percent of these housewives were themselves heads of the household without husbands or jobs. These and other kinds of descriptive data are available on the Negro subcommunity of Portland in the census reports, but it is worth noting what the characteristics of our Negro sample were like.

Ten percent of the Negro sample had been laid off at the time they were interviewed, five times the proportion of white citizens in our sample in a similar situation. Although only 10 percent of the Negro respondents owned their own homes, compared to one third of the white respondents, half of them were in the process of paying off a mortgage. Slightly more than half of the Negro respondents had children in public school, while an additional 13 percent had preschool-age children. That they were interested in the *de facto* school segregation question is evidenced by the response of 43 percent of them to the effect that they had talked with friends and acquaintances about the matter of a possible change in school policy to eliminate it. One percent had taken a more active part in the matter. This compares to 23 percent and 1 percent, respectively, of the white citizens who reported comparable degrees of participation. Nine percent of the Negro sample reported belonging to the NAACP, while 4 percent reported membership in the Urban League.

Their involvement in school affairs compares favorably with that of white citizens, which is an exceptional pattern, given the educational, income, and other differentials between Negroes and whites. They report a rate of discussion of public school matters with family, friends, teachers, and school officials equal to or somewhat higher than the rate of such discussion by white citizens. This is the case even though one third of the Negro sample admits to being not registered to vote compared to one fifth of the white sample.

The interest of Portland Negroes in education was not anticipated. A variety of items attest to the fact that the Negro stress on education is not that of a spectator but of someone who is personally more involved. For example, in response to questions as to whether the public schools ought to increase their programs of preparing children to get along with others, and vocational training for children not going on to college, 96 percent and 90 percent of the Negro respondents approve each increase, respectively (compared to 83 and 84 percent of the much more highly educated white respondents, respectively). After being asked about their attitudes toward fifteen programs of innovations in, or greater use of local public school programs, both Negro and white respondents were asked whether they would be willing to see the local school district spend more money than at present to carry out those programs they saw as most important. Sixty-eight percent of the Negro, and 56 percent of the white, respondents answered affirmatively. Although their respective economic situations were very different, a slightly greater proportion of Negro than white respondents with preschool or school-age children thought "realistically" that at least one of their children would go on to college (although a somewhat smaller proportion of Negro than white parents thought that all of their children would go on to college).

Although a slightly smaller proportion of Negroes than whites felt that school officials would understand their problems and do what they could about them (46 percent to 56 percent, respectively) rather than try to "pass the buck" or ignore them, Negroes—much more than whites—would like to have more influence in school affairs than they feel they have currently. Three out of every five Negroes feel that way, compared to one out of five whites.

In summary, the Negroes in our sample as in the Portland School District generally are a disadvantaged group economically and educationally compared to the relatively affluent white citizens in the community. Yet, it is clear that the local public schools have captured the interest and concern of the Negro citizen; he is involved in a manner unexpected of, and unusual for, comparably disadvantaged Negro citizens of other cities. His interest includes, but extends beyond the *de facto* segregation situation. He values education, particularly for his children, in a way that other minority groups have in the past, and which, some white citizens assert or imply, the Negro in the United States does not. He does in Portland, in any event. His expectations are not only optimistic or hopeful in regard to his children's future education; they are so much so that for the most part he is bound to be frustrated—given what projections can be made from current trends. It is not risky to predict, on the basis of these and unreported data, that the Portland Negro's concern about, and active participation in, public school affairs is likely to increase rather than decrease in the future, and that the *de facto* segregation policy matter may provide a focus partly for its intrinsic significance and partly for its symbolic meanings, for even more active demonstration of that concern in the future.

The White Citizen

Attitudes toward Integration

Are the white citizens of Portland prejudiced toward Negro citizens? Do whites feel that Negroes ought to live in segregrated or integrated neighborhoods?

A substantial majority (72 percent) of white citizens regard Negroes as by nature equal to whites in intelligence, although one quarter regard Negroes as having inferior native intelligence. A bare majority (54 percent) of the white citizens regard Negroes as by nature equal to whites in morality. Forty-one percent of the whites regard Negroes as natively inferior in this regard. (Portland's white citizens' attitudes in regard to Negro native intelligence are better than those of the nation's white citizens. Fifty percent of the latter believe that Negroes have less native intelligence than whites—compared to the 24 percent figure in Portland, but the national figure includes a more prejudiced set of white southerners. See the *Newsweek*-Lou Harris poll.*)

Whites are divided evenly on the matter of segregating Negroes residentially: 45 percent are in favor of segregated living patterns, 45 percent are in favor of mixing neighborhoods and 10 percent are uncertain or say that they think it ought to be up to Negroes to decide themselves. (Portland whites may be quite close to the northern white attitude in general in this regard: 42 percent of the nation's whites say that integrated neighborhoods are desirable—which figure, however, includes respondents from the South as well. See *Newsweek*-Harris poll.*) It should be noted, furthermore, that the question was asked in general and not in terms of what the respondents felt about having Negroes living in their own neighborhood, in the same block, or next door. (This is an area that needs further exploration and intensive measurement.) The findings indicate that if the two items on native intelligence and morality are regarded as indicators of prejudice (in the dictionary sense of prejudging a person on the basis of characteristics attributed to a larger category of which he is a member), 54 percent of the white citizens are not prejudiced in either regard, 24 percent are prejudiced on one of the two items (usually morality), while only 22 percent are prejudiced on both items. Tolerance and intolerance might be the terms applied to white sentiments towards Negroes in segregated or integrated neighborhoods. Looking at the patterns of prejudice and intolerance in the white subcommunity of Portland, we find—using the same data—that the unprejudiced and tolerant people constitute 28 percent of the total sample; the unprejudiced but intolerant constitute 20 percent of the sample; the somewhat prejudiced (on one item—usually morality) but still intolerant constitute 10 percent; the somewhat prejudiced but intolerant constitute 12 percent; the prejudiced and intolerant 13 percent; and the prejudiced but tolerant constitute 7 percent.

That there is a direct relationship between prejudice and intolerance is clear. On the other hand it is also clear that the absence of prejudice is far from a guarantee of tolerance, just as the presence of at least some prejudice does not automatically lead to intolerance, at least of this verbally reported attitudinal character. The fact that 17 percent of the white population, although believing Negroes to be inferior on intelligence and/or morality, still approve of an integrated city is indicative of the possibilities of pursuing policies of toleration and accommodation without having to change every prejudiced person's basic beliefs. At the same time the balance in white citizen's segregation-integration sentiments gives pause to any notion that substantial changes can be made without finding extensive disagreement and resistance.

Turning now to white citizens' attitudes towards race-related school policies, we may ask the same questions as we asked about our Negro respondents:

Do whites feel that it would be better for Negro children to go to schools that have more white pupils? Do whites approve or disapprove of a policy of transporting some children by bus to schools outside of their neighborhoods as a way of reducing *de facto* segregation?

White citizens' approval of mixed neighborhoods is substantially more than the support they give to more integration in the public schools. Half of the white respondents (49 percent) actually disagree that there should be more school integration, while 31 percent agree, and 19 percent are uncertain. Support for a busing policy

---

*[*Op. cit.*]

falls off even more sharply among whites: one fifth approve (only 2 percent "strongly," compared to 41 percent strongly approving among Negro respondents), 74 percent disapprove, while only 7 percent do not have a definite opinion.

It is well known that people with mild attitudes are unstable attitudinally in regard to a variety of policy matters at the local community as well as at the national level. To the extent that any kind of busing policy or its equivalent is considered in attempting to alleviate the school *de facto* segregation situation, one of the more urgent tasks revealed by these findings would be an increase in the number of strong supporters of such a policy among the white citizens. The strong opponents outnumber the strong supporters of this ambiguously worded busing policy by a ratio of 17:1, and it is those who feel strongly that are frequently the most relevant in determining shifts in, or the maintenance of, attitudes of the majority of citizens.

Is there any relationship between prejudiced views of the Negro, and white citizens' attitudes toward (1) more Negro children in school with white children or (2) toward a busing policy on the part of the white citizens of Portland?

As we saw, prejudice did relate directly, although not perfectly, to white citizens' attitudes toward neighborhood segregation. Prejudice also relates to white attitudes toward one of these two school policy perspectives. Almost twice the proportion of unprejudiced than prejudiced white citizens agree that it would be better for Negro children to go to schools that have more white pupils (38 percent to 20 percent, respectively). The relationship between prejudice and the school busing policy is weak at best, and with these numbers of respondents—statistically insignificant.

As with prejudice and preferred racial residential housing patterns, prejudice—as measured by these two items on Negro-white native intelligence and morality— accounts for only a small portion of the opposition to the instant school-policy matters. (A longer, more reliable measure of prejudice would be warranted in any further studies to make more valid assessments of the extent of prejudice and the magnitude of its relationship to the foregoing and other policy attitudes.) We shall now examine the impact of other kinds of "prejudices" as well as other factors that conceivably relate to these race-related attitudes on school policy.

To what extent, if at all, are white attitudes toward residential segregation related to race-related attitudes on school policy?

There is a clear-cut relationship in the Portland white sample between housing tolerance and approval of Negro children going to schools that have more white pupils. Three quarters of those who are intolerant of Negroes living in white neighborhoods are intolerant of greater racial mixing in the schools, whereas less than half of those who are tolerant about integrated neighborhoods are intolerant of additional school integration. Clearly, not all who are tolerant about interracial living patterns in the city are in favor of additional integration in the public schools—in fact, almost half are not. Yet, the two matters are not unrelated, as these findings indicate.

Attitudes toward additional integration in the public schools are in turn related to attitudes toward busing of children to remedy *de facto* school segregation. Although slightly less than a majority of those who in principle favor additional numbers of Negro children going to school with white children approve of a busing policy, the ratio of those who disapprove to those who approve of such a transportation policy among those who are opposed to Negro children going to schools with more white pupils is 15:1. While busing at the moment is not a favored policy on the part of white citizens, the attitude toward it is very much affected by the attitude toward the general question of *de facto* segregation.

Although these attitudes are interrelated in that tolerance of mixed neighborhoods relates to tolerance of additional mixing in schools, which in turn is related to attitudes toward a busing policy, the overall interrelationship is not simple. For example, tolerance of mixed neighborhoods has apparently only a slight relationship to attitudes towards the busing policy. In fact, if we ask whether the two are related when tolerance of mixed schools is taken into account (controlled) at the same time, the answer is negative. One of the implications of these findings is that if tolerance relative to mixed neighborhoods increased, it is not at all certain that a busing policy would be any more approved, but it is likely that such an increased tolerance would be associated with an increased tolerance of mixed schools. If more supportive attitudes toward a busing policy were desired, efforts might best be directed to that end and to increasing tolerance of more mixed schools. If more supportive attitudes toward mixed schools were desired, efforts might best be directed to that end and to increasing tolerance of mixed neighborhood living patterns.

Interpreting the causal flow between and among such attitudes is speculative at best in the absence of systematic natural experimental studies. It should be pointed out, however, that it is easy to fall into what might be termed a logical trap. Since *de facto* segregation is ordinarily pointed to as a function of segregated living patterns, we ordinarily ask, as we did above, what the relationship is between housing and neighborhood segregation attitudes and attitudes toward school segregation, implying the former as the cause of the latter. The fact that almost half of those approving mixed neighborhoods are opposed to more mixing in the schools, and the fact that one quarter of those approving segregated neighborhoods actually approve more mixing in the schools should give us pause. (The absence of a perfect relationship, apart from measurement errors, etc., suggests that we might look at such other factors as whether respondents have children in school, which we will do below.) In fact, we find that two thirds of those who approve greater mixing of the races in public schools also approve mixed neighborhood living patterns, whereas less than 40 percent of those who disapprove of the former approve of the latter.

The implication is that attitudes toward tolerance of school integration affect (cause; shape; influence) tolerance of biracial neighborhood patterns. It is not impossible that the cause and effect sequence flows in part in that direction. If so, a program directed to developing tolerance of more integrated public schools might have the effect of reducing resistances to more desegregated, open neighborhood living patterns. The finding that attitudes in such matters are interrelated, forces one to ask the question about what causes what, and to suggest that it is possible to think about breaking down what in many cities has become a circular avoidance of responsibility. School officials point to landlords and real estate people as those "basically" responsible, while the latter point to the demands by those who have been educated in the local public schools for housing in all-white areas as "basically" responsible for a current *de facto* school segregation situation. The findings in point relative to the interrelatedness of racial attitudes suggest that partial efforts by various groups in their own spheres of authority are not necessarily bound to be without impacts on attitudes in other spheres.

Effect of Socioeconomic Factors

The present study affords an opportunity to explore some of the factors underlying, determining, or associated with school policy attitudes, with tolerance and intolerance relative to neighborhood racial patterns, and with prejudice itself. We shall first examine components of socioeconomic status, or what might be referred to as indicators of social class position, as they may relate to the foregoing images and perspectives.

Do white citizens prejudice, intolerance, and/or race-related school policy attitudes vary according to occupation, education, and/or income?

The data indicate that the concept of social class is not a particularly useful one in trying to understand white race-related images and attitudes in Portland. This is important to know in two regards. If social class groupings varied in identifiable ways, the tasks of reaching those especially resistant to possible policy changes would be easier than otherwise. Of perhaps even greater importance are the traditional community policy-making and policy-changing roles of upper-social class groupings in many communities. Those from upper-class positions most actively involved in community politics not only may find themselves receptive fellows as informal opinion leaders, but accommodating race relations attitudes on the part of whites in many communities have been most pronounced in this upper-middle to upper-class segment that serves disproportionately in the community's active policy-making stratum.

If social (or socioeconomic) class were a relevant concept in understanding white citizens' attitudes and perspectives in regard to racial matters in Portland, the relationship of each of the three indicators—occupation, education, and income—to race-related perspectives would tend to be similar. Whatever the socioeconomic perquisites of particular class categories, and however open a social class system might be, the interrelatedness of such "class" characteristics might be expected to produce in Portland (as it has in many—but not all—other communities) a relatively clear-cut differentiation of class categories on racial matters. This does not happen, even though there are strong relationships in Portland as elsewhere between educational level, occupation, and income.

A category that in many other communities has been known to resist racial accommodation policies is the "working class"—the unskilled, semiskilled, and skilled blue-collar workers. We find that if we classify the white citizen respondents by their own or their spouse's occupation as blue-collar, white-collar (clerical, sales, etc.) or business and professional, blue-collar workers are if anything slightly less prejudiced; somewhat more intolerant of mixed neighborhoods (50 percent of the blue-collar workers think Negroes ought to live by themselves, compared to 46 percent and 38 percent of the white-collar and business and professional people, respectively; insignificantly more opposed to and more uncertain about sending Negro children to schools with more white pupils, and no different than the other occupational categories on the busing policy.) White citizens' attitudes toward Negroes on such matters as these cut across occupational lines.

As income goes up, the highest degree of prejudice goes down (as measured by our two-item views of Negro intelligence and morality index), but the proportion of white citizens without any prejudice on our index remains almost constant. Income level makes almost no difference on tolerance of neighborhood integration; actually those making less than $4,000 per year are more in favor of neighborhood integration than any higher income category. There is a definite, strong, negative relationship between income level and attitudes toward Negro children going to schools with more white pupils. Those who make less than $6,000 per year approve more than those who have higher incomes. In fact, the relatively small category of white citizens who make $10,000 per year or more are most opposed to that policy and, insignificantly, most opposed to a policy of busing even though that high-income category produces the only noticeable, albeit very small, proportion of people who "strongly approve" a busing policy. Apparently it is not the poor whites of Portland who constitute, at the moment, the major centers of active resistance.

We asked also about income expectations ten years hence. There is a small proportion of white citizens who expect to be making less than at present (9 percent of the sample). They are distinctly more opposed to Negro children going to school with more white pupils than are those who expect to have the same or more income ten years hence (63 percent of the former are opposed to more school integration compared to 46 percent of the latter). Although a majority of both categories disapproves the idea of a busing policy, twice the proportion of those who expect to have at least the same incomes ten years hence approve a busing policy than those who are pessimistic about their future incomes (21 percent to 11 percent, respectively). These findings suggest that even the state of the economy, or personal pessimism or optimism, affects white citizens' attitudes toward aspects of race relations. (Future studies might find it desirable to explore this area further with larger numbers of respondents and additional batteries of questions. There is another finding that suggests that actual occupational mobility, apart from income expectations, relates to racial attitudes. The upwardly mobile—those who have better jobs now than they had in recent years—are actually more prejudiced, more intolerant of integrated neighborhoods, and more opposed to additional school integration than are either those with stable occupations or the downwardly mobile—a somewhat unexpected finding. That upwardly mobile group constitutes 13 percent of the working force in our sample. White housewives are another interesting category. They are no less prejudiced or tolerant than others in regard to neighborhood integration, but they are much more uncertain about—and less opposed to—having Negro children attend schools that have more white pupils. They are also more in favor of a busing policy as well as more uncertain about (rather than being opposed to) that policy compared to the rest of the sample. Further research could clarify such relationships.)

Turning now to formal educational level, we find that the college educated white citizens are somewhat less prejudiced than the less well educated, but the differences are small. There is a much greater difference in regard to attitudes toward mixing neighborhoods. Fifty-seven percent of those who have been to college for at least one year are in favor of mixing neighborhoods, whereas 60 percent of the white citizens who have stopped their education short of high school are in favor of segregated neighborhoods.

The respondents with at least some high school education (53 percent of the sample) lean to segregation: 48 percent to 42 percent, with 10 percent uncertain. The more accommodating attitudes of the more highly educated white citizens do not extend, however, to school policy attitudes. The absence of an expected relationship here suggests a variety of questions about the efforts and effects of curricula at both the elementary and high school levels in regard to education about the Negro, about political democracy, and the like. This is not to suggest that in other cities those with comparable degrees of formal education are any more tolerant than in Portland. The results of research in other settings are not clear-cut, nor has there been very much research to establish the relationship between educational level on the one hand, and racial tolerance on the other. Long-range research might well inquire into the conditions under which carefully controlled programs of education about minority groups affect prejudice and intolerance of students, and into the conditions of family, peer group, and neighborhood attitudes toward racial and other minorities as these might effect the consequences of educational programs, and so on.

Do white citizen prejudice, intolerance, and/or race-related school policy attitudes vary with age?

As age increases, prejudice by whites toward Negroes steadily increases. As age increases, intolerance by whites toward Negroes living in mixed neighborhoods remains constant, except among those sixty-five years of age and older who are slightly more intolerant than those younger. Relative to the question of having Negro children go to schools with more white pupils, there is no direct relationship between age and attitude. The very youngest adults and the elderly are both more in favor of more integrated schools than the middle-aged, with the elderly the most undecided of any age category. This is also the pattern with the busing policy attitude. On the latter item, those under thirty-four years of age have almost as many supporters of such a policy as the elderly, but they also contain the highest proportion of those who "strongly disapprove" of such a policy. These data indicate, at the very least, that any policy based on the assumption that over time the younger white citizens will prove to be considerably more tolerant than the older generation is on a very shaky foundation, indeed. Given the higher proportion of better educated people among the young than the old, the assumption that the newer generation is likely to be considerably more tolerant than their elders in regard to race-related school policy is equally shaky, in the light of these findings and of those on education and racial attitudes, above. These findings lead us to a question as to whether race-related school policy attitudes are associated with having children in school or not.

(One of the few optimistic notes in the *Newsweek*-Harris poll* of white attitudes toward Negroes, was their statement that "Young white Americans are turning out to be significantly less prejudiced than their grandfathers." We hope that our interpretation of their analysis is incorrect, but it seems that to strike that optimistic note they—purposefully?—omitted the findings on the "fathers" of those young white Americans. In a table, they report that the nationwide percentage of whites who believe that Negroes have less intelligence is 50 percent. On that same page they report that "The stereotype that Negroes have less native intelligence commands support among 48 percent of the elders but only 28 percent of the younger group." The preceding sentence suggests that their elder category includes those over the age of fifty while the younger group contains those between twenty-one and thirty-four years of age. If this is the case, and in the light of their nationwide percentage of 50, it would appear that considerably more than 50 percent of the whites between the ages

---

*[Op. cit.,]

of thirty-five and forty-nine years in the nation are prejudiced on this item. If this is the case, Portland is not as atypical as the *Newsweek* interpretation might suggest in regard to the asserted difference between the young and the old. In fact, on the same prejudice index—based on the Negro native intelligence and morality items—we do find a small, linear relationship among the white citizens of Portland between age and prejudice.)

Do white citizens' prejudice, intolerance, and/or race-related school policy attitudes vary by the school status of their children?

The white citizens with preschool age children (9 percent of the sample) are the least prejudiced, equal to those with at least one child currently in grade or high school, on tolerance of mixing Negro-white neighborhoods (slightly and insignificantly more tolerant than those without children or those with children beyond school age), considerably more in favor of Negro children going to school with more white pupils, than any other category, and much more in favor of a busing policy than any other category. In fact, the parents of preschool age children are more approving of a busing policy than any other category on this factor or any other factor yet considered. They are the only category with an equal number of supporters and opponents of that policy, with the bulk undecided (30 percent approved, 30 percent disapproved, 40 percent were undecided). The numbers of such people in the sample were so small that no great confidence can be given to that finding, but it appears that further investigation of that possibility is warranted. Whether there tend to be changes in racial attitudes when children enter school is something that may, or may not, occur.

The white respondents with at least one child in school were somewhat less prejudiced in their views of Negro intelligence and morality than those with no children or with children beyond school. They were no less tolerant of mixed neighborhoods than others. However, they were the least supportive of a policy of Negro children going to schools with more white pupils and they were more opposed to a busing policy than any of the other three categories. This suggests that the situation of one's children, whether in school currently or not, is related to such school policy attitudes. To pursue this further, we asked the following question:

Do white citizen prejudice, intolerance, and/or race-related school policy attitudes vary by the fact or degree of integration in the schools attended by their children?

With the information as to what schools each white resident's children were attending, and with the ratio of Negro to white children in each of the Portland schools, it was possible to classify each respondent as having no children in public schools, having children in currently all-white public schools, or having children in integrated schools (the last category for some purposes subdivided into schools that had less than 1 percent Negro enrollment, between 1 percent and 5 percent Negro enrollment, and more than 5 percent Negro enrollment). When a respondent had children in two or more schools with different proportions of Negroes enrolled, the higher proportion was used to classify the respondent. Although the number of respondents in the category of children in all-white public schools is very small (13 people), the findings are extremely interesting (they exclude parents with children in Catholic schools).

The white citizens with children in all-white schools are the most prejudiced, while those with children in integrated schools are somewhat less prejudiced than those with no children in school. The same pattern holds for tolerance in neighborhood living patterns: 50 percent of those respondents with children in integrated schools approve of mixed neighborhoods, compared to 43 percent and 31 percent of respondents with no children in schools and respondents with children in currently all-white schools, respectively. The proportion of those favoring mixed neighborhoods rises from 51 percent to 55 percent among those with children in schools with under 1 percent Negro enrollment to those with from 1 percent to 5 percent Negro enrollment. It drops off to 39 percent for those respondents with children in schools with relatively heavy Negro enrollment (5 percent or more), which is still a higher degree of tolerance than for the respondents with children in all-white schools.

The percentages of the total white sample in these categories are as follows: 61 percent have no children in public schools currently; 4 percent have children only in all-white schools; 13 percent have children in schools with between 1 percent and 5 percent Negro enrollment; and 6 percent have children in schools with over 5 percent Negro enrollment. Four percent of the sample had children only in Catholic schools, and the status of 2 percent of the sample was not ascertained.

The pattern of white citizens with children in integrated public schools being more tolerant than either those with children in all-white schools or those without children in the schools (i.e., those without children, with preschoolers only, or with postschoolers) holds only in part in regard to attitudes towards having Negro children go to school with more white pupils. The most tolerant on this policy are those without children currently in school, which is partly a function of the earlier mentioned tolerance of parents of preschoolers, and apparently a function of the greater tolerance in this regard on the part of people who are not involved personally in the issue (in the sense of not having children in school). However, those respondents with children in integrated schools are no less tolerant on the school integration policy matter than those whose children attended all-white schools; the former are actually somewhat less opposed, being more uncertain than are the latter.

When we turn to the busing policy question, we find that the white citizens without children in school are the less disapproving, while those with children already in integrated schools are the most disapproving. To what extent the sentiments of the latter are due to a feeling that integration of the kind they already have might be accomplished through some other policy than busing or to a dislike of the possibility that the degree of integration in their own children's schools might be increased too much with such a policy, or to other factors, is unknown. (Further research might examine such questions, as well as finding out to what extent a larger sample of whites would or would not reveal the aforementioned kinds of patterns, and what the possible implications are of the differences, if real, between those whose children are attending integrated schools and those whose children are in all-white schools regarding their racial-school attitudes. An oversampling in the areas most likely to produce cases of white parents with children in schools integrated to varying degrees might be most useful.) This analysis led to an even more suggestive set of findings regarding the possible effects of residential location and racial attitudes.

Effect of Neighborhood Integration

Is the degree of white citizen prejudice, tolerance, and/or race-related school policy attitude associated with the degree to which they are living in integrated neighborhoods?

The answer to this question is "yes." The patterns are interesting and deserve to be treated at length. First, however, the manner in which the underlying hypothesis was tested will be described.

The closest that our data would permit an assessment of the degree of integration in the white respondents' neighborhoods was through the use of the 1960 census data on racial composition of dwelling units by blocks in the city of Portland. Since those data are three years old, our findings may be somewhat off, but since this is simply an exploratory analysis with but preliminary findings, we will ignore that possibility for the moment. When drawing the sample, the census tract and block numbers of each respondent were noted, making it possible to code each respondent as being in one of the following categories: living in a block with no Negroes; living in a block with fewer than 5 percent of the dwelling units occupied by Negroes; living in a block with more than 5 percent of the dwelling units occupied by Negroes. The distribution of the white and Negro population of Portland and the size of the sample made any finer categories too small for purposes of analysis. In our white sample we found that for those respondents for whom these block data were available, 76 percent were living on all-white blocks, 11 percent were living in blocks with up to 5 percent Negro occupancy, and 12 percent were living in blocks with more than 5 percent of the dwelling units occupied by Negroes. Of the total sample, 15 percent were living in blocks outside of the city limits but within the Portland School District, and it is for these respondents that we do not have available the racial composition of blocks. They are treated as a separate category below.

Prejudice by whites toward Negroes is associated with the degree to which they are living in integrated neighborhoods in the following manner. The largest proportion of unprejudiced white citizens is found in the integrated blocks with less than 5 percent Negroes. The next highest proportion is found in the blocks outside of the city, which also have the smallest proportion of the most prejudiced people. Then come the all-white blocks in the city, with the most heavily populated Negro blocks having the smallest proportion of unprejudiced whites.

The ranking is similar in regard to attitudes toward segregated versus integrated neighborhoods. The most intolerant respondents are living in the most integrated blocks, followed by the respondents in the all-white blocks, while the respondents living in sparsely integrated blocks are nearly identical with those living in the blocks outside of the city but within the school district—both categories having a majority of white citizens in favor of integrated neighborhoods.

The tolerance of the white respondents who live on lightly integrated blocks is maintained on the matter of school policy involving Negro children going to schools with more white pupils. The respondents from the outlying areas of the school district are less in favor of additonal school integration than are those from either of the other categories. Those from the all-white blocks, those from the most heavily Negro blocks, and those from the outlying areas are in the majority against such a school policy. Even though there are only thirty respondents from the sparsely integrated blocks, given the numbers in the other categories, these findings could have occurred by chance less than once in a thousand times. (This means that the odds are greater than 1,000 to 1 that the finding is not due to a chance drawing of this particular set of respondents from the many sets than can be drawn when selecting a random sample.)

Although statistically insignificant (i.e., the odds are such that it might best be regarded as possibly a finding peculiar to the sample drawn by chance), a similar pattern is found for school busing policy attitudes. The respondents from the blocks that are integrated, although sparsely, are much more inclined to favor a school busing policy to accomplish a breakdown of *de facto* school segregation than any other category. The ratio of opponents to supporters of busing is about 1.5:1. Those from outside the city, those from blocks that have the heaviest Negro populations, and those from all-white blocks have the following ratios of opponents to supporters of school busing: 6.5:1, 5.5:1, and 4:1, respectively, in the same rank order in which they were opposed to additional desegregation in the schools (the previous item).

The tentative conclusion that we would draw from the foregoing findings is that, contrary to what many people would expect, the greatest degree of tolerance and support for racial accommodation school policies is in those areas where there is already a degree of residential integration. This is an unexpected finding to some degree because it is in such areas where the most vocal opposition is sometimes heard to both housing and school integration. What is intriguing about these findings is the possibility that to some unknown extent such tolerance may have developed after, or been reinforced by, integration of the neighborhood or block. If so, this would be supportive evidence for the proposition that social contact can contribute to racial accommodation rather than cause racial strife. The *Newsweek*-Harris poll* affirms the proposition that social contacts decrease prejudice naturally, but their interpretation begs even more the kind of question that we must raise about our findings. This is the question as to whether the greater degree of racial tolerance on the part of whites in integrated neighborhoods is to some extent due to the more tolerant whites moving to, or remaining in, desegregated blocks whereas more intolerant whites remain in, or move to, all-white blocks or outlying areas which presumably have more all-white neighborhoods.

While the kinds of social contacts referred to in the *Newsweek*-Harris poll are quite likely to have been shaped by such dynamics, we think that this is not as likely to be the case with residential living choices, particularly on the part of less advantaged, less well-educated people. To test this indirectly, we divided the respondents in each block category by their level of education and examined their attitudes on additional desegregation to the public schools. Not only were the college educated more in favor of that policy than the highly educated in any other category, but so, too, were the high school educated. While those among the highly educated who were tolerant might not have moved away after their blocks were desegregated or did not let desegregated blocks interfere with their decision to locate there as a matter of principle, we suspect that those with less than a college education were less likely to have acted on such principles.

Such indirect tests are basically still conjectures. An alternative hypothesis that we cannot properly test because of inadequate numbers of respondents is that perhaps those living in sparsely integrated blocks are more of a renter group than those living in either the all-white blocks or the more outlying areas of the school district, and perhaps that is one of the reasons for the aforementioned findings. (The latter may

---

*[*Op. cit.*]

also for the most part be living in all-white blocks, but we do not have the data to be sure.) We have found that white respondents who are renting (30 percent of total sample) are slightly less prejudiced, more tolerant, more disposed to approve Negro children going to schools with more white pupils and even to support a busing policy than white citizens who are buying or already own their homes.

Whatever the actual reasons for the findings on the differential racial attitudes of white citizens according to their location in various kinds of racial or biracial environments, and however tentative such findings must be at this stage, they do point to the inadequacy of assuming without question that visible vocal resistances to residential integration are sufficient evidence that such integration automatically leads to a worse race relations situation. These findings also cast some doubt on the assumption that the attitudes of whites in heavily Negro, ghetto-type areas is the norm for whites in all integrated areas. To the extent that they may be valid, they even provide some further grounds for considering how the schools might assist in the process of reducing the proportion of all-white blocks in the district through a process of educating white pupils to be less resistant to biracial patterns and/or through policies designed to reduce the proportion of Negroes in the heavily Negro sections and blocks of the district. To the extent that the schools as part of their goal to educate for democratic citizenship were successful in reducing the proportion of heavily Negro blocks and schools, the effects might be twofold: increasing white tolerance in the areas of reduced Negro concentrations, and increasing white tolerance in the newly integrated areas.

The impact of racial attitudes on residential location decisions and the impact of changing racial compositions of neighborhoods and blocks on the racial attitudes of white citizens in Portland might well be the subject of further research. It might be possible, for example, to assess the racial attitudes of white citizens living on blocks and in neighborhoods that have been desegregated since 1960, to assess the racial attitudes of those who moved into such areas after they were integrated, and then to compare them to the attitudes of white citizens living in all-white areas. It might also prove possible and illuminating to compare matched sets of Negro respondents who live in sparsely and heavily integrated areas of Portland on a variety of attitudinal items of interest. It would be useful to have a large sample of white citizens living in the outlying, more suburban parts of the Portland School District, as well as samples of citizens living in the suburbs and in other communities in adjacent school districts, in order to assess whether such populations are as intolerant as our inadequate data suggest.

A Concluding Note

The findings reported herein must be regarded as tentative and preliminary, partly because of the limitation of the Negro sample to the specified census tracts, and partly because the survey was undertaken for other reasons. Nevertheless, confidence can be placed in one general finding; namely, the attitudes, perspectives, and policy predispositions of the white and Negro citizens of Portland conflict at various points. Portland, as the nation as a whole, is manifesting the kinds of race relations problems and tensions that are rooted in vast social and psychological distance between the two races. School policy making, as with policy making in regard to other matters that concern race relations, is better made to the extent that racial differences in attitudes and perspectives are understood and acknowledged rather than glossed over or denied. It is also important to discard our tendencies to conceive of the sentiments of a racial group, or of subcategories thereof, in the terms that a friend or acquaintance of the other race—whichever that may be—reports as his sentiments or as the sentiments of the members of his racial category. Findings from even small random samples tend to be more reliable than findings from a few friends or informants. This does not mean that self-selected or elected representatives of racial groups or categories cannot adequately represent the policy attitudes or demands of their constituents. Nor does this mean that action must wait until reliable information has been collected on every point from selected samples. It does mean that whatever studies can be done systematically in the near future, and whatever experimental studies can be set up for longer-term research, need to be carefully considered for the findings they may contain that bear on very difficult policy decisions. We trust that this report contains at least some such findings.

Our final word is one of caution to the effect that racial attitudes may change over time. This is particularly the case with policy matters that are race related. How policies are developed, how they are communicated and in what terms, how much active support is given by even small numbers of policy supporters—these and other factors may all change considerably a set of policy attitudes over a given period of time. One might consider the desirability and feasibility of setting up a longer-term mapping or measurement operation which could chart the shifts in, or stability of, race-related policy perspectives on the part of selected sets of citizens. Such an operation would provide Portland with the kind of data that few if any other cities possess in regard to the state and climate of race relations particularly in regard to school policy matters.

A Personal Postscript: March, 1965

Almost one and one-half years after the completion of the first study, printed above, it was possible to obtain in another connection reinterviews with two thirds of both the Negro and white samples and interview 250 more Negro respondents drawn at random from the same Portland area. That study occurred after the passage of the Civil Rights Act by the congress, just before the national presidential election for the white respondents, and just after that election and the issuance of the Committee on Race and Education's report to the Portland School Board. The latter report suggested a series of improvements for the predominantly Negro schools including an open enrollment plan, which at this time has become district policy, but no busing of masses of Negro students at public expense to end *de facto* school desegregation. To the surprise and dismay of many white civic leaders, the Portland chapter of the NAACP disapproved that plan—after our 1964 surveys—on the ground that it avoided such policies as drawing new attendance lines, closing down the worst almost all-Negro schools, and transporting Negro children to less predominantly Negro schools at public expense, which in their view would constitute the most effective and immediate attacks on *de facto* school segregation.

The results of the 1964 surveys confirm the results reported in the earlier study. Negro citizen attitudes, as measured in the later, much larger sample, were substantially identical with those of the earlier, much smaller sample. Even after the publication of the committee's report and contrary to the reported decrease in support for school busing in the North as a whole, almost three quarters of these Portland Negro respondents approved of a busing policy in the 1964 study. White opposition rose to a new high (toward 80 percent disapproval).

The Negro revolt nationally as well as in Portland may have had some positive effects on the racial perspectives of white citizens. For example, our findings reveal that the proportion of whites viewing Negroes as the same as themselves on morality rose from 54 percent to 67 percent from 1963 to 1964, respectively. Even more dramatically, the figure of 45 percent of white citizens saying that Negroes ought to live in mixed Negro-white neighborhoods as of 1963 rose to 63 percent in 1964.

The local educational turmoil over *de facto* school segregation policy may have had some other impacts in Portland on the policy perspectives of both whites and Negroes. There was a small but noticeable increase in uncertainty ("don't know") on the part of whites by 1964 who had earlier in the 1963 study disagreed with the proposition that it would be better for Negro children to go to schools that have more white pupils. Negro citizens, for reasons that are not clear but perhaps have to do with the complexity of the political issue over school policy, similarly evidenced an increase in uncertainty and disapproval of that general notion.

In any event, and in summary, the 1964 survey underlined the policy gulf over school desegregation and improvement policies between the white and Negro communities in Portland, Oregon, particularly over the issue of transportation out of the ghetto. That policy preference has not become something that Negro citizens (and a few white groups) have been willing to trade for model schools inside the ghetto or something that the school authorities have been willing to institute on a mass basis at public expense. Sooner, rather than later, we would hope, the schools might join with other community institutions in a direct, massive destruction of *de facto* segregation in various areas of Portland life rather than cling to a principle that racial integration in schools or wherever is not a vital part of the process of education itself. At the same time that a policy deadlock seems to have occurred in the school area, our findings suggest that the white citizens of the city have gained increasing respect and some additional tolerance for Negroes as fellow citizens and potential neighbors, perhaps making it more likely that the *de facto* school segregation issue can be resolved more quickly than it otherwise might be.

"NEGRO DIALECT" AND THE MOTIVE TO ACHIEVE

Rufus F. Baehr *is associate professor of psychology, Chicago City College, Wilson Campus. This study is based on his* Need Achievement and Dialect in Lower Class Adolescent Negroes *(unpublished Ph.D. dissertation, University of Chicago, 1964).*

Language may be considered an index of social status and a possible vehicle of mobility. The immigrant was keenly aware of this. He regarded his substandard language as a barrier and the acquisition of standard language an avenue for change in status. Today, the Negro American may be faced with a similar problem. The success of his efforts at mobility may depend, at least in part, upon the nature of his speech and language patterns. Altering these patterns may depend upon intelligence and

From *Integrated Education*, **February/March 1966. Reprinted by permission of the author.**

perhaps specific language ability. But it may also be a function of motivation—more specifically, of the *motive to achieve.*

In the present study, we deal with dialect and the motive to achieve. If the dialect and motivation of the lower-class adolescent Negro are examined, the young lower-class Negro with high motive to achieve may be expected to have at his command more of the dialect preferred by those in higher status than the lower-class young Negro of the same intelligence but with low motive to achieve. The central purpose of this study is to explore the relationship between the need to achieve and the dialect of the lower-class adolescent Negro.

Dialect differences are important to the linguist and are the focus of considerable study. Standard English is considered the socially preferable dialect and is spoken by the prestige groups of the community, the upper- and middle-class families; while substandard English is spoken by members of the lower social status groups. What becomes the prestige dialect will depend upon the region. In the United States there are three geographic types of standard English: northern, midland, and southern.

The term "Negro dialect" is often indiscriminately applied to Negro speech. This popular stereotype of "Negro dialect" is based upon the notion that Negro pronunciation is highly uniform and differs quite markedly from that of the white population. However, the linguist does not use racial membership as a means of identifying dialect differences, and besides, research clearly shows that Negro speech varies with region and social class position.

Issues and Hypotheses

1. The focal issue and central hypothesis of this study was: There is a positive relationship between the motive to achieve as measured by McClelland's method* and the nature of dialect of the lower-class adolescent Negro. With intelligence, grade-point average in school, sex, and other relevant variables constant, adolescent Negroes who are high in motive to achieve will manifest less southern speech than those who are low in motive to achieve.

2. With respect to sex differences, the speech of the lower-class adolescent Negro girl will contain more southern dialect than the lower-class adolescent Negro boy. The rationale for this prediction is based upon the theoretical formulations and observations of some linguists regarding the conservative influence of women on speech. According to this assumption, women are said to be the "preservers of the traditional language" and do not experiment with new linguistic forms. It may also be argued that the girls stay closer to home than boys, and as a result, they are more influenced by their parents' speech and less exposed to other speech possibilities.

3. With respect to the question of dialect and school achievement there is a positive relationship between grade-point average and diminution of southern speech. The rationale for this prediction has its source in several possibilities. First, the same motives that underlie superiority in language use may also underlie superiority in academic achievement. Second, reduction of southern speech among those who do well in school may simply indicate that accepted pronunciation is learned as subject matter is learned. Hence, the student who is successful in his schoolwork

---

*[Editor's Note: Psychologist David A. McClelland uses projective tests to elicit from subjects data on the strength of their need to achieve.]

would be expected to succeed in learning the preferred dialect of his community. Third, there is the matter of "halo effect." The teacher's judgment of the student's academic worth may be influenced by the student's greater use of middle-class speech.

4. With respect to the general question of the effect of the motive to achieve on behavior, is there evidence in the present study of other types of relationships between motive to achieve and relevant manifest performance? For example, is there evidence in the data that there is a difference in productivity between the high and low in motive to achieve as measured in this study? There are numerous studies showing that McClelland's method seems to work for males but not for females. Is this the case also with the present sample?

Sample

A public high school located on Chicago's west side served as the setting for the study. The sample consisted of sixty-three students in their junior year of high school. In addition to grade level, the sample was selected in accordance with the following requirements: an intelligence score of one hundred or better, membership in the lower class, birth and residence in Chicago, with parents born in a southern state. Information about family size and birth order was also collected. The sample was evenly divided between boys and girls.

Instruments

1. The measure of the motive to achieve. The McClelland TAT pictures were to measure the strength of the achievement drive. The test was administered in accordance with the procedures described by McClelland.

2. The measure of dialect. Two speaking situations were chosen, one achievement-oriented and the other neutral. An instrument was developed to be used for the achievement-oriented situation. The test consisted of words and statements designed as stimuli to elicit from the informant other words which could then be assessed for presence or absence of southern dialect. It was presented to the subjects as a vocabulary test and each informant was urged to do as well as he could. The neutral speaking situation consisted of an informal interview which followed the vocabulary test. The distinction between the two speaking situations was that the latter was informal and conversational, and dealt with what can be called "small talk." Both speaking situations were recorded on tape for later analysis.

Variables Noted

The material on the tape recordings was coded and grouped into eight categories that identify some of the major characteristics of southern American pronunciation. There were seven linguistic variables: changing vowels to diphthongs; changing diphthongs to pure vowels; raising and lowering vowels; the loss of consonants; the substitution of one consonant for another; dissimilation; and nasality. Drawl, the eighth variable, is considered paralinguistic.

The intensity of southern pronunciation was determined by noting each occurrence of southern speech in the achievement-oriented and neutral testing situations. The larger the number of the occurrences the greater the evidence of southern dialect.

The reliability of the instrument was checked by Dr. Juanita Williamson, a professional linguist.

Procedure

Four steps were followed in data collection.

1. Students in the junior class were asked to fill out a short questionnaire designed to give information about the birthplace of the student and of his parents as well as an estimate of the educational attainment of the parents.
2. The personnel folders of those students meeting the requirements of the study were checked for further information, such as parents' occupations.
3. The weekly morning division period was the time used to administer McClelland's TAT pictures.
4. Each student's speech was recorded under achievement-oriented and neutral conditions. The interview occurred during the regular school day but at a time that would not interfere with class attendance. The rooms used for recording were equipped for that purpose. The sample was collected over a period of three semesters.

Results

1. In the neutral speaking situation, no relationship between motive to achieve and dialect was found. This same result was obtained for boys, for girls, and for the total sample.
2. In the achievement-oriented speaking situation there was a highly significant relationship between motive to achieve and dialect for boys, with intelligence, grade-point average, and other variables held constant. Boys with high achievement showed less southern dialect than the boys with low motive to achieve. This finding did not hold for the girls.
3. With respect to sex differences in dialect there is a difference between boys and girls on one dialect trait—changing vowels to diphthongs—this being more significantly characteristic of the girls' than of the boys' speech. This finding supported the hypothesis in both testing situations. Differences in the other seven dialect variables showed no consistent trend and in any event did not reach statistical significance.
4. With respect to the relationship between dialect and school achievement, a distinction must be made between the achievement-oriented and neutral speaking situations. With respect to the achievement-oriented speaking situation, the results for the boys showed a trend in the direction of low southern dialect being related to better school achievement. This trend was not found for the girls. With respect to the neutral speaking situations, a small but significant relationship was found between greater use of middle-class speech and academic success. Again, the findings held for the boys but not for the girls.
5. With respect to the relationship of motive to achieve to other aspects of behavior: (a) during the interview the output (as measured by number of pages of transcription) of boys with high motive to achieve was significantly greater than that of the boys with low motive to achieve. This did not hold for the girls. (b) The grade-point average of the boys with high motive to achieve scores was somewhat (and significantly) higher than that of boys with low motive to achieve. Again, this did not hold for the girls.

Discussion of Results

The concepts of *imitation* and *identification* may be applied to account for the findings with respect to the central issue of the study. Identification implies the following: An individual (usually a child) gives his allegiance to an adult (usually a parent) and internalizes the ideas, values, attitudes, beliefs, gestures, and other expressive patterns of the individual with whom he identifies. With respect to language learning, one might anticipate the initial speech of the child to be that of the parents and then to be modified gradually as other identifications are made. In the present case, the adolescent with high motive to achieve identifies with individuals who may speak a different dialect.

In addition to identification, there is imitation which helps to account for a different type of language learning behavior. Where behavior is a result of identification, it is unconscious or in a sense unpremeditated; behavior resulting from imitation is subject to conscious control. The behavior can be turned on and off at will in compliance with the demands of a particular situation. It is possible, of course, to mistake an imitative dialect for the dialect the individual has learned through identification.

With respect to the first two findings, the use of southern dialect under neutral speaking conditions by the boys with high motive to achieve scores suggests that the characteristics of middle-class speech used by them in the achievement-oriented situation were not part of their normal speaking habits. Rather, these were speech traits which the highly motivated achievers were successfully able to imitate. Hence, the lower-class adolescent Negro boy who is high in motive to achieve can make use of a dialect other than his own, especially when it is instrumental in goal attainment.

The low-need achievers in both testing situations were high in southern dialect, which suggests they made little attempt to imitate the dialect of the middle class.

Recent studies by French and Lesser[1] may help to clarify the lack of relationship between high motive to achieve and dialect, as well as other similar inconclusive findings reported for the girls. French and Lesser hold that the dynamics of the achievement motive are more complex in women than in men. The achievement scores of women are more predictive of performance when their value orientations (intellectual or woman's role) are known and when the appropriate stimulus figure (male or female) is used. If the achievement motivation scores of the girls in this sample had been obtained in accordance with these suggestions, the results might have been more consistent with the findings for boys.

The reduction of drawl by the boys in both the achievement and neutral speaking situations is the only evidence that suggests some kind of permanent change in southern speech for those scoring high in motive to achieve. Two interpretations may be offered to explain why high motive to achieve is so strongly associated with the imitation of middle-class speech norms and so weakly associated with the identification of middle-class speech norms. One interpretation is that the lower-class adolescent Negro boy who is high in motive to achieve is forced into a dilemma: He either maintains the desirable acceptance and recognition by his peer group or he

[1] Elizabeth G. French and Gerald S. Lesser, "Some Characteristics of the Achievement Motive in Women," *Journal of Abnormal and Social Psychology*, February, 1964.

adopts the ways of those in higher status with whom he may hope to be identified as a function of his achievement needs. He may resolve this conflict in his speech by modifying only the least noticeable aspects of his dialect and retaining the highly audible elements.

Instead of emphasizing the conservative effect that possible rejection by one's peer group may have upon language learning, an alternative explanation might focus upon the conservative effects of intergroup tension which grow out of class and racial differences. When the lower-class adolescent high in motive to achieve experiences more defeats than rewards from those in higher prestige positions, the experiences necessary for the development of permanent identification are absent. If such conditions prevail, one might expect to find the high-need achiever predominantly imitative in his use of standard English.

The findings with respect to sex differences and dialect support the hypothesis that the speech of the lower-class adolescent Negro girl contains more southern dialect. In addition to the two explanations already offered to account for this phenomenon, a third might be suggested. Since only one out of the eight dialect traits (greater use of diphthongs by the girls) supported the hypothesis, the evidence might indicate that some speech traits are defined by the culture as more feminine. The assumption that there are linguistic forms which the culture considers to be either masculine or feminine is a possible area of investigation. If such linguistic forms exist, then personality structure may be significantly related to individual departure from the norms.

There is some evidence to suggest that boys who are better students also show less evidence of southern speech. Since the relationship is slight, these findings must be considered as tentative, but they may serve as a guideline for further research and inquiry. With respect to the girls, the data show them to be superior to the boys in English as graded in school, but this success in academic English was not matched by greater use of middle-class speech.

The data, which show boys high in motive to achieve talking longer during the interview than boys low in motive to achieve, add a new dimension to the understanding of verbal productivity. Verbal productivity seems to be related to motive to achieve on the spoken as well as the written level of communication. Considering the fact that intelligence and educational differences (factors that may influence verbal productivity) are controlled, the above evidence seems to indicate that verbal productivity is a function of the achievement motive.

Because the dialect of a lower-class child can be a hindrance to his normal academic development, the classroom teacher needs to take a second look at the role of speech in the life of the student. The following proposals are an attempt on the part of the author to formulate several teaching objectives that might help the lower-class child value his dialect and at the same time avoid some of its pitfalls. First of all, the classroom teacher should recognize and accept the dialect of each student, knowing that it is a part of his cultural background. To depreciate the dialect of anyone is to attempt to separate the individual from his social heritage. Sound educational procedure builds upon the resources the child brings to the learning situation. Rejection of any part of these resources is alien to good educational practice. Acceptance of dialect differences on the part of those in authority supports the psychological conditions necessary for the academic growth of the student.

Secondly, teaching of English grammar should take into consideration the speech habits of the pupil. Often there are points of cleavage between the speech of the lower-class child and the objectives of an English class. The problem of subject-verb agreement is just one of many areas of difficulty. For the lower-class child, the learning expectations in an English class are similar to those of learning a foreign language. Thus the task of learning English grammar is not simply a task of extending mastery over the written dimension of one's native tongue. If the English teacher draws upon the rationale and methodology of linguistics, the problems unique to the lower-class child will be more easily recognized and dealt with in a more explicit and systematic way.

With respect to practical considerations, the lower-class student should be made aware of the fact that successful advancement in his community may require the learning of an additional dialect, that is, learning the preferred dialect of his community. Placing the emphasis upon learning a new dialect avoids the pitfall of requiring the student to turn his back upon the dialect of his childhood in order to learn a new dialect. In reality, the student needs both.

The future of our democratic society is dependent, in part, upon the success of the classroom teacher in facilitating the movement of the lower-class child into the mainstream of our culture. Language learning is an integral part of this endeavor.

LOWER-CLASS NEGRO MOTHERS AND THEIR CHILDREN

Robert R. Bell, *assistant professor of sociology, Temple University, is editor of* Sociology of Education *(Dorsey, 1962). The following article is based on a paper read before the annual meeting of the American Psychological Association on September 5, 1964.*

What aspirations do lower-class Negro mothers have for their children? Often, it is assumed that lower-class mothers, reflecting limited personal experience and education, lack the hope and imagination to stimulate their children to higher aspiration levels. For example, the concept of "deprivation" often implies fatalism by lower-class parents for themselves and their children. When the middle and lower class are compared, differences exist in child-rearing and socialization. But there has been little research as to whether or not the lower class is homogeneous in its values and aspirations toward education.

Recently, the writer conducted a study in Philadelphia designed in part to study the aspirations of Negro mothers for their children's future. (This study was partially supported by the Philadelphia Center for Community Advancement.) In the lower-class Negro family, the mother has long been recognized as the most important adult figure, especially in reference to her children. In our population study the mother was the only common parent figure, because no husband/father was present in 27 percent of the families. The population to be discussed consists of 202 Negro mothers, each with a minimum of two children, one of whom was either in nursery school or kindergarten. The mothers lived in three elementary school districts, almost totally Negro and on the basis of demographic data classified as lower class. The interviewing

From *Integrated Education,* **December 1964/January 1965. Reprinted by permission of the author.**

was done by two Negro female graduate students using a schedule consisting of 102 items. The interview schedule was designed to get at various aspects of the Negro woman's self-role image; i.e., background data, her views of her marriage and her wife role, patterns and techniques of child-rearing, her feelings about the schools, and her expectations for her children when they reach their adult years.

Four Negro subgroups were defined on the basis of education and number of children. The use of education is supported by the findings of a number of researchers who have found education to be one of the best single indices of Negro social class differences. The size of family (number of children) has also been correlated with social class differences by various researchers. Therefore, amount of education and number of children provide a two-variable index for attempting to distinguish Negro social class differences. These two variables were used to divide the Negro mother population into the following four subgroups:

- Group A: Low education (0-8 years) and large number of children (seven or more). Thirty-seven *low-status* mothers.
- Group B: Low education (0-8 years) and small number of children (six or fewer). Forty-three *middle-status* mothers.
- Group C: High education (nine or more years) and large number of children (seven or more). Twenty-nine *middle-status* mothers.
- Group D: High education (nine or more years) and small number of children (six or fewer). Ninety-three *high-status* mothers.

In the discussion of data that follows, the major focus is on the differences between the "low-status" and "high-status" mothers.

Aspirations

In the discussion that follows, the aspirations given by the Negro mothers for their children's futures are examined for internal consistency *within* three response categories as well as for logical relationships between the three categories.

Education and Occupation

In the first aspirational category the mothers were asked how many years of education they would like to see achieved by both son(s) and daughter(s). For the sons there was a statistically significant difference between the educational aspirations given by the "low-status" and "high-status" mothers. In the "low-status" mother group, 44 percent wanted a college education for their sons as compared to 65 percent of the "high-status" mother group. For daughters there was also a significant difference, with 39 percent of the "low-status" mothers and 61 percent of the "high-status" mothers wanting a college education.

The mothers were also asked what kind of occupation they would like to see their son(s) and daughter(s) fill when they reached their adult years. The occupational responses given by the mothers were classified as "office and clerical," "skilled," "professional," and "don't know." In occupational aspirations for sons the responses given by the "low-status" and "high-status" mothers showed no significant differences. They were equally likely to respond "professional" (47 percent), but the "low-status" mothers were slightly higher in giving "skilled" occupation for their sons than were the "high-status" mothers (21 percent as against 12 percent). For the daughters there was a significant difference in one type of job aspiration with 38 percent of the "low-status" mothers responding "office or clerical" as contrasted to 21 percent of the "high-status" mothers.

Marriage and Parenthood

Educational and occupational items are the measures most commonly used to determine aspirational levels. Yet, other adult role expectations may also be important not only as independent measures but also because they may influence the achievement of educational and occupational goals. For example, if a mother holds high educational and occupational aspirations for her children and at the same time thinks they should marry young and have a large family, there is often by implication, a contradiction in her aspirations. Therefore, one might expect that those mothers who have high educational and occupational aspirations for the children would also hold aspirations for them of older age at marriage and to have fewer children.

The mothers were asked what they thought would be the best ages for their children to marry. Ages given for son(s) showed significant differences between the two mother groups. Fifty percent of the "low-status" mother group responded twenty-one years of age or under as compared to only 17 percent of the "high-status" mothers; and in the older marriage range, 37 percent of the "low-status" mothers and 63 percent of the "high-status" mothers gave twenty-four years of age and older as the best age for a son to marry.

There were also significant differences between the two mother groups regarding the best age for daughters to marry. Thirty-five percent of the "low-status" mothers and 7 percent of the "high-status" mothers answered nineteen years of age or younger, and at the older age range 10 percent of the "low-status" and 27 percent of the "high-status" mothers suggested twenty-four years of age or older as the best age for a daughter to marry.

The mothers were also asked what would be the ideal number of children for sons and daughters to have when they grow up. There were significant differences in the ideal number given by "low-status" and "high-status" mothers for their son(s). Sixty-one percent of the "low-status" mothers and 41 percent of the "high-status" mothers said that two or fewer children were the best number for a son. At the other extreme 21 percent of the "low-status" and 36 percent of the "high-status" mothers suggested four or more children for their sons. The difference in ideal number of children for daughters as given by the mothers was not statistically significant, but the direction of difference was the same as that given for sons. Sixty percent of the "low-status" and 50 percent of the "high-status" mothers said two or fewer children, and 19 percent of the "low-status" and 33 percent of the "high-status" mothers said four or more children.

These findings raise the question that if the "high-status" mothers suggest a higher ideal number of children for both their sons and daughters than did the "lower-status" mothers, is there a conflict with their higher aspirational level for their children? It is suggested that there may be no contradiction for several reasons. First, the range of ideal number of children suggested by the "high-status" mothers is not greater than commonly found in the many studies of fertility ideals. Second, with the older age at marriage suggested by the mothers, parenthood generally would not occur until after the achievement of educational aspirations. Third, the small number of children suggested by the "low-status" mothers may be a reflection of their personal problems with their own large families, leading to the belief that if their children have small families they might escape some of the same problems.

The American Dream

The mothers' aspirations for their children in such areas as education, occupation, age at marriage, and number of children was generally influenced by the realities of personal experience and interpretation. Yet, a part of the value system related to aspirations for children also includes more abstract or less experiential values—what may be called "American dream" values. The already discussed aspirational values may be defined as essentially concrete. We would expect the two mother groups to be less differentiated in their acceptance of more general abstract "American dream" values than they were with the more concrete aspirational items.

While the mothers were asked specific questions in reference to educational aspirations for their children they were also asked a more general question about education. The mothers were asked what kind of education they thought a young man needed these days to be successful. On this item there were significant differences between the responses of "low-status" and "high-status" mother groups. Fifty percent of the "low-status" and 32 percent of the "high-status" mothers said "high school" or "technical education," with the rest in each group saying "college." This item as a general value is closely related to the more concrete item on educational aspirations for their sons. The number of years' schooling they would like to have their son(s) receive and the kind of education they think a young man needs to be successful are essentially the same. This would suggest that the general ideal held for educational success by each of the two mother groups was influenced by what each sees as the reality of the situation; that is, what each mother group defines as the educational level they would like to see their sons achieve.

A second question focused on a more abstract value by asking the mother if she believed any young man with ability and hard work could hope to earn $10,000 a year. There were no differences between the "low-status" and "high-status" mothers in their responses to this question, with 72 percent of the "low-status" and 74 percent of the "high-status" mothers answering "yes." For the "low-status" mother group their high acceptance of this aspect of the "American dream" would suggest that on the abstract level they verbalize high aspirations although in the more concrete aspirational areas they do not.

A third question focused on one other aspect of the "American dream." The mothers were asked what they believed to be most important for a man to get ahead in his job: (1) hard work and ambition; (2) playing up to the boss; or (3) to socialize with the boss. There were significant differences in the responses of the two mother groups with 69 percent of the "low-status" and 95 percent of the "high-status" mothers giving the traditional "American dream" response of "hard work and ambition." Even with the differences in responses between the two mother groups, it is of interest that two thirds of the "low-status" mothers gave the traditional response.

The data on two of the items suggests there are differences between the "low-status" and "high-status" mothers in their acceptance of general "American dream" values. While there is a common acceptance of those values by the "low-status" mother group, it seems possible that for them the abstract values have minimal force and are influenced by more concrete values to a greater degree than among the "high-status" mothers.

Discussion

We have suggested that it is possible to distinguish significant subgroups within the Negro lower class. This is indicated by our data on variables that help distinguish social class levels and in the differences between the two mother subgroups in stated aspirations for their children.

Can it be said that *if* the "low-status" and "high-status" Negro mother groups were representative of extremes in our lower-class population, the other two mother groups ("middle-status": Group B, low education and small family, and Group C, high education and large family) should fall between in the aspirational responses given for their children? When a comparison was made between the responses of the Group B and Group C mothers on the eleven aspirational items only one showed a significant difference. Because of the lack of difference between the Group B and Group C mothers the two groups were combined. It was found that on all eleven aspirational items the combined BC ("middle-status") mother group fell between the "low-status" and "high-status" mothers. Furthermore, on only two of the eleven items were there significant differences between the combined BC mother group and *either* the "low-status" or "high-status" mothers.

While the two extreme groups used for comparison were designated as "low-status" and "high-status" groups, it was assumed that the overall mother population studied was within the Negro lower class. While there are probably some exceptions within the "high-status" mother group it is suggested that even for that group the greatest majority are within the upper range of the Negro lower class. This suggestion is based on a comparison of our "high-status" mothers with other studies of Negro social class where the research descriptions of the Negro middle class are generally different.

It must be recognized that the aspirational values discussed in this paper were verbalized only by mothers. However, given the importance of the family and especially the mother in the Negro lower-class family, her values and aspirations in reference to her children are often meaningful and influential for the children's futures. It seems reasonable to assume that the closer the mother's aspirations for her children are to the bottom level of the lower-class value range the less likely are her children to be greatly influenced by other agencies and persons reflecting more middle-class values. Therefore, the relative positions of Negro mothers in the lower class may be related to different aspirational values transmitted to their children, and may also contribute to a way of life which makes any alternative aspirational levels difficult for their children to internalize and successfully achieve.

On the one hand, our findings suggest the danger in writing off whole populations simply because they come from "deprived homes." Educators would be wise to avoid this practice and in fact many might be surprised at the different levels of aspirations to be found even among persons at the bottom level of the lower class. On the other hand, however effective the school program, there also must be anawareness of value forces operating on the child when away from school. Within the family context this implies educational values presented to the child and how these values support or subvert those being developed in school programs. It is an important function of the sociologist to provide possible insights, through conceptual and empirical studies of the heterogeneous character of the lower class, that may lead to a broader understanding of the nonschool aspirational values that influence the child. A more broadly based interdisciplinary approach may contribute to greater success in the future for lower-class educational programs.

SECURING TEACHERS FOR SLUM SCHOOLS

William W. Wayson *is assistant professor of educational administration, Syracuse University. This article is adapted from an address to the annual meeting of the American Association of School Administrators, February 19, 1964.*

In considering the problem of securing teachers for the schools in the inner city, we must conclude that teachers and laymen consider them as situations (1) in which most of my readers would not want to teach, (2) to which you would not send your child, (3) in which many would not let their daughters teach, (4) in which most teachers fear to teach, and (5) from which most teachers wish to escape.

Most objective observations of the careers followed by teachers in large cities show that these generalizations are widely held; yet, the public statements of educators often imply that none is true.

Objective observations also reveal that schools in the inner city are (1) not so bad as they are popularly believed to be and (2) are not so good as politicians and administrators would have us believe. Not many of these schools are "blackboard jungles"; but at the same time, few of them represent equal educational opportunity.

These schools pose grave staffing problems. On their staffs are many inexperienced or temporarily licensed teachers. They are the locus of high rates of out-transfer and low (if any) in-transfer. Teachers typically seek "promotions" from the inner-city schools to more desirable neighborhoods. It is a common stereotype among both professionals and laymen that the teachers in these schools are incompetent, insufficiently trained, or unambitious. Such stereotypes prevent solving staffing problems in conventional ways. Many beginning teachers fear assignment to slum schools. If they are assigned to such schools, they often regard it as an initiation ritual that must be survived if one is to succeed in the city system. They tend to transfer out of the inner city as soon as they have opportunity.

However, there are teachers who stay in these schools and one can find teachers who have been there for many years. If we knew why they stay, we should know much more about slum schools and we might learn ways to reduce the teacher shortages there.

A study recently conducted at the Midwest Administration Center at the University of Chicago* dealt with the reasons teachers stay in the slum school. In a large midwestern city, 27 white and 15 Negro teachers who had been in slum schools for more than five years and sixteen white and four Negro teachers transferring from

---

From *Integrated Education,* **February/March 1966. Reprinted by permission of the author.**

*[Editor's Note: See two articles by William W. Wayson: "Expressed Motives of Teachers in Slum Schools," *Urban Education,* Vol. I (1965), and "Sources of Teacher Satisfaction in Slum Schools," *Administrator's Notebook,* May, 1966.]

the same schools were interviewed. All respondents were asked why they had stayed in the school as long as they had. They talked about the sources of satisfaction in their jobs.

The responses were analyzed both to identify the attractive features of the slum school and to compare the responses given by stayers and leavers. Responses given by white and Negro teachers were also compared.

All of the reasons for remaining were categorized into ten types that were developed after a study of the characteristics of slum schools and were refined on the basis of the interviews. It was theorized that as more fishermen are found near the sea, more of certain types of teachers would be found in slum schools. The ten response categories were

1. According to principal—loyalty to a principal who caters to the needs and desires of teachers.
2. Altruism—the wish to fulfill intrinsic needs of others. The needs are expressed by the other; teacher strives to meet them.
3. Constraints—being compelled by organizational rules or other pressures to remain in the situation.
4. Despotism—wishing to dominate, especially by force.
5. Group belongingness—being accepted by a group of peers.
6. Inertia—unwillingness to change or to face an unknown situation.
7. Missionary zeal—the wish to give others something good that they are felt to lack. The teacher decides what is good.
8. Personal esteem—wanting to be personally admired by others.
9. Professional appraisal—the desire to be recognized by a superior.
10. Professional autonomy—seeking freedom from outside pressures or interference in the classroom.

Table 1 contains the results of the analysis of the interview data. The findings indicate that most attractive features of the inner-city schools are their isolation from community pressures, the absence of extra-classroom obligations such as PTA meetings and after-school faculty meetings, and the characteristics of slum children that are perceived as complementary to the expressed needs of teachers. The least attractive features, as expressed by the leavers, are the children's academic ineptness and their deviation from middle-class modes of behavior and personal appearance.

It may be seen that stayers and leavers give different reasons for teaching in the slum school. Their responses in the interviews indicated that they viewed pupils differently; they had different professional aspirations; and they described the role of the teacher differently. The differences are described below. The descriptions are generalized and abstracted. They do not accurately portray any individual teacher; however, the descriptions are useful for generalizing the findings of the study, and they illuminate some issues related to the staffing problems of the slum school.

Most of the leavers were young and had no experience in other schools. They had to teach no more pupils, their classes were no larger than those of the stayers, and they lived no farther from the school. They had lower-middle-class backgrounds as did the stayers.

The leavers desired *professional appraisal*. They wanted recognition from professional superiors and gained little satisfaction from having pupils or parents

Table 1
Types of Motives Expressed by Each Subgroup
in Percentages

Type of Motive (As ranked by total sample)	Teachers Giving at Least One Response in Category			
	White		Negro	
	Stayer n = 27 (%)	Leaver n = 16 (%)	Stayer n = 15 (%)	Leaver n = 4 [a] (%)
1. Personal esteem	58 [b]	19	33	25
2. Missionary zeal	33	31	33	25
3. Professional autonomy	37	13	27	25
4. Inertia	37 [b]	6	13	25
5. Constraints	4	6	40 [d]	75
6. Group belongingness	7	25	27	0
7. Accommodating principal	22 [b]	0	13	25
8. Professional appraisal	7	38 [c]	0	25
9. Altruism	22 [b]	0	7	0
10. Despotism	7	13	0	0
Unclassified	0	6	0	0

[a] Negro leavers were too few in number to compare. They are shown only as a matter of interest.
[b] White stayers exceeded white leavers, significant at 0.05 level.
[c] Leavers exceeded white and Negro stayers, significant at 0.05 level.
[d] Negro stayers exceeded white stayers at 0.05 level and white leavers at 0.10 level.

praise them. They wanted pupils to acquire academic skills and knowledge and they did not like having to meet the child's emotional and physical needs. They were frustrated by the low academic achievement of disadvantaged pupils. They wanted to teach children "who could learn." Leavers resisted "watering down" the curriculum. They felt that middle-class parents would be more aggressive than parents in the slum; they felt that suburban pupils would achieve enough to compensate for the greater pressure. They liked not having after-school and evening meetings in the slum school, but were willing to attend such meetings to get higher professional appraisal. Some of them expressed *missionary zeal* but felt that it was impossible to change the disadvantaged pupil and his parents.

More teachers were leaving schools in changing neighborhoods. Schools with stable enrollments, whether the pupils were white or Negro, had few teacher transfers.

There were few Negro leavers. Three of the four interviewed felt that they could not get positions in other neighborhoods. Their expressed attitudes about the slum school were quite similar to those expressed by white teachers.

Most of the stayers had taught in other types of schools. They had begun in small rural schools and had moved, sometimes in several steps, to schools in larger districts and finally into the city. They taught the same number of pupils, traveled the same distances, got along just as well with the principal as did the leavers. Like leavers, they had lower-middle-class backgrounds, but fewer of them were born in the city.

Stayers gave one or more of the following types of reasons for teaching in the slum school: personal esteem and altruism, inertia, professional autonomy, and accommodating principal. Two thirds of them expressed one or more of the latter three reasons. They indicated that slum schools afford much autonomy, but these teachers seemed to want freedom from pressures more than freedom to initiate new practices in their instruction. Teachers did not visit pupils' homes, and parents did not come to the school. Neither parents nor superiors questioned the actions of these teachers and they were happy with the arrangement.

Nearly half the stayers gained satisfying personal recognition from pupils. The slum child was reported to be "grateful," and he expressed affection for teachers who established rapport with him. Former pupils often returned in later years to see a friendly teacher. Stayers tended to feel that they had great personal influence upon their pupils, particularly the few (often very few) of their former pupils who were successful in life. Their classroom goals were not achievement oriented (the study did not reveal whether their pupils achieved any more or less than other pupils), rather their goals centered upon close personal relationships with the pupils. About one fifth of the stayers expressed altruism, usually showing a maternal feeling toward the slum child. About equal percentages of stayers felt that they had enough success to justify their efforts.

Negro stayers expressed motives that were similar to those given by white stayers. Negroes felt constrained by racial barriers to their placement in better neighborhoods, but they did not blame the current administration for their limited opportunities.

There was no attempt in this study to assess the success or the effectiveness of the teachers. Merely staying in school is not a measure of effective teaching. Teaching must be evaluated by other criteria that were beyond the scope of the present study to determine. The study did reveal certain personal characteristics as those characteristics were related to the teacher's staying or leaving the slum school.

There are many limitations to the study described above; however, objective studies of staffing problems in the slum school are few in number and the present findings add to what is known. Informal interviews and observations in the schools of two other cities convince me that the findings of the study are valid and that the staffing problems as described do not vary appreciably from one city to another. On the basis of contacts with teachers from those cities, conversations with personnel from other cities, and extensive reading about inner-city schools, I feel that certain changes need be made in staffing procedures if the educational program for disadvantaged youngsters is to be noticeably improved. Giving all possible credit to organizational changes, compensatory materials, new buildings, crash programs, and publicity, one must come face-to-face with the fact that the single most important feature of the educational program for the disadvantaged youngster is the teacher; thus, it is to personnel practices that the administrator must look to make greatest improvement in the program.

Probably the chief implication of the study is that city school administrators (indeed administrators in all communities) would do well to study the sources of satisfaction in their schools and then to ask, "What kind of people are attracted to such an environment?" Staffing practices and procedures should then be evaluated upon the most probable impact of such persons upon the pupils they serve. Failure to consider the environmental impact upon personnel results in a higher incidence of assigning the wrong people to the wrong classrooms.

An obvious place to begin to attack staffing problems is in the preservice training of teachers. Teachers-in-training should get course content, observational experiences, and intern experiences that better equip them to meet the demands of the inner city. There should be close cooperation between public schools and universities to develop, operate, and evaluate preservice programs. The programs at Hunter and Yeshiva Colleges and the Urban Teacher Preparation Program at Syracuse University (despite some problems inherent in each) are prototypes. However, special programs will not attract large numbers of prospective teachers, and the programs are so few in number that they will not noticeably reduce the staffing needs in large cities. Despite their usefulness and desirability, preservice training efforts will never meet the demand.

We must then proceed with the in-service development of existing staffs both to prevent their leaving the school and to increase their effectiveness. Especially in schools in changing neighborhoods, in-service education for teachers is too conventional, too little, and too late. In-service programs in the inner city school and in those schools in changing neighborhoods should be systematically directed toward the teaching-learning problems that typify the pupils served. These programs will have to deal with the sociological and psychological characteristics of the total teaching-learning process among disadvantaged children.

The program would also be improved substantially if there were more interaction between the teacher and the home. Parents whose children most need help do not come to the school. If one understands life in the lower-status home, he can understand why this should be so and he knows that there will be no increase in the number of parents who come to the school. The only viable alternative is that the school must go to the home. It is rare to find a teacher or an administrator in city slums, even though he may have worked there many years, who has visited many homes. Indeed, most of them know very little, if anything, about the homes or about the neighborhood. Lack of direct knowledge about the homelife of the youngsters they serve forces teachers to act on the basis of all manner of stereotypes, most of which are untrue for at least two thirds to three quarters of the pupils and some of which are untrue for all of the pupils. Educators in the Banneker School District in St. Louis learned that better education results from communication between teachers and parents. There teachers left the school and went to homes. In the process teachers found that their apprehensions about visiting homes were ill-founded. It is of importance to our discussion that even though parents may have changed somewhat in this interchange, teachers changed their orientation to disadvantaged pupils and their learning problems.

Steps must be taken to create a climate for change in the city system. It is a cliche, nevertheless true, that the large system resists change and maximizes the dysfunctional characteristics of bureaucracy. Such systems encourage resistance to change and discourage innovative and experiment-minded teachers and administrators. Creating a climate for change depends very much upon the appointment and placement of building principals. With a few outstanding exceptions in each city, current appointive procedures have made principals' offices collectively the greatest deterrent to change in the system. Due to bureaucratic modes of promotion, the second greatest deterrent to change in the city is in the central office staff. New procedures must break the lockstep of present practices and must be directed to identifying, recruiting, and selecting at least enough innovative and rebellious administrators to prevent stagnation within the system. Such administrators may be self-confident enough to face problems realistically with positive rather than defensive measures.

The suggestions made above deal with effecting deep and abiding changes in individuals *in process* of becoming effective teachers for deprived children. There are some administrative and organizational changes that might attract competent staff members and make their contributions to the educational program more effective.

First, and perhaps most controversial, we might (as Conant suggested) pay a premium to teachers in slum schools. It is well established that money is neither a good nor a sufficient motivator for work but it is an important inducement. Teachers' organizations oppose paying a premium for many reasons, some of them valid, many of them based on unsound premises. Though experience in some cities, such as Syracuse, shows that few if any teachers can be induced to teach in the slum school even *if extra money is offered,* it seems foolish, in view of the great need, to refuse to use money to attract even a few additional teachers. We must recognize three facts: (1) the practice of using salaries to attract and hold teachers is well established in the intersystem competition for personnel especially among the best known suburban districts in the country, (2) economic competition and differential ability to pay among school districts has brought about a wide discrepancy in the salaries paid to teachers in each state, even within counties; and (3) the teacher in the slum school does not receive many of the noneconomic rewards (such as hobnobbing with "good people" or having bright pupils to show off) that are so competitively sought by many of the same people who oppose paying her more. If none of these arguments moves the opposition, one can still assert that the teacher in the inner city deserves more on the well-established and often-practiced principle of extra-pay-for-extra-duty; for the job of the teacher in the disadvantaged neighborhood, if defined as it must be if the program is to improve, will require extra duty. Extra duty will evolve from the in-service programs, the establishment of rapport with the home, the search for more effective methods, and the meeting of nonacademic but educationally necessary demands from pupils.

Two other administrative changes require the reversal of traditional and compelling forces in the career development of metropolitan teachers and change agent. First, one might find more than sufficient arguments for giving teachers some assurance that their assignment in the inner city would have a foreseeable end to it, after which they would be guaranteed placement in a school serving more advantaged and academically talented pupils if they desired such placement. It is feasible that the teachers, when no longer faced with the prospect of endless tenure in the less desirable school, might not surrender to the seemingly insurmountable problems there and would utilize their best efforts to teach disadvantaged children. Furthermore, better morale results when professional workers have an opportunity to change the content of their jobs. Assuring transfer from the slum will run directly counter to the present practices that promote teachers out of the school and stigmatize those who remain.

A second attack upon current career patterns would take the form of policies and procedures to use only experienced teachers in the slum school. That this would require administrative ingenuity and courage is taken for granted; however, it has much to recommend it. Beginning teachers placed in the slum school have to solve two serious sets of problems simultaneously. Either set taken alone is enough to eliminate teachers from the system; encountered together they probably eliminate a large number of otherwise salvable teachers. One set of problems is involved in the process of *becoming a teacher;* they are difficult for every beginning teacher. A second set of problems arise from adjusting to the foreign environment of the slum school—a taxing task. If teachers could resolve their career-entrance problems in a school that is less threatening, they might then be better able to adjust to slum schools. Disadvantaged children would also be exposed to more expert teaching.

One obvious procedural change would be the assignment of all beginning teachers to schools in the outlying zones of the city (thus giving the added advantage of having no great number of them in any one school). A second change would be the assignment of experienced teachers to the slum schools. Teachers' organizations in some cities have opposed attempts to make such changes. Perhaps the new federal corps of teachers will be a means for accomplishing the same purposes.

Evidence is mounting that city school systems may be too large to accomplish their educational tasks. One commonly hears it said that no administrator could succeed in New York and Chicago. If the allegation is true, then it is clear that policy making and decision making must be decentralized. We must, it seems to me, reconstitute city school systems into smaller autonomous districts under boards of education responsible for developing local educational policies but deriving necessary financial resources from a metropolitan taxing authority that encompasses all the districts. Within the smaller districts, many curriculum decisions should be delegated to individual faculties or groups of faculties, and individual staffs should be encouraged to experiment with unique programs and processes. State recognition that city school systems need to be divided would not be a retrenchment from the principle that most school districts are too small; it is realization that the relationship between school size and educational quality reaches a point of diminishing returns. Experiences of the past decade indicate that the returns diminish rapidly as cities grow beyond populations of 500,000.

Any of the suggestions made here would raise concomitant problems if enacted. Such problems as could not be anticipated would have to be treated as they arose. Administrators will never escape problems (though they may ignore them for some time). Their task is to seek means of removing obstacles to sound educational programs for as many pupils as possible. Such obstacles are abundant and recently have become more apparent in the slum school. Improving urban education demands realistic appraisal of the metropolitan school complex and requires extraordinary and fundamental changes in personnel practices. No other change, however fully financed or publicized, can have so great an impact.

LEARNING EFFECTS OF INTEGRATION IN NEW ROCHELLE

T. G. Wolman *is administrative assistant for research and program development with the New Rochelle public school system. The following article was presented to the annual meeting of the American Psychological Association, September 4, 1964, under the title, "Some Initial Effects of Integrated Schooling on the Reading Achievement Scores of Transfer Students in New Rochelle Elementary Schools."*

New Rochelle, New York, is a city of some 83,000 residents, approximately 20 miles from Manhattan and situated in a country traditionally regarded as part of New York's more bucolic surroundings. It is, nevertheless, more of a microcosmic than a semirural community. Its population is heterogeneous in every sense: socially, economically, professionally, and ethnically.

Until June, 1963, when a controversial elementary school was permanently closed, there were twelve elementary schools, two junior high schools, and a comprehensive high school for its 12,000-plus public school population. One of these elementary schools was more than a half-century old and Negro children constituted 98 percent of its student body. An historic court decree required the abolition of *de facto* segregation by permitting optional transfers from this school for Negro students. Approximately half the parents of this body elected to make use of this prerogative until June, 1963, when a decision of the superintendent of schools and the board of education closed the building.

During the summer of 1963, a survey was conducted to observe what effects, if any, the integration of the first transfer students had had on academic achievement. Some of these students had already had one and some two years at other schools. Grade equivalent scores for reading comprehension on the Metropolitan Achievement Tests were selected as the measure of growth, although it was clearly understood that this served to measure only one aspect of possible change. No direct measurements of changes in self-esteem, motivation, and effort were available.

When the scores of transfer students from grades one through five were evaluated, the mean-grade equivalent scores showed a pattern of growth consistent with those for comparable socioeconomic and ethnic groups. Differences were not statistically significant. When one considers the factors militating *against* success in achievement for these transfer students, their ability to sustain a working level *at least* comparable to nontransfer pupils must be credited. The challenges to be met by these youngsters were several: adjust to new school staff and physical surroundings, the novelty of being bused to and from school, anxiety and apprehension as to acceptance by a largely white peer group, and the general aura of a political struggle to which many of them had been exposed directly and indirectly.

That these problems *must* have had potent impact on their ability to work is now almost axiomatic. Katz, Clark, Deutsch and others have, in their recent papers, all

From *Integrated Education,* December 1964/January 1965. Reprinted by permission of the author.

amply demonstrated the actuality of these and other factors in academic effort.* It was inferred, therefore, that this initial period of integration had been essentially positive, that the overall reading ability of these children had not been impaired and was at least sustained during this first stage of transfer.

Statistical analysis of the differences between the means of the reading scores for the transfer group and the nontransfer group (ethnically and socioeconomically comparable) and the white group (socioeconomically but not ethnically comparable) were found to have statistical significance. All of these groups, however, when compared at the fourth-grade level with a group of students from an exclusively white school population from affluent backgrounds, demonstrated statistically significant lower scores. In addition, 80 percent of the children from the upper-income white group achieved better than two years' growth in reading scores in a two-year period, while the other groups (low-income white and Negro) did *not* exceed 25 percent of their pupils with this extent of gain.

Here, too, as suggested in other studies, the socioeconomic milieu of students seems to serve as an intrinsic determinant of academic prowess.

Concerned next with the question of age and the point at which schools might be maximally influential in establishing the foundations for educational competence, we surveyed the kindergarten group. And it was here that more striking evidence of the positive effects of integrated schooling was demonstrated. The percentage of transfer children who achieved higher scores in the Metropolitan Reading Readiness Test was significantly higher than either of the two other nontransfer groups.

Here, too, however, the effect of social and economic conditions on the scholastic potential of very young children is evident. Youngsters from upper-income families continued to show greater competence. We can assume that exposure to favorable learning circumstances at an early enough age can have a salutary and compensatory effect on the educational potential of minority and otherwise deprived children.

The educational inferences for schools seemed to us to be clear. The need for early identification of reading problems, prekindergarten training, in-service education for teachers and administrators, better school-community relations with less accessible families, curriculum revision, and more appropriate texts and learning materials was easily inferred.

New Rochelle's school system has begun to expand its educational scope. Under the vigorous leadership of its superintendent, Dr. David G. Salten, the board of education and enterprising members of the system's administrative and teaching staff, efforts are being made to advance the progress of students with special learning needs. These efforts range from preschool to high school levels, from student to staff, from private philanthropies and teaching volunteers to government support, and from immediate changes of a preventive and remedial nature to research and extended observation.

---

*[Editor's Note: See, for example, Irwin Katz, "Review of Evidence Relative to Effects of Desegregation on the Intellectual Performance of Negroes," *American Psychologist,* June 1964; Kenneth B. Clark, *Dark Ghetto,* Harper & Row, New York, 1965; and Martin Deutsch, "Some Psychosocial Aspects of Learning in the Disadvantaged," *Integrated Education,* June-July 1965.]

There is much we have learned from the first years of integrated schooling that may promise more effective education for the disadvantaged. Most important, the program is part of a total plan for educational excellence which does not single out the underprivileged as its sole or primary focus but concerns itself with the academic development of all the system's pupils as well.

FAMILY AND EDUCATIONAL EXPERIENCES OF DISPLACED NEGRO CHILDREN

Robert L. Green *is associate professor of education, Michigan State University, and has served as director of the Citizenship Education Program, Southern Christian Leadership Conference.* **Marilyn E. Hayes** *is an instructor at Michigan State University. This is part of a cooperative research project, The Educational Status of Children in a District Without Public Schools, by Robert L. Green, Louis J. Hoffman, Richard J. Morse, Marilyn E. Hayes, and Robert F. Morgan. The project was supported by a grant from the Office of Education, U.S. Department of Health, Education, and Welfare, 1964.*

In the spring of 1959, the Prince Edward County, Virginia, Board of Supervisors voted not to reopen their public schools rather than to comply with the 1954 United States Supreme Court decision ordering public school integration. As a result of this school closure, Prince Edward County's Negro children were without public school education from fall, 1959, until fall, 1964, when the schools reopened in the context of limited integration. Organizations such as the American Friends Service Committee were able to send some of these children to school outside the county for periods ranging from one to four years; however, these instances were relatively few when compared to the total school age population, most of whom remained without public education and its commensurate opportunities for broadening social and academic contacts.

Prince Edward County, predominantly rural, possesses only one urban center, Farmville, with a population of approximately 5,000. A large percentage of the Negro population resides in the more remote areas of the county. Negro residents of the town are often isolated from the mainstream of social and cultural activities. It was a plausible assumption that those Negro children who had spent some time outside of the county would manifest certain different occupational aspiration, education aspiration, social outlook, and attitude toward their community and themselves than would those who had remained at home in the rather narrow confines of the county for the entire four-year period. Of special significance was the fact that some of those young people who had been away to school had lived in racially mixed neighborhoods, some with Caucasian families, and had attended integrated schools. In most instances, contact with a different society than that characterized by Prince Edward County was provided. The purpose of this report is to document and assess effects of a more open social milieu on young people previously the victims of the ultimate in educational deprivation.

From *Integrated Education,* **February/March 1966. Reprinted by permission of the authors.**

In order to determine the possible effects of such change, interviews were conducted with selected Negro students at Moton High School in Farmville, Virginia, after these young people had been back in the Prince Edward County school for one year. Eight students were interviewed for a period of one hour each. The ages ranged from sixteen through nineteen, represented by three females and five males. The interviewees were asked to discuss their experiences while away at school; their attitudes toward the schools, neighborhoods, and people with whom they came in contact; and the perceived attitudes of others toward them. The interviews were structured around a series of basic but open-ended questions.

Several of the subjects had lived with two or more families during the course of their education outside the county. At some time during their residence away from home, four of them had lived with white families; three had lived in an all-Negro neighborhood; four had lived in a mixed area; one had lived in an all-white neighborhood. Two of the students had attended biracial institutions where they had "lived in," and one subject continued to reside with his mother who had gone outside the county in order to continue teaching when the Prince Edward schools closed. In all instances where the subjects resided with host parents, a professional, middle-class, and reasonably affluent environment was encountered. Several of the subjects had been able to travel about the country with the host parents (both within and outside the state in which they were living temporarily). While traveling about, the young people accompanying the host families were generally well accepted by both Negroes and Caucasians.

Most of the interviewees indicated that they had had little or no difficulty adjusting to a new home, new people, a new neighborhood, and a new school. In general, they did not feel "strange" with respect to the changed environment or the individuals in it and were accepted and very well treated by their peers, their teachers, and the families with whom they resided. The young people away from home found so many opportunities to engage in interesting activities both within and outside the school matrix that they did not have much opportunity for loneliness. One student who had attended school in Dayton, Ohio, expressed the view held by the majority of those interviewed:

> I felt as though I was at home. The family was very good to me, and I fitted in very well with both the adults and the children in the family. I worked in well with the neighborhood and with the new school. No one made me feel strange, and relationships with other people (both Negro and white in the case of mixed neighborhoods and integrated schools) were not strained. I didn't feel much different there than I had at home.

However, there were two exceptions to the above. One girl who was twelve years old when she was sent to school in Morristown, New Jersey, had experienced difficulty in adjusting to peers and to the town in which she lived. A young man (aged nineteen when interviewed) had attended school in Baltimore, Maryland, for one year and had at first experienced some difficulty. His neighborhood was all white, and he felt somewhat uncomfortable living with white people. He was so well accepted by the family with whom he stayed, however, that he was soon able to overcome what he termed his "color-consciousness." This interviewee's experiences are especially interesting and informative. The interview is offered here *in toto*:

The American Friends arranged for me to go away to school after I told them I wanted to go away. As far as expenses go, I had $8.00 per week as an allowance from the people with whom I stayed. These people took care of all my expenses because they wanted to. They were quite prosperous people. I used to do odd jobs in the neighborhood such as shoveling snow for money from other people, but the family with whom I stayed wanted me to keep all that I made and still gave me the $8.00 per week allowance. This family had four children of their own—three boys and one girl—all small children. This was a white family, Quakers, and the man worked at the Social Security Bureau.

It was hard for me at first to adjust because I had to get used to staying with a white family. Nothing like this had ever happened to me in Prince Edward County where Negroes just didn't stay that close to white people, and I felt rather strange about it at first. For one thing, the white family with whom I stayed cooked differently than I was used to, and I had to learn to eat a different kind of food. The kids in the family took a while to learn how to act toward me, but they weren't unaccepting; they just had to get used to me, I guess. They liked me, but they didn't know quite what to make of me at first.

The family traveled a lot and this was one of the reasons it was very nice staying with them. I saw a lot of interesting things by traveling around with them. We went out of the locality almost every weekend. Sometimes we would go up to New York City. Often we would visit historical sites in the area. The man of the family was very interested in history and spent a lot of time visiting these sites. At Thanksgiving I went to California with them for two days and visited their relatives out there. Often we camped as we traveled, and I enjoyed this a great deal. We stayed for a week in Kansas one time and visited their relatives and also went to some of the schools in Kansas to observe how they were teaching and what these schools were like. While I was in Kansas I also visited the American Friends Service Committee University.

The neighborhood in which I lived was all white. At first, the people would "look" at me, but I soon became friendly with some of the neighbors and would even baby-sit for their children. The children in the neighborhood became friendly toward me after a while, but they had to get used to my being there and didn't try to become friendly right at first. I went to an integrated school about four or five miles away from where I lived. School was pretty hard, and I really had to get down to work and study. Ann and John (the man and woman of the family with whom I stayed) were very concerned about grades and I had to do well. My teachers were all white except two. The majority of the school was white. In the school, most of the Negro kids would look at me and didn't know what to make of my living with a white family. On the whole, though, I got on very well with the kids, both white and Negro, in the school. I really liked that school and wish I could have stayed there.

The family with whom I lived was Quaker. I really liked the Quaker worship. I am Baptist, myself, but I went to the Quaker services while I was in Baltimore. I liked to go there also because I liked the Quakers as people, and because I had a chance to meet people.

As I mentioned, it was a bit difficult at first getting acquainted in the neighborhood. Sue, the girl next door, did not know how to accept me at first, but we became good friends later. Many of the adults in the neighborhood never did accept me fully. Some of them were old southern people, and they did not really like me very much, possibly because I was friendly with a white girl and I guess they just couldn't understand or accept this. They were polite, but that was all.

The family with whom I stayed was so very nice. They kind of softened me up and helped me and made me want to help someone else in turn. I don't know just what it was, but they did something to me that has changed my outlook. I was a bit "hard-headed" before, and usually thought more of myself than of anyone else. But their helping me made me see that it is good to help other people too. Going away to school and staying with this family was the greatest thing that ever happened to me. After living with a white family I found that I was not color-conscious anymore, where I had been before. The only time I really thought about color was when we were traveling—sometimes strangers would really stare at us and this reminded me again that I was Negro. I was never made to feel that way by the family with whom I stayed, though.

I intend to join the Peace Corps when I finish a 26-week training program in electrical appliances which I am starting as soon as I graduate this June. I think it is a good idea to have some kind of a trade at which I can work if I ever need to. I doubt if this trade will help me much in the Peace Corps, but I still want to have it. I would like to go to some part of India with the Corps, and I hope I can do some work in human relations and agriculture while there. I want to help people in any way that I can, and this seems to be the way that I can do this best.

The young man in the above interview had experienced some difficulty in adjusting to being accepted by Caucasian members of the community. Most of the subjects did not indicate serious difficulty in this respect, and most of them appeared to be almost astonished by their favorable reception. One girl who had attended and lived at Berea College in Kentucky as one of three Negro students in her dormitory found herself to be very well accepted by the white students and teachers and hoped to return there to pursue a degree in nursing. One young man who had attended an academy in Virginia expressed amazement that both Negro and white students at this school, northern and southern alike, could sit down and objectively discuss racial issues without a "show of prejudice," as he expressed it.

Many of the host families had children of approximately the same age as the students; possibly this rendered it easier to make the adjustment to the new environment. Some of our subjects found that the younger children in the host family "were about the same age as my own brothers and sisters at home, and I felt toward them as I did toward my own family." In most instances, the girls helped the host mother of the house and related very well to her, thinking of her as a friend and companion. The boys also related well to the host fathers and perceived them as firm friends as well as parental figures. Boys and girls alike had their own tasks to perform in the home, and the families with whom the young people stayed apparently endeavored in this manner to foster a strong sense of responsibility toward work and school—believing, perhaps, that if the young people had duties to perform in the home, they would feel themselves to be more valid members of a family unit.

In this study, a concern was also with the influence that the host parents might have exercised in regard to choice of vocation on the part of the subjects. Many of the students have selected future occupations that were the same as, or closely related to, those of the host parents. Apparently the interviewees have chosen their host parents as reference figures with respect to vocations and even personal style of life. Because of their close contact with members of the professions, they came to realize that occupations heretofore perceived as unattainable might one day be open to them. Most of the young people who indicated a preference for professional occupations did not come from families with a professional background. One or both parents possessed only a grade-school education. Of the mothers, three had a grade-school education; two had completed high school; two had completed college. Of the fathers, five had a grade-school education; one had completed high school; and one had completed college. Occupationally, the mothers of these children consisted of two teachers, a worker in the school cafeteria, a cook who had been a secretary, a driver of a school bus, one domestic, and two full-time housewives. Of the fathers, one owned his own upholstery business, four were laborers (one in the local shoe factory, one on the railroad, one in construction, and one in the mines), one was a minister, and one was a farmer. In contrast, the young people indicated that they intended to pursue the following occupations upon graduation from high school: a political affairs major at George Washington University, a social worker in Prince Edward County, a Peace Corps volunteer, a mortician, an electrical or mechanical engineer, a corporation attorney, a nurse, and a secretary. Members of families with whom these young people had stayed at some time included the following occupations (some children resided with more than one host family while away at school): five housewives, one secretary, one teacher, one vice-president of a university, one employee in the Social Security Bureau, one mortician, one member of the advertising field, two electrical engineers, one technical writer in electronics, one machinist, and one lieutenant in the United States Navy. Some of our subjects had lived with families whose members included young people who were college graduates or who were at the time attending a university, whereas the subjects' own families had not included older children in college. A majority of the subjects expressed a desire to enter college, and where this was not explicitly mentioned, occupations were chosen that would necessitate training beyond high school including that provided by college.

There are other data bearing on the contention that the occupations of the host parents may be a factor in upgrading the educational and occupational aspirations of those young people who had been outside of the county to school.[1] For example, our findings indicate that those children who had attended schools outside the county for all or part of the four-year period expressed significantly higher educational and occupational aspirations than those young people who had not received formal schooling and who had remained in the county.

> The finding that the "education" group expressed significantly higher educational and occupational aspirations than the "no education" group seems to point to this important role the school plays in orienting children toward higher educational and occupational aspirations. The less informed "no education" group, exposed to fewer persons, particularly Negroes who have made such achievements, consequently aspired to lower levels of education and low-level occupations.[2]

Without exception, the subjects interviewed were very positive that they would be able to realize their goals. Their greatest concern was not with how they were going to finance their education, but with maintaining a sufficiently high grade-point average both in high school and in college. The children were very definite regarding what they wanted to do occupationally and expressed clearly and succinctly why they had chosen a particular vocation as a life work. All subjects, despite high goals, were realistic regarding the amount of education required to achieve that particular occupational goal.

Regarding opportunity itself, most of the subjects wished to leave the county in order to attend school and to work where they would have more and better opportunities for doing so. Many wanted to return to the cities or towns in which they had stayed while away at school, and if there was a college located in that city, they wished to attend it. They indicated that they already knew people in these areas, that they had friends there, and they had made contacts with individuals who might help

---

[1] Robert L. Green, Louis J. Hoffman, Richard J. Morse, Marilyn E. Hayes, and Robert F. Morgan, *The Educational Status of Children in a District Without Public Schools*, Cooperative Research Project No. 2321, United States Department of Health, Education, and Welfare, 1954.

[2] Green, *et. al., op. cit.*, p. 168.

them realize their goals. Once having been away from Prince Edward County, they tended to view the county in a different perspective. They noted even more acutely now its limitations and its lack of socioeconomic opportunities, and they wished to leave as quickly as possible after completing high school. Some considered themselves to have become sophisticated beyond whatever few advantages the county might have to offer and felt that life in the county was uninteresting and lacking in real challenge. As one interviewee expressed it, "A person can only stand still here." Only one child recognized that the county itself might possibly possess a challenge to a Negro: this was a girl who wanted to become a social worker so she could return to Prince Edward County and work toward making it a happier and better place in which to live. She felt that this would be doing a service not only to her people but to the state of Virginia as a whole, and that the upgrading of Negro life and opportunity would contribute to the betterment of all. "I might not live to see this come about," she stated, "but my grandchildren will. And somebody has to be willing to start."

During the interviews, probes were made to determine the young peoples' feelings about the schools they had attended while outside the county. The majority of the subjects interviewed considered school away from home as "OK, about the same as school anywhere, because we had lessons to do and homework to complete, and we had to study hard." The interviewees found the new schools to be more difficult than the Prince Edward County schools. One girl rated the school she had attended as so excellent in all respects that she would have liked to continue there. All of the schools attended by our subjects while living with host parents were biracial, both as to student body and faculty, and many, although not all, were in the North. An aspect of the new schools often discussed was the extensive and interesting variety of activities (basketball, football, various clubs and teams, etc.). These had been present only to a very limited degree in Prince Edward County. With the exception of one student, the students related very well to all their teachers, both Negro and white.

These interviews, although based on a limited number of subjects, illustrate what has already been apparent in the total body of data collected from Prince Edward County.[3] Living away from home in an environment different from what they had been used to produced new, more positive experiences; new, more positive reactions.

SCHOOL INTEGRATION AND ABSORPTION OF NEWCOMERS

> **David Gottlieb,** *former deputy director of research and evaluation, Job Corps, Office of Economic Opportunity, and now professor of human development and chairman of community services, College of Human Development, Pennsylvania State University, is co-author of* The American Adolescent *(Dorsey, 1964). This article is based on a paper delivered to the forty-second annual meeting of the American Orthopsychiatric Association, March 18, 1965.*

A young Negro student recently enrolled in a predominantly white urban high school said: "I wanted in and my folks wanted me to come here. This is a new school and they have a fine science program. But, man, is this place cold."

---

[3] *Ibid.*

From *Integrated Education,* **August/November 1965. Reprinted by permission of the author.**

His use of the term "cold" was in reference to his perception of the social climate of his school.

The continuing desegregation of American high schools will have far-reaching social, economic, and political implications. Social research on the detrimental effects of *de jure* segregation was an important argument in the supreme court decision of 1954.* The evidence presented in this case generated considerable controversy among social scientists as well as those actually involved in the education of the young. More recently, the attention of social scientists and the public has focused more on *de facto* segregation in high schools. Here, too, research findings, as well as general observations, are contradictory.

The specific aim of the research presented here was to assess the types of student social systems which emerge in high schools with varying racial compositions. The purpose of this investigation was not to come up with the ideal racial balance or to see which racial formula most efficiently produces high scores on standardized tests. Rather our concern is with noting what occurs *within* the *social* system of the high school as a result of the racial composition of the student body and faculty.

Data to be presented here were obtained from three high schools located in a large midwestern city. Each school has more than 1,500 students. There are two major differences among these schools. They vary in the racial composition of the school population and they differ greatly in physical appearance and educational facilities. As might be anticipated, the oldest school with the poorest facilities had the largest Negro population.

School A has a predominantly white student body and faculty. Negro students make up 6 percent of the population; Negro faculty, less than 3 percent. School B has what many would call a racially balanced student population—47 percent Negro. Ninety percent of the faculty is white. School C is virtually all Negro in student composition with white students making up less than 2 percent of the student body. The faculty in this school is about one-fourth Negro.

While there is some variation in the socioeconomic background of the students, they all tend to come from working-class families. The reported median educational level of the parents was 9.9 years for School A, 8.9 years for School B, and 8.6 years for School C.

While racial composition is a crucial factor in this research, it should be kept in mind that we are talking about an ever-changing variable. As is the case in many urban areas, public schools undergo steady and frequently dramatic changes in racial composition. Since these data were collected, there have been changes in Schools A and B. Both have experienced the exodus of white students and a growing enrollment of Negro students. Only School C has remained stable since the pattern of urban residential mobility rarely includes whites moving into Negro neighborhoods.

Involvement in School Activities

The degree to which students are integrated within the social setting of the school can be determined in part by their involvement in the various extracurricular activities offered by the school. Only in School A were Negro students less likely to be involved in extracurricular activities than their white peers. In addition, School A shows the

*[Editor's Note: See Appendix A, "Text of Supreme Court Rulings (*Brown* v. *Board of Education*, ...).")]

least variation between the proportion of students in each racial group involved in these activities. As there is a progression from a small minority of Negro students, School A, to a growing Negro student population, schools B and C, there is a decline in the activity participation of white students. This decline reaches its lowest point in School C, where white students are only a small percent of the student population. Data reflect a departure on the part of the white population, and an increased involvement on the part of the Negro population; this finding evinces the importance of examining in greater detail the social processes by which Negro adolescents begin, maintain, and enhance their involvement in the social system of the high school. These data enable us to determine whether (1) there is an undifferentiated mass exodus on the part of white students who have already been in the system, or whether (2) there is a gradual giving up and taking on of certain roles and functions by both racial groups in the school. It will be shown that as racial change takes place, the withdrawal of whites from the system is hardly an undifferentiated mass exodus; on the contrary, there is definite structure in the changes in roles and functions of Negro and white students in the social system of the high school. It will be shown that Negro and white students develop distinct social systems that result in both racial groups maintaining their own forms of racial segregation.

In terms of increasing Negro participation in the high school, we would anticipate the following:

1. In situations where there is an already established social system of white students, the incoming Negro group will enter first into those activities that call for a minimum of social or unstructured interpersonal contact between the races. That initial participation with the school will be limited to those activities that are not perceived as prestige-giving by the white majority or the Negro minority.
2. As the proportion of Negro youths within a school increases and they become a sizable segment of the population, there will be the emergence of two separate systems. In this case there will be clearer distinctions between the races with respect to the type of activity in which the student is involved and the prestige attributed to those engaged in the activity.
3. When there has been a total changeover in population and the Negro youth constitute the social system, there will be a decline in their concentration in certain activities. In addition, they will show greater variation in the kinds of activities which they perceive as giving one prestige with his peers. In this case, their behavior within the school will not be too different from any other group of adolescents of similar backgrounds and high schools.

In looking at the type of school activity engaged in by the students in each of the sample schools, we find that while there is some variation between students of the same race in different schools, the most frequent pattern is for variation between Negro and white youths in the same school. In School A, comparison of both males and females from both racial groups shows that there are five out of ten activities in which the differential of involvement exceeds 5 percent. Of particular interest are the activities in which both groups of students are more likely to be involved. For the Negro males in School A, athletics, band or orchestra, vocational clubs, and chorus are the primary areas for involvement. For the white males, the five activities most frequently noted are athletics, student government, band or orchestra, hobby clubs, and school newspaper. The two activities in which both groups have a high rate of involvement are athletics and band-orchestra which are highly structured activities requiring little interpersonal contact. Student government, school newspaper, and hobby clubs, on the other hand, demand a closer and more consistent contact frequently taking place in a relatively informal setting.

The pattern among the females in School A is not too different from that observed among the males. The one exception is the Negro female involvement in hobby clubs; this high level of involvement, however, can be explained by the fact that the club to which the Negro girls are referring is a school-sponsored popular music group organized by the Negro girls.

In School B there are seven groups among the males and eight among the females where differences in activity involvement exceed five percent. In addition, there are similarities between Schools A and B in the types of activities in which both racial groups are involved. Finally, the findings for School B lend support to the proposition that with an increase in the Negro population there will be indications of the emergence of two separate systems.

For School C, the school with few white students, the Negro students show a greater spread in activity involvement. As suggested earlier, in a school in which the process of racial change is completed and the Negro student body does in fact become the social system, there will be less concentration in specific activities and a more even diffusion in all activities within the school. Although the white group in School C is quite small, it is interesting to note that it is very much like the minority Negro group in School A in that these white students cluster within but a few activities.

In discussing the various consequences of change in racial composition, we noted that in addition to variation in activity involvement there would be differences in the prestige attributed to various roles held by students within the system.

Leadership in the Social System

In order to get some measure of the status structure, each student was asked, "Who, in your estimation, are the real leaders in your school?"

Beginning with School A, we find that among both the Negro males and females there is a contradiction between the activities in which they are involved and the activities which they see as important to leadership. Student council, for example, was an activity in which Negro students showed limited participation. Yet, they perceive it as important to student leadership. Athletics, on the other hand, attracts Negro students but is given little weight as a means to student status. Finally, Negroes place greater emphasis on being a "good student" than white students. This would be anticipated, given our initial position, that Negroes in a minority situation will seek entrance into the system through more formal activities. In this case, Negro students show stronger dependency on the formal system by seeking rewards from adults in the system through taking on the role of the "good student."

In School B, where we would predict the emergence of two separate social systems, we find greater consensus between both Negroes and whites as to what leads to leadership and activity involvement. Negroes are more likely than whites to be involved in athletics, and they see this activity as important to leadership. Conversely, whites are lower on athletic activities and give athletics less status. Student government involvement is higher for whites, and they are more likely to see it as a means of leadership than are the Negro students.

The Racial Composition of Informal Peer Groups

It is a well-established empirical finding that a racial or ethnic minority will usually show higher self-preference than a racial or ethnic majority. Lundberg and Dickson have shown that Negro high school students show greater self-preference than whites, and that their self-preference is greatest for friendship choices, as intermediate for work, and is least for leadership.[1]

In the present study, sociometric data were collected only for friendship choices. All students were asked to name their three best friends. From this data, the self-preference levels of each race-sex group in each school were determined.

As expected, Negroes show higher self-preference than whites. Within each racial group, girls show higher racial self-preference than boys.

It was stated earlier that, in a minority situation where there is an already established social system of white students, the incoming Negro group will enter first into those activities that call for a minimum of social contact with whites. Indeed, the Negro minority in School A does show a high level of self-preference in their choice of friends. In this situation, their participation in the school and in other activities is largely limited to those activities that require a minimum of cross-race interaction. This high level of self-preference persists in the situation where the Negro population is greater, in School B, with the emergence of two separate social systems. In addition, from analysis of School B's sociometric choices, we found a decline in the proportion of cross-race choices made by white students. This is further evidence that there are two separate social systems in School B, one Negro and one white.

The Negro minority at School A and the white minority at School C both showed a marked tendency to choose as their three best friends persons not in the school. The percent of choices made within the school shows the increasing alienation of whites from the school as the proportion of Negroes increases. In School A, the whites are about twice as likely to choose within the school as are the Negroes. In School B, there is no marked difference in in-school choices among Negroes and whites. In School C, the Negroes become most committed to the school, and the whites highly alienated. This enables us to make the following proposition: the level of commitment of students to their high school varies directly with the proportion of students in the school who are of their own race.

Based on the present findings, several conclusions can be drawn.

Regardless of the actual racial composition of the school, there appears to be a minimum of interaction between Negro and white students. Despite the presence of both racial groups in a single school, the pattern is for the emergence of two separate social systems established along racial lines.

[1] George A. Lundberg and Lenore Dickson, "Interethnic Relation in a High School Population," *American Journal of Sociology*, Vol. 38 (1952), pp. 1-10; George A. Lundberg and Lenore Dickson, "Selective Association Among Ethnic Groups in a High School Population," *American Sociological Review*, Vol. 17 (1952), pp. 23-35. A recent study by St. John confirms this result: see Nancy Hoyt St. John, "De Facto Segregation and Interracial Association in High School," *Sociology of Education*, Vol. 37 (1964), pp. 334-338.

A form of racial segregation continues with Negro students less likely than whites to be involved in those academic and extracurricular activities associated with entrance into college and professionally oriented occupations.

It would appear then that it is not sufficient merely to mix students if we seek to make integration a meaningful and worthwhile experience. There is a great difference between the biracial and the integrated school. The former is accomplished by the "mixing" of students of different races. For example, by busing in a group of Negro students, we have a biracial situation but not necessarily a school setting where students are equally *involved* in all aspects of the school program.

The meaningful integration of schools cannot be accomplished within the current framework and structure of many of our urban public school systems. As changes have occurred in the population of the urban school, so must changes take place in the functions of urban schools in order to absorb newcomers into the system.

General Recommendations

The concluding section of this paper will deal with certain strategies that might be applied in order to maximize and maintain integration within our urban schools. Each of the alternative strategies presented here is based on the proposition that most people, regardless of race or class, view school and formal education as making the difference between the good life and a life of social and economic deprivation. Commitment to this belief, across all population lines, has in fact done much to dispel the popular notion that concern for the education of its youth is the exclusive sentiment of only the more affluent American parent.

Given this concern and commitment it would seem that the more attractive the school becomes in terms of the educational benefits it offers, the less salient other factors will be to the clientele of the school.

A visible example is found in the work of the North Carolina Advancement School, organized in 1964. This residential school is located in Winston-Salem, North Carolina. Briefly, the program is directed at adolescents who have been identified as academic underachievers. They come to live and study at the Advancement School for a period of three months. During the initial planning stages, much concern was expressed by both educational and behavioral science consultants as to the conflict that would arise within the school since this was to be an interracial program. Local school superintendents presented a similar view maintaining that white parents, as well as some Negro, would not allow their children to room with others of a different race.

These prophesied developments, however, were not forthcoming. Some two hundred students have entered the school and not one has withdrawn for racial reasons nor has any student refused to share a room with someone because of race. The school is totally integrated, with race not playing a part in where students live or study. Race is not the variable that predicts involvement in various aspects of the social system nor does it account for variations in the types of educational programs in which the student is enrolled.

The staff of this school has initiated a policy that successfully fulfils the educational desires adults have for their children. This does not mean that the school has necessarily changed parental attitudes. Rather, parents are placed in a position where they must decide which is more important—the perceived end value of this program or personal feelings about racial segregation. It is apparent by the actions of the parents that perceived educational benefit for their children places other feelings in a secondary position.

Given this commitment to the importance of education on the part of parents, it would seem that a program directed at enhancing the status of the urban school might, in part at least, lessen the barriers to school integration. The following alternative strategies are suggested with this goal in mind.

1. We should supplement the busing of children with a program of busing teachers. Local school systems should identify outstanding teachers and bring them into schools undergoing racial integration. This could be done on a rotating basis with teachers representing different skills and talents involved in different phases of the integration program. This in-migration of experienced teachers will serve three purposes: (a) to give added necessary help to Negro youth who frequently find themselves in academic difficulty when moving from a segregated to interracial school setting. (b) the presence of these special teachers would make clear that school administrators do not mean to abandon the school because of a change in racial composition, and (c) this approach would tend to offset the too-typical pattern of the exodus of experienced white teachers that seems to come with the arrival of Negro students.

2. Added support in the way of new and exciting educational innovations should be given to these schools. The latest in educational and teaching technology should not be confined to schools being built in the suburbs and fringes of the city but must find its place in urban schools as well.

3. Work with the newcomer once he arrives in the school. The absorption process should include the integration of newcomers into all phases of the school system. Every effort should be made to enroll Negro students in all extracurricular activities. This means that Negro students should be made aware of how one gains entrance into the student newspaper, student council, debate and science clubs, and the like. Segregation in extracurricular school activities minimizes interaction between racial groups and restricts opportunity for exposure to new and different activities for incoming students.

4. The absorption process must include the breaking-down of curricular stereotype where Negro youths ultimately end up in vocational educational programs as opposed to the college preparatory route. In part, the heavier enrollment of Negroes in terminal high school curriculums arises from their lack of knowledge as to other alternatives available to them. The deprivation of their background minimizes their understanding of both the scope of the occupational world and the educational courses required for goal attainment. It is important, then, that students not only understand how the system works but what it takes to make it within the system.

5. Recognizing the fact that too frequently urban schools do not have the professional personnel to fulfill needed programs, other resources could be utilized. There is certainly sufficient evidence that there are, for example, college students eager and able to assist in the socialization process. A variety of colleges already have well-organized student groups working within public school systems in order to assist teachers and counselors.

6. The organization of peer tutorial programs. In this case, students more accomplished in certain educational areas than their peers could assist in the learning process. There would be some value in structuring such a program along racial lines. Empirical research makes it clear that Negroes, especially in relation to whites and in task-oriented situations, have relatively low self-concepts. There is also general agreement between the self-concept of Negroes and the concept that whites have of Negroes. This situation may be explained by the fact that in most everyday activities involving Negroes and whites, Negroes play the subordinate role. As a result, Negro youth have few prestige-role models to absorb and emulate. At the same time, white youth have only limited contact with Negroes who do hold prestige positions with the exception of athletes and entertainers.

The carry-over of this social concept phenomenon is found in other phases of this research where we find that both Negro and white students see Negro teachers as having less ability in helping the student attain his goals than do white teachers.

In order to bring about some change in these racial perceptions, the peer tutorial system would be structured so that higher achieving Negro youth would be "teaching" white youth. Hopefully, through this experience, Negro youth would enhance their own self-concept and white youth might develop a more positive concept of the Negro.

7. Along similar lines it is obvious that Negro teachers and administrators must be distributed through the school system in a manner unlike that which is found in the community we studied. The placement of Negro personnel should not be based on the number of Negro students in the school. It is important that both Negro and white students have greater contact with Negro teachers and administrators.

The suggestions made here do not directly touch upon the business of the formal learning process itself. Little is being said about the type of curriculum or pedagogical techniques to be employed. Our approach has been to view the school as a social system where participants interact and this interaction is closely related to attitudes, expectations, roles, and status. These factors cannot and should not be separated from cognitive learning. It is for this reason that every effort must be made not only to understand the dynamics of the social system but to initiate intervention techniques which will produce a system that maximizes goal attainment for all students.

BIBLIOGRAPHY FOR PART FIVE

Armor, David. "The Racial Composition of Schools and College Aspirations of Negro Students," in *Racial Isolation in the Public Schools.* Vol. II, Appendix C2. Washington, D.C.: Government Printing Office, 1967.

Ausubel, David P. "A Teaching Strategy for Culturally Deprived Pupils: Cognitive and Motivational Considerations," *School Review* (Winter 1963).

Birch, Herbert G. "Intelligence, Ethnic Origin, and Integration," in *Proceedings of the Third Annual Invitational Conference on Urban Education, 1964.* New York: Graduate School of Education, Yeshiva University, n.d.

Blake, Elias, Jr. "Color Prejudice and the Education of Low Income Negroes in the North and West," *Journal of Negro Education* (Summer 1965).

————, *A Comparison of Intraracial and Interracial Levels of Aspiration*. Ph.D. dissertation, University of Illinois, 1960. *Dissertation Abstracts*, XX, 1960, p. 4586.

Bloom, Richard, Martin Whiteman, and Martin Deutsch. "Race and Social Class as Separate Factors Related to Social Environment," *American Journal of Sociology* (January 1965).

Bond, Horace Mann. *A Study of Factors Involved in the Identification and Encouragement of Unusual Academic Talent among Underprivileged Populations*. Atlanta: Atlanta University, 1967.

Boyd, G. F. "The Levels of Aspiration of White and Negro Children in a Non-Segregated Elementary School," *Journal of Social Psychology*, Vol. 36 (1952).

Cramer, M. Richard, Charles E. Bowerman, and Ernest Q. Campbell. *Social Factors in Educational Achievement and Aspirations among Negro Adolescents*. 2 vols. Chapel Hill (N.C.): Institute for Research in Social Science, 1966.

Davis, Allison. "Cultural Factors in Remediation," *Education Horizons* (Summer 1965).

Elliott, Merle H., and Alden W. Badal. "Achievement and Racial Composition of Schools," *California Journal of Educational Research* (September 1965).

Goodman, Mary Ellen. *Race Awareness in Young Children*, rev. ed. New York: Collier Books, 1964.

Gordon, Edmund W., and Doxey A. Wilkerson. "A Critique of Compensatory Education" in *Compensatory Education for the Disadvantaged*. New York: College Entrance Examination Board, 1966.

Gottlieb, David. "Teaching and Students: The Views of Negro and White Teachers," *Sociology of Education* (Summer 1964).

Kaplan, Henry K., and Anthony J. Matkom. "Peer Status and Intellectual Functioning of Negro School Children," *Psychology in the Schools* (April 1967).

Katz, Irwin. "Review of Evidence Relative to Effects of Desegregation on the Intellectual Performance of Negroes," *American Psychologist* (June 1964).

————. "Status of Research on School Desegregation," *IRCD Bulletin* [Yeshiva University] (September 1965).

Kurokawa, Minako. "Childhood Accident as a Measure of Social Integration," *Canadian Review of Sociology and Anthropology*, III (1966).

Lortie, Dan C. "Towards Educational Equality: The Teacher and the Educational Park," in *Racial Isolation in the Public Schools*, Vol. II, Appendix D2.4. Washington, D.C.: Government Printing Office, 1967.

Miller, Sidney, and others. *A Comparative Study of Attitudes and Factors Influencing the Decision of Negro Parents of Seventh Grade Students to Participate in the Seattle School Transfer Program to Improve Racial Balance*. Seattle School of Social Work, University of Washington, 1965.

Morland, J. Kenneth. "A Comparison of Race Awareness in Northern and Southern Children," *American Journal of Orthopsychiatry* (January 1966).

————. "The Development of Racial Bias in Young Children, *Theory into Practice*, II (1963).

———. "Racial Recognition in Nursery School Children in Lynchburg, Virginia," *Social Forces* (December 1958).

———. "Racial Self-Identification: A Study of Nursery School Children," *American Catholic Sociological Review* (Fall 1963).

Orum, Anthony M. "A Reappraisal of the Social and Political Participation of Negroes," *American Journal of Sociology* (July 1966).

Pearl, Authur. "[Ability] Grouping Hurts the Poor," *Southern Education Report* (December 1966).

Pederson, Lee A. "Non-Standard Negro Speech in Chicago," in William A. Stewart (ed.), *Non-Standard Speech and the Teaching of English.* Washington, D.C.: Center for Applied Linguistics, Modern Language Association for America, 1964.

Pettigrew. Thomas F. "Adult Consequences of Racial Isolation and Desegregation in the Schools," in *Racial Isolation in the Public Schools,* Vol. II, Appendix C5. Washington, D.C.: Government Printing Office, 1967.

Platoff, Joan. Preschool Prototype: An Integrated Semi-Cooperative Nursery School," *Young Children* (March 1966).

Romano, Edith. *Implementing Intercultural Education: A Frame of Reference.* Syracuse (N.Y.): Central New York School Study Council, Syracuse University.

Scott, Ralph. "First to Ninth Grade IQ Changes of Northern Negro Students," *Psychology in the Schools* (April 1966).

St. John, Nancy Hoyt. "De Facto Segregation and Interracial Association in High School," *Sociology of Education* (Summer 1964).

———. "The Effects of Segregation on the Aspirations of Negro Youth," *Harvard Educational Review* (Summer 1966).

Shores, J. Harlan. "What Does Research Say about Ability Grouping by Classes?" *Illinois Education* (December, 1964).

Singer, Dorothy. *Interracial Attitudes of Negro and White Fifth-Grade Children in Segregated and Unsegregated Schools.* Ed.D. dissertation, Columbia University, 1966 (University Microfilm, 67-2836).

Webster, Staten W. "The Influence of Interracial Contact on Social Acceptance in a Newly Integrated School," *Journal of Educational Psychology,* LII (1961).

Wilson, Alan B. "Residential Segregation of Social Classes and Aspirations of High School Boys," *American Sociological Review* (December 1959).

Zanoff, Richard B. "The Attitudinally Disadvantaged Teacher," *Urban Review* (December 1966).

Part Six

Comparative Aspects

The comparative perspective is valuable for Americans because it helps them see their own problems more clearly. Racism, although not peculiar to America, has taken a distinctive shape in this country. In no other modern western country is it as imbedded in everyday life. South Africa is the only possible exception to this statement. As the article on that country demonstrates, officially sponsored racism in the educational system has taken giant strides in recent years. In New Zealand and Australia, however, color is a prominent but not a pervasive national problem. England is somewhere between: In numbers, the "color problem" touches about one million persons or two percent of the population. In intensity, however, certain of what are increasingly called "American" overtones have made their appearance.

What makes color so explosive on the contemporary world scene is its connection everywhere with poverty and powerlessness. Efforts to remedy both have not made general headway in recent years. American events can be evaluated within this same framework. But wherever we look in the world of color, education is regarded as a necessity second only to food. Throughout the new African nations, the schools and universities are growing by leaps and bounds and yet remain insufficient. This hunger for schooling is a response to the need for new skills but also is symbolic of the drive for intellectual independence.

SCHOOL INTEGRATION IN ENGLAND

At the time of this debate, **Sir Edward Boyle** *was British Minister of Education. This article was taken from* Hansard *(Nov. 27, 1963, cols. 437-444).*

As the Honorable Gentleman the Member for Huddersfield, East (Mr. J. P. W. Mallalieu) said in introducing this debate, we have been discussing for some time earlier today the question how many immigrants should be admitted. Now we are dealing with the certainly no less important question how we can achieve integration between the communities who live in this country, and I think that perhaps especially in the week of President Kennedy's death I must at the start state to the House my own belief that the problem of racial relations, and of integration versus segregation, will continue for generations to be one of the most important facing the free world. I am, therefore, very grateful to the honorable Gentleman for having enabled us to have a debate on this subject.

I completely agree with the honorable Gentleman when he says that all experience suggests that children are, by nature, free of racial prejudice. I heard a very wise teacher in Birmingham say at a conference recently that we shall achieve integration in this country when the children of different races attend one another's birthday parties in their homes as a matter of course. I think that that is true. Children of different races tend to play and learn together very easily if adults do not put them off with their own fears and superstitions. The school is, therefore, of great importance as the obvious instrument for achieving integration.

I am not, of course, directly responsible for running the schools, but my approach to this is a very simple one. It seems to me that I am responsible quite clearly to this House for all children who are resident in this country, whatever their intelligence, whatever their race or color, and receiving education according to their age and ability.

After all, one of the strongest arguments we all use when we advocate educational advance is this. We say very truly today that our children tend to be more equal as physical specimens than they ever were before, and that today the average child of one and a half or two years of age is a much better physical specimen than the average child of that age in the past, but the opportunities children have in their homes for learning and gaining knowledge of England can be very unequal; and just as they can be unequal as between native children, as one says so often, so there are greater inequalities of opportunity between native children and immigrant children. It is, to my mind, for that reason that this is a subject which must certainly be taken very seriously indeed.

So far as I can influence these matters at all it is my own hope that schools will not become segregated. That is to say, I do not wish to see in this country—and I am sure no one in this House wishes to see—*laissez faire* acceptance of what one might call *de facto* segregation between immigrant schools and native schools. I am sure that that is wrong for two reasons.

In the first place, in the interests of general policy for racial integration, it is my view that efforts must be made to prevent individual schools from becoming only

From *Integrated Education,* **June/July 1964.**

immigrant schools. Secondly, there is the educational point of which we must not lose sight. If possible, it is desirable on educational grounds that no one school should have more than about 30 percent of immigrants. I have the greatest admiration for the hundreds, indeed thousands, of admirable teachers in the country who are coping with the problem. I will mention them particularly in one context. But I am sure that the education problems that one gets above the level of 30 percent immigrant children become infinitely harder and perhaps impossible to tackle.

Let us be under no illusions as to how difficult the problem is from the point of view of local education authorities.

It is easy enough for us in the House to pronounce general principles, but I have every sympathy with a local authority and its staff who actually have to tackle the problem. For example, one must realize the difficulty in places where nearly a whole neighborhood is taken over by immigrant families. The school serving the neighborhood will cease to have a sufficient supply of native children, and it is both politically and legally more or less impossible to compel native parents to send their children to a school in an immigrant area if there are places for them in other schools.

Moreover, even when native parents continue to live alongside immigrants, they will often seek to transfer their children to more distant nonimmigrant schools if their local school has more than about 30 percent of immigrant children. That is the sort of problem that a local authority has to tackle.

When I speak of the importance of all children receiving a proper education, I mean all children—that is to say, immigrant children and native children. One must recognize the perfectly legitimate anxiety of many of the parents of what I call the native children; one must recognize the reasonable fear of many parents that their children will get less than a fair share of the teachers' attention when a great deal of it must of necessity be given both to language teaching and to the social training of immigrant children.

So I say, on the general principle, by all means let us stand firmly in this House against segregation between native schools and immigrant schools. I hope that the House will never be attracted by the spuriously respectable doctrine which has gone by the name of "separate but equal." In practice, immigrant schools, if separate, will never be equal. But let us realize at the same time the legitimate fears of the parents of native-born children and let us very fully realize the particular problems, administrative problems not least, with which any local authority will be faced.

It is fair to say that lately public attention has centered on the particular instance of this problem as it has affected Southall, in Middlesex. I want to mention this subject because I addressed a meeting of parents there on 15th October. In a political life of about thirteen years in this House, it was one of the best public meetings that I have attended. We had about four hundred people in a large hall. I talked for twenty-five minutes, we had a long question time, and I thought the spirit of the meeting was admirable and the questioning extremely thoughtful and constructive. Nothing more disreputable happened than, as *The Times* fairly reported, a British Union banner being rather unceremoniously unfurled and a rather damp paper parcel being undone at the end and very few leaflets being given out. The spirit of the meeting was absolutely admirable.

My department is due to meet the Middlesex and Southall education authorities in December to work out arrangements for distributing Indian and Pakistani children over the schools of the borough. I must regretfully tell the House that one school, Beaconsfield School, must be regarded now as irretrievably an immigrant school. The important thing to do is to prevent this happening elsewhere.

To look on the brighter side, I must say that the schools of Southall have coped extremely well with this problem. There has been a real burden on Beaconsfield Road School. The two headmistresses, both of whom I met, have done a really first-class job and I was struck at the meeting by how admirable were the contributions made by the teachers who were present.

I am certain that the spirit in Southall is extremely good on this subject. The aim is to lessen the concentration in Beaconsfield Road School, but, at the same time, that particular area has changed its character so much that the problem there might be insuperable when it comes to preventing it becoming an immigrant school.

I have also been to a conference in Birmingham on this subject. I attended at my own request. I am greatly impressed by the manner in which Birmingham is tackling this question. But anyone who knows the Director of Education, Sir Lionel Russell, will not be surprised. The education committee has done extremely well and is getting good cooperation from the leaders of the West Indian community. I know just how well those leaders are helping the authority.

I want to make one or two remarks about the practical steps that can be taken. I take account of the need for extra teachers to cope with immigrants by giving the authorities concerned additions to their teacher quotas. I announced to Southall that we have made deliberately a small addition there. It is always difficult with a quota, however. The more exceptions one makes the less fairly the system tends to work. But I am sure that it is right that we should bear in mind the need for extra teachers to cope with immigrants.

I certainly will support any authority which tries to spread immigrant children by introducing zoning schemes. This must be a matter of cooperation rather than compulsion, but I can promise any authority which attempts to spread immigrant children my strongest support insofar as it lies with me.

As far as I can fit this in with my other engagements, I shall always be ready to travel to various parts of the country where this is a real problem to see whether there is help I can give or to answer parents' questions, because this is a highly important subject both for the present and the future.

We shall certainly do all we can to disseminate advice and information about teaching of immigrant children. Her Majesty's inspectors aim to do this all the time in their normal contacts with teachers and authorities and the pamphlet which will be published on 29th November is the fruit of a number of years of study.

Finally, I have asked the under-secretary in the schools branch of my department to take special responsibility for advising me on these matters, and I am considering whether it might not be possible to strengthen this particular branch of the Ministry so as to ensure that adequate work is done in collecting and disseminating information on this subject. I agree entirely that there are a number of interesting experiments, not least at Huddersfield, and that it is very important that this knowledge should be as widely shared as possible.

This is a subject which I think would well merit a longer debate on a number of occasions. Let us remember that the present immigrant settlers will produce an increasing number of children. Immigrant children as they reach maturity may well reproduce in larger numbers than perhaps some other parts of the population. This is not just a short-term matter, but a long-term question as well. It affects secondary as well as primary education. In my constituency I know that there is a feeling among some teachers that we tend to think relatively not enough about it in the secondary education context.

I have every sympathy for those who feel difficulties in a new community, and I ask all concerned to think not just about the immediate problem of today, not just to compare the problem of today with the Britain of ten years ago, but above all, to see that in tackling it we help to build the sort of Britain and the sort of local communities we all wish to see for the future.

[Editorial note: On December 6, 1963, the author met with representatives of the Middlesex County Council and the Southall Divisional Executive, as well as head teachers and parents. A press release from the Ministry of Education reported: "There was general agreement that the best approach to the problem was to spread the immigrant school population more widely in the area, in order to keep the proportion as nearly as possible no higher than one-third in any school. There was discussion of the methods available to the local authority—with the cooperation of parents—for bringing this about and of the ways in which the Ministry might be able to help."]

EDUCATION FOR AFRICANS IN SOUTH AFRICA

Len Bloom, *formerly a member of the psychology department at the University College of South Wales and Monmouthshire, is now with The University of Zambia.*

South Africa is an authoritarian state with a modern industrial and urban sector, and like all authoritarian states, its educational system and policy are intimately linked with the governing ideology.

The central problem in South African educational policy is to reconcile the needs of a modern economy and a racialistic ideology. More concretely: How far, if at all, can Apartheid be maintained in a society whose economic system demands increasing integration of blacks and whites? How can rigid stratification be preserved without too drastically limiting the growth of the literate and skilled African population that is demanded by the economic system?

Thus, we are faced with a number of paradoxes. The education of Africans is inferior in quality and in quantity to that of other groups, yet there is a thin trickle of Africans who have been permitted—and have managed—to go beyond primary schooling to complete university or professional courses. There has been a steady (though grossly inadequate) increase of the total amount spent upon African education; yet the *per capita* cost is very low, and the heavy wastage after the early stages of primary schooling is tolerated. South Africa is severely short of skilled and professional people, yet there is a mass of laws and customs that effectively bar all but a tiny number of Africans from higher occupations.

These paradoxes are partially resolved if one recalls that the total population of South Africa is about 17.5 million, of whom about 67 percent (12 million) are

From *Integrated Education,* **August/November 1965. Reprinted by permission of the author.**

Africans, 20 percent (3 million) are whites, 10 percent (1.75 million) are colored (of mixed descent) and the rest, about 3 percent (0.5 million) are of Indian descent.[1]

The whites feel outnumbered and have a powerful feeling of group isolation. During the three turbulent centuries of South Africa's modern history, the whites have built an "impenetrable armour around themselves—the armour of racial purity and self preservation,"[2] which expresses itself politically in the concept of white supremacy, baasskap. Dr. H. J. Verwoerd recently said that "it is true that there is white control today. There is white supremacy—white baasskap."[3]

Coupled with subjective feelings of white group-consciousness, there is the assumption that Africans are racially different from whites. Eiselen, the main architect of Apartheid, argues that the African "is a person of a different type" between whom and the whites there are such sharp and deep biosocial differences that no understanding between the groups can ever form.[4] The terms of reference of the Commission on Native Education (headed by Dr. Eiselen) included "the formulation of the principles and aims of education for Natives as an independent race, in which their past and present, their inherited racial qualities, their distinctive characteristics and aptitude [sic], and their needs under everchanging social conditions are taken into consideration."[5] Bantu education was introduced in 1953, and was based upon the racialistic and separatist principles of the Nationalist Government's ideology. The new system placed African education directly under state control, and moreover not under the control of the central educational authority but under the political control of the department concerned with African affairs.

According to the government spokeman, the defects of the old system were that the schools "were unsympathetic to the country's policy . . . by ignoring the segregation or 'apartheid' policy. . . . By blindly producing pupils trained on a European model, the vain hope was created among Natives that they could occupy posts within the European community. . . . This is what is meant by the creation of unhealthy 'White Collar Ideals.' "[6]

Later in the same speech, Dr. Verwoerd specified the requirements of Bantu education, including the following:

- "The school must equip him [the African] to meet the demands which the economic life of South Africa will impose upon him."
- "The Bantu teacher . . . must learn not to feel above his community, with a consequent desire to become integrated into the life of the European community. . . . He tries to make his community dissatisfied because of such misdirected ambitions which are alien to his people."
- "Care will now be taken that the Native population in the cities will no longer be privileged in educational matters. . . ."

---

[1]M. Horrell (compiler), "A Survey of Race Relations in South Africa," South Africa Institute of Race Relations, Johannesburg, 1965.

[2]N. J. J. Olivier, "Apartheid—A Slogan or a Solution," *Race Relations*, No. 90, South Africa Institute of Race Relations, Johannesburg, 1953.

[3]Reported in *The Star*, Johannesburg, April 8, 1965.

[4]W. W. M. Eiselen, reported in *Bantu*, Department of Information, Pretoria, 1960.

[5]*Ibid.*

[6]H. J. Verwoerd, "Bantu Education: Policy for the Immediate Future," Department of Information, Pretoria, 1954 (Hansard, 1953, V, II).

- "The Bantu must be guided to serve his community in all respects. There is no place for him in the European community above the level of certain forms of labour."
- ". . . Education should start with both feet in the reserves and have its roots in the spirit and being of Bantu society."
- "Above all, good race relations cannot exist when education is given under the control of people who . . . believe in a policy of equality."

Practices of Bantu Education

In quality and quantity, the education of Africans has declined disastrously during the twelve years of the system. The numbers of persons in the four population groupings and the percentages they comprise of the total population are shown in Figure 1. In 1962, the numbers of pupils and students were Africans, about 1,770,000; whites, about 811,000; coloreds, about 351,000; and Indians and others, about 144,000. Only in the case of whites is there the same proportion of pupils and students as there are young people of school age.

Figure 2 shows that at least 31 percent of the African population is of school age; yet, as shown in Figure 3, only 14.8 percent are receiving education; that is, less than half of the Africans of school age are in school. Thus, after some twelve years, the African school population still needs to be doubled to equal the proportion corresponding to age distribution.

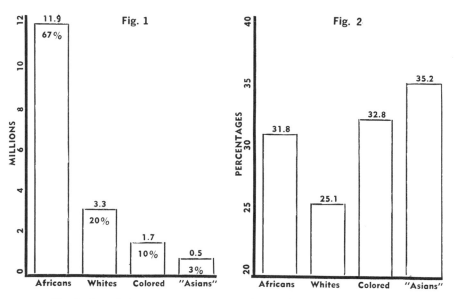

Fig. 1—Population groupings in South Africa, 1964 (estimated). (Source: M. Horrell, "A Survey of Race Relations in South Africa," South Africa Institute of Race Relations, Johannesburg 1965, p. 135.)

Fig. 2—Population groupings in South Africa; proportion within each group of school age (7-20 years), 1961. (Source: M. Horrell, "A Decade of Bantu Education," South Africa Institute of Race Relations, Johannesburg, 1964, p. 282.)

Figures 4 and 5 show the extent to which pupils continue beyond primary schooling, and here again there is a marked disadvantage for the Africans. Whereas 35 percent of all white pupils were receiving secondary education in 1962, only 3 percent of the Africans were. About 284,000 whites were receiving secondary education compared with about 56,000 Africans. At university level, whereas some 6.5 percent of the white pupils were receiving education of Post-Standard 10 or above, only 0.10 percent of the Africans were.

This sharp decline in advanced education for Africans can be related to the general patterns of discrimination against them. There is a desperate shortage of school space, so the average African teacher has twice the number of pupils as a white teacher. In 1962, 5,000 African schools were forced to run double sessions. There are still many inadequately qualified African teachers who are overworked in teaching the crucial (and, because of the system, inevitably neglected) primary grades.

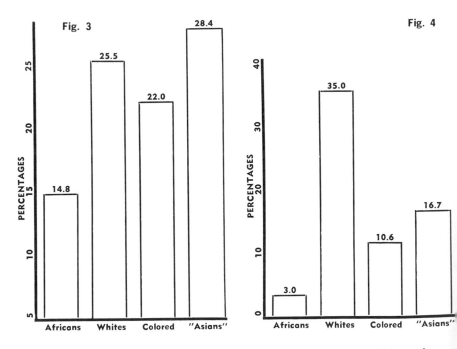

Fig. 3—Population groupings in South Africa: proportion within each group of students in schools, 1962. (Source: E. G. Malherbe, "Manpower Training: Educational Requirements for Economic Expansion," South Africa Institute of Race Relations, Johannesburg, 1965, p. 7.)

Fig. 4—Population groupings in South Africa: proportion of students in each group receiving secondary education, 1962. (Source: E. G. Malherbe, "Manpower Training: Educational Requirements for Economic Expansion," South Africa Institute of Race Relations, Johannesburg, 1965, p. 7.)

Unlike the white schools, the African school boards must bear half the costs of erecting post and higher primary schools, and many boards find it very difficult to raise enough funds. In the comparatively wealthy area of Soweto in Johannesburg, of the 133 schools only 8 are secondary schools, and only 4 provide education to matriculation level.[7]

Other reasons are founded in poverty: many parents cannot afford to pay school fees and other expenses, particularly now that African schoolchildren (unlike whites) must pay most expenses and provide their own midday meals. Many children must go out to work who should be attending school.

Since 1953 there has been a steady decline in the *effective* amount spent upon education for Africans. A former director of education for the province of Natal comments: "By international standards South Africa should be spending 5 to 6 percent of its national income on the education of its children. . . . But on the education of the African two thirds of our children we are now spending . . . less than one third of 1 percent of our national income."[8] Although the gross expenditure has risen this has not kept pace with the rise in enrollment, the rise in costs, and the needs to improve the system. In 1953-1954 the cost per African pupil was the paltry sum of 17.08 rands (about $23.80), which had by 1963-1964 declined to 13.37 rands (about

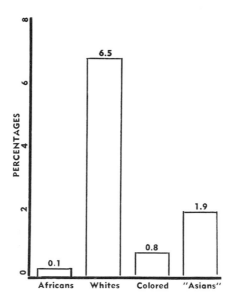

Fig. 5

Fig. 5—Population groupings in South Africa: proportion of students in each group receiving postsecondary education, 1962. (Source: E. G. Malherbe, "Manpower Training: Educational Requirements for Economic Expansion," South Africa Institute of Race Relations, Johannesburg, 1965, p. 7.)

[7]Horrell, *op. cit.*

[8]W. G. McConkey, "Financial Curb on Bantu Education," *The Natal Mercury*, Durban, April 11, 1962.

$18.33).[9] This figure is about one eleventh of the amount per head spent upon educating white pupils.

From 1946 to 1963 there was no change in the salary scales of African teachers. Many African teachers earn little more than semiskilled and less well-educated workers, and an African teacher earns at the top notch about one half the salary of his white professional equal. A white male assistant teacher in a secondary school *starts* at R2,640 (about $3,696); no African teacher can earn more than R1,788 (about $2,503).[10]

In African schools there is a severe shortage of qualified and specialist teachers, particularly in science and mathematics, and many schools are grossly overcrowded and underequipped. In 1961, there were, on the average, more than fifty-seven African pupils per class, compared with a teacher-load in white schools of twenty-two.[11] This situation works to the detriment of the African child who wants to become a doctor—one of the few professions open to him.

The Quality of Bantu Education

Most educationalists agree that education for Africans is markedly inferior to that for other South Africans. In general, the syllabi are designed to stress the world of the tribe and the countryside, and to praise of the virtues of Apartheid. Too much time is spent on mother-tongue teaching, "practical" subjects such as gardening and sewing, and political indoctrination. The fiction is maintained through the educational system that Africans are, by and large, subordinates by nature, doomed to be unskilled and semiskilled workers, rooted in the countryside and never-to-be-fully townsmen. The history and social studies syllabi stress the virtues of white colonialists who brought "civilization," and the inferiority of the culture of the ancestors of present-day Africans.

A recent official instruction to African teachers defined white South Africans as "fearless, honest and sincere who should be studious because they are the most important whites in the world."[12]

This, writes a former director of education for Natal, is "the baasskap pattern in education": education for servitude.[13]

Most significant has been the steady decline of African matriculants since 1953. In 1953, there were 547 of whom 47.3 percent passed. In 1961 there were 635 (a negligible increase), of whom only 23 percent passed. In 1962 there were nearly 900 candidates in all schools (at state aided *and* at private schools and at correspondence colleges), and the overall pass was 40.5 percent. The results in various subjects reveal general trends that indicate the poor quality of much of Bantu education. "The results in English A, Afrikaans B, and mathematics have been poor." In Physical Science the passes have centered about 49 percent, and Zoology at about 58 percent.[14]

---

[9]Horrell, *op. cit.*

[10]M. Horrell, "A Decade of Bantu Education," South Africa Institute of Race Relations, Johannesburg, 1964.

[11]*Ibid.*; McConkey, *op. cit.*

[12]Reported in the *Rand Daily Mail*, July 24, 1964.

[13]McConkey, *op. cit.*

[14]Horrell, ". . . Bantu Education," *op. cit.*

Briefly: In the academic year 1963-1964, of the 1.7 million African pupils at school, only 150 qualified for university entrance, which is about the same as those at the (white) Pretoria Boys' High School.[15]

University and professional education is segregated as strictly as preuniversity, and there has been a rigid restriction of Africans either to their "tribal college" or to the correspondence courses of the University of South Africa. Of the 1,408 African university students in 1961, more than 1,100 were taking correspondence courses through the University of South Africa, or taking its degrees at their "tribal college." In 1961 there were 112 Africans studying medicine about 8 percent), 60 studying science (about 4 percent) and 3 studying engineering (about 0.2 percent). By far the larger proportion were studying for Arts degrees and diplomas.[16]

In 1963 in technical colleges there were only 385 Africans; at technical schools there were only 1,957.[17]

Adult education is now in the control of the Department of Bantu Education, and although the general literacy rate for Africans has been estimated at between 40 percent and 50 percent, in 1963-1964 the government only paid R1,000 as a subsidy towards the costs of night schools and continuation classes.[18]

Conclusions

Is Bantu education "education for success" as the government describes it or is it "education for barbarism"?[19]

Malherbe in a 1965 survey of the manpower needs of South Africa, points to the fundamental failure of Bantu education: "What is remarkable is that the number of Bantu completing high school in 1961-1962 with either a matriculation or a school-leaving certificate was only 452; i.e., 0.1 percent of the economically active Bantu population." The figure for coloreds was 14 times higher, for Indians 57 times and for whites 189 times higher.[20] This is not due to any inherent inferiority of Africans, but a direct result of the network of discriminatory economic, legal, political, and social practice that effectively bars their advancement.

The objections to the present system may be summarized as follows:

1. There has been a steady drop in the per capita expenditure.
2. There has been a steady dwindling of Africans going on to advanced technical and professional education, in proportion to their population.
3. Bantu education promotes tribalism and makes it increasingly difficult for an African to participate in the industrialized world of the modern economic system as an equal with the whites in South Africa.
4. The increase in university enrollment is misleading: It is largely because of the increase in nondegree correspondence classes being followed, and does not reflect any increase in Africans studying for the specialized skills of a modern economy.

[15]Reported in the *Rand Daily Mail*, July 24, 1964.

[16]Horrell, "...Bantu Education," *op. cit.*

[17]*Education for Success*, Department of Information, Pretoria, 1965.

[18]Horrell, "...Bantu Education," *op. cit.*

[19]I. B. Tabata, *Education for Barbarism in South Africa*, Pall Mall Press, London, 1960.

[20]E. G. Malherbe, "Manpower Training: Educational Requirements for Economic Expansion," South Africa Institute of Race Relations, Johannesburg, 1965.

5. Bantu education (coupled with political and social repression) has forced many young Africans to leave their country to seek higher education, specialized training, and better opportunities, with a long-term dangerous lowering of the general level of education, and ultimately endangering the economic and social advance of a potentially wealthy country.

Among many white South Africans there is broad agreement with Dr. Verwoerd that "Bantu education should not clash with Government policy. . . . If the native in South Africa today . . . is being taught to expect that he will live his adult life under a policy of equal rights, he is making a big mistake.[21] That some 11.9 million of the population are treated as third-best to the ruling 3 million is to ensure that the struggle for equality shall be impeded.

ABORIGINAL EDUCATION IN AUSTRALIA

A. T. Duncan *is staff tutor, Department of Adult Education, University of Sydney. This is the text of an address presented to the Conference on Aboriginal Education, University of Sydney, August 19-20, 1966.*

During the past two or three decades, many Australians have become aware of what has been called "The Aboriginal Problem." In Federal Parliament efforts are being made to revise those sections of the Australian Constitution that discriminate against Aborigines. Even in 1966 Aborigines are excluded from the Commonwealth census. In the United States the federal government has taken the lead in overcoming discrimination against Indians and Negroes but in this country our federal constitution expressly states that the Aboriginal question is one for each individual state and that the Commonwealth cannot take any action except in the Northern Territory. It is significant that the definition of an Aborgine varies from state to state and indeed, an Aborigine who moves around Australia requires a constitutional lawyer to accompany him to ensure that he does not infringe various state laws. There is little doubt that the constitutional amendments will eventually be passed but how soon will depend on public support.

In almost every state changes have been made recently in the acts that govern Aboriginal welfare and in South Australia a bill has been introduced that will make racial discrimination an offense. In the federal industrial courts action is being taken to provide equal pay for Aboriginal workers in some industries, although it may be a long time before all Aboriginal workers receive equal pay. In N.S.W. there is now no discriminatory legislation against Aborigines except where they reside on special Aboriginal reserves. However, there is a growing awareness that the mere removal of discriminatory legislation is not the total answer to the question and that positive action is required to meet the needs of indigenous minority.

---

[21]Verwoerd, "Bantu Education . . . ," *op. cit.*

From *Integrated Education,* **December 1966/January 1967. Reprinted by permission of the author.**

In New South Wales a joint parliamentary committee is undertaking a comprehensive survey of the situation in this state and many people hope that their report will ensure that N.S.W. will take the lead in tackling the real problems that are involved.

There are still many people in Australia who proudly proclaim that we have no racial problem in this country. They argue that unlike many overseas countries, Australia has a homogeneous, uniracial society which provides equal opportunities for all. The fact that the indigenous people in Australia represent only 1 percent of the total population appears to be sufficient grounds to ignore the existence of our colored minority. On the other hand, there is a growing tide of public awareness that the Aboriginal question is extremely complex and, with the relatively high Aboriginal birthrate and the concentration of the Aboriginal population in the more scarcely settled areas of the continent, positive action is required to prevent the very type of situation that has developed overseas.

Most people are aware that there are two major areas of concern in discussing the Aboriginal question.

There is the fundamental question concerning the advancement of the tribal full-blood Aborigines in Northern Australia. This is an extremely complex issue and we can only hope that our administrators learn the lesson from history and prevent the development of the situation that has occurred in the southern states. This may be a pious hope, but there is an indication that a positive program will be evolved to meet the real needs of these people.

This paper is concerned with our cultural minority in the southern states, the Aborigine and part-Aborigine who has lost his own culture, but who, as yet, has not taken his full place in our society. I use the term Aborigine to include all those who identify themselves as Aborigines, regardless of the degree of skin pigmentation or admixture of Aboriginal blood since a social definition of this kind is the only valid definition for this social question. I might add that I will use the term Europeans when referring to non-Aborigines and here I do not mean New Australians, but rather all Australians who have arrived in this country since the day of Governor Phillip.

In the southern states, Aborigines comprise an educationally, economically, and socially disadvantaged minority in the community. They are easily identified by skin pigmentation and to pretend that they are "poor whites" is to ignore their racial heritage, increase their feelings of inferiority, and aggravate rather than improve the situation. Aborigines have made it quite clear that they have no wish to be black replicas of white Australians and it is only when they have regained their pride in their own racial heritage that they will become full members of the Australian community. To tell them that they must not be Aborigines to be good Australians is one of the major barriers that are preventing their integration into our society.

There are certain social and historical reasons why Aborigines today in fact form a very large part of the deprived sector of the community. Historically, the loss of traditional, economic pursuits which followed the alienation of land by European settlers, led to the policy of segregation when Aborigines lived in segregated groups on the outskirts of settlement. This policy of segregation was continued until 1939. From 1931 such people as Professor A. P. Elkin and others were forceful in their demands that a new and more positive policy should be introduced. Elkin rejected the idea of absorption but it is unfortunate that absorption has appeared to be a definite element in the new Australian policy of assimilation. Since the time of the first settlement we have tried many policies. They have included laissez faire, segregation, protection, and now assimilation. All these policies have had only limited success and perhaps the major reason for this is that they have been imposed by non-Aborigines rather than developed in consultation with the Aborigines to ensure their active cooperation and interest.

Although a great deal has been done to improve the situation of the Aborigines, we must remember that there has been a marked rise in educational standards and in affluence of the European sector of the community during this century and that this has not been matched by a similar rate of educational and economic development in the Aboriginal community. Despite efforts to raise the socioeconomic level of Aborigines, the gap between the two sectors of the community has continued to widen, accentuating the depressed conditions under which most Aborigines live. Lacking the knowledge and skills necessary to enable them to compete in an industrial society, many Aborigines have given up hope and have become apathetic and distrustful of all attempts by Europeans to improve the situation.

Most Aborigines are unskilled or seasonal workers on low income and live in a depressed socioeconomic environment. The poverty in which they live is self-perpetuating unless positive steps are taken to meet the cultural deprivation which they face. If we look particularly at the question in N.S.W. we find that there are relatively few Aborigines who are other than unskilled laborers. There are very few middle-class Aborigines and no upper-class Aborigines.* In fact, well over 90 percent of the Aborigines are in the working class and, unfortunately, in the lower section of this working class because they tend to seek positions where little skill is required. It is rather an indictment of our treatment of the Aborigines when in 1966 we have newspapers proudly proclaiming that an Aborigine has graduated from the University. In New Zealand, many Maoris graduate each year and no one will convince me that Aborigines have less intelligence than Maoris or Europeans or any other race of people. There is no scientific evidence to support such a proposition. Like all races of mankind, some Aborigines are bright, some are dull, and the vast majority are average. Surely we must be concerned that even bright Aboriginal children fail to reach their full potential and obtain even normal qualifications.

Without educational qualifications Aborigines cannot hope to compete in our industrialized society. They cannot hope to improve their job status and economic position. Unless they, too, have the opportunity for social mobility, they will continue to live under depressed socioeconomic conditions and will continue to require welfare services from the community. It seems strange that Australia is spending a great deal of time and effort to attract skilled workers to this country but continues to ignore the untapped potential of our indigenous population. With effective guidance Aborigines must become an asset, rather than a liability to the community and the key to economic and social advancement is in the field of education.

One of the basic assumptions in Australian education is that we should provide equal educational opportunities for all. Even if we were to achieve this goal, this will

---

*[Editor's Note: These classifications are based on the schema worked out by William Lloyd Warner, whereby social classes are divided into six subclasses based on occupation, income, and housing.]

still not meet the real needs of those who are culturally deprived. At this point in time, Aborigines are unequal, and to treat them equally will perpetuate their inequality. From the first day at school the disadvantaged child faces serious difficulties with vocabulary, concept formation, language, and perceptual discrimination. This is not because of a lack of innate intelligence or ability, but because of the lack of social experience before the child commences school. When we add the physical disadvantages of an impoverished environment and a lack of intellectual stimulation in the home, it is not difficult to realize why Aboriginal students quickly fall behind in their formal schoolwork. Their failure leads to feelings of frustration and dissatisfaction so that absences and poor attendance lead to a further deterioration of their standards. By the time the majority reach high school, they are classified as slow learners and have little hope of obtaining normal educational qualifications. This is not a problem that is unique to the Australian Aborigines. It is found with disadvantaged minorities throughout the world. In the United States for example, Hildegard Thompson, who is the Chief of the Branch of Education for the Bureau of Indian Affairs, wrote in 1964 with regard to the Indians in the United States:

> On the basis of their citizenship, Indians today are entitled to educational services on the same basis and from the same sources as other residents of their respective states. However, unusual circumstances and severe disadvantages of some Indian groups require special attention to give them equal advantages with others in a normal public school setting. The Bureau's educational function is directly related to the special attention necessary to give Indians educational opportunities commensurate with the demands of twentieth century living.

In New Zealand Mr. Allan Grey of the Maori Education Foundation wrote last year:

> The problem that gave rise to the Maori Education Foundation as stated at its inception was: Maori pupils were underachieving, dropping out of school, failing at school, reluctant to learn, behavior problems at school. Today the task is to gear schooling to attract those who are emotionally and socially handicapped in today's schooling. Many of these people are actually making a scholastic jump that we see as being from the eighteenth to the twentieth century and they are doing this in one generation. This transition involves a difficult adaption, for it represents not only a shift from a simpler culture into a more complex one but also into a society which is mechanized, anonymous, impersonal, individualized, and in which they are aliens.

Surely if we look at the words of Hildegard Thompson and Grey, these could be stated quite obviously about Australian Aborigines. The point must be made again that the Aboriginal question is not a unique problem that faces Australia and is in fact but a part of the worldwide problem of equalizing opportunities for the culturally deprived. The solutions and partial solutions that have been adopted in many countries overseas must be investigated and examined to see if they can be applied to the Australian situation.

I have mentioned that Aborigines start school behind scratch. In New Zealand, the Maori play centers are doing a great deal to meet this situation. It is significant that the play centers use Maori mothers as instructors and it has been found that these mothers have continued to take an active interest in the child's education long after they leave the play center. Indeed, many Maori mothers try to keep up with their children as they continue their school career. It has been found that the mothers of many secondary pupils have now enrolled in evening classes to continue their own education which had previously been rather limited.

In New York, the Department of Psychiatry of the New York Medical College has developed a preschool enrichment program for disadvantaged children. The most significant result of this program has been a marked increase in interest and enthusiasm towards school-oriented activities not only by the children but also by the parents. This must only result in improved school achievement. Aboriginal children who have attended preschool kindergartens run by the "Save the Children Fund" are now doing much better in school. In some cases there could be greater involvement by parents, as overseas experience suggests that this is a very important feature of long-term solutions.

It is well known that the survey by the N.S.W. Teachers' Federation indicated that only 9 percent of Aboriginal children remained beyond second year, so that over 90 percent of Aboriginal students lack the necessary educational qualifications required for the skilled trades, clerical work, or the professions. In a survey undertaken by a research worker in Sydney recently, some 138 adult Aborigines were interviewed. Of these only 9 had passed the Intermediate Certificate. These were the people who had come to Sydney to improve their socioeconomic status but how can they complete effectively in the metropolitan area?

Since Aborigines do not have less intelligence than Europeans, this high drop-out rate and wastage of talent presents a serious problem to the community. How can we ensure that Aborigines remain at school to develop their full potential? How can we ensure that Aboriginal children will really profit from their school experience and attain normal standards of achievement? Lacking the necessary fundamental research in Australia we must, of necessity, turn to overseas experience where a great deal has been done to meet the needs of the culturally deprived. In New York, Dr. John J. Theobald, the superintendent of schools, carried out an interesting research project with one hundred underprivileged Negro children who were ready to leave school. As well as providing special financial assistance through scholarships, Dr. Theobald introduced a carefully planned enrichment program into the school. Among the dramatic results of this project was the interesting fact that the average IQ of the children concerned rose from 81 to 101 over a period of eighteen months.

Similar projects have been developed in other parts of America with very encouraging results. The Bureau of Indian Affairs has a special branch concerned with the education of Indians in the United States. In Canada, the Indian Affairs Branch of the Department of Citizenship and Immigration has been particularly successful in the development of band councils and in general community development among tribal groups. Under the Indian Act, band councils may make bylaws about health, traffic, game management, public works, and other matters on the reserves and many band councils have complete control over the disbursement of band funds.

Throughout North America, many universities take special interest in the problems of cultural minorities and have done a great deal to stimulate community development.

The University of Auckland in New Zealand has for many years conducted regional Maori Leadership Conferences. As a direct result of these conferences, the Hunn Report on the Maroi situation led to major changes in policy. It is important to realize that these changes have been made in full consultation with, and the active cooperation of, Maori leaders and perhaps this may be one of the major reasons for the success of New Zealand's policies for their indigenous minority. In the United Kingdom a great deal of research has been carried out on the problems facing the West Indians who have entered Britain and also on many aspects of cultural deprivation.

In Australia we speak of an Aboriginal problem as if it was a burden that Australia alone must bear. Surely we must realize that other countries have groups of people who are culturally deprived but perhaps a major difference is that in other countries positive projects are being implemented to meet the situation. We still tend to adopt a paternalistic attitude and think in terms of welfare and social services rather than positive educational programs. We should be reminded of the words of Cicero when writing to Atticus in the first century BC: "Do not obtain your slaves from Britain because they are so stupid and so utterly incapable of being taught that they are not fit to form a part of the household of Athens."

In Sydney today there are many Aboriginal youths who drift in and out of employment and whose work record leaves much to be desired. A similar situation became apparent in Chicago three years ago. The late President John F. Kennedy made $1 million available to the Office of Manpower, Automation, and Training to develop what became known as the JOBS Project. This project was designed to train 1,000 currently unemployable youths to reach the necessary educational level for employment, to develop the attitudes required for employment, to acquire some job skill experience, and finally to be placed in employment.

The Project's report in October, 1963, indicated that of the 1,559 students enrolled, 33 percent had not completed training but the majority of these had either found suitable employment on their own or had returned to full-time schooling. This is one of many successful projects which could well be implemented in N.S.W.

Although we have not carried out a great deal of research in Australia, it is obvious that we can, and indeed must, benefit from overseas experience.

In summary, we must admit that the Aboriginal question is extremely complex, with many interrelated facets. It is clear, however, that education is one of the major keys that may be used to ensure that our indigenous minority can achieve equality in every sense of the word. Although it would be foolish to suggest that any particular country has solved the problem of the culturally deprived, it would be equally foolish to ignore many of the major advances that have been made overseas. Many Aborigines fail to realize their full educational potential. We cannot wash our hands and point out that our educational system has been designed to suit the majority and that their failure is their own fault. If we do this we are failing in our responsibilities and to quote Richard and Hephzibah Hauser in their book *The Fraternal Society:* "The test of a nation's civilization is the manner in which it deals with its most impoverished, underprivileged minority group."

In this country this group is the Australian Aborigines.

EDUCATION OF THE CANADIAN INDIAN AND ESKIMO

J. Roby Kidd *is chairman of the adult education department, The Ontario Institute for Studies in Education, Toronto, Canada. This is part of an address given to the Conference on Aboriginal Education, University of Sydney, August 19-20, 1966.*

The history of the relationship with the indigenous people in Canada is a very tangled one and on the whole an unhappy but an improving one. There is a great deal of bloodshed associated with it; there were years, centuries even, of the worst kinds of paternalism; there were great misunderstandings, there are epic stories of devotion and service by some government officials and many church people, there is also a lot of romantic nonsense about the noble savage; we have gone through all of these phases. There are now about a quarter of a million Indians in Canada; they are scattered right across the country, but are most numerous in the northern and more remote areas. This quarter-million lives in 550 different bands or distinct groups mainly on about 2,500 different reservations or settlements. The total land acreage is substantial; it is six million acres; about 75 percent of all Indians are either on these settlements or reservations or live close to them. In accepting these figures, one must remember that our statistics are not always accurate. There is a phenomenon: (and this is sad commentary on us) the phenomenon of "passing" of so many people of Indian origin, men and women who cease to report that they are Indians, who feel that they must no longer divulge this for some reason or other.

Until about World War II, most Canadians ignored the Indians and Eskimos. If they had an attitude, it was a reasonably benevolent one: these people were dying out, these were the "vanishing Canadians," and we ought to be decent to them while they still existed. Then we discovered, and this was a bit of a shock to some of us, that they were not going to die out. They were tough people and they were on the increase, and they still are. Accordingly, we had to turn around and face the matter squarely. The result is a 150-degree shift in our policy over the last fifteen years.

These people have ten main languages. Four of them are found east of the Rockies. One or two of these are magnificent languages, limited in range, limited in concept, but admirable for their purpose. Six of the linguistic groups are west of the Rockies in the Pacific area. The people who lived in the Atlantic provinces of Nova Scotia, New Brunswick, and Prince Edward Island—even Newfoundland, used to live by hunting and occasionally by fishing. They are now becoming primarily farmers or miners. They also manage wood lots; some of them work in lumbering. I mention these occupations because the question is always asked if indigenous people do have a particular kind of vocation, is it possible for them to learn something else. In every single case, or almost without exception, these men and women have learned or are learning different vocations.

The Indians in the central region (many of them) are agriculturalists. The six nations of the Iroquois were notably successful in developing agriculture from the earliest days. In the northern parts of Canada they were primarily hunters and trappers.

From *Integrated Education,* **December 1966/January 1967. Reprinted by permission of the author.**

In the prairie provinces most Indians lived by hunting the buffalo. Their economy, indeed their whole life, was based on the buffalo which provided most of the things that they needed. Those in the northern parts were mainly trappers. Now agriculture and forestry have been introduced into this area; so Indians are now taking part in farming, in logging, and also in mining. Some Indians still pursue trapping and a great many of the guides for hunting parties are Indians. On the Pacific coast the Indians were fishers and hunters, but here too, forestry, agriculture, and dairy farming have been introduced and of course fishing is still carried on.

All of the Indians now have the vote, all of them now receive family allowances and other welfare services. Those Indians still living on the reserves do not pay any personal income tax; they do not pay property taxes. Of course, if they are off the reserves they pay taxes like anybody else. Each of the reserves is governed by a band council. These councils are in most cases elected, but there are cases where the old practice of passing on the chieftainship by inheritance still continues. One of the most difficult problems that has been faced is the use of alcohol. Some of our Indians misused it in the same way that their paler-skinned brothers misused it, so there were very stringent laws about the sale of alcohol to Indians. However, the problem is being faced more realistically. Changes are coming in a phased way and discrimination in this respect is being eliminated. We must note that band councils often have the control over alcohol, not just the "bootlegger" or some other outside persons.

Now a word or two about the Eskimo. Unlike the Indian, who because of this history, and our treatment of him, had lost much of his culture and most of his self-confidence and self-respect, the Eskimo is a free being; he lives simply. He has lived in a stone-age culture but he has always been the best man in his own milieu. When others entered the polar environment, they had to depend on him, so he has been free and independent and always a very agreeable person to deal with because of his dignity and self-assurance. There is a great deal of attention given to the Eskimo these days in literature and television. More and more the Eskimos are coming to the South and influencing Eskimo policy. There are even instances of Eskimos going out as our representatives to other countries. We recently sent an Eskimo girl as our main representative to Ghana and I hope that this kind of practice will continue.

The humor that Eskimo people display is very refreshing. The first time we had a conference on the Eskimos in Canada, one Eskimo sat quietly at the back while non-Eskimos talked and argued learnedly about the problem. He listened to one superintendent of a hospital after another talk about the number of Eskimos who had come to their hospitals, but had gone back to the North as soon as they were able to, because they did not seem to like the South very well. Then the little Eskimo stood up and said: "I am an Eskimo. I have noticed that almost everyone who leaves a hospital wants to go home!" Then he said: "I have lived two years in the South—in Civilization. It's not *too* bad."

Eskimos have a written language; the Canadian Eskimos are able to communicate with the Eskimos in Alaska and Russian-Siberian territories. There is also the beginning of communication and contact between our Eskimos and those in Greenland. Let me refer now to the tremendous advances that have been made in Greenland. I think this is one of the fine stories on the development of indigenous people comparable to that of the Maoris. It would be very interesting to have comparisons made now of progress in Greenland and New Zealand. The Greenland

Eskimos have not only a written language, but a substantial literature. Most of their social services are in the hands of their own people with, of course, the help and cooperation of the Danes. The Eskimos of Greenland are a small group of strong, confident, and effective people.

What are the main changes that have come about in Eskimo policy over the past fifteen-year period? First of all, there have been changes in attitude and changes in attention.

Canadians no longer take their North for granted, nor do they take for granted these indigenous people. They know that a long program of reeducation and reorganization is at hand. Newspapers, churches, farm groups, business organizations, trade unions, and others regularly attend to the matter in annual meetings, in publications, and in policy statements. Much of the change has come about through the creation of the Indian Eskimo Association, a private body in which churches, government officials, trade unions, cooperatives, women's groups, and many others have membership. This organization has helped focus support for the work of the government officials in the North and has helped officials realize that their work is supported. It helps them understand that not everyone outside of government is entirely critical of the record in the past, although much must now be changed. Government personnel used to fear any contact with ordinary people, believing, it seems, that there would always only be complaints, and there would be questions asked in Parliament and their jobs would be in danger. Now there is much greater collaboration between the nongovernmental organizations and the government officials.

Secondly, there is a much greater degree of collaboration as well between the interested churches. The churches have long had an honorable record of working in the North, but they worked as separate denominations and too often there has been competition or no association at all. Much of this is changing, and has changed. Thirdly, there has been an active program of public education in many of the communities into which the Indians are moving. What used to happen is that a problem would arise where Indians would be found drunk on Saturday night, or there would be prostitution, and some good people would say: "Let us solve this disgraceful condition by chasing off the Indians to another town. Let them get drunk there," or by building a bigger jail or hostel for the girls. These temporary measures did not really solve anything. Wherever a problem of this kind has arisen the association has organized a seminar for community leaders in an attempt to achieve understanding of the whole problem, and all that might be done, rather than trying to deal with it with the usual "tooth-pulling" kind of measure.

Another activity of the association has been to press for an inquiry by the senate of Canada. A lengthy investigation by the senate into the whole matter of indigenous people was held. For this, many organizations, all Indian bands, and some of the Eskimo people presented comprehensive briefs over a six-month period. This investigation became a public education program of some consequence and was followed by major changes in legislation.

Education for Indians, or for Indian children, has improved and has increased. There are four kinds of schools, or rather four approaches in the provision of schools. One is to enroll more of the Indian children in the local schools and 22,000 are now in non-Indian schools as against 4,000 in 1954. An increasing number of special Indian schools have been built in areas where the population is almost totally Indian. The last count was 56,000 children in Indian schools which is double what there had been in 1954. There are also schools for the migrant people, for Eskimos who are out hunting half the year and for some of the Indians who spend many months out trapping. Schools have also been planned in camps where families reside for the winter months and intensive work is given during those months when it is possible to reach them. Because of the high incidence of TB for Indians and Eskimo people and the number of them that have been in hospitals, special schools and vocational training courses have also been developed in these hospitals and sanatoriums. Considerable development in adult education has taken place as well. The provision of base libraries and traveling libraries for the scattered bands, and the distribution throughout the North of documentary films to bring about understanding of conditions for employment, as well as general information about Canada and the world, are examples of this effort. There have been a good many "leadership" schools, somewhat like those carried on by the University of Auckland with the Maoris, for Indian chiefs and other band leaders. Many of the schools are centered around specific skills.

There has been an improvement in on-the-job training offered specifically to indigenous peoples coming into the city and some vocational training has also been provided on the reserves. A special counseling and placement service, a part of the National Employment Service, has been developed for indigenous people. With economic development has come some provision of special credit to cooperative production and marketing societies among the Indians. The closeness of association of a band or a tribe has been the base for the organization of these credit unions and cooperatives and in many cases these have become quite strong. Particularly have cooperatives been useful in the marketing of handicrafts. The stone carvings of the Eskimos which you may have seen and many of the handicrafts of the Indians have been marketed by cooperatives. The great success story of the moment is the cooperative that has only one product: the Ookpik. You may never have heard of the Ookpik; this is a kind of Eskimo mythical owl but it already has produced half a million dollars worth of revenue and is probably now the symbol of Canada rather than the beaver or maple leaf.

There has also been emphasis on development not only by the government services, but by nongovernment agencies. The churches were there already, and the women's institutes of Canada have organized about twenty-five institutes of women in the North with many Indians as members. The trade unions have begun to organize so there are now a good many unions in the mining areas with Indian membership. The cooperative movement has been sending its leaders to help in organization for some time. There has been an attempt to bring about better understanding by the Canadian people about the whole situation, through planned programs such as the conferences of the kind that I mentioned earlier, conferences held nationally, regionally, and in local communities. Educational radio and television broadcasts have helped. So have attempts to eliminate some of the worst of the textbooks which had been repeating libels and lies for generations. By the way, there has even been some improvement in movies since Indians are now allowed to win a few of the battles! Education about Indian affairs within the trade unions and among groups of managers, business people, and employers has also become more common.

There have been errors in our past education policies. I have forgotten who it was who said he did not worry about his enemies, he needed to be defended from his friends. Some of the friends of the Indians have made some of the worst blunders.

When schools were developed, originally they were built fairly near to where Indians lived. Boys and girls were drawn off the reservations or away from the settlement into this school and segregated from their families and the Indian community for five to eight years. Two things happened. Many boys and some girls, who have great capacity, would pass right through the school and would lose all contact with Indian life. These schools became, as it were, trapdoors for the release or the loss of the leaders of these Indian communities. Boys who did not do well, who were not brilliant enough to win scholarships, would go back to the reservation spoiled—or almost spoiled—for the kind of life that was there, and no longer valuing what their parents considered of basic importance. Naturally, tensions and difficulties were created. It is little wonder that the abuse of alcohol and other forms of escape from pressures became fairly prevalent. Rarely were the parents or the whole community involved in this education process which was on an individual basis. Attempts are now being made to reach whole families and reach whole groups, with the education of the parents in the Indian community going on at the same time as the education of the children. This is an elementary notion: it is the A of ABC, but it dawned on some of us rather late.

I can remember a telephone call from a man I did not know. He was a priest who had been responsible for the development of Indian-Eskimo work of his church for ten years. He had been to a conference run by UNESCO and had learned one important lesson. It was that the proper approach in education was to the whole family and not just to the children. He telephoned me from his ship since he had heard about our association and our work in adult education. He said "I have been wrong all my life, now I will have to adopt a different approach." It is an obvious point, but some of us did miss this rather elementary but important point.

We used to be late in getting Indian children started, and by the time we had them in schools they were already limited in their speech and in their concepts. More attention is now given to the provision of enriching experiences for the family, for the mother, and for the children in the earlier years. Another error was that we expected too little from the Indian children. Much of our instruction consisted of stunts and tricks and the lowest level of vocational training. I learned a little about this from my own son who has been out teaching recently. He did not "know any better" so he made quite a lot of progress. He was in the far North with Frontier College—this is an organization that sends young college men to teach in the summer. They work all day on the road gang or building dams to earn money and at night they organize classes. It's a good test for a teacher. He was working almost entirely with Indians and they taught him a great deal—how to play better baseball, about the sun dance, about their beliefs and their ideology; and, having taught him so much, they were quite ready to learn from him. He started classes in elementary reading, writing, and arithmetic, but since he had also been a philosophy student at the university, he put on a course he called "Logic." Nobody told him he could not do that and these men who had worked ten hours a day in the sun and then taken elementary work between seven and nine, trooped into the smoky, railway boxcar in substantial numbers, to talk about ideas. He found they were far more articulate and far more able to express themselves about their own thoughts, dreams, aspirations, and ideas than he was.

Quite often we have limited these people by having too little respect for them. In the field of craft, while we did make a market for curios, most of the designs of our Indians were debased by making opportunities for them to market funny little knickknacks for the tourist trade. Sometimes we have done this even with good artists. The first professor at the University of Alaska of Eskimo origin is Ronald Senungetuk, a magnificent artist. He creates rather free forms, but if you look at them closely, you can see there is an Eskimo origin to them. Since he is a free artist, some of the best friends of the Eskimos in Alaska are a bit perturbed about this because *he is not Eskimo enough,* born though he was in an igloo. This was also true in Puerto Rico. I had a great friend who was organizing a ceramics factory, or rather a working studio in Puerto Rico. The Spanish Indians who came there in the early stages used to go to Woolworth's and buy some articles which they used to trace designs for their pottery. Naturally this practice had to be broken when my friend was brought in to take over the direction of the center. Some anthropologists from the university arrived and said to my friend. "You have a great opportunity, the most magnificent designers in this whole hemisphere were Indians, the Aztecs and the Mayas and the Incas. Now you can get these Indians to design like the Incas and the Aztecs and the Mayas, and we will help you, we have all the designs for you." Now, my friend was a very vulgar man, and he said, "Get to hell out of here," and chased them off the premises. He said, "You do not have any trust in the people today to design. Please leave us alone." He had the patience and the toughness to fend off opposition over the next twelve to eighteen frustrating months. Well, they helped each other to throw away their carbon paper and begin to feel and see and observe and then express designs, magnificent designs. You can trace their Indian ancestry in them all right, but these are new designs being freshly done by Spanish Indians of today.

Let me now come to a few general principles that I think apply more or less to most of the indigenous people in many areas. One is the need for a national program. Regional and local efforts are essential, but in Canada we had to make national plans because many of our Indians are migrant people and not stopped by provincial and state boundaries. We have had to deal with a whole situation involving education and economics and health and defense and art and beauty. So it is a national program as well as a local and provincial one. Secondly, we have had sometimes to use law, and a series of acts have been passed in Canada in the last twenty years to make discrimination in employment, in housing, in recreation, and in other things very difficult. We have had to do this not only for the benefit of indigenous people but for the rest of us. Law has been a very good source and foundation for much of the education that has been carried out. Thirdly, and this perhaps the most important, we have had to educate ourselves. The great problem of the indigenous people is not with the indigenous people, it is with the rest of the Canadians. Serious efforts have been made to understand and to realize that patience is needed, that solutions will not be magical and will not come overnight. We have had to realize the importance, or economic value if you wish, of Indian and Eskimo people, particularly in their own environment. In Alaska where I have occasionally been a consultant, millions of dollars have been spent to bring in workmen from Georgia and Minnesota and other places. These highly paid workmen go in for a year or two, some of them stay, but the rest just go back to the South. Now a little money is being spent on the vocational training of Indians and Eskimos who are already there and who are doing very well, thank you, in these vocations. Many of these indigenous people have provided special skills that were badly needed. If you were to see the high steel being erected in almost any great building in New York or in most of the other cities around, you would note that workers are Indian people, the Cawgnawauga Indians, who have developed an astonishing specialized skill in working hundreds of feet in the air on the steel frames. These are two examples, there can be many more possibilities.

Another principle which is obvious to you and which has been discussed here, is the need to build up the pride and self-confidence in the indigenous people, and for this the arts, music, and sports are very important. In Canada we realized this rather late in the day; we foolishly believed that if we solved the economic and political problems then we could get around many years later to such things as dancing and art. However, these are the first things to do. Arts and sports and other avenues through which people attain confidence and strength are part of the first task along with jobs. A further principle is the necessity to look at the whole situation of education, jobs, counseling, job placement, and training together in one related program. There is not just one simple kind of solution. Another principle to which I have already referred is the need to deal with family groups, with the joint family, or with the whole tribe or the whole of the society, not just with individuals.

A further principle or practice is that while we must use experts (and I do not wish to sound derisive of anthropologists and sociologists from whom we have learned a great deal) we do not make much progress unless there is involvement and participation by the indigenous peoples themselves in the planning. If it is an economic program, or an educational program, or a political program, involvement and deep participation by the people themselves is essential. Related to this is that we do not make much progress until we have indigenous people who are the teachers, the lawyers, the social workers, and the interpreters who are working in their group. Two more points. It is not enough to value a romantic historical being, the "noble savage"; it is essential to value the human beings who are living with us today. Lastly, these people expect to serve and we need to expect service from them, as we would of any other citizens.

SOCIALLY HANDICAPPED—THE MAORIS OF NEW ZEALAND

S. R. Morrison *is director of University Extension, University of Auckland, Auckland, New Zealand. The article is the text of an invited communication to the Conference on Aboriginal Education, University of Sydney, August 19-20, 1966.*

There are probably few nations that do not contain clearly identifiable groups that are handicapped in some way in their ability to benefit from the schooling that is provided. They may be the children of bargees in England or Maoris in New Zealand or Aborigines in Australia. The handicaps may arise from historical, economic, or racial circumstances or because of cultural and intellectual distances that have created social differentation, parochial morality, poor ambition, or blasted hopes. We have ample evidence to show that handicaps of this kind not only affect the acceptance of opportunity, but also performance, and subsequent station.

It was the recognition of this in so many children of socially handicapped groups that led to the glib and unscientific reasoning which I do not doubt is still current in

From *Integrated Education,* **December 1966/January 1967. Reprinted by permission of the author.**

Australia. In your country it will be expressed like this: "The children of Aborigines can be educated only so far. After that they fall behind the children of white Australians." It is, therefore, a waste of effort. If those who say this are kindly Australians they may add that Aboriginal children are happier if their schooling is not as sustained as that given to others.

Because so many Maori children—but by no means all—do fall behind in performance at school in New Zealand, we have been concerned to discover what can be done to remove the disadvantages. It is about their attempts to do something about the disadvantages, the handicaps, that I write to you and I will try to relate the experience to any socially handicapped community or race such as the Aboriginal people of Australia.

European settlement on any scale in New Zealand dates from the 1840s. By the middle of the century—the 1850s and 1860s—the obvious threat to the traditional Maori economy based on agriculture, hunting, and fishing was obvious to their leaders. The Maori wars were an attempt to stop further encroachment. The tribes who had rebelled were defeated but not conquered. They did, however, lose much of their land by confiscation. There ensued for nearly seventy years a period of withdrawal. Contact with European settlers was marginal in many areas. The Maori population as a whole remained as rural communities living in most cases quite remote from centers of European settlement.

Then came the years of the establishment of the welfare state, 1935-1938, with provision for old-age and sickness pensions, unemployment benefits, child endowments for all children, and full employment. These welfare measures were available to all New Zealanders. At the same time the state began to negotiate compensatory money grants to the tribes who had had their lands confiscated.

During and particularly after the World War II years, younger Maori men and women began to move to centers of population looking for jobs. Today nearly 40 percent of all Maoris live in urban areas and the process is, if anything, being accelerated. Approximately the same time division separated the period of schooling by insisting on the elimination of all elements of Maori culture from the curriculum of all schools. Children were even strapped if detected speaking Maori in the playground.

There is no doubt that this policy stemmed from a firm conviction that this insistence on uniform schooling would remove the handicaps of Maori children. Probably the strong tradition for equality in New Zealand was reinterpreted in the period of the full establishment of social welfare 1935-1939 and certainly educationists began to question the wisdom of eliminating all traces of Maori culture from the school curriculum. A few even began to challenge the view that social handicaps would thus be removed.

During this period Maori arts and crafts were introduced as part of schooling, particularly in Maori schools. In most rural areas where there was a significant Maori population, the schools were not under education boards but directly controlled by the department of education with a separate inspectorate and separate financial provision. But even in these schools the Maori elements incorporated in school education were not extensive.

Today there is increasing attention in all primary schools. All children learn something of Maori history and arts and crafts. Most Maori children (about 80 percent) now attend schools under education board control and the policy of the department of education is to convert by consent the remaining schools for Maoris which the department controls.

It was not until the 1950's, however, that any research was made upon the comparative effects of schooling, although many teachers of Maori children inclined to the view that Maori children tend 'to "fade out" as they proceed with their schooling. The research, still in the main tentative, seemed to show that by the age of fourteen the Maori child had fallen behind, on the average, by about one year. This crude measure told us little, as it was known that attendance, for various reasons, was often irregular. A later research seemed to point to a "racial" weakness in reading and comprehension, the skills that depended upon the child's control of the English language and that are basic to all learning in a school. Again the research was limited and inadequate, and administrators turned their attention to physical factors. In the year 1961 the then Secretary of Maori Affairs, G. K. Hunn, prepared a report in which he suggested a crash program to quickly remove the disadvantages that are peculiar to Maori children in seeking to maintain equality with the white child in school. The state took up the suggestion enthusiastically and launched the Maori Education Foundation as a remedy for all the social handicaps. The state granted £200,000 and a pound-for-pound subsidy on all moneys raised. The Maori people responded well to the vigorous campaign and probably the bulk of the money raised came from Maori sources. Today, this fund stands at nearly £900,000 and the interest is used in two ways. Most, over 80 percent, is expended upon providing to Maori parents grants so that their children, who cannot by reason of remoteness easily attend the neighborhood secondary school, may attend one with boarding facilities and for an extensive development of preschool education by establishing play centers after Maori parents have learned a little about child development.

This may seem a very limited program and indeed it is. It must be remembered, however, that it is not part of the Foundation's function to take over anything which is an education department responsibility. The Foundation was to provide the extra facilities that seemed to be needed.

It is as yet too soon for any firm judgment upon the success or otherwise of the Foundation. This much, however, can be said with conviction. The physical factors, the logistics of schooling, have now been solved. There are equal facilities in the racial sense. Inequalities today arise from rural and not racial situations.*

The Maori play centers also flourish and multiply although their success in removing any of the social handicaps is yet to be measured. Perhaps the most important result of the establishment of the Foundation has been the increased awareness of Maori parents. For a time, at least, education was nearly a crusade. This is also true of the play centers. These are entirely run by Maori parents (mostly mothers), who must have gained an increased appreciation of the educative process. Something of this increased awareness was reflected in a "back to school" movement among Maori parents. Very few Maori parents ever went as far in their schooling as to pass School Certificate (four years secondary examination) or University Entrance which comes after School Certificate. Some hundreds or more Maori parents decided

---

*[Editor's Note: A contrasting judgment on this matter may be found in Roger Oppenheim, "Maori Children in Auckland Schools," *The New Era* (England), December, 1964.]

to enroll in evening classes and a few passed the examination in one year. All who studied must have been better fitted as parents and in nearly all cases this was the vocational aim.

I have tried to show that two changes have been made in Maori schooling. First, and this has been going on for thirty years now, a deliberate attempt has been made to foster Maori history and arts and crafts in schools attended by Maori children and now generally. There is little doubt that this relatively minor change has considerable value in reducing a little the social distance between teacher and pupils, in increasing parental appreciation, in providing a sort of emotional bond for Maori pupils in particular, and in offering an area of limited success.

Then came the Maori Education Foundation which has concentrated in the Maori upon the disabilities of distance. To this should be added the preschool venture. Some of us, however, think that the most difficult handicaps are yet to be removed, and before this can be done we need to know more than we do about the Maori family, its structure and relationships, the school community relationships, and the roles of teachers. I would suggest that this, too, must be discovered in Australia. One study in New Zealand has produced this picture of personality development in Maori children. A high degree of independence on the part of the preschool child; participation in widespread but loosely organized and unsupervised play groups of prime importance as socializing agents and as a source of values and status; inconsistent and often sharp attempts at discipline by parents; a growing exposure to European influences; increasing awareness of seniority group status; fairly short-lived adolescent rebellion followed by stern imposition of adult role behavior and standards. Here we see several parallels with patterns that are characteristic of Negro American children but fewer with the more closely knit families of Mexican and Puerto Rican children in similar circumstances. The consequences, as interpreted by those who made the survey are: deeply felt needs for responsiveness, expression, and conformity and deep fears of failure, social isolation, emotional commitment, and out-group rejection.

The extent to which this picture is a precise diagnosis is a subject for experts. The important fact is its direct contrast with the view widely held by Europeans including teachers in New Zealand to whom the Maori is a warm, friendly, happy-go-lucky, uncomplicated person. I do wonder to what extent the picture above parallels the personality development of the Aboriginal child and in what ways it differs. I would hazard a guess that the stereotype of the Aboriginal child is probably as remote from the real picture as is the one in New Zealand.

I began by saying that there are social handicaps that arise from, among other things, the cultural and intellectual distances that separate children from children of another culture and teachers from these children. Where there is a minority culture, both teacher and the majority of school pupils will, in the case of Australia and New Zealand, be white and middle class. What must be discovered, or the Aboriginal or Maori child will remain handicapped, is what differences there are between us and them, between our children and their children, and then what changes in attitude and curriculum and method will be required to remove the social handicaps.

The Maori Education Foundation has helped. The next step awaits a body of knowledge so that we will know better what to do. We hope that the days of faith and charity are over, useful as they were.

BIBLIOGRAPHY FOR PART SIX

Alport, E. A. "The Integration of Oriental Jews into Israel," *World Today* [London] (April 1967).

Burgin, Trevor, and Patricia Edson. *Spring Grove—The Education of Immigrant Children.* London: Oxford University Press, 1967.

Butkevich, M. N. "Why a Student Does Not Arrive at the 'Finish,' " *Soviet Review* (Spring 1966).

Cameron, John. "The Integration of Education in Tanganyika," *Comparative Education Review* (February 1967).

Connelly, Bob. "What's Lacking in the Integration Kit?" *The Saskatchewan Bulletin* (May 1964).

Danziger, K. "The Psychological Future of an Oppressed Group," *Social Forces* (October 1963).

DeVos, George, and Hiroshi Wagatsuma. *Japan's Invisible Race: Caste in Culture and Personality.* Berkeley and Los Angeles: University of California Press, 1966.

Dilling, H. J. "Educational Achievement and Social Acceptance of Indian Pupils Integrated in Non-Indian Schools of Southern Ontario," *Ontario Journal of Educational Research* (Autumn 1965).

Harre, John. *Maori and Pakeha: A Study of Mixed Marriages in New Zealand.* London: Pall Mall Press, 1966.

Horrell, M. *A Decade of Bantu Education.* Johannesburg: South Africa Institute of Race Relations, 1964.

Oppenheim, Roger. "Maori Children in Auckland School," *The New Era* [England] (December 1964).

Porter, John. "Social Class and Educational Opportunity," in *The Vertical Mosaic: An Analysis of Social Class and Power in Canada.* Toronto: University of Toronto Press, 1965.

Segal, Ronald. "The Dying Minds," [UNESCO] *Courier* (March 1967).

Tajfel, Henri, and John L. Dawson (eds.). *Disappointed Guests: Essays by African, Asian and West Indian Students.* London: Oxford University Press, 1966.

Van Den Berghe, Pierre L. *Race and Racism: A Comparative Perspective.* New York: Wiley, 1967.

Vernon, P. E. "Educational and Intellectual Development among Canadian Indians and Eskimos," *Educational Review* [England] (No. 1, 1966).

Wright, Theodore P., Jr. "Muslim Education in India at the Crossroads: The Case of Aligarh," *Pacific Affairs* (Spring-Summer, 1966).

Appendixes

APPENDIX A

Text of Supreme Court Rulings

May 17, 1954: *Brown* v. *Board of Education,* 347 U.S. 483

Mr. Chief Justice Warren delivered the opinion of the Court.

These cases come to us from the States of Kansas, South Carolina, Virginia, and Delaware. They are premised on different facts and different local conditions, but a common legal question justifies their consideration together in this consolidated opinion.

In each of the cases, minors of the Negro race, through their legal representatives, seek the aid of the courts in obtaining admission to the public schools of their community on a nonsegregated basis. In each instance, they had been denied admission to schools attended by white children under laws requiring or permitting segregation according to race. This segregation was alleged to deprive the plaintiffs of the equal protection of the laws under the Fourteenth Amendment. In each of the cases other than the Delaware case, a three-judge federal district court denied relief to the plaintiffs on the so-called "separate but equal" doctrine announced by this Court in *Plessy* v. *Ferguson,* 163 U.S. 537 [1896]. Under that doctrine, equality of treatment is accorded when the races are provided substantially equal facilities, even though these facilities be separate. In the Delaware case, the Supreme Court of Delaware adhered to that doctrine, but ordered that the plaintiffs be admitted to the white schools because of their superiority to the Negro schools.

The plaintiffs contend that segregated public schools are not "equal" and cannot be made "equal," and that hence they are deprived of the equal protection of the laws. Because of the obvious importance of the question presented, the Court took jurisdiction. Argument was heard in the 1952 Term, and reargument was heard this Term on certain questions propounded by the Court.

Reargument was largely devoted to the circumstances surrounding the adoption of the Fourteenth Amendment in 1868. It covered exhaustively consideration of the Amendment in Congress, ratification by the states, then-existing practices in racial segregation, and the views of proponents and opponents of the Amendment. This discussion and our own investigation convince us that, although these sources cast some light, it is not enough to resolve the problem with which we are faced. At best, they are inconclusive. The most avid proponents of the post-War Amendments undoubtedly intended them to remove all legal distinctions among "all persons born or naturalized in the United States." Their opponents, just as certainly, were antagonistic to both the letter and the spirit of the Amendments and wished them to have the most limited effect. What others in Congress and the state legislatures had in mind cannot be determined with any degree of certainty.

An additional reason for the inconclusive nature of the Amendment's history, with respect to segregated schools, is the status of public education at that time. In the South, the movement toward free common schools, supported by general taxation, had not yet taken hold. Education of white children was largely in the hands of private groups. Education of Negroes was almost nonexistent, and practically all of the race were illiterate. In fact, any education of Negroes was forbidden by law in some states. Today, in contrast, many Negroes have achieved outstanding success in the arts and sciences as well as in the business and professional world. It is true that public school education at the time of the Amendment had advanced further in the North, but the effect of the Amendment on Northern States was generally ignored in the congressional debates. Even in the North, the conditions of public education did not approximate those existing today. The curriculum was usually rudimentary; ungraded schools were common in rural areas; the school term was but three months a year in many states; and compulsory school attendance was virtually unknown. As a consequence, it is not surprising that there should be so little in the history of the Fourteenth Amendment relating to its intended effect on public education.

In the first cases in this Court construing the Fourteenth Amendment, decided shortly after its adoption, the Court interpreted it as proscribing all state-imposed discriminations against the Negro race. The doctrine of "separate but equal" did not make its appearance in this Court until 1896 in the case of *Plessy* v. *Ferguson, supra,* involving not education but transportation. American courts have since labored with the doctrine for over half a century. In this Court, there have been six cases involving the "separate but equal" doctrine in the field of public education. In *Cumming* v. *County Board of Education,* 175 U.S. 528, and *Gong Lum* v. *Rice,* 275 U.S. 78, the validity of the doctrine itself was not challenged. In more recent cases, all on the graduate school level, inequality was found in that specific benefits enjoyed by white students were denied to Negro students of the same educational qualifications. *Missouri ex rel. Gaines* v. *Canada,* 305 U.S. 337; *Sipuel* v. *Oklahoma,* 332 U.S. 631; *Sweatt* v. *Painter,* 339 U.S. 629; *McLaurin* v. *Oklahoma State Regents,* 339 U.S.

637. In none of these cases was it necessary to reexamine the doctrine to grant relief to the Negro plaintiff. And in *Sweatt* v. *Painter, supra,* the Court expressly reserved decision on the question whether *Plessy* v. *Ferguson* should be held inapplicable to public education.

In the instant cases, that question is directly presented. Here, unlike *Sweatt* v. *Painter,* there are findings below that the Negro and white schools involved have been equalized, or are being equalized, with respect to buildings, curricula, qualifications and salaries of teachers, and other "tangible" factors. Our decision, therefore, cannot turn on merely a comparison of these tangible factors in the Negro and white schools involved in each of the cases. We must look instead to the effect of segregation itself on public education.

In approaching this problem, we cannot turn the clock back to 1868 when the Amendment was adopted, or even to 1896 when *Plessy* v. *Ferguson* was written. We must consider public education in the light of its full development and its present place in American life throughout the Nation. Only in this way can it be determined if segregation in public schools deprives these plaintiffs of the equal protection of the laws.

Today, education is perhaps the most important function of state and local governments. Compulsory school attendance laws and the great expendituresfor education both demonstrate our recognition of the importance of education to our democratic society. It is required in the performance of our most basic public responsibilities, even service in the armed forces. It is the very foundation of good citizenship. Today it is a principal instrument in awakening the child to cultural values, in preparing him for later professional training, and in helping him to adjust normally to his environment. In these days, it is doubtful that any child may reasonably be expected to succeed in life if he is denied the opportunity of an education. Such an opportunity, where the state has undertaken to provide it, is a right which must be made available to all on equal terms.

We come then to the question presented: Does segregation of children in public schools solely on the basis of race, even though the physical facilities and other "tangible" factors may be equal, deprive the children of the minority group of equal educational opportunities? We believe that it does.

In *Sweatt* v. *Painter, supra,* in finding that a segregated law school for Negroes could not provide them equal educational opportunities, this Court relied in large part on "those qualities which are incapable of objective measurement but which make for greatness in a law school." In *McLaurin* v. *Oklahoma State Regents, supra,* the Court, in requiring that a Negro admitted to a white graduate school be treated like all other students, again resorted to intangible considerations: " ... his ability to study, to engage in discussions and exchange views with other students, and, in general, to learn his profession." Such considerations apply with added force to children in grade and high schools. To separate them from others of similar age and qualifications solely because of their race generates a feeling of inferiority as to their status in the community that may affect their hearts and minds in a way unlikely ever to be undone. The effect of this separation on their educational opportunities was well stated by a finding in the Kansas case by a court which nevertheless felt compelled to rule against the Negro plaintiffs:

Segregation of white and colored children in public schools has a detrimental effect upon the colored children. The impact is greater when it has the sanction of the law; for the policy of separating the races is usually interpreted as denoting the inferiority of the negro group. A sense of inferiority affects the motivation of a child to learn. Segregation with the sanction of law, therefore, has a tendency to [retard] the educational and mental development of negro children and to deprive them of some of the benefits they would receive in a racial[ly] integrated school system.

Whatever may have been the extent of psychological knowledge at the time of *Plessy* v. *Ferguson,* this finding is amply supported by modern authority. Any language in *Plessy* v. *Ferguson* contrary to this finding is rejected.

We conclude that in the field of public education the doctrine of "separate but equal" has no place. Separate educational facilities are inherently unequal. Therefore, we hold that the plaintiffs and others similarly situated for whom the actions have been brought are, by reason of the segregation complained of, deprived of the equal protection of the laws guaranteed by the Fourteenth Amendment. This disposition makes unnecessary any discussion whether such segregation also violates the Due Process Clause of the Fourteenth Amendment.

Because these are class actions, because of the wide applicability of this decision, and because of the great variety of local conditions, the formulation of decrees in these cases presents problems of considerable complexity. On reargument, the consideration of appropriate relief was necessarily subordinated to the primary question—the constitutionality of segregation in public education. We have now announced that such segregation is a denial of the equal protection of the laws. In order that we may have the full assistance of the parties in formulating decrees, the cases will be restored to the docket, and the parties are requested to present further argument on Questions four and five previously propounded by the Court for the reargument this Term. The Attorney General of the United States is again invited to participate. The Attorneys General of the states requiring or permitting segregation in public education will also be permitted to appear as *amici curiae* upon request to do so by September 15, 1954, and submission of briefs by October 1, 1954.

It is so ordered.

May 31, 1955: *Brown* v. *Board of Education,* 349 U.S. 294

Mr. Chief Justice Warren delivered the opinion of the Court.

These cases were decided on May 17, 1954. The opinions of that date, declaring the fundamental principle that racial discrimination in public education is unconstitutional, are incorporated herein by reference. All provisions of federal, state, or local law requiring or permitting such discrimination must yield to this principle. There remains for consideration the manner in which relief is to be accorded.

Because these cases arose under different local conditions and their disposition will involve a variety of local problems, we requested further argument on the question of relief. In view of the nationwide importance of the decision, we invited the Attorney General of the United States and the Attorneys General of all states requiring or permitting racial discrimination in public education to present their views on that question. The parties, the United States, and the States of Florida, North Carolina, Arkansas, Oklahoma, Maryland, and Texas filed briefs and participated in the oral argument.

These presentations were informative and helpful to the Court in its consideration of the complexities arising from the transition to a system of public education
freed of racial discrimination. The presentations also demonstrated that substantial
steps to eliminate racial discrimination in public schools have already been taken, not
only in some of the communities in which these cases arose, but in some of the states
appearing as *amici curiae,* and in other states as well. Substantial progress has been
made in the District of Columbia and in the communities in Kansas and Delaware
involved in this litigation. The defendants in the cases coming to us from South
Carolina and Virginia are awaiting the decision of this Court concerning relief.

Full implementation of these constitutional principles may require solution of
varied local school problems. School authorities have the primary responsibility for
elucidating, assessing, and solving these problems; courts will have to consider
whether the action of school authorities consitutes good faith implementation of the
governing constitutional principles. Because of their proximity to local conditions and
the possible need for further hearings, the courts which originally heard these cases
can best perform this judicial appraisal. Accordingly, we believe it appropriate to
remand the cases to those courts.

In fashioning and effectuating the decrees, the courts will be guided by equitable
principles. Traditionally, equity has been characterized by a practical flexibility in
shaping its remedies and by a facility for adjusting and reconciling public and private
needs. These cases call for the exercise of these traditional attributes of equity power.
At stake is the personal interest of the plaintiffs in admission to public schools as soon
as practicable on a nondiscriminatory basis. To effectuate this interest may call for
elimination of a variety of obstacles in making the transition to school systems
operated in accordance with the constitutional principles set forth in our May 17,
1954, decision. Courts of equity may properly take into account the public interest in
the elimination of such obstacles in a systematic and effective manner. But it should
go without saying that the vitality of these constitutional principles cannot be allowed
to yield simply because of disagreement with them.

While giving weight to these public and private considerations, the courts will
require that the defendants make a prompt and reasonable start toward full
compliance with our May 17, 1954, ruling. Once such a start has been made, the
courts may find that additional time is necessary to carry out the ruling in an effective
manner. The burden rests upon the defendants to establish that such time is necessary
in the public interest and is consistent with good faith compliance at the earliest
practicable date. To that end, the courts may consider problems related to administration, arising from the physical condition of the school plant, the school transportation system, personnel, revision of school districts and attendance areas into compact
units to achieve a system of determining admission to the public schools on a
nonracial basis, and revision of local laws and regulations which may be necessary in
solving the foregoing problems. They will also consider the adequacy of any plans the
defendants may propose to meet these problems and to effectuate a transition to a
racially nondiscriminatory school system. During this period of transition, the courts
will retain jurisdiction of these cases.

The judgments below, except that in the Delaware case, are accordingly reversed
and the cases are remanded to the district courts to take such proceedings and enter
such orders and decrees consistent with this opinion as are necessary and proper to

admit to public schools on a racially nondiscriminatory basis with all deliberate speed the parties to these cases. The judgment in the Delaware case—ordering the immediate admission of the plaintiffs to schools previously attended only by white children—is affirmed on the basis of the principles stated in our May 17, 1954, opinion, but the case is remanded to the Supreme Court of Delaware for such further proceedings as that Court may deem necessary in light of this opinion.

It is so ordered.

APPENDIX B

Major Developments: A Chronology (1954-1967)

1954
* In *Brown v. Board of Education of Topeka,* the U.S. supreme court held that segregated schools deprive citizens of equal protection of the laws as guaranteed in the Fourteenth Amendment.

1955
* The U.S. supreme court directed federal district courts to enforce school desegregation "with all deliberate speed."

1957
* Federal troops were ordered into Little Rock, Arkansas, to enforce a federal court order to desegregate Central High School.

1958
* A New York City court held, in Skipwith, that a parent cannot be prosecuted for child neglect because he refused to send the child to a segregated, inferior school.

1959
* Prince Edward County, Virginia, closed its public schools rather than permit them to be desegregated.

1960
* The Board of Regents of the State of New York became the first statewide body to adopt a policy that racial imbalance, whatever its cause, was educationally harmful and must be eradicated.

1962
* In the New Rochelle, New York, case a federal court found that the school board had deprived children of equal protection of the laws by gerrymandering school attendance boundaries.
* Civil rights advocates concentrated on open enrollment and redistricting of attendance boundaries as chief remedies for school segregation.

1963
* First in Boston and then in Chicago, large-scale pupil boycotts of school systems were organized by civil rights groups as a protest against school segregation.
* During the spring, city authorities in Birmingham, Alabama, used in-

discriminate violence to suppress civil rights demonstrations. National revulsion led to a new intensity of civil rights organization throughout the country.

- Illinois adopted the Armstrong Act which required a periodic redrawing of school attendance boundaries to reduce segregation and prevent any additional segregation (held unconstitutional by the state supreme court in 1967).

1964

- The New York state official Allen Report on New York City's public schools called previous efforts to desegregate the city's schools a failure and called for new organizational approaches such as school complexes and middle schools.
- The high point of public demonstrations and marches by civil rights groups.
- The federal Civil Rights Act was enacted. Title IV provided federal funds to help school boards carry through desegregation programs. Title VI forbade the use of federal aid funds for racially discriminatory purposes.

1965

- Massachusetts adopted the first state law to encourage racially balanced schools. State aid was to be withheld from school districts refusing to remedy imbalance. Special state subsidies were offered to school districts seeking to establish racially balanced schools.
- Increasingly, civil rights groups started to call for "*quality* integrated" education, thus extending their concern to concrete changes in the classroom.
- The federal Elementary and Secondary Education Act was Passed. Title I, directed at remedying the special problems of educationally deprived children, contained no provision requiring a desegregated framework for compensatory education.
- For five days, federal aid to Chicago schools was deferred by federal authorities because of indications that Title VI of the Civil Rights Act was being violated (political pressures forced revocation of the deferral decision).
- Educational parks began to take precedence over open enrollment and boundary changes as remedies preferred by civil rights advocates.

1966

- Ghetto parent protest at Intermediate School 201 in East Harlem set off a spreading movement for genuine community controls over the appointment of school personnel and academic achievement of students.
- The U.S. Office of Education published *Survey of Equal Educational Opportunities* (the "Coleman Report"), the largest-scale study yet made of racial differentials in American elementary and secondary education.
- A collective bargaining contract between a teacher union and the school board of Ecorse, Michigan, permitted teachers to be transferred or denied transfer in the interest of staff integration.
- The doctrine of separate-and-equal schools gained support from some advocates of black nationalism, especially in certain northern urban centers. Meanwhile the desegregation movement gained strength in the South.
- The National Education Association and the American Federation of

1966 *(Continued)*

Teachers increasingly concerned themselves in educational programs regarding integration, with particular attention focused on Negro history.

1967

- The U.S. Commission on Civil Rights published *Racial Isolation in the Public Schools,* an extensive documentation of the educational advantages of racial integration.
- The federal district court of Washington, D.C. found school segregation in the District of Columbia to be unlawful. Singled out were the track system, unequal money expenditures on white and Negro schools, and maldistribution of experienced teachers (*Hobson* v. *Hansen*).
- The U.S. court of appeals, fifth circuit, held in Jefferson County case that school boards in states that once required school segregation had a positive obligation (not merely an option) to integrate schools; later in the year, the U.S. supreme court affirmed this decision.
- Ground was broken in East Orange, New Jersey, and in Pittsburgh, Pennsylvania, for erection of educational parks, major efforts to combine instructional innovation, urban renewal, and racial integration.
- The mayor of New York City recommended decent decentralization of the school system of his city into thirty to sixty community school districts, financed centrally but each administered by an eleven-member board on which elected parents formed the majority.

Index